Get More and Do More at Dummies.com®

Start with **FREE** Cheat Sheets

Cheat Sheets include
- Checklists
- Charts
- Common Instructions
- And Other Good Stuff!

P9-CQU-051

To access the Cheat Sheet created specifically for this book, go to
www.dummies.com/cheatsheet/ireland

Get Smart at Dummies.com

Dummies.com makes your life easier with 1,000s
of answers on everything from removing
wallpaper to using the latest version
of Windows.

Check out our
- Videos
- Illustrated Articles
- Step-by-Step Instructions

Plus, each month you can win valuable prizes
by entering our Dummies.com sweepstakes. *

Want a weekly dose of Dummies?
Sign up for Newsletters on
- Digital Photography
- Microsoft Windows & Office
- Personal Finance & Investing
- Health & Wellness
- Computing, iPods & Cell Phones
- eBay
- Internet
- Food, Home & Garden

Find out "HOW" at Dummies.com

Sweepstakes not currently available in all countries; visit Dummies.com for official rules.

Ireland FOR DUMMIES®

6TH EDITION

by Liz Albertson

WILEY

Wiley Publishing, Inc.

Ireland For Dummies®, 6th Edition

Published by
Wiley Publishing, Inc.
111 River St.
Hoboken, NJ 07030-5774
www.wiley.com

Copyright © 2011 by Wiley Publishing, Inc., Indianapolis, Indiana

Published simultaneously in Canada

WILEY

About the Author

Liz Albertson worked as an editor for Frommer's Travel Guides for four years before making the leap to the other side of the computer as the author of *Ireland For Dummies*. When she isn't researching and writing, Liz spends much of her time in Ireland sitting in on traditional music sessions, fiddle in hand. During the school year, Liz teaches middle school Science and English in New York City, where she lives with her husband, Hugh, and her adopted African cichlid fish, Rocky. Liz welcomes feedback and suggestions for the next edition of the book at ejalbertson@yahoo.com

Dedication

Dedicated to my Beloved Bunchukks.

Author's Acknowledgments

I raise endless pints to Christine Ryan, my amazing and patient editor, and to my favorite travel companions in the world: my husband, my mom, and my dad.

Publisher's Acknowledgments

We're proud of this book; please send us your comments through our Dummies online registration form located at www.dummies.com/register/.

Some of the people who helped bring this book to market include the following:

Editorial

Editors: Christine Ryan,
Eric T. Schroeder

Copy Editor: Elizabeth Kuball

Cartographer: Guy Ruggiero

Editorial Assistant: Andrea Kahn

Senior Photo Editor: Richard Fox

Cover Photos:
Front: ©The Irish Image Collection /
SuperStock, Inc. Back: ©Steve
Vidler / SuperStock, Inc.

Cartoons: Rich Tennant (www.the5th
wave.com)

Composition Services

Project Coordinator: Patrick Redmond

Layout and Graphics: Claudia Bell,
Jennifer Henry, Heather Pope,
Lavonne Roberts, Julie Trippetti

Proofreaders: Laura Albert,
Cara L. Buitron

Indexer: Estalita Slivoskey

Publishing and Editorial for Consumer Dummies

Diane Graves Steele, Vice President and Publisher, Consumer Dummies

Kristin Ferguson-Wagstaffe, Product Development Director, Consumer Dummies

Kelly Regan, Editorial Director, Travel

Publishing for Technology Dummies

Andy Cummings, Vice President and Publisher, Dummies Technology/
General User

Composition Services

Gerry Fahey, Vice President of Production Services

Debbie Stailey, Director of Composition Services

Contents at a Glance

Maps at a Glance

Table of Contents

Introduction

Relatively tiny Ireland (84,434 sq. km/32,600 sq. miles) unfolds to offer travelers a wide variety of experiences. You'll find landscapes that range from those famed rolling green hills to stark, rugged cliffs; restaurants that serve the best in modern fusion ("New Irish") cuisine and pubs that serve Irish stew made from a recipe that's hundreds of years old; theaters showcasing the best in contemporary dance and festivals devoted to traditional Irish music. This guide highlights the best of Ireland's diverse offerings so that you can plan the trip of your dreams.

About This Book

Ireland For Dummies features need-to-know information, from how to access the best airline deals to helpful tips on how to organize and maximize your time in a destination. Each section of the book features a selective, streamlined choice of accommodations, restaurants, and attractions in all price ranges.

Please be advised that travel information is subject to change at any time — this is especially true of prices. You may want to e-mail or call ahead for confirmation when making your travel plans. The author, editors, and publisher cannot be held responsible for the experiences of readers while traveling. Your safety is important to us, however, so we encourage you to stay alert and be aware of your surroundings. Keep a close eye on cameras, purses, and wallets, all favorite targets of thieves and pickpockets.

Conventions Used in This Book

In this book, I included lists of hotels, restaurants, and attractions. As I describe each, I often use abbreviations for commonly accepted credit cards. The following is a list of the credit card abbreviations used in this book:

AE: American Express

DC: Diners Club

MC: MasterCard

V: Visa

Prices over €10 or £10 are rounded to the nearest euro or pound. In the dining sections, the listed prices are the range of prices for main courses at dinner, unless otherwise noted.

Each hotel or restaurant review is accompanied by a dollar-sign designation, which is designed to help you get a sense of the price at a glance. The following is the key to the dollar-sign designations for accommodations and restaurants.

Hotel Category	Euros	British Pounds	U.S. Dollars
$	€70 or less	£56 or less	$112 or less
$$	€71–€120	£57–£96	$113–$192
$$$	€121–€180	£97–£144	$193–$288
$$$$	€181 or more	£145 or more	$289 or more

Restaurant Category	Euros	British Pounds	U.S. Dollars
$	€15 or less	£12 or less	$24 or less
$$	€16–€23	£13–£19	$25–$37
$$$	€24–€29	£20–£23	$38–$46
$$$$	€30 or more	£24 or more	$47 or more

Foolish Assumptions

As I wrote this book, I made some assumptions about you and what your needs may be as a traveler. Here's what I assumed about you:

✔ You may be an experienced traveler who hasn't had much time to explore Ireland and wants expert advice when you finally do get a chance to enjoy that particular locale.

✔ You may be an inexperienced traveler looking for guidance when determining whether to take a trip to Ireland and how to plan for it should you decide to go.

✔ You're not looking for a book that provides all the information available about Ireland or that lists every hotel, restaurant, or attraction available to you. Instead, you're looking for a book that focuses on the places that will give you the best or unique experience in Ireland.

If any of these criteria match your needs, then *Ireland For Dummies* gives you the information you seek!

How This Book Is Organized

This book is divided into seven parts, described in the following sections.

Part 1: Introducing Ireland

This part introduces you to the splendor of Ireland and helps you get an idea of what you'd like to see and where you'd like to go. The book starts with a chapter devoted to the very best that Ireland has to offer. Chapter 2 includes all sorts of information about Ireland, from a look at the island's history to translations of local lingo to culinary information. Chapter 3 provides brief descriptions of the regions covered in this guide so that you get a sense of where you'd like to go. In Chapter 3, I also discuss various approaches to touring the country, and hash out the pros and cons of visiting during different seasons. I also give you a rundown of the many festivals, events, and celebrations held in Ireland throughout the year. In case you'd like some guidance on how to plan your itinerary, I offer four different suggested itineraries in Chapter 4.

Part 11: Planning Your Trip to Ireland

Part II answers all your practical questions about planning and getting ready for a trip to Ireland. Chapter 5 deals with money, providing rough guidelines on what things cost, helping you decide how to carry your money, and listing loads of money-saving tips. Chapter 6 outlines the different ways to get to Ireland, and Chapter 7 deals with the various options for getting around the island. After you plan how to get there, you can turn to Chapter 8, which gives you the lowdown on the different types of accommodations in Ireland, as well as tips on how to save on lodging costs. Chapter 9 includes tips for travelers with special needs and interests, including seniors, travelers with disabilities, gay and lesbian travelers, students, outdoorsy travelers, and more. Before you go out and start buying your travel-size toothpaste, check out Chapter 10 for information on getting a passport, figuring out insurance, and staying in touch once you get to Ireland.

Part 111: Dublin and the East Coast

Part III is devoted to Dublin and the surrounding counties: Meath and Louth to the north and Wicklow, Wexford, Waterford, Kilkenny, and Tipperary to the south.

Chapter 11 covers Dublin, the Republic of Ireland's bustling, vibrant capital city. This fat chapter is packed with information on the best restaurants, hotels, attractions, shopping, and nightlife in the city. If the choices overwhelm you, check out the one-, two-, and three-day suggested itineraries.

Counties Meath and Louth, just north of Dublin, are home to a treasure trove of prehistoric sights, including the remarkable burial mounds at Knowth and Newgrange; you'll find more information about these areas in Chapter 12. Chapters 13 and 14 cover the beautiful southeastern counties of Wicklow, Kildare, Wexford, Waterford, Tipperary, and Kilkenny; these counties offer a diverse array of attractions, including some of Ireland's most beautiful gardens, medieval towns, stunning mountain and coastal scenery, and the popular House of Waterford Crystal.

Part IV: Counties Cork and Kerry

Part IV covers two counties, Cork and Kerry, which together attract the lion's share of visitors to Ireland with their stunning mountain and coastal scenery. The gorgeous sea- and landscapes and cute towns of West Cork are covered in Chapter 15, as is bustling Cork City. Chapter 16 features the best of beautiful Killarney National Park and the breath-taking Ring of Kerry and Dingle Peninsula.

Part V: The West and the Northwest

This part bundles the entire western and northwestern areas of Ireland into one package that incorporates a tremendous variety of landscapes and towns. Chapters 17 through 20 are filled with information on gorgeous natural wonders, including the sheer Cliffs of Moher and the Slieve League cliffs; the rocky, wildflower-studded Burren; the beautiful Aran Islands; the wild landscape of Connemara and County Mayo; and much more. You get the lowdown on some of the best cities and towns in this area, including the sweet Mayo town of Westport and the artsy and dynamic city of Galway.

Part VI: Northern Ireland

Part VI covers the separate country of Northern Ireland, which may be last in this book but is not least in terms of natural beauty and interesting cities. Chapters 21 through 23 guide you to the most beautiful natural wonders, including the Mourne Mountains and the hexagonal basalt columns of the Giant's Causeway. They also give you all the information you need to explore the hot-and-happening city of Belfast and the historic city of Derry.

Part VII: The Part of Tens

The Part of Tens features some fun extras, including a list of Irish food and drink that you shouldn't miss during your trip, and my top ten suggestions of what to buy in Ireland.

At the back of this book, I've included an appendix — your Quick Concierge — containing lots of handy information you may need when traveling in Ireland, such as phone numbers and addresses of airlines, car rental companies, and more. Check out this appendix when searching for answers to lots of little questions that may come up as you travel. You can find the Quick Concierge easily because it's printed on yellow paper.

Icons Used in This Book

Keep an eye peeled for these icons, which appear in the margins throughout this book:

This icon highlights money-saving tips and/or great deals.

This icon highlights the best hotels, restaurants, attractions, activities, shopping, and nightlife in Ireland.

This icon gives you a heads-up on annoying or potentially dangerous situations, such as tourist traps, unsafe neighborhoods, rip-offs, and other things to beware of.

This icon highlights attractions, accommodations, restaurants, or activities that are particularly hospitable to families.

This icon points out accommodations, restaurants, and attractions that have excellent environmental practices.

This icon points out useful advice on things to do and ways to schedule your time.

Where to Go from Here

Now you're ready to go! Put a Chieftains CD on the stereo; pour yourself a glass of Guinness; and get ready to fling yourself headlong into the historic, friendly, beautiful experience that is Ireland today.

Part I

Introducing Ireland

The 5th Wave   By Rich Tennant

WHILE ON VACATION IN IRELAND, BILL AND DENISE WATCH A LOCAL FAMILY WORKING ON THE TRADITIONAL THATCHED ROOF COTTAGE, THATCHED ROOF SATELLITE DISH, AND THATCHED ROOF JEEP CHEROKEE.

In this part . . .

*I*reland is a traveler's dream, with diverse and spectacular scenery, vibrant towns and cities humming with activity, a culinary scene that makes the most of the country's fresh ingredients and artisanal products, a wide array of attractions, great music, and more than its share of superb accommodations, from upscale hotels to cozy B&Bs. Chapter 1 whets your appetite with brief descriptions of some of Ireland's best scenery, restaurants, accommodations, and more.

Read through Chapter 2 for background information on Ireland, including a look at Irish history, Irish cuisine, and local lingo, plus a list of some fun and interesting Irish books, movies, and music.

In Chapter 3, I provide brief descriptions of the regions covered in this guide, discuss various approaches to touring the country, and hash out the pros and cons of visiting during different seasons. I also include a calendar of events so you can schedule your trip to coincide with the festivals and celebrations that interest you.

Overwhelmed by the wealth of things to see and do in Ireland? Chapter 4 includes some suggested itineraries.

Chapter 1

Discovering the Best of Ireland

In This Chapter

▶ Enjoying Ireland's best travel experiences

▶ Finding Ireland's best hotels, restaurants, and pubs

▶ Exploring Irish history at the best castles and archaeological sites

*T*his chapter gives you the lowdown on the very best that Ireland has to offer, from the best food on the island to the most gorgeous seascapes to the best spots to hear traditional Irish music.

Throughout the book, the Best of the Best icon refers you to the items mentioned in this chapter.

The Best Travel Experiences

With all that Ireland has to offer, it's tough to come up with a list of favorite experiences; but here are some of the adventures I keep daydreaming about long after I'm home:

✔ **Listening to traditional Irish music:** What could be better than relaxing to live traditional music in an atmospheric pub? The Traditional Irish Musical Pub Crawl in Dublin is a terrific introduction to the musical style. See Chapter 11.

✔ **Taking in the Book of Kells and Trinity College:** This ninth-century book of the four gospels glows with ornate Latin script and stunning Celtic knots and designs. The book is found in a museum at lovely Trinity College. See Chapter 11.

✔ **Filing into Newgrange Tomb:** You'll feel like a lucky explorer as you descend into the cool, dim chamber of this 5,000-year-old *passage tomb* (an underground chamber thought to have religious or ceremonial importance). See Chapter 12.

✔ **Rambling around the Wicklow Mountains (Wicklow):** In the lush and rolling Wicklow Mountains, you'll find leafy woodlands,

Ireland

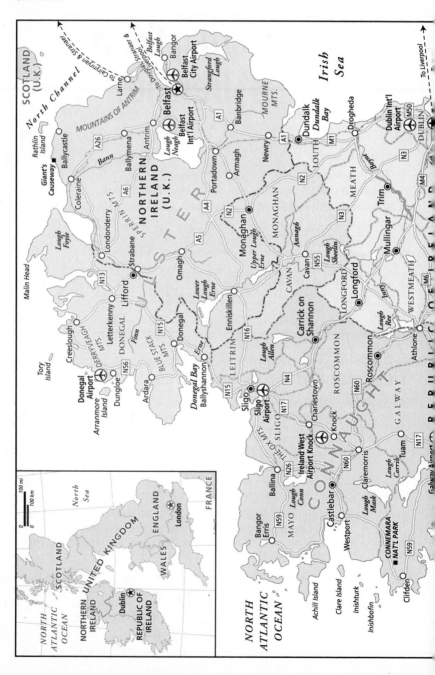

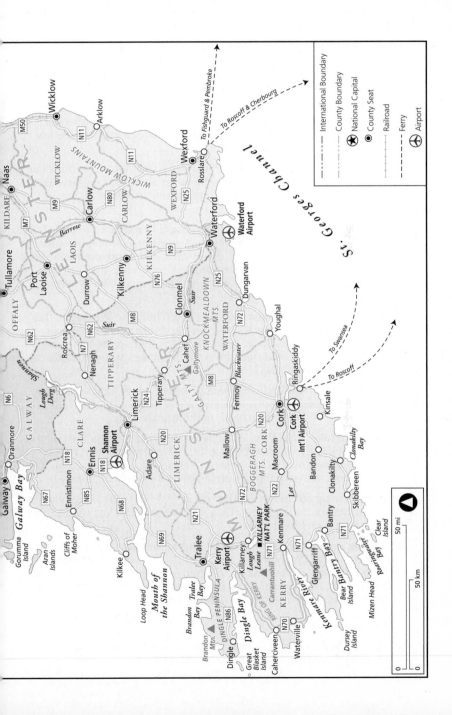

shimmering lakes, verdant fields, and plenty of trails on which to enjoy the surroundings. See Chapter 13.

✔ **Strolling through Powerscourt Gardens:** These gardens have many facets, including a mossy grotto, a formal garden with an impressive fountain and statuary, a rose garden that bursts into a riot of color in season, and peaceful woodlands. See Chapter 13.

✔ **Touring the House of Waterford Crystal:** This fascinating tour takes you behind the scenes to watch the evolution of Waterford Crystal pieces, from their beginnings as molten crystal to the finished product. See Chapter 14.

✔ **Exploring Killarney National Park:** Use a bike, horse, jaunting car, or your own two feet to explore the silver streams, sapphire lakes, dense woodlands, and heather-covered mountains here. See Chapter 16.

✔ **Driving the Ring of Kerry and the Dingle Peninsula:** Driving along both of these peninsulas, each vista you encounter is more spectacular than the one before it. Seascapes, cliffs, and mountain views are the order of the day on the Ring of Kerry, while the Dingle Peninsula has hills, farms, sandy beaches, craggy cliffs, loads of ruins, and more seascapes. See Chapter 16.

✔ **Hiking through the Burren:** Hiking is the ultimate way to see this strange and stunning rocky plateau, filled with wildflowers that poke up through cracks in the rock, rivers that spring up from below the ground, and ruins from the Stone Age through medieval times. See Chapter 17.

✔ **Exploring Ireland's islands:** Taking a ferry out to explore one (or more) of Ireland's islands is like an adventure within an adventure. See Chapter 18 for information on the Aran Islands.

✔ **Taking a hike:** There's nothing like wandering through the countryside to really experience Ireland. Two of my favorite hikes are a ramble along County Cork's Sheep's Head Way, and a jaunt out of Port, north of Donegal Bay. See Chapters 15 and 20.

✔ **Adventuring out to the Skelligs (Kerry):** A boat ride is the best way to appreciate these rocks, which jut dramatically from the frothing sea below. See Chapter 16.

✔ **Gazing awestruck at the Cliffs of Moher and Slieve League:** The breathtaking Cliffs of Moher plummet down to the Atlantic 288m (760 ft.) below. The vistas are stunning — you can see all the way to the Aran Islands in Galway Bay when the weather is clear. If you can't get enough of cliffscapes, Slieve League are the highest in all of Europe, towering dizzily over the turbulent Atlantic. See Chapters 17 and 20.

✔ **Seeing the Derry and Belfast political murals:** These murals are moving testaments of the Troubles. The best way to view them in context is with a driving or walking tour. See Chapters 21 and 22.

- **Clambering around the Giant's Causeway:** You can climb around this natural wonder — a stretch of tightly packed six-sided basalt columns of varying heights — like you're on a StairMaster gone crazy. See Chapter 22.

- **Going to market:** Markets in Ireland are colorful, interesting, and filled with some of the best local and artisanal foods around. My favorite markets are in Dublin; Bantry, in West Cork; and Belfast. See Chapters 12, 15, and 22.

The Best Luxury Lodgings

The following hotels and manor houses made my list of favorites because they offer a unique atmosphere, outstanding service, uncommon luxury, a particularly Irish flavor, or perhaps all the above:

- **The Merrion (Dublin):** This place is a classic, with lovely architectural details and a welcoming staff. See Chapter 11.

- **The Ritz-Carlton Powerscourt (Wicklow):** It's a Ritz-Carlton. Among lush, rolling green hills. Need I say more? See Chapter 13.

- **Waterford Castle (Waterford):** Don your crown and head to this castle on its own island, with an interior featuring tapestries, antiques, and stone fireplaces. See Chapter 14.

- **Killarney Park Hotel (Kerry):** Luxury, luxury, and more luxury are on tap at this hotel, with a gorgeous Victorian-style lobby, spacious guest rooms furnished with antiques and lush fabrics, and an outstanding staff. See Chapter 16.

- **Dromoland Castle (Clare):** This just may be the fairytale castle you've dreamt of, with towers aplenty, and grand public spaces. See Chapter 17.

- **Dolphin Beach House (Galway):** Perhaps my all-time favorite place to stay in Ireland, Dolphin Beach House offers dazzling views, an interior that was clearly designed by someone with a skilled artistic eye, and two of the nicest hosts I've ever come across. *Caution:* People have a hard time leaving. See Chapter 18.

- **The g (Galway):** Okay, so it's expensive (really expensive), but this place boasts theatrical surroundings, a wonderful spa, friendly staff, and possibly the most comfortable beds on the Emerald Isle. See Chapter 18.

- **Templehouse (Sligo):** A stay at Templehouse is like a visit to a close relative . . . who just happens to own a sprawling manor house on 400 hectares (1,000 acres). See Chapter 19.

- **Ashford Castle (Mayo):** Live out a medieval tale with a stay in this luxurious castle. Public rooms feature large gilt-framed oil paintings, medieval coats of armor, and oak paneling, while antiques and carved-wood furniture are the order of the day in guest rooms. The hotel offers all sorts of activities, from horseback riding to fishing. See Chapter 19.

✔ **Malmaison (Antrim):** This boldly funky Belfast boutique hotel provides extraordinarily friendly service to celebrities and the rest of us. See Chapter 22.

The Best Moderately Priced Accommodations

Want a great bargain without sacrificing comfort and style? Check out the following options. Many are B&Bs — one of my favorite lodging choices in Ireland because you get the company and advice of a friendly local along with your room.

✔ **Kilronan House (Dublin):** Cormac, the warm proprietor of this guesthouse, couldn't be more helpful. Rooms are simple and bright, and the setting is a grand Georgian house about a ten-minute walk from downtown Dublin. See Chapter 11.

✔ **McMenamins Townhouse (Wexford):** Kind hosts, soothing rooms, a central location, and a spectacular breakfast make this place one of Ireland's best B&Bs. See Chapter 14.

✔ **Foxmount Country House (Waterford):** It's easy to feel like the lord or lady of this manor as you stroll the stunningly landscaped grounds and settle into your cozy, elegant room. See Chapter 14.

✔ **The Old Presbytery (Cork):** The only way that this place could be more relaxing would be if a masseuse came with each room. The huge beds are filled with snow-white blankets and pillows, many rooms have tubs or Jacuzzis, and the staff is among the friendliest and most helpful around. See Chapter 15.

✔ **Sandycove House B&B (Cork):** Lie on your fluffy duvet and gaze out at the crescent of beach framed by cliffs in the background and your hosts' adorable pet donkey in the foreground. Ahhh, this is what vacation is about. See Chapter 15.

✔ **Milestone B&B (Kerry):** Owners Barbara and Michael Carroll make this B&B a standout, helping every guest to plan his or her perfect Dingle Peninsula itinerary. See Chapter 16.

✔ **Berry Lodge (Clare):** The views of farmland and sea are gorgeous, and the bedrooms are comfy and bright, but the real reason to stay here is the unbelievably delicious cuisine served at dinner. See Chapter 17.

✔ **Devondell House (Galway):** This sweet B&B is a slice of home (with a terrific breakfast) right outside of Galway City. See Chapter 18.

The best of the Irish awards

As you make your way around Ireland, you'll discover that the Irish absolutely love awards. Almost every restaurant and lodging has some sort of sign or sticker indicating that the place is lauded by one organization or other. In fact, there are even awards for the best public bathrooms in each county. You heard it here first: One of Ireland's top toilets is in Lismore, in County Cork. The esteemed public bathroom is located at the foot of the road leading toward the castle.

✔ **Sea Mist House (Galway):** *Peace* and *tranquility* are the words that come to mind at this B&B in the middle of the bustling little town of Clifden. See Chapter 18.

✔ **The Merchant's House (Derry):** Slip back in time with a stay at this beautifully restored Georgian B&B, featuring high ceilings, intricate plasterwork, and a museum-quality Georgian-style dining room. See Chapter 21.

✔ **Killead Lodge (Antrim):** This serene B&B is a welcome oasis after a day exploring Belfast. Rooms are comfortable and bright, and the breakfast is top-notch. See Chapter 22.

✔ **Slieve Croob Inn (Down):** You can't beat the location of this comfortable inn, nestled in rolling green hills a few minutes away from the Mourne Mountains. Hiking trails start practically at the front door. See Chapter 23.

The Best Restaurants

Feel like sitting down to an elegantly prepared slice of Irish salmon with lemongrass and ginger? Or is Irish stew more your style? No matter what you're craving, you won't go hungry in Ireland. Here are my favorite places to dig in:

✔ **L'Gueulton (Dublin):** French-influenced cuisine is perfectly prepared from fresh ingredients at this casually elegant (and popular) restaurant. See Chapter 11.

✔ **The Winding Stair (Dublin):** At this lovely restaurant, overlooking the River Liffey, you'll find Irish classics all dressed up for 21st-century Dublin. Think spring lamb chops with mint crème fraîche. See Chapter 11.

✔ **Man Friday (Cork):** There's no fancy footwork at this seafood-and-meat-centric restaurant, just excellent ingredients cooked in a way that allows their flavor to shine, such as the black sole cooked on the bone. The interior is warm, romantic, and cozy, lit by lantern-style lamps. See Chapter 15.

✔ **Mary Ann's (Cork):** This warm and buzzing pub in the tiny West Cork town of Castletownshend serves up some up the best fish I've ever had. See Chapter 15.

✔ **Out of the Blue (Kerry):** This cheerful, Mediterranean-style restaurant offers some of the freshest fish in town. See Chapter 16.

✔ **The Lighthouse Café (Kerry):** The view from the picnic benches will knock your socks off, as will the unbelievable seafood chowder and other casual dishes. See Chapter 16.

✔ **The Long Dock (Clare):** Go for a traditional dish in the cozy pub (bacon and cabbage with parsley sauce, perhaps?), or order the fresh-caught fish that was just swimming in the nearby bay that morning. See Chapter 17.

✔ **Cava (Galway):** Traditional tapas in Ireland? Yup, and they're fantastic, served up in an airy, relaxing space. See Chapter 18.

✔ **Cayenne (Antrim):** There's a reason that all those folks are crowded into the entranceway of this restaurant: The fusion cuisine here is daring and luscious, featuring such bold dishes as an appetizer of cinnamon quail with carrot, honey, and ginger salad. See Chapter 22.

The Best Castles

You can step back in time and unleash your inner lord or lady at any of the following castles:

✔ **Dublin Castle (Dublin):** Art and history lovers alike will appreciate a tour of Dublin's castle, which has been used in various capacities for the past 800 years. See Chapter 11.

✔ **Cahir Castle (Tipperary):** This 13th- to 15th-century defensive castle, the setting for the movie *Excalibur,* is one of the best-preserved medieval castles in Ireland. See Chapter 14.

✔ **Kilkenny Castle (Kilkenny):** A storybook-castle exterior, a beautiful interior boasting 1830s furnishings, and expansive grounds are the charms of this medieval castle. See Chapter 14.

✔ **Bunratty Castle and Folk Park (Clare):** Built in 1425, and featuring an interior that's furnished as it was in the 15th century, Bunratty Castle is one of Ireland's most popular attractions. For the full castle experience, book a seat at one of the medieval banquets held here. See Chapter 17.

✔ **Dunluce Castle (Antrim):** Perched over the crashing waves of the ocean, the stone ruins of 17th-century Dunluce Castle are some of the most picturesque in Ireland. Window openings and doors frame the sea and sky, and you can still see the remains of the giant stone fireplaces. See Chapter 22.

Travel: A study in serendipity

This is probably the most difficult chapter to write, because some of my Ireland bests are one-of-a-kind moments, which lack admission fees and open hours — a late-night Irish music session, a great conversation with a Dublin taxi driver, the sun breaking out of the clouds to illuminate a faraway hill. You'll have these bests too, experiences unique to your trip. Dog-ear this book, mark off everything you want to experience, and make reservations for the best restaurants, but don't forget to be open to those serendipitous experiences that make travel so magical.

The Best Ruins and Archeological Sites

History buffs will have a field day at any of the following attractions:

- ✔ **Newgrange (Meath):** Check out the stones carved with geometric designs before you climb down a passageway into the heart of this 5,000-year-old burial chamber. See Chapter 12.

- ✔ **Glendalough (Wicklow):** A monastic community founded in the sixth century, Glendalough functioned as a community of learning for almost 900 years. Today you can see the remains of a cathedral, a graveyard, and a remarkably well-preserved round tower. See Chapter 13.

- ✔ **Jerpoint Abbey (Kilkenny):** One of the best-preserved monastic ruins in the country, this 15th-century Cistercian Abbey is home to Celtic crosses and stone carvings of knights and dragons. See Chapter 14.

- ✔ **Rock of Cashel (Tipperary):** Once the province of the high kings of Munster, many of the ruins on this limestone outcropping are tied to St. Patrick, who is said to have explained the Holy Trinity to pagans on this site. See Chapter 14.

- ✔ **Gallarus Oratory (Kerry):** This tiny seventh-century church, built without any sort of mortar, is one of Dingle Peninsula's many interesting archaeological sites. See Chapter 14.

- ✔ **Dún Aengus (Galway):** Set on a sheer cliff overlooking the Atlantic Ocean, this giant, well-preserved prehistoric stone fort stretches over 4.4 hectares (11 acres). See Chapter 18.

- ✔ **Carrowmore Megalithic Cemetery and Carrowkeel Megalithic Cemetery (Sligo):** A tour of Carrowmore, the largest group of megalithic tombs in Ireland, paints a vivid picture of life on the island thousands of years ago. An exploration of Carrowkeel is otherworldly, as you hike around the vast, practically untouched collection of megalithic tombs, stopping to crawl down the passageways of several of the tombs. See Chapter 19.

The Best Scenic Drives

Ireland's landscape is so stunning that almost every drive is a scenic drive. Here's a list of my favorite excursions:

- ✔ **The Vee drive:** This drive provides panoramas of lush mountains and farmland laid out like a quilt below. See Chapter 14.

- ✔ **The coastal drive from Skibbereen to Mizen Head:** Cliffs and sea-scapes are the stars of this drive, which ends at wild-and-wooly Mizen Head, where the Atlantic waves crash on Ireland's south-westernmost point. See Chapter 15.

- ✔ **The Ring of Kerry:** Give yourself at least an entire day for this winding drive, because you'll be pulling over every couple minutes to take pictures of the ever-changing seascapes, mountain views, and charming villages along the way. I recommend getting off the Ring drive at some point to explore the beautiful mountains in the interior. See Chapter 16.

- ✔ **The Slea Head Tour on the Dingle Peninsula:** This round-trip circuit will make your jaw drop. Highlights include the towering cliffs of Slea Head, incredible views of the Atlantic Ocean and the nearby Blasket Islands, and hills covered in a patchwork of small fields. See Chapter 16.

- ✔ **The Connemara drive:** The spectacular drive west from Galway on N59 affords picture-perfect views of the silent bogs, lush wood-lands, and glistening lakes of Connemara. See Chapter 18.

- ✔ **The drive around Lough Gill:** Take along a book of Yeats's poems as you make the drive around this peaceful blue lake. The lake itself and its many islands (including the famed Lake Isle of Innisfree) feature prominently in the poet's works. See Chapter 19.

- ✔ **The Clew Bay drive:** This dazzling drive (one of my absolute favor-ites in Ireland) takes you past the pyramid-shaped peak of Croagh Patrick, through moody bogland, and along glassy Killary Fjord. See Chapter 19.

- ✔ **The peninsula north of Donegal Bay:** Make sure that you find the twisty little road to Port as you cruise around this peninsula. See Chapter 20.

- ✔ **The A2 along the Antrim coast:** As you wind along the Antrim coast, you'll pass cliffs, beautiful seascapes, small seaside towns, and the incredible Giant's Causeway. See Chapter 22.

The Best Pubs

It's no secret that the Irish have a bit of a reputation for spending long nights at the pub. Check out a few of these inviting options, and maybe you'll understand why:

- ✔ **Cobblestone (Dublin):** This is the real deal — a cozy pub filled with locals and ringing to the rafters with traditional Irish music played by excellent musicians. See Chapter 11.

- ✔ **Jack Meade's (Waterford):** Crackling fires, loud laughter, a warren of small rooms, and terrific pub food conspire to make Jack Meade's a gem in the Waterford countryside. See Chapter 14.

- ✔ **The Long Valley (Cork):** Belly up to the long bar here to drink pints, munch on giant sandwiches, and shoot the breeze with the friendly regulars. See Chapter 15.

- ✔ **The Bulman (Cork):** This pub has it all — crackling fires, good company, live traditional Irish music, great seafood dishes, and a view of beautiful Kenmare Bay. See Chapter 15.

- ✔ **Dick Mack's (Kerry):** One of Ireland's quaintest pubs, Dick Mack's used to double as a cobbler's shop, and one side of the place still holds the leather-working tools of the trade. The interior hasn't changed in years, and the music is terrific. See Chapter 16.

- ✔ **The Poet's Corner (Clare):** A warm, always-humming bar located in the Old Ground Hotel, this place offers some of the best traditional Irish music in Ennis, a town known for its formidable traditional music scene. See Chapter 17.

- ✔ **Crane Bar (Galway):** In a city full of excellent traditional Irish music, this is the place to go for the very best. See Chapter 18.

- ✔ **Nancy's (Donegal):** Cozy and welcoming, Nancy's fulfills all my fantasies of stepping into Middle Earth for an evening at a Shire pub. See Chapter 20.

- ✔ **Crown Liquor Saloon (Antrim):** This is one of the most beautiful Victorian pubs in all Ireland, outfitted with carved wood, brass fittings, and gas lamps. You'll be drooling into your Guinness. See Chapter 22.

Chapter 2

Digging Deeper into Ireland

- -

In This Chapter

▶ Taking a short course in Irish history

▶ Discovering the mythological and literary giants of Ireland

▶ Noting language differences

▶ Eating your way through Ireland

▶ Getting the lowdown on pubs

▶ Appreciating Irish music

▶ Absorbing books and movies about Ireland

- -

Sure, you need reviews of hotels, restaurants, and attractions when you travel. But for a rich experience, you also need to know about the history and culture of your destination. This chapter gives you the lowdown on Irish history, language, food and drink, music, and other facets of Irish culture.

History 101: The Main Events

Ireland has an intriguing and complex history fraught with invasions, battles, and rebellion.

Invaders welcome

From the beginning, Ireland put out a doormat welcoming invaders, or so it seems. Ireland was first inhabited by Mesolithic hunters and fishermen who appeared in the country around 7500 B.C., most likely from continental Europe. They were followed by a wave of Neolithic farmers who arrived 4,000 years later, around 3500 B.C. Around 450 B.C., or perhaps even earlier, the Celts arrived, most likely from the Iberian Peninsula. The Celts conquered the earlier settlers and spread much of the Gaelic culture and language that still thrives today. Nine hundred years later, in the fifth century A.D., Christian missionaries, including the famed St. Patrick, arrived from various parts of Europe and converted much of the Irish population to Christianity.

In the late eighth century, Norse Vikings from Denmark and Norway landed on several Irish coasts. The Vikings raided and plundered their way through Ireland, setting up coastal bases that evolved into the country's first cities — Dublin, Wexford, Waterford, Cork, and Limerick. The Vikings were routed in 1014 by the armies of High King Brian Boru, the first leader to preside over all Ireland.

Peace reigned for a century or so. But in 1169, Celtic Diarmuid MacMurrough, the dethroned king of Leinster (the southeastern portion of Ireland) called on the Anglo-Normans, under the leadership of Strongbow, to help him seize back his kingdom. The Anglo-Normans were Vikings who had settled in Normandy in France and had control over much of Britain. With their superior military, they had no trouble capturing much of Ireland for themselves. Strongbow's prize for his troubles was the hand of MacMurrough's daughter, Aoife, in marriage.

Rebels with a cause

In the 14th and 15th centuries, the Celts (also called the Gaels) rose up against both the British and the Anglo-Norman invaders. They succeeded in containing the British in an area around Dublin known as the Pale, but they had no luck in ridding the island of the powerful Norman overlords. In fact, through intermarriage and the adoption of Irish language and culture, the Normans were becoming as Irish as the Irish themselves. Some of the most popular surnames in Ireland today — Fitzgerald, Burke, Joyce — are actually Norman.

In the 16th century, the British launched a reconquest of Ireland under Henry VIII, who declared himself king of Ireland and forced the Irish chieftains to acknowledge his sovereignty. Henry's daughters, Mary and Elizabeth, sent a steady flow of British settlers into Ireland during their reigns. Due to Henry VIII's split with the church in Rome, Catholic persecution began in Ireland.

In 1601, Gaelic troops joined with a Spanish army to try to squelch the English army, but the English forces triumphed under Lord Mountjoy, and English law was introduced to much of the island, including Ulster, previously the most Gaelic part of Ireland. Defeated, many of the O'Neills and O'Donnells, the most powerful Gaelic clans in Ulster, fled from Ireland. The English government pronounced the O'Neill and O'Donnell lands forfeit to the crown and sent Protestant English and Scottish settlers to develop farms and towns in the area. Naturally, the Irish Catholic inhabitants of Ulster strongly resented the imposition of these Protestant settlers, and thousands were massacred when the Catholics rebelled in 1641. The 17th-century bitterness between the Protestant settlers and the Catholic natives is one of the roots of the modern Troubles in Northern Ireland.

In 1649, eight years after the Catholic rebellion, the ruthless Puritan English leader Oliver Cromwell arrived in Ireland with the goal of taking the whole of Ireland under English control. Cromwell's army butchered thousands; by 1652, he controlled the country. Cromwell dispossessed every Catholic landowner east of the River Shannon, whether Irish or Old English. Connacht and County Clare, west of the Shannon, were used as a "reservation" for Catholics who had not fled the country. Though Catholics caught a glimpse of hope when Catholic King James II came to the throne, it was a brief peek that ended as the Glorious Revolution brought Protestant William of Orange to the throne. James launched the unsuccessful siege of the Protestant walled city of Derry, during which the inhabitants of Derry slammed the city gates shut and remained inside for 105 days, subsisting on rats and other vermin. In what is arguably the most important battle in Irish history, James was trounced by William at the Battle of the Boyne in 1690, giving Protestant England complete control over Ireland.

Penal Laws were enacted that forbade Catholics from owning land, practicing law, holding public office, bearing arms, and even practicing Catholicism (though this last tenet was not strictly enforced). These laws were in effect for almost 100 years. They were finally repealed in 1783 due to unrest in rural areas of the country, the need for Irish Catholic recruits to fight in the American War of Independence, and the liberal philosophies of the European Enlightenment.

The French Revolution in 1789 threw kindling on the fire of rebellious feelings that were already smoldering among the Catholics; and in 1798, war between Britain and France gave Ireland a window of opportunity for another rebellion. Irishman Wolfe Tone conspired with the French to drive the British out of Ireland, but his rebellion failed, claiming more than 30,000 Irish lives. Captured by British forces, Tone slit his own throat rather than face execution by his enemies.

In 1828, 30 years after Tone's rebellion, Daniel O'Connell ran for a member of Parliament position, even though, as a Catholic, he would not be allowed to hold office. O'Connell was elected by a landslide, and the British prime minister, striving to avoid a civil war in Ireland, passed the Catholic Emancipation Act, allowing Catholics to sit as members of Parliament. O'Connell spent his time in Parliament fighting tooth and nail for the rights of Catholics, earning him the nickname "The Great Liberator." O'Connell also strove to dissolve the union between Ireland and Britain. O'Connell's progress was stopped in its tracks when the Great Famine struck in 1845. O'Connell died in 1847.

The population of Ireland, over eight million in 1841, depended on the potato as its main diet staple. When a fungus killed off potato crops for five successive years, beginning in 1845, the island was thrown into turmoil. More than one million people died of starvation; another million abandoned Ireland for the shores of the United States, beginning a stretch of Irish emigration that would keep up until the 1930s. While famine tore through the rest of Ireland, Protestant Ulster began to experience an Industrial Revolution, and Belfast blossomed from a small town into an industrial city. Catholics and Protestants both joined the working class in Belfast, and riots between the two groups, spurred by their rancorous history, were common.

The Irish flag

Ireland's flag — three thick vertical strips of green, white, and orange — was first used by Irish Nationalists in 1848. The green represents Ireland's Nationalist majority (mostly Catholic), the orange represents the Unionist minority (mostly Protestant), and the white stands for the hoped-for peace between them.

Exhausted by the famine, Ireland didn't see a new leader for almost 30 years, until the 1870s and 1880s, when Charles Stewart Parnell emerged on the scene. Parnell, Ireland's representative to the British Parliament, succeeded in uniting different factions of Irish Nationalists, and began the legislative struggle for home rule. (Ireland would have its own Parliament while still being part of Britain.) Parnell was well on his way to realizing this goal when the news broke in 1890 that he was living with the estranged wife of one of his followers. The Irish Catholic hierarchy turned against him as an adulterer, as did his fellow Nationalist members of Parliament. Parnell never regained his popularity and died in 1891.

In the 1900s, Nationalists reunited under leader John Redmond, who managed to pass a Home Rule bill in 1914. However, Redmond promised that Nationalist Ireland would support the English in World War I. Although some of his followers agreed with this plan, others did not and broke away to create the separatist Irish Volunteers. The Volunteers staged Ireland's most famous rebellion: On Easter Monday in 1916, 1,500 freedom fighters, led by Patrick Pearse and James Connolly, seized Dublin's General Post Office. They hoisted the tricolor flag from the roof of the post office, and Pearse read the Proclamation of the Irish Republic from the front steps. This rebellion led to swift retaliation by the British. After six days of battle, the rebels were overwhelmed. Connolly, Pearse, and 13 other leaders of the Rising (as the rebellion was called) were taken to Kilmainham Gaol (jail), tried, and shot. The Irish were outraged at the savage executions, and the murdered patriots became martyrs.

In 1918, two years after the Easter Rising, the Nationalist party of Sinn Fein (pronounced shin fane) won the general election in Ireland and declared an independent Irish Parliament. The British were not pleased with this turn of events, and Ireland plummeted into a civil war for independence, led by Michael Collins. A truce was reached in 1921, followed by the Anglo-Irish Treaty, which gave autonomy to 26 of Ireland's 32 counties. The remaining six counties continued on as part of the United Kingdom and became known as Northern Ireland. Many Irish, eager to finally reach peace, accepted the treaty; others, led by Eamon de Valera, refused. A civil war broke out in 1922 between the pro-treaty and anti-treaty factions. The pro-treaty side emerged victorious in May 1923, and the six counties remained part of Britain. The other 26 counties officially cut all ties with Britain when the Republic of Ireland Act was passed in 1948.

There was a nervous peace in Northern Ireland for the first half of the 20th century. However, in the late 1960s, Catholics in Northern Ireland began to campaign against religious discrimination in jobs, politics, and housing. Civil rights meetings spiraled into violence, paving the way for the creation of the Irish Republican Army (IRA), a Nationalist paramilitary group that organized several terror attacks. This was the beginning of the period known as the Troubles. Violence continued on both sides up until the Belfast Agreement (also known as the Good Friday Agreement) of 1998, when the Irish voted to make a fresh start with a new government in Belfast. Unfortunately, the new government was suspended in 2000 because paramilitary groups did not disarm by the deadline. In July 2005, the prospects for a lasting peace were strengthened when the paramilitary Provisional Irish Republican Army (PIRA) announced that it had decommissioned all weapons. Sadly, violent incidents have been cropping up again for the last few years. The climate is much better than it was during the Troubles, but it's still not solidly peaceful. For the latest on the political situation in Northern Ireland as you plan your trip, visit www.irishcentral.com/news/nuzhound.

The last decade of the 20th century saw a huge and rapid change in Ireland, as the strong Celtic Tiger economy, fueled by a booming high-tech industry, infused money into the Republic and the North. You couldn't look down a street in Dublin without seeing a building crane, and swanky new hotels popped up at a feverish rate.

What a difference a few years makes. Ireland was hit hard by the global recession. Many of those trendy hotels started to show wear and tear as fewer visitors came to Ireland, and young people have been leaving in droves to find employment abroad. As of this writing, it looks like things are on the upswing. I have my fingers crossed.

Who's Who in Irish Mythology

Some of the folks I describe in this section lived more verifiably real lives than others, but all have entered the mythology to such an extent that you're likely to hear them mentioned at some point in your trip.

- **Children of Lir:** In this legend, the wicked new wife of King Lir (pronounced leer) puts a spell on his children to turn them into swans for 900 years. There are several endings to this story; in one, the swans turn back into humans upon hearing a church bell. A sculpture depicting the Children of Lir is the centerpiece of Dublin's Garden of Remembrance, and it's illegal to kill a swan in Ireland.

- **Cuchulainn (pronounced coo-*cul*-in):** The famous mythical Celtic warrior could grow to such enormous size and strength that he could kill scores of men with one swing of a sword. Many legendary stories are told of his feats. A statue stands in Dublin's General Post Office depicting Cuchulainn in bloody action.

✔ **Queen Medb or Maeve (pronounced mave):** Cuchulainn's enemy, whom legend credits with stealing the prize bull of Ulster, among other exploits. Is she real or a myth? See the sidebar "The mystery of Queen Maeve," in Chapter 19.

✔ **Finn MacCool:** This perhaps-mythical Irish hero is immortalized in poems by his son Osian and in many Fenian ballads, named after the Fionn (also known as Fianna), professional fighters whom Finn was said to have led in the third century. Finn and his men's claims to fame are defending the country from foreign aggressors and hunting for food. Finn is frequently accompanied by his dog, Bran.

✔ **Osian (pronounced o-*sheen*):** Finn MacCool's son, a great leader and warrior, as well as a talented poet. His name means "fawn"; according to legend, his mother spent part of her life as a deer.

Who's Who in Irish Literature

The Irish are fiercely proud of their rich literary tradition (and rightly so!), and many writers have places of honor around the country. You can't go to County Sligo without tripping over sights related to poet William Butler Yeats; and repeated references to the novels of James Joyce fill Dublin. Theaters around Ireland resonate with the words of playwrights O'Casey, Shaw, Synge, Beckett, and other Irish wordsmiths.

Contemporary Irish literary luminaries include poet Seamus Heaney; playwrights Brian Friel, Conor McPherson, and Martin McDonough; and writers Roddy Doyle, Edna O'Brien, Colm Tóibín, among many, many others.

Following are some bite-size bios of the literary wonders you're most likely to hear about.

✔ **Samuel Beckett (1906–1989):** Most of playwright and novelist Beckett's work deals with lonely and bewildered people in search of an unknown something. The best-known and most performed of his plays is *Waiting for Godot,* which centers on two men waiting endlessly for the arrival of a mysterious character named Godot.

✔ **Brendan Behan (1923–1964):** Behan's youth was full of run-ins with the law, including a stint with the IRA in his teens. The playwright, columnist, and novelist is perhaps most famous for *The Borstal Boy,* a novel based on his experiences in jail and reform school; *The Quare Fellow,* a play that draws on his experiences in prison; and *The Hostage,* a play about the events surrounding an IRA member's execution.

✔ **James Joyce (1882–1941):** Though he moved to Continental Europe at age 22, Joyce's four major works — *Portrait of the Artist as a Young Man, Dubliners, Finnegan's Wake,* and *Ulysses* — are all set in Dublin. Joyce is known for his experimentation with language, and his books are rich in wordplay.

✔ **Sean O'Casey (1880–1964):** This famous playwright shocked the-atergoers with controversial plays based on his early, poverty-stricken days and the fight for Irish home rule. Best known are *Juno and the Paycock,* the story of a poor family during the 1916 Rising, and *The Plough and the Stars,* which deals with different perspectives on the 1916 Rising.

✔ **George Bernard Shaw (1856–1950):** Socialist Shaw explored moral and social problems with wit and intellect. His most famous plays include *Pygmalion,* the story of Eliza Doolittle; *Major Barbara,* about a Salvation Army major questioning charity and capitalism; and *St. Joan,* about Joan of Arc.

✔ **John Millington Synge (1871–1909):** A noted Abbey Theatre playwright, Synge is best remembered for plays that explore the rural life of western Ireland. *Riders to the Sea* focuses on life in a fishing community on the Aran Islands; in *Shadow of the Glen,* a man fakes his death in order to find out if his wife is cheating on him; and in *Playboy of the Western World,* a man is celebrated as a hero for killing his father.

✔ **Oscar Wilde (1854–1900):** Wilde is best known for his plays, including *An Ideal Husband,* a political melodrama, and *The Importance of Being Earnest,* a hilarious comedy of manners.

✔ **William Butler Yeats (1865–1939):** Poet and playwright Yeats co-founded Dublin's Abbey Theatre. Many of his poems take the landscapes and mythology of Ireland as their themes, while others riff on the struggle for Irish home rule and on love and romance.

Word to the Wise: The Local Lingo

English is the main language in use in Ireland, but between slang words, Gaelic phrases and regional accents, it can sound like a foreign tongue at times. Read these handy glossaries so that you don't need to keep one of those polite but puzzled smiles on your face while talking with locals.

The Irish language in contemporary Ireland

Irish Gaelic (usually called "Irish" in Ireland) and English are the official languages of Ireland. Almost the entire population speaks English, and about 95 percent of the population uses English as its primary language. About a million and a half of Ireland's five million residents can speak at least a few words of Irish Gaelic (the language is now taught in all public schools), and about 600,000 people use Gaelic as their first language. Gaelic-speaking areas are called *Gaeltacht* (pronounced *gale*-tokt) and are concentrated in the west of Ireland, though there are pockets elsewhere.

Irish slang translation: Yer man

In your travels, you'll probably hear people referring to *yer man* (as in, "I was talking to *yer man* the other day . . ."). You may well wonder who this incredibly popular person is. Well, he's the fella Americans call *this guy* (for example, "I was talking to *this guy* the other day . . .") and British call *this bloke*. You may also hear the feminine counterpart, *yer won*.

Learning the lingo

Some of the following terms are slang, and some are authentic Irish Gaelic. Note that in Northern Ireland, the word *wee* is peppered liberally into speech. It literally means "little," but it isn't used that way in Northern Ireland; in fact, you may hear a sentence like "Oh, I used to live in New York, down by the wee Empire State Building." Also see Chapter 7 for terms related to driving in Ireland.

- **Cheers:** Thanks.
- **Class:** Great, as in "Lauren is class at playing the tin whistle."
- **Craic, crack (pronounced crak):** Good times; fun (Gaelic).
- **Dear:** Expensive.
- **Dodgy:** Suspect, as in "I wouldn't eat those clams. They smell dodgy."
- **Fáilte (pronounced *fal*-cha):** Welcome (Gaelic).
- **Fir:** Men (Gaelic, sometimes used on bathroom doors).
- **Footpath:** Sidewalk.
- **Garda:** Police officer. (Plural is *gardaí* [pronounced *gar*-dee].)
- **Go away (or go 'way):** Wow!
- **Grand:** Great, as in "Would you like some more Guinness?" "Thanks, that'd be grand."
- **Hash:** Pound sign (on telephone keypads and the like).
- **Lads:** A group of people, regardless of gender (often used to address a group, like "y'all" in the American South).
- **Lift:** Elevator.
- **Mna (pronounced muh-*nah*):** Women (Gaelic, sometimes used on bathroom doors).
- **Off-license:** Liquor store.
- **Petrol:** Gasoline.

- ✔ **Poitín (pronounced pot-*cheen*):** Moonshine; homemade whiskey.

- ✔ **Ring:** To telephone, as in "I'll ring you later."

- ✔ **Stroke:** Slash (as in "girls/women").

- ✔ **Quay (pronounced key):** Waterfront; wharf.

- ✔ **Sin é (pronounced shin-*aye*):** Done (Gaelic).

- ✔ **Slainte! (pronounced *slon*-cha):** Cheers! (Gaelic).

- ✔ **Take-away:** Fast food; to go.

- ✔ **Till:** Cash register.

- ✔ **Tins:** Canned goods.

- ✔ **Windscreen:** Windshield.

Avoiding misunderstandings

In Ireland (especially Northern Ireland), holding your pointer and middle fingers up in a *V* with your palm facing inward is the same as raising your middle finger to someone. Careful when ordering two pints!

The following words and phrases have definitions that are quite different in Ireland than they are in other parts of the world:

- ✔ **Cute hoor (pronounced whore):** In Ireland, *cute* is often used to mean someone who is sly or devious, and a *cute hoor* is a devious person. The phrase is often used to describe politicians.

- ✔ **Fag:** Cigarette.

- ✔ **Fanny:** Female genitalia.

- ✔ **Flaming:** Drunk.

- ✔ **Ride:** Sex or an attractive person. So, if you're looking for someone to drive you somewhere, ask for a lift.

- ✔ **Take the piss out of (as in, "We were just taking the piss out of him"):** Messing with or teasing; other terms for this are *slagging* or *taking the mickey.*

Taste of Ireland: Irish Cuisine and Dining

If you think of shepherd's pie and Guinness stew when you think of Irish cuisine, you're right. But that's just a tiny bit of the story: A stroll down a row of restaurants is like paging through a book about the world's cuisines, featuring everything from pasta to curries to sushi.

Along with these ethnic eateries is a bevy of restaurants creating New Irish cuisine — innovative dishes that showcase the best of Ireland's fresh produce and incorporate international influences. Typical dishes?

How about fresh Irish salmon served with wasabi-infused mashed pota-toes or local free-range beef with a Thai curry sauce?

If you're in the market for traditional Irish dishes, your best bet is a pub, where you find hearty offerings such as Irish stew, thick vegetable soups, and ploughman's lunches (cheese, pickles, and bread). But even pub grub reflects the influences of the last few decades. The dishes are better than ever, many chefs use as much local produce as possible, and international twists are found in many dishes. Most traditional pubs also squeeze salads and other healthy options onto the menu.

 If you have your heart set on eating at a posh restaurant in one of the larger cities during the summer or on a weekend (or on a summer week-end!), making reservations is a good idea.

See Chapter 24 for my top ten traditional Irish meal and beverage suggestions.

Minding your manners: Irish meal times and dining customs

You may notice that the Irish, like many Europeans, keep their knives in their right hands and lift food on their forks with their left hands.

In Ireland, breakfast begins around 7 a.m. and finishes at 10 or 11 a.m. Lunch goes from noon to about 3 p.m., with 1 to 2 p.m. being the busiest time. Dinner is usually served from about 6 to 10 p.m., sometimes going until 11 p.m. on weekends.

Your server won't bring the check (called the "bill" in Ireland), until you ask for it.

For information on tipping, see Chapter 5.

Deciphering the menu

Here are a few food terms that you may not have run up against before:

- ✔ **Aubergines:** Eggplants.
- ✔ **Bangers:** Sausages.
- ✔ **Boxty:** Potato pancakes filled with meats and vegetables.
- ✔ **Champ:** Mashed potatoes with green onions.
- ✔ **Chipper:** Fast-food fish-and-chips shop.
- ✔ **Chips:** French fries.
- ✔ **Colcannon:** Mashed potatoes with cabbage.
- ✔ **Coriander:** Cilantro.
- ✔ **Courgette:** Zucchini.

- **Crisps:** Potato chips.

- **Fry or fry up:** A traditional Irish fried breakfast.

- **Darne:** A slice of fish (often on the bone).

- **Dublin coddle:** A thick stew made with sausages, bacon, onions, and potatoes.

- **Goujons:** Small strips or chunks of chicken, fish, or red meat.

- **Mange tout:** Snap peas.

- **Marie Rose sauce:** A ketchup-and-mayonnaise-based sauce.

- **Mash:** Mashed potatoes.

- **Minerals:** Soft drinks.

- **Prawns:** Shrimp.

- **Rasher:** Canadian-style bacon. (American-style bacon is referred to as *crispy bacon* or *American bacon*.)

- **Rocket:** Arugula (a gourmet salad green).

- **Salad:** Aside from its universal meaning, *salad* also indicates a garnish of lettuce and tomato on a sandwich.

- **Shepherd's pie:** Ground beef and vegetables topped with mashed potatoes.

- **Sultanas:** Similar to raisins.

- **Take-away:** Carryout or takeout food.

- **Tray bake:** Fresh-baked brownies, blondies, lemon squares, and so on.

Living the Pub Life

Visiting Ireland without setting foot into a pub would be like going to Egypt and missing the pyramids. Pubs serve as the beating heart of communities around Ireland, offering great *craic* (fun), witty conversation, laughter, fabulous music (often traditional Irish), great pub food, and, of course, drinks.

Pubs originated centuries ago, when groups of friends would gather in someone's living room or kitchen to chat and perhaps play some music, dance, and drink some home-brewed liquor. Word of the friendliest places spread, attracting more and more people, and the houses gradually became known as *public houses,* shortened to *pubs.*

There is as wide a variety of pubs as there are folks who drink in them: music pubs; literary pubs; sports pubs; actors' pubs; even political pubs, where revolutionaries met in secret to plan uprisings. Pub designs also run the gamut. Most familiar are those shiny Victorian dark-wood pubs that show up in cities around the world. But there are also pubs that look like someone's well-loved living room, with tattered, mismatched furniture and dusty books; and, on the other end of the spectrum, modern, streamlined pubs that look an awful lot like clubs.

In many pubs, you may notice small partitioned areas called *snugs.* These small compartments are great places for quiet conversation or to get away from the crowd. But that's not what they were for originally. Until the late 1960s, it was impolite for women to drink in public, so they were confined to the snugs.

Pubs can now make their own hours, which means that many are staying open later than they used to. Most pubs are open all day, closing between midnight and 2 a.m.

Paying attention to pub etiquette

If you're drinking with a group, think rounds. Everyone (including guests) takes turns buying drinks for the group, even if "the group" is a bunch of people you've just met.

The larger size glass is called a *pint,* and the smaller one (which measures a half-pint) is called a *glass.*

Bartenders don't expect a tip unless they've provided table service. Instead, it's customary to buy the bartender a drink every once in a while.

The Irish version of "cheers" is *slainte* (pronounced *slon*-cha), meaning "health."

If you're hanging out in a traditional music session and someone asks you to perform, he probably really means it. If you're up for it, recite a poem or sing a song — doesn't matter if it's not Irish. Also, although clapping is great after a tune is finished, it can sometimes be distracting to musicians if many people are clapping along in rhythm.

There are worse things than being locked in a pub

Very occasionally, a publican decides to allow patrons to stay in a pub after closing hours. This is called a *lock-in* because the doors are locked and the curtains pulled so that no one else can come in and allegedly so that the *gardaí* (police) will not think that anyone is in the pub. Lock-ins are great fun and an excellent way to get to know locals. One of my best nights (mornings?) in Ireland was spent in a pub in a tiny Clare town, learning new Irish tunes from several fantastic musicians until about 5 a.m. Lock-ins are much more common in small towns and rural pubs than in big-city pubs.

Guinness versus Murphy's

Wondering what the difference is between Guinness and Murphy's Stout? Employees at St. James's Gate, where Guinness is brewed, have an idea. According to rumor, a drawing inside the brewery shows a donkey drinking from a trough labeled "Guinness." Behind the donkey is another trough, into which the animal is urinating. This trough, of course, is labeled "Murphy's." I assume Murphy's has its own ideas about its rival.

Savoring the black stuff: Guinness

The pints of Guinness in Ireland taste nothing like Guinness elsewhere. Call it the home-court advantage, or credit the fact that the stuff is as fresh as all get-out in Ireland, but it's a fact that the Guinness you drink in Ireland is a high cut above the Guinness anywhere else.

Five words to live by: A good pint takes time. Barkeeps draw the pint about three-quarters and let it sit for about two minutes. Then, by pushing the tap forward so the stout comes out even more slowly than the first draw, they fill the glass the rest of the way (some fill the glass in a three-step process). This is how you get the best creamy, white head on top. Even when you finally get the pint in your hands, don't drink just yet. Wait until it has settled completely and turned a deep ruby, almost black. You also can tell a good pint of Guinness by the circle of foam that it leaves on the inside of the glass with each sip.

Sampling other Irish brews

As hard is it may be to believe, Guinness doesn't have a complete monopoly on Irish beer. Some of the other popular Irish brews are Harp, a light; Smithwick's, a dark ale; Kilkenny, a red ale with a sweet malty taste and a creamy head like Guinness; Murphy's Amber, a light ale; Murphy's Stout, which is a bit sweeter than Guinness; and Bulmers Cider, a sweet, entirely too drinkable hard cider.

Sipping some Irish whiskey

Monks did a lot for Ireland. They painstakingly crafted the Book of Kells. They protected Irish antiquities during invasions. But ask your average man on an Irish street, and he may say that the best thing monks did for Ireland was invent whiskey. Irish whiskey is known all over the world for its smoothness and quality, and it has brought Ireland huge revenues over the centuries. The original Gaelic term for whiskey, *uisce beatha* (pronounced *ish*-ka *ba*-ha) means "water of life."

Irish whiskey has a distinctive smoothness, which results from triple-distillation (American whiskey is distilled only once; Scotch, twice).

If you're interested in the distillation of Irish whiskey, three historic and popular distilleries are open for tours: **Old Bushmills Distillery,** County Antrim (☎ 028-2073-3218); **Old Jameson Distillery,** Dublin (☎ 01-872-5566); and **Old Midleton Distillery,** Cork (☎ 021-461-3594).

Sampling poteen

You may have heard of a potent potable called poteen and wondered just what it is. Well, *poteen* (or potcheen, or poitín in Gaelic) is a distilled, clear, potato-based whiskey that's basically the Irish equivalent of moonshine, originally made from potatoes. Though it has been produced illegally since being banned in 1661, some companies have started to produce a legal poteen (which still contains a huge amount of alcohol), so you may see it around Ireland.

Appreciating Irish Music

This should say something about the importance of music in Ireland: It's the only nation in the world with a musical instrument as a national symbol. The Tara Harp appears on all official documents of the Irish government.

Traditional Irish music (often called *trad*) has been around for centuries and is an integral part of Irish culture, woven into the daily lives of many Irish people. In fact, you'd be hard-pressed to find an Irish person who doesn't know at least a few tunes or songs. Irish traditional music is a living tradition, and new tunes and songs are constantly incorporated into the repertoire.

The best place to hear Irish music is in a pub. Offerings range from scheduled ballad singers to pick-up traditional instrumental *sessions,* sometimes open to anyone who shows up. Ballad singers sing a range of Irish songs, accompanying themselves on guitar, from upbeat tunes about a night of boisterous drinking to slow songs about the death of an Irish freedom fighter. Instrumental sessions can range from small, planned, miked sessions to giant acoustic sessions open to anyone who wants to play. In instrumental sessions, you often find *tin whistles* (also called *penny whistles* — thin, recorder-type instruments), wooden Irish flutes, *fiddles* (the same as violins; just played differently), *bodhráns* (handheld goatskin drums; pronounced *bow*-rons), mandolins, *uilleann pipes* (the Irish version of bagpipes; pronounced *ill*-un), *concertinas* (small accordion-type instruments), and accordions. Other instruments that show up include *bones* (animal bones used for rhythmic accompaniment), guitars, banjos, harmonicas, *bouzuki* (a type of mandolin), and harps.

If you've been turned on to Irish traditional music and you want to find sessions near your home, check out the geographic search feature on www.thesession.org.

Turlough O'Carolan

Turlough O'Carolan (1670–1738) is a famous harper and composer (sometimes referred to simply as "Carolan"). After smallpox blinded him in his teens, he learned to play the harp, and for the rest of his years, he traveled throughout Ireland as an itinerant musician and bard, composing tunes for patrons across Ireland. He wrote more than 200 compositions that are still played today, more than 300 years later.

Background Check: Recommended Books and Movies

Ireland has produced a wealth of wonderful literary figures and has its share of great filmmakers. The books and movies in the following sections should enhance your appreciation and understanding of the island. Also see "Who's Who in Irish Literature," earlier in this chapter.

Fiction

For a look at Dublin in the beginning of the 20th century, wrap your mind around the works of James Joyce, including his famous novels *A Portrait of the Artist as a Young Man, Finnegan's Wake,* and *Ulysses,* and his short-story collection, *Dubliners.*

Roddy Doyle offers a funny and sometimes poignant look at contemporary Ireland in his novels, which include *Paddy Clarke Ha Ha Ha; A Star Called Henry;* and the trilogy *The Commitments* (the basis of the movie), *The Snapper,* and *The Van.*

Other contemporary novels to check out include the following:

- *Finbar's Hotel,* edited by Dermot Bolger, is composed of seven intertwining short stories by seven well-known Irish novelists.
- Niall Williams's *Four Letters of Love* is a mystical, poetic, romantic novel set in Galway.
- *Juno and Juliet,* by Julian Gough, is a beautifully written contemporary novel about a pair of twins away for college in Galway.

Autobiography

If you haven't read it yet, pick up *Angela's Ashes,* Frank McCourt's wrenching memoir about his impoverished childhood in Limerick.

Written by former IRA member Ernie O'Malley, *On Another Man's Wound: A Personal History of Ireland's War of Independence* is a fascinating collection of memoirs about Ireland's fight for independence between 1916 and 1921.

Starting your Irish music collection

The following four CDs are a great beginning — or addition — to your Irish musical library:

✔ *Lake Effect: Liz Carroll* (2002): Chicago-born Liz Carroll is one of my favorite fiddle players. She uses stunning ornamentation and variations in her playing, and composes fabulous new tunes.

✔ *Music at Matt Molloy's* (1992): This CD is as close as you can get to an Irish music session in your living room without inviting a bunch of musicians over. Crack open a can of Guinness and listen to the wild reels, jigs, and songs, all recorded live in Chieftain musician Matt Molloy's Pub in Westport, County Mayo.

✔ *Solas* (1996): This CD features some of the most beautiful and spirited playing of Irish supergroup Solas. Singer Karan Casey's voice is as clear and pure as spring water, giving life to the English and Gaelic songs that pop up between the instrumental tunes.

✔ *The Well-Tempered Bow: Liz and Yvonne Kane* (2002): This CD, by fiddle-playing sisters from Connemara, contains lovely tunes played with grace and style.

Great Blasket Island, off the coast of the Dingle Peninsula, was home to a small and very traditional Irish community up until the 1950s. This island of storytellers produced several excellent writers. In *Peig: The Autobiography of Peig Sayers of the Great Blasket Island,* the eponymous author relates the hardships and joys of life on the island. *Twenty Years A-Growing,* by Maurice O'Sullivan, is a beautifully written, innocent book about growing up on Great Blasket.

McCarthy's Bar: A Journey of Discovery in the West of Ireland, by Pete McCarthy, is a hilarious travelogue about journalist Pete McCarthy's ramblings around Ireland.

Also in the humorous vein, *Round Ireland with a Fridge,* by Tony Hawks, is about, well, a guy who travels around Ireland with a refrigerator.

Poetry

Poetry is where you hit the jackpot in Ireland. The gorgeous, mystical poems of William Butler Yeats are a wonderful introduction to the mythology, history, and landscapes of Ireland. *Collected Poems: 1909–1962* is the best anthology of Yeats's work.

For beautifully spun poems about farming, rural life, and the Irish landscape, pick up Patrick Kavanagh's *Collected Poems.*

Seamus Heaney's poems about the land are rhythmic and powerful, sounding like music when read aloud. *Opened Ground: Selected Poems 1966–1996* is a great sampler of his poems, and *The Haw Lantern, Death of a Naturalist, The Spirit Level,* and *District and Circle* — all collections — are gems.

History and politics

A Short History of Ireland, by John O'Beirne Ranelagh, gives an overview of Irish history from pre-Christian times to 1998. If you'd like something more comprehensive, pick up the *Oxford History of Ireland* by R. F. Foster. For a look at Irish nationalism, check out *The Green Flag* by Robert Kee.

There are quite a few books out about the political situation in Northern Ireland. Among the best are *We Wrecked the Place,* by Jonathan Stevenson, which features interviews with both Loyalist and Unionist militants, and *The Troubles: Ireland's Ordeal 1966–1996 and the Search for Peace,* by Tim Pat Coogan, a history with a Republican slant.

How the Irish Saved Civilization, by Thomas Cahill, is a lively history of how Irish monks and scribes preserved the great written works of the West when the rest of Europe was immersed in the Dark Ages.

Movies

The Quiet Man (1952) is a version of Shakespeare's *The Taming of the Shrew,* set in a small Irish village. John Wayne plays a boxer returning to the village to woo beautiful Maureen O'Hara. In *Ryan's Daughter* (1970), filmed on the Dingle Peninsula, a married woman grapples with her love for a World War I British officer.

On the comedy front, *The Commitments* (1990) is the often-humorous story of a motley crew of working-class Dubliners who form a soul band. You'll laugh through *Waking Ned Devine* (1998), which captures a tiny Irish village turned upside down when one of their own wins the lottery and then promptly dies. *The Boys and Girls of County Clare* (2003) is a funny, quirky, and sweet film about two brothers competing against each other in a traditional Irish music competition. All the great traditional music featured is reason enough to watch the movie.

The Secret of Roan Inish (1996), a magical film that kids and adults alike enjoy, centers on a *selkie* — a half-woman–half-seal creature from Celtic mythology — and her impact on an Irish family. In the same magical realism vein, *Into the West* (1992) tells the story of two Irish gypsy boys who travel from the slums of Dublin to the west of Ireland in pursuit of their lost horse.

For a realistic and sweet look at Dublin today, rent *Once* (2006), a modern-day realistic musical (with a gorgeous soundtrack) about two young Dubliners who build a relationship through music.

Quite a few excellent movies have been made about Irish politics. *Michael Collins* (1996) depicts the life of Collins, leader of the IRA, from the Easter Uprising of 1916 to his assassination six years later. *In The Name of the Father* (1993) deals with a man wrongly convicted for an IRA bombing. *The Boxer* (1997) is the story of an ex-IRA man and former boxer building a new life in Belfast. *The Wind That Shakes the Barley* (2006) is an excellent film about two brothers during the Irish War of Independence (1921–1922) and the subsequent Civil War (1922–1923).

Chapter 3

Deciding When and Where to Go

*W*ould you rather gaze at the rainbows that show up during the spring in Ireland or enjoy the solitude of the countryside during the winter? Do you want to experience Galway's Arts Festival in July or Cork City's Jazz Festival in October? This chapter can help you decide when to visit Ireland and gives you tips for planning your itinerary.

Going Everywhere You Want to Be

Should you fly into Shannon or Dublin? Is Northern Ireland worth a visit? This section is designed to help you make informed choices about where to spend your precious vacation time.

Experiencing the vibrant Dublin area

People often fly into Dublin airport and set off for the western part of the country before their plane even comes to a complete stop. Big mistake! **Dublin,** with its restaurants, shops, clubs, pubs, and museums, is a vibrant city with plenty to hold your attention (see Chapter 11). South and west of Dublin, counties **Wicklow** and **Kildare** (see Chapter 13) offer green hills, loads of outdoor activities, and some of the most beautiful gardens in Ireland. And just north of Dublin, counties **Meath** and **Louth** contain magnificent prehistoric ruins (see Chapter 12).

Touring the southeastern counties

The southeastern counties of **Wexford, Waterford, Kilkenny,** and **Tipperary** offer the famous House of Waterford Crystal, the bustling harbor town of Wexford, the medieval streets and storybook castle of

Kilkenny Town, verdant farmland, the 800-year-old Rock of Cashel, and more. Sound good? It is — read Chapter 14 to find out more.

Swinging by the southern and southwestern counties

Cork City is a bustling place, with terrific restaurants and a healthy arts scene, plus an array of diverse attractions nearby, including a wildlife park and the Blarney Stone. West County Cork offers quaint towns, including **Kinsale,** an upscale seaside spot know for great food, plus stunning cliff, beach, and island scenery without big crowds.

County Kerry has long been Ireland's hottest tourist spot, offering awe-inspiring vistas of the sea, cliffs, and green mountains (often viewed on a drive around the **Ring of Kerry** or the **Dingle Peninsula**), plus a number of lively towns and a rich offering of Gaelic culture.

Wandering the western counties

The West offers the wonderful city of **Galway,** with its great restaurants and pubs and hot arts scene. Then there's the incredible scenery, including the **Cliffs of Moher** in **Clare;** the wild, mountain-filled landscape of **Connemara;** the moonscape of the Burren; the woods, lakes, and beaches of **Sligo;** and the craggy coastline of **Donegal.**

Rambling through Northern Ireland

When you cross that invisible border between the Republic and Northern Ireland, the first thing you're likely to notice is that you don't notice anything different. The landscape is as green, and the people are as friendly. Highlights are the rolling **Mourne Mountains,** the spectacular **North Antrim** coast, the hopping city of **Belfast,** and the history-rich city of **Derry.**

Scheduling Your Time

Check out Chapter 4 for some suggested itineraries.

I recommend touring Ireland with a car and moving from place to place over the course of your vacation. If you take this approach, plan your itinerary so that you make a circuit, starting and finishing in the city where you arrive and depart Ireland.

 If you want to visit both the East and the West of Ireland and you have limited time, I highly recommend flying into Dublin and out of Shannon, or vice versa.

Revealing the Secrets of the Seasons

This section presents the highlights and drawbacks of the four seasons.

Summer

The most popular and arguably the best time to tour Ireland is the summer.

Summer is great because

- ✔ Ireland is just plain gorgeous during this time of year. Temperatures often stay comfortably warm and breezy during the day and drop to that perfect light-sweater temperature at night. Don't hold me to this forecast — you'll still get caught in the rain, but it will be a more bearable experience in summer.

- ✔ Summer is when all attractions are open and offer the longest hours; some attractions close during the off season.

But keep in mind that

- ✔ Many major attractions, hotels, and restaurants are likely to be jam-packed. If you're averse to crowds, this is not the time to go.

- ✔ Lodging prices are at their highest during this time.

Fall

Fall is probably the most underrated time to visit Ireland — days are mild, with not too much rain, and most of the seasonal attractions are open through the end of September.

Fall is great because

- ✔ In late September or early October, hotel prices start to drop. Even some restaurants offer menus with lower prices.

- ✔ You won't find the overwhelming crowds you do in summer. Plus, you're more likely to have the chance to hang out with Irish folks, because they're back from their summer holidays.

But keep in mind that

- ✔ Weather can be a little dicey sometimes, with cold temperatures and rain beginning to settle in.

- ✔ Some attractions close or limit their opening hours after August or September.

Winter

Although winter is not the ideal time to travel to Ireland, there are a few benefits to going in this harsh season.

Winter is great because

- ✔ Prices are at their lowest all across the country, and you're likely to find the cheapest fares of the year to get to the country.

- ✔ You're liable to have the run of the country. And the landscape is still beautiful — winter doesn't take as hard a toll on Ireland's plants and trees as it does in many areas of North America.

But keep in mind that

- ✔ The temperature doesn't dip to extreme lows, but Ireland's winter forecast is often cold, rainy, and windy.

- ✔ Lots of places close (or have shorter hours) for the season, including many attractions and some small hotels and B&Bs.

Spring

Spring is a fantastic time to travel in Ireland.

Spring is great because

- ✔ The warmer temperatures, flower-filled scenery, and longer days combine to make wonderful circumstances for touring the country.

- ✔ The locals are fresh from their own break from visitors and are ready to start playing host.

But keep in mind that

- ✔ The weather can be rainy in the spring (though rain showers usually last only part of the day).

- ✔ Some attractions and B&Bs are not open yet, and some still have abbreviated hours.

Walking on Sunshine and Singing in the Rain: Ireland's Climate

Ireland has a pretty moderate climate; it's rare to get a scorching summer day or a bitterly cold winter day. Table 3-1 lists the monthly average high and low temperatures and precipitation.

The key to dressing for Ireland is layers because, as the Irish like to say, you often end up getting all four seasons in one day.

From the true-stereotypes file: It rains often. No matter what time of the year you go, chances are slim that you'll make it back without having an encounter with a shower, so pack a raincoat or umbrella. Rain falls most often in winter, and the West is the wettest area of Ireland.

Table 3-1	Ireland's Average Monthly Temperatures and Precipitation											
	Jan	Feb	Mar	Apr	May	June	July	Aug	Sept	Oct	Nov	Dec
High (°F/°C)	46/8	47/8	51/10	55/13	60/15	65/18	67/20	67/19	63/17	57/14	51/10	47/8
Low (°F/°C)	34/1	35/2	37/3	39/4	43/6	48/9	52/11	51/11	48/9	43/6	39/4	37/3
Rainfall (in./cm)	2.8/ 7.0	2.0/ 5.0	2.1/ 5.4	2.0/ 5.1	2.2/ 5.5	2.2/ 5.6	2.0/ 5.0	2.8/ 7.1	2.6/ 6.6	2.8/ 7.0	2.5/ 6.4	3.0/ 7.6

Weather and temperature aren't the only factors involved in deciding when to go. The amount of daylight varies greatly from season to season. Ireland is situated at such a high latitude that summer days are blissfully long (sunset as late as 11 p.m.), but winter days are short (sunset as early as 4:30 p.m.). *Remember:* The more daylight there is, the more sights you get to see.

Perusing a Calendar of Festivals and Events

Just about any time you visit Ireland, some sort of event or festival is sure to be going on. I've sorted through and picked the highlights. You may notice the absence of January and February on the list in this section. These two months are the slowest in Ireland in terms of festivals and events.

Dates often fluctuate from year to year, so I generally list the rough time of the month when the event occurs, rather than the specific dates. For dates, call the event's number or visit its Web site.

Also, check the months before and after the one that you'll be in Ireland, as many festivals are on the cusp of two months, and some (such as the Wicklow Gardens Festival) stretch over several months.

Sports fans: Check out the golf, horse-racing, hiking, and fishing sections in Chapter 9 for events of particular interest to you.

March

The feast day of the patron saint of Ireland is celebrated at the **St. Patrick's Festival** (☎ 01-676-3205; www.stpatricksday.ie), a six-day festival of music, street theater, and fireworks, with a huge parade down O'Connell Street. Usually begins on March 12, with the parade falling on March 17.

Irish dancers from around the world compete in the **World Irish Dancing Championships** (☎ 01-814-6298; www.worldirishdancing.com). Location varies. Late March or early April.

April

The **Pan Celtic Festival** (www.panceltic.ie) celebrates all the Celtic nations and features music, dancing, sports, parades, and more. Location varies. Late April or early May.

May

During the **Wicklow Gardens Festival** (☎ 0404-20-070; www.visitwicklow.ie/gardens), many beautiful private gardens and estates open to visitors on select dates. May through August.

Stand rough-side to the world's most famous masters at the **Irish Open.** This golf championship attracts the best of the best. The venue changes from year to year, so check online or with the Irish Tourist Board. Mid- to late May.

Smithwick's Cat Laughs Comedy Festival (☎ 056-776-3837; www.thecatlaughs.com), in Kilkenny, features stand-up comedians from all over the world. Late May or early June.

June

Classical music by internationally renowned musicians is presented in beautiful buildings and mansions during the **KBC Music in Great Irish Houses** (☎ 01-664-2822; www.musicgreatirishhouses.com), in various locations around Ireland. Mid-June.

Overlapping with the famous Bloomsday celebration, the **Dublin Writers Festival** (☎ 01-222-5455; www.dublinwritersfestival.com) honors writers from all over the world with readings by Irish and visiting writers, a poetry slam, a jazz and poetry night, and events planned specifically for children. Early June.

Dublin's **Bloomsday Festival** (☎ 01-605-7700; www.visitdublin.com/bloomsday) commemorates Leopold Bloom, the main character in James Joyce's 900-plus page novel *Ulysses,* which takes place in Dublin on June 16, 1904. Guided walks take in Joyce-related sights. June 16.

Dublin's **Darklight Festival** (☎ 01-445-6483; www.darklight.ie) presents creative new films, with a special emphasis on animation. Mid- or late June.

Held at the Curragh Racecourse in County Kildare, the **Dubai Duty Free Irish Derby** (☎ 045-441-205; www.curragh.ie) is Ireland's version of the Kentucky Derby. Book tickets as far in advance as possible. Late June.

July

Oxegen (www.oxegen.ie), held in County Kildare, is a huge multiday outdoor summer rock festival. Mid-July.

Galway Arts Festival (☎ 091-509-700; www.galwayartsfestival.ie) and **Galway Races** (☎ 091-753-870; www.galwayraces.com) are both held in Galway City. The Arts Festival boasts two weeks of terrific music, theater, visual arts, and more. The famous Galway Races follows the Arts Festival. Second half of July.

August

The **Dublin Horse Show** (☎ 01-668-0866; www.dublinhorseshow.com) showcases the best-bred Irish horses, and features jumping competitions (for the horses) and plenty of balls and celebrations (for the people). Early August.

The **Kilkenny Arts Festival** (☎ 056-775-2175; www.kilkennyarts.ie) features all sorts of music, films, readings, visual arts, and more. Early to mid-August.

The **Puck Fair** (☎ 066-976-2366; www.puckfair.ie) is three days of parades, concerts, street entertainment, and general debauchery in the small town of Killorglin. The festivities center on the crowning of "King Puck," a wild goat captured by locals before the fair. August 10 through August 12.

The **Rose of Tralee International Festival** (☎ 066-712-1322; www.roseoftralee.ie) consists of five days of concerts, entertainment, horse races, and a beauty pageant to pick the new Rose of Tralee. Late August.

September

Lisdoonvarna (☎ 065-707-4005; www.matchmakerireland.com) is a huge singles festival, featuring lots of music, dancing, and matchmaking. Throughout September.

Tickets to the live matches of the **All-Ireland Hurling and Football Finals** (☎ 01-819-2300; www.crokepark.ie and www.gaa.ie), held at Croke Park in Drumcondra, outside Dublin, are virtually impossible to get, but the games are televised, and the excitement shouldn't be missed. Get thee to a pub. Mid-September.

Besides eating, events at the **Galway Oyster Festival** (☎ 091-587-992; www.galwayoysterfest.com) include dancing, an oyster-shucking competition, an oyster tasting, and more. Late September.

Ireland: Home of Halloween

Many of the traditions that exist around Halloween originated among the Celts thousands of years ago. The Celts marked the beginning of winter on November 1, and they believed that the boundaries between the spirit world and the living world were more permeable than usual at this time. In order to scare off the spirits, many Celts wore masks (the roots of our contemporary costume tradition). And, in order to satisfy the spirits, many would leave offerings of food by the entrances to their homes (the origin of today's treats).

October

The **Kinsale International Gourmet Festival** (☎ 021-477-3571; www. kinsalerestaurants.com), held in the foodie town of Kinsale, County Cork, features special menus at local restaurants, plus visiting star chefs. Mid-October.

The **Belfast Festival at Queen's** (☎ 028-9033-4455; www.belfast festival.com) is an all-out arts festival hosted by Queen's University, featuring ballet, dance, film, opera, jazz, and traditional and classical music. Mid- to late October.

The popular **Wexford Festival Opera** (☎ 053-912-2400; www.wexford opera.com), in Wexford Town, features performances of 18th-, 19th-, and 20th-century operas, plus classical concerts. Mid- to late October.

The **Guinness Cork Jazz Festival** (www.guinnessjazzfestival.com), in Cork City, has an excellent lineup of top jazz musicians. Late October.

Halloween (Samhain) is celebrated with fireworks, bonfires, costumes, and the eating of *barnbrack* (fruit bread). To find out where the festivities will occur, just look for the field or lot where kids are stacking up wood scraps. The people of Derry and the people of Dublin are expert Halloween revelers. October 31.

November

A wide array of films is shown all over Cork City during the **Corona Cork Film Festival** (☎ 021-427-1711; www.corkfilmfest.org). Mid-November.

December

On **St. Stephen's Day,** people all over Ireland have been reviving the old tradition of "hunting the wren." In past centuries, groups of boys would chase down and kill a wren, and then parade it from house to house while singing songs and collecting money and treats. Usually, the money would be used to hold a large dance for the entire village. Nowadays, kids and adults travel from house to house with a fake or caged wren, playing music, singing, and collecting money for charities or community projects. December 26.

Chapter 4

Following an Itinerary: Four Great Options

*I*reland is a jewel box, with vibrant cities, charming towns, and stunning landscapes and seascapes. If you're overwhelmed by the bounty of choices and the different routes around the country, the four itineraries in this chapter may help provide some structure.

These itineraries are intended for travelers with a car, but you can follow them by bus as long as you keep on top of the schedules.

Seeing Ireland's Highlights in One Week: The Whirlwind Tour

This itinerary takes you through many places that are on the beaten visitor track, so if you prefer to visit remote, untouched places, this isn't the route for you.

Day 1: Dublin

Fly into **Dublin** (most flights arrive in the morning). Get settled in your hotel or B&B, and then visit the **Dublin Tourism Centre,** if you'd like to scope out some free literature on day trips, tours, and so on. Head over to **Trinity College** to see the **Book of Kells** and explore the campus. If you like, take the **Historical Walking Tour** that leaves from the front gates of Trinity. Grab a quick lunch, and then catch the **Dublin Bus Tour;** it has narration, and allows you to hop on and off at the top sights in Dublin. As the name implies, you can hop off the bus to explore an attraction and then continue your journey on a later bus. Highlights of the bus tour include the **Guinness Brewery,** the **National Museum,** and **St. Stephen's Green.** After your bus tour, have dinner before heading to

Oliver St. John Gogarty's Pub for the **Musical Pub Crawl,** or to Duke's Bar to begin the **Literary Pub Crawl.** See Chapter 11.

Day 2: Dublin to Kinsale

Pick up your rental car and head out early in the morning through Wicklow, perhaps stopping to take in beautiful **Powerscourt Gardens** and peaceful **Glendalough.** Make your way to the seaside town of **Kinsale** for a terrific dinner.

Day 3: Kinsale to Killarney

Head off to Killarney in the morning, possibly spending some time on the **Beara Peninsula** or the **Sheep's Head Peninsula** along the way. Check into your hotel, and then set out to explore gorgeous **Killarney National Park.** For more on County Kerry, turn to Chapter 16.

Day 4: Killarney to Dingle

Drive up to the beautiful **Dingle Peninsula,** where I recommend taking the **Slea Head Drive.** Before flopping into bed, check out the traditional music scene in town. For information on County Kerry, see Chapter 16.

Day 5: Dingle Peninsula to Galway City

Right after breakfast, make your way north (use the Tarbert-Kilrush ferry to cut down on driving time) to the **Cliffs of Moher.** Spend the afternoon exploring the wildflower-studded Burren, and then drive to Galway City for a great dinner and some excellent traditional Irish music at the **Crane Bar.** See Chapters 17 and 18.

Day 6: Galway City to Connemara

Leave Galway City early to give yourself plenty of time to explore the breathtaking **Connemara** landscape. Spend the night in the lively town of **Clifden** — the Dolphin Beach House is well worth the splurge for your last night in Ireland.

Day 7: Connemara to Shannon

Head back to Shannon for your flight home.

Seeing Ireland's Highlights in One Week: The Relaxed Tour

The previous one-week tour is jam-packed. If you want a more leisurely weeklong visit, I recommend spending your first two nights in Dublin, the next two on the Dingle Peninsula (Dingle Town makes a great base), the next one in Clare (base yourself in Ballyvaughan for the best of the Burren), and the final two nights in Connemara (County Galway), before heading to Shannon for the flight home.

Suggested Itineraries

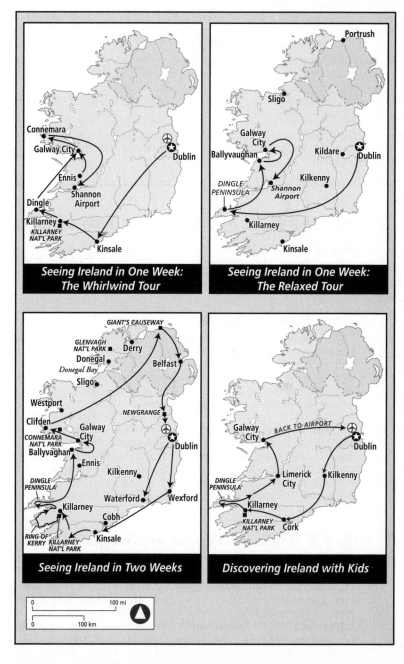

Seeing Ireland in One Week: The Whirlwind Tour

Seeing Ireland in One Week: The Relaxed Tour

Seeing Ireland in Two Weeks

Discovering Ireland with Kids

Discovering the magic of Ireland off the beaten path

Some of the most magical moments of your trip to Ireland may be those times when you turn down that little road toward a tiny farming village, or when you happen into a roadside pub where fires are roaring and fiddles are tuning up for an evening of music, or when you spontaneously decide to take a stroll down to a peaceful, glimmering lake for a picnic.

This book helps you discover the highlights of the country, but I can't emphasize enough the wonderful rewards that often result from following your instincts in getting off the well-trod path.

Touring the Best of Ireland in Two Weeks

This tour features the best that Ireland has to offer. It covers a lot of ground, so someone in your party should feel quite comfortable driving. If you'd like to spend more time in fewer places, I recommend cutting out the Wicklow/Wexford/Waterford section of the tour.

Days 1 and 2: Dublin

Fly into **Dublin.** Get settled in your hotel or B&B, visit the **Dublin Tourism Centre,** and then head over to **Trinity College** to see the **Book of Kells** and take the **Historical Walking Tour** that leaves from the front gates. Grab a picnic lunch and eat in **St. Stephen's Green,** and then ramble over to the **National Museum.** After dinner, head off to Oliver St. John Gogarty's Pub for the **Musical Pub Crawl.**

The next day, catch the **Dublin Bus Tour.** You can hop off the bus to explore the attractions that interest you most; my favorite is **Kilmainham Gaol,** though many people pick the **Guinness Storehouse** as their first choice. Alternatively, spend the day exploring **Newgrange** and **Knowth,** the ancient passage tombs in County Meath. Say goodbye to Dublin with a splurge at **L'Gueulton** or the **Winding Stair** before pub-hopping. See Chapter 11.

Day 3: Dublin to Wexford or Waterford

Choose your own adventure: Head down to charming **Wexford Town,** which has a plethora of great small attractions, including the **Dunbrody Famine Ship** and the lovely **Hook Peninsula.** Or hit Waterford City to take a behind-the-scenes tour at the **House of Waterford Crystal.** On your drive south, take some time to explore County Wicklow, where top attractions include **Powerscourt Gardens** and peaceful **Glendalough.** See Chapters 13 and 14 for information on these counties.

Day 4: Wexford/Waterford to County Cork

Spending the morning and early afternoon exploring Wexford or Waterford before heading off to County Cork around lunchtime. You many want to base yourself in **East Cork,** where highlights include the colorful seaside town of **Cobh** and **Fota Wildlife Park.** If you're staying in Cork City, hit the **English Market,** one of the best in Ireland.

Alternately, you could continue on to West County Cork to explore **Mizen Head,** Ireland's most southwesterly point; the **Beara Peninsula;** or the **Sheep's Head Peninsula.** All three peninsulas are lovely; the Sheep's Head, with great hiking and walking, is my personal favorite of the three. The **Bantry** area is a nice place to spend the night. See Chapter 15 for more about County Cork.

Days 5 and 6: County Cork to the Ring of Kerry

Head up to the famed **Ring of Kerry.** I recommend taking your time for the drive, booking one night's accommodations on the Ring itself.

The next day, complete the Ring of Kerry and head to Killarney to spend the day at **Killarney National Park.** Spend the night in Killarney. See Chapter 16 for information about County Kerry.

Days 7 and 8: The Ring of Kerry to the Dingle Peninsula

Head up from the Ring of Kerry to the **Dingle Peninsula.** A beautiful landscape, excellent traditional Irish music, interesting ruins, the **Slea Head Drive,** and the adorable **town of Dingle** conspire to make this one of my favorite places in Ireland. See Chapter 16.

Day 9: The Dingle Peninsula to County Clare

Head up to County Clare today, taking the Tarbert to Kilrush car ferry to save yourself some driving time. Spend your time gazing at the sheer Cliffs of Moher, and explore the otherworldly moonscape of the **Burren. Ballyvaughan** makes a nice base. See Chapter 17.

Day 10: County Clare to Galway City

Explore the **Burren** until 2 or 3 p.m., when it's time to hit Galway City for dinner and the hopping pub scene. See Chapter 18.

Days 11 and 12: Galway City to Connemara

Head out from Galway City to explore the stunning, moody landscape of **Connemara.** The lively town of **Clifden** makes a terrific place to spend your two nights. See Chapter 18 for information on County Galway.

Day 13: Connemara to Belfast

Start off early for your drive through breathtaking **County Mayo** to the **Giant's Causeway** in Northern Ireland, and then continue on to hot-and-hopping **Belfast** for the night. See Chapter 18.

Day 14: Belfast to Dublin

If you have time, explore Belfast a bit in the morning before driving down to Dublin for your flight home.

Discovering Ireland with Kids

Ireland is a family-friendly place, and with a little planning, you can have a terrific time with your kids.

Day 1: Dublin

Fly into **Dublin** (most flights arrive in the morning), and head to your hotel or B&B — **Jurys Inn Christchurch** is a particularly family-friendly option. Kids will love **the Viking Splash Tours,** which take visitors cruising (sometimes literally) around Dublin in WWII amphibious vehicles. For lunch, satisfy everyone's sweet tooth at the **Queen of Tarts**. In the afternoon, explore **Phoenix Park and Zoo** if it's nice out, or hit the **National Museum**. A fun dinner pick is **Elephant & Castle**. See Chapter 11 for more on Dublin.

Day 2: Dublin to Cork City

Today is a long-ish driving day, but you can break it up with stops at lovely **Powerscourt Gardens** and a visit with the exotic animals at Fota Wildlife Park. See chapter 15.

Day 3: Cork City to Killarney

Spend the morning browsing for picnic supplies at the **English Market** and have lunch on the **UCC Campus**. On your way out of town, stop to ring the bells at **St. Anne's Church (Shandon Church)**. Meander along West Cork's coastline, perhaps stopping for a boat trip to **Cape Clear Island** or a jaunt out to Ireland's most southwestern point at Mizen Head. End your day in Killarney, in County Kerry. See Chapter 15 for more about County Cork, and Chapter 16 for County Kerry.

Day 4: Killarney

Head out to **Killarney National Park** for walks, pony cart rides, and boat trips among the park's stunning lakes, mountains, and forests. See Chapter 16 for more on County Kerry.

Days 5 and 6: Killarney to Dingle Town

Stick around County Kerry for an excursion to the **Dingle Peninsula.**
Kids (and parents) shouldn't miss a visit with Fungie, Dingle Bay's resident dolphin. Spend two nights in hopping little Dingle Town. See Chapter 16 for information on County Kerry.

Day 7: Dingle Town to Adare

Take the breathtaking **Conor Pass** route as you leave the Dingle Peninsula and head up to Newmarket-on-Fergus to spend your last night living the castle dream at **Dromoland Castle** in County Clare before departing the next day from nearby Shannon Airport. See Chapter 17 for information on Counties Clare and Limerick.

Part II
Planning Your Trip to Ireland

The 5th Wave   By Rich Tennant

"This afternoon I want everyone to go online and research Native American culture, history of the old west, and discount airfares to Ireland for the two weeks I'll be on vacation."

In this part . . .

*B*efore you can start planning your trip to Ireland, you'll want to do some legwork. How much will it cost? What are your options for getting there? What about your choices for getting around? What kinds of accommodations are available? The chapters in this section give you the answers to all these questions and more.

Of course, there's the bottom line. Chapter 5 features information on currency in Ireland, how to plan your budget, what things cost, and how to save money.

Chapter 6 gives you the lowdown on how to get to Ireland, and Chapter 7 covers the nitty-gritty of getting around the country.

After you figure out how you're getting to Ireland, turn to Chapter 8 for tips on booking accommodations.

Consult Chapter 9 for tips on special needs and special interests. Chapter 10 tells you everything you need to know in order to tie up loose ends before you leave.

Chapter 5

Managing Your Money

. . . .

In This Chapter
▶ Budgeting for your trip
▶ Discovering how to save big bucks
▶ Figuring out currency in Ireland and Northern Ireland
▶ Traveling with ATM cards and credit cards
▶ Getting some tax back

. . . .

*Y*es, we are climbing our way out of a recession, but fret not, because this guide —and this chapter in particular — gives you lots of money-saving tips, and subsequent chapters offer accommodations and dining selections that won't tap your wallet like a keg of Guinness on St. Patrick's Day. Read on for tips on creating a budget and cutting costs.

Planning Your Budget

Generally speaking, you should factor the following into your budget:

▰ **Airfare:** Airfare to and from Ireland varies depending on where you're flying from, the time of year (summer being the most expensive), and the totally arbitrary whims of the airline gods. On average, airfare from New York to Ireland and back runs about $750. (See Chapter 6 for tips on getting the best airfare deals.)

▰ **Transportation:** Transportation costs vary depending on whether you're busing or training it or renting a car. Driving costs around $120 per week for a small car, plus gas, which is about double the cost of gas in the U.S. Bus fares can cost anywhere from $2 to $25 per person, depending on your destination. Trains are slightly more expensive. (See Chapter 7 for more information.)

▰ **Lodging:** An average double hotel room runs about $120. Rooms on the inexpensive end in hotels and rooms in bed-and-breakfasts (B&Bs) go for about $70, while those on the high end can reach $350 or more. Lodging prices are fluctuating wildly right now, as accommodations cycle between trying to make a profit by charging higher prices, and trying to woo travelers with bargains.

✔ **Meals:** A good per-person allowance for a simple lunch is $12; for dinner, between $20 and $35. Breakfast is included with most accommodations. However, some hotels in the larger cities offer rooms without breakfast at a lower rate. This is often a great choice because you can get an inexpensive breakfast at a local cafe.

✔ **Attractions:** A fair amount to budget for sights is $20 per person per day. Buying a Heritage Card is worth it, if you're planning to see a lot of sights (see "Cutting Costs — But Not the Fun," later in this chapter).

✔ **Shopping:** Gauge your buying tendencies and factor them in. A perk of buying in Ireland: You can get the VAT on your purchases refunded (see "Taking Taxes into Account," later in this chapter).

✔ **Nightlife:** Pubs are the most popular place to spend the evening, and they're as free as the air you breathe, except for all those pints of Guinness (about $5.50 each).

Table 5-1 offers the average costs of some common items.

Table 5-1	What Things Cost in Ireland
Item	**Cost in U.S. Dollars**
Pint of Guinness	$5.50
Soda in a restaurant	$2.50
Chocolate bar	$1.50
Double room at an expensive hotel	$300
Double room at a moderate hotel	$125
Double room at a moderate B&B	$75
Lunch for two at a pub	$28
Dinner for two at an expensive restaurant (with wine and tip)	$120
Walking tour	$13

Note: Prices for food and accommodations in Dublin are slightly higher than the prices listed here.

The ins and outs of restaurant tipping

Almost all restaurants in Ireland leave the service charge (tip) up to you. Most Irish tip about 12 percent to 15 percent. Note that your bill *will* include the value-added tax (VAT), which is 13.5 percent in the Republic of Ireland and 17.5 percent in Northern Ireland. It is not customary to tip bartenders unless they're providing you with table service. For taxi service, most people round up to the nearest euro or pound and kick in a little extra for especially great service. Hairdressers and barbers customarily get a 10 percent tip, while spa technicians don't expect tips.

Cutting Costs — But Not the Fun

Worried that you won't be able to afford your trip? Well, you can rent *Leap Year,* read *Angela's Ashes,* listen to a Chieftains CD, and just pretend you're in Ireland, but what fun is that? Instead, make your vacation a bargain by cutting a few corners. I scatter various money-saving tips throughout this book, but I also present a list of general money-savers here, organized by category.

✔ **Accommodations:** Cut some corners in the lodging department with these tips:

- **Stay in B&Bs.** I can't emphasize enough how wonderful the B&B experience is. Not only do B&Bs usually cost less than staying in a hotel in the same area, but you also frequently get a friendly insider perspective from your hosts.

- **Check out self-catering accommodations.** By renting an apartment or house (called *self-catering accommodations* in this guide) for a week or more, you can save money overall on accommodations (especially if you're traveling with a group) and on food because you can prepare your own meals in the kitchen. (See Chapter 8.)

- **Get out of town.** In many places, hotels and B&Bs just outside the most popular areas can be a great bargain. You may be able to find a great deal just a short cab, bus, car ride, or walk away. And, as an extra bonus, hotels that are off the beaten path usually offer free parking.

- **Ask if your kids can stay in your room with you.** Although many accommodations in Ireland charge by the head, some allow kids to stay for free. Even if you have to pay $10 or $15 for a rollaway bed, in the long run you'll save hundreds by not booking two rooms.

- **Never make a phone call from a hotel.** The marked-up fees that hotels charge are scandalous. Use a cellphone, Skype, or Google Voice (see information in Chapter 10).

🖙 **Attractions:** Save money as you tour Ireland's sights:

- **Get your hands on a Heritage Card.** A Heritage Card gives you free admission to more than 65 attractions throughout Ireland. You can buy the card at any participating attraction, purchase it over the phone with a Visa or MasterCard (☎ **1-850-600-601** in Ireland, 01-647-6000 outside Ireland), or buy it online at www.heritageireland.com.

- **Pick up those free, coupon-packed visitor pamphlets and magazines.** Detailed maps, feature articles, dining and shopping directories, and discount and freebie coupons pack these pocket-size giveaways. Tourist offices have up-to-date free magazines and pamphlets with information about the surrounding area. Just ask.

🖙 **Food:** Grab your grub for less with these suggestions:

- **Take advantage of free breakfasts.** Most accommodations include a substantial free Irish breakfast. Eat up, and then pick up a light lunch to get you through the afternoon.

- **Get a great deal with a room-only rate.** Larger hotels sometimes offer the option of a room rate without breakfast, which can save you up to $25 (!) in some places. You can easily find one or more cafes serving breakfast in cities and most towns.

- **Try expensive restaurants at lunch or pre-theater times.** Lunch and early-bird menu prices are usually a fraction of prices during regular dinner hours, and the menu often boasts many of the same specialties. Early-bird fixed-price are usually taken between 5:30 p.m. and 7:30 p.m.

- **Picnic.** A real waterfall on a warm day easily trumps that fake waterfall in the nearby restaurant. Grab some food from a market or grocery store and dine alfresco.

🖙 **Special prices:** Taking advantage of discounts and group rates can cut your costs substantially:

- **Always ask for discount rates.** Membership in AAA, frequent-flier plans, trade unions, AARP, or other groups may qualify you for savings on car rentals, plane tickets, hotel rooms, and even meals. Students, teachers, kids, and seniors are also often entitled to discounts (see Chapter 9). Ask about discounts; you may be pleasantly surprised.

- **Take advantage of family prices.** Most attractions in Ireland offer significantly reduced family rates for parents and up to four kids. Look for family prices on the rate board at attractions, or just ask.

- **Try a vacation package.** Packages allow you to book a combination of airfare, hotels, ground transportation, and sometimes sightseeing, all of which are bundled together for significant discounts. (See Chapter 6 for more on vacation packages.)

✔ **Ground transportation:** Getting around Ireland can be cheaper than you think.

- **Book your rental car at weekly rates, when possible.** Doing so often saves you money over daily rates.

- **Walk in cities and towns.** You can easily explore most cities by foot, even Dublin and Belfast. So save the cab fare, and hoof it. As a bonus, you'll get to know your destination more intimately, because you'll be exploring at a slower pace.

✔ **Travel costs:** Getting to Ireland can eat up a large chunk of change, but planning ahead can ease the financial bite.

- **Go in the off season.** Traveling between November and April saves you a lot on your airfare and the cost of accommodations. Christmas week is the exception, when many Irish in other countries come home to visit, and the airlines cash in. (See Chapter 6 for more information on airfares.)

- **Travel midweek.** If you can travel on a Tuesday, Wednesday, or Thursday, or at a less popular time of day, you'll often get a cheaper airfare.

Making Sense of the Currency in Ireland

The Republic of Ireland uses the euro currency, which is the currency of many countries across Europe. Euro notes come in denominations of €5, €10, €20, €50, €100, €200, and €500. The euro is divided into 100 cents. Coins come in 1¢, 2¢, 5¢, 10¢, 20¢, 50¢, €1, and €2 pieces. The word *euro* is usually used in the singular, so €30 is *30 euro*.

Northern Ireland is part of the United Kingdom, which uses the pound sterling as its currency. Pound notes in Northern Ireland are found in denominations of £5, £10, £20, and £50. The pound is divisible by 100 pence (abbreviated as *p*). Coins in circulation are 1p, 2p, 5p, 10p, 20p, 50p, £1, and £2.

The exchange rate fluctuates daily. For up-to-the-minute currency conversions, visit www.xe.com.

Handling Money

Credit cards, ATM cards, and cash are all easy to use in Ireland. The very best way to get cash in Ireland is from ATMs (usually called *cash points*), which are available in all but the tiniest villages. All the airports have ATMs, so you can take out money as soon as you land in Ireland.

Using ATMs and carrying cash

The easiest and best way to get cash away from home is from an ATM, usually called a *cash point* in Ireland. Before you leave home, be sure you know your personal identification number (PIN) as a number (as opposed to memorizing it as a word); in Ireland, ATM keys occasionally lack letters. In addition, be sure to find out your daily withdrawal limit. Also, remember to transfer the money that you think you'll need during your vacation to your checking account, because many Irish ATMs don't let you access your savings account. Finally, it's well worth it to take out larger amounts of cash than you usually might in order to minimize the charges for using a bank that's not your own.

Charging ahead with credit cards

In addition to offering relatively good exchange rates, credit cards allow you to withdraw cash advances at banks or ATMs, provided you know your PIN. If you've forgotten yours, or didn't even know you had one, call the number on the back of your credit card and ask the bank to send it to you. It usually takes five to seven business days, though some banks will provide the number over the phone, if you provide personal identifying information.

Keep in mind that almost all credit card companies assess a 1 percent to 3 percent "transaction fee" on *all* charges that you incur abroad (whether you're using the local currency or your native currency). But credit cards are still a smart way to pay when you factor in such things as exorbitant ATM fees and higher traveler's check exchange rates and service fees.

Chip and PIN: Cool new credit card machines

If you're paying with a credit card at a restaurant, chances are that a credit card reader will be brought to your table. In the Republic and Northern Ireland, most people have credit cards with an embedded microchip that is activated by the reader when they enter their four-digit PIN. Most U.S. and Canadian cards don't have microchips as of this writing, so you must swipe your card, enter the tip on the machine, press Enter, and then sign your receipt just as you did back in the old days.

Credit card companies recommend that you notify them of any impending trip abroad so that they don't become suspicious and block your charges when the card is used numerous times in a foreign location. Even if you don't call your credit card company in advance, you can always call the card's toll-free emergency number if a charge is refused — a good reason to carry the phone number with you. But perhaps the most important lesson here is to carry more than one card with you on your trip; a card may not work for any number of reasons, so having a backup is the smart way to go.

Visa and MasterCard are the most widely accepted credit cards in Ireland, with American Express coming in at a distant second, and Diners Club following at a very distant third (you rarely find a B&B that accepts Diners Club). Discover is accepted very rarely in Ireland.

Some restaurants and hotels put your credit card transaction through in your home currency. This may result in an unfavorable exchange rate, so ask establishments to put your charges through in euro in the Republic of Ireland and pounds in Northern Ireland.

Exchanging money

You get the best exchange rates by using an ATM or credit card, though exchanging cash is also easy in Ireland. You can exchange money anywhere you see a bureau de change sign.

Taking Taxes into Account

All prices for consumer items in Ireland (except books and children's clothing) include a VAT of about 21 percent. Happily, travelers from the U.S. and Canada are entitled to a refund of this tax.

Here's how it works: Many stores have stickers reading tax free for tourists, indicating that they're part of the Global Refund (www.global refund.com) or Premier Tax Free (www.premiertaxfree.com) network. When you make a purchase in one of these stores, get a refund check, fill it out, and then hand in your completed checks at the VAT-refund counter in the airport (in the departure hall in Dublin or the arrivals hall in Shannon). If you're running late, you can get the checks stamped by Customs officials and then send them in to Global Refund or Premier Tax Free. If you forget to get your checks stamped while in Ireland, a notary public or police officer can stamp them for you when you get home. Some stores will give you the VAT refund at the register. In this case, you'll be given papers to mail before you leave the country.

You also can get the VAT refunded by stores that aren't part of the Global Refund or Premier Tax Free network; just get a full receipt that shows the shop's name, the address, and the VAT paid, and then get the receipt stamped at the Customs office when you're leaving Ireland. You can then mail the receipts back to the store where you made the purchase, and it will refund your VAT with a check sent to your home. Unfortunately, the VAT system is not always reliable, and travelers are sometimes left without a check even if they follow all the instructions to the letter.

Dealing with a Lost or Stolen Wallet

Be sure to contact all your credit card companies the minute you discover your wallet is gone, and file a report at the nearest police precinct. Your credit card company or insurer may require a police report number or record of the loss.

Most credit card companies have an emergency toll-free number to call if your card is lost or stolen; they may be able to wire you a cash advance immediately or deliver an emergency credit card in a day or two. Call the following emergency numbers in Ireland:

- ✔ **American Express: ☎ 1-336-393-1111** (collect) in the Republic and Northern Ireland

- ✔ **Diners Club: ☎ 303-799-1504** (collect) in the Republic, **☎ 0-870-1900-011** or 01-252-513-500 in Northern Ireland

- ✔ **MasterCard: ☎ 1-800-55-7378** in the Republic, **☎ 0800-96-4767** in Northern Ireland

- ✔ **Visa: ☎ 1-800-55-8002** in the Republic, **☎ 0800-89-1725** in Northern Ireland

If you need emergency cash when banks and American Express offices are closed, you can have money wired to you via **Western Union** (**☎ 800-654-238;** www.westernunion.com).

Identity theft or fraud is a potential complication of losing your wallet, especially if you've lost your driver's license along with your cash and credit cards. Notify the major credit-reporting bureaus immediately; placing a fraud alert on your records may protect you against liability for criminal activity. The three major U.S. credit-reporting agencies are **Equifax** (**☎ 888-766-0008;** www.equifax.com), **Experian** (**☎ 888-397-3742;** www.experian.com), and **TransUnion** (**☎ 800-680-7289;** www.transunion.com).

Finally, if you've lost all forms of photo ID, call your airline and explain the situation. They may allow you to board the plane if you have a copy of your passport or birth certificate and a copy of the police report you filed.

Chapter 6

Getting to Ireland

* * *

In This Chapter

▶ Going by air
▶ Finding the least expensive airfare
▶ Selecting an escorted tour
▶ Picking an independent package deal

* * *

*B*ecause those jet-packs that we've been promised still haven't materialized, you need to begin your vacation to Ireland with a flight. This chapter explores the ins and outs of selecting one. In addition, I cover package and escorted tour options. If you're coming from another location in Europe, you may want to consider a ferry trip. **Direct Ferries** (☎ **1-800-932-151** in the Republic of Ireland; www.directferries. co.uk) provides fares and timetables for all the ferries to and from Ireland.

Flying to Ireland

The sections here offer tips on winging your way over to the Emerald Isle.

When you book your flight, let the ticket agent know the ages of any kids coming along. Some airlines offer child-companion fares and have a special kids' menu upon request. Flight attendants are usually happy to warm up baby food and bottles if you ask.

Picking an arrival airport

Your options for major international airports in the Republic of Ireland are **Dublin Airport** (☎ **01-814-1111;** www.dublinairport.com), located 11km (7 miles) outside Dublin on the East Coast of Ireland (via the N1), and **Shannon Airport** (☎ **061-71-2000;** www.shannon airport.com), located 24km (15 miles) west of Limerick, on the West Coast (via the N18). In Northern Ireland, **Belfast International Airport** (☎ **028-9448-4848;** www.belfastairport.com) is located 31km (19 miles) west of the city. Choose your arrival airport based on fares and on the proximity of the airport to the starting point of your itinerary.

If you want to see both the East and the West of Ireland and you have limited time, I highly recommend flying into Dublin and out of Shannon, or vice versa. It won't cost you any more than booking a round-trip to and from the same airport, and it's a great time-saver.

Finding out which airlines fly to Ireland

In addition to Aer Lingus (which is Gaelic for — guess what? — *airline*), a few U.S. airlines fly to Shannon and Dublin airports. Comparing fares from more than one airline is a good idea.

Here's a list of the major airlines that fly direct to Ireland from North America. Airline destinations change, so check the Web sites to find the departure and arrival points that are most convenient for you.

- ✔ **Aer Lingus** (☎ **800-474-7424** in the U.S. and Canada, 0871-718-5000 in the U.K., 0818-365-000 in Ireland; www.aerlingus.com) has direct flights from Boston, New York, Chicago, and Orlando to Shannon and Dublin

- ✔ **Air Canada** (☎ **888-247-2262** in the U.S. and Canada; www.air canada.com) has direct flights from Toronto to Shannon.

- ✔ **American Airlines** (☎ **800-433-7300;** www.aa.com) has direct flights out of Chicago to Dublin.

- ✔ **Continental** (☎ **800-231-0856;** www.continental.com) has direct flights out of Newark, New Jersey, to Shannon, Dublin, and Belfast.

- ✔ **Delta Air Lines** (☎ **800-221-1212;** www.delta.com) has direct flights out of Atlanta and New York to Dublin, and out of New York to Shannon.

- ✔ **United Airlines** (☎ **800-864-8331;** www.united.com) has direct flights from New York and Philadelphia to Dublin.

Many North American airlines fly to London, where you can catch a connecting flight to Ireland. Some North American travelers take advantage of this option, because a flight to London and a connecting flight to Ireland are sometimes cheaper than a direct flight to Ireland. Your best bets for inexpensive flights between London and Ireland are from **Ryanair** (☎ **01-248-0856;** www.ryanair.com), **bmi** (☎ **800-788-0555** in the U.S., 800-788-0555 in the U.K.; www.flybmi.com), and **Aer Lingus** (☎ **800-474-7424** in the U.S. and Canada, 0871-718-5000 in the U.K., 0818-365-000 in Ireland; www.aerlingus.com).

Getting the Best Deal on Your Airfare

Competition among major airlines is unlike that of any other industry. Every airline offers virtually the same product (basically, a coach seat is a coach seat is a . . .), yet prices can vary by hundreds of dollars.

If you can book your ticket far in advance, stay over Saturday night, and are willing to travel midweek (Tues, Wed, or Thurs), you can qualify for the least expensive price — usually a fraction of the full fare. Obviously, planning ahead pays.

Search the Internet for cheap fares. The best Web sites for low fares are **Airfarewatchdog** (www.airfarewatchdog.com), **Expedia** (www.expedia.com), **Orbitz** (www.orbitz.com), and **Travelocity** (www.travelocity.com). In the U.K., also try www.travelsupermarket.com. Meta search sites (which search many sites for deals instead of just their own site) include **SideStep** (www.sidestep.com) and **KAYAK** (www.kayak.com). **Lastminute.com** is a great source for last-minute flights and getaways. Watch local newspapers for promotional specials or **fare wars,** when airlines lower prices on their most popular routes.

Frequent-flier membership doesn't cost a cent, but membership may entitle you to better seats, faster response to phone inquiries, and more prompt service if your luggage is lost or stolen, your flight is canceled or delayed, or you want to change your seat (especially after you've racked up some miles). And you don't have to fly to earn points: **Frequent-flier credit cards** can earn you thousands of miles for doing your everyday shopping. There are many, many frequent-flier programs, so investigate the details for your favorite and most convenient airlines, and then apply for the card that gives you the best rewards for that airline. To play the frequent-flier game to your best advantage, consult the community bulletin boards on **FlyerTalk** (www.flyertalk.com) or go to Randy Petersen's **Inside Flyer** (www.insideflyer.com), where Petersen and friends review all the programs in detail and post regular updates on changes in policies and trends.

Joining an Escorted Group Tour

Though escorted group tours may be right for some people, I strongly encourage you to travel on your own. Ireland is a destination that invites lingering, whether you're having a late-night pub chat or taking an extended driving break to explore a beach, and escorted tours tend to visit the maximum number of sights in the minimum amount of time. That said, if you want someone else to take care of all your vacation details for you (both before and during your trip), and you enjoy traveling with a large group, you may be a good candidate for an escorted tour. The tour company organizes everything except airfare — transportation, accommodations, meals, and more — and a guide travels with your group throughout your vacation. You know your costs up front, and, in the case of the tamer tours, you don't get many surprises.

If you decide to go with an escorted tour, I strongly recommend purchasing travel insurance, especially if the tour operator asks to you pay up front. But don't buy insurance from the tour operator! If the tour operator doesn't fulfill its obligation to provide you with the vacation you paid for, there's no reason to think that it'll fulfill its insurance obligations either. Get travel insurance through an independent agency. (I tell you more about the ins and outs of travel insurance in Chapter 10.)

Depending on your recreational passions, I recommend one of the following tour companies.

- ✔ **CIE Tours International** (☎ 800-243-8687; www.cietours.com): CIE offers a large selection of tours. The 12-day Irish Classic makes a circuit around the country; at press time, it cost $2,160 with airfare and $1,758 without airfare.

- ✔ **Cosmos** (☎ 800-276-1241; www.cosmosvacations.com): The budget arm of Globus offers a slightly less upscale and less expensive version of Globus trips. As we went to press, the nine-day Irish Explorer tour cost $1,079 to $1,199 (airfare not included).

- ✔ **Globus** (☎ 866-755-8581; www.globusjourneys.com): Globus offers a variety of upscale tours. At press time, the 13-day Scenic Ireland tour cost $2,100 to $2,240 (airfare not included).

- ✔ **Tauck World Discovery** (☎ 800-788-7885; www.tauck.com): Tauck offers deluxe tours of Ireland that house you in the finest hotels in the Emerald Isle. At press time, the 13-day Best of Ireland tour cost $5,000 (airfare not included).

Choosing an Independent Package Tour

With an independent package tour of Ireland, you're paying for airfare, hotel/B&B vouchers, and car rental in one bundle, and your itinerary is entirely up to you. The price of car rental, accommodations, and airfare from a packager is often less than the price would be if you bought each component yourself. That's because packages are sold in bulk to tour operators, who resell them to the public. It's kind of like purchasing your vacation at a warehouse store — the tour operator is the one who buys the 1,000-count box of garbage bags and resells them ten at a time at a cost that undercuts the local supermarket.

The value of a package tour really depends on airfares at the time that you want to visit Ireland. If fares are high, independent packages are often a good value; if there are airfare deals to be had, I would skip the independent package.

Many B&B owners in Ireland are frustrated by the rock-bottom prices that they must offer through the voucher system. Many choose not to accept vouchers, so your B&B options will be more limited if you purchase a package.

The airlines themselves are great sources for package deals. **Aer Lingus** (☎ **800-495-1632;** www.aerlingusvacationstore.com) offers some excellent air/land packages, as do most major airlines, including **American Airlines Vacations** (☎ **800-321-2121;** www.aavacations. com), **Delta Vacations** (☎ **800-800-1504;** www.deltavacations.com), **Continental Airlines Vacations** (☎ **800-829-7777;** www.covacations. com), and **United Vacations** (☎ **888-854-3899;** www.unitedvacations. com). In addition, several big **online travel agencies** — lastminute.com, Orbitz, and Travelocity — also do a brisk business in packages. If you're unsure about the pedigree of a smaller packager, check with the Better Business Bureau (www.bbb.org) in the city where the company is based. If a packager won't tell you where it's based, don't fly with that packager.

For independent packagers, **Brian Moore International Tours** (☎ **800-982-2299;** www.bmit.com), whose five-night Amazing Ireland package includes round-trip airfare, car rental, and four nights of B&B vouchers and one night in a castle hotel ($849–$999 per person at press time) is a great choice, as is **CIE Tours International** (☎ **800-243-8687;** www. cietours.com), whose packages also include car rental, B&B vouchers, and airfare (a six-night package was $970 per person at press time). For luxury packages that combine fine accommodations and car rental, check out **Destinations Ireland** (☎ **800-832-1848;** www.destinations-ireland.com), where a recent ten-day Luxury Castles & Manors tour started at $1,990 per person.

The travel section of your local newspaper and the ads in the back of national travel magazines such as *Travel + Leisure, National Geographic Traveler,* and *Condé Nast Traveler* are also good places to find packages.

Chapter 7

Getting Around Ireland

In This Chapter
▶ Renting a car in Ireland
▶ Taking the bus
▶ Traveling by train

*Y*our main choices for transportation around Ireland are trains, buses, or a car. For most trips, I recommend renting a car, because you can get to the less-accessible areas of Ireland, you can tour at your own pace, and many drives are attractions in and of themselves. In addition, if you're traveling in a group, renting a car is often the most economical option. For those who would rather not drive the winding roads, trains and buses are a great option — they're relatively inexpensive, run frequently, and have big windows so you can see the countryside rolling by.

Seeing Ireland by Car

I think the best way to see Ireland is by car. However, driving in Ireland can be harrowing at times, due to the narrow width of some roads, the prevalence of manual-transmission rental cars (which can be hard to manage, if you're used to an automatic), and the fact that the Irish drive on the left side of the road, which can take some getting used to.

For route-planning help and specific driving directions, go to www. aaireland.ie and click "AA Route Planner." I find that the best driving maps are the **Ordnance Survey Ireland** maps, available at some book-stores or travel shops, online at www.osi.ie, and by calling ☎ **01-802-5300.** If you're using a **GPS** (called a *sat-nav* in Ireland), be aware that the calculated time of arrival is frequently wrong, especially if you're traveling on narrow, curvy local roads on which you'll rarely reach the speed limit. Finally, go to www.dummies.com/cheatsheet/ireland for a handy mileage chart that will help you plan your itinerary.

Booking a rental car

In the off season (Oct–Mar), you should have little difficulty getting a car on short (or even no) notice. But if you're traveling in summer, book your rental car at least a few weeks in advance.

Some of the major rental-car companies operating in Ireland are **Alamo, Argus, Auto-Europe, Avis, Budget, Dan Dooley, Hertz, Murray's Europcar,** and **National.** The toll-free numbers and Web sites for these companies are listed in the Quick Concierge.

If you fly into Dublin and plan to spend some time there, wait to get a car until you're ready to head out to the countryside. Dublin is relatively walkable, and the lack of parking makes having a car more of a nuisance than a help. However, if you're planning to leave town straightaway, or if you fly into Shannon Airport, getting a car upon arrival is a good idea.

Most rental-car companies allow you to drop off cars at places other than where you picked them up, and most don't charge a drop-off fee (but some do, so be sure to ask). However, some companies don't allow you to pick up a car in the Republic and drop it off in Northern Ireland, or vice versa.

Saving money on your rental

Car rental rates depend on the size of the car, how long you keep it, where and when you pick it up and drop it off, where you take it, and a host of other factors. A few tips:

- ✔ If you're keeping the car for five or more days, the weekly rate is almost always less expensive than the daily rate.

- ✔ Check whether the rate is cheaper if you pick up the car at a location in town rather than at the airport.

- ✔ Find out whether age is an issue. Some companies charge drivers younger than 25 or older than a certain age extra (or won't rent to them at all).

- ✔ If you see an advertised price in print or online, be sure to ask for that specific rate, otherwise you may be charged the standard (higher) rate. Don't forget to ask for AAA, AARP, and trade unions membership discounts.

- ✔ Check your frequent-flier accounts. You may be able to get a discount on a rental while adding miles to your account.

- ✔ Use the Internet to comparison-shop. You can check rates at the major rental agencies' Web sites, and compare deals at www.car rental.com. Plus, all the major travel sites — **Expedia** (www.expedia.com), **Orbitz** (www.orbitz.com), and **Travelocity** (www.travelocity.com), for example — have search engines that can dig up discounted car-rental rates.

In addition to the standard rental prices, other charges apply to most car rentals. You'll have to pay taxes, and you're required to have a *collision damage waiver* (CDW), which covers costs if the car is damaged or stolen. See "Getting the scoop on driver's licenses and insurance" for information on additional insurance options. Some companies offer *refueling packages,* in which you pay for your initial full tank of gas up front and return the car with an empty tank. The prices can be competitive with local gas prices, but you don't get credit for any gas remaining in the tank. If you don't use this option, you pay only for the gas you use, but you have to return the car with a full tank or face high charges for any shortfall.

Considering your rental options

You may think you want a larger vehicle, but keep in mind that many roads are nail-bitingly narrow. So, try to get the smallest car you think you'll be comfortable in. Another thought: Smaller is cheaper.

Unlike the United States, where it's standard for rental cars to have an automatic transmission, the standard in Ireland is a manual transmission (stick shift). You can get an automatic — but it usually costs at least 50 percent more than a manual (prices vary widely, so shop around).

Boots, bonnets, and other brouhaha

To save you confusion about the words and phrases that the Irish have for car-related and driving-related things, here's a list of the most commonly used (and confused) terms:

- ✔ **An Lár:** City center.
- ✔ **Bonnet:** Hood.
- ✔ **Boot:** Trunk.
- ✔ **Car park:** Parking lot or garage.
- ✔ **Dual carriageway:** Divided highway.
- ✔ **Footpath or path:** Sidewalk.
- ✔ **Gear stick:** Stick shift.
- ✔ **Lay-by:** Pullout from the main road.
- ✔ **Motorway:** Highway.
- ✔ **Petrol:** Gasoline.
- ✔ **Roundabout:** Traffic circle (or a rotary, if you're from New England). These are common, especially entering and leaving cities. Make sure you go left and yield to the right!
- ✔ **Sat-nav:** In-car GPS system.
- ✔ **Windscreen:** Windshield.

Because the driver's side is on the right side of cars in Ireland, the stick shift is controlled by your left hand, not your right.

Paying for a rental car

Some companies require a deposit when you make your reservation, generally on a credit card.

Don't be shocked if the rental company charges you a gas deposit on your card, too. Just be sure to fill the tank before drop-off, and the deposit will be taken off (good thing, because the deposit is always way higher than the actual cost of the gas).

Gas, called *petrol* in Ireland, is costly. The prices that petrol stations advertise may seem decent to U.S. citizens until you realize that they're priced per liter, not gallon. Generally you pay twice what you would in the United States. This is another good reason to get a smaller car: better gas mileage.

Getting the scoop on driver's licenses and insurance

If you're from the United States, Canada, the U.K., Australia, New Zealand, or a European Union (EU) country, all you need to legally drive a car in Ireland is a valid driver's license from your country of residence.

Your personal auto insurance most likely doesn't extend to rental cars in Ireland. You must get a CDW with your rental car (this is usually included in the price quoted); this insurance reduces your financial responsibility in the case of an accident. The car-rental companies also offer additional *liability insurance* (if you harm others in an accident), *personal accident insurance* (if you harm yourself or your passengers), and *personal effects insurance* (if your property is stolen from your car). Definitely consider the liability insurance and the personal accident insurance (ask your rental agent for more information). Unless you're toting around the Hope diamond (and you don't want to leave that in your car trunk anyway), you probably can skip the personal effects insurance. Check with your credit card company, as some companies will cover auto insurance.

If you plan on taking the car into Northern Ireland from the Republic, be sure to inform the rental company, and ask whether additional insurance is required.

Figuring out the rules of the road

Here are some important traffic rules, laws, and explanations of signage that will help you get around safely and legally.

✔ Perhaps most important, remember that you're driving on the left-hand side of the road. On the highway, you merge to the right while slower traffic stays on the left. Left turns do not cross oncoming traffic, but right turns do. Often, North American visitors accidentally drive on the right after they've been in Ireland for a few days, and have stopped constantly reminding themselves to stay on the left. To avoid this, you may want to stick a note on the steering wheel that says left. Inside the car, the steering wheel is on the right side, and the gearshift is operated with your left hand; the positions of the gas, clutch, and brake are the same as in North American vehicles.

✔ Speed limits throughout the Republic of Ireland are listed in kilometers per hour, while speed limits in Northern Ireland are in miles per hour. In the Republic, the speed limit on local and regional roads (indicated by an L or R in front of a number) is 80kmph, while the speed limit on national roads (indicated by an N in front of a number) is 100kmph. The speed limit on highways, known as motorways (indicated by an M in front a number) is 120kmph. Standard 80-, 100-, and 120kmph signs are indicated only by a black circle with a slash through it (with no numbers). When the speed limit is something other than the standard for that type of road, there will be a sign with a red circle and the speed limit written inside in black. You often see these signs when entering towns, where the speed limit is always reduced to 50kmph. In Northern Ireland, the speed limit on motorways and divided highways (dual carriageways) is 70 mph, while the speed limit on other roads is 60 mph, going down to 30 mph in cities and towns.

✔ A sign that is a red circle with a red X through the middle means no stopping or parking during posted hours.

✔ A circle rimmed in red with a white center means that you have arrived at a pedestrians-only street, where cars are forbidden.

✔ In a *Gaeltacht* (Gaelic-speaking area), you may encounter Gaelic road signs. The most common are go mall or taisteal go mall, which mean "go slowly," and géill slí, which means "yield."

✔ When entering a roundabout (traffic circle), yield to traffic coming from your right.

✔ Seat belts must be worn by drivers and passengers.

✔ Using a cellphone while driving is illegal in Ireland.

✔ Drinking and driving is a serious offense and is dealt with harshly. The legal blood alcohol limit is currently 0.05 percent in the Republic and 0.08 percent in Northern Ireland. Legislation is in the works to reduce the limit to 0.05 percent in Northern Ireland as well.

✔ There is no official border crossing between Northern Ireland and the Republic. Travelers may come and go as they please.

If you have any further questions about traffic laws, visit the Web site for the **Road Safety Authority** (www.rsa.ie).

Understanding parking rules and regulations

There's no law that prohibits you from parking a car facing traffic. You'll often see cars on one side of the road parked in both directions, which makes it tough to tell if you're going the wrong way on a one-way street. In larger towns, there are usually a few parking garages (called *car parks*). For street parking, you often have to buy *parking disks,* which are paper disks that indicate how long you've been in the spot, or use "Pay & Display" machines, where you enter the amount of time that you'll be parked, pay, and then print out a receipt to put in your window. You can buy parking disks at machines marked *P* and at local shops. Purchase a disk, and then display it in the window.

Traveling by Bus

Buses are a great way to see Ireland for a variety of reasons: They make many more stops than trains, you get a great view of the countryside from the huge windows, they're comfortable, they're pretty inexpensive, and they offer plenty of storage for luggage. Downsides to bus travel are that you're not free to stop whenever you want, and most buses don't have bathrooms.

Getting to know the major bus companies

Bus Éireann (☎ 01-836-6111; www.buseireann.ie) is the country's principal public coach line, with a vast network of routes throughout the Republic and into Northern Ireland. Bus Éireann is pretty much a tool of transportation rather than tourism, so it doesn't always stop right near popular sights. The trick is to get to a town near the attraction that you want to see and then take local transportation from there. Call or visit the Web site for prices, timetables, routes, and other information. You can purchase tickets at bus stations, on the bus, or online for a 10-percent discount.

In Northern Ireland, **Ulsterbus** and the luxurious **Goldline** are the area's bus services, with routes that include stops at or near the region's attractions. You can contact both lines at ☎ 028-9066-6630, or find information online at www.translink.co.uk. You can buy tickets at the station, on the bus, or, in some cases, online.

Taking a bus tour

Bus Éireann offers guided sightseeing tours that cover a number of top attractions. Routes become more limited in the off season, so call ahead to find out when each tour is offered. The major day trips out of Dublin are Glendalough, Wicklow, and Powerscourt Gardens (see Chapter 13) and Newgrange and Boyne Valley (see Chapter 12). You also can book seasonal trips out from Cork, Galway, and Sligo. For more information, visit www.buseireann.ie or call ☎ 01-836-6111.

Riding the Rails

Ireland has an excellent rail system that connects the major cities of the Republic and Northern Ireland. The advantages of train travel are that it's fast and comfortable. On the downside, trains are more expensive and travel to fewer destinations than buses, and stops are quick, so you have to be ready to jump off with all your luggage the moment the train pulls into the station.

Trains between major cities run several times daily. For information about destinations, times, and fares, and to purchase tickets, call **Irish Rail** (Iarnród Éireann), at ☎ **1-850-366-222,** or visit www.irishrail. ie. Tickets are available online, by phone, and at train stations in major towns and cities. In Northern Ireland, **NI Railways** information is available at ☎ **028-9066-6630** or www.nirailways.co.uk. You can purchase tickets at the train station; some types of tickets also are available online.

There are some excellent packages that combine train travel to a destination with bus tours that explore non-rail-accessible destinations such as the Burren, Connemara, and the Ring of Kerry. Some of these offerings include hotel accommodations. **Railtours Ireland** (☎ **01-856-0045;** www.railtoursireland.ie), which operates in association with Iarnród Éireann (Irish Rail), is one of the finest tour operators, offering tours that range from half a day to six days.

Bus and Rail Passes for Extended Travel

The following bus and rail deals are available through **Bus Éireann** (☎ **1-850-366-222;** go to www.buseireann.ie, click on "Timetables/More info," and then click on "Tourist Travel Passes"). For a flat price, you get a pass allowing you unlimited use of trains and buses. You can buy the passes online.

- ✔ **Irish Explorer Bus & Rail:** Eight days out of fifteen consecutive days combined rail and bus in the Republic of Ireland only (includes Intercity, DART, and Suburban Rail, plus all Bus Éireann services) for €245 adults, €122 kids 15 and under.

- ✔ **Irish Rover Bus Only:** Good for all Bus Éireann services plus all Ulsterbus services in Northern Ireland. Three days out of eight consecutive days for €84 adults, €49 kids 15 and under. Eight days out of fifteen consecutive days for €190 adults, €103 kids 15 and under. Fifteen days out of thirty consecutive days for €280 adults, €152 kids 15 and under.

- ✔ **Open Road Pass:** This pass provides unlimited travel on all Bus Éireann buses in the Republic. There are many options for this pass, from tickets that can be used on three days out of a consecutive six (€54) to tickets that can be used on 15 days out of a consecutive 30 days (€234).

Irish Rail Routes

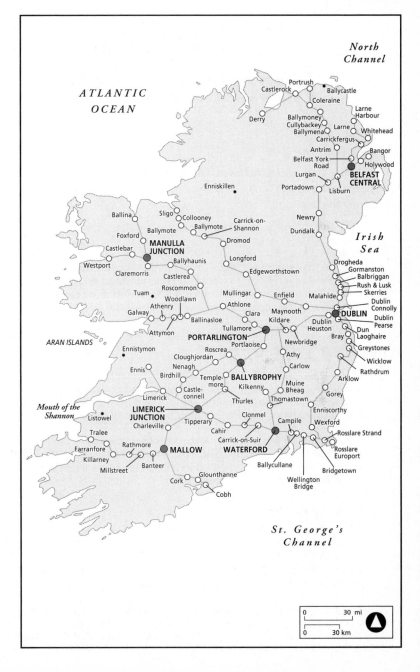

Chapter 8

Booking Your Accommodations

A re B&Bs the best value? Where can you find discounts on lodging? How much does a swanky hotel cost? Read on for answers to all your burning accommodations questions, and don't miss the information on scoring accommodations deals (see the end of this chapter).

Knowing Your Options

From grand manor houses to cute and charming B&Bs, Ireland has accommodations for a range of budgets and tastes. Anywhere you stay, you're likely to encounter the warmth and friendliness that are so much a part of Irish culture. People here take a lot of pride in their hospitality.

Some terms to be aware of as you hotel-hunt: *En suite* means that the room has a private bathroom, a *double room* has one shared bed (could be anything from a double bed to a king-size bed), while a *twin room* has two smaller (single or double) beds.

Opting for hotels

Among hotels, the range of accommodations is wide — from ornate castles with butlers to posh minimalist spaces to small and simple family-run lodges. Many of the larger and chain hotels provide fitness equipment, 24-hour desk staff, and in-house pubs and restaurants, but don't count on these amenities in smaller independent hotels.

The **Irish Hotel Federation's** Web site and brochure lists thousands of hotels, manor houses, inns, and castles. You can click through the listings online (www.irelandhotels.com), or call ☎ 01-808-4419 to order a copy of the guide (€10).

Getting the best room

Asking one or two questions can go a long way toward making sure you get the best room in the house.

✔ If you're staying in a city or on a main street, ask for a room at the back of the hotel or guesthouse, which you'll definitely appreciate when the pubs get going late at night.

✔ Ask for a corner room. These rooms are usually larger and quieter and have more windows and light than standard rooms, and they don't always cost more.

✔ Inquire about the location of restaurants, bars, and clubs in the hotel — all sources of annoying noise.

If you aren't happy with your room when you arrive, talk to the front desk. If they have another room, they should be happy to accommodate you, within reason.

If you enjoy the familiarity of chain hotels, the following chains (listed in order from upscale to budget) have several locations in Ireland: Doyle Collection Hotels (www.doylecollection.com), **Marriott** (Marriott.com), Jurys Hotels and Inns (www.jurysinns.com), Premier Inn (www.premierinn.com), and Travelodge (www.travelodge.com).

Choosing B&Bs or guesthouses

The terms *bed-and-breakfast* (B&B) and *guesthouse* are often used interchangeably, though I've noticed that guesthouses often seem to have more rooms than B&Bs and a rotating hired staff instead of being family-run. However, there are cases where the opposite is true, so read reviews and check Web sites to get a sense of the accommodations.

Though they're not for everyone (misanthropes need not apply), I think that B&Bs and guesthouses are the best lodging options in Ireland. Because they're small (on average about three to ten guestrooms), they give you an opportunity to get to know the owners, who, more often than not, are friendly and knowledgeable about the area. Another big advantage of choosing a B&B over a hotel is the price. The cost of a double room is usually much lower than at a hotel, averaging between €60 and €120. B&Bs run the gamut from simple and cheerful spots to rest your head, to grand manor houses that offer all the amenities of a posh hotel. Though the vast majority of B&Bs have private bathrooms *(en suite)*, you may encounter a few that have shared bathrooms.

Try to book your B&B at least a week in advance of your trip. The best B&Bs fill up quickly during the summer, and you'll have fewer options during the off season because many B&Bs (especially in rural areas) close from late fall to early spring.

As with hotels, the very best rates for B&Bs and guesthouses are usually found by booking through the accommodations' Web sites. If you can't reserve online, the next best option is to call.

Keep in mind that some B&Bs and guesthouses don't accept credit cards, so make sure you have enough cash on hand when it's time to check out. Most guests leave about a €1 per night if rooms are cleaned by an outside employee. If rooms are cleaned by your host, a tip is not necessary.

Fáilte Ireland, the Irish Tourist Board (☎ 800-742-6762 in the U.S.; www.discoverireland.ie), and the **Northern Ireland Tourist Board** (☎ 028-9023-1221; www.discovernorthernireland.com) have brief descriptions and contact information for thousands of B&Bs and guesthouses all over Ireland. In addition to online listings, both tourist boards publish free booklets listing hundreds of B&Bs; you can find the booklets in most tourist offices. For upscale options, including some of the oldest and most beautiful houses in Ireland, check out **Hidden Ireland** (☎ 01-662-7166; www.hidden-ireland.com) and **Manor House Hotels** (☎ 01-295-8900; www.manorhousehotels.com). For B&Bs on working farms, check out **Irish Farmhouse Holidays** (www.irishfarmholidays.com). If you're interested in working on a farm in Ireland, check out **World-Wide Opportunities on Organic Farms** (www.wwoof.org).

Enjoying self-catering accommodations

Self-catering accommodations are like having a home in Ireland. You'll be provided with a furnished space, but usually there isn't a regular housekeeping service, desk staff, or breakfast. You'll almost always have a kitchen, so it's easy to cook your own meals. If you're making the trip with children, this may be a great option, in terms of both convenience and cost.

With self-catering, you pay one price for a week or a few days. Compared to the amount of money you pay for hotels and B&Bs on a nightly basis, the price is usually a bargain. Plus, food costs decrease when you're buying your own and cooking it yourself.

Don't buy into the stars

The Irish Tourist Board and the Northern Ireland Tourist Board rank hotels, guesthouses, and bed-and-breakfasts from one to five stars based on the amenities and facilities offered. These ratings give you a rough idea of what you can expect in terms of room service, Wi-Fi, and so on, but they don't say much about the character, décor, and cleanliness of the accommodations or about the owners and staff. A down-at-the-heels hotel could be given four stars just because it has a restaurant and business center, while a beautifully-furnished, well-run B&B could end up with only two stars because it lacks these amenities.

The drawback is location. Although some self-catering cottages and apartments are in *great* locations, the trouble is that they don't move: Rent one and you're in one place for a few days to a week; to see the sights around the country, you have to drive to them and then drive "home" again. Of course, this is fine if you plan to spend all your time in one area. But making day trips to sights in far-flung parts of the country may be tough.

The variety of self-catering options is as diverse as types of hotels. You can stay in actual thatched-roof cottages or classy modern units. To get you started, the following organizations deal solely with self-catering accommodations. In addition, you can get ideas for accommodations through the tourist board in the area you want to visit.

✔ **Cottages in Ireland** (☎ **028-9036-0500**; www.cottagesin ireland.com) has properties in gorgeous locations in Northern Ireland.

✔ **The Irish Landmark Trust** (☎ **01-670-4733**; www.irish landmark.com) restores historic properties to provide some of the coolest self-catering options in Ireland — think staying in a lighthouse. Book way in advance, as these accommodations are very popular.

✔ **Rent an Irish Cottage** (☎ **061-41-1109**; www.rentacottage.ie) organizes self-catering in cottages all over Ireland.

✔ **Self-Catering Ireland** (☎ **1-850-200-236**; www.selfcatering-ireland.com) is the most comprehensive reservation service, offering three- and four-star self-catering apartments throughout Ireland and Northern Ireland.

✔ **Trident Holiday Homes** (☎ **01-201-8440**; www.tridentholiday homes.ie) offers a good selection of rentals all over Ireland.

Staying at a hostel

Hostels have a reputation for being the accommodations of choice for the micro-budgeted, and if you have an image in your head of hostels full of young, tireless travelers who don't mind going long stretches without showers or food, you're partly right — though only partly. Today, hostels serve all kinds of independent travelers who cherish flexibility and good value (in a nice hostel, a dorm-room bed runs about €18, while a double room averages €42). Most hostels have facilities to accommodate couples and families. I can't vouch for every hostel in Ireland, but the ones that I've visited have been clean and well kept.

Some Irish hostels offer community kitchens, and dorm-style rooms, with anywhere from four to dozens of people per room (some have single-sex dorm rooms while others are coed). However, more and more Irish hostels now have double and family rooms, and even private single rooms. Bathrooms are usually shared.

Hostels provide a blanket and pillow, and some beds have sheets, but to be safe, bring your own sleep-sack — two twin sheets sewn together. Also bring a lightweight travel towel, because some hostels don't provide towels. If you're staying in a dorm-style room, remember to lock up money, valuables, and important documents. If there are no security lockers, you may want to consider taking these items to bed with you.

Most hostels take reservations. If you're planning to do a hostel tour of Ireland, you'll really benefit from joining **Hostelling International** (www.hihostels.com) before you depart. Fees are about $28 per year for adults. With a membership card, you get discounts at affiliated hostels, as well as reductions at some attractions, shops, and restaurants. If you're from the U.S., contact **Hostelling International U.S.A.** (☎ 301-495-1240; www.hiusa.org) for membership.

To find hostels in the Republic of Ireland, check out **An Óige,** the Irish Youth Hostel Association (☎ 01-830-4555; www.anoige.ie). For hostels in Northern Ireland, contact or visit **Hostels International Northern Ireland** (☎ 028-9032-4733; www.hini.org.uk).

Seeking out alternatives

If you're looking for something a little different from the usual hotel or B&B, try one of these options:

- ✔ **Caravans (trailers/motor homes):** For information on renting or buying a caravan or trailer, contact the **Irish Caravan & Camping Council** (www.camping-ireland.ie).

- ✔ **University housing:** Check with local tourist boards or directly with universities to find out whether they have unused dorm space in campus housing to rent. Cities with large universities include Dublin, Galway, Cork, and Limerick. Housing is usually available only during the summer and Christmas holidays.

Figuring Out Accommodations Prices

To make it easy for you to quickly gauge lodging prices in this guide, in Table 8-1, I list the cost of a *double room* for each option and the corresponding dollar sign. If you're traveling alone, count on paying a bit more than half the price listed for a double.

Most of the accommodations I list in this book include a full Irish breakfast.

Table 8-1		Key to Hotel Dollar Signs
Dollar Sign(s)	*Price Range*	*What to Expect*
$	€70 or less	Small bed-and-breakfasts often fall into this category, offering cozy rooms and homemade breakfasts. You may miss high-end amenities (usually no pool, restaurant, or the like), but you're sure to appreciate the friendly hosts and hostesses who operate these spots.
$$	€71–€120	B&Bs and hotels both fall into this price range. The more expensive B&Bs are often a bit classier and refined than those in the preceding category, with gourmet breakfasts, prime locations, antiques-filled rooms, and so on. Hotels in this range are usually stylish and offer extras such as hair dryers, irons, and microwaves.
$$$	€121–€180	Higher-class still, these accommodations are pretty plush. Think grand manor houses, castles, and top-tier business hotels, boasting perks such as fine linens, beautiful antiques and furniture, excellent in-house restaurants, and polished service.
$$$$	€181 or more	These top-rated accommodations (most often manors, castles, and luxury hotels) feature luxury amenities such as golf courses, spas, and in-room hot tubs.

Finding the Best Room Rate

The **rack rate** is the maximum rate a hotel charges for a room. It's the rate you get if you walk in off the street and ask for a room for the night. You sometimes see these rates printed on the fire/emergency exit diagrams posted on the back of your door. Hotels are happy to charge you the rack rate, but you almost always can do better.

Hotel room rates change frequently as occupancy rates rise and fall. B&B rates may fluctuate a bit, but they tend to stay more stable than hotel rates. In most of Ireland, hotels and B&Bs charge the uppermost rate during the high season of mid-June through August and the lowest during the off season of November through March. Weekends are often more expensive than midweek. (See Chapter 3 for more on the seasons in Ireland.)

Almost all Irish hotels and many B&Bs promise to match and possibly undercut the rates offered by booking agencies, so booking online directly with the hotel or B&B is the best option. In the context of the recession, booking hotels online **one or two days before your stay** seems to be the way to score good deals. Hotels have been slashing their prices at the last minute when many rooms are left empty. It's a little nerve-wracking to wait until the eleventh hour to book your hotel, but you may be rewarded with deals — such as my recent find of a double room that had been reduced from €350 to €85. What a difference a couple of lean years make! Definitely browse the hotel or B&B's Web site for package deals and specials. If you're booking online, either print out your confirmation page, or write down your confirmation number.

If you're unable to reserve online, your next move should be to call both the hotel's direct number *and* the toll-free number, and book through whichever one offers the better deal. You also can check out Expedia, Orbitz, and Travelocity for discounted packages and rates, though they're often the same or more expensive than those that you'll find directly from the hotel.

Be sure to mention membership in AAA, AARP, frequent-flier programs, or any other corporate rewards programs you can think of when you call to book. You never know when an affiliation may be worth a few dollars off your room rate.

See Chapter 6 for information on package tours, which often include airfare and accommodations sold together for a discounted price.

Chapter 9

Catering to Special Travel Needs and Interests

*I*n this chapter, I run through some services for travelers with special needs and interests, give some tips, and note some challenges of travel in Ireland. I also offer resources for travelers with special interests such as genealogy research, golfing, hiking, biking, and fishing.

Traveling with the Brood: Advice for Families

Ireland is a wonderful place to travel with a family; the language, food, and culture are familiar enough to be comforting, but different enough to be exciting. As a general rule, kids are more than welcome at attractions, accommodations, and restaurants.

You can find good family-oriented vacation advice on the Internet from sites such as **Family Travel Forum** (www.familytravelforum.com), a comprehensive site that offers advice, deals, and customized trip planning; **Family Travel Network** (www.familytravelnetwork.com), an award-winning site that offers travel features, deals, and tips; **Traveling Internationally with Your Kids** (www.travelwithyourkids.com), a comprehensive site offering sound advice for long-distance and international travel with children; and **Family Travel Files** (www.thefamily travelfiles.com), which offers an online magazine and a directory of off-the-beaten-path tours and tour operators for families.

Most attractions and some public transportation companies in Ireland and Northern Ireland offer reduced fees for kids. And most attractions have **family group prices** (usually for two adults and two or more kids) that are a great bargain. Be sure to ask. (See more money-saving tips in Chapter 5.)

Car-rental companies provide necessary car seats, and all vehicles have rear seatbelts. The law requires that kids always buckle up.

For a small additional fee, you often can add a portable bed to your room at a hotel, guesthouse, or B&B so that your kids can stay in the same room as you. Check with the concierge or manager.

Throughout this book, I point out kid-friendly accommodations, dining options, and attractions — just look for the Kid Friendly icon.

Making Age Work for You: Advice for Seniors

Members of **AARP**, 601 E St. NW, Washington, DC 20049 (☎ **888-687-2277**; www.aarp.org), get discounts on select hotels, airfares, and car rentals. Anyone over 50 can join. **Golden Ireland** (☎ **064-662-6511**; www.goldenireland.ie) features hotel and accommodations discounts for visitors older than 55.

In Ireland, people older than 60 qualify for reduced admission to theaters, museums, and other attractions, as well as discounted fares on public transportation.

Senior discounts are sometimes listed under the term *OAP,* which stands for *Old Age Pensioner* and means the same thing that *senior* does in the United States.

Many reliable agencies and organizations target the senior market. **Road Scholar** (formerly Elderhostel; ☎ 800-454-5768; www.roadscholar.org) arranges educational travel in the United States and in more than 80 countries around the world. Tours are now open to adults of any age. American tour operator **CIE Tours** (☎ 800-243-8687; www.cietours.com) offers discounts to adults 55 and older on some of its tours.

A recommended publication offering travel resources and discounts for seniors is the quarterly magazine ***Travel 50 & Beyond*** (www.travel50andbeyond.com).

Accessing Ireland: Advice for Travelers with Disabilities

Ireland has accessibility regulations for public areas. Most sidewalks have ramps, and some accommodations are wheelchair-accessible. Getting around in cities and towns isn't too hard, with the exception of areas with cobblestone streets. Though services are getting better, some of Ireland's attractions aren't very accessible. Not every museum has closed captions for video presentations, and not every castle has an entrance ramp. Calling ahead to find out about accessibility at attractions and B&Bs (many of which aren't wheelchair-friendly) is always a good idea. You can feel fairly confident that most restaurants and newer hotels are entirely accessible. For further information, the Access department of the **National Disability Authority,** 25 Clyde Rd., Dublin 4 (☎ **01-608-0400;** www.nda.ie), can connect you with information on wheelchair-friendly attractions, restaurants, and accommodations. For tips on travel in the North, contact **Disability Action** (☎ **028-9029-7880;** www.disabilityaction.org).

Many travel agencies offer customized tours and itineraries for travelers with disabilities. **The Guided Tour, Inc.** (☎ 215-783-5841; www.guidedtour.com) conducts annual trips to Ireland for developmentally challenged travelers, and **Trips, Inc.: Special Adventures** (☎ **800-686-1013** in the U.S.; tripsinc.com) leads a variety of trips for travelers with all sorts of disabilities. For travelers with physical disabilities, **Flying Wheels Travel** (☎ **877-451-5006;** www.flyingwheelstravel.com) provides individualized travel arrangements, as well as escorted tours. Travelers in wheelchairs should also check out **Accessible Journeys** (☎ **800-846-4537;** www.disabilitytravel.com).

Organizations that offer assistance and advice to disabled travelers include **MossRehab** (www.mossresourcenet.org), the **American Foundation for the Blind** (☎ **800-232-5463;** www.afb.org), the **Society for Accessible Travel and Hospitality** (☎ **212-447-7284;** www.sath.org), and **Emerging Horizons** (www.emerginghorizons.com).

Studying Up on Ireland: Advice for Students

With half its population under 35, Ireland is accustomed to catering to students. Most attractions have reduced student admission prices, and many transportation companies offer students discounts. Usually, you just need to present your university ID card. A handful of attractions and companies require the presentation of an official student ID card (instead of your regular university ID), so check out the **International Student Exchange Card** (www.isecard.com) or the **International Student Identity Card** (www.isiccard.com) if you want to make sure you get every last bargain.

In the United States, **STA Travel** (☎ **800-781-4040;** www.statravel.com) offers information and booking for all sorts of student travel discounts. In Canada, **Travel CUTS** (☎ **866-246-9762;** www.travelcuts.com) does the same.

Following the Rainbow: Advice for GLBT Travelers

Ireland is becoming more and more gay-friendly. Same-sex travelers can almost always book double rooms without receiving odd looks, and the larger towns and cities — Dublin, Cork, Belfast, and Galway — hold well-attended gay-pride events. That said, some people are homophobic, so use your judgment regarding public displays of affection. Most antigay crimes in Ireland seem to occur at night around groups who have been drinking heavily. The majority of reported attacks occur in the Dublin 1, Dublin 7, and Dublin 8 areas.

Your guide to all things gay and lesbian is the *Gay Community News* (www.gcn.ie), which also publishes a free monthly newspaper devoted to the gay community. The paper is available in gay-oriented venues, especially bookshops, all over Ireland. **Queer ID** (www.queerid.com) has a great listing of gay events, clubs, and more, mostly in Dublin. **Outhouse,** 105 Capel St., Dublin 1 (☎ 01-873-4932; www.outhouse.ie), offer all sorts of information for GLBT travelers.

Good guides to Europe with a gay slant are *Spartacus International Gay Guide* (www.spartacusworld.com/gayguide), which focuses on men, and the *Damron* guides (www.damron.com), which offers separate, annual books for gay men and lesbians.

Exploring Your Special Interests

Whether your tastes run to tracing family history or casting a line for salmon, here are some suggestions for travelers with special interests.

Doing genealogy research

The Ireland Tourist Board publishes a book called *Tracing Your Ancestors in Ireland,* which is available free from any Irish Tourist Board office and online at www.irishgenealogy.ie. The best online sites to begin your search for records pertaining to your Irish ancestors are **Ancestry.com;** the **Irish National Archives** (www.national archives.ie), which has a database of many of Ireland's records; and **Irish Ancestors** (www.ireland.com/ancestor), where you can pay to register and then begin your search with any information that you currently have (surnames, places of birth, and so on).

First-time ancestor-hunters are encouraged to get started by visiting the **National Library,** Kildare Street, Dublin 2 (☎ 01-603-0200; www.nli.ie), where staff at the free genealogy advisory service can counsel you on how and where to begin your search. A great place to start exploring documents is at the **National Archives,** Bishop Street, Dublin 8 (☎ 01-407-2300; www.nationalarchives.ie), in the Republic, and at the

Public Record Office of Northern Ireland, 66 Balmoral Ave., Belfast (☎ **028-9025-5905;** www.proni.gov.uk).

You also can hire someone to research your roots for you. The National Library maintains a list of independent genealogy researchers (go to www.nli.ie, click on "Family History Research," and then "Commissioning Research"). **ENECLANN,** Unit 1b, Trinity College Enterprise Center, Pearse Street, Dublin 2 (☎ **01-671-0338;** www.eneclann.ie), is one of the finest services.

When available, I've listed genealogy services specific to each region in the "Fast Facts" listings at the end of each chapter.

Rambling your way around Ireland by foot

Hiking (usually called *walking* or *hill-walking* in Ireland) is one of the very best ways to soak up the beauty of Ireland, whether you take off on a weeklong trek or go for an afternoon stroll. Check out www.walking ireland.ie for information on trails, events, festivals, and tour operators. The best way to get information on the various hikes in an area is to visit the local tourist information office (listed in the "Fast Facts" section of each chapter).

An excellent site for information about day hikes (including loop hikes) is **Coillte Outdoors** (www.coillteouttdoors.ie). Also, check out the very well-done **Discover Ireland** (www.discoverireland.ie/walking) and **Walking Ireland** (www.walkingireland.ie) for hikes all over Ireland, and **Walk Northern Ireland** (www.walkni.com) for hikes in the North.

For more information on walking and hiking in Northern Ireland, visit **Northern Ireland's Tourist Board** Web site (www.discovernorthern ireland.com), and enter "Walking" in the search bar. The Tourist Board's publication *Walk Northern Ireland,* which encompasses hikes of all kinds, is a great resource, available at the Tourist Board offices and as a hard copy from most major tourist offices in Northern Ireland. Also available at major tourist offices (and in a shortened format online at www.walkni.com) are guides to all of Northern Ireland's Waymarked Ways.

For detailed information on Ireland's long-distance marked trails (many of which are composed of a series of day hikes), visit **Waymarked Ways of Ireland** (www.irishtrails.ie). You usually can pick up trail maps at the larger tourism offices, or you can order them directly from **EastWest Mapping** (☎ **053-937-7835;** eastwestmapping.ie) or **Ordnance Survey Ireland** (☎ **01-802-5300;** www.osi.ie).

You also can get a hold of a number of excellent walking/hiking guidebooks, including *Walking in Ireland* (sometimes sold as *Hiking in Ireland;* Lonely Planet), *Northern Ireland: A Walking Guide* (Collins Press), the excellent area-specific hiking guides by Kevin Corcoran (O'Brien Press), and, my personal favorite, *The Independent Walkers Guide to Ireland* (Interlink Publishing).

A number of companies offer hiking vacation packages in Ireland, either with a leader or self-guided. **Backroads** (☎ 800-462-2848; www.backroads.com) and **Country Walkers** (☎ 800-464-9255; www.countrywalkers.com) offer guided hiking trips. **Hidden Trails** (☎ 888-987-2457; www.hiddentrails.com) offers self-guided and guided hiking tours in several regions in Ireland.

Teeing off on the greenest greens

Golf is the biggest sporting attraction in Ireland. For information on many of Ireland's golf courses, visit www.irishgolfcourses.co.uk. You can find more golfing information at the Golfing Union of Ireland's Web site (www.gui.ie).

Specialty Ireland (☎ 052-617-0630; www.specialtyireland.com) offers guided tours of Ireland's top courses, while **Golf International** (☎ 800-833-1389 or 212-986-9176; www.golfinternational.com) sets up both escorted tours and customized self-guided tours. Many companies offer golf packages with accommodations included. Some of the best-known are **Carr Golf Travel** (☎ 800-882-2656 in the U.S., 01-822-6662 in Ireland; www.carrgolf.com) and **World Golf** (☎ 800-882-2656; www.worldogolf.com).

Bicycling around Ireland

Stunning scenery, short distances between towns, and some relatively flat roads make Ireland a wonderful place for cycling. **Backroads** (☎ 800-462-2848; www.backroads.com) and **VBT** (☎ 800-245-3868; www.vbt.com) offer guided bike vacations that include bikes, gear, luggage transportation, food, and accommodations. **Irish Cycle Tours** (☎ 066-712-8733; www.irishcycletours.com) offers both guided and self-guided tours. For semi-independent cycling (you receive a bike and route details, accommodation is prearranged, and your luggage is transported from hotel to hotel), contact **Irish Cycling Safaris** (☎ 01-260-0749; www.cyclingsafaris.com) or **Celtic Cycling** (☎ 051-850-228; www.celticcycling.com).

If you want to create your own itinerary, you can rent a bike from an Irish company that permits one-way rentals. **Rent-A-Bike Ireland,** Roches Street, Limerick (☎ 061-416-983; www.irelandrentabike.com), located not far from Shannon Airport, and **Eurotrek Raleigh** (☎ 01-465-9659; www.raleigh.ie) are two reliable options.

Fishing Ireland's waters

Ireland may be the best place in Europe to cast your line for salmon, sea trout, and brown trout. There are a few exceptions to the dates listed here, but in most cases salmon season is January 1 to September 30, wild brown trout season is February 1 to September 30, and sea-trout season is March 15 to September 15. The coarse fishing is excellent, and sea angling presents an amazing variety (anything from bluefin tuna to the finest mackerel may appear at the end of your rod). Coarse fishing and sea angling take place all year. Find details about fishing and fishing licenses from the top-notch **Fishing in Ireland** (☎ 01-278-7022; www.fishinginireland.info). Check out **Great Fishing Houses of Ireland** (www.irelandfishing.com) for information on hotels and guesthouses that have sole access to lakes and ponds, and offer fishing equipment and guides (often called *ghillies* in Ireland). In Northern Ireland, you must get a rod license and a permit; contact the **Department of Culture, Arts, and Leisure** (☎ 028-9051-5119; www.dcal-fishing ni.gov.uk).

Cruising around Ireland and surfing the Irish waves

Ireland's clear waters, Gulf Stream, winding rivers, and large *loughs* (lakes) make this a terrific place to get out onto the water. Northern Ireland is home to some fabulous canoeing opportunities (see www.canoeni.ie for details). For information on sailing in Northern Ireland, visit www.discovernorthernireland.com/Sailing-in-Northern-Ireland-T15533. In the Republic, visit www.iwai.ie for information about day trips and boat rentals. If a multiday cruise along the Shannon and Erne rivers appeals to you, I recommend checking out the **Shannon Princess barge** (☎ 087-251-4809; www.shannonprincess.com).

The charming fishing village of Kinvarra, County Galway, hosts **Cruinniú na mBad** (literally, "Gathering of the Boats") in August. The festival focuses on races among the majestic "hooker" sailboats that used to carry turf from port to port. Visit www.festivalpig.com/Cruinniu-na-mBad.html for exact dates and times.

Here's the equation for Ireland: island + nice high winds = an excellent surfing destination that keeps growing in popularity. For information on where to hang ten, visit www.isasurf.ie.

Horseback riding

What could be more romantic than clip-clopping through the Irish countryside on horseback? For a list of horseback-riding (*horse-riding* in Ireland) outfitters, contact or visit the Web site of the **Association of Irish Riding Establishments** (☎ 045-854-518; www.aire.ie) in the Republic, or the **British Horse Society** (☎ 0844-848-1666; www.bhs.org.uk) in Northern Ireland. For a selection of horseback-riding vacation outfitters, check out **Equestrian Holidays Ireland** (www.ehi.ie).

Spectator sports

Spectator sports are hugely popular in Ireland. Many pubs have the local game on — whether it's football (known as *soccer* in the U.S.), Gaelic football, rugby, hurling, or horse racing. Seeing a live sporting event is a quintessential Irish experience.

Road bowling

If you're meandering along on a country lane and you come upon a group of people hurling shot-put-type balls along the road, you aren't hallucinating. You're lucky enough to have encountered road bowling, an old Irish game that is sort of a golf-bowling hybrid. Players roll and throw the ball in an attempt to reach a designated finish line with the fewest possible shots. The game is most popular in County Cork and County Armagh.

Horse racing

Steeplechases are run year-round. The flat season (races without hurdles) is from mid-March through early November. The Irish Tourist Board draws up an Irish Racing Calendar every year, and you can contact or visit **Horse Racing Ireland** (☎ **045-455-455;** www.hri.ie) for information. Some of the highlights are the Dublin Horse Show in early August; a Christmas racing festival in Dublin; the Irish Grand National, at Fairyhouse in County Meath; the Galway Races; and the Irish Derby.

Greyhound racing

Greyhound racing takes place around the country, usually Monday through Saturday at 8 and 10 p.m. The largest racetracks are the **Shelbourne Park Stadium** in Dublin and **Kingdom Greyhound Stadium** in Tralee. For more information, visit the **Irish Greyhound Board** (www.igb.ie).

Rugby, soccer, hurling, and Gaelic football

These four sports are played throughout the country. *Gaelic football* is a rough-and-tumble sport that combines the best aspects of American football, soccer, and rugby.

Hurling is a fast-paced and thrilling game akin to field hockey or lacrosse played with a stick called a *hurley stick*. It's well worth seeking out a game, as the sport is unique to Ireland and a ton of fun to watch.

You can get Gaelic football and hurling schedule information from the **Gaelic Athletic Association** (☎ **01-836-3222;** www.gaa.ie). You can get schedules and information for soccer from the **Football Association of Ireland,** 80 Merrion Sq., Dublin 2 (☎ **01-8999-589;** www.fai.ie). For rugby schedules and information, contact **Irish Rugby** (☎ **01-647-3800;** www.irishrugby.ie).

Chapter 10

Taking Care of the Remaining Details

In This Chapter

▶ Figuring out passports

▶ Looking at travel and health insurance

▶ Keeping in touch with friends and family at home

▶ Bringing the correct electrical adapters

▶ Knowing what to expect regarding airline security

*N*ow that you're all excited to go to Ireland, here are some tips on such things as passports, insurance, calling home, and bringing the right electrical adapters.

Getting a Passport

The following list offers passport information for citizens of Australia, Canada, New Zealand, the United States, and the United Kingdom.

 Allow plenty of time before your trip to apply for a passport; processing times vary, but you should allow several weeks. Be aware that kids need their own passports.

- ✔ **For residents of Australia:** Contact the **Australian Passport Information Service** at ☎ **131-232,** or visit www.passports.gov.au.

- ✔ **For residents of Canada:** Contact the central **Passport Office,** Department of Foreign Affairs and International Trade, Ottawa, ON K1A 0G3 (☎ **800-567-6868;** www.ppt.gc.ca).

- ✔ **For residents of New Zealand:** Contact the **Passports Office,** Department of Internal Affairs, 47 Boulcott St., Wellington, 6011 (☎ **0800-225-050** in New Zealand, or 04-474-8100; www.passports.govt.nz).

- ✔ **For residents of the United Kingdom:** U.K. residents don't usually need a passport to visit the Republic of Ireland. The one exception is travel with Ryanair, which requires passports for all passengers (including children). However, U.K. residents traveling to the Republic via plane or ferry must present a valid photo ID (driver's license, International Student Card, and so on). For U.K. passport information visit your nearest passport office, major post office, or travel agency, or contact the **Identity and Passport Service (IPS),** 89 Eccleston Sq., London, SW1V 1PN (☎ **0300-222-0000;** www.ips. gov.uk).

✔ **For residents of** the **United States:** To find your regional passport office, check the U.S. Department of State Web site (http:// travel.state.gov/passport) or call the **National Passport Information Center** (☎ 877-487-2778) for automated information.

Playing It Safe with Travel and Medical Insurance

The types of insurance travelers are most likely to need are trip-cancellation insurance and medical insurance. The cost of travel insurance varies widely, depending on the cost and length of your trip, your age and health, and the type of trip you're taking.

Figuring out trip-cancellation insurance

Trip-cancellation insurance will help you retrieve your money if you have to back out of a trip or depart early, or if your travel supplier goes bankrupt. Trip-cancellation insurance traditionally covers such events as sickness, natural disasters, and Department of State advisories. More comprehensive options include lost-luggage insurance; medical insurance; expanded hurricane coverage; and "any-reason" cancellation coverage, which costs more but covers cancellations made for any reason.

Minor health advisories for Ireland

A few years ago, a handful of towns (notably Ennis and Galway) had issues with bacteria in their drinking-water supplies. Most people affected only experienced mild gastrointestinal symptoms, though those with compromised immune systems felt the effects to a greater degree. Everything seems to be back to normal, and you can visit www. epa.ie to check on current water safety.

Ticks, which can carry Lyme disease, are found in fields and woodland throughout Ireland. Consider wearing socks and closed-toe shoes during outdoor activities, and check your body carefully for the tiny black bugs. If you find an embedded tick, use tweezers to pull the tick out, making sure that you remove all body parts. If you experience a rash (often in the shape of a bull's-eye) and/or flu-like symptoms (headache, muscle aches, fatigue), see your doctor to get tested for Lyme disease, which can be treated easily with antibiotics.

Be sure to weigh your personal situation and your comfort level with risk when considering trip-cancellation insurance. I've never bought travel insurance, but a friend with several children always does. It gives her peace of mind to know that she could cancel her trip to take care of her kids without losing a lot of money.

Before you look into trip insurance, check the insurance provided by your credit card company and renter's or homeowner's insurance — both already may provide coverage for many aspects of traveling. You can get estimates for various providers through **InsureMyTrip.com** and **SquareMouth** (www.squaremouth.com). Enter your trip cost and dates, your age, and other information, for prices from more than a dozen companies.

Considering medical insurance

For overseas travel, you may want to look into **medical insurance.** As with trip-cancellation insurance, consider your personal situation and your comfort with risk. If you're considering both trip-cancellation and medical insurance, check the details of each policy to make sure that you aren't paying twice for the same services. As far as prices for simple medical treatment, a visit to a walk-in clinic and an antibiotic prescription in Ireland currently costs around €65.

Several **U.S.** health plans do cover services overseas after certain deductibles are met, but some (including Medicare and Medicaid) don't provide any coverage. In almost all cases, you have to pay up front and then apply for reimbursement. The vast majority of plans don't cover medical evacuation, though some credit cards do.

Canadians should check with their provincial health plan offices or call **Health Canada** (☎ 866-225-0709; www.hc-sc.gc.ca) to find out the extent of their coverage and what documentation and receipts they must take home in case they're treated overseas.

Travelers from the **U.K.** to the Republic should carry their free European Health Insurance Card (EHIC), which covers any unforeseen medical services provided in EU countries. For information on obtaining a card, call ☎ **0800 6789-1011,** or go to ec.europa.eu/social.

Australian visitors are covered via Australia's Reciprocal Health Care Agreements for hospital stays in the Republic of Ireland and for all National Health Service treatments (except dentistry) in the U.K. Visitors from **New Zealand** are covered in the U.K. for emergency medical care but not in the Republic.

If you require additional medical insurance, check out various plans on **InsureMyTrip.com** and **SquareMouth** (www.squaremouth.com). **MEDEX** (☎ **800-527-0218;** www.medexassist.com) is a popular provider. **Air Ambulance Card** (www.airambulancecard.com) is a prepaid card that covers air ambulance transportation from any destination to your home hospital.

Staying Healthy When You Travel

Getting sick will ruin your vacation, so I strongly advise against it. However, if you do need medical care, both the Republic and Northern Ireland offer up-to-date, comprehensive medical facilities and services. For information on purchasing medical insurance for your trip, see the preceding section.

Talk to your doctor before leaving on a trip, if you have a serious and/ or chronic illness. For conditions such as epilepsy, diabetes, or heart problems, wear a **MedicAlert identification tag** (☎ **888-633-4298;** www. medicalert.org), which alerts doctors to your condition and gives them access to your records through MedicAlert's 24-hour hot line.

The United States **Centers for Disease Control and Prevention** (☎ **800-311-3435;** www.cdc.gov) provides up-to-date information on health hazards by region or country and offers tips on food safety.

Calling the Folks Back Home

This section helps you figure out the best ways to stay in touch while you're away from home.

Using a cellphone in Ireland

Cellphones are definitely the most economical way of staying in touch by phone while you're in Ireland. Pay phones are few and far between, and calls on hotel phones may require you to take out a second mortgage. Though you can rent a cellphone, the most cost-effective option usually is purchasing an Irish phone or an Irish SIM card if you know that your phone is compatible with the Irish Global System for Mobile (GSM) system. If your GSM phone is "unlocked," you can change services by switching SIM cards. If you don't know whether your phone is locked or unlocked, call your carrier to find out. Most will unlock your phone, if you tell them you're traveling internationally. To find out if your phone is compatible with the Irish GSM system and for more details about unlocking your phone, visit the "Road Warrior Resources" section of **The Travel Insider** (www.thetravelinsider.info).

In Dublin, you can find prepaid phones and SIM cards (Vodafone and O2 are the best) at several electronics shops; at the centrally located **Vodafone** store at 48 Grafton St. (☎ **01-670-5205**); and at the **O2 Experience** store at 30 Mary St. (☎ **01-874-4027**), on Dublin's north side. If you fly into Shannon, the easiest place to buy a phone or SIM card is at **Vodafone,** in the SkyCourt shopping mall (☎ **061-708-869**), off the N18 in the town of Shannon.

Numbers beginning with 800 or 850 within Ireland are called *freephone numbers* and are toll-free, but calling a toll-free number in Ireland from the United States (and vice versa) is not free. In fact, doing so costs the same as a regular overseas call.

Using a U.S. calling card

AT&T, MCI, and Sprint calling cards all operate worldwide, so using any of them in Ireland is no problem. Each card has a local access number, which saves you the cost of dialing directly to the United States. When you want to use your card in the Republic of Ireland, just call ☎ 1800-55-0000 for **AT&T,** ☎ 1800-55-1001 for **MCI,** or ☎ 1800-55-2001 for **Sprint.** In Northern Ireland, call ☎ 0-800-89-0011 for **AT&T,** ☎ 0800-279-5088 for **MCI,** and ☎ 0800-89-0877 (land lines) or 0500-890-877 (cellphones) for **Sprint.** The operator will then explain how to make the call.

If you have a calling card with a company other than one of the three I named, contact the company before you go on the trip to see whether it has a local access number in Ireland. Also, it's a good idea to call your card company before you go on your trip to see whether it has a discount plan for calling overseas.

Using an Irish calling card

You can purchase Irish calling cards in most supermarkets and convenience stores. The cards (which are often receipt-type slips of paper) provide you with a local access number and PIN for low-cost calls overseas. Check out the cards to make sure that you buy the one with the best deals for your calling destination — different cards focus on different areas of the world.

Using Skype or Google Voice

If you have a computer and Internet access while traveling, a broadband-based telephone service such as Skype (www.skype.com) or Google Voice (www.google.com/voice) is a fantastic way to make free or low-cost calls. If the person you're calling has Skype or Google Voice installed, you can talk for free through your computers. You also can use Skype or Google Voice to call people on their cellphones or land lines; fees for these calls are typically low. You need a headset with microphone to use Skype and Google Voice, unless you're using the Skype iPhone application, which allows you to use your phone as you normally do.

Accessing the Internet Away from Home

You have a number of ways to check your e-mail and access the Internet on the road.

With your own computer

The majority of hotels, guesthouses, and B&Bs in Ireland now offer free wireless access for their guests. Remember to ask for the password if the wireless network is locked. Larger hotels tend to offer wireless on a pay-as-you-go basis; you open your browser, pay the wireless service by credit card, and then have access to the Internet through the wireless service for the amount of time for which you've paid. Other hot spots for free wireless access are cafes, restaurants, and museums.

Without your own computer

Most larger towns and cities in Ireland have Internet cafes. I list the address and telephone number of a local Internet cafe in the "Fast Facts" section of each chapter. Tourist information centers and your hotel information desk or B&B proprietor will almost always be able to help you locate an Internet cafe.

If you're staying in a hotel that serves business travelers, you'll often find a business center with computers. Be aware that using a computer in the business center is almost always much more expensive than using one at an Internet cafe.

Sending and Receiving Snail Mail in the Republic and Northern Ireland

You do know you'll be hard-pressed to get someone to pick you up at the airport if you don't send home any postcards, right? Post offices in the Republic are called *An Post* (www.anpost.ie) and are easy to spot: Look for a bright green storefront with the town or city name across it. Ireland's main postal branch, the **General Post Office (GPO),** on O'Connell Street, Dublin 1 (☎ **01-705-8833**), is in the heart of Dublin and is the hub of all mail activity; it's open Monday through Saturday 8:30 a.m. to 6 p.m. Major branches, located in the bigger towns and cities, are usually open Monday through Friday 9 a.m. to 5:30 p.m. and Saturday 9 a.m. to 1 p.m. Minor branches, which are in every small town, are usually open Monday through Friday 9 a.m. to 1 p.m. and 2 or 2:30 to 5:30 p.m., and Saturday 9 a.m. to 1 p.m. Irish post offices sell phone cards and lottery tickets, and you can even change money at main branches.

From the Republic, mailing an air-mail letter or postcard costs 80¢. It usually takes mail about a week to get to the United States.

In Northern Ireland, the post offices and post boxes are bright red. The general hours are the same as those of *An Post.* The cost to send a letter or a postcard starts at 65p.

If you need mail sent to you while on your trip in Ireland, have the sender address the mail with your name, care of the General Post Office, Restante Office, and the town name (for example, Joe Smith, c/o General Post Office, Restante Office, Galway, Ireland). Your mail will be held there for you to pick up for 30 days. Only larger post-office branches provide this service.

Figuring Out Electricity in Ireland

Electricity in the Republic of Ireland operates on about 220 volts; in Northern Ireland, on about 240 volts. Many travel appliances, such as shavers, irons, and most laptops, have a nice feature called *dual voltage* that adapts to the change, but unless your appliance gives a voltage range (such as 110v–240v), don't chance it. To use appliances that don't have dual voltage, you need a transformer or converter, which you can buy at travel stores or on Amazon (www.amazon.com).

Sockets in the Republic of Ireland and the U.K. require a unique three-pronged plug, so you need to purchase a plug adapter unless you're from the U.K. You can find adapters easily; some sources include your local hardware store, the airport, and online vendors such as Amazon. com. Make sure that you *don't* purchase the standard-plug European adapters — they don't work in the U.K. or the Republic.

Keeping Up with Airline Security

With the federalization of airport security in the United States, security procedures are more stable and consistent than ever. Generally, you'll be fine if you arrive at the airport **1 hour and 15 minutes** before a domestic flight and at least **2 hours** before an international flight. Dublin Airport is notorious for strict check-in cut-off times, so absolutely arrive no later than 90 minutes before your departure from Dublin.

To get into Ireland, you need a valid passport (unless you're from the U.K. — read the passport information at the beginning of this chapter).

In 2003, the Transportation Security Administration (TSA) phased out **gate check-in** at all U.S. airports. And **E-tickets** have made paper tickets nearly obsolete. Most airlines require you to check in at **electronic kiosks** at the airport, or you can beat the lines with **online check-in.** Online check-in involves logging on to your airline's Web site, accessing your reservation, and printing out your boarding pass. **Curbside check-in** is also a good way to avoid lines, although a few airlines still ban curbside check-in; call before you go.

Speed up security by **not wearing metal objects** such as big belt buckles. If you have metallic body parts, a note from your doctor may prevent a long chat with the security screeners. Keep in mind that only **ticketed passengers** are allowed past security, except for folks escorting disabled passengers or children.

Federalization has stabilized **what you can carry on** and **what you can't.** Travelers in the U.S. are allowed one carry-on bag, plus a "personal item" such as a purse, briefcase, or laptop bag. Now that so many airlines charge a fee for checked luggage, more and more travelers are opting to carry all of their luggage onboard. Carry-on hoarders can stuff all sorts of things into a laptop bag; as long as it has a laptop in it, it's still considered a personal item. The TSA has a list of restricted items; check www.tsa.gov/travelers/airtravel for details. If you want to pack gels and liquids in your carryon rather than in your checked luggage, the containers must be 3 ounces or smaller and must be sealed in a 1-quart resealable clear plastic bag. One bag is permitted per passenger. Medications, baby food, formula, and breast milk are exempt from these restrictions but must be presented at the security checkpoint.

Airport screeners may decide that your checked luggage needs to be searched by hand. You can purchase luggage locks that allow screeners to open and relock a checked bag if hand-searching is necessary. Look for Travel Sentry–certified locks at luggage or travel shops, AAA branches, or Amazon.com. For more information on the locks, visit www.travel sentry.org.

Part III
Dublin and the East Coast

"Okay, we got one cherry lager with bitters and a pineapple slice, and one honey malt ale with cinnamon and an orange twist. You want these in steins or parfait glasses?"

In this part . . .

Dublin City and the surrounding areas offer attractions that run from quiet mountain towns to hot, trendy clubs. Vibrant Dublin City is home to several excellent museums, an array of fabulous restaurants serving everything from fish and chips to gourmet New Irish meals, and a varied and hopping nightlife scene. Just north of the city are counties Meath and Louth, where you find some of Ireland's most magnificent ancient ruins (see Chapter 12). To the south and west are Wicklow and Kildare, two counties filled with gardens and estates, mountains, horses (especially in Kildare), and loads of that gorgeous Irish green. You won't want for outdoor activities in these parts. Head to Chapter 13 for details.

The southeastern counties of Wexford, Waterford, Tipperary, and Kilkenny offer an array of places to see and things to do. Some highlights are driving along the coast in Wexford, watching Waterford Crystal being created, exploring the Rock of Cashel in Tipperary, and wandering the medieval streets of Kilkenny. Turn to Chapter 14 for more information.

Chapter 11

Dublin

In This Chapter

▶ Arriving in Dublin and finding your way around
▶ Deciding where to stay and where to eat
▶ Discovering Dublin's top attractions
▶ Shopping for the best Irish goods
▶ Hitting the finest of Dublin's 1,000-plus pubs

*W*alking down a street in Dublin filled with hip young things heading for an after-work pub visit, it appears that you could be in any cosmopolitan city in the world. But spend a few hours strolling around Dublin, and you start to get a sense of the city's 1,000-year-plus history. Those hip young things are crowding into pubs that natives from two centuries ago would recognize, and talking on iPhones as they walk down cobblestone streets that have felt the weight of countless wagon wheels. This coexistence of old and new is a major part of Dublin's appeal. You find yourself visiting an 800-year-old church on your way to dinner in a hot new Asian restaurant, or watching a Celtic-punk band at a pub where James Joyce used to drink.

Dublin has undergone major changes in the past 20 years or so. The strong software and communications economy (dubbed the Celtic Tiger) pumped money into the city, and the European Economic Community (now the European Union) showered grants on Ireland in general and on Dublin in particular. Though the Celtic Tiger seems to be playing dead, Dublin remains one of Europe's trendiest cities. Dublin's population has gotten younger and more ethnically diverse, and up until the recession the 20- and 30-something Dubs helped create and support vibrant, cutting-edge arts, dining, clubbing, and shopping scenes. Though some restaurants, clubs, and hotels have fallen victim to tough economic times, many have adapted, with top restaurants creating reasonably priced early-bird menus and luxury hotels offering deep discounts.

Getting to Dublin

Dublin is one of Ireland's two main international gateways, so if you're flying to the country, there's a good chance you'll be touching down here. Dublin also is well connected to the rest of the country by bus, train, and ferry routes.

By plane

Dublin International Airport (☎ **01-814-1111;** www.dublinairport. com) is 11km (7 miles) north of the city, about a 25- to 45-minute drive from the city center (*An Lar* in Gaelic). Aer Lingus, Air France, American Airlines (operated by Aer Lingus), Continental, Delta, and United fly directly into Dublin from the United States. Aer Lingus, Air France, bmi, Lufthansa, and Ryanair have regular flights from England. See Chapter 6 for more on flights into Ireland.

In the arrivals concourse, you'll find a travel information desk that can help you figure out how to get to your destination, desks for the major car-rental companies (listed in Chapter 7), and ATMs.

Taxis are available outside the arrival terminal's main entrance — just look for the signs. The fare to downtown Dublin is about €20 to €30, and the trip takes 25 to 45 minutes, depending on traffic. Not all locals tip, but those who do usually tip about 10 percent.

AirCoach (☎ **01-844-7118;** www.aircoach.ie) runs 24 hours a day, at 10- to 30-minute intervals (one hour intervals 12:30–4:30 a.m.), between Dublin Airport and various stops in Dublin's city center and south side. The one-way fare is €7 adults, €1 kids. The bus trip from Dublin Airport to the city center takes about 40 minutes, barring traffic jams. **Dublin Bus** (☎ **01-873-4222;** www.dublinbus.ie) has several routes from the airport, including Airlink routes 747 and 748, which provide service to many points in the city center. If your hotel or B&B is not in the city center, check with the information desk in the arrivals hall to figure out which bus to take. The Airlink runs every 10 to 15 minutes daily between 5:15 a.m. and roughly 11 p.m. One-way tickets are €6 adults, €3 kids.

If you're flying out of Dublin Airport, give yourself more than enough time to get to the airport and through check-in and security. Flights close an hour before departure and many people (including me) have missed flights departing from Dublin Airport.

By ferry

A number of ferry companies have routes to Dublin from harbors in Wales and England. See Chapter 6 for a listing of ferry companies and the ports that they serve. Ferries dock at **Dublin Ferryport** (☎ **01-887-6000**) or at **Dun Laoghaire** (pronounced dun *leer*-ee) **Ferryport,** less than 13km (8 miles) from Dublin. Public transportation into the city is available from both ports.

By train

Iarnród Éireann (pronounced ee-*arn*-rod *air*-an), also know as **Irish Rail** (☎ **1-850-366-222;** www.irishrail.ie), runs between Dublin and the major towns and cities of Ireland, including Belfast in Northern Ireland. Trains arrive at one of three stations: Connolly Station on Amiens Street (primarily serving trains from the North and Northwest, including Northern Ireland); Heuston Station on Kingsbridge, off St. John's Road (serving trains from the South, Southwest, and West); and Pearse Station on Westland Row, Tara Street (serving trains from the Southeast). The **Dublin Area Rapid Transit** (DART; ☎ 1-850-366-222; www.irishrail. ie) commuter trains connect the city to the suburban towns north (as far as Dundalk) and south of the city (as far as Arklow).

By bus

Ireland's bus system, **Bus Éireann** (☎ 01-836-6111; www.buseireann. ie), runs between Dublin and most cities and towns in the Republic. The city's bus terminal, called **Busáras,** is next to the Customs House on Store Street, which is on the north side of the river, three blocks east of O'Connell Street.

By car

The N1, M1, N2, and N3 lead into Dublin from the north; the N4, M4, M7, and N7 lead in from the west; and the M11/N11 leads into the city from the south. The M50 is Dublin's beltway, surrounding three sides of the city and linking most major routes into and out of town. After you get into Dublin, you should return your rental car or leave it in your hotel parking lot, and use your feet, public transportation, and taxis to see the city. If you have to bring a car into the city, several parking garages (known in Ireland as *car parks*) are available. On the north side of the Liffey, parking choices include a lot off Marlborough Street (at Cathal Brugha Street) and one off Jervis Street (at Lower Ormond Quay), among others. There are even more choices on the south side of the Liffey, including one at Fleet Street (off Temple Bar), and one at Stephens Green Shopping Centre.

Orienting Yourself in Dublin

The thin ribbon of the River Liffey divides Dublin into north and south sides. On the north side, the main thoroughfare is wide O'Connell Street, which leads up to Parnell Square. Along the river on the south side is hopping Temple Bar, which is filled with pubs, arts venues, and restaurants. Nearby Nassau Street runs along the Trinity College campus and intersects with Grafton Street, a bustling pedestrian street that leads up to St. Stephen's Green, a popular park. See the neighborhood breakdown in this section for more details.

A few words on street names: They have a tendency to change when you least expect it. One minute, you're on Aungiers Street; the next, you're on South Great George's Street. Did you make a turn without knowing it? No, that's just how the streets are in Dublin, so trust your sense of direction.

All Dublin addresses include a digit after the word *Dublin,* as in *General Post Office, O'Connell Street, Dublin 1.* These numbers are postal codes, similar to U.S. zip codes. Most of central Dublin is located within postal codes 1, 2, and 8. Odd numbers are north of the River Liffey, and even numbers are south of it.

Introducing the neighborhoods

Here's a breakdown of Dublin's central city neighborhoods, from trendy Temple Bar to posh Merrion and Fitzwilliam squares:

- ✔ **O'Connell Street area (north side of the Liffey):** Although this area once thrived as the most fashionable part of the city, it became an aging starlet in the latter half of the 20th century. Over the past few years, efforts have been made to restore buildings and generally rejuvenate the locale. Though you'll still find fast-food joints and tacky souvenir shops between stately buildings, such as the **General Post Office** and **Gresham Hotel,** the silvery sky-scraping **Millennium Spire** (affectionately called "the stiletto in the ghetto") is a reminder that things are changing. O'Connell Street's center median is home to impressive statues of noted Irishmen, and at the top of the street, you find the serene **Garden of Remembrance,** the excellent **Dublin City Gallery,** the **Hugh Lane,** and the interesting **Dublin Writers Museum.** A few blocks to the east of O'Connell Street are the famous **Abbey Theatre** and the **James Joyce Centre;** to the west are the bustling shopping streets of Henry, Moore, and Abbey.

- ✔ **Quartier Bloom, the Italian Quarter, and Millennium Walk (north side):** You only *thought* you booked your ticket to Ireland. This area of the north side, just over the Millennium Bridge, is Dublin's own Little Italy, featuring Italian wine bars and restaurants in addition to a few non-Italian restaurants.

- ✔ **Trinity College area (south side):** Across O'Connell Bridge on the south side of the River Liffey stands **Trinity College,** home to the **Book of Kells.** This sprawling campus of green lawns and Hogwarts-style old buildings sits in the heart of the city and is surrounded by classy bookstores and shops.

- ✔ **Temple Bar (south side):** Tucked into a spot between Trinity and Dublin Castle is the funky and fashionable Temple Bar, where you find pubs, hip shops, restaurants, and arts venues along cobbled alleys. This area hosts a number of excellent weekend markets, including a book market, a fashion market, a furniture market, and an organic food market. A few years ago, this area was known for a lack of locals and countless rowdy stag and hen (bachelor and bachelorette) parties, but cultural offerings are luring Dubs back.

- ✔ **Old City–historical area (south side):** This historical area boasts narrow streets and ancient buildings, some dating as far back as Viking and medieval times. Some highlights are **Dublin Castle, Christ Church Cathedral, St. Patrick's Cathedral,** and the **old city**

walls. A bit farther on is the **Guinness Storehouse.** South Great Georges Street and the streets that surround it are filled with great shops, restaurants, and pubs.

✔ **St. Stephen's Green and Grafton Street (south side):** This area begins at the bottom of the pedestrian Grafton Street, with its many trendy clothing stores and its variety of street performers, and finishes up in St. Stephen's Green, Dublin's favorite park. This pretty part of town has plenty of upscale shops and cafes and is always teeming with people.

✔ **Merrion and Fitzwilliam squares (south side):** These two square parks are surrounded by some of Dublin's most beautiful Georgian town houses, each with a distinctive, brightly colored door. Some were once the homes of Dublin's most famous citizens, but today, many of them house professional offices. Some big names from Dublin's past lived on Merrion Square, including the poet William Butler Yeats, Irish nationalist leader Daniel O'Connell, and writer Oscar Wilde.

✔ **Docklands and Grand Canal Dock:** If you want to see the most recently developed (and developing) area in Dublin, walk east of O'Connell Street along the River Liffey. On the north side, you'll find a beautiful new convention center that looks a whole lot like a pint glass, the giant O_2 indoor concert venue, and one of the most moving sculpture installations I've ever seen, portraying men and women during the Great Famine. Cross over the gorgeous new Samuel Beckett Bridge to the south side to see the super-modern new Grand Canal Theatre building.

Finding information after you arrive

Dublin Tourism (☎ **01-850-230-330** from Ireland, 066-979-2083 outside Ireland; www.visitdublin.com) runs two walk-in visitor centers around the center of the city and one at the airport. The largest and best visitor center is in the **Church of St. Andrew** on Suffolk Street, Dublin 2, and is open September through May Monday through Saturday 9 a.m. to 5:30 p.m., Sunday 10:30 a.m. to 3 p.m.; and July and August Monday through Saturday 9 a.m. to 7 p.m., Sunday 10:30 a.m. to 3 p.m. The others are at the **Arrivals Hall,** Dublin Airport (Open: Daily 8 a.m.–10 p.m.), and at **14 O'Connell St.,** Dublin 1 (Open: Mon–Sat 9 a.m.–5 p.m.).

For information on events once you get to Dublin, pick up a copy of *InDublin* magazine (www.indublin.ie), available at the visitor centers and around Dublin.

Getting Around Dublin

The best way to see Dublin is to lace up a good pair of shoes and hoof it. The center of the city is compact and easily walkable. For attractions that are not within walking distance, take advantage of the excellent bus network. Even if you ignore the rest of this book, heed these words: *Don't explore Dublin by car.* The slow traffic and confusing streets are a study in frustration, and parking is expensive and out of the way.

Remember that the Irish drive on the left side of the road, so look right first before stepping into the street.

By bus

Dublin Bus, 59 Upper O'Connell St., Dublin 1 (☎ **01-873-4222;** www. dublinbus.ie), operates double-decker buses, regular buses, and *imps* (mini buses) throughout Dublin city and its suburbs, with city center fares only 50¢ and suburban fares under €5. The destination and bus number are posted in the windshield; buses going toward the city center read an lar, which is Irish Gaelic for "center city." You find bus stops every two or three blocks, and most bus routes pass down O'Connell Street, Abbey Street, and Eden Quay on the north side of the river and down Westmoreland Street, Nassau Street, and Aston Quay on the south side. Most buses run every 10 to 15 minutes Monday through Saturday from about 6 a.m. to about 11:30 p.m. and Sunday from about 10 a.m. to about 11 p.m. A late-night bus service runs on a limited route Friday and Saturday nights from midnight to 4:30 a.m. The fare is a flat €5, and buses depart from College Street, Westmoreland Street, and D'Olier Street. If you don't have a bus pass, the buses accept exact change only. If you pay more than the required amount, you get a coupon for a refund that you can redeem at the Dublin Bus headquarters at 59 Upper O'Connell St.

The three-day Freedom ticket, which gives you unlimited local bus access for 72 hours, discounts at attractions, and a free ride to and from the airport, is a great deal if you're planning on using the bus a lot. The unlimited one-day, three-day, five-day, and seven-day Rambler bus passes are also a great bargain. Passes are available at convenience stores and supermarkets all over the city center, online at www.dublin bus.ie, and at Dublin Bus headquarters, 59 Upper O'Connell St.

By taxi

To get a taxi in Dublin, go to a taxi rank, where cabs line up along the street; or hail a cab by sticking out your arm. If the cab's roof light is on, it means that the cab is unoccupied and ready to pick up passengers. If possible, take a cab with a meter and a roof sign; unmarked cabs may overcharge you. Ask for the estimated fare before you begin your journey. There are taxi ranks at large hotels, train stations, the bus station, the O'Connell Street median near the General Post Office, opposite St. Stephen's Green shopping center, and near Trinity College on Dame Street. You also can call a cab; reliable companies include **Castle Cabs** (☎ **01-831-9000**) and **National Radiocabs** (☎ **01-677-2222**). Most locals tip drivers around 10 percent.

In Ireland, passengers usually sit up front with the driver, rather than in the back seat, chauffeur style.

Looking for a greener option? Check out Dublin's new motor-assisted, pedal-powered, two-passenger **Ecocabs** (www.ecocabs.ie), which offer rides around the city center (within about a 3.2km/2-mile radius of O'Connell Bridge). Did I mention that they're free? Yup, companies pay to advertise on the cabs, which pays all expenses, so they don't cost you a cent!

By train

The **DART** commuter train (☎ 1-850-366-222; www.irishrail.ie) connects the city to suburbs and coastal towns both north (as far as Howth) and south (as far as Greystones) and is quite a bargain for a day trip to a nearby town. The three stops in Dublin's city center are Connolly Station, Pearse Street Station, and Tara Street Station. It's not usually worth it to take the DART within the city center, because the three stops are within such easy walking distance of one another. Most DART trains run every 5 to 20 minutes Monday through Saturday from about 6 a.m. to about 11:45 p.m. There is usually not much service on Sundays. Tickets are on sale in each station and online. Go to www.dummies.com/cheatsheet/ireland for a DART map. The shortest journeys come in at €1.45 each way, with trips to nearby seaside towns costing around €3.50 each way.

By car

If you're completely ignoring my advice and driving in Dublin, remember to avoid parking in bus lanes or along curbs with double yellow lines — these are easy ways to get your tires clamped by parking officials. To park on the streets in Dublin, buy a Pay-and-Display ticket at one of the vending machines along the street, and display it in the window of your car. See p. 73 for information on parking lots (called *car parks* here).

By Luas (tram)

Luas (☎ 1-800-300-604; www.luas.ie) is Dublin's sleek, shiny light-rail tram system. The Luas (pronounced lewis) is a great way to get to attractions that are outside of the immediate city center, including the National Museum of Decorative Arts; the Cobblestone Pub, in Smithfield; and the O$_2$ concert venue. The Red Line makes traveling to Heuston and Connolly rail stations a cinch. One-way fares run between €1.50 and €2.50, depending on your destination. You can buy tickets from the machines at each stop.

By bike

You can rent a city-worthy bike from one of the 40 locations run by **dublinbikes** (☎ 1-850-777-070; www.dublinbikes.ie). You use an automated ticket terminal at one of 14 locations to buy your pass, and then you can rent your bike from any of the 40 locations. You'll pay a flat €2 for a three-day ticket, plus service charges ranging from 50¢ for one hour to €6.50 for four hours. The first 30 minutes on all bikes are free of service charges, so if you're taking a short journey, you'll pay only €2. A few of the most central ticket terminals are on the east and south sides of Stephen's Green and on Dame Street at Parliament Street. You can return your bike to the same location or any of the other locations.

Spending the Night in Dublin

There's no denying it: Dublin is a hip and cosmopolitan city, and a hip and cosmopolitan city breeds trendy (and expensive) hotels. If you're looking for luxury, Dublin offers an embarrassment of riches. If that trust fund hasn't turned up yet, your accommodations options are more limited, because central Dublin lacks the cozy, inexpensive B&Bs found in abundance across the rest of Ireland. But fear not: This section includes accommodations options ranging from deals for budget travelers to extravagant hotels, where penthouse accommodations cost €1,000 or more. See Chapter 8 for more tips and information on finding and booking various types of accommodations.

Unlike accommodations in the rest of the country, some Dublin hotels don't significantly lower prices during the off season (Oct–Apr). However, many lodgings offer weekend or midweek packages, so ask.

Some of the accommodations listed here have free or discounted parking. Rates include breakfast, unless otherwise noted.

Dublin's top accommodations

Ariel House
$–$$ Ballsbridge, Dublin 4

Sure, it's located in a leafy residential area that's about a 20-minute walk from the center of the city (or a super-quick ride on the nearby DART train), but this romantic hotel is worth any tradeoff in convenience. Rooms in the 1850s house are high-ceilinged, spacious, and gorgeously furnished with Victorian and Georgian antiques and period-style wallpaper and fabrics. Picture velvet drapes, canopy beds (in many of the rooms), and lovely framed prints and portraits. Don't come expecting museum-quality surroundings, however; furnishings have a well-worn quality that you might expect in a rich Irish great-aunt's house. Try to avoid bedrooms in the basement — they can be stuffy and a little dark. The drawing room is elegant and welcoming — you may be inspired to take out your quill pen and write some postcards in front of the crackling fire. Ariel House's beauty is more than skin deep; the staff are some of the friendliest and most knowledgeable in Dublin, making this hotel, like Kilronan House (reviewed later in this section), one of the best choices for first-time Dublin visitors. Book online for deep discounts.

50–54 Lansdowne Rd. ☎ *01-688-5512. Fax: 01-688-5845.* www.ariel-house.net. *DART: Lansdowne Road. Parking: Free on-site. Rack rates: €70–€100 double. MC, V.*

Azalea Lodge
$$ Drumcondra, Dublin 9

I can't count the number of times I've heard "Azalea Lodge" from visitors in response to my question: "What's your favorite moderately priced bed-and-breakfast in Dublin?" You'd be hard-pressed to find kinder hosts than Bernadette and Padraig Sweeney, who do everything within their power to make your visit pleasant and fun. Breakfast is excellent, with fresh fruit, home-baked scones, and, with prior notice, vegetarian options for those who prefer their Irish breakfast meat-free. Rooms are large and clean, painted in soothing colors and featuring snow-white linens. Though the B&B is outside of the city center, there is a bus that stops right across the street that will get you into Dublin's heart in about 15 minutes. A number of lively pubs nearby give visitors a more authentic encounter with pub life than many joints in Temple Bar.

If you're looking for a lower-cost B&B, try the nearby ABC Guesthouse (see p. 116); for similar options that are closer to the city center, look into Kilronan House (see p. 113) or Waterloo House (see p. 115).

67 Upper Drumcondra Rd. ☎/*fax* **1-837-0300**. *www.azalealodge.com. Parking: Free on-site. Rack rates: €100–€110 double. MC, V.*

Brooks Hotel
$$$ Old City, Dublin 2

This is my top choice for those seeking a full-service hotel in Dublin's city center. The location is incredible, on a bustling and trendy little street within a few minutes' walk of Grafton Street, St. Stephen's Green, Temple Bar, and Trinity College. The staff and concierge go out of their way to make sure that you have a pleasant stay. When I asked if there was a good Laundromat in the area, the concierge actually walked me to the best nearby option, insisting on carrying my bulging laundry bag. It's well worth it to reserve a renovated room (termed *deluxe*), which have a contemporary look, with king-size beds dressed in cloud-white and deep plum colors, air-conditioning (still a rarity in Irish hotels), and warm lighting. The older rooms are just as clean as the renovated rooms, but they definitely feel worn and a bit ragged. Some rates include breakfast, but others don't (if yours doesn't, take advantage of Lemon Crepe and Coffee Co., around the corner on South William Street). The only negative that I can think of is that rooms that face Drury Street can get some noise at night, although compared to the decibel level in Temple Bar hotels, this place is a monastery. Check the Web site for some great packages and specials.

The Westbury Hotel (see p. 116) is a great similar option.

Drury Street. ☎ **01-670-4000**. *Fax: 01-670-4455. www.brookshotel.ie. Bus: 7a, 7d, 11, 11a, and 11b. Parking: Free on-site. Rack rates: €127–€210 double. Some rates do not include breakfast. AE, MC, V.*

Dublin Accommodations and Dining

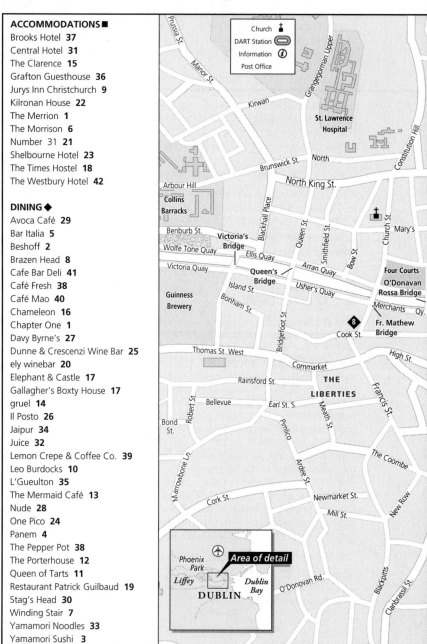

ACCOMMODATIONS■

Brooks Hotel **37**
Central Hotel **31**
The Clarence **15**
Grafton Guesthouse **36**
Jurys Inn Christchurch **9**
Kilronan House **22**
The Merrion **1**
The Morrison **6**
Number 31 **21**
Shelbourne Hotel **23**
The Times Hostel **18**
The Westbury Hotel **42**

DINING◆

Avoca Café **29**
Bar Italia **5**
Beshoff **2**
Brazen Head **8**
Cafe Bar Deli **41**
Café Fresh **38**
Café Mao **40**
Chameleon **16**
Chapter One **1**
Davy Byrne's **27**
Dunne & Crescenzi Wine Bar **25**
ely winebar **20**
Elephant & Castle **17**
Gallagher's Boxty House **17**
gruel **14**
Il Posto **26**
Jaipur **34**
Juice **32**
Lemon Crepe & Coffee Co. **39**
Leo Burdocks **10**
L'Gueulton **35**
The Mermaid Café **13**
Nude **28**
One Pico **24**
Panem **4**
The Pepper Pot **38**
The Porterhouse **12**
Queen of Tarts **11**
Restaurant Patrick Guilbaud **19**
Stag's Head **30**
Winding Stair **7**
Yamamori Noodles **33**
Yamamori Sushi **3**

Church
DART Station
Information
Post Office

Prussia St.
Manor St.
Kirwan
Grangegorman Upper
St. Lawrence Hospital
Constitution Hill
Brunswick St.
North
North King St.
Arbour Hill
Collins Barracks
Benburb St.
Wolfe Tone Quay
Victoria's Bridge
Ellis Quay
Blackhall Place
Queen St.
Smithfield St.
Bow St.
Church St.
Mary's
Victoria Quay
Queen's Bridge
Arran Quay
Four Courts
O'Donavan Rossa Bridge
Island St.
Usher's Quay
Guinness Brewery
Bonham St.
Merchants Qy.
Bridgefoot St.
Fr. Mathew Bridge
Cook St.
Thomas St. West
Cornmarket
High St.
Rainsford St.
THE LIBERTIES
Francis St.
Robert St.
Bellevue
Earl St. S.
Meath St.
Bond St.
Pimlico
Ardee St.
The Coombe
Marrowbone Ln.
Cork St.
Newmarket St.
New Row
Mill St.
Blackpitts
Clanbrassil St.

Phoenix Park
Liffey
DUBLIN
Dublin Bay
Area of detail
O'Donovan Rd.

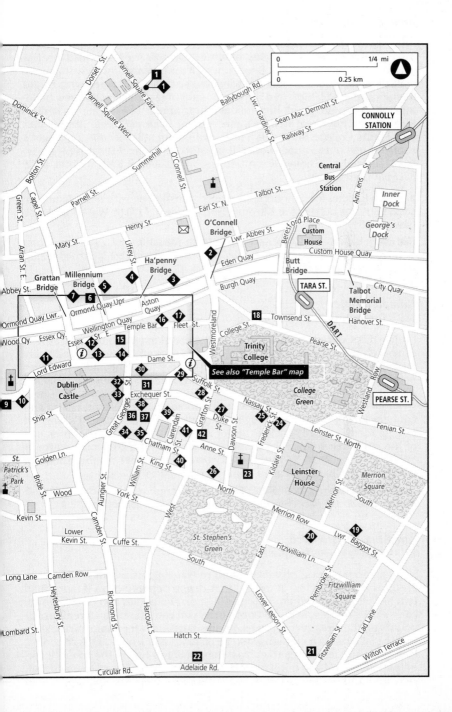

Grafton Guesthouse
$$ Old City, Dublin 2

This guesthouse is a good value, offering neat, cute rooms at relatively low prices (for Dublin, anyway). Rooms (which range from tiny to average) are simply decorated with kitschy touches, such as wallpaper with bright flowers and mod lamps, and the continental breakfast (served a few buildings over) is quite good. But the best thing about this place is its central location, on hip Great George's Street, near Grafton Street, Temple Bar, and Trinity College. Service is a little rushed but still friendly. Try to get a room on one of the upper floors, if possible — some of the rooms on the lower floor can be noisy. Reception is now located at Kelly's Hotel, at 36 S. Great George's St.

If you're looking for a moderately priced guesthouse with more hands-on staff, you'd be better of at Kilronan House (see p. 113) or Waterloo House (see p. 115).

See map p. 110. 26–27 S. Great George's St. ☎ *01-648-0010.* www.graftonguest house.com. *DART: Tara Street Station. Bus: 16A. Parking: Garage parking nearby, about €24 per day. Rack rates: €85–€110 double. MC, V.*

Hampton Hotel
$$$ Donnybrook, Dublin 4

I think this Georgian building has some sort of magical ability to attract top-notch staff. The hotel has changed hands but still draws the genuinely warm, attentive, and helpful staff that it always has. They'll even deliver popcorn to your room when you borrow a DVD! The spotless rooms are playful and contemporary, with fun, bold wallpaper backing each bed; sleek electric "fireplaces"; and velvety pomegranate-colored chairs and couches in larger rooms. Though all the rooms are beautiful, it's worth it to upgrade to a more spacious Select room or, if your budget allows, one of the gorgeous suites. The hotel is located about a 20-minute walk (or quick bus trip) from St. Stephen's Green, in the quiet neighborhood of Donnybrook. Check online for some terrific special offers.

19–29 Morehampton Rd. ☎ *01-668-0995.* www.hamptonhotel.ie. *Bus: 10, 46a, 746. Parking: Free on-site. Rack rates: €100–€150 double. Breakfast not included. AE, MC, V.*

Jurys Inn Christchurch
$$ Old City (near Temple Bar), Dublin 8

You can't beat Jurys for value, if you're traveling as a family: This hotel group is one of the few in Ireland that doesn't charge extra if more than two people share a room. Three adults, or two adults and two children, can share a room, and if you book early, you can get some incredible discounts on the already-low prices. Rooms here are rather uninspiring standard hotel fare, with modern wood furnishings and white-tiled bathrooms. However, any lack of character is compensated for by the friendly and helpful staff, and the hotel's central location at the top of Dame Street, right near Christ Church Cathedral and Dublin Castle (ask for a room with a view of the cathedral). There is a restaurant and a casual cafe downstairs. Don't pay extra for the breakfast here; you can do better on your own (Queens of Tarts, on Cow's Lane, or Lemon Crepe & Coffee Co., at 66 S. William St., are two of my favorites).

See map p. 110. Christ Church Place, right off Dame Street. ☎ **01-454-0000.** *Fax: 01-454-0012.* www.jurysinns.com. *DART: Tara Street Station. Bus: 49, 50, 51B, 54A, 56A, 65, 77, 77A, 78A. Parking: €14 per night at the connected public parking lot. Rack rates: €70–€110 for up to three adults or two adults and two children. You may get significant discounts if you book for more than one night and if you book early. Breakfast not included. AE, MC, V.*

Kilronan House
$$ St. Stephen's Green, Dublin 2

This small family-run guesthouse is one of the best places to stay if this is your first visit to Dublin. Cormac, the hotel's friendly proprietor, is like a warm and funny uncle, and makes a point to sit down with each guest to help plan an itinerary and to field questions about the city. Located on a quiet street within an easy ten-minute walk of St. Stephen's Green, the Georgian townhouse features many original details, such as beautiful crown molding, large bay windows, Waterford chandeliers, and hardwood floors in the public areas. The spacious bedrooms are simply furnished, brightly painted and filled with natural light — ask for one with a skylight. An excellent breakfast, featuring several choices, is served in the elegant dining room.

See map p. 110. 70 Adelaide Rd. ☎ **01-475-5266.** *Fax: 01-478-2841.* www.dublinn.com. *DART: Pearse Street. Bus: 14, 15A, 15B, 44, 44N, 48A, 48N. Parking: Free on-site. Rack rates: €75–€135 double. AE, DC, MC, V.*

The Merrion
$$$$ Old City, Dublin 2

Trendy hotels are certainly fun, but if you want a classic hotel with substance, book here. Voted the number one Dublin hotel by readers of *Condé Nast Traveler* in 2009, the Merrion is housed in a row of meticulously restored Georgian buildings that were once home to high-society occupants, including the Duke of Wellington. The intricate woodwork and plasterwork throughout the hotel are museum-worthy, and the turf fires and enveloping couches in the drawing rooms invite lingering. The guest rooms are airy and sophisticated, decorated with Irish antiques and beautiful fabrics of the finest quality, and bathrooms are outfitted in marble. Service is top-notch; the staff is welcoming, friendly, and happy to share their considerable knowledge. A handful of visitors have complained that the front-desk staff are stuffy, but I've never had that experience — even when I accidentally walked into the wrong entrance for the Art Tea, soaking wet and bedraggled from a surprise rain shower. I would skip the extra charge for breakfast and opt for one of the many nearby cafes instead.

Upper Merrion Street. ☎ **01-603-0600.** *Fax: 01-603-0700.* www.merrionhotel. com. *Bus: 25, 25a, 25b. Parking: Valet €20 per day. Rack rates: €200–€270 double. Breakfast not included. DC, MC, V.*

The Morrison
$$$ North Liffey, Dublin 1

A supermodel who has let herself go a bit, the Morrison was once Dublin's paramount example of modern, minimalist style. However, a lack of upkeep has left the rooms a bit tired-looking. Happily, this supermodel gets by on personality, with an incredible staff that's willing to bend over backward to make sure that you enjoy your stay. The location is another bonus; minutes from Temple Bar but without the late-night hubbub that keeps Temple Bar hotel denizens awake. Rooms are large and clean, with very comfortable beds. Check the Web site for some excellent packages and discounts.

See map p. 110. Ormond Quay (in front of the Millennium Bridge). ☎ **01-887-2400.** *Fax: 01-874-4039.* www.morrisonhotel.ie. *DART: Connolly Station. Parking: On-site public parking €14 per day. Rack rates: €120–€195 double. Rates are much lower midweek than weekends. Breakfast not included. AE, MC, V.*

Mt. Herbert Hotel
$–$$ Ballsbridge, Dublin 4

Family pride may play a part in the excellent maintenance of this hotel: John Loughran, the director, grew up here when his parents were in charge, and he seems to take pleasure in providing guests with a comfortable stay. Located in a residential section of Dublin, only a short DART ride away from the heart of the city, Mt. Herbert offers sleek, slightly Asian-influenced public areas that retain some of their original Georgian architectural features. Bedrooms are clean, contemporary, and simple, with pine furnishings and sparkling white linens. Service is friendly and helpful.

Herbert Road. ☎ **01-614-2000.** *Fax: 01-660-7077.* www.mountherberthotel.ie. *DART: Lansdowne Road. Parking: Free on-site. Rack rates: €70–€110 double. Most rates do not include breakfast. MC, V.*

Number 31
$$$–$$$$ St. Stephen's Green, Dublin 2

Designed by Sam Stephenson, one of Ireland's most famous modern architects, this guesthouse is tucked away behind a vined wall on a peaceful little lane about a ten-minute walk from St. Stephen's Green. Inside, the style is a marriage of modern design and classic Georgian grace. The spacious rooms are simply and artistically furnished, and feature little modern surprises such as a burnished gray mirrored wall or a sunken bathtub sporting turquoise mosaic tiles. Sitting in the glass-walled conservatory munching on fresh-made granola, poached pears in vanilla syrup, and delightful hot breakfast dishes (I loved the eggs with salmon) may make you want to move in permanently. Your hosts, Deirdre and Noel Comer, are warm and helpful.

See map p. 110. 31 Leeson Close, off Lower Leeson Street, near the junction with Fitzwilliam Street. ☎ **01-676-5011.** *Fax: 01-676-2929.* www.number31.ie. *Bus: 70X, 92. Parking: Free on-site. Rack rates: €175–€200 double. AE, MC, V.*

Shelbourne Hotel
$$$$ St. Stephen's Green, Dublin 2

Fingers were crossed when this grande dame of Dublin was taken over by the Marriott chain and closed for a massive renovation. Happily, the Shelbourne's stately character is still intact, and the desk staff and concierge are as helpful as ever. The hotel seems to be feeling the effects of the recession, and as a result is charging quite a bit for "extras" (Wi-Fi is €20, and breakfast is a whopping €30). Rooms are traditionally furnished with floral prints and antique-style furnishings and boast some nice amenities, including 300-thread-count sheets and flat-screen TVs. Several travelers have found that paying for a Heritage Room, which allows access to the grand-sounding Heritage Lounge, is not worth it due to measly snack offerings and a sometimes-unpleasant staff. Peek into Room 121, where history was made when the Irish constitution was drafted here in 1922.

See map p. 110. 27 St. Stephen's Green. ☎ **01-663-4500.** *Fax: 01-661-6006.* www. marriott.com. *Bus: 10, 10A, 11, 11A, 140. Parking: Valet €25 per day. Rack rates: €175–€300 double. Breakfast (€30) is not included in some rates. AE, DC, MC, V.*

The Times Hostel
$ Old City, Dublin 2

This place should run classes on how to keep budget travelers happy. The hostel is in a prime location, right near Trinity College, and the bedrooms, bathrooms, and spacious kitchen and common room are kept spotless. To sweeten the deal, the hostel offers all sorts of perks, including complimentary phone calls to 40 countries, a gratis dinner on Tuesdays, a lovely free continental breakfast (plus pancakes on Sunday), and free Wi-Fi. The staff knows the area well, and they lead walking tours and pub crawls for guests. Long live this fabulous hostel!

8 College St. ☎ **01-675-3652.** www.timeshostels.com. *Bus: 16 16a. Parking: Very limited street parking only. Rack rates: €66–€76 double. MC, V.*

Waterloo House
$$ St. Stephen's Green area, Dublin 4

I admit it: I was sort of skeptical that a place like this existed. It's an honest-to-goodness B&B, near Dublin's city center, which is a rare breed, indeed. Occupying a restored Georgian building on a quiet, leafy street, Waterloo House is about a 15-minute walk from St. Stephen's Green and the top of Grafton Street. The bedrooms, painted in warm colors and featuring comfy beds, are neat as a pin, and the excellent full Irish breakfast (including home-baked bread) is served in the pretty conservatory. Your hostess, Evelyn Corcoran, is kind and helpful, as is her staff.

8–10 Waterloo Rd. ☎ 01-660-1888. www.waterloohouse.ie. Bus: 10. Parking: Free on-site. Rack rates: €80–€130 double. MC, V.

Runner-up hotels

ABC Guesthouse

$ North Dublin, Dublin 9 This guesthouse, located a 20- to 30-minute walk or quick bus trip north of the city center, gets rave reviews for its kind and helpful hosts, delicious Irish breakfast, and great value. The bus into the center of the city stops right in front. *57 Upper Drumcondra Rd. ☎ 01-836-7417. www.abchousedublin.com. Parking: Free on-site. Rack rates: €60–€90 double. MC, V.*

Central Hotel

$$$ Old City, Dublin 2 You're basically paying for location here. If you're a late-night party animal, this is a great choice for very centrally located, no-frills accommodations. Otherwise, book elsewhere — the street noise from this area is louder than a teenage heavy-metal band. *See map p. 110. 1–5 Exchequer St. ☎ 01-679-7302. Fax: 01-679-7303. www.central hoteldublin.com. Bus: 10. Parking: Nearby public parking €8.50 during the day and €8 overnight. Rack rates: €90–€190 double. Midweek rates are much lower than weekend rates. Breakfast not included. MC, V.*

The Clarence

$$$ Temple Bar, Dublin 2 This hotel offers a terrific location at the doorstep of the lively Temple Bar area, the classy Octagon Bar, and great service. Plus, it's touched by fame: The hotel is partly owned by Bono and The Edge of U2. Unfortunately, it's a bit overpriced for what you get. Rooms on the River Liffey side of the hotel are much quieter. Skip the appallingly high-priced breakfast — instead, visit a nearby cafe (the Queens of Tarts on Cow's Lane is a great option). *See map p. 110. 6–8 Wellington Quay. ☎ 01-407-0800. Fax: 01-407-0820. www.theclarence.ie. Bus: 26, 66, 66A, 66B, 66D, 67, 67A. Parking: Valet €25 per day. Rack rates: €140–€190 double. Breakfast not included. AE, DC, MC, V.*

The Westbury Hotel

$$$$ Old City, Dublin 2 This place is a bit pricey, but travelers adore the central location and the stylish bedrooms, decked out with Frette linens, iPod docking stations, large flat-screen TVs, and your own personal espresso machine. The staff is warm, friendly, and helpful. *See map p. 110. Grafton Street. ☎ 01-679-1122. www.doylecollection.com. Bus: 90, 746, 747, 748. Parking: On-site €20 per day. Rack rates: €161–€230 double. Breakfast not included. AE, DC, MC, V.*

Dining in Dublin

You can't swing a cat in Dublin (not that you'd want to) without hitting a pleasant place to eat. The city is chock-full of great restaurants for all budgets and tastes. The trend in Dublin (as in the rest of the country) is toward creative dishes made with the freshest Irish products available (think Irish free-range beef served with a sauce featuring local mushrooms and herbs). Being a diverse city, Ireland's capital is also home to eateries that offer cuisines from across the globe. Looking for Indian or Mediterranean? You've got it. Or is it French, Tex-Mex, or Creole that's tempting your taste buds? No problem.

If you're craving traditional Irish fare — stew, fish and chips, shepherd's pie — point yourself in the direction of a pub (which shouldn't be too difficult). See my recommendations later in the section in the "Traditional Irish dishes" sidebar.

During the summer and on weekends, I recommend that you make a reservation for many of the more popular and upscale restaurants. Restaurants tend to be busiest from 7:30 to 9 p.m. I indicate when reservations are necessary in the following listings.

Tough economic times have given birth to a wonderful perk: Early-bird fixed-price menus! The majority of restaurants in Dublin, even the most posh, now offer these two- or three-course menus. The menus usually feature three or four selections from the a la carte menu for each course. At the Winding Stair, where main courses by themselves can come in at €27, the three-course early-bird menu totals €30. Early-bird menus usually are served starting at 5 p.m. or 5:30 p.m., with last orders at 7 p.m. or 7:30 p.m. You'll find similar deals at lunch.

Dublin diners tend to dress in smart-casual clothes when going out to a fancy restaurant. At all but the most chichi places, even a nice pair of jeans is fine.

Great lunch options

A wide range of lunch options in Dublin means that there's something to suit every budget and mood, from visitors looking to linger over lamb stew in a Victorian pub (see the "Traditional Irish dishes" sidebar, later in this chapter) to those who want to grab a sandwich and go.

If there are restaurants that interest you but seem prohibitively expensive for dinner, check their lunch offerings, which are often just as good and much less expensive.

My favorite lunch spot in Dublin is the **Pepper Pot** in the Powerscourt Townhouse Centre, 59 S. William St. (☎ **087-790-3204**), where you can people-watch from a balcony while munching on fresh, seasonal lunch dishes and baked goods. I loved my recent Niçoise salad, featuring new

Temple Bar

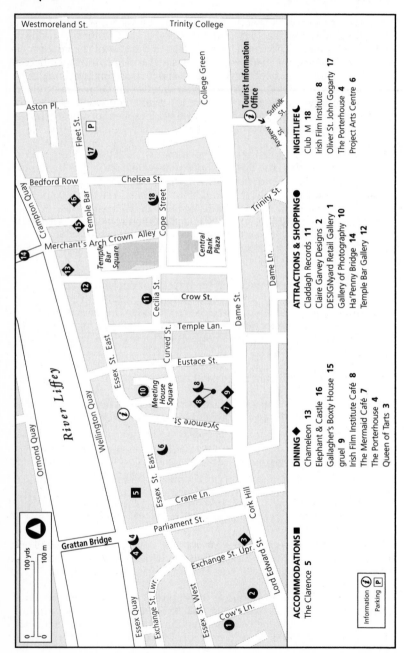

ACCOMMODATIONS ■
The Clarence **5**

DINING ◆
Chameleon **13**
Elephant & Castle **16**
Gallagher's Boxty House **15**
gruel **9**
Irish Film Institute Café **8**
The Mermaid Café **7**
The Porterhouse **4**
Queen of Tarts **3**

ATTRACTIONS & SHOPPING ●
Claddagh Records **11**
Claire Garvey Designs **2**
DESIGNyard Retail Gallery **1**
Gallery of Photography **10**
Ha'Penny Bridge **14**
Temple Bar Gallery **12**

NIGHTLIFE ☏
Club M **18**
Irish Film Institute **8**
Oliver St. John Gogarty **17**
The Porterhouse **4**
Project Arts Centre **6**

Information ⓘ Parking Ⓟ

season baby potatoes and topped with a semi-soft-boiled egg. Don't miss the blissful desserts.

In the Powerscourt Townhouse Centre on South William Street, you'll find **Cafe Fresh, (☎ 01-671-9669),** the home of great vegetarian cooking in Dublin. At **Avoca Cafe,** 11–13 Suffolk St. (☎ **01-677-4215**), you get beautiful food served by beautiful men. Another nice sit-down option is **Cafe Bar Deli,** in the former location of Bewley's Oriental Cafe, on 12 S. Great Georges St. (☎ 01-677-1646), which serves up simple, inexpensive fare in sumptuous surroundings of stained glass, dark wood, marble tables, and crystal chandeliers. In Temple Bar, I love the cafe at the **Irish Film Institute,** 6 Eustace St. (☎ 01-679-5744). On Dublin's north side, **Panem,** Ha'penny Bridge House, 21 Ormond Quay Lower (☎ 01-872-8510), is a popular spot for a light Italian lunch.

Want to grab a quick bite between attractions? Baggot Street has many spots for a good takeout lunch. You'll find options from Cornish pasties to sushi to Spar supermarket's selection of high-quality packaged sandwiches and salads. St. Stephen's Green, conveniently located right down the road, makes a perfect picnic spot. Near Trinity, a speedy lunch option is **Nude,** 21 S. Suffolk St. (☎ 01-672-5577), which sells delicious pasta, salads, sandwiches, and other quick bites made with organic ingredients.

 Finally, I can't think of a better sightseeing pick-me-up than a freshly made crepe folded around banana slices and Nutella. Follow the crowds to the deservedly popular **Lemon Crepe & Coffee Co.,** 66 S. William St., Dublin 2 (☎ **01-672-9044**).

Dublin's top restaurants

Bar Italia
$$ **Millennium Walkway/Bloom's Lane   ITALIAN/PIZZA**

This isn't the place for a romantic dinner; the restaurant is so noisy with chatter and laughter that your companion may mistake your sweet nothings for "Please pass the peas." However, the buzz doesn't distract diners from digging into such delicious classic southern Italian dishes as delicate gnocchi in marinara sauce, fabulous pizzas, and an out-of-this-world bruschetta with garlic, tomatoes, and basil. The setting is classy, with white walls, candles, and light wood, and the service is good. Most dishes are at the lower end of the price range listed here.

See map p. 110. Ormond Quay, on Bloom's Lane/Millennium Walkway. ☎ **01-874-1000**. *Bus: 37. 39, 39a, 70, 145. Reservations recommended. Main courses: €9–€18 (more for steaks). AE, DC, MC, V. Open: Mon–Thurs noon to 10:30 p.m., Fri–Sat noon to 11 p.m., Sun 1–9 p.m.*

(A very) Little Italy in Dublin

Two for the price of one! You buy a ticket to Ireland and get a free trip to a mini Italy. Quartier Bloom/Millennium Walkway, right over the Millennium footbridge on the north side of the Liffey, has become home to a handful of authentic Italian wine bars, Italian restaurants (see the review of Bar Italia earlier in this chapter), and a cafe serving panini, Italian pastries, and coffee (Caffé Cagliostro; ☎ 01-888-0834). There is even a hip little piazza and a contemporary Roman arch. Check out the mural near the center of Bloom's Lane, a riff on da Vinci's Last Supper in which Jesus and his apostles are replaced by people plucked randomly from Dublin's sidewalks (Jesus is played by an Indian graduate of Trinity College).

Beshoff
$ O'Connell Street area, Dublin 2   FISH AND CHIPS

If there were an Olympic category for best *chipper* (fish-and-chips shop), and I were the judge, Beshoff would get the gold. The fish here is as fresh as can be, its juices sealed in by a fried golden-brown crust; the *chips* (fries) are cut fresh each day and are thick and deliciously dense. If you like salt and vinegar to begin with, you'll love how they complement fish and chips, so ask for them. If you feel the same way about fish that my friend Shannon does — "If it comes from the sea, let it be" — take heart and order the chicken option.

Beshoff's rival is **Leo Burdocks,** 2 Werburgh St., Dublin 8 (☎ **01-454-0306**). I think Beshoff is better, but let me know your vote.

See map p. 110. 6 Upper O'Connell St. ☎ *01-872-4400. DART: Tara Street Station. Bus: 1, 2, 3, 121, 122, 123. Main courses: €4–€7. No credit cards. Open: Sun–Wed 9 a.m.–9 p.m., Thurs 11:15 a.m.–10 p.m.*

Café Mao
$$ Grafton Street area, Dublin 2   ASIAN FUSION

Take a seat outside or in the airy interior of this excellent restaurant, and settle down for a long, casual meal, and some great people-watching. The menu roams Asia and is full of flavorful dishes, including tender salmon teriyaki with vegetables, an awesome Malaysian chicken curry, and the intriguing sour orange vegetable curry. Don't miss the superb pumpkin spring rolls, served with a sweet and zingy plum sauce. The €20 three-course menu is a steal.

See map p. 110. 2–3 Chatham Row. ☎ *01-670-4899. Bus: 7, 10, 11, 11A, 11B, 46A, 46B. Main courses: €14–€19. AE, MC, V. Open: Mon–Sat noon to 11 p.m., Sun 2–9 p.m.*

Chameleon
$$-$$$ Temple Bar, Dublin 2 INDONESIAN

If you like tapas-style dining, you'll love *rijst-tafel,* a meal composed of several small Indonesian dishes. The kind staff will guide you through your options, from a four-dish seafood choice to an eight-dish vegetarian extravaganza. I loved the Kimodo menu, especially the lamb meatballs served in a spiced coconut sauce and the sesame fried vegetables. There are excellent stand-alone dishes if that's more your style, including the popular *sambal udang* — Tiger shrimp with chili, garlic, tamarind, shallots, and pineapple. The rooms are candlelit and cozy, with gleaming wood, rich red walls, silk pillows, and Indonesian art. The music selection is fabulously eclectic; our server told us that the owner is almost as proud of his iPod playlists as he is of his food. If you have a large group, book the Opium Room and share a feast.

1 Lower Fownes St., right near the Liffey. ☎ *01-671-0362. Bus: 39, 39a. Main courses: €14–€18 a la carte; €25–€35 rijst-tafel; early-bird four-course menu (served Tues–Thurs 5–7:30 p.m. and Fri–Sat 5–6:30 p.m.) €18. MC, V. Open: Tues–Fri and Sun 5–10:30 p.m., Sat 1–11 p.m.*

Chapter One
$$$$ North Side, Dublin 8 NEW IRISH

Voted the best restaurant in Dublin, the Michelin-starred Chapter One is devoted to crafting creative, impeccably prepared dishes with the finest of ingredients. The menu changes often, but you may encounter such decadent and inspired creations as Galway rock oysters served with chilled horseradish velouté, Riesling jelly, apples, and ginger; or cod with crushed Jerusalem artichokes and Morteau sausage, served with preserved lemon butter and leeks. Die-hard foodies may want to book the tasting menu at the chef's table (€80), while budget-watchers may be more interested in the two-course lunch (€30) or three-course pre-theater menu (€38, served 6–7 p.m.). The setting is a lovely brick and stone room with a green Connemara marble bar, and the service is excellent.

In the basement of the Dublin Writers Museum, 18–19 Parnell Sq. ☎ *01-873-2266. Bus: 46e, 145. Main courses: €32–€34. AE, MC, V. Open: Tues–Fri 12:30–2:30 p.m. and 6–10:30 p.m., Sat 6–10:30 p.m.*

Dunne & Crescenzi Wine Bar
$$ Trinity area, Dublin 2 ITALIAN

This was one of the first of Dublin's crop of Italian wine-bar restaurants, and it's still one of the very best. Located on a quiet street, the interior is warm and sophisticated, with tea lights illuminating the tables and hundreds of wine bottles lining the dark wood shelves. The classic Italian dishes are beautifully executed; the *caprese* salad with fresh mozzarella, tomatoes, and basil tastes like something you might eat under an olive tree in a Tuscan courtyard; the squid-ink pasta dish is packed with fresh clams, mussels, and shrimp; and the antipasta plates are legendary. The wine list, as you might expect, is outstanding, and the service is kind and unhurried.

14–16 South Frederick St. ☎ **01-675-9892.** *Bus: 4, 5, 7, 7a, 7d, 8. Main courses: €12–€23. AE, MC, V. Open: Mon–Sat 7:30 a.m. to midnight, Sun 9:30 a.m.–10 p.m.*

Elephant & Castle
$$ Temple Bar, Dublin 2   AMERICAN

Locals and visitors alike pile into this immensely popular, buzzing joint in the heart of Temple Bar, which serves exceptional burgers, salads, omelets, and other American diner fare. Burger-slingers around the world should cross their fingers that Elephant & Castle doesn't open a branch in their town, because these juicy, flavorful burgers are some of the best I've ever tasted. Garlic-philes must try the garlic burger, with roasted garlic cloves, garlic butter, and aioli; another winner is the burger with horseradish, black pepper, and sour cream. Or go for a tasty omelet or a fresh, generous salad. And don't miss the beverage list, which offers everything from elderflower soda to fresh limeade. This warm, relaxed restaurant, with its wood booths and funky paintings and photos (my favorite is a painting of a sign shop, reading "Advertise with SIGNS. We make them."), is the perfect place to watch the crowds of people who parade down Temple Bar. Elephant & Castle recently started offering some nice "upscale" dishes, but I recommend sticking with the fantastic basics.

See map p. 110. 18 Temple Bar St. ☎ *01-679-3121. DART: Tara Street Station. Bus: 7B, 7D, 11, 14A, 16, 16A, 46, 46A, 46B, 46C, 46D, 51N, 58X, 67N, 69N, 116, 121, 122, 150, 746. Main courses: €9–€20 (more for steak). AE, MC, V. Open: Mon–Fri 8 a.m.–11:30 p.m., Sat–Sun 10:30 a.m.–11:30 p.m.*

ely winebar
$$$ St. Stephen's Green area, Dublin 2   NEW IRISH

Though this restaurant has more than 400 choices on its wine list (from a lovely glass of Spanish white for €6.50 to a bottle of Bordeaux that comes in at €1,820), it is the least snobby wine bar you can imagine. Servers are friendly and relaxed, and they're skilled at matching your dish with a wine that appeals to you. Set in a restored Georgian town house adorned with contemporary furnishings, this is not just a wine bar with good food; the classy, unpretentious dishes would be reason enough to visit even if the restaurant served only water. The owners are devoted to local, seasonal, and organic sources (the beef and pork come straight from the couple's family farm in the West of Ireland). My husband and I battled it out over the last of our gorgeously presented cucumber and crab salad, and I loved my pan-fried arctic char with olive oil crushed potatoes, grilled asparagus, and saffron cream as much as he loved his organic burger with caramelized shallots and blue cheese. The bangers and mash are legendary, and if it's on the dessert menu don't miss the ely mess, a jumble of berries, cream, and meringue. Upstairs is more relaxed, while downstairs is more boisterous.

Traditional Irish dishes

If you ask a Dub where to find the best beef-and-Guinness stew or shepherd's pie, you may be met with a blank expression. With such a wide range of restaurants to choose from, you have to know where to look to find traditional Irish dishes. Here are some good bets:

- **Brazen Head,** 20 Lower Bridge St. (☎ 01-677-9549), is Dublin's oldest pub and serves all the classics.

- **Davy Byrne's,** 21 Duke St. (☎ 01-677-5217), was made famous through James Joyce's *Ulysses.* You can't go wrong here — follow in Leopold Bloom's footsteps and order a gorgonzola cheese sandwich or hunker down to a bowl of Irish stew.

- **Gallagher's Boxty House,** 20–21 Temple Bar (☎ 01-677-2762), serves up traditional Irish potato pancakes stuffed with various fillings.

- **The Porterhouse,** 16–18 Parliament St. (☎ 01-679-8847), is a beautiful new bar linked with the excellent Porterhouse brewery. The bar features ceiling-high shelves of lit glass bottles and a great traditional menu with a few modern twists (the fish and chips features "mint-infused" mushy peas).

- **Stag's Head,** 1 Dame Court, off Dame Street (☎ 01-671-3701), is a beautiful Victorian pub serving some of the best traditional Irish dishes in the city.

See map p. 110. 22 Ely Place. ☎ *01-676-8986. Bus: 7, 7A, 8, 10, 11, 13. Main courses: €15–€32; early-bird two- or three-course menu €25–€29 (served Mon–Sat 5–7:30 p.m.). AE, MC, V. Meals served: Mon–Wed noon to 10 p.m., Thurs noon to 10:30 p.m., Fri noon to 11 p.m., Sat 5–11 p.m.*

gruel
$$ Dublin 2   NEW IRISH/WORLD

"Please sir, may I have some more?" I'm sure the friendly staff at gruel would happily accommodate little Oliver Twist's appeal, though after seeing the gigantic portions here, he may reconsider his request. Every city should have a place like gruel — a bright, casual restaurant that serves inexpensive, hearty, creative dishes. Groups of friends and couples chat over fresh salads, homemade soups, and main courses that change daily but may include the likes of vegetable *tagine* served with couscous and mint yogurt, and bangers and mash with onion jam. Many repeat customers are devotees of the ever-changing "Roast on a Roll," a crunchy roll filled with freshly roasted meat and interesting garnishes. As you wait for your food, check out the art exhibits on one wall, the posters for upcoming concerts on another wall, and the funky pink fireplace graced with Campbell's Tomato Soup cans.

See map p. 110. 68a Dame St. ☎ *01-670-7119. Reservations not accepted. DART: Tara Street Station. Bus: 49, 56A, 77, 77A, 123. Main courses: €8–€15. No credit cards. Open: Mon–Wed and Fri 11:30 a.m.–9:30 p.m., Thurs and Sat 11:30 a.m.–10:30 p.m., Sun 11:30 a.m.–9 p.m.*

Il Posto
$$–$$$ Dublin 2 ITALIAN

Everything about this place is warm, inviting, and elegant, from the friendly service to the orange-and-cream paintings on the wall to the candles on each table. The delicious and filling food, served in giant portions, just adds to the general feeling of ease and comfort. The menu features many creatively put-together "nouveau" Italian dishes, such as the duo of duck breast and lamb's liver with braised balsamic lentils and walnuts, served with a red-wine-and-cinnamon poached pear and a toffee *jus*. The seafood dishes, including the grilled whole sea bass with rosemary-and-garlic oil and crushed black olives, are especially delicious. The early-bird set menu, served from 5:30 to 7 p.m. daily, is a good deal.

See map p. 110. 10 St. Stephen's Green. ☎ *01-679-4769. Reservations recommended. Main courses: €14–€25. AE, MC, V. Open: Mon–Sat noon to 2:30 p.m. and 5:30–11 p.m.*

Jaipur
$$–$$$ Grafton Street area, Dublin 2 INDIAN

You know you're in for a delicious Indian meal as soon as you take a bite of the complimentary airy *pappadum,* which are served with a trio of sauces: sweet pineapple chutney, tangy cilantro sauce, and a spicy red sauce. The atmosphere is refined and romantic, with exotic fresh flowers on each table and candlelight casting a golden glow on the faces of the couples and small groups of friends dining here. The menu is filled with great options, from traditional Indian favorites, such as chicken tikka masala, to more unusual choices such as nalli gosht — tender roast lamb with the chef's special spices. Be sure to order the pulao rice — fluffy, spiced basmati rice — to complement your main dish.

See map p. 110. 41 S. Great George's St. ☎ *01-677-0999. Reservations recommended. DART: Tara Street Station. Bus: 16A. Main courses: €13–€23. AE, MC, V. Open: Daily 5:30–11:30 p.m.*

Juice
$$ Old City, Dublin 2 GLOBAL/VEGETARIAN

Juice is a casual, friendly little slice of health-conscious California in the heart of Dublin. Small groups of friends and solo diners drop in to chat, flip through the newspaper, or write in their journals over generous portions of vegetarian and vegan dishes that take their inspiration from cuisines all over the planet. You find everything from miso soup to spicy bean burgers to crepe-like pancakes served with fresh fruit and organic maple syrup shot through with mango puree. And as the name not-very-subtly suggests, you also find all kinds of juices, which are so fresh, they taste like you just inserted a straw directly into the fruit or vegetable. High ceilings, curved walls, a metal panel covered with Christmas lights, and candy-colored glass flower vases and votive holders give this place a warm, funky air that invites lingering, especially on a cool, rainy day (not that Dublin has any of those).

See map p. 110. 73–83 S. Great George's St. ☎ **01-475-7856.** *DART: Tara Street Station. Bus: 16A. Main courses: €12–€16. AE, DC, MC, V. Open: Mon–Fri 10 a.m.– 11 p.m., Sat–Sun 11 a.m.–11 p.m.*

L'Gueuleton
$$$ Old City, Dublin 2   FRENCH

This popular restaurant boasts a French-cuisine-inspired menu, polite service, and a casually elegant atmosphere that hums with conversation and laughter. Choosing a single dish from the offerings can be difficult. The menu changes often, but dishes on a recent night included Toulouse sausages; duck with potatoes, sweetened chicory, and green peppercorns; and roast John Dory with fennel confit and baby spinach. Everything is prepared with an eye to preserving the character and flavor of the ingredients. The atmosphere is a happy marriage of stylish and casual; diners pull up mismatched chairs to tables adorned with tea lights and small bowls filled with cracked pepper and sea salt, and there is a cute garden in the back for warm-weather dining. The unfortunate combination of being all the rage and not accepting reservations means that you might have a wait if you arrive during prime Dublin dinner hours. A kind-of-strange thing: They don't serve any soda.

See p. 110. 1 Fade St. (right off of South Great George's Street). ☎ **01-675-3708.** *Reservations not accepted. Bus: 16A. Main courses: €15–€27. MC, V. Open: Mon–Sat 12:30–3 p.m. and 6–10 p.m., Sun 1–3 p.m. and 6–9 p.m.*

The Mermaid Cafe
$$$ Dublin 2   NEW IRISH

This is one of my favorite restaurants in Dublin, because it serves innovative dishes made with some of the freshest, most flavorful ingredients around. The menu changes seasonally, offering the likes of Irish Angus rib-eye steak with sage-and-mustard mashed potatoes and garlicky beans; yellowfin tuna with plum tomatoes, capers, mint, and wasabi mayonnaise; and a salad of asparagus and quail eggs with shaved parmesan and greens. The crowd is always buzzy and chic; businesspeople descend on the restaurant at lunch, while dinner sees more couples and small groups. The surroundings are cozy and modern, featuring contemporary art, white wood walls, high-backed pine chairs, and solid pine tables. Save room for the unbelievable desserts, including pecan pie served with maple ice cream and the Eton Mess, a jumble of cream and fruit. The two- and three-course lunch and early-bird dinner deals are excellent.

See map p. 110. 70 Dame St. ☎ **01-670-8236.** *Reservations recommended. DART: Tara Street Station. Bus: 68, 69, 69X. Main courses: €17–€26. MC, V. Open: Mon–Sat 12:30–3 p.m. and 6–11 p.m., Sun noon to 3:30 p.m. and 6–9 p.m.*

One Pico
$$$$ **Grafton Street area, Dublin 2** **FRENCH/NEW IRISH**

This is my number-one pick for sealing a business deal in Dublin. A classy crowd (including quite a few businesspeople) fills this elegant restaurant, decorated with dusky purples and golds, to sample star chef Eamonn O'Reilly's inventive, mouthwatering creations. Like the chefs at the Winding Stair, Chapter One, and the Mermaid Cafe (all reviewed in this section), O'Reilly creates adventurous dishes with fresh Irish produce, though his menu seems to have more of a French influence than the menus at those three restaurants. The menu changes often, featuring such delights as a starter of seared scallops served with black olive gnocchi, cauliflower puree, chorizo, and star anise foam, and an Irish Angus beef filet with artichoke puree, boiled asparagus, Pomme Anna (thinly sliced potatoes layered with butter), and cabernet sauvignon sauce. The fish dishes are some of the best in the city. Whatever you do, be sure to try the desserts; Cookies & Cream, a haute re-creation of some of the world's most beloved cookies, was one of my recent favorites. The two- to three-course fixed-price lunch (€25), pre-theater dinner (€26, served Mon–Thurs until 6:45 p.m.), and fixed-price dinner (€39, served all night Mon–Thurs and until 6:45 p.m. Fri–Sat) are excellent values.

See map p. 110. 5–6 Molesworth Place, Schoolhouse Lane (off St. Stephen's Green). ☎ *01-676-0300. Reservations recommended. DART: Pearse. Bus: 10, 11A, 11B, 13, or 20B. Main courses: €24–€32 (steak €36). AE, DC, MC, V. Open: Mon–Sat 12:30–11:30 p.m.*

Queen of Tarts
$ **Dublin 2** **BAKERY/CAFE**

I'd hate to think what would happen to my waistline if I lived near these two bakeries and cafes (right around the corner from one another). Savory lunch tarts (such as a goat cheese, tomato, olive, and pesto combo), salads, sandwiches, and toothsome homemade soups attended by a thick slice of brown bread are served in a cheerful, casual yellow room. But the excellent lunch fare is just the opening act for the glorious desserts, including a tangy blackberry-and-apple crumble offset by sweet cream that I could eat every day.

See map p. 110. 4 Corkhill (part of Dame Street across from Dublin Castle) and nearby on Cow's Lane. ☎ *01-633-4681. DART: Tara Street Station. Bus: 49, 56A, 77, 77A, 123. Main courses: €6–€12. Baked goods: €2.50–€5.50. No credit cards. Open: Mon–Fri 8 a.m.–7 p.m., Sat 9 a.m.–7 p.m., Sun 10 a.m.–6 p.m. (until 7 p.m. for the Dame Street branch).*

Restaurant Patrick Guilbaud
$$$$ **Dublin 2** **FRENCH**

Perhaps the finest haute cuisine in Dublin is served in this bright, cream-colored room, which sports abstract paintings. The ever-changing menu combines fresh Irish and French ingredients with French cooking techniques and pure creativity for some real stunners. The chefs are mad (but brilliant) scientists, devising such heavenly creations as caramelized veal sweetbread glazed with licorice and parsnip sauce, served with a lemon confit; and roast Atlantic cod served with seaweed butter and a carrot and star anise salad. If you really want to relive Dublin's Celtic Tiger days, order up the €80 (you read that right) Annagassan blue lobster with green apple and lime *jus*. Desserts are appropriately complex and impressive; a recent menu listed a plate of five different cold and hot dark-chocolate confections. The €50 three-course lunch is a great deal (relatively speaking, of course).

See map p. 110. In the Merrion Hotel, 21 Upper Merrion St. ☎ *01-676-4192. Reservations highly recommended. DART: Westland Row. Bus: 48A. Main courses: €46–€60 (lobster is more). AE, DC, MC, V. Open: Tues–Fri 12:30–2:15 p.m. and 7–10:15 p.m., Sat 1–2:15 p.m. and 7–10:15 p.m. The latter times indicate last orders rather than closing times.*

Winding Stair
$$$ Dublin 2   NEW IRISH

I think the Winding Stair is the best restaurant in Dublin, serving Irish classics that have been turned on their heads with top-notch cooking skills and the light-handed addition of unorthodox ingredients. Molly Malone might be impressed by the interesting role that her famed cockles and mussels play in a dish of Kilkeel hake filet served with sweet potatoes, tomatoes, cockle and mussel stew, and Dublin Bay prawns; and traditionalist Irish grannies throughout the country may do a double-take in response to the mint crème fraîche that accompanies the spring lamb chops. The chefs are obsessed with finding the top sources for their local and seasonal ingredients, from the Irish Aberdeen beef (which is accompanied by sticky onions, garlic butter, and homemade French fries) to the fromage heaven that greets you on the Irish Cheese Board. Don't miss the desserts, especially the unbelievable sticky pear and ginger cake. The setting, on the top floor of a beloved bookstore, is casual and airy, with views over the Liffey River through ceiling-high windows. You may find yourself elbow-to-elbow with your fellow patrons, but with the good spirits, laughter, and transcendent food you should hardly mind. A fixed-price lunch menu (€18–€23) is offered daily, and fixed-price dinners (€25–€30 for three courses) are offered each night as long as the table is vacated by 8 p.m.

See map p. 110. 40 Ormond Quay (near the Ha'penny Bridge). ☎ *01-872-7320. Reservations highly recommended. DART: Tara Street Station. Bus: 68, 69, 69X. Main courses: €22–€27. AE, MC, V. Open: Sun–Thurs noon to 5 p.m. and 5:30–10:30 p.m., Fri–Sat noon to 3:30 p.m. and 5:30–10:30 p.m.*

Yamamori Sushi and Yamamori Noodles
$$$ Old City, Dublin 2   NOODLES/SUSHI/JAPANESE

Throughout my travels in Ireland, I'm always on a quest to find sushi that meets my New York–bred sushi-snob requirements. And although this new branch of Yamamori (Yamamori Sushi) doesn't compare to sushi bars where people drop $250 for the very best in raw fish, the sushi here is really, really good. Groups of friends and couples chat over sushi selections as well as fabulous cooked dishes such as yaki soba and tempura. The space has retained the original stone and brick walls, and practically defines the word *airy,* with high ceilings, slices of sky visible through the many skylights, and a small bamboo-filled courtyard. There's a great wine list, but during the summer you're practically required to order a mango mojito.

If you're craving Japanese cooked dishes only, the original Yamamori (Yamamori Noodles) is another great option. In a large space decorated with white lanterns and a glass panel sandwiching delicate cherry-blossom-shaped lights, diners gather over super-fresh bowls of delectable ramen big enough to drown in, as well as other Japanese dishes, such as wok-fried noodles; rare tuna loin served with a trio of soba, rice, and green tea noodles; and various teriyaki plates.

See map p. 110. Yamamori Noodles: 71–72 S. Great George's St. ☎ *01-475-5001. DART: Tara Street Station. Bus: 16A. Yamamori Sushi: 38–39 Lower Ormond Quay.* ☎ *01-872-0003. Main courses: €17–€25 (lobster more). AE, MC, V. Open: Yamamori Noodles daily 12:30–11:30 p.m.; Yamamori Sushi Sun–Wed 12:15–11 p.m., Thurs–Sat 12:15–11:30 p.m.*

Exploring Dublin

Dublin is packed with things to see and do. An exploration of the city is like a journey through history, as you discover medieval churches, Viking ruins, an 18th-century college campus, and museums containing artifacts such as 3,000-year-old Celtic gold jewelry. Modern Dublin is evident in sights ranging from a portrait of U2 singer Bono in the National Gallery to a slew of über-trendy shops.

 If you're in Dublin for a short time, one of the best ways to take in as many attractions as possible is to use the Dublin Bus Tour. The bus visits 23 of Dublin's most popular attractions; and you can hop off the bus to see an attraction, and then board another bus when you're finished. See the review in "Seeing Dublin by Guided Tour," later in this chapter, for more details.

Dublin is relatively compact, but it still makes sense to look at a map and plan to see attractions in the same area on the same day.

No need to break the bank sightseeing; all the parks in Dublin are free, as are many other attractions listed here. You also can get combined tickets to some attractions, which could save a few euro (see reviews for further information).

With the **Dublin Pass** you pay a flat price and get free admission to 31 Dublin and Dublin-area attractions, plus discounts on several tours and at a handful of restaurants, shops, and entertainment venues. What the Dublin Pass folks don't tell you, however, is that many of the 31 attractions listed, including the national museums and the Chester Beatty Library, are free to *all* visitors. The one-day pass can be a good deal if you know that you want to go to the Guinness Storehouse as well as many other attractions that have an admission fee, but I can't see how the multiday passes pay for themselves. To decide if the pass is right for you, think about how much you can pack into a day, and check the admission prices for the attractions that you know you want to see. The one-day pass is €35 adults, €19 kids 5 to 15. The pass is available at any Dublin tourism office (☎ 01-605-7700), including the office at the arrivals concourse at Dublin Airport, and at www.dublinpass.ie.

Families should be aware that most attractions in Dublin and the rest of Ireland offer family rates — low, flat rates that usually cover two adults and up to four children.

The top attractions

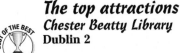

Chester Beatty Library
Dublin 2

The Chester Beatty Library is one of those gems that often gets overlooked in favor of the more flashy attractions of Dublin. But this extensive collection of books, artwork, manuscripts, and religious objects from around the world is well worth a few hours of precious vacation time. On the first floor, you find an exhibit called *Arts of the Book,* an awe-inspiring and diverse collection of ancient books, from Egyptian Books of the Dead to medieval illuminated manuscripts. Narrated videos of craftspeople at work are found throughout the gallery, shedding light on crafts such as bookbinding, papermaking, and printmaking. The second floor is dedicated to books and objects from many of the world's religious traditions. A beautifully created audiovisual presentation explores religious practices and belief systems around the world. The treasures on this floor are numerous, including a Hindu cosmological painting from 18th-century Nepal; a standing Tibetan Buddha; and some of the earliest New Testament and Gospel texts, including the Gospel of St. John, written on Greek papyrus, circa 150 to 200. Temporary exhibits have been fascinating, from an exhibition devoted to Chinese snuff bottles to a show featuring the best contemporary Irish calligraphers. If you're spiritually satiated but physically hungry, the on-site Silk Road Cafe is excellent. Allow one and a half to two hours for your visit.

See map p. 130. Dublin Castle. ☎ 01-407-0750. www.cbl.ie. Bus: 13, 16, 19, 123. Admission: Free. Open: May–Sept Mon–Fri 10 a.m.–5 p.m., Sat 11 a.m.–5 p.m., and Sun 1–5 p.m.; Oct–Apr Tues–Fri 10 a.m.–5 p.m., Sat 11 a.m.–5 p.m., and Sun 1–5 p.m.

Christ Church Cathedral
Dublin 8

Christ Church Cathedral, an Anglican/Episcopal church, has existed in various forms in this spot for almost a thousand years. The Vikings built a simple wood church at this location in 1038. In the 1180s, the original foundation was expanded into a cruciform, and the Romanesque cathedral was built in stone. The church you see today is the result of restoration and rebuilding on the 1180s building during the 1870s. The cathedral

Dublin Attractions

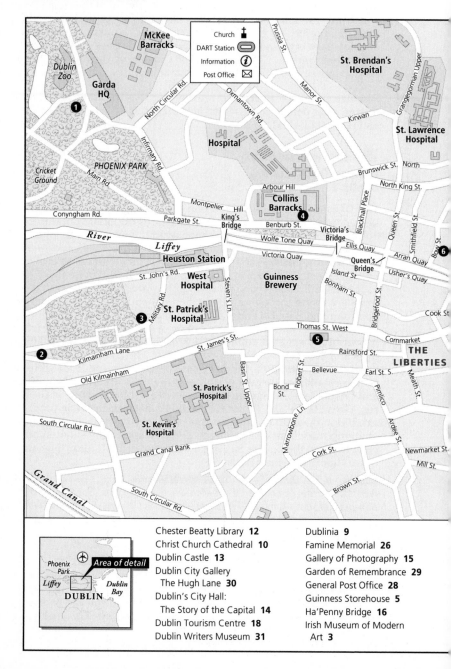

Church ✝
DART Station
Information ⓘ
Post Office ✉

McKee Barracks
Dublin Zoo
Garda HQ
Dublin Zoo
North Circular Rd.
Oxmantown Rd.
Manor St.
Prussia St.
St. Brendan's Hospital
Grangegorman Upper
Kirwan
St. Lawrence Hospital
Hospital
Brunswick St. North
Infirmary Rd.
Cricket Ground
PHOENIX PARK
Main Rd.
North King St.
Montpelier Hill
Arbour Hill
Collins Barracks
Blackhall Place
North King St.
Queen St.
Smithfield St.
Conyngham Rd.
Parkgate St.
King's Bridge
Benburb St.
Victoria's Bridge
Bow St.
River
Liffey
Heuston Station
Wolfe Tone Quay
Ellis Quay
Arran Quay
St. John's Rd.
West Hospital
Victoria Quay
Queen's Bridge
Usher's Quay
Steven's Ln.
Guinness Brewery
Island St.
Bonham St.
Bridgefoot St.
Cook St
Military Rd.
St. Patrick's Hospital
Thomas St. West
Commarket
Kilmainham Lane
St. James's St.
Rainsford St.
THE LIBERTIES
Old Kilmainham
St. Patrick's Hospital
Basin St. Upper
Robert St.
Bellevue
Earl St. S.
Meath St.
South Circular Rd.
St. Kevin's Hospital
Bond St.
Pimlico
Ardee St.
Grand Canal Bank
Marrowbone Ln.
Cork St.
Newmarket St.
Mill St.
Grand Canal
South Circular Rd.
Brown St.

Phoenix Park
Area of detail
Liffey
DUBLIN
Dublin Bay

Chester Beatty Library **12**
Christ Church Cathedral **10**
Dublin Castle **13**
Dublin City Gallery
  The Hugh Lane **30**
Dublin's City Hall:
  The Story of the Capital **14**
Dublin Tourism Centre **18**
Dublin Writers Museum **31**

Dublinia **9**
Famine Memorial **26**
Gallery of Photography **15**
Garden of Remembrance **29**
General Post Office **28**
Guinness Storehouse **5**
Ha'Penny Bridge **16**
Irish Museum of Modern
  Art **3**

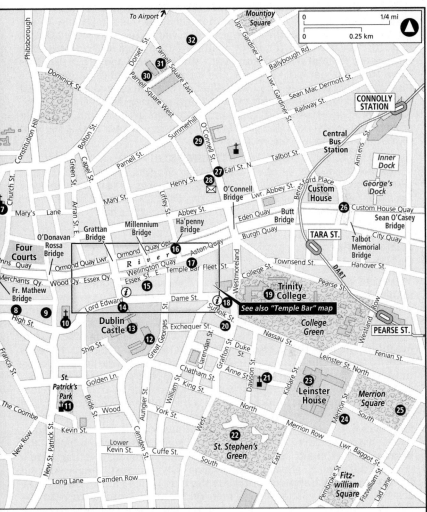

James Joyce Centre **32**
James Joyce Statue **27**
Kilmainham Gaol **2**
Merrion Square **25**
The Millennium Spire **28**
Molly Malone Statue **20**
The National Gallery **25**
National Museum of
  Archaeology & History **23**

National Museum of
  Decorative Arts & History **4**
National Museum of Natural
  History **24**
Old Jameson Distillery **6**
Phoenix Park & Dublin Zoo **1**
Science Gallery **19**
St. Ann's Anglican Church **21**
St. Audoen's Church **8**

St. Michan's Church **7**
St. Patrick's Cathedral **11**
St. Stephen's Green **22**
Temple Bar Gallery **17**
Trinity College and the
  Book of Kells **19**

provides an informative self-guided tour brochure when you enter, or you can take the self-guided audio tour (€4 adults, €3 seniors and students). Don't let all the soaring architecture and intricate stonework above you distract from the beautiful 13th-century tile floor. Also, take time to see the tomb of Strongbow, the Norman leader whose troops captured Dublin in 1170. The highlight for many visitors is the medieval crypt, which houses the cathedral's Treasury, with silver objects and other precious items, plus my personal favorite, the mummified rat and cat found in a pipe of the organ in the late 1860s. Visitors are welcome at services; just call or check the Web site for times. Choral services (Wed–Thurs 6 p.m., Sat 5 p.m., Sun 11 a.m. and 3:30 p.m.) are especially beautiful. Note that admission is reduced if you visit Dublinia (reviewed later in this section) first. Allow 45 minutes for your visit.

See map p. 130. Christ Church Place. ☎ *01-677-8099.* www.cccdub.ie. *DART: Tara Street Station. Bus: 49, 50, 65, 77. Admission: €6 adults, €4 seniors, €3 students, free for kids accompanied by a parent. Audio tour: €4 adults, €3 seniors and students. Open: June–Aug Mon–Sat 9:45 a.m.–6:15 p.m., Sun 12:30–2:30 p.m. and 4:30–6:15 p.m.; Sept–May Mon–Sat 9:45 a.m.–4:15 p.m., Sun 12:30–2:30 p.m.*

Dublin Castle
Dublin 2

This is not your typical storybook castle. The original building was erected in the 13th century, but many additions were made over the following 800 years. Today, the castle looks like an encyclopedia of European architectural styles, from the 13th-century Norman Record Tower to the 19th-century Gothic Church of the Holy Trinity. The castle hosts official state functions, such as the president's inauguration, and the clock tower is home to the excellent Chester Beatty Library (reviewed earlier in this section). Guided tours (listed as 50 minutes long, but often extended) take you through many of the impressively furnished State Apartments, including the Drawing Room, which features a breathtaking Waterford Crystal chandelier; the Throne Room, where Queen Victoria ordered servants to lop several inches off the legs of the throne so that her feet wouldn't dangle as she spoke to her subjects; and Patrick's Hall, which boasts the banners of the Knights of St. Patrick and historical ceiling paintings. You'll end up in the moat, gazing at the original city and castle walls. Art and history lovers alike should appreciate the tour, which focuses on both the aesthetics of the castle and its history. It would be ideal to read the "History 101" section in Chapter 2 before your tour if you need to brush up on your Irish history. After the tour, don't miss the Church of the Holy Trinity, with its beautiful carved oak panels and stained-glass windows. Note the statue of Justice in the courtyard. See how she faces away from the city? Cynical Dubliners will tell you that was intentional. During official government functions, the State Apartments may be closed. Allow an hour for your visit.

See map p. 130. Cork Hill, off Dame Street. ☎ *01-645-8813. Bus: 50A, 54, 56A, 77, 77A, 77B. Tours: €4.50 adults, €3.50 seniors and students, €2 kids 11 and under. Visits to the interior are by guided tour only. Open: Mon–Sat 10 a.m.–4:45 p.m., Sun 2–4:45 p.m.*

Exploring Temple Bar

In the 1970s, artists of all kinds began setting up shop in Temple Bar, and the area, which had hitherto been in decline, became a hotbed for cutting-edge visual and performing arts. Though the 1980s were rough for Temple Bar, the area rallied during the economic boom of the early 1990s and, with its high concentration of pubs, became *the* place for visiting partiers (you couldn't find a Dub in the vicinity at night). Temple Bar has reached a nice equilibrium; it's a hub for visual arts, film, and theater, and though it's still packed and loud at night, the vibe most nights tends more toward jubilant partying than get-completely-smashed-and-scream-a-lot partying.

Temple Bar is especially fun to visit when the Food Market, Book Market, or Designer Market are taking place (see the "This little traveler went to market" sidebar in the "Shopping in Dublin" section, later in this chapter).

Check out a few of my favorite spots in Temple Bar (shown on the "Temple Bar" map):

- ✔ The **Gallery of Photography,** Meeting House Square (☎ 01-671-4654), has a great permanent exhibit of early-20th-century Irish photography and puts on excellent temporary exhibits by contemporary Irish and international photographers.

- ✔ **The Irish Film Institute,** 6 Eustace St. (☎ 01-679-5744; www.irish film.ie), is one of the hippest places in Dublin, showing a terrific selection of old and independent films. The cute cafe here serves the best nachos in Dublin, as well as more substantial fare. During the summer, the institute projects films on an outdoor screen in Meetinghouse Square on Saturday nights.

- ✔ **Temple Bar Gallery,** 5–9 Temple Bar (☎ 01-671-0073 www.templebar gallery.com), houses several studios and exhibits new works by up-and-coming artists.

- ✔ **Project Arts Centre,** 39 E. Essex St. (☎ 01-881-9613; www.project artscentre.ie), presents new and often avant-garde art exhibits, theater, and dance.

The **Temple Bar Information Centre,** 12 East Essex St. (☎ 01-677-2255; www.temple bar.com), has all sorts of information on Temple Bar, including the lowdown on the area's many free outdoor events.

Guinness Storehouse
Dublin 8

Though the actual Guinness Brewery is closed to the public, the Guinness Storehouse will fill you in on everything you've ever wanted to know about "black gold." This temple to Guinness is housed in a 1904 building that was used for the fermentation process — when yeast does its magic to turn the combined hops, barley, and water into beer. The core of the building is a seven-level, pint-glass-shaped structure that could hold approximately 14.3 million pints of Guinness. The Storehouse explores every facet of Ireland's favorite beverage, from the ingredients that go into each batch to the company's advertising campaigns to the role of Guinness in Irish culture. Though there is a sense of unabashed propaganda to the whole attraction, the exhibits are beautifully done in a cool, modern design. There is a lot to see, but you'll definitely want to make time for the ingredients exhibit, which features a veritable beach of barley and a waterfall of Irish water; the intriguing audiovisual journey through the Guinness brewing and packaging process (taste the toasted barley, if it's available); the fun Pour-Your-Own-Pint room where you receive a hands-on education in pulling the perfect pint; and the fun display of Guinness advertisements through the years (I always laugh at the old doctor's endorsement of Guinness, which notes that the beverage "cures insomnia"). The top-floor Gravity Bar is (literally) the Storehouse's crowning glory, offering 360-degree views of Dublin through floor-to-ceiling windows. Bartenders dispense a free pint of black stuff to every visitor over the age of 18 or one of several sodas to visitors who prefer their bubbles without alcohol. Book your visit to the Storehouse online to bypass lines and receive a 10 percent discount on your ticket price. Allow two and a half hours for your visit.

See map p. 130. St. James's Gate, on Market Street. ☎ *01-408-4800.* www.guinness-storehouse.com. *Bus: 51B, 51C, 78A, 123. Luas: James's Street. There is a complimentary parking lot on Crane Street. Admission: €15 adults, €11 seniors and students 18 and over, €9 students 17 and under, €5 kids 6–12, free for kids 5 and under. Price includes a free pint of stout or a soda. Open: July–Aug daily 9:30 a.m.–8 p.m. (last admission 7 p.m.), Sept–June daily 9:30 a.m.–6 p.m. (last admission 5 p.m.).*

The Ha'Penny Bridge
Dublin 1 and 2

This famous footbridge has connected the north side of the river directly to Temple Bar since 1816. Its name comes from the half-penny toll that it once cost to cross the bridge. (The poet William Butler Yeats and others were not fans of the toll and walked down to O'Connell Bridge to avoid it.) You can't miss the bridge — it's bright white and arches high over the River Liffey, and at night, it gleams with the warm glow cast by the streetlamps that line the bridge. The Ha'Penny offers views up and down the River Liffey, which can be quite picturesque, especially in the evening. If you want a view of the Ha'Penny stretching over the Liffey, walk to the Millennium Bridge, a shimmery little wisp of a bridge directly west of the Ha'Penny. You'll find a peaceful boardwalk along the north side of the river. You can see the bridge in five minutes.

See map p. 130. Over the River Liffey between O'Connell and Millennium bridges, across from Liffey Street Lower.

The bridges of Dublin County

Seventeen bridges cross the River Liffey in Dublin, including Ha'Penny (see the listing in this section) and plans are in the works for more. **Fr. Mathew Bridge** (which crosses from Church Street to Bridge Street Lower and is also known as the Old Bridge), is quite interesting historically. Though the present bridge is only about 200 years old, a bridge has occupied this space since 1014 and the 15th-century version was lined with shops, inns, houses, and even a chapel. For sheer modern architectural beauty, my vote goes to the **Samuel Beckett Bridge,** which swoops up in an abstracted interpretation of a harp and can rotate 90 degrees to let ships pass.

Kilmainham Gaol
Dublin 8

From the 1780s to the 1920s, many Irish rebels against the British crown (such as Charles Stewart Parnell, Joseph Plunkett, and James Connolly) were imprisoned at Kilmainham Gaol (pronounced *jail*), some for years and others only for the short period before they met the firing squad. Used as the set for the 1993 Daniel Day Lewis film *In the Name of the Father,* the jail has been restored and offers visitors access to the site via excellent guided tours. A short audiovisual presentation about the jail and Irish political history is shown in the chapel where Plunkett was allowed to marry Grace Gifford just hours before being shot for his part in the 1916 Rising. Perhaps the most haunting part of the tour is the visit to the stark courtyard where firing squads executed many of the rebels from the 1916 Rising, including Connolly, who was so badly injured during the fighting that he couldn't stand up by himself and had to be strapped into a chair to be shot. After the tour, check out the intriguing exhibits about the political history of Ireland and the history of the jail. Perhaps I'm stating the obvious, but the tour may not be suitable for kids. Also, the jail is quite cold during the winter, so layers are the way to go. Allow 90 minutes for your visit.

See map p. 130. Inchicore Road, Kilmainham about 5.6km (3½ miles) from the center of Dublin. ☎ *01-453-5984. Bus: 51B, 78A, 79, 79A. Access by guided tour only. Tours: €6 adults, €4 seniors, €2 students and kids. Open: Apr–Sept daily 9:30 a.m.–6 p.m. (last admission 5 p.m.); Oct–Mar Mon–Sat 9:30 a.m.–5:30 p.m. (last admission 4 p.m.), Sun 10 a.m.–6 p.m. (last admission 5 p.m.). Tours leave every hour on the hour.*

Merrion Square
Dublin 2

This is my favorite of Dublin's parks. Thick with old trees and brilliant, splashy flowers during the warm months, Merrion Square's park is filled with little nooks and paths that make it seem many times larger than it is. Take one path, and you're walking in a lush, dense forest filled with birdsong; make a turn, and there's a sun-dappled field with school kids kicking around a soccer ball; turn again, and you're greeted by a couple picnicking on a bench in a formal garden area. Lining the square are textbook Georgian row houses, characterized by their brightly painted doors, elegant brass door knockers, and *fanlights* (half-moon-shaped windows over the doors). Around the square are plaques that identify the former homes of poet William Butler Yeats (no. 82), playwright Oscar Wilde (no. 1), and Catholic liberator Daniel O'Connell (no. 58). On Sundays, some of the city's top artists hang their works for sale from the rails surrounding the square. Allow 30 minutes for your visit.

See map p. 130. Merrion Square takes up the block directly behind the National Gallery. Take Nassau Street on the south side of Trinity College and continue east for a few blocks until it becomes Merrion Square North. DART: Pearse Street Station and head south on Westland Row and Merrion Street Lower. Bus: 4, 5, 7, 7A, 44, 45, 49x. Admission: Free. Open: Daylight hours.

The National Gallery
Dublin 2

This fine collection of Western European art (mostly paintings) from the Middle Ages through the 20th century is often overlooked by visitors planning their itineraries in Dublin, which is a shame, because the collection is varied and interesting. The museum has an extensive collection of Irish works from the 18th century through today and boasts 17th-century treasures such as Caravaggio's *The Taking of Christ,* Vermeer's *Lady Writing a Letter,* and Rembrandt's *Rest on a Flight into Egypt.* A gem of the museum is a large room (no. 21) devoted to the works of the Yeats family, with a focus on the mystical, vivid paintings of Jack Yeats (brother of William Butler). The star of the Portrait Gallery just may be a portrait of U2's Bono, by Louis le Brocquy. If you're in the museum on Saturday or Sunday, take advantage of the free guided tours. Allow 90 minutes for your visit.

See map p. 130. Merrion Square West at Clare Street. ☎ *01-661-5133.* www.national gallery.ie. *DART: Pearse Street Station and head south on Westland Row and Merrion Street Lower. Bus: 5, 7, 7A, 44, 45, 49X, 77X. Admission: Free, although special exhibits may have a fee. Open: Mon–Wed and Fri–Sat 9:30 a.m.–5:30 p.m., Thurs 9:30 a.m.–8:30 p.m., Sun noon to 5:30 p.m. Free guided tours available Sat–Sun afternoon (call for times — they vary).*

National Museum of Archaeology
Dublin 2

This grand museum, featuring a huge rotunda and beautiful mosaics, is home to many of Ireland's most dazzling and important artifacts from 7000 b.c. through the medieval period. The stars of the museum's collection are in the *Treasury,* where you find the gorgeous Tara Brooch and Ardagh Chalice, plus masterpieces of craftsmanship from Ireland's Iron Age; and in *Ireland's Gold,* where elegant gold ornaments dating from 7000 to 2000 b.c. are displayed. The other exhibits, including *Prehistoric Ireland, Viking Ireland, Medieval Ireland,* and the somewhat-out-of-place *Ancient Egypt* also boast interesting and beautifully presented objects. Be sure to check out the *Kingship and Sacrifice* exhibit, which features the awesome "Bog

Bodies" — well-preserved human bodies from the Iron Age unearthed in 2003. Allow a couple hours for your visit.

See map p. 130. Kildare and Merrion streets. ☎ **01-677-7444.** *DART: Pearse Street. Bus: 7, 7A, 10, 11, 13. Admission: Free. Open: Tues–Sat 10 a.m.–5 p.m., Sun 2–5 p.m. Guided tours available (call for times).*

National Museum of Natural History
Dublin 2

A visit to this museum should give pause to everyone who believes that kids these days are interested only in texting or playing video games. There are no bells and whistles here, and yet the kids I've observed can't get enough of the awe-inspiring collection of stuffed and preserved animals, from the beautifully preserved Irish birds on the first floor to "Spoticus" the giraffe upstairs. Known among Dublin natives as "the dead zoo," the museum opened in 1857 and the traditional Victorian character of the exhibits has hardly changed at all. Wood-framed glass cases, old labels, and details like the cringe-worthy bullet hole in the head of a polar bear shot by a 19th-century Irish explorer conspire to draw old-style museum buffs from around the world. Don't miss the second floor; the staircase is at the back of the first floor through an open door. In addition to the thousands of breathtaking stuffed and preserved animals, the museum also features exquisite glass models of microscopic sea life created by a father-and-son team in the late 19th century (closed at press time, but worth a stop if it's open again by the time you visit).

On Merrion Square. ☎ **01-677-7444.** *Admission: Free, though donations are welcome. Open: Tues–Sat 10 a.m.–5 p.m., Sun 2–5 p.m.*

St. Patrick's Cathedral
Dublin 8

St. Patrick's Cathedral, the national cathedral of the Church of Ireland, derives its name from the belief that in the fifth century, St. Patrick baptized converts to Christianity in a well that once existed on this land. Though there have been churches on this spot since the 12th century, the glorious church that stands today was built in the early 13th century, with restorations to the west tower in 1370 and the addition of a spire in 1749. Volunteers provide an informative map pamphlet that guides you through the church, explaining the highlights of the interior. You can visit the moving memorial of author and social critic Jonathan Swift, who served as the dean of the cathedral and is buried next to his beloved friend Stella; and pay your respects to the memorial to Turlough O'Carolan (1670–1738), one of Ireland's finest and most prolific harpers and bards, who composed many tunes that are still played by Irish musicians today. Don't miss the choir, which is adorned with the colorful medieval-style banners and helmets of the Knights of St. Patrick. Beautiful matins (Mon–Fri 9 a.m., Sun 11:15 a.m.) and evensongs (Mon–Fri 5:30 p.m., Sun 3:15 p.m.) are sung here. Your ticket includes admission to *Living Stones,* an exhibit that uses objects to explore the cathedral's place in history and in the world today. Allow 45 minutes for your visit.

See map p. 130. Patrick's Close. ☎ **01-453-9472.** www.stpatrickscathedral. ie. *DART: Tara Street Station. Bus: 49, 49A, 49X, 54A, 54N. Admission: €5.50 adults, €4.50 seniors and students; services free. Open: Mar–Oct Mon–Fri 9 a.m.–5:30 p.m., Sat 9 a.m.–6:30 p.m., Sun 9–11 a.m., 12:30–3 p.m., and 4:30–6:30p.m.; Nov–Feb Mon–Sat 9 a.m.–5:30 p.m., Sun 9–11 a.m. and 12:30–3 p.m. Last admission is always 30 minutes before closing.*

St. Stephen's Green
Dublin 2

Sitting in this beautiful, centrally located park on a sunny Saturday, you'll probably see about half of Dublin's population promenading by, pushing strollers, lugging shopping bags, munching on sandwiches, and so on. The 11-hectare (27-acre) park encompasses several different landscapes, from a large duck pond shaded by the trailing leaves of weeping willows, to formally laid-out flower gardens, to open green spaces that beg you to settle down for a picnic. During the summer months, you can enjoy the frequent lunchtime concerts. Allow about 45 minutes for your visit, more if you want to join the rest of Dublin on nice days at lunchtime.

See map p. 130. St. Stephen's Green takes up the a few blocks at the top of Grafton Street (in the opposite direction of Trinity College). ☎ **01-475-7816.** *DART: Tara Street Station. Bus: 10, 11, 13, 14, 14A, 15A, 15B. Luas: St Stephen's Green (Green Line). Open: Mon–Sat 7:30 a.m. to dusk, Sun 9:30 a.m. to dusk.*

Trinity College and the Book of Kells
Dublin 2

Trinity College, founded in 1592 by Elizabeth I, looks like the ideal of an impressive, refined, old-world college, with Georgian stone buildings and perfectly manicured green lawns. The campus sits in the middle of the busy city, but within its gates, everything is composed and quiet. As you enter the main gate, look to your left to see the cross-denominational Christian chapel. Directly opposite, on your right, is the college exam hall (during exam time, you may see students sprinting there from the chapel). On your left, next to the chapel, is the dining hall. As you wander the cobbled paths around Trinity, you can imagine the days when former students Oscar Wilde, Samuel Beckett, Jonathan Swift, and Bram Stoker (a great athlete at Trinity) pounded the same pavement on their way to class. During nice weather, students lounge on the well-kept greens or on benches for picnics or studying. There is nothing finer than taking a picnic lunch (try fish and chips from Beshoff, reviewed earlier in this chapter) to Trinity's little hidden garden or cricket and rugby pitch (walk past the Old Library, and make a right at the pretty garden with benches). It's well worth it to take a guided tour of the Trinity campus. The 30-minute tours are offered about eight times a day, Monday through Saturday, mid-May through September; they leave from the desk at the Front Arch Entrance to the university. The price is €10 and includes admission to the Book of

Kells (which costs €9, so if you're planning to see the Book, the tour is really only €1 extra).

For visitors, the jewel in Trinity College's crown is the **Book of Kells,** housed in the Old Library. This manuscript of the four gospels of the Bible was painstakingly crafted by monks around a.d. 800. The gospels are written in ornate Latin script, and the book is filled with stunning, vivid illustrations, including intricate Celtic knots and fantastical animals (you'll see only one page of the book on your visit — a different page is displayed each day). The engaging exhibit that leads to the Book of Kells (and three other ancient Irish religious texts) gives historical context and reveals the techniques used in the creation of the books. Upstairs is the Long Room, which has gallery bookcases filled with Trinity's oldest books and was used as a model for the Hogwarts dining hall in the Harry Potter movies. It also boasts the oldest known harp of its kind in Ireland, made of oak and willow, and houses excellent exhibitions built around intriguing books from the Trinity collection; a recent one focused on documents related to Irish men and women living in India during the 19th century.

Finally, if you're a science lover, check out the new Science Gallery (see p. 144) while you're on the Trinity campus. Allow about two and a half hours for your visit.

See map p. 130. Main entrance on College Street at the eastern end of Dame Street. Walk two blocks south of the River Liffey from O'Connell Street Bridge; entrance is on your left. Walk through the front entrance arch, and follow signs to the Old Library and Treasury. ☎ 01-896-1000 for Trinity College information, 01-896-2320 for Book of Kells information. DART: Tara Street Station. Bus: 1, 2, 3, 25, 25a, 26, 27x, 44, 44c, 48a, 49x, 50x, 66, 66a, 67, 67a, 77. Admission: College grounds free; Old Library and Book of Kells €9 adults, €8 seniors, students, kids 12–17, free for kids 11 and under. Tours of Trinity: €10 (includes admission to the Book of Kells). Open: May–Sept Mon–Sat 9:30 a.m.–5 p.m., Sun 9:30 a.m.–4:30 p.m.; Oct–Apr Mon–Sat 9:30 a.m.–5 p.m., Sun noon to 4:30 p.m. Closed for ten days during Christmas holiday.

More cool things to see and do

The following sections list other great attractions in Dublin, including churches, museums, and historic buildings.

More monuments and historic buildings

- ✔ **General Post Office,** north of the River Liffey, halfway up the left side of O'Connell Street, Dublin 1 (see map p. 130; ☎ 01-705-8833): The bullet holes scarring the pillars of the General Post Office (GPO) testify to the violent battle between Irish patriots (also called Republicans) and English forces during the Easter Rising of 1916. The Republicans commandeered the building, and leader Pádraig Pearse read the Proclamation of the Irish Republic from the front steps. The patriots held their ground for a week before shelling from the British forces drove them to surrender. Thirteen of the Republican leaders were executed shortly thereafter, and the interior of the post office was burned to the ground. Rebuilt in 1929, this is now Dublin's main post office. In addition to comprehensive postal services, a small, well-done museum has recently been created. Offerings include exhibits on the 1916 Rising, the history of mail and the post office in Ireland (more interesting than you may think), and postage-stamp art and design, where you have an opportunity to design your own stamp. Before you leave, check out the statue of the ancient mythic Irish hero Cuchulainn, dedicated to those who died during the Rising.

Admission to the post office is free; museum admission is €2. The post office is open Monday through Saturday from 8:30 a.m. to 6 p.m.; the museum is open Monday through Friday from 10 a.m. to 5 p.m., Saturday 10 a.m. to 4 p.m. Last admission is 30 minutes before closing. Allow ten minutes if you're not visiting the museum, 40 minutes if you are.

✔ **Famine Memorial,** Custom House Quay, in the Docklands, Dublin 1: The wasted figures walking along the River Liffey catch many off guard until they realize they've come upon Dublin's Famine Memorial, one of the most haunting memorials I've ever seen. You need only five minutes for a visit.

✔ **Glasnevin Cemetery and Museum,** Finglas Road (see map p. 147; ☎ 01-830-1133; www.glasnevintrust.ie; Bus: 19, 19A, or 13 [from O'Connell Street to Harts Corner, a five-minute walk from the cemetery] or 40, 40A, 40B, or 40C [from Parnell Street to the main cemetery entrance]): This cemetery, founded in 1832 as a burial ground for people of all faiths, is the final resting place of many famous Irish citizens, including political heroes Michael Collins and Charles Stewart Parnell and playwright Brendan Behan. There are stunning Celtic crosses throughout the cemetery. A heritage map lists who is buried where (pick one up at the visitor center or print one from www.glasnevintrust.ie). Better yet, take one of the superb guided walking tours, offered three times daily by historian Shane MacThomáis. The newly opened **Glasnevin Museum** features two large exhibits, one on burial practices and one on the many historical figures buried in the cemetery.

Admission to the cemetery is free; tours cost €5. Museum admission is €6. The museum is open Monday through Friday from 10 a.m. to 5 p.m., Saturday and Sunday from 11 a.m. to 6 p.m. Tours meet daily at the main entrance of the cemetery at 11:30 a.m., 12:30 p.m., and 2:30 p.m. (call in winter to make sure tours are running). Allow an hour or two for your visit.

✔ **James Joyce Statue,** halfway up O'Connell Street, just at the top of Earl Street North, Dublin 1 (see map p. 130): This statue pays homage to the wiry, bespectacled man whose words capture the essence of old Dublin. You can see the statue in a few seconds, unless you decide to recite a sentence or two from *Finnegan's Wake,* which could take a month.

✔ **The Millennium Spire,** O'Connell Street, Dublin 1, in front of the main post office (see map p. 130): This 120m-high (394-ft.) spike of stainless steel is meant to represent 21st-century Dublin. The spire replaces Nelson's Pillar, which was erected during the British occupation of Ireland. Because parts of the north side of the Dublin have become run down, Dublin's local wags have termed the spire "The Stiletto in the Ghetto." You just need enough time to gaze up in vertiginous awe and snap a photo.

✔ **Molly Malone Statue,** corner of Nassau and Grafton streets (see map p. 130): Sing along, now: "In Dublin's fair city, where the girls are so pretty, I first set my eyes on sweet Molly Malone. . . ." Inspired by the traditional song "Cockles and Mussels," this statue is a tribute to Molly Malone, who represents all the women who have hawked their wares (shellfish or otherwise) on Dublin's busy streets in the past. Affectionately known as "The Tart with the Cart," Molly welcomes shoppers at the head of Grafton Street. You can see the statue in about 30 seconds, unless you take time to sing the whole song.

More museums

✔ **Dublinia,** St. Michael's Hill, at the corner of High Street and Winetavern Street, across from Christ's Church (see map p. 130; ☎ 01-679-4611; www.dublinia.ie; Bus: 49, 50, 65, 77 or Dublin Bus Tour): Try on some chain mail, rummage through the apothecary's drawers to find a cure for what ails you, and sniff through the spice merchant's wares at the Medieval Fair, one of several exhibits at Dublinia, a hands-on museum that illustrates life in medieval Dublin from 1170 to 1540. Though the wall text is comprehensive and geared to adults, kids older than 4 or 5 should enjoy the interactive activities and walk-through scenes, and kids and adults alike will likely be intrigued by the medieval artifacts found during excavations in Dublin.

Admission to Dublinia is €6.95 adults, €5.95 seniors and students, €4.95 kids. It's open March through September daily from 10 a.m. to 5 p.m. (last admission 4:15 p.m.), October through February daily from 10 a.m. to 4:30 p.m. (last admission 3:45 p.m.). Allow an hour for your visit.

✔ **Dublin City Gallery The Hugh Lane,** Parnell Square North (see map p. 130; ☎ 01-222-5550; www.hughlane.ie; Bus: 3, 7, 10, 11, 13, 16, 19, 46A, 123; Luas: Abbey Street): Travelers who enjoy contemporary and modern art should pay a visit to The Hugh Lane. The museum features an interesting and varied collection, including many works by Irish artists. Some of my favorite pieces are *Eve of Saint Agnes,* a stained-glass masterpiece; Renoir's *Les Parapluies;* and paintings by Jack B. Yeats and Louis le Brocquy. Check to see if the museum is hosting any temporary exhibits, and don't miss Francis Bacon's studio, which was disassembled in London and then painstakingly reconstructed at the museum.

Admission is free, but there's a suggested donation of €2. It's open Tuesday through Thursday from 10 a.m. to 6 p.m., Friday and Saturday from 10 a.m. to 5 p.m., and Sunday from 11 a.m. to 5 p.m. Allow about an hour for your visit.

✔ **Dublin's City Hall: The Story of the Capital,** Dame Street across from Parliament Street (see map p. 130; ☎ **01-222-2204;** Bus: 50, 54, 56A, 77, 77A, 123): Located in Dublin's beautiful city hall, this exhibit gives a good overview of Dublin history through audiovisual presentations, text, and objects. Even if you decide not to go through the exhibit, the rotunda, featuring frescoes representing the early history of Dublin, is worth a peek.

Admission is €4 adults, €2 seniors and students, €1.50 kids. It's open Monday through Saturday from 10 a.m. to 5 p.m. (last admission 4 p.m.). Allow about 45 minutes for your visit.

✔ **Dublin Writers Museum,** 18 Parnell Sq. N., Dublin 1 (see map p. 130; ☎ **01-872-2077;** www.writersmuseum.com; DART: Connolly Station; Bus: 10, 11, 11A, 11B, 13, 16, 16A, 19, 19A, 121, 122): Who said to U.S. Customs officials: "I have nothing to declare — except my genius?" That would be witty Oscar Wilde. Wilde's life and literature are presented at this museum, along with the biographies, works, personal effects (including Samuel Beckett's telephone), letters, and portraits and photographs of Ireland's literary luminaries from ancient times through the 20th century. Exhaustive and interesting text on the walls relates the biographies of the writers and explains Ireland's literary movements. The audio tour gives brief descriptions of the writers and includes snippets of text read by actors, and music appropriate to the display you're perusing. You can contemplate the words of the literary giants over a snack in the tranquil Zen Garden or have a complete meal at the museum's restaurant. Numerous lectures, performances, readings, and children's programs are also on offer (call for details or check the Web site). Literature lovers tend to adore this museum — others, not so much.

Admission is €7.50 adults, €6.30 seniors and students, €4.70 kids 11 and under. It's open Monday through Saturday from 10 a.m. to 5 p.m. (last admission 4:15 p.m.), Sunday from 11 a.m. to 5 p.m. (last admission 4:15 p.m.). Allow a couple hours for your visit if you want to read all the text, 45 minutes if you want to zip through.

✔ **Irish Museum of Modern Art,** Military Road, Kilmainham, Dublin 8 (see map p. 130; ☎ **01-612-9900;** www.imma.ie; Bus: 26, 51, 79, 123; Luas: Red line to Heuston Station): Sitting grandly at the end of a tree-lined lane, this is one of Ireland's most magnificent 17th-century buildings, built in 1680 as a hospital for injured soldiers. The building is so impressive that when it was finished, many people lobbied to use it as the campus for Trinity College. Be sure to check out the Baroque chapel, with its wood carvings and stained glass. The permanent collection includes an exciting array of Irish and international works, from photographs by Marina Abramovic to paintings by Sean Scully. The temporary exhibitions are usually first-rate.

Admission is free, though some special exhibitions have a fee. It's open Tuesday and Thursday through Saturday from 10 a.m. to 5:30 p.m., Wednesday from 10:30 a.m. to 5:30 p.m., Sunday from noon to 5:30 p.m. Last admission is always at 5:15 p.m. Allow about an hour for your visit.

✔ **James Joyce Centre,** 35 N. Great George's St., Dublin 1 (see map p. 130; ☎ 01-878-8547; www.jamesjoyce.ie; Bus: 123): "The supreme question about a work of art is out of how deep a life does it spring?" writes James Joyce in *Ulysses.* Joyce fans can begin to plumb the depths of the writer's life at this museum, which features a re-creation of Joyce's bedroom, portraits of the Joyce family, interactive displays about each of the writer's books, and a comprehensive library and archives. Walking tours of Joyce's Dublin are offered Tuesday, Thursday, and Saturday at 11 a.m. (if at least four people show up) and at 2 p.m. (€10 adults; €8 seniors and students). Though I enjoy many of the displays, this museum often leaves me wanting more — more exhibits, more depth in the exhibits, and more ways to know about Joyce's life and works.

Admission is €5 adults; €4 seniors, students, and kids 9 and younger. It's open Tuesday through Saturday from 10 a.m. to 5 p.m., Sunday from noon to 5 p.m. Allow an hour for your visit.

✔ **The National Museum of Decorative Arts and History,** Collins Barracks, Benburb Street, Dublin 7 (see map p. 130; ☎ 01-677-7444; www.museum.ie; Luas: Red Line to museum; Bus: 25, 25A, 66, 67, 90): This well-designed museum, housed in 18th-century army barracks, exhibits some of Ireland's finest decorative objects. Galleries are organized by theme — Scientific Instruments, Irish Period Furniture, Irish Silver, and so on — and feature engaging descriptions of the history of the various items. My favorite exhibit is the *Curator's Choice,* which comprises 25 diverse objects chosen by the museum's curators because of the intriguing stories that they tell. Fashion buffs won't want to miss *The Way We Wore,* an exhibit displaying Irish fashions over the past 250 years.

Admission is free. The museum is open Tuesday through Saturday from 10 a.m. to 5 p.m., Sunday from 2 to 5 p.m. Allow two hours for your visit.

✔ **Old Jameson Distillery,** Bow Street, Dublin 7 (see map p. 130; ☎ 01-807-2355; DART: Connolly Street; Luas: Smithfield): Want to learn about the history of whiskey? Interesting guided tours visit part of Jameson's now-unused Bow Street distillery. You can watch a short film about Irish whiskey and follow the life of this spirit from raw materials through distillation to finished product. The tour finishes off with a blind whiskey tasting for a lucky handful of volunteers and a dram of Jameson's for all other visitors of legal age. On the bottom floor of the distillery, keep an eye out for Smithy the cat, who kept the distillery mouse-free. The distillery store sells all kinds of Jameson products, including some addictive whiskey fudge.

Admission is €14 adults, €10 seniors and students 18 and older, €8 kids 17 and younger. It's open daily from 9 a.m. to 6:30 p.m. (last tour 5:30 p.m.). Allow 45 minutes for your visit.

✔ **Science Gallery,** Pearse Street (at the back of Trinity College), Dublin 2 (see map p. 130; ☎ **01-896-4091;** Bus: 1, 2, 3, 25, 25a, 26, 27x, 44, 44c, 48a, 49x, 50x, 66, 66a, 67, 67a, 77): Trinity College's new Science Gallery hosts intriguing exhibits that blur the line between art and science. One of my favorite past exhibits explored the concept of light, with offerings from a life-size playable Pong game projected on an old building across the street to an interactive artist's rendition of the Northern Lights.

Admission is free, but there's a suggested donation of €5. It's open Tuesday through Friday from noon to 8 p.m., Saturday and Sunday from noon to 6 p.m. The museum may be closed when a new exhibit is being installed.

More parks (and a zoo!)

✔ **Garden of Remembrance,** the east side of Parnell Square at the top of O'Connell Street, Dublin 1 (see map p. 130): This small, peaceful park is dedicated to the men and women who died in pursuit of Irish freedom from British rule during the country's many uprisings. Near the entrance is a still reflecting pool with a mosaic at its bottom depicting broken weapons — symbols of peace. Farther back, the large statue near the fountain portrays the myth of the Children of Lir, who were turned into swans by their selfish and cruel stepmother. The park's location is significant — it is where several leaders of the 1916 Easter rebellion were held overnight before being taken to Kilmainham Gaol and put to death.

The park is open April through September daily from 8:30 a.m. to 6 p.m., October through March daily from 9:30 a.m. to 4 p.m. Admission is free. Allow 20 minutes for your visit.

✔ **National Botanic Gardens,** off Botanic Road, Glasnevin, Dublin 9 (see map p. 147; ☎ **01-804-0300;** Bus: 4, 13A, 19, 83): With a huge plant collection (more than 20,000 species), this is a must for anyone who has a green thumb (or aspires to have one). Highlights include a rose garden, an alpine area, and an arboretum. The huge greenhouses (called *glass houses* in Ireland) shelter tropical plants and other exotic species. Guided tours are offered Sundays at noon and 2:30 p.m.

Admission is free, but parking costs €2. The gardens are open mid-February through mid-November daily from 9 a.m. to 6 p.m. (greenhouses close at 5 p.m.), mid-November through mid-February daily from 9 a.m. to 4:30 p.m. (greenhouses close at 4 p.m.). Allow about an hour for your visit.

✔ **Phoenix Park and Dublin Zoo,** Park Gate, Conyngham Road, Phoenix Park Visitor Centre, Dublin 8 (see map p. 130; Park Visitor Centre ☎ **01-677-0095,** Dublin Zoo ☎ **01-474-8900;** www.dublin zoo.ie; Bus: 37, 38, or 39 to Ashtown Cross Gate [for the park], or 10, 10A, 25, 15A, 26, or 66, 67, 68, 69 [for the zoo]): This is one of Europe's largest enclosed city parks — five times the size of London's Hyde Park. You can drive through it, but if the weather's nice, don't pass up the chance to walk, because Phoenix Park is more than just a green spot for picnic lunches: Enclosed within it are the homes of Ireland's president and the U.S. ambassador. Other sights include the Papal Cross, where Pope John Paul II said Mass to a million Irish in 1979, and Ashton Castle, a 17th-century tower house that's now the visitor center. The park is home to a herd of deer who have lived here since the 1660s.

The Dublin Zoo is the world's third-oldest zoo. A wide variety of animals, from lions to red pandas, are housed here in large habitats that have been designed to give the animals as much freedom as possible. The zoo runs several successful breeding programs, so baby giraffes, tiger cubs, and the like are often on view. Be aware that because the animal enclosures are large, seeing the zoo requires a lot of walking.

Admission to the park is free; the zoo is €15 adults, €13 students, €12 seniors, €11 kids 3 to 15, and free for kids 2 and under. The park is open all day every day; the zoo is open March through September daily from 9:30 a.m. to 6 p.m., November through January daily from 9:30 a.m. to 4 p.m., February daily from 9:30 a.m. to 5 p.m., and October daily from 9:30 to 5:30 p.m. Last admission is one hour before closing, and the African Plains area closes half an hour before the rest of the zoo. Allow 90 minutes for a leisurely look at the park; add two or three more hours if you're visiting the zoo.

More cathedrals and churches

✔ **St. Ann's Anglican Church,** Dawson Street at Molesworth Street, Dublin 2 (see map p. 130; ☎ **01-676-7727;** www.stann.dublin. anglican.org; DART: Tara Street Station; Bus: 10, 11A, 11B, 13, 20B): In this church, Bram Stoker, the writer of the creepy novel *Dracula,* married Florence Balcombe, witty playwright and Oscar Wilde's first love. Wolfe Tone, the famous rebel, also was married here. Highlights are the gorgeous stained-glass windows and ornate plasterwork.

Admission is free and the church is open Monday through Friday from 10 a.m. to 4 p.m. Allow 20 minutes for your visit.

✔ **St. Audoen's Church,** Cornmarket, off High Street (see map p. 130; ☎ **01-677-0088):** There are actually two churches of the same name off Cook Street, but you're looking for the smaller and older of the two. St. Audoen's is situated right next to the only remaining gate of the Old City, which was built in 1214. The only medieval church in Dublin that still holds services, St. Audoen's features a doorway from 1190; a 13th-century nave; and three of the oldest church bells in Ireland, cast in 1423. A nicely done exhibit explains the history of the church. Tours are available if you book in advance.

Admission is €2 adults; €1 seniors, students, and kids. The church is open June through September daily from 9:30 a.m. to 5:30 p.m. (last entry and tour at 4:45 p.m.). Allow 45 minutes for your visit.

✔ **St. Michan's Church,** Church Street, Dublin 7 (see map p. 130; ☎ 01-872-4154; DART: Tara Street Station; Bus: 134): Unless you plan to make your next vacation a tour of the ancient pyramids, this may be your best chance to see actual mummies. It's hard to believe, but the combination of cool temperatures and dry air at this location preserves bodies, and the vaults below the church contain the remains of such historical figures as Henry and John Sheares, leaders of the Rebellion of 1798, and a man thought to have been a Crusader. It's definitely a creepy experience, as arms and legs are visible through the seams of the coffins, and four bodies are completely exposed. The church itself is also worth a look, boasting an organ believed to have been played by Handel, and detailed wood carvings of instruments above the choir area. Call before going — the church can occasionally be closed without notice.

Admission is €4 adults, €3.50 seniors and students, €3 kids 11 and under. The church is open March 17 through October Monday through Friday from 10 a.m. to 12:45 p.m. and 2 to 4:30 p.m., Saturday from 10 a.m. to 12:45 p.m.; November through March 16 Monday through Friday from 12:30 to 3:30 p.m., Saturday from 10 a.m. to 12:45 p.m. Allow 30 minutes for your visit.

Seeing Dublin by guided tour

As you can tell by the collection of Best of the Best icons in this section, I'm a great fan of guided tours in Dublin. The city is rich in history, and it's fascinating to take tours with different themes. Each tour pulls back a different curtain to reveal new facets of the city. If you're very short on time, I recommend taking the Dublin Bus Tour during the day and the Musical Pub Crawl in the evening.

If you want something more independent than the guided tours listed in this section, check out one of the Dublin Tourism Board's free self-guided podcast tours of the city. There are 11 tours, including the **Georgian Trail,** which covers five 18th-century squares, surrounded by period homes; the **Viking and Medieval Trail,** concentrating on the medieval area of Dublin; and the **In the Steps of Ulysses** route, which follows the steps of Joyce's famous character. Download the podcasts by visiting www.visitdublin.com (enter "iWalks" in the Search box). Give yourself an afternoon for each tour.

Attractions around County Dublin

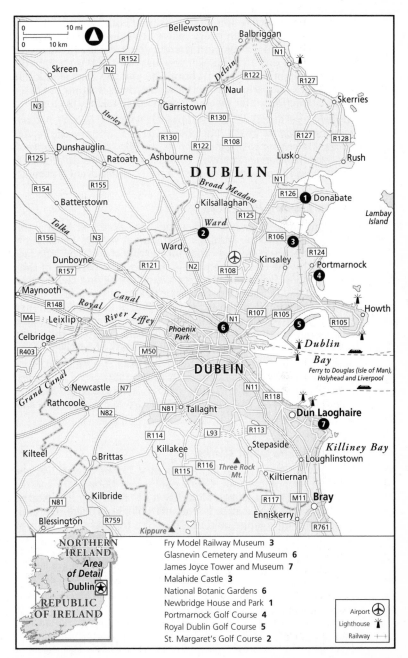

Fry Model Railway Museum	**3**
Glasnevin Cemetery and Museum	**6**
James Joyce Tower and Museum	**7**
Malahide Castle	**3**
National Botanic Gardens	**6**
Newbridge House and Park	**1**
Portmarnock Golf Course	**4**
Royal Dublin Golf Course	**5**
St. Margaret's Golf Course	**2**

Dublin Bus Tour

I highly recommend this tour, which is perfect if you want some guidance but also want the freedom to take as much time as you want checking out the sights. Pretty much every major attraction the city has to offer is at one of the 23 bus stops, and there's commentary throughout. The tour takes an hour and 15 minutes if you just ride the bus straight through, but your bus ticket is valid for 24 hours, so you can (and should!) hop on and off to check out various attractions, stretching the tour out to a whole day. Some attractions offer discounts for people taking this tour.

All tours leave from Dublin Bus, 59 Upper O'Connell St., Dublin 1, but you can join the tour at any stop. ☎ 01-703-3028. www.dublinsightseeing.ie. Admission: €16 adults, €14 seniors and students; up to two kids 13 and under travel free with an accompanying parent (otherwise, €6 kids 5–14). Bus runs daily 9 a.m.–5 p.m. (A bus stops at each stop every 10 minutes 9 a.m.–3 p.m. and every 15 minutes 3–5 p.m.)

Dublin Literary Pub Crawl

Literature has never been more fun! Two excellent Irish actors perform humorous tidbits by Dublin's best-known writers as they guide you to pubs of literary fame and other interesting stops. You'll be laughing hysterically by the end of the tour — and not just because of the numerous pints you've consumed. There's a quiz at the end (with prizes), so pay attention. If you haven't gotten your tickets at the tourist office on Suffolk Street, you should arrive at the Duke Pub at least half an hour before the tour begins to ensure a spot. For small groups who want more literature and fewer libations, a new Literary Walk (without the pubs) is being offered by advance reservation (call ☎ 01-87-263-0270).

Tours leave from upstairs at the Duke Pub, 9 Duke St., off Grafton. Purchase tickets at the tourist office on Suffolk Street (☎ 01-670-5602), online, or upstairs at the Duke Pub at 7 p.m. www.dublinpubcrawl.com. Admission: €12 adults, €10 students. Tours: Apr–Oct daily 7:30 p.m., Nov–Mar Thurs–Sun 7:30 p.m. The crawl lasts just over two hours.

Hidden Dublin Ghost Walks

Finally! With its long and storied history, Dublin always has been a prime location for a ghost tour. Other companies popped up and disappeared quickly, but Hidden Dublin looks like it's here to stay. The **Northside Ghost Walk** explores the haunted history of Dublin's northside; the tour is spooky, historically interesting, and fun. If you're the type who can watch horror movies with your front door unlocked, you'll want to book on the macabre **Haunted History** walk, which genuinely scares many people. The Northside Ghost Walk is appropriate for kids 12 and older who are relatively scare-proof, while the Haunted History tour is strictly adults only.

Northside Ghost Walk leaves from Mary Street, opposite McDonald's Mon–Wed and Sat 8 p.m. Haunted History leaves from the little square next to City Hall, on Dame Street Thurs–Sun 8 p.m. Call to confirm that meeting points and times haven't changed. ☎ 085-102-3646. www.hiddendublinwalks.com. Admission: €12. Discount offered for those who book online. All walks are 90 minutes.

Historical Walking Tours of Dublin

Walk this way for outstanding historical tours of the city. On the "Original Tour," nicknamed the "Seminar on the Street," Trinity history students and graduates give a relatively in-depth, fascinating account of Irish history as they guide you to some of the city's most famous sites, including Trinity College, the Old Parliament House, Dublin Castle, City Hall, Christ Church, and Temple Bar. During the summer, the company adds several special tours, including "Piety, Penance & Potatoes," a sexual history of Ireland; "From Nelson to the Needle," a tour of Dublin's statues and monuments; and "A Terrible Beauty," a tour focusing on the birth of the Irish state (1916–1923).

Tours leave from the front gate of Trinity College on College Street. ☎ **087-688-9412.** www.historicalinsights.ie. *Admission: €12 adults, €10 seniors and students, free for kids 13 and under. "Original Tour": May–Sept daily 11 a.m. and 3 p.m., Apr and Oct daily 11 a.m.; Nov–Mar Fri–Sun 11 a.m. Special tours: May–Sept daily (call to find out which days and times).*

Traditional Irish Musical Pub Crawl

This pub crawl is a fabulous experience for anyone even remotely interested in Irish music. Two excellent musicians guide you from pub to pub, regaling you with Irish tunes and songs; cracking many a joke; and filling you in on the instruments used in Irish music, the history of the music, and the various types of tunes and songs. The musicians who present this tour care deeply about Irish music and create an experience that is as authentic as possible. Get thee to the Dublin Tourist Office (on Suffolk Street), the phone, or the Internet to order tickets; or show up early at the pub to assure yourself a spot on the tour. Musicians: You may have a chance to perform at the end of the crawl.

Tours leave from the upstairs at Oliver St. John Gogarty's Pub in Temple Bar (corner of Fleet and Anglesea streets). ☎ **01-478-0193.** www.discoverdublin.ie. *Admission: €12 adults, €10 students. Tours: Apr–Oct daily 7:30 p.m., Nov–Mar Thurs–Sat 7:30 p.m. Arrive early or book ahead. The tour lasts about two and a half hours.*

Viking Splash Tours

Two things make this tour stand out from the competition: First, you're riding around in a World War II amphibious vehicle (called a *duck*) that, at one point, leaves the normal tourist trail to sail along the Grand Canal. Second, the Viking theme doesn't just color the historical information related along the tour; all riders are given Viking helmets and encouraged to roar at "rival" tour groups. I promise, kids will not be bored. Book online or by phone to ensure that you get a ticket.

Tours leave from the north side of St. Stephen's Green at Dawson Street. ☎ **01-707-6000.** www.vikingsplash.ie. *Admission: €20 adults, €18 seniors and students, €10 kids 4–12; kids 3 and under are not permitted. Tours: Daily every 30 minutes 10 a.m.–5:30 p.m. Call to confirm, as times may vary, especially during the winter. The tour lasts 75 minutes.*

Green on green: Dublin's top golfing spots

These courses are all within easy reach of Dublin. Try to reserve your tee time at least one day in advance.

✔ **Portmarnock,** Portmarnock, County Dublin (see map p. 147; ☎ 01-846-2968; www.portmarnockgolfclub.ie): This par-72 links course incorporates the rugged landscape of the region and has been home to several major championships. The course is open April through October daily, and the fees are €180; November through March, it's open weekends only, and the fees are €120.

✔ **Royal Dublin,** North Bull Island, Doillymount, Dublin 3 (see map p. 147; ☎ 01-833-6346; www.theroyaldublingolfclub.com): Situated on manmade North Bull Island in Dublin Bay, only 6.4km (4 miles) from the center of Dublin, this par-72 championship links course has offered exciting play amid great scenery for more than 100 years. The links are located along the seaside. The course is open every day except Wednesday, but only a few tee times are offered on weekends. From March through December, the fees are €125; in January and February, you can play for €100.

✔ **St. Margaret's,** Stephubble, St. Margaret's, County Dublin (see map p. 147; ☎ 01-864-0400; www.stmargaretsgolf.com): One of the hosts of the Irish Open, this is a relatively new, challenging, and exciting par-73 inland course with an infamously difficult finishing hole. The course is open daily. April through October, fees are €50 Monday through Thursday, €65 Friday through Sunday; November through March, fees are €45 Monday through Thursday, €55 Friday through Sunday. Discounts are often available when you book online.

Attractions a little out of town

Dublin Bus, 59 Upper O'Connell St., Dublin 1 (☎ 01-703-3028), runs a tour that covers Dublin's northern coastline on a double-decker bus. The "North Coast and Castle Tour" explores the coastline, with stops at the gorgeous seaside town of Howth and at Malahide Castle. It leaves daily at 10 a.m. and 2 p.m. Prices are €26 adults, €13 kids 5 to 14, free for kids 4 and under. Call for reservations or book online at www.dublin sightseeing.ie.

Wild Wicklow Tours (p. 185) and Mary Gibbons tours (p. 173) are excellent ways to see the neighboring counties of Wicklow and Meath, respectively.

If you're planning to visit the Joyce Tower, Malahide Castle, and Fry Railway, buy a ticket that covers the admission fees for all the attractions. These tickets are available at each of the attractions.

DART out of town

I love the DART train (see p. 107). It's inexpensive, runs very frequently, and takes you through the pretty countryside surrounding Dublin. In the mood for a little seaside jaunt? Spend a handful of euro and end up in the charming town of Greystones. Want to have a look at the location where James Joyce set the first scene of *Ulysses?* Hop on the DART and head south to Sandycove. See Chapters 12 and 13 for more about the areas surrounding Dublin City.

Check the "Attractions around County Dublin" map for the location of the following sights:

✔ **James Joyce Tower and Museum,** near the corner of Georges Street, Dun Laoghaire (see map p. 147; ☎ **01-280-9265;** DART: Sandycove Station; Bus: 7 and 7a): This tower was made famous in the first scene of *Ulysses:* Stephen Dedalus stays here with Buck Mulligan. Located on a rocky beach in the quaint town of Sandycove, the tower was built, along with 11 others, in 1804, as protection against a possible invasion by Napoleon. Joyce actually did stay in the tower with his friend Oliver St. John Gogarty (who inspired the fictional Mulligan) at the start of the century, and now the place is officially known as Joyce Tower. It houses such Joycean effects as letters, a walking stick, and a cigar case. Lovers of Joyce and *Ulysses* will have a great time here; less enthusiastic fans may be disappointed by the small size of the exhibit and may want to stick to the James Joyce Centre (see p. 130).

Admission is €6 adults, €5 seniors and students, €4 kids 11 and under. It's open April through August Tuesday through Saturday from 10 a.m. to 1 p.m. and 2 to 5 p.m., Sunday from 2 to 6 p.m. You can visit at other times by arrangement. Allow 45 minutes for your visit.

✔ **Malahide Castle,** Malahide (see map p. 147; ☎ **01-846-2184;** Irish Rail: Malahide Station from Connolly Station; Bus: 42): This castle was witness to the longevity of one of Ireland's great and wealthy families, the Talbots, who resided here from 1185 to 1973. You can tour the castle with an audio guide. The architecture of the house is varied, and period furniture adorns the rooms. There's a large collection of Irish portraits, many from the National Gallery, and the Great Hall chronicles the Talbots with portraits of family members. One tragic legend tells of the morning of the Battle of the Boyne in 1690, when 14 members of the family shared a last meal; by the end of the battle, all had been killed. The grounds are spectacular — be sure to check out the Botanic Gardens. Kids will have a great time at the Fry Model Railway Museum (see the next review), located on the castle grounds.

Admission is €7.50 adults, €6.30 seniors and students, €4.70 kids 11 and under; combined tickets are available for the castle and the Fry Model Railway Museum. It's open April through September, Monday through Saturday daily from 10 a.m. to 5 p.m.; October through March, Monday through Saturday from 10 a.m. to 5 p.m., Sunday from 11 a.m. to 5 p.m. The last tour leaves 30 minutes before closing. Allow 90 minutes for your visit.

✔ **Fry Model Railway Museum,** Malahide Castle (see map p. 147; ☎ 01-846-3779; Irish Rail: Malahide Station from Connolly Station; Bus: 42): Located on the grounds of Malahide Castle (see the previous review), the Fry Model Railway Museum will entertain kids of all ages. This unique collection of handmade trains spans the history of train travel in Ireland and runs over an area covering over 230 sq. m (2,500 sq. ft.), with stations, bridges, trams, buses, and a mini representation of the River Liffey. The collection was assembled by railway engineer Cyril Fry during the 1920s and 1930s.

Admission is €6 adults, €5 seniors and students, €4 kids 11 and under; combined tickets are available for the castle and museum. It's open April through September, Tuesday through Saturday from 10 a.m. to 1 p.m. and 2 to 5 p.m., Sunday from 1 to 5 p.m. Last admission is always at 4:30 p.m. Allow an hour for your visit.

✔ **Newbridge House and Park,** Donabate (see map p. 147; ☎ 01-843-6534; Irish Rail: Donabate Station from Connolly Station; Bus: 33B): Walking around Dublin, you see plenty of examples of Georgian exteriors, but here's your chance to see a fine Georgian interior. Each gorgeous room in the manor house features original furniture and objects. The extensive park grounds are home to a kid-friendly animal farm.

Admission to the house is €7 adults, €6 seniors and students, €3.50 kids 11 and under; to the farm, it's €3.50 adults, €2.50 seniors, students, and kids 11 and under. Both are open April through September, Tuesday through Saturday from 10 a.m. to 1 p.m. and 2 to 5 p.m., Sunday from 2 to 6 p.m.; October through March, Saturday and Sunday from noon to 5 p.m. The last tour starts an hour before closing. Allow 90 minutes for your visit.

Suggested one-, two-, and three-day sightseeing itineraries

If you just have **one day** and you really want to pack the sightseeing in, I recommend taking the **Dublin Bus Tour** so that you can see as many attractions as possible in the most efficient way. Take in **Trinity College** and the **Book of Kells** first, and then wander around the excellent shopping areas of Grafton Street and Nassau Street. Grab a fish-and-chips lunch at **Beshoff**, and picnic in **Merrion Square** or **St. Stephen's Green**. In the afternoon, visit the nearby **National Museum**. Treat yourself to a delicious dinner at the **Winding Stair** before meeting up with the

Traditional Irish Musical Pub Crawl. If you're still craving more traditional music after the pub crawl, end your day at the **Cobblestone**.

If you have **two days,** follow the itinerary in the preceding paragraph. On
the morning of the second day, take the **Historical Walking Tour.** Then
head over to the **Chester Beatty Library** to gaze at the gorgeous books
and art housed within. Eat lunch in one of the pubs recommended in the
"Traditional Irish dishes" sidebar, earlier in this chapter, and then head
out to see **St. Patrick's Cathedral, Dublin Castle,** and the **Guinness
Storehouse** (all outlined in "The top attractions"). Drop into the **Queen
of Tarts** for an afternoon treat on your way back to Temple Bar. Stroll
the Grafton Street area, and have dinner at **L'Gueuleton** before joining
up with the **Literary Pub Crawl.**

If you have **three days,** follow the itineraries in the preceding two para-
graphs. Then DART out of the city to Bray or Greystones, and hike the
Bray Head trail. After all that hiking, you deserve dinner at **Chapter One**
before heading off to see a show at the famous **Abbey Theatre.**

Shopping in Dublin

Dublin is the shopping capital of Ireland. Within the city limits, you can
easily find all sorts of famous Irish items, including Donegal tweed,
Waterford Crystal, Belleek china, and Claddagh rings, as well as gorgeous jewelry and clothes, books, musical instruments, CDs, and much
more.

Locating the best shopping areas

There are three main shopping areas in Dublin. The **Grafton Street area**
(including Duke, Dawson, Nassua, South William, Wicklow, and other
nearby streets) on the south side of the River Liffey, offers a variety of
shopping options. Bustling Grafton Street itself is lined with trendy big-
name clothing stores and is home to **Brown Thomas,** Ireland's ultrafash-
ionable department store. The side streets off Grafton are home to
upscale and funky boutiques and stores. Nearby Nassau Street is the
place to find the best in Irish crafts, from sweaters to crystal.

If you're looking for the funky fashions, jewelry, art, and music, head to
the **Temple Bar area.**

On the north side of the River Liffey is the **Henry Street–Mary Street
area,** off O'Connell Street, where you'll find stores that populate many
large cities worldwide, including Gap, The Body Shop, and others.
Moore Street, just off the main shopping drag, offers a daily open-air
market with plenty of the freshest (and cheapest) fruits and vegetables
in the city. This is where you'll hear the perfected lilt of the vendors
hawking their wares — a Dublin attraction in its own right.

Dublin Shopping

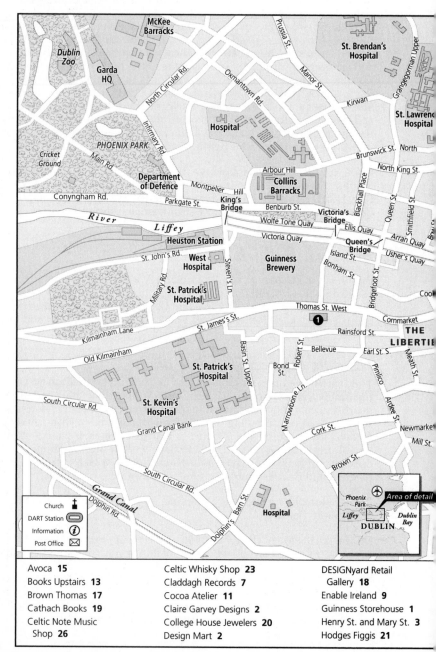

Avoca **15**
Books Upstairs **13**
Brown Thomas **17**
Cathach Books **19**
Celtic Note Music
  Shop **26**

Celtic Whisky Shop **23**
Claddagh Records **7**
Cocoa Atelier **11**
Claire Garvey Designs **2**
College House Jewelers **20**
Design Mart **2**

DESIGNyard Retail
  Gallery **18**
Enable Ireland **9**
Guinness Storehouse **1**
Henry St. and Mary St. **3**
Hodges Figgis **21**

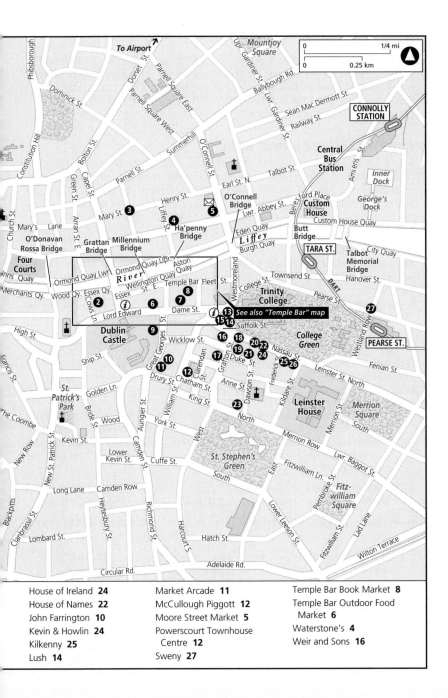

House of Ireland **24**
House of Names **22**
John Farrington **10**
Kevin & Howlin **24**
Kilkenny **25**
Lush **14**

Market Arcade **11**
McCullough Piggott **12**
Moore Street Market **5**
Powerscourt Townhouse
  Centre **12**
Sweny **27**

Temple Bar Book Market **8**
Temple Bar Outdoor Food
  Market **6**
Waterstone's **4**
Weir and Sons **16**

Teenagers: You may want to drag your parents to the **Market Arcade,** on South Great George's Street, between Exchequer Street and Fade Street, for music, fun clothes, jewelry, and a grungy coffee shop.

Powerscourt Townhouse Centre, 59 S. William St., Dublin 2 (☎ 01-679-4144), is a grand restored Georgian town house with a variety of shops, ranging from clothes boutiques to art galleries. It's fun to wander through, even if you're not interested in buying anything. This is *the* place to go for antique jewelry.

Finding Ireland's best wares

Ireland is known the world over for its handmade products and fine craftsmanship, and Dublin, as Ireland's commercial center, is a one-stop source for the best of Irish products. If you're traveling to a town or city where a certain craft is produced, you may want to hold off on purchasing that craft in Dublin, as markups can be significant.

Antiques

High-quality antiques dealers are concentrated on **Francis Street,** between Thomas Street West and the Coombe. Several shops at the Powerscourt Townhouse Centre, 59 S. William St., sell beautiful antique jewelry. Also see Cathach Books in the next section, and John Farrington in the "Crafts and jewelry" section.

Books

Like any section of a city that surrounds a college campus, there are loads of good bookstores near Trinity College. You can find works of Irish writers here that may be hard to find at home.

- ✔ **Books Upstairs,** 36 College Green and Dame Street, across from the Trinity College front entrance, Dublin 2 (☎ 01-679-6687), has a comprehensive collection of Irish fiction and nonfiction, a sizable gay and lesbian selection, some fiction bargains, and a friendly and helpful staff.
- ✔ **Cathach Books,** 10 Duke St., off Grafton Street, Dublin 2 (☎ 01-671-8676), sells rare editions of Irish literature, plus old maps of Ireland.
- ✔ **Hodges Figgis,** 56–58 Dawson St., Dublin 2 (☎ 01-677-4754), is a giant bookstore offering a wide selection of books.
- ✔ **Waterstone's,** Jervis Centre, Mary Street, Dublin 1 (☎ 01-878-1311), and 7 Dawson St. (☎ 01-679-1415), is pretty much the Barnes & Noble of the Emerald Isle.

Chocolate

Cocoa Atelier, 30 Drury St. (☎ 01-675-3616), is like the Wonka Factory for sophisticated adults, with handmade chocolates, truffles, and caramels in all sorts of flavors, plus melt-in-your-mouth French-style macaroons.

Clothes

You won't want for clothing stores in Dublin; here are a few of my favorites:

- ✔ **Avoca,** 11–13 Suffolk St. (☎ 01-677-4215), sells the Irish-designed and -made Anthology line of clothes, with all the vivid colors and funky lace, beads, and ribbons that a 20- or 30-something girl could want. Other offerings include all sorts of household goods, edibles, and clothes for hip babies (such as a onesie that says, "It girl"). Break up your shopping trip with a snack at the store's excellent cafe.

- ✔ **Brown Thomas,** 88–95 Grafton St., Dublin 2 (☎ 01-605-6666), sells the latest in upscale fashion.

- ✔ **Claire Garvey Designs,** 6 Cow's Lane, Dublin 2 (☎ 01-671-7287), is where fairy queens would buy their clothes. Garvey creates shimmery, sheer pieces, many with lace-up bodices and beads, and her recent line features punk influences. Looking like a goddess doesn't come cheap.

- ✔ **Enable Ireland,** South Great George's Street, Dublin 2 (next to Juice; ☎ 01-478-2763), sells used clothes from silver vinyl pants to girls' flowery dresses. All profits go to Enable Ireland, which helps people with disabilities lead independent lives.

- ✔ **Kevin & Howlin,** 31 Nassau St., Dublin 2 (☎ 01-633-4576), sells authentic hand-woven tweed jackets, scarves, ties, and hats.

Crafts and jewelry

If you're in the market for contemporary Irish crafts and jewelry, point yourself in the direction of Nassau Street, on the edge of Trinity College, which is lined with shops selling Irish items. For antique jewelry, visit the Powerscourt Townhouse Centre, 59 S. William St. Also see "Souvenirs and gifts," later in this chapter.

- ✔ **College House Jewellers,** 44 Nassau St., Dublin 2 (☎ 01-677-7597), stocks gorgeous Celtic-style jewelry and has a comprehensive collection of Claddagh jewelry, from classic to modern.

- ✔ **DESIGNyard Retail Gallery,** 48–49 Nassau St., Dublin 2, (☎ 01-474-1011), stocks exquisite and generally affordable contemporary Irish-designed jewelry and sculpture. The shop is known for its engagement and wedding ring collection.

- ✔ **John Farrington,** 32 Drury St., Dublin 2 (☎ 01-679-1899), is a good bet for vintage jewelry, from Georgian silver earrings to Victorian lockets.

- ✔ **Weir and Sons,** 96 Grafton St., at Wicklow Street, Dublin 2 (☎ 01-677-9678), which has been around since 1869, sells fine jewelry, china, silver, leather, and watches.

This little traveler went to market

One of the best ways to experience Dublin is to hit the markets. Here are some of the best:

✔ **Designer Mart,** Cow's Lane, Old City, Temple Bar, is the place to find hip, handmade clothing, crafts, and jewelry. It runs every Saturday from 10 a.m. to 5:30 p.m.

✔ **Moore Street Market,** Moore Street, is a bustling market full of vendors selling fresh vegetables, fruits, and flowers. Some vendors still hawk their wares in a lilting, singsong voice reminiscent of the Molly Malones of the past, and banter is part of many transactions. African and Asian stores have moved onto the street, making for an even richer market experience. It runs Monday through Saturday from 9 a.m. to 5 p.m.

✔ **Temple Bar Book Market,** Temple Bar Square, is a smallish outdoor used-book market. Grab some lunch at the outdoor food market, and browse through the offerings. It runs every Saturday and Sunday from 11 a.m. to 6 p.m.

✔ **Temple Bar Outdoor Food Market,** Meetinghouse Square in Temple Bar, is an orgy of Irish gourmet and organic food, including delicacies such as Chez Emily's chocolates, artisanal breads and cheeses, and gorgeous produce. It runs every Saturday from 10 a.m. to 4:30 p.m.

Irish music and musical instruments

If you fell in love with the sounds of the traditional session you heard at the pub last night, head to one of these stores to pick up a CD, or even a tin whistle or *bodhrán* (pronounced *buh*-rahn; a goatskin drum) of your very own.

✔ **Celtic Note Music Shop,** 12 Nassau St., Dublin 2 (☎ **01-670-4157**), is a great place to find any type of Irish music, from traditional to contemporary rock. Prices here are slightly lower than at Claddagh Records. Celtic Note occasionally hosts free midday in-store concerts by hot traditional Irish bands.

✔ **Claddagh Records,** 2 Cecilia St., Temple Bar (☎ **01-677-0262**), sells the best traditional Irish and world music CDs. The staff here is exceedingly knowledgeable, so this is the place to go if you're not sure what you're looking for.

✔ **McCullough Piggott,** 11 S. William St., Dublin 2 (☎ **01-677-3138**), sells all sorts of instruments and the tutorial books and CDs that help you play them. The staff is incredibly nice and helpful.

Souvenirs and gifts

Also see the recommendations in "Crafts and jewelry," earlier in this chapter.

- **Celtic Whiskey Shop,** 27–28 Dawson St., Dublin 2 (☎ **01-675-9744**), sells everything from the best-known brands of whiskey, such as Bushmills, to rare bottlings from distilleries that have closed their doors. They host frequent tastings in the store to whet your palate.

- **Guinness Storehouse,** St. James's Gate, Dublin 8 (☎ **01-408-4800;** www.guinness-storehouse.com), stocks all things Guinness, from posters and slippers to clocks and candles.

- **House of Ireland,** 37 Nassau St., at the corner of Dawson Street, Dublin 2 (☎ **01-671-1111**), is one-stop shopping for authentic Irish goods such as crystal, china, hand-knit Aran sweaters, and more.

- **House of Names,** 26 Nassau St. (☎ **01-679-7287**), creates and sells wall shields and plaques; clothing; and jewelry with the crest, coat of arms, and motto of most European family names. Here's hoping you have one of those cool dragons on your coat of arms.

- **Kilkenny,** 5–6 Nassau St. (☎ **01-677-7066**), boasts original Irish designs, including glass, knitwear, jewelry, and a large selection of gorgeous pottery.

- **Lush,** 166 Grafton St., across from the entrance to Trinity College (☎ **01-677-0392**), is not particularly Irish, but when your giftees open their packages of colorful homemade soaps, bubble baths, shampoos, and more, they won't care. All the items here look good enough to eat, and you probably *could* eat them, because they're all made with as many natural ingredients as possible.

- **Sweny,** 1 Lincoln Place, at the top of Westland Row (no phone), is the pharmacy where Leopold Bloom buys lemon soap in *Ulysses,* and you'll make a Joyce fan very, very happy with his or her own bar of lemon soap, packaged in brown paper and tied with string. My mom actually yelped upon receipt of her gift. The pharmacy looks almost as it would have in Joyce's day, and it hosts Joyce-related events.

Hitting the Pubs and Enjoying Dublin's Nightlife

James Joyce put it best in *Ulysses:* "Good puzzle would be to cross Dublin without passing a pub." With more than 1,000 pubs in the city (the "Dublin Nightlife" map helps locate them), there's something to suit everyone, whether your taste runs to Victorian pubs with globe lamps and polished mahogany bars or to local watering holes with worn couches and clocks that read the wrong time. See the section "Enjoying the Music," later in the chapter, for details on pubs that feature great traditional Irish music.

For a night of food and great storytelling, reserve a place for **"Food, Folklore, and Fairies"** at the Brazen Head. The event runs from 7 to 10

Dublin Nightlife

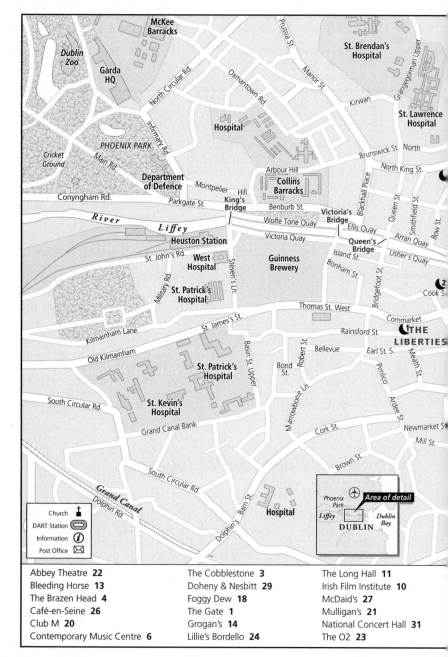

Abbey Theatre **22**
Bleeding Horse **13**
The Brazen Head **4**
Café-en-Seine **26**
Club M **20**
Contemporary Music Centre **6**

The Cobblestone **3**
Doheny & Nesbitt **29**
Foggy Dew **18**
The Gate **1**
Grogan's **14**
Lillie's Bordello **24**

The Long Hall **11**
Irish Film Institute **10**
McDaid's **27**
Mulligan's **21**
National Concert Hall **31**
The O2 **23**

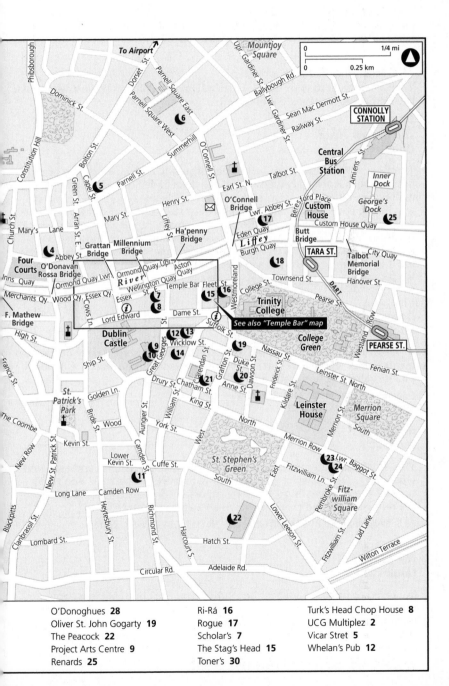

O'Donoghues **28**

Oliver St. John Gogarty **19**

The Peacock **22**

Project Arts Centre **9**

Renards **25**

Ri-Rá **16**

Rogue **17**

Scholar's **7**

The Stag's Head **15**

Toner's **30**

Turk's Head Chop House **8**

UCG Multiplez **2**

Vicar Stret **5**

Whelan's Pub **12**

p.m. Tuesday through Friday, and prices are €44 adults, €40 students, and €37 kids, including a meal. You can book online at www.irish folktours.com, or by phone at ☎ 01-492-2543.

Hitting the pubs

Take a cab back to your hotel, if you're leaving a pub after dark. Much of the crime in Dublin is alcohol-fueled.

The Brazen Head
Dublin 8

The Brazen Head claims to be the oldest pub in Dublin. That may or may not be true, but certainly many a pint has been pulled here since its opening in 1661 (an older pub, from 1198, stood on this site before the "new" pub was built). The unusual name comes from a story about a bold woman who was so curious during one of the country's many rebellions that she stuck her head out of the window — only to have it chopped off! Though it's a bit touristy, it's a beautiful Victorian pub, lit by lanterns. There's music every night beginning at 9:30 p.m., and an excellent storytelling show.

20 Lower Bridge St. ☎ *01-677-9549. Bus: 78A, 79, 90.*

Doheny & Nesbitt
Dublin 2

A poster-child of Victorian pubs, Nesbitt's boasts *snugs* (cozy compartments), dark wood, and bartenders full of wisdom. The clientele is heavy on journalists, economists, and politicians.

5 Lower Baggott St. ☎ *01-676-2945. Bus: 10, 11, 11A.*

Grogan's
Dublin 2

This small, unpretentious pub is filled with artists, writers, and assorted characters. The walls are covered with works by local artists. You're sure to meet some interesting folks here, especially on weekend evenings when the pub is so packed that the crowd spills into the street.

15 S. William St. ☎ *01-677-9320. Bus: 16, 16A, 19, 19A, 65, 65B, 83, 112.*

The Long Hall
Dublin 2

Rumored to have the longest bar in the city, the Long Hall is a gorgeous, ornate specimen of a pub. There's a vast array of antique clocks, Victorian lamps, a mahogany bar, and plenty of snugs to get lost in. The crowd is mostly locals, and the tiny TV (almost never on) and lack of music make it a terrific place for a long chat.

51 S. Great George's St. ☎ *01-475-1590. Bus: 50, 50A, 54, 56, 77.*

Café-en-Seine: The antipub?

Café-en-Seine, 40 Dawson St., Dublin 2 (☎ **01-677-4567**), looks like it was flown over intact from 19th-century Paris. This popular spot has a gorgeous Art Deco interior, with a glass atrium, brass chandeliers, murals, and large mirrors. You can get light bites, pastries, and coffees by day and wine, beer, and cocktails by night. The crowd can be a bit snooty, making for excellent people-watching.

McDaid's
Dublin 2

Attention, writers and literature-lovers: This was bad-boy playwright Brendan Behan's favorite watering hole, and the old-style pub still attracts those who love the world of words.

3 Harry St., off Grafton Street. ☎ **01-679-4395.** *Bus: 10, 11, 13B, 14, 14A, 15, 15A, 15B, 15C.*

Mulligan's
Dublin 2

This is an authentic old Dublin pub and favorite watering hole for the journalists of the nearby *Irish Times* newspaper. JFK drank here as a young European correspondent for the Hearst newspapers in 1945, and again when he visited as president. It's mentioned in *Ulysses,* and locals say it serves one of the best pints of Guinness in town.

8 Poolbeg St. (off south quays near O'Connell Bridge). ☎ **01-677-5582.** *Bus: 5, 7, 7A, 7X, 8.*

The Stag's Head
Dublin 2

The Stag's Head is a Victorian classic, with gleaming rich auburn wood, frosted globe lamps, and stained-glass windows. It's popular with Trinity students, journalists, theater folk, and everyone else. Try to score a seat in the small, opulent room on the right in the rear. The food here is terrific.

1 Dame Court (look for the mosaic stag head inlaid into the sidewalk on Dame Street, pointing the way). ☎ **01-679-3701.** *Bus: 21A, 50, 50A, 78, 78A, 78B.*

Toner's
Dublin 2

This is a great, old, authentic Dublin pub with a high *craic* (fun) factor. You'll find everyone from older folks enjoying a drink to boisterous rugby fans celebrating their team's victory.

139 Lower Baggott St. ☎ **01-676-3090.** *Bus: 10.*

Enjoying the music

Dublin has a hot music scene, featuring everything from jazz to rock to traditional Irish music.

Traditional Irish music venues

In addition to visiting the pubs in this section, I suggest the **Traditional Irish Music Pub Crawl** (listed in "Seeing Dublin by guided tour," earlier in this chapter). Also, see the Brazen Head (reviewed earlier in this chapter).

✔ **The Cobblestone,** 77 North King St., at Red Cow Lane (☎ 01-872-1799), a dim pub filled with instruments and photographs of traditional Irish musicians, hosts a lively, mostly Irish crowd and friendly sessions each night, with some exceptional musicians. No fuss, no show, no hip location — just the best traditional Irish music in Dublin. This is the real thing.

✔ **Hughes,** 19 Chancery St. (☎ 01-872-6540), is an unpretentious pub with excellent music several nights a week.

✔ **Oliver St. John Gogarty,** 58 Fleet St., Temple Bar (☎ 01-671-1822), is a popular pub named for surgeon, wit, and writer Oliver St. John Gogarty, who was the model for Buck Mulligan, a flip character in *Ulysses.* The interior screams Irish pub, with its décor of old books and bottles and portraits of traditional-Irish-music greats. The pub is always packed with travelers from all over the world, and you find live Irish music daily from 2:30 p.m. until the wee hours.

Rock, jazz, and other music venues

Dublin is by no means all jigs and reels all the time. The hopping live-music scene encompasses rock, jazz, country, folk, blues, classical, and more. The following venues consistently offer fantastic concerts:

✔ **The Contemporary Music Centre** (☎ 01-673-1922; www.cmc.ie) offers the very best new music from Irish composers at various venues.

✔ **The National Concert Hall,** Earlsfort Terrace, Dublin 2 (☎ 01-417-0000; www.nch.ie), is Dublin's best venue for classical music performances. The concert hall also hosts other types of music, including opera and traditional Irish music.

✔ **The O₂,** Eastlink Bridge, North Wall Quay (☎ 819-8888; www.theo2.ie), is Dublin's gorgeous new top venue for internationally known rock and folk acts, seating up to 6,000 people in arena seating.

✔ **Vicar Street,** 8 Thomas St., Dublin 8 (☎ 01-454-6656), is a small concert venue that hosts excellent (and often well-known) rock, jazz, folk, and traditional music.

✔ **Whelan's,** 25 Wexford St., Dublin 2 (☎ **01-478-0766;** www.whelans
live.com), has a cozy wooden interior; a nice atmosphere; and a
great lineup of well-known rock, folk, and traditional musicians.

Clubbing your way through Dublin

As in most European capitals, clubbing is taken seriously in Dublin,
and dress is pretty important, especially at the trendiest, most popular
clubs — don't be surprised it you're turned away because you're wearing jeans or athletic shoes. Often, there are cover charges (usually €5–
€25), and you may need to show an ID. Clubs usually open just when
regular buses stop running (about 11:30 p.m.), so expect to take a cab or
the Nitelink bus back to your hotel.

Here are some of the best clubs in Dublin at the moment:

✔ **Club M,** Cope Street, Temple Bar (☎ **01-671-5274**), packs 'em in
Monday, Friday, and Saturday for friendly, sweaty, all-night DJ
dance parties. This place has a reputation as a pickup joint.

✔ **The Dragon,** South Great Georges Street (☎ **01-478-1590**), is a gay
bar that hosts popular dance parties on the weekends.

✔ **Lillie's Bordello,** Adam Court, off Grafton Street (☎ **01-679-9204**),
is still one of the hottest Dublin clubs after many years, with a
lipstick-red interior and the members-only (you can pay to be a
member) Library room.

✔ **Ri-Rá,** 1 Exchequer St. (☎ **01-671-1220**), fills up every night with
dancers getting down to funk, jazz, rock, and other grooves.

Checking out Dublin's excellent theater scene

Dubliners have long held theater in high reverence, and the city has a
thriving theater scene that encompasses everything from the plays of
Synge to new multimedia projects.

Ireland's most famous playhouse, the **Abbey Theatre,** 26 Lower Abbey
St., Dublin 1 (☎ **01-878-7222;** www.abbeytheatre.ie), is best known
for staging superb productions of works by some of Ireland's best-loved
playwrights, including Sean O'Casey and J. M. Synge. The Abbey's sister
theater, the **Peacock,** 26 Lower Abbey St., Dublin 1 (☎ **01-878-7222;**
www.abbeytheatre.ie), boasts excellent productions of new plays.
The **Gate,** 1 Cavendish Row, on Parnell Square, Dublin 1 (☎ **01-874-
4045;** www.gate-theatre.ie), does a beautiful job with European,
Irish, and American classics and new plays. The theater is particularly
lauded for its productions of Samuel Beckett's work. **Project Arts
Centre,** 39 E. Essex St., Dublin 2 (☎ **01-881-9613;** www.projectarts
centre.ie), is the place to go for new and experimental theater. The
brand-new **Grand Canal Theatre,** on Cardiff Lane, on the south side of
the Samuel Beckett Bridge (☎ **01-677-7999;** www.grandcanaltheatre.
ie), is a huge theater hosting visiting musicals, ice shows, and major
concerts.

Going to the movies

Or, as the Irish say, "the cinema." There are lots of places to catch a flick in Dublin. **Cineworld Cinema,** midway down Parnell Street in Parnell Center, Dublin 1 (☎ **01-520-880-444;** www.cineworld.ie), is a streamlined and very modern multiplex, with 12 screens showing the latest commercial movies. The **Irish Film Institute** (IFI), 6 Eustace St., Temple Bar, Dublin 2 (☎ **01-679-3477;** www.irishfilm.ie), shows up-and-coming Irish independent cinema, European exclusives, and classics. A place for true film buffs, the IFI is as hip as it gets. There is a cafe, a lively bar, and a book and video/DVD shop on the premises. (Note that most American VCRs and DVD players can't play videos and DVDs purchased in Ireland.)

Fast Facts: Dublin

Area Code

The area code for Dublin city and county is **01.** If you're calling from outside of the country, you can drop the 0.

Dentists

A Dental Emergency Clinic is located at 24–26 Dame St. (☎ 01-670-9256).

Doctors

Usually, your hotel or B&B is able to get you an appointment with its house doctor. There is a drop-in medical clinic at 111 Lower Baggot St. (☎ 01-676-2175). Also see "Hospitals."

Embassies and Consulates

United States, 42 Elgin Rd., Ballsbridge, Dublin 4 (☎ 01-630-6200); Canada, 7/8 Wilton Terrace, Dublin 2 (☎ 01-234-4000); United Kingdom, 29 Merrion Rd., Dublin 4 (☎ 01-205-3700); Australia, 15 Ailesbury Rd., Ballsbridge (☎ 01-269-4577).

Emergencies

Dial ☎ **999** for police, fire, or ambulance.

Hospitals

The two best hospitals for emergency care in Dublin are St. Vincent's Hospital, Elm Park, off Merrion Road, Dublin 4 (☎ 01-221-4000), on the south side of the city; and Beaumont Hospital, Beaumont Road, Dublin 9 (☎ 01-809-3000), on the north side.

Information

Dublin Tourism (☎ 01-605-7700; www.visitdublin.com) runs three walk-in visitor centers around the center of the city. The largest and best is on Suffolk Street, Dublin 2. The others are in the arrivals concourse at the Dublin airport; at Exclusively Irish, and at 14 O'Connell Street, Dublin 1.

Temple Bar has its own information Web site at www.templebar.ie.

Internet

Dublin has a number of Internet cafes, including Global Internet Cafe, 8 Lower O'Connell St., Dublin 1 (☎ 01-878-0295).

Maps

Good maps are available at the Dublin Tourism Centre, Suffolk Street, and online through the Tourism Centre's Web site at www.visitdublin.com. Type "maps" in the Search box.

Newspapers/Magazines

The major newspaper in Ireland is the *Irish Times* (www.irishtimes.com). The best events listings are found at www.hotpress.com.

Pharmacies

The Temple Bar Pharmacy, 21 Essex St. E., Dublin 2 (☎ 01-670-9751), is a central pharmacy with extended hours.

Police

Dial ☎ **999** in case of emergencies. You can contact the police headquarters at Phoenix Park, Dublin 8 (☎ 01-666-0000). Police in Ireland are known as Garda or Gardai (pronounced *gard*-ee), or the Guards.

Post Office

The General Post Office (GPO) is located on O'Connell Street, Dublin 1 (☎ 01-705-7600). Its hours are Monday through Saturday 8:30 a.m. to 6 p.m. Branch offices, called *An Post* and noted with green storefront awnings, are generally open Monday through Saturday from 9 a.m. to 6 p.m.

Safety

Late-night crime is not uncommon, so don't walk back to your hotel alone after dark. Take a taxi.

Smoking

Smoking is not permitted in public buildings and is banned in restaurants and bars. Many hotels and some B&Bs offer smoking rooms.

Taxis

To get a taxi in Dublin, go to a taxi rank or hail a cab by sticking out your arm. If you need to call a cab, try Castle Cabs (☎ 01-831-9000) or National Radiocabs Co-op (☎ 01-677-2222).

Chapter 12

Easy Trips North of Dublin: Counties Meath and Louth

In This Chapter

▶ Exploring 5,000-year-old tombs

▶ Checking out Celtic high crosses

▶ Visiting the 800-year-old castle featured in *Braveheart*

▶ Biking or walking a trail rich in history and mythology

Collectively, Counties Meath and Louth are known as the ancient land of the Celts. They contain some of the country's finest prehistoric and mythical sites, including ancient sacred burial mounds, land that was revered by the Irish high kings of yore, and Celtic high crosses.

County Meath has some of the most important ancient religious attractions in Ireland — the prehistoric tombs of **Newgrange** and **Knowth,** and the **Hill of Tara,** a site sacred to ancient Irish kings. This region has been fought over by the country's many invaders, and all those invaders, from the Normans to the English, have left their marks here. The heart of the area is the River Boyne, home of the famous Battle of the Boyne, in which Protestant William of Orange defeated Catholic King James II, changing the course of Irish history. The history-rich towns of **Kells, Slane,** and **Trim** (with minor attractions including Slane Castle and Trim Castle) are the best places to stay in County Meath itself, though my favorite town in the area is **Carlingford,** which is relatively close to Meath's major attractions despite being located in County Louth.

County Louth is rich in mythology; legends such as Cuchulainn (pronounced coo-*cul*-in), Queen Maeve, and the great warrior Finn MacCool are associated with the area (see Chapter 2 for the stories behind these figures). The most beautiful area of Louth is the far northern area, encompassing the **Cooley Mountains** and **Cooley Peninsula,** and the delightful heritage town of **Carlingford.**

You easily can take day trips from Dublin to both counties, which you may well think of as one destination because they're both small. But I encourage you to set up camp for a night, especially in Carlingford.

Counties Meath and Louth

ATTRACTIONS
Carlingford Adventure
  Centre **1**
Causey Farm **11**
Cooley Peninsula **2**
Hill of Tara **8**
Monasterboice **4**
Newgrange & Knowth **6**
Old Mellifont Abbey **5**
Táin Way **2**
Trim Castle **10**

ACCOMMODATIONS
Ballymascanlon House
  Hotel **3**
Bellinter House **7**
Shalom Bed and
  Breakfast **1**
Tigh Catháin **9**

DINING
Ghan House **1**
Khan's Spices **10**
Kingfisher
  Bistro **1**
Vanilla Pod **12**

SHOPPING
Crystal Antiques **1**

NIGHTLIFE
McManus' **3**
P.J.'s (O'Hare's) **1**

Getting to and around Meath and Louth

Most visitors to Louth and Meath arrive by car, often on a day trip from Dublin. Take the M1 north toward Dundalk and follow the signs for most of the major towns and attractions mentioned in this chapter. To get around the Cooley Peninsula, take the R173, which loops the peninsula and hooks up with the M1 at Navan.

Irish Rail (☎ **1-850-366-222;** www.irishrail.ie) stops in the County Louth towns of Drogheda and Dundalk from Dublin.

Bus Éireann (☎ 01-836-6111; www.buseireann.ie) has year-round routes to Navan, Kells, Slane, Drogheda, Dundalk, Carlingford, and other smaller towns throughout the area.

Mary Gibbons organizes an excellent bus tour that departs from Dublin to take in several of Meath's ancient sights (see "Exploring Meath and Louth: The Top Attractions," later in this chapter, for details).

Spending the Night in Meath and Louth

In addition to its cooking school and restaurant, the Ghan House, in Carlingford (see "Cooking up a storm") offers charming, spacious accommodations. For hotel locations, see the "Counties Meath and Louth" map.

Ballymascanlon House Hotel
$$$ Dundalk, County Louth

This authentic Victorian mansion retains an old-world ambience, with spacious rooms that are tastefully decorated with antiques and Victorian touches. This is a great place for active folks — there's an 18-hole course on the grounds; a leisure center that boasts a pool, a gym, a Jacuzzi, and tennis courts; and acres of gardens and parkland to explore. Don't miss the 4,000-year-old Proleek dolmen on the property. An elegant restaurant serves lunch and dinner, and 24-hour room service is available. Check the Web site for frequent discounts and packages.

The hotel is 2 miles north of the town of Dundalk on Ballymascanlon Road. Take Exit 18 off the M1, and then take the Ballymascanlon Road at the roundabout. ☎ *042-935-8200. Fax: 042-937-1598.* www.ballymascanlon.com. *Parking: Free on-site. Rack rates: €160 double. MC, V.*

Bellinter House
$$$$ Navan, County Meath

Let's see. . . . What would a typical day be like at the grand Bellinter House? You could sleep late in your room, featuring lovely Georgian details, and then head down to the well-appointed breakfast room. Perhaps read for a while in one of the lounges, which marry traditional Georgian elements with hip, modern design. Then walk the extensive grounds, heading to the indoor or outdoor infinity pool (the outdoor option overlooks a herd of horses munching in a field). Then stop by the spa, which offers a complete menu of treatments, from head massages to full body wraps. Then will it be cocktails, a nice dinner made with fresh Irish ingredients, a dip in the hot tub, or a game of billiards in the Games Room? In short, this is a luxurious destination perfect for those looking for relaxation. The rooms in the main house are the most sumptuous.

Off the road to Kilmessan, near Navan. ☎ *046-903-0900.* www.bellinterhouse. com. *Parking: Free on-site. Rack rates: €148–€298 double. MC, V.*

Shalom Bed and Breakfast
$ Carlingford, County Louth

Shalom means "peace" (among other things) in Hebrew, and that's just
what you'll find here. This B&B is located across the road from the shores
of sparkling Carlingford Lough (pronounced lock), which is rimmed by the
Mourne Mountains. Conveniently, the bustling town of Carlingford is an
easy five-minute walk from the house. Rooms are simple and spacious,
painted with bright colors and featuring contemporary fabrics and sweet
little touches such as Japanese lanterns and chocolate bars on the in-
room tea trays. Friendly owners Kevin and Jackie Woods make every
effort to help you plan your visit. Self-catering apartments are available.

*Upon entering Carlingford on R173, make a right turn just past the Four Seasons
Hotel.* ☎ **042-937-3151.** `www.jackiewoods.com`. *Parking: Free on-site. Rack
rates: €58–€80 double. No credit cards.*

 Tigh Catháin
$ Trim, County Meath

This classic Irish B&B, offers a breakfast featuring homemade preserves
and eggs from owner Marie Keane's hens, and large bedrooms sporting
perfectly pressed floral and white linens. The cottage boasts pretty gardens and a grassy backyard, and it's right outside the lovely little heritage
town of Trim. Marie will make you feel right at home.

Longwood Road (R160), about 1km (⅔ mile) outside Trim. ☎ **046-943-1996.** `www.`
`tighcathaintrim.com`. *Parking: Free on-site. Rack rates: €70–75 double. No
credit cards. Closed Nov–Jan.*

Dining Locally in Meath and Louth

Locations are indicated on the "Counties Meath and Louth" map. If
you're touring Newgrange and Knowth, the cafeteria at the visitor center
is a good place for lunch. For good pub fare, try P.J.'s.

 Khan's Spices
$$ Trim, County Meath   INDIAN

Who knew that some of the best Indian food in Ireland would be found in
the cute little town of Trim? All the classics are here, from chicken tikka
masala to lamb biryani (a rice and lamb dish laced with saffron), and
they're executed beautifully. Service is kind and attentive, and the owner
and servers are happy to point you in the direction of a dish that will suit
your tastes. The setting feels both relaxed and royal (perhaps they're
channeling nearby Trim Castle?), with burgundies, dark wood, and ornate
chairs that could pose as mini-thrones.

In Emmett Yard on Emmett Street, off of Castle Street (near Trim Cathedral). ☎ **046-
943-7696.** *Main courses: €8–€16. MC, V. Open: Mon–Thurs 5–11 p.m., Sun 5 p.m. to
midnight.*

Cooking (or eating) up a storm

Ghan House (☎ 042-937-3682; www.ghanhouse.com), a grand Georgian house, is home to one of the best restaurants in these parts, and it also offers all sorts of popular one- and two-day cooking classes and demonstrations, from an Italian cooking course to a quick class on making Halloween treats. The cherries on top are the luxurious guest rooms (€130–€200 double). Check the Web site for fabulously priced bed, breakfast, and dinner packages.

Kingfisher Bistro
$$$ Carlingford, County Louth   NEW IRISH

How does Thai-spiced pork with sticky rice, curry oil, sweet soy, and hot-and-sour onions sound? Or are you more intrigued by the roast duck breast with star anis jus, served with celeriac mash and asparagus? The Kingfisher creatively combines the best of Irish raw materials with influences from around the world. The intimate dining room blends modern and rustic styles, with pine floors, Edward Hopper–style paintings, glass candleholders, and an open kitchen. Friendly service and a relaxed atmosphere invites lingering.

McGees Court, on Dundalk Street. ☎ *042-937-3716. Main courses: €17–€26. MC, V. Open: Mon–Sat 6:30–9 p.m., Sun 12:30–3 p.m. and 6–9 p.m.*

Vanilla Pod Restaurant
$$$ Kells, County Meath   NEW IRISH

Yes, it's in a hotel, but this is no we're-too-tired-to-go-out-so-we'll-have-a-burger-here kind of place. The large room is stylish and welcoming, decorated with small paintings and sconces that hold tea lights. The dishes are also stylish and welcoming — the kind of cuisine that is creative without being fussy or wacky. Think oven-baked salmon with dill hollandaise or duck roasted in honey and balsamic vinegar, with a touch of the restaurant's namesake vanilla. Families take note: For every main course ordered by an adult, you get a kid-size main course for free. The offer is in effect Monday through Saturday between 5:30 p.m. and 6:45 p.m., and Sunday between 12:20 p.m. and 6:45 p.m.

Headfort Arms Hotel, Kells, off the N3 (Navan Road), just east of downtown Kells. ☎ *046-924-0084. Main courses: €17–€25. MC, V. Open: Mon–Thurs 5:30–10 p.m., Fri–Sat 5:30–11 p.m., Sun 12:30–9:30 p.m.*

Exploring Meath and Louth: The Top Attractions

The knowledgeable Mary Gibbons narrates superb bus tours of Meath, which include visits to Newgrange and the Hill of Tara, and a drive along the beautiful and historical Boyne River and through the village of Slane. For more information and to reserve your place, call **Mary Gibbons Tours** at ☎ **086-355-1355,** or visit www.newgrangetours.com. Tours cost €35 adults, €30 students and kids. Tours last about seven hours, and leave Monday through Saturday from Dublin (there are pick-ups between 8:15 a.m. and 10:30 a.m. at several Dublin hotels).

Newgrange and Knowth
Donore, County Meath

The Brú na Bóinne Visitor Centre provides access to the wondrous prehistoric passage-tombs of Newgrange and Knowth. Newgrange is a huge, impressively intact round mound — 200,000 tons of earth and stone covering a magnificent and well-preserved 5,000-year-old burial chamber. Take a walk around the tomb to see the ancient stone carvings — spirals, diamonds, and other designs. No one knows what these carvings symbolize. One theory is that they're mathematical symbols; another is that they were produced under the effects of hallucinogenic drugs. Over the entrance stone to Newgrange is an opening that allows light to slowly creep into the burial chamber during the five days surrounding the winter solstice, filling the room with a warm, golden glow for about 15 minutes. You enter the tomb through a low arch and make your way Indiana Jones–style down the long and narrow stone passage to the cool, dark central burial chamber, where you see more stone carvings and may be party to a very special surprise (no hints — you have to go see for yourself).

Knowth is a tomb of similar size to Newgrange, used from the Stone Age through the 1400s. The main tomb is attended by many smaller satellite tombs, and the stones surrounding the tomb sport beautiful designs. You can't enter the central chamber at Knowth, but you can climb into a small anteroom to gaze down the long entry passageway. Be sure to take the opportunity to climb on top of the tomb to see the Boyne Valley laid out before you.

If you have to choose between Newgrange and Knowth, I recommend Newgrange because you can actually enter the central chamber. But if you can, see both.

You can access Newgrange and Knowth only through the visitor center; purchase tickets there and take the minibus shuttle to the sites. If you have extra time, check out the offerings in the visitor center, which include interpretive displays about the society that created the tombs, as well as an audiovisual presentation that provides an interesting introduction to the tombs. Arrive early to ensure a ticket — this is a very popular site, and tickets are limited. Also, be aware that the last shuttle bus for the tombs leaves 1¾ hours before the visitor center closes. On your way out, sign up for the lottery to be one of the 50 lucky people who gets to watch the winter solstice from inside Newgrange. Allow three hours if you're exploring both Newgrange and Knowth; two hours if you're exploring only one tomb.

2km (1¼ miles) west of the village of Donore. From Dublin, take the M1 to the Donore exit, near Drogheda, travel to the village of Donore, and then turn right, passing Daly's Bar and Restaurant. The parking lot will be about 1km (⅔ mile) farther, on your right. ☎ *041-988-0300. Admission: Newgrange €6 adults, €5 seniors, €3 students and kids; Knowth €5 adults, €3 seniors, students, and kids. Open: June to mid-Sept daily 9 a.m.–7 p.m., May and last half of Sept daily 9 a.m.–6:30 p.m., Feb–Apr and Oct daily 9:30 a.m.–5:30 p.m., Nov–Jan daily 9 a.m.–5 p.m. Knowth is open only Easter to Oct. The last shuttle bus always leaves to explore the sights 1¾ hours before the visitor center closes.*

Trim Castle
Trim, County Meath

This 800-year-old citadel has a round tower, crenellated walls, and a three-story castle keep built in an unusual cruciform shape. You may recognize it from the movie *Braveheart*. I recommend poking around the ruins for about half an hour and then taking the excellent 45-minute tour of the castle keep, where you'll learn about the castle's history, see ancient graffiti, and get a dazzling view of the surrounding countryside from the parapet. Tours fill up quickly, and visitors arriving earlier in the day usually have a shorter wait than those who arrive later in the day. A grisly side note: While excavating the ruins of Trim Castle in the early 1970s, archaeologists discovered the remains of ten headless men. Based on historical records, the unfortunate fellows are thought to have been beheaded in the 15th century for committing robbery. Allow 90 minutes for your visit.

Located in the center of the town of Trim. ☎ *046-943-8619. Admission: €4 adults, €3 seniors, €2 students and kids. Tours: €1. Open: Easter to Sept daily 10 a.m.–6 p.m., Oct daily 9:30 a.m.–5:30 p.m., Nov–Jan Sat–Sun 9 a.m.–5 p.m., Feb to Easter Sat–Sun 9:30 a.m.–5:30 p.m. The last tour always leaves one hour before closing time.*

Newgrange: Tomb or womb?

Some scholars have suggested that Newgrange was created to symbolize rebirth and was designed to represent the female reproductive system. The word *brú* in Old Irish means "womb" so *Brú na Boinne* may be translated as "Womb of the Moon" or "Womb of the Bright Cow." Proponents of this theory suggest that the mound itself symbolizes the womb, while the passage represents the birth canal. Some also point out that the three-armed spiral, carved into several stones at Newgrange, has associations with fertility.

Other Cool Things to See and Do

- ✔ **Biking around Louth:** One of the most pleasant bike rides in this area travels along quiet roads on the Cooley Peninsula for about 20km (12 miles). **On Your Bike Hire** (☎ 087-239-7467; www.onyourbikehire.com) provides bike rentals and information on several routes, including the one on the Cooley Peninsula. If you're up for something more strenuous (and much, much longer), the Táin Trail cycling route travels 575km (357 miles) past some major historical sights, including castles, ruins, Celtic crosses, and areas associated with the ancient Irish epic of the Cattle-Raid of Cooley. Parts of the route can be quite strenuous, so make sure you're up to the challenge. For more information, call or visit the **Dundalk Tourist Office,** on Jocelyn Street in Dundalk (☎ 042-933-5484).

- ✔ **Carlingford Adventure Centre,** Tholsel Street, Carlingford, County Louth (☎ 042-937-3100; www.carlingfordadventure.com): This place offers the staff, equipment, and instructions for great outdoor activities. Among the many options are windsurfing, kayaking, and sailing on Carlingford Lough, and trekking and rock climbing in the Cooley Mountains. It's open year-round.

- ✔ **Causey Farm,** off the R164, 1.6km (1 mile) outside Fordstown (past Girley Church), Navan, County Meath (☎ 046-943-4135; www.causey.ie.): Want to get your hands dirty while having some old-fashioned Irish fun? The Causey Farm gives you and your kids the opportunity to watch a sheepdog demonstration, milk a cow, and try your hand at the *bodhrán* (Irish drum), among several other offerings. Admission is €14 per person, €50 families; kids 2 and under are free. Currently, family programs start at 2 p.m. on Tuesdays and Fridays in July and August. Call in advance to book, and again to make sure that the time and dates haven't changed. Allow about three hours for your visit.

- ✔ **Driving the Cooley Peninsula,** outside Dundalk, County Louth: This peninsula offers a gorgeous scenic drive with impressive views of the Irish Sea and Carlingford Lough. The peninsula is the mythic home of legendary heroes, namely Cuchulainn and Finn MacCool (see Chapter 2 for the stories of these heroes), and is somewhat undiscovered by visitors, so you're likely to have it mostly to yourself. You'll encounter *dolmen* (Neolithic tombs), forests, mountains, rivers, ruins, and quaint fishing villages. The largest village, Carlingford, is a good place to stop for a stretch or for the night. Walk around the ruins of Carlingford's King John's Castle (especially impressive in the evening), and stroll along Carlingford Lough, a natural fjord from the Ice Age that separates the Republic and Northern Ireland in this area.

  The R173 loops around the peninsula. You can hook up with the R173 near Navan off the M1 or N52. Allow two to three hours for your drive.

✔ **Hiking the Táin Way:** This 40km (25-mile) hiking route encircles the Cooley Peninsula, offering stunning mountain and sea views, sites of mythological importance, and medieval buildings. You'll climb through hills, skirt the Carlingford Lough, and hike through forests. Most people take two days for this hike, which is mostly gentle with a few relatively steep inclines. You can easily break up the route into shorter sections if you're interested in a day hike. For more information and walking guides, visit or contact the Dundalk Tourist Office on Jocelyn Street in Dundalk (☎ 042-933-5484). For a detailed map of the route, order from **EastWest Mapping** at ☎ 053-937-7835 or www.eastwestmapping.ie.

✔ **Hill of Tara,** south of Navan, off the main Dublin road (N3), County Meath: The hill of Tara was the ceremonial and political seat of the Irish high kings, who presided over a lively national assembly held every three years to pass laws and resolve disputes. The last assembly was thought to have been held in a.d. 560, and it is said that 242 kings were crowned on the hill at Lia Fáil, the Stone of Destiny, which is still standing. This site takes some imagination to enjoy, because most of the remnants of this pre-Christian ceremonial center are mounds and depressions where buildings once stood, plus a few old building stones. A late–Stone Age passage tomb also exists on the site. Take advantage of a guided tour (available on request, so just ask) and the audiovisual presentation in the visitor center to get a better feel for the site. There are dazzling views from the hill.

Admission is €3 adults, €2 seniors, €1 students and kids. It's open from May 27 through mid-September daily 10 a.m. to 6 p.m. Last admission is one hour before closing. For more information, call ☎ 046-902-5903 from May 27 through mid-September, or ☎ 041-988-0300 from mid-September through May 27. To get there from Dublin, take the N3 toward Navan, and look for signs beginning about 15km (9 miles) before reaching Navan, near the village of Kilmessan. Allow 45 minutes for your visit.

✔ **Monasterboice,** off the main Dublin road (M1) near Collon, County Louth: Two remarkable tenth-century decorated High Crosses keep a solemn watch over the ruins of a sixth-century monastery and a graveyard. High Crosses combine Celtic and Christian symbols and designs and were thought to have been used to mark the boundaries of monastic lands or to commemorate a miraculous event. Many were decorated with biblical scenes and are thought to be teaching tools to help illiterate citizens better understand the bible. The first cross that you encounter, known as Muiredach's Cross, depicts the Last Judgment and many Old Testament scenes (check out the interpretive panel opposite the Cross). The other cross (sometimes called the West Cross) is one of the largest in Ireland. The remains of a round tower and church ruins are other highlights. Admission is free, and it's open during daylight hours year-round. Allow 30 minutes for your visit.

✔ **Old Mellifont Abbey,** Tullyallen, off the R168, 10km (6 miles) northwest of the village of Drogheda, County Louth: Founded by St. Malachy in 1142, Mellifont was the first Cistercian monastery in Ireland. This historic house of worship was suppressed by Henry VIII, then became a pigsty (literally), and later was the headquarters for William III during the Battle of the Boyne. The site is peaceful and tranquil, set along the banks of the River Mattock. The unique octagonal *lavabo* (a washing trough for religious ceremonies) remains intact, along with several of the abbey's arches. The visitor center contains examples of masonry from the Middle Ages. You can visit the site for free at any time, but the visitor center is open May through September daily 10 a.m. to 6 p.m. (last admission one hour before closing). When the visitor center is open, you can take a guided tour (€3 adults, €2 seniors, €1 students and kids). For more information, call ☎ **041-982-6459** mid-May through September or ☎ **041-988-0300** October through mid-May. Allow 45 minutes for your visit.

Shopping

Crystal Antiques, on Dundalk Street, in Carlingford (☎ **042-937-83012**), sells all sorts of interesting and relatively inexpensive objects, from old spice jars to magic lanterns.

Hitting the Pubs

The "Counties Meath and Louth" map shows the locations of the following pubs.

McManus'
Dundalk, County Louth

This family-run establishment is like three pubs in one. The Music Bar usually hosts traditional music sessions on Mondays and Fridays, and spontaneous sessions are not uncommon at other times. On cold days, make your way to the back Kitchen Bar, an intimate room with brick interior and a cast-iron stove. Coal and turf fires warm the pub year-round.

Seatown Place (near St. Patrick's Church off the main road). ☎ **042-933-1632.**

P.J.'s (also known as O'Hare's and as The Anchor Bar)
Carlingford, County Louth

Part-grocery, part-pub, O'Hare's was one of a dying breed of pubs that combined a local watering hole with a neighborhood convenience store. That part of the pub is still preserved, and new owners have added a spacious Lounge Bar as well as an award-winning pub-food menu (go for the local oysters). Traditional Irish music sessions take place on many

Tuesdays and Wednesdays. Before you leave, check out the leprechaun in the glass case, and judge its authenticity for yourself.

Located on the Tholsel Street (the main street) in Carlingford. ☎ **042-937-3106.**

Fast Facts: Counties Meath and Louth

Area Codes

042 and **046** for Meath; **042** and **041** for Louth.

Emergencies/Police

Dial ☎ **999** for all emergencies.

Genealogical Resources

In Meath, contact the Meath Heritage Centre, Castle Street, Trim (☎ 046-943-6633; www.meathroots.com). For records in Louth, contact the Louth County Library, on Roden Place, in Dundalk (☎ 042-933-5457; www.louthcoco.ie).

Hospitals

Louth County Hospital is off Dublin Road (N1) in Dundalk (☎ 042-933-4701).

Information

For visitor information in Dundalk, go to the tourist office at Jocelyn Street (☎ 042-933-5484). In Carlingford, the Tourist Information Center is in the Old Dispensary in town (☎ 042-937-3033).

Post Office

Comprehensive post offices are located at 95 Clanbrassil St., Dundalk, Louth (☎ 042-932-5200), and on Dundalk Street in Carlingford (☎ 042-937-3171).

Chapter 13

Easy Trips South of Dublin: Counties Wicklow and Kildare

. . . .

In This Chapter

▶ Wandering through some of Ireland's most beautiful gardens

▶ Visiting the ruins of an early monastery

▶ Hiking the Wicklow Mountains

▶ Checking out the racehorses at the National Stud

. . . .

*I*mmediately south of bustling Dublin, you find the beginnings of all that famous Irish green. County Wicklow's people pamper all that lush greenery to produce stunning gardens (many with gorgeous manor houses crowning the properties). You also can hike through the verdant hills and valleys in the rolling Wicklow Mountains. County Kildare's citizens tend to feed their greenery to the horses — the county is home to dozens upon dozens of horse farms, including the National Stud, where some of Ireland's strongest and fastest racehorses are born and rest between training sessions.

County Wicklow

County Wicklow is known as "The Garden of Ireland," and it's easy to see why. The county begins just barely out of Dublin City's limits, and the cityscape begins to give way to rural roads and peaceful hill and coastal scenery. Wicklow's northeastern coast is studded with resort areas and harbor towns, where you can have a fine seafood dinner and a walk along one of the many beaches. **Greystones,** a peaceful, hip little hamlet, is my favorite of the towns in this area. Then, there are the famed gardens and manor houses of the area, including the must-see Powerscourt Gardens. Inland, the velvety valleys, purple bogs, and wooded glens of the Wicklow Mountains beckon. To really get a feel for the area, take a walk on a stretch of the **Wicklow Way,** a signposted walking path that follows forest trails, sheep paths, and county roads from Rathfarnam, just outside Dublin, all the way to Clonegal (a total of about 130km/80 miles), skirting quaint villages along the way. If you want to stay right in the mountains, the towns of **Roundwood** and **Laragh** are great choices.

If you love gardening, try to plan your visit to Wicklow between the beginning of May and the end August, not only so that you can see the gardens in their full glory, but also so that you can take advantage of the **Wicklow Gardens Festival** (www.visitwicklow.ie/gardens), during which many delightful private gardens are open to the public. You're guaranteed to return home with a head swimming with gardening ideas.

Getting to and around County Wicklow

If you're arriving by car, take the N11 (which becomes M11 periodically) south from Dublin toward Arklow. You can turn off along this route to reach most major towns and attractions. **Dublin Area Rapid Transit** (DART; ☎ 1-850-366-222; www.irishrail.ie) extends as far as Greystones and is an easy, inexpensive way to get to the northern, coastal Wicklow towns. The **Irish Rail's** Dublin (Connolly Station) – Rosslare Harbour train line (☎ 01-850-366-222; www.irishrail.ie) has stations in Dun Laoghaire, Bray, Greystones, Wicklow, Rathdrum, and Arklow. **Dublin Bus** (☎ 01-873-4222; www.dublinbus.ie) runs from City Centre to Dun Laoghaire, Dalkey, and the Bray DART station. **Bus Éireann** (☎ 01-836-6111; www.buseireann.ie) travels year-round to several towns in the area, including Wicklow, Arklow, Rathdrum, Glenealy, and Avoca, among others.

Spending the night in County Wicklow

Glendalough Hotel
$$$ Glendalough

Occupying a woody area overlooking the ruins of the monastery complex at Glendalough, this hotel, built in the 1800s, is a great launching point for an exploration of Glendalough and the Wicklow Mountains National Park. The public rooms are beautifully furnished with antiques. The good-size, pastel bedrooms are nothing to write home about, but you'll probably be exploring the area the whole day anyway. Check the Web site for special offers and discounts, which run often.

On the 755. Take the R755 off the N11. ☎ *0404-45-135. Fax: 0404-45-142.* www. glendaloughhotel.com. *Parking: Free on-site. Rack rates: €140–€180 double. AE, MC, V.*

Hunter's Hotel
$$$ Rathnew

This family-run inn, at 300 years old, is one of Ireland's oldest coaching inns, offering views of lush gardens and nearby mountains. If you prefer sleek, modern accommodations with amenities such as Wi-Fi, you won't like this place; if you appreciate a quirky, classic inn where you can

Counties Wicklow and Kildare

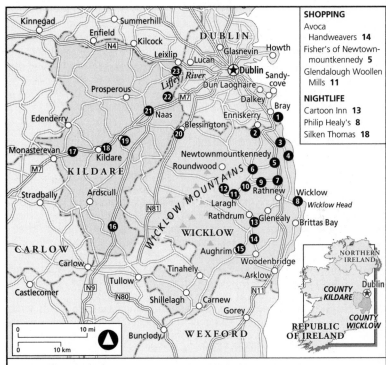

SHOPPING
Avoca
  Handweavers **14**
Fisher's of Newtown-
  mountkennedy **5**
Glendalough Woollen
  Mills **11**

NIGHTLIFE
Cartoon Inn **13**
Philip Healy's **8**
Silken Thomas **18**

ACCOMMODATIONS
Barberstown Castle **22**
Cherryville House **17**
Glendalough Hotel **12**
Hunter's Hotel **9**
Ritz Carlton Powerscourt **2**
Slievemore **3**
Wicklow Way Lodge **11**

DINING
Bates Restaurant **13**
The Conservatory Tea House **11**
Harbour Restaurant **21**
The Hungry Monk Wine Bar &
  Restaurant **3**
The Moone High Cross Inn **16**
Poppies Country Cooking **2**
The Roundwood Inn **6**
Sugar Tree Café & Fern House Café at
  Avoca Handweavers **14**
Strawberry Tree **15**

ATTRACTIONS
Avon Rí Adventure Centre **20**
Castletown House **23**
The Curragh **19**
Glendalough Equestrian Centre **10**
Glendalough Round Tower and Monastery **12**
Irish National Stud, Japanese Garden &
  St. Fiachra's Garden **18**
Kildare Country Club **22**
Kilruddery House and Garden **1**
Meeting of the Waters **13**
The Moone High Cross **16**
Mt. Usher Gardens **7**
National Garden Exhibition Centre **4**
National Sea Life Centre **1**
Powerscourt Estate Gardens **2**
Powerscourt Waterfall **2**
Russborough House **20**
Steam Museum & Walled Garden **22**
Sugar Loaf Mountain **2**
Wicklow Mountains National Park **11**

imagine travelers of the past writing love letters in the quaintly named Smoke Room, you'll love it. Rooms are huge, with antique furniture and warm lighting. Irish dishes, such as Wicklow lamb with fresh vegetables from the hotel's gardens, are served in the restaurant. Blazing fires add to the charm. Check out the window in the bar where honeymooners used to scratch messages with their diamond engagement rings.

Newrath Bridge. Take the N11 from Dublin, and take a left in Ashford village by the bridge and opposite Ashford House pub. Hunter's is 2km (1½ miles) from Ashford. ☎ *0404-40-106. Fax: 0404-40-338.* www.hunters.ie. *Parking: Free on-site. Rack rates: €130–€190 double (see Web site for specials). MC, V.*

Ritz Carlton Powerscourt
$$$$ Enniskerry

It's got Ritz Carlton in the name, so you know it's going to be good. Set on the expansive Powerscourt Estate, the grand Palladian-style building is a five-minute drive or a 15-minute bike ride from lush Powerscourt Gardens. The perfectly groomed grounds of the hotel feel like an extension of the formal gardens. The guest rooms may distract you with their cloud-like feather beds, rain-forest showers, and bathroom radiant-floor heating, but don't forget you have exploring to do! Thankfully, these devilish amenities are countered by the benevolent spa, golf courses, and complimentary bikes, which assure that you do leave your room at some point. Frequent guests advise that if you're unhappy with anything, you should tell the friendly and incredibly accommodating staff who will work to solve the problem. Though you may not expect it from such a luxurious property, the hotel recently won a silver award for its Environmental Action Plan focusing on energy reduction and eco-friendly waste and water management.

On Powerscourt Estate. Follow the signs from Enniskerry to Powerscourt Gardens, turn into the Gardens, and then follow the signs to the hotel. ☎ *01-274-8888. Fax: 01- 274-9999.* www.ritzcarlton.com. *Parking: Free on-site self-parking, €20 overnight valet. Rack rates: €245–€275 double. Lower rates available without breakfast.*

Slievemore
$ Greystones

You could spend all day gazing at Greystone's pretty harbor from Slievemore, an impeccable, whitewashed B&B run by a pleasant couple. Rooms are bright, spacious, and sweet, with sparkling-clean bathrooms. A delicious and filling breakfast is served in the back conservatory, where you can watch robins flit by as you munch your bacon. It's an easy walk to Slievemore from the DART station, so you don't even need a car to enjoy this darling seaside town and this excellent B&B. Check to see if harbor construction is still taking place at the time of your visit; at press time, views were obstructed and the sounds of construction were not exactly soothing.

The Harbour. Follow signs south out of Bray to Greystones village. ☎ *01-287-4724.* www.slievemorehouse.com. *Parking: Free on-site. Rack rates: €75 double. No credit cards.*

Wicklow Way Lodge
$ Laragh

If you're doing any hiking along the Wicklow Way, you can't beat this welcoming B&B, nestled in the Wicklow Mountains, minutes from hiking trails. And even if you've left your hiking boots in the trunk of your car, you'll love the friendly hosts (Marilyn and Seamus know this area inside and out); the hearty and delicious breakfast (the porridge, served with generous dollops of brown sugar and cream, is legendary); and the airy, high-ceilinged, sparkling-clean rooms. In the rooms, expect simple, modern décor, comfortable beds (important after a day on the trails), and stunning views of the Wicklow Mountains through huge windows.

From Laragh, turn left at the sign for St. John's Church. ☎ **01-281-8489.** *www. wicklowwaylodge.com. Parking: Free on-site. Rack rates: €70–€80. MC, V.*

Dining locally in County Wicklow

If you're in the mood for an excellent Italian-influenced dinner, check out **Bates Restaurant,** in the same building as the Cartoon Inn (see p. 191).

The Hungry Monk Restaurant & Wine Bar
$$ Greystones ECLECTIC

Excellent wines, glowing candles, dark wood furnishings, and simple hearty food are the catalysts for the convivial atmosphere at the wine bar downstairs. Clink your wineglasses over plates of well-prepared fish, steak, or perhaps the excellent Wicklow Mountain lamb burger, served with tzatziki. Vegetarians will appreciate the "Sheperdless" Pie. Keep your eyes peeled for the various works of art with monks as their subject. Groups may want to reserve early in order to snag the large, candelabra-lit table. The more formal restaurant upstairs offers a great-value fixed-price menu from Thursday through Sunday.

Church Road. ☎ **01-287-5759.** *Reservations recommended. Main courses: €15–€21; two-course fixed-price menu €24, three-course fixed-price menu €28. MC, V. Open: Restaurant Thurs–Sat 5:30–11 p.m., Sun 12:30–7:30 p.m.; wine bar Mon–Sat 5–11 p.m., Sun 12:30–9 p.m.*

Poppies Country Cooking
$ Enniskerry CAFE

The name says it all. This is simple country cooking at its best, with such tasty options as vegetable quiche, a chicken and mushroom tart, and the amazing beef-and-Guinness pie. There is another location in Dun Laoghaire for those who can't get enough of Poppies.

The Square. ☎ **01-282-8869.** *Main courses: €5–€11. MC, V. Open: Mon–Sat 8 a.m.–7 p.m., Sun 9 a.m.–7 p.m.*

The Roundwood Inn
$$ Roundwood PUB FOOD/GERMAN FOOD

Forget about greasy fish and chips; the Roundwood Inn offers Irish classics as well as German dishes. Stars of the menu include Wiener schnitzel, roast suckling pig, and an exceptional Irish stew. If you want a less expensive meal, check out the terrific pub grub in the bar, including Galway oysters, crab bisque, and again, that awesome Irish stew. The inn was built in the 18th century and is furnished with dark wood and an open fireplace.

Main Street. Out of Bray, take the R755 to Roundwood. ☎ **01-281-8107.** *Reservations recommended for dinner. Main courses: €9–€18. AE, MC, V. Open: Pub daily noon to 9:30 p.m.; restaurant Fri–Sat 7:30–9 p.m., Sun 1–3 p.m.*

Strawberry Tree
$$$$ Aughrim NEW IRISH

This is the only restaurant I know of in Ireland that uses wild and organic ingredients exclusively. The menu changes all the time, and dishes are flavorful and unfussy. Recently, offerings included a beef filet with beet root and balsamic *jus,* and luscious tarragon pasta with wild mushrooms. In addition to the regular menu, the restaurant offers a Big Table Experience, in which local artisan products of all sorts are presented family style at a long table that can accommodate up to 40 people. The room is formal and elegant.

The BrookLodge & Wells Spa, Macreddin Village. Take the R753 to Aughrim and follow the signs. ☎ **0402-364-44.** *Main courses: Fixed-price dinner €65. AE, MC, V. Open: Mid-July to Aug daily 7–9:30 p.m., June to mid-July and Sept Tues–Sun 7–9:30 p.m., Apr–May and Oct Wed–Sun 7–9:30 p.m., Nov–Mar Thurs–Sun 7–9:30 p.m.*

Sugar Tree Cafe and Fern House Cafe at Avoca Handweavers
$–$$$ Avoca ECLECTIC

If you thought that the cafe here was just a decent place to get some tea and baked goods while blowing your budget on Avoca's beautiful woven items, think again. Located in the back of the shop, this cheerful, spacious cafe serves some divine lunch choices, from salads, soups, and sandwiches to main courses such as smoked trout and honey-glazed ham. The low lunch prices make it easy to justify buying that extra woolen throw. If you're in the mood for sit-down service or a heartier meal, trot over to the store's **Fern House Cafe,** where you'll find a varied menu of delights, from the Moroccan Mezze Plate, with bean and root vegetable tagine, couscous, hummus, tzatiki, edamame puree, and pita; to pasta with crab, zucchini, cherry tomatoes, chili flakes, garlic, and cream. The Fern House setting feels like a conservatory, with high ceilings and lemon and orange trees growing inside.

At Avoca Handweavers, Avoca. ☎ **01-274-6990.** *Main courses: Sugar Tree Cafe €10–€15, Fern House Cafe €19–€27. MC, V. Open: Sugar Tree Cafe Mon–Fri 9 a.m.–5 p.m., Sat 10 a.m.–5 p.m., Sun 10 a.m.–5:30 p.m.; Fern House Cafe Mon–Wed 9:30 a.m.–5:30 p.m., Thurs–Sat 9:30 a.m.–9:30 p.m., and Sun 9:30 a.m.–6 p.m.*

The Conservatory Tea House
$$ **Laragh** CAFÉ/NEW IRISH

Calling this lovely cafe a "teahouse" sells it short. In addition to cakes, tarts, and baked goods that taste as good as they look (and they're quite beautiful), the lunches here are out of this world. The chef changes the menu frequently to take advantage of the freshest ingredients and to play with her new ideas. You may find wild venison, a blue cheese and leek tart, or pumpkin risotto. The owner is planning on adding dinner to the offerings soon; it's worth a call to find out if dinner is being served when you're in town.

The Old School House in Laragh, right outside the village off Sallygap Road. ☎ **0404-45-302.** *Main courses: €5–14. Open: June–Aug Wed–Mon 10 a.m.–6 p.m., Sept–May Wed–Mon 10 a.m.–4 p.m. Check for dinner hours, which should be added soon.*

Exploring County Wicklow

Here are some of the best ways to enjoy the emerald landscape of County Wicklow.

Organized tours

A number of operators offer bus tours of Wicklow, while others take advantage of the area's beauty to offer horseback and hiking tours.

Bus Éireann (☎ **01-836-6111;** www.buseireann.ie) offers day tours of the Wicklow area from Dublin. The **Glendalough and Powerscourt Gardens Tour** (€32 adults, €29 seniors and students, €23 kids) takes visitors along the south coast of Dublin, through the Wicklow Mountains and the towns of Laragh and Roundwood, with stops at Powerscourt Gardens, and Glendalough. Tours leave from Busaras, on Store Street, June through September at 10 a.m. daily, returning at 5:45 p.m. Admission to Powerscourt and Glendalough is included in the price. To get to Store Street, take Lower Abbey Street off of O'Connell Street and follow the street until it turns into Memorial Road, where you'll find the junction with Store Street.

The Wild Wicklow Tour (☎ **01-280-1899;** wildwicklow.ie), which uses a small Mercedes coach that goes where the big and bulky buses can't, packs in many of the highlights of Wicklow. First, you drive through several seaside towns south of Dublin, including Dalkey, home to many of Ireland's rich and famous, including Van Morrison, Enya, and Bono. You'll stop at Avoca Handweavers, which sells colorful woolen items, funky clothing, and housewares, as well as delicious hot drinks and snacks. Next, you hit one of Wicklow's top attractions, the enchanting sixth-century monastic settlement of Glendalough, where you'll take a stroll along the Upper Lake, working up an appetite for your pub lunch. Your day ends with a visit to Sally Gap, which has stunning views of the surrounding mountains, and Lough Tay (*lough* is pronounced lock), a quietly magnificent mountain lake. This area appeared in *Excalibur,* *Braveheart,* and *P.S. I Love You.* I particularly recommend this tour because the guides are friendly, fun, and informative, and they allow you time to explore a bit on your own. The full-day tour picks up passengers at various hotels around Dublin between 9 a.m. and 10 p.m. (tell them where you're staying, and they'll tell you the closest pickup point) and returns to Dublin between 5 and 5:30 p.m. Prices are €28 adults, €25 seniors, students, and kids; the price covers everything except food and drinks. Advance reservations are required.

The top attractions

Glendalough Round Tower and Monastery
Glendalough

This secluded, leafy site, centered on two peaceful lakes, has been a sacred one since at least the sixth century, when St. Kevin founded a monastery here. The area flourished as a community of learning for almost 900 years. The entire complex was sacked by Anglo-Norman invaders in the 14th century, and most of the buildings were destroyed. However, you still can explore many ruins around the Upper Lake and Lower Lake, including the remnants of a seventh- to ninth-century cathedral; a graveyard full of beautifully designed Celtic crosses; and the highlight, a stunningly preserved 31m (103-ft.) round tower capped with a belfry. Drop into the well-done visitor center to get a sense of the context of this site. I highly recommend the peaceful walk from the Lower Lake to the less-visited Upper Lake. Note that although the visitor center has an admission fee, you can visit the grounds and the ruins themselves for free. Allow 90 minutes for your visit.

Glendalough. ☎ *0404-45-325. Take the N11 to the R755 from Dublin, the R752 to the R755 from Wicklow. Admission: Grounds and ruins free; visitor center €3 adults, €2 seniors, €1 students and kids. Open: Grounds and ruins always open; visitor center mid-Oct to mid-Mar daily 9:30 a.m.–5 p.m., mid-Mar to mid-Oct daily 9:30 a.m.–6 p.m. (last admission 45 minutes before closing).*

Hiking around Wicklow

This is prime hiking (or "walking" as the Irish refer to it) territory, with loads of marked trails set aside just for hikers, beautiful scenery, gentle hills, and mild weather. You can find detailed directions for many hikes at the well-done www.wicklowwalks.com. One of my favorite hikes follows the 8km (5-mile) path that snakes along gorgeous cliffs between **Bray and Greystones.** Allow about two hours one-way for your hike. The route begins (or ends, depending on your point of view) by the harbor in Greystones. In Bray, the trail head appears on the left as you follow the promenade and climbs up Bray Head. Another great hike in the hills circles heart-shaped **Lough Ouler.** The hike starts and ends at the parking lot at the top of the Glenmacnass waterfall, and takes 3 to 4 hours. The path can be hidden at times, so use a map or print out instructions from www.wicklowwalks.com. For great views (some frequent hikers say they've seen Wales from here), take the one- to two-hour hike up **Sugar Loaf Mountain.** To get to the trail head, take the N11 and exit at

Kilmacanoge. Immediately take the left up the narrow road to the GAA grounds. You'll find the trail head alongside the GAA grounds.

The Wicklow Way is a 122km (76-mile) trail extending from Marlay Park in County Dublin to Clonegal in County Carlow, running through forests, over hills, around bogs and farms, along country roads and old stone walls, skirting charming villages. You can walk the whole trail in six or seven days, staying in towns along the way, or just drop in for a day hike. The walk from the Deerpark parking lot near the River Dargle to Luggala is a gorgeous **day-hike option**, as is the 9.1km (5¾-mile) hike from Annamoe to Glendalough. You can get information on hikes at Wicklow Mountains National Park (described later in this section) or at several Wicklow tourist offices. Check out the Wicklow Trail Sheets, available at Wicklow tourist offices, for shorter hikes. You can buy a detailed map of the Wicklow trails at the National Park visitor center, from **EastWest Mapping** (☎ **053-937-7835;** www.eastwestmapping.ie), or from **Harvey Maps** (☎ **44-786-841-202;** www.harveymaps.co.uk).

Mt. Usher Gardens
Ashford

More than 5,000 species of plants from all over the world populate these informal gardens, which were named the best gardens to visit in Ireland by *Gardeners' World Magazine.* Located along the River Vartry, these 8 hectares (20 acres) started as a humble potato patch in 1860. What a difference 150 years makes: This place has blossomed into a wild ocean of flowers, trees, meadows, and waterfalls, with small suspension bridges crossing the river, and birds and wildlife flitting above and through the exotic greenery. The spot where a mini suspension bridge spans a little waterfall just may be one of the most romantic spots in Ireland. Also on the premises is a branch of the excellent Avoca Cafe and a courtyard filled with shops. Allow 90 minutes for your visit.

Off the main Dublin-Rosslare Road (M11/N11). Look for the signs. ☎ *0404-40-205. Admission: €7.50 adults, €6 seniors and students, €3 kids 5–16. Open: Mar–Oct daily 10:30 a.m.–5:20 p.m.*

National Garden Exhibition Centre
Kilquade

What a brilliant idea: This garden complex features a collection of 22 unique small gardens designed by some of Ireland's garden-design superstars. The effect of wandering from garden to garden is much like that of exploring an eclectic manor house—in one garden "room" you may be surrounded by lush, vivid flowers and a babbling fountain, while in the next "room" you may encounter a single tree ringed by a Stonehenge-like circle of bleached wooden planks. Some of my favorite details in the gardens include the use of mirrors in the Oriental Reflections garden (look for the hidden one at the stream), the fictional story that inspired the Water's Edge Garden, and the stone faces set into the wall in the Celtic Stone garden. The Centre's Copper Kettle Cafe is a lovely place to sip tea and munch on fresh pastries while you fantasize about plans for your garden at home. Tickets to the gardens are sold in the garden center's main store. Allow about an hour for your visit, more if you plan to have a snack at the cafe.

Kilquade, County Wicklow. From Dublin, turn left off N11 at the sign for Kilquade. From Wicklow, take a left at the sign for Greystones, go under N11 and then get back on the N11, following signs for Wicklow/Wexford. Turn left at the sign for Kilquade. ☎ **01-281-9890.** *www.gardenexhibition.ie. Admission: €5 adults, €3.50 seniors and students, free for kids. Open: Mon–Sat 9 a.m.–5 p.m., Sun 1–5 p.m.*

Powerscourt Estate Gardens
Enniskerry

These gardens are the finest in Wicklow County, which is saying a lot, because the county is known for its abundance of exceptionally beautiful gardens. First laid out from 1745 to 1767, the gardens were redesigned in Victorian style from 1843 to 1875. The gardens have many different facets, among them a wooded glen graced with a stone round tower that was modeled on Lord Powerscourt's dining-room pepper pot, a magical moss-covered grotto, a formal Italianate area with a circular pond and fountain presided over by sculptures of winged horses, and a walled garden where blazing roses cling to the stone. Don't miss the moving pet cemetery, with sweet monuments to various pets owned by the Powerscourt family, from faithful dogs to a particularly prolific dairy cow. I recommend following the route around the entire estate, which should take you a good one to two hours, after which you can refresh yourself and take in the stunning views at the Terrace Cafe, which serves light, fresh snacks and lunches. Powerscourt Waterfall is down the road (see "Other cool things to see and do," later in this chapter).

Off the main Dublin-Wicklow Road (N11). By car: Take the N11 out of Dublin (it becomes the new motorway M11), and follow the signs for the garden. By bus: 44C from Dublin to Enniskerry (then a 2.4km/1½-mile walk to the garden). ☎ **01-204-6000.** *Admission: Garden €8 adults, €7 seniors and students, €5 kids 5–15, free for kids 4 and under. Open: Daily 9:30 a.m.–5:30 p.m. or dusk, whichever comes earlier.*

Wicklow Mountains National Park
Glendalough

This park, covering nearly 20,000 hectares (50,000 acres), encompasses forest, hills, and large mountain bogs, and protects such wildlife as the rare peregrine falcon. The park centers on beautiful Glendalough (reviewed earlier in this section) and includes Glendalough Valley and the Glendalough Wood Nature Reserve. A tough stretch of the Wicklow Way (described earlier in this section) runs through the park. An information office (open daily at the Upper Lake at Glendalough during the summer and on weekends from about September through about June) offers information on hiking in the park, including route descriptions and detailed maps, and organizes free nature walks and events, including bat walks, astronomy nights, deer watches, and more (call or check the Web site for the schedule). In addition, the Web site allows you to download and print

The ideal picnic spot

Just beyond Avondale House is the famed **Meeting of the Waters,** where the Avonmore and Avonbeg rivers come together. This spot is so beautiful, it inspired Thomas Moore to write: "There is not in the wide world a valley so sweet / as the vale in whose bosom the bright waters meet." Pack some fruit, bread, cheese, and wine and head to the picnic spot in Avondale Forest Park, 5km (3 miles) south of Rathdrum heading toward Arklow on the R752 (which becomes the R755 as you leave Rathdrum).

out guides to several hikes. If you'd like to purchase a map before you arrive, order one from **EastWest Mapping** (☎ 053-937-7835; www.east westmapping.ie) or **Harvey Maps** (☎ 44-786-841-202; www.harvey maps.co.uk). Allow one to three hours for your visit.

Take the N11 to R755 from Dublin; the R752 to R755 from Wicklow. The Information Point is located by Upper Lake, R756 off R755. ☎ **0404-45-425** *or 0404-45-656.* www. wicklownationalpark.ie. *Open: All day every day.*

Other cool things to see and do

I find that in addition to hiking, horseback trail rides are an excellent way to enjoy the gentle beauty of this region. Also see the description of Wicklow Mountains National Park (earlier in this chapter).

- ✔ **Avon Rí Adventure Centre** (☎ 045-900-670): This company offers all sorts of outdoor activities, including orienteering, Segway-riding, mountain biking, and canoeing, kayaking, sailing, and windsurfing on the sparkling Blessington Lakes. The center is located at the Blessington Lake Short Resort. To get there, drive to Blessington (off the N81), go through the village, pass the turn for Naas, and take the next left. Prices and opening times vary, so call ahead.

- ✔ **Glendalough Equestrian Centre,** Glendalough Estate, Annamoe, near Roundwood (☎ **0404-45569;** www.glendaloughadventure. ie): These stables are terrific for any level of horseback riders, offering independence without forcing you to leave your comfort zone. Trail rides feature small groups (six is usually the maximum) and although your horse knows the way, it's not one of those big-group nose-to-tail rides in which each horse plods along regardless of your input. The Equestrian Centre is located on the gorgeous Glendalough Estate, and trail rides will take you through mossy pine forests, past meadows (we saw a tranquil herd of deer), along the babbling Avonmore River, and, on longer rides, onto adjacent Scar Mountain. Instructors are friendly and skilled, and will offer tour options based on your experience, interests and ability. To get there, take the M11 to Kilmacanogue and then take the road sign-posted for Roundwood/Glendalough. Continue through Roundwood village, following the signs for Annamoe. At the sharp left-hand bend at Annamoe Antiques, take a right onto the old road flanked by stone walls and drive about 0.4km (1/4 mile) up to the stables. Prices vary; a two-hour trail ride costs €45 per person.

If you're looking for a place closer to Dublin, try **Brennanstown Riding School** in Hollbrook, Kilmacanogue, near Bray (☎ 01-286-3778; www.brennanstownrs.ie).

✔ **Killruddery House and Garden,** off the main Dublin-Wicklow Road (N11), Killruddery, Bray (☎ 087-419-8674): Killruddery is the oldest surviving formal garden in Ireland, laid out in the 1680s in the French style of the time. Highlights are the outdoor theater, exotic shrubs, orangery featuring Italian statues, and pond. Lest you think this place is all upper-class elegance, know that there is also a working farm on the premises, where you can visit sheep and cows, and watch crops being planted and harvested. The gardens and farm are certainly the draw here, but the grand Elizabethan-revival house is also worth a visit. The house has been in the family of the Earls of Meath since 1618 and features a stunning conservatory. Check the Web site for information on events and activities, from a film festival to a Father's Day treasure hunt. Stay tuned for major changes here, including the addition of a new visitor center, a kitchen garden, and a farm shop. Admission to the house and garden is €10 adults, €8 seniors and students, €3 kids; for the garden only, it's €6 adults, €5 seniors and students, and free for kids 12 and under. The house is open May, June, and September daily from 1 to 5 p.m.; the garden is open April weekends from 12:30 to 5 p.m. and May through September daily from 12:30 to 5 p.m. Allow about an hour for your visit.

✔ **National Sea Life Centre,** Strand Road on the boardwalk, Bray (☎ 01-286-6939; www.sealifeeurope.com): This aquarium brings you face to face with thousands of seawater and freshwater creatures, including sharks, a playful giant octopus, piranhas, and rays. Kids will have a ball picking up ocean dwellers at the touch tank and hanging out as various creatures are fed. It's worth planning your visit around the feedings, talks, and demonstrations by the aquarium's staff (check the Web site for times). Tickets are deeply discounted on the Web site, so buy them online, if you can. The center is a ten-minute walk from the Bray DART station. Admission is €12 adults, €11 seniors and students, €9 kids 3–14, and free for kids 2 and under. It's open March through October daily from 10 a.m. to 6 p.m. (last admission 5 p.m.); November through February Monday through Friday from 11 a.m. to 4 p.m., Saturday and Sunday from 10 a.m. to 5 p.m. Allow two hours for your visit.

✔ **Powerscourt Waterfall,** off the main Dublin-Wicklow Road (N11), Enniskerry (☎ 01-204-6000): This pretty waterfall, located in a leafy glen, is Ireland's highest. On a nice day, get some ice cream and enjoy the view. Don't expect solitude; there are usually a handful of visitors here at any given time. Admission is €5 adults, €4.50 seniors and students, €3.50 kids 15 and under. It's open May through August daily from 9:30 a.m. to 7 p.m.; March, April, September, and October daily from 10:30 a.m. to 5:30 p.m.; and November through February daily from 10:30 a.m. to 4 p.m.

✔ **Russborough House,** off the N81, Blessington (☎ **045-86-5239**): This house, built in the mid-1700s in the Palladian style, is home to the world-famous Beit Collection of paintings, which includes pieces by Reynolds, Rubens, and Guardi. The furnishings of the house — including tapestries, silver, bronzes, porcelain, and ornate furniture — are also works of art. Visits are by guided tour only. The grounds are open for exploration, and there is a restaurant, a shop, a hedge maze, and a children's playground. The house has been quite unlucky in the past, with four art robberies over the past 30 years and a significant fire in 2010; here's hoping the next 30 years bring good luck instead.

To get there from Dublin, take the N7 to Naas, and pick up the R410. The house is located where the R410 meets the N81. Admission to the grounds is free. The house tour costs €10 adults, €8 seniors and students, €5 kids 11 and under. The tours are offered May through September daily from 10 a.m. to 6 p.m. (with the last tour starting at 5 p.m.). Allow an hour for your visit.

Shopping in County Wicklow

Avoca Handweaver, Avoca Village (☎ **0402-35-105**), is the oldest hand-weaving mill in Ireland (dating to 1723) and sells colorful knitwear, including tweed and knit clothing and blankets, beautiful trendy/bohemian clothing, and a wide range of fine Irish crafts. There is also another large Avoca store in Kilmacanogue, near Bray (☎ **01-274-6939**). This branch of Avoca also houses the lovely Fernwood and Sugar Tree cafes (see p. 184). Located in a converted schoolhouse, **Fisher's of Newtownmountkennedy,** in the big pink building on the R765, off the N11, Newtownmountkennedy (☎ **01-281-9404**), has tons of men's and women's clothes and accessories, both elegant and country-casual, plus cool items such as hip flasks and pool cues. **Glendalough Woollen Mills,** on the R755 between Laragh and Rathdrum (☎ **0404-45-156**), is housed in an old farmhouse and sells handmade knitwear and jewelry inspired by ancient Celtic designs.

Hitting the pubs

Cartoon Inn
Rathdrum

Make sure you don't snort Guinness through your nose as you laugh at the cartoons on the wall of this pub, many of which were drawn by famous cartoonists. Ireland's now-defunct annual Cartoon Festival used to be held in Rathdrum in early summer. There's a fabulous Italian restaurant here, called Bates Restaurant, as well as a nice informal cafe, so come for lunch or dinner.

28 Market Sq. ☎ 0404-46-774.

Johnnie Fox's
Glencullen, County Dublin

One of Ireland's oldest pubs, Johnnie Fox's is also one of the liveliest drinking establishments in these parts. You're virtually guaranteed entertainment with your pint, whether it be in the form of a rollicking, impromptu traditional Irish music session; a chat with people you've just met that night; or a storyteller. For something more organized, check out the Hooley Night show, which includes a four-course dinner, loads of excellent traditional Irish music, and a top-notch traditional dancing show. The Hooley takes place most nights and runs from 7:30 p.m. to midnight.

In Glencullen, on the R116, County Dublin. ☎ **01-295 5647.**

Phil Healy's
Wicklow

This unpretentious spot is where locals meet for a leisurely drink and chat. The high ceilings make it feel open and airy, but the pub has plenty of nooks to settle into if you want to have a quiet conversation.

Fitzwilliam Square. ☎ **0404-67-380.**

Fast Facts: County Wicklow

Area Codes

County Wicklow's area codes (or city codes) are **01, 0404, 0402,** and **045.**

Emergencies/Police

Dial ☎ **999** for all emergencies.

Information

There are several tourist offices in the area. The tourist office in Fitzwilliam Square,

Wicklow (☎ 0404-69-117; www.visit wicklow.ie) is open Monday through Saturday year-round and can provide reservation services.

Hospital

Wicklow District Hospital is on Glenside Road in Wicklow Town (☎ 0404-67-108).

County Kildare

Welcome to horse country. A land of gentle hills and open grasslands, County Kildare is home to hundreds of stud farms, including the mother of them all, the Irish National Stud, where some of the finest racehorses in Ireland are born and rest between training. Of course, one needs a place to race all these fine horses, so the county boasts three large racetracks, including the Curragh, where the Irish Derby is held each year.

Getting to and around County Kildare

By car, take the N7 (which turns into the M7) from Dublin or Limerick to get to several towns in County Kildare, or take the N4 to Celbridge and then use the R403. **Irish Rail** (☎ 1-850-366-222; www.irishrail.ie) has daily service to Kildare town, and **Bus Éireann** (☎ 01-836-6111; www.buseireann.ie) services Kildare, Naas, Straffan, Newbridge, and other towns throughout the area.

Spending the night in County Kildare

Barberstown Castle
$$$$ Straffan

This one is a classic. Once owned by Eric Clapton, this lavish, old-style hotel centers around a 13th-century castle keep with Victorian and Elizabethan extensions. Guest rooms are elegant, with antiques, reproductions, four-poster beds in each room, and sumptuous fabrics. Afternoon tea is available in the sitting room, and the gardens surrounding the hotel are perfect for an evening walk. The staff always has time to chat and offer any help that you need.

From Dublin, take the N7 to Kill, where you turn for Straffan. From the west, take N4 to Maynooth, where you turn for Straffan. ☎ 01-628-8157. www.barberstown castle.ie. *Parking: Free on-site. Rack rates: €230–€260 double. AE, MC, V.*

Cherryville House
$ Monasterevan, near Kildare Town

The beef cattle on this farm may not be as graceful as the horses that populate County Kildare, but it's still fun to stay on a working farm. In addition to the cattle, you may run into the free-range hens, ducks, and outdoor cats. The 130-year-old farmhouse feels peaceful and quiet, even though you're just a short drive from several area attractions. Rooms are spotless and soothing, and your kind hostess, Ruby, knows a ton about the area.

On Cherryville Cross, off R445 east of the village of Monasterevan. ☎ 045-521-091. www.kildarebedandbreakfast.com. *Parking: Free on-site. Rack rates: €70 double. MC, V.*

Dining locally in County Kildare

Also see "Hitting the pubs," later in this chapter.

Harbour Restaurant
$$ Naas   CONTINENTAL

Don't let the nondescript exterior fool you; one foot in the door, and you'll know you're in for a meal that will keep you going all day long or satisfy you after a day spent exploring. The chefs create great versions of down-to-earth dishes such as rack of lamb with rosemary *jus,* while also fashioning more adventurous options such as a whiskey-flavored lobster terrine.

Limerick Road. Take the N7 from Dublin to Naas. ☎ **045-87-9145.** *Main courses: €11–€20. AE, MC, V. Open: Daily 7 a.m.–10 p.m.*

The Moone High Cross Inn

$$ Moone PUB GRUB

Take a seat and enjoy the friendly atmosphere at this authentic pub and restaurant from the 18th century, which serves beef stew; shepherd's pie; and other simple, delicious, well-prepared dishes. Be sure to check out the old photographs and local curios around the pub.

Bolton Hill, 7.5km (5 miles) south of Ballytore. ☎ **059-862-4112.** *Main courses: €10–€20. MC, V. Open: Lunch in the pub daily noon to 3 p.m., dinner in the restaurant Thurs–Sun 6–9 p.m.*

Exploring County Kildare

The top attractions

Castletown House

Celbridge

This stately house was built in the early part of the 18th century for William Connolly, the then speaker of the Irish House of Commons. Its grandeur is staggering, and it remains a standout in Irish architecture. The mansion was built in the Palladian style, a Renaissance style meant to copy the classicism of ancient Rome. The interior is decorated with Georgian furnishings, and the main hall and staircase are covered with intricate plasterwork. Run by the state and open to the public, the house is worth the drive — about 16km (10 miles) northeast of Naas. Access is by guided tour only. The land surrounding the house is great for a peaceful stroll. Check the Web site for concerts and events here. Allow 90 minutes for your visit.

From Dublin, take the N4 west. Get off at Exit 6 for the R449 and stay in the left-hand lane, which merges with Hewlett Packard Road. You'll see the gates to the house on the right. Located on the R403 just before you reach the village of Celbridge. By bus: 67 and 67A from Dublin to Celbridge and then a 15-minute walk. ☎ **01-628-8252.** *Admission: Tours €4.50 adults; €3.50 seniors, students, and kids; free for kids 4 and under. Open: Mid-Mar to Nov 30 Tues–Sun with tours departing from 10 a.m.–4:45 p.m.*

The Curragh

Newbridge

This racetrack, the country's best-known, is often referred to as the Churchill Downs of Ireland. You can catch a race here at least one Saturday a month from May through September. In late June, the Curragh is host to the famous Irish Derby.

On the Dublin-Limerick Road. Take the N7 from Dublin or Naas. By train: Daily service gets you near Newbridge; a complimentary shuttle bus taken you to and from the Curragh. Bus Éireann (☎ 01-836-6111) offers a round-trip bus from Dublin on race days. ☎ 045-44-1205. www.curragh.ie. Admission: €15–35 for most races. Call ahead for upcoming dates. Races usually begin at or around 2 p.m.

Irish National Stud, Japanese Gardens, and St. Fiachra's Garden
Tully

What could be more pleasant than strolling around a collection of rich green fields on a sunny day, gazing at the strongest and fastest racehorses in Ireland? You can tour the yards on your own with an informative brochure or take one of the interesting 45-minute guided tours (daily at noon, 2:30 p.m., and 4:30 p.m.). The prize-winning stallions are a must-see; check out the plaques on their stables, stating the name of the horse and the highlights of his career. Though it's tempting, don't touch the stallions — they're known to kick and bite without provocation. Don't miss the mare and foal paddocks, and the Foaling Unit near the Sun Chariot Yard, where pregnant mares give birth and hang out with their newborn foals for a few days.

The fields and paddocks wrap around lovely St. Fiachra's Garden, designed to honor the spirituality of sixth- and seventh-century Irish monastic communities. One of the highlights is the 5,000-year-old sunken oak forest, where branchless trees stand sentry, preserved by the bog that surrounds them. Another beautiful feature is the Waterford Crystal Garden, where Waterford crystal pieces, ferns, fossils, and orchids are secreted away within one of the monastic cells. The Japanese Gardens are more interesting than stunning; the path follows the "journey of life," from the Cave of Birth to the Gateway of Eternity. It's fun to follow the explanation for each section of the path in your brochure. Allow two to three hours for your visit.

Outside of the town of Kildare. Take the N7 from Dublin or Naas. By train: Daily service into Kildare Railway Station, where you can get a free shuttle bus or a taxi. ☎ 045-52-1617. www.irish-national-stud.ie. Admission: €11 adults, €8 seniors and students, €6 kids 15 and under. Open: Mid-Feb to Dec 23 daily 9:30 a.m.–5 p.m.

More cool things to see and do

✔ **Kildare Country Club (K-Club),** 27km (17 miles) west of Dublin in Straffan (☎ 01-601-7200; www.kclub.ie): There are two courses here: The Palmer Ryder Cup Course is an 18-hole championship golf course designed by Arnold Palmer, which hosted the Ryder Cup in 2006, and the Palmer Smurfit Course, an inland links course that uses plantings native to the area to give it a less formal, more natural look.

Par for both courses is 72. Fees for the Ryder Course are €240 in May, July, and August; €305 in June and September; €175 in April, March, and October; and €150 from November through February.

For the Smurfit Course, fees are €190 in May, July, and August; €220 in June and September; and €175 from October through April.

✔ **The Moone High Cross,** on the southern edge of Moone village, signposted off the N9: This 1,200-year-old high stone cross boasts beautiful carvings of Celtic designs, as well as biblical scenes.

✔ **Steam Museum and Walled Garden,** off the Dublin-Limerick Road (N7), Lodge Park, Straffan, near Celbridge (☎ **01-627-3155** in summer, 01-628-8412 in winter): Anyone with an interest in steam locomotion will enjoy this museum, housed in a restored church. The collection of model trains and 18th-century locomotive engines includes Richard Trevithick's Third Model of 1797, the oldest surviving self-propelled machine in existence. Another room contains stationary engines from the Industrial Age. You can find plenty of steam-locomotion literature in the shop. Sundays are the best day to visit, because most of the engines are powered up that day. If it's nice out, check out the 18th-century walled garden.

To get there, take the N7 from Dublin or Naas. There is also daily train service into Kildare Railway Station. Admission is €7.50 adults; €5 seniors, students, and kids. It's open June through August Wednesday through Sunday from 2 to 6 p.m., May and September by arrangement only. Allow an hour for your visit.

Hitting the pubs

Also see the Moone High Cross Inn, reviewed in "Dining locally in County Kildare," earlier in this chapter.

Silken Thomas
Kildare

Silken Thomas is an entertainment complex with three bars (including a warm and welcoming thatched-roof, oak-beamed pub and a glistening Victorian-style hangout) and a state-of-the art club. Fortify yourself with some of Silken Thomas's delicious pub grub, including steaks, sandwiches, and soups, or a more formal dinner in the Chapter 16 restaurant. The pub's name comes from a member of the Fitzgerald family known for wearing luxurious clothing and being accompanied by standard-bearers carrying silken banners.

The Square. ☎ 045-52-2232.

Fast Facts: County Kildare

Area Codes

Kildare's area code is **045**.

Emergencies/Police

Dial ☎ **999** for all emergencies.

Genealogical Resources

Get in touch with the Kildare Library, on Main Street in Newbridge (☎ 045-433-602).

Hospital

Naas General Hospital (☎ 045-849-500) is in Naas town's center, off the R445.

Information

The main tourist office is at 38 S. Main St., Naas (☎ 045-898-888).

Chapter 14

The Southeast: Counties Wexford, Waterford, Tipperary, and Kilkenny

. . . .

In This Chapter

▶ Traveling back in time at the Irish National Heritage Park

▶ Discovering the wonders of the Hook Peninsula

▶ Touring the Waterford Crystal Factory

▶ Visiting Ireland's version of the Rock (the Rock of Cashel, that is)

▶ Exploring medieval streets and buildings in Kilkenny

. . . .

*W*exford, Waterford, Tipperary, and Kilkenny are among Ireland's Southeast counties, and are often referred to as the "sunny Southeast" because they generally enjoy more sunshine than the rest of the country. This area has many sights that are well worth exploring, from the celebrated House of Waterford Crystal and Rock of Cashel to lesser-known attractions such as a re-creation of a ship that carried passengers to America during the Great Famine, and tours of an 800-year-old lighthouse. Though the landscape here is not as dramatic as it is in the West of Ireland, the Southeast is no slouch, with sandy beaches, rounded mountains, and crystal-clear rivers. The major towns in the Southeast are some of the oldest in Ireland, and an afternoon spent exploring the twisting streets of Kilkenny or Wexford is an attraction in its own right.

Eight attractions in the Southeast, including the House of Waterford Crystal, the Jameson Distillery, and the Dunbrody Famine Ship, have formed a partnership to offer discounts to travelers. When you visit one of the attractions, you receive 20 percent off your visit to the other seven attractions.

County Wexford

County Wexford is one of the unsung treasures of Ireland, offering myriad peaceful beaches, rolling hills, meandering rivers, the 1,200-year-old town of Wexford, and, in my opinion, some of the friendliest people in all of Ireland. If you're looking for don't-miss attractions, you may find Wexford disappointing, but if you're interested in wandering along beaches and down the winding streets of Wexford Town, chatting with locals, and visiting a number of interesting historical sites and gardens, you're in for a treat.

The county's largest town is **Wexford Town** (see the map of the same name), a sweet and pretty harbor town that attracts Ireland's yuppies for weekend trips (lots of chichi clothing stores stand amid the main street's cute bakeries and pubs). Along with cute and bustling **New Ross,** Wexford Town is a great base for exploring the county.

County Wexford was the heartbeat of the 1798 rebellion, when Irish rebels took a brave stand against the strong arm of the Brits, and it was at Vinegar Hill, near Enniscorthy, where 20,000 rebels were massacred by English cannons, effectively ending that rebellion. As a result, you may encounter a ferocious pride in Irish freedom in these parts.

Getting to and around County Wexford

If you're driving from Dublin, take the N11 (which becomes M11 periodically) or the N80 south to Wexford Town; from Wexford Town, take the N25 west to New Ross. Most attractions are along the route between Wexford Town and New Ross. A fast and cost-effective shortcut across Waterford Harbour between Passage East, which is about 16km (10 miles) east of Waterford City, and Ballyhack, about 32km (20 miles) southwest of Wexford Town, is provided by **Passenger East Car Ferry** (☎ 051-38-2480; www.passageferry.ie). The ferry runs April through September Monday through Saturday from 7 a.m. to 10 p.m., Sunday and public holidays from 9:30 a.m. to 10 p.m.; October through March Monday through Saturday from 7 a.m. to 8 p.m., Sunday and public holidays from 9:30 a.m. to 8 p.m. Fares are €8 one-way and €12 round-trip for a car and passengers, €2 one-way and €3 round-trip for walk-ons. Bicyclists can bring along bicycles for no extra fee.

The Dublin (Connolly Station)–Rosslare Europort line of **Irish Rail** (☎ 1-850-366-222; www.irishrail.ie) has stations in Rosslare, Wexford, and Enniscorthy. **Bus Éireann** (☎ 01-836-6111; www.buseireann.ie) travels year-round to Wexford, Enniscorthy, Rosslare, New Ross, and other towns throughout the area.

Ferries connect Britain and Rosslare Harbour, which is 19km (20 miles) south of Wexford Town. **Stena Line** (☎ 01-204-7777; www.stenaline.ie) has passenger and car ferries from Fishguard, Wales to Rosslare Harbour Ferryport. **Irish Ferries** (☎ 0818-300-400; www.irishferries.ie) has service to Rosslare from Pembroke, in Wales, and from Roscoff and Cherbourg, in France.

The Southeast

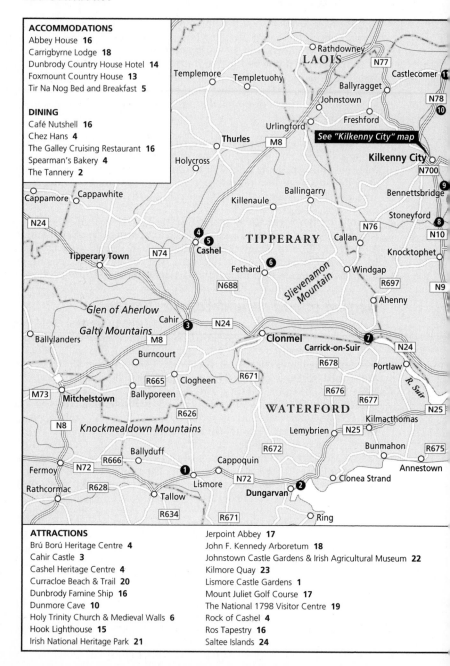

ACCOMMODATIONS
Abbey House **16**
Carrigbyrne Lodge **18**
Dunbrody Country House Hotel **14**
Foxmount Country House **13**
Tir Na Nog Bed and Breakfast **5**

DINING
Café Nutshell **16**
Chez Hans **4**
The Galley Cruising Restaurant **16**
Spearman's Bakery **4**
The Tannery **2**

ATTRACTIONS
Brú Ború Heritage Centre **4**
Cahir Castle **3**
Cashel Heritage Centre **4**
Curracloe Beach & Trail **20**
Dunbrody Famine Ship **16**
Dunmore Cave **10**
Holy Trinity Church & Medieval Walls **6**
Hook Lighthouse **15**
Irish National Heritage Park **21**

Jerpoint Abbey **17**
John F. Kennedy Arboretum **18**
Johnstown Castle Gardens & Irish Agricultural Museum **22**
Kilmore Quay **23**
Lismore Castle Gardens **1**
Mount Juliet Golf Course **17**
The National 1798 Visitor Centre **19**
Rock of Cashel **4**
Ros Tapestry **16**
Saltee Islands **24**

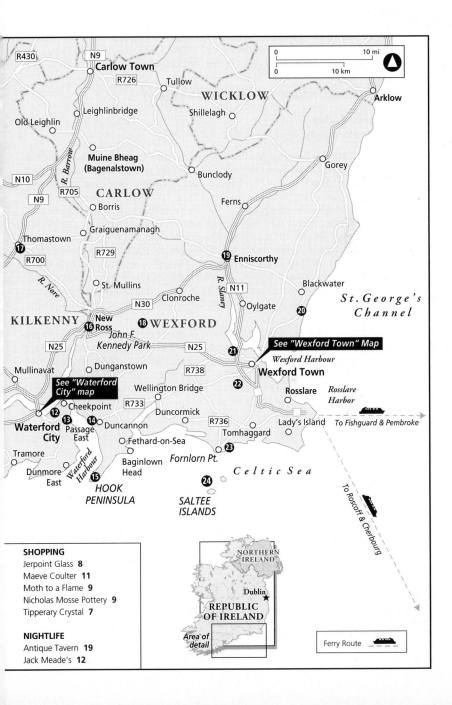

SHOPPING
Jerpoint Glass **8**
Maeve Coulter **11**
Moth to a Flame **9**
Nicholas Mosse Pottery **9**
Tipperary Crystal **7**

NIGHTLIFE
Antique Tavern **19**
Jack Meade's **12**

Walking is the best way to get around County Wexford's towns. Even the largest town, Wexford, is easily walkable. You'll find street parking in most of the towns in the area. It may be either Pay-and-Display (you buy a ticket from one of the machines on the street) or Disc parking (you purchase a parking disc from any of the nearby shops).

Spending the night in County Wexford

Carrigbyrne Lodge
$ **Raheenakennedy, near New Ross**

Your hosts, Ian Neville and Noëlle O'Connor, and their three young children, Aoife, Conor, and Ben, will make sure that you're comfortable and happy at this down-to-earth three-room country bed-and-breakfast. Everything is easygoing and uncluttered here — you're welcome to linger over your top-notch Irish breakfast in the morning sunshine that floods the breakfast room, and you can pad down to make yourself a cup of tea or hot chocolate at any time. Plus, how could you not feel relaxed when you wake up to green fields and a browsing pet horse outside the window of your spacious, simply decorated room? Though Carrigbyrne feels quite rural, the hopping town of New Ross (which offers several excellent attractions) is only a 15-minute drive away. Kids are more than welcome here; in fact, you may have to pull them away from bouncing on the trampoline or playing soccer with the Neville/O'Connor kids.

Raheenakennedy. Take the N25 to New Ross. At the bridge in New Ross, turn right and follow the N25 toward Wexford. At the Horse and Hound Pub, take a right toward Old Ross and follow the sharp bend around the house (right-hand side) on the corner, and then take a right turn at the signpost for Carrigbyrne Lodge B&B. ☎ **051-428-741.** www.carrigbyrnelodgebandb.com. *Parking: Free on-site. Rack rates: €60–€75 double (kids stay free). No credit cards.*

Dunbrody Country House Hotel
$$$$ **Arthurstown**

Recipe for an exceptional country hotel: Take one Georgian mansion surrounded by acres of gardens and woodland, add 22 rooms that seamlessly blend stately, classic surroundings with inspired contemporary touches, and sprinkle in fresh flowers and roaring fires. Now you'll need to add the icing: A world-class on-site cooking school offering all sorts of courses, a lauded restaurant (The Harvest Room), and a posh spa (lime, ginger, and salt exfoliation anyone?). Top with a friendly potbellied pig named Delago. Now just sit back on the patio, order from the extensive cocktail menu, chat with other guests, and enjoy.

Arthurstown. Take the R733 through Wellingtonbridge and Ramsgrange, and find the hotel right before you enter the village of Arthurstown. ☎ **051-389-600.** www.dunbrodyhouse.com. *Parking: Free on-site. Rack rates: €175–€325 double. Check online for special rates and packages. AE, MC, V.*

Wexford Town

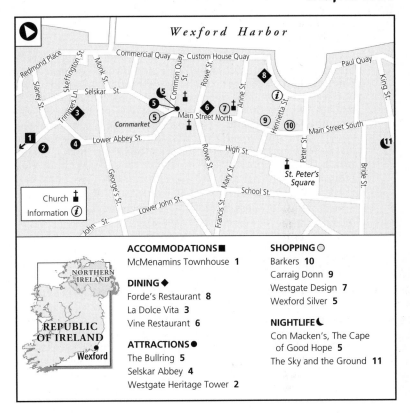

ACCOMMODATIONS■
McMenamins Townhouse **1**

DINING◆
Forde's Restaurant **8**
La Dolce Vita **3**
Vine Restaurant **6**

ATTRACTIONS●
The Bullring **5**
Selskar Abbey **4**
Westgate Heritage Tower **2**

SHOPPING○
Barkers **10**
Carraig Donn **9**
Westgate Design **7**
Wexford Silver **5**

NIGHTLIFE☾
Con Macken's, The Cape
of Good Hope **5**
The Sky and the Ground **11**

McMenamin's Townhouse
$$ Wexford Town

You'll feel at home immediately at this welcoming Victorian B&B, run by sweet and charming Kay and Seamus McMenamin, who offer what just may be Ireland's best breakfast. The good-size bedrooms are furnished in a tasteful Victorian style. The linens are scented with lavender, and the beds are so comfortable that you'd be tempted to sleep in each morning if it weren't for the scent of Kay's gourmet breakfast wafting up the stairs. A former restaurant owner and chef, Kay treats her guests to an array of breakfast choices, from fresh-caught fish to lamb's kidney served in sherry sauce for the adventurous. Sides, such as homemade marmalade made with whiskey, oranges, and brown sugar and thick, tangy homemade yogurt, accompany your breakfast. The B&B is in Wexford Town, not far from the bus and train station, so it's great for those without a car.

6 Glena Terrace, Spawell Road, Wexford Town. ☎ **053-914-6442.** *www.wexford-bedandbreakfast.com. Parking: Free on-site. Rack rates: €90 double. MC, V.*

Dining locally in County Wexford

Café Nutshell
$$ New Ross IRISH/CAFE

Do as the families, groups of friends, and couples of New Ross do, and pop into this casual cafe, furnished with blond wood and graced with framed paintings and posters. The Irish classics and classics-with-a-twist use top-notch local vegetables, meats, cheeses, and fish. Don't miss the freshly made soups (the Golden Summer Vegetable soup is a must-try), juices and smoothies (my husband recommends the no. 5, a banana, coconut, and yogurt concoction), and the seafood platter with wasabi-lime mayo. Or just order an appetizer, and then go straight for the homemade desserts, which range from a cloud-like pavlova to cupcakes that look like they jumped out of the pages of a children's book. A deli and natural foods store upfront are good bets for snacks on the run.

8 South Street, New Ross. ☎ *051-422-777. Main courses: €8–€20. Open: Cafe Mon–Sat 12:30–5 p.m., store Mon–Sat 9 a.m.–5:30 p.m.*

Forde's Restaurant
$$$ Wexford Town NEW IRISH

This inventive restaurant took Wexford Town by storm when it opened in 2003, placing in the top 100 restaurants in Ireland. The quiet room looks as though it was decorated by hip royalty, with dramatic wine-colored walls, standing cast-iron candleholders, ivory candles, and mirrors. The hip/dramatic theme extends to the menu, which offers local meats and produce with interesting modern twists, such as a potato side dish folded into a spring-roll wrapper. Menu standouts include fresh Dublin Bay shrimp pan-fried with ginger and lemongrass, and the prime filet of steak with garlic butter. You can wash it all down with a glass from the comprehensive wine list. Service is attentive and unobtrusive.

Crescent Quay. ☎ *053-912-3832. Reservations recommended. Main courses: €20–€29; early bird €24. MC, V. Open: Daily 6–10 p.m.*

The Galley Cruising Restaurant
$$–$$$$ New Ross IRISH

Picture this: You're cruising along a glassy river, taking in the picturesque shoreline. You wander in from the outdoor deck to sit down to a beautifully prepared five-course meal featuring fresh local produce. What could be more relaxing? Lunch and tea cruises last two hours; dinner cruises, between two and three hours. You have two or three options for each course, with the emphasis on Continental favorites such as chicken stuffed with cheese and served in a white wine sauce or salmon bathed in hollandaise. Dress is casual.

New Ross Quay. West on the N25 from Wexford. ☎ *051-421-723.* www.river cruises.ie. *Cost of cruise: €25 lunch, €12 afternoon tea, €40 dinner. MC, V. Reservations required. Cruises depart June–Aug daily at 12:30 p.m. (lunch), 3 p.m.*

(afternoon tea), and 6:30 or 7 p.m. (dinner). Cruises may go out in Apr or May if there is enough interest. Call and ask. You also can pay just for the cruise if you don't want to eat; without food, prices are €12 lunch, €10 tea, and €25 dinner.

La Dolce Vita
$$ Wexford Town ITALIAN

Do the streets look deserted around lunchtime? That's because everyone's packed into this restaurant and deli for beautifully crafted Italian salads, pasta dishes, and heartier fare such as saltimbocca or sausage with braised lentils. Lunch proved so popular that owner Roberto Pons has decided to open for dinner on Friday and Saturday. The walls of the simply furnished restaurant are lined with gourmet Italian products, so pick up a bottle of olives or a fine chocolate bar before you hit the road.

6–7 Trimmers Lane, off North Main Street. ☎ **053-917-0806.** *Main courses: Lunch €9–€12, more for dinner. Reservations recommended for dinner. MC, V. Open: Mon–Thurs 9 a.m.–5:30 p.m., Fri–Sat 9:30 a.m.–9:30 p.m.*

Vine Restaurant
$$ Wexford Town THAI

This Thai restaurant comes up again and again when I ask people in Wexford about their favorite place to eat. You can chow down on all sorts of Thai specialties in a beautiful high-ceilinged room with funky décor. You can't go wrong with any of the dishes flavored with Thai herbs and spices; the duck with tamarind is particularly delicious.

109 N. Main St. ☎ **053-912-2388.** *Main courses: €14–€22. DC, MC, V. Open: Tues–Sun 6–10 p.m.*

Exploring County Wexford

The excellent one-hour **walking tour** of Wexford Town reveals this area's fascinating history, including stories of the many groups who fought against British rule. Tours usually leave from the White's Hotel, on Abbey Street, Monday through Friday at 11 a.m. (call ☎ **053-916-1155** to confirm), and cost €5 adults, €3 seniors and students.

For a view of Wexford from the River Barrow, see the review of the **Galley Cruising Restaurant,** in the "Dining locally in County Wexford" section; you can opt to take the cruise and skip the meal.

The top attractions

Dunbrody Famine Ship
New Ross

Thousands of people haunted by the Great Famine left Ireland for an uncertain new life in America aboard the *Dunbrody,* a three-masted ship built in 1845. Though the original ship was lost at sea, an exact replica of the *Dunbrody* was created in 2001. A tour guide will take you through the ship, outfitted to look as it did during the time of the Great Famine. The ship comes to life through the details, from the crystal decanter sitting on the captain's dining table, to the list of fines for crew offenses (use of foul language would see you docked one day's pay) to the waste buckets that steerage passengers used. You'll meet two actors playing passengers on the vessel; one portrays a mother traveling with her husband and four children in steerage, and another takes the role of a mother who is traveling first-class with her family. This portion of the tour could easily turn corny, but the actors do a lovely, subtle job of portraying their characters. Take time after the tour to explore the ship on your own, including a visit to the hold. Allow an hour for your visit.

If you're interested in the history of New Ross and/or textile arts, walk across the street to the Ros Tapestry (see p. 209).

Docked in New Ross. ☎ **051-425-239**. www.dunbrody.com. *Admission: €7.50 adults, €6 seniors, €4.50 students and kids. Open: Apr–Sept daily 9 a.m.–6 p.m., Oct–Mar daily 9 a.m.–5 p.m.*

Exploring the Hook Peninsula

There's so much to see on this small foot of land in southwest County Wexford that it's worth spending the afternoon driving the Hook Head Drive and walking parts of the lovely 201km (125-mile) Slí Charman (Wexford's Coastal Pathway). There are many beaches along the route. I love **Baginbun Head,** near Fethard-on-Sea on the east side of the peninsula, which has a warren of rock formations to clamber on (check out the tide pools for sea life), some sandy patches for sunbathing, and good swimming and snorkeling.

My favorite attraction along the peninsula is the **Hook Lighthouse,** situated at the end of the R734 at the tip of the Hook Peninsula (☎ **051-397-054;** www.hookheritage.ie), which has operated almost continuously for the past 800 years. It's definitely worth it to take the roughly 30-minute guided tour of the lighthouse. In the upper living quarters, check out the reddish tinge to the wall; it's thought that the builders of the lighthouse used ox or cow blood as part of their cement. Tours are €6 adults, €4 seniors and students, €3.50 kids 5 to 16, free for kids 4 and under. To reward yourself for climbing the 115 steps to the balcony of the lighthouse, grab a light lunch or snack at the bustling cafe. Inspired by the scenery? You can create your own painting on-site. For €3 to €5, you get access to paints, slate, paper, a smock, and an art instructor to help you develop your painting.

Castle and history fans will enjoy the detailed historical tour and displays at **Ballyhack Castle** (☎ **051-389-468;** Open: June–Sept 10 a.m.–6 p.m.), built in the 1450s. Admission is €2 adults; €1.20 seniors, students, and children. For an independent adventure, you can browse around the quiet ruins of 16th-century **Slade Castle;** Richard Rice, of Slade House (☎ **086-822-8801**), will give you the key.

Duncannon Fort (☎ **051-38-9454;** Open: June–Sept 10 a.m.–5:30 p.m.), built to fend off attacks from the Spanish Armada, makes an interesting stop, especially for those interested in military history. If you stop here, definitely take the tour (€4 adults, €2 seniors and kids) and check out the Cockleshell Art Gallery. The **ruins of Dunbrody Abbey** (3km/4 miles beyond Duncannon; Open: May to mid-Sept 10 a.m.–6 p.m.) are also worth a stop. Don't miss the well-done adjoining **hedge maze,** one of only two full-size hedge mazes in Ireland. Admission to the abbey is €2 adults, €1 kids. Admission to the maze is €4 adults, €2 kids.

Tintern Abbey, Ballyhack, and Duncannon are off the R733. To get to Hook Head, go south toward Fethard on the R734 from New Ross. If you'd like to hike, you can pick up the coastal walk, Wexford Coastal Path (Slí Charman), at several points along the drive. To start the walk at the beginning, park in Fethard and hop onto the trail head.

Irish National Heritage Park
Ferrycarrig

Set on 14 hectares (36 acres), this intriguing living-history park traces the region's history from its earliest Stone Age settlements through the Celtic, Viking, and Norman periods. The 16 historical sites feature re-creations of castles, boats, homes, and the landscape during each period, many featuring costumed interpreters, bringing the past off the pages of books and into three dimensions. Exhibits are hands-on, making this a great place for kids. Allow two hours for your visit.

Off Dublin-Wexford Road (N11). A few miles west of Wexford off the N11 at Ferrycarrig. ☎ *053-912-0733. www.inhp.com. Admission: €8 adults, €6.50 seniors and students, €4.50 kids13–16, €4 kids4–12. Open: May–Aug 9:30 a.m.–6:30 p.m. (last admission 5 p.m.), Sept–Apr 9:30 a.m.–5:30 p.m. (last admission between 3 and 4 p.m.).*

John F. Kennedy Arboretum
New Ross

Plant-lovers will enjoy meandering down self-guided trails through gardens featuring more than 4,500 species of trees and exotic shrubs from five continents. Bird-lovers will enjoy the waterfowl that frequent the arboretum's pond. Allow 90 minutes for your visit.

Off Duncannon Road (R733). ☎ *051-38-8171. Admission: €3 adults, €2 seniors, €1 students and kids. Open: May–Aug daily 10 a.m.–8 p.m., Sept and Apr daily 10 a.m.–6:30 p.m., Oct–Mar daily 10 a.m.–5 p.m. (last admission 45 minutes before closing).*

Johnstown Castle Gardens and Irish Agricultural Museum
Wexford Town

The fairy-tale gardens here offer 20 hectares (50 acres) of trees and flowers, plus hothouses, lakes with mute swans, and sculptures and other ornamental structures, all surrounding a lovely 19th-century castle. On the grounds is a museum focusing on the important role of farming in Wexford's history, with exhibits on farm transport, dairy farming, and farmhouse furniture, and a comprehensive look at the role of the potato in Ireland and during the Great Famine. A highlight is the exhibit depicting the typical Irish kitchen in 1800, 1900, and 1950. Allow two hours for your visit.

Johnstown Castle Estate, Bridgetown Road, off Wexford-Rosslare Road (N25). A couple of miles east of Wexford off the R733. ☎ **053-917-1247.** *Admission: Garden (only charged May–Sept) €6 per car, €2 adults on foot; museum €6 adults, €4 students and kids. Open: Gardens daily 9 a.m.–4:30 p.m.. Museum Apr–Oct Mon–Fri 9 a.m.–5 p.m., Sat–Sun 11 a.m.–4:30 p.m.; Nov–Mar Mon–Fri 9 a.m.–5 p.m. (closed for lunch 1–2 p.m.).*

Wexford Wildfowl Reserve
North Slob, Ardcavan (right outside of Wexford Town)

This national nature reserve, located in amusingly named North Slob, draws many species of ducks, swans, and other waterfowl from October through April, while autumn and spring see quick feeding stopovers from additional migratory birds. Over 9,000 Greenland White-Fronted Geese call the area home during the winter; during the summer, up to 240 mute swans make the reserve their home. Blinds and an observation tower are set up for birders, and the reserve has a visitor center with an audiovisual show and exhibits. Allow an hour to an hour and a half for your visit.

North Slob, just 4.8km (3 miles) east of Wexford Town. ☎ **053-912-3129.** *Admission: Free. Open: Daily 9 a.m.–5 p.m.*

More cool things to see and do

- ✔ **The Bullring,** off Quay Street, Wexford Town: The first declaration of an Irish Republic was made here in 1798, and a statue memorializes the men who fought for Irish independence at that time. The name of the area comes from the bloody sport of bull-baiting that took place here in the 17th century. You can see the statue in a few minutes.

- ✔ **Curracloe Beach and a cycling trip,** 11km (7 miles) northeast of Wexford Town on the R742: This beach is where the opening scenes of *Saving Private Ryan* were filmed. It is home to many migratory birds and is a popular swimming destination during the summer. A nature trail leads you through the sand dunes here. From Wexford, the road up through Curracloe to Blackwater makes an excellent day-long bike trip. Visit **Hayes Cycle Shop,** 108 S. Main St., Wexford Town (☎ **053-912-2462**), to rent a bike and get directions. Allow a couple hours to swim or a full day if you bike here.

- ✔ **The National 1798 Visitor Centre,** Mill Park Road, Enniscorthy (☎ **053-923-7596;** www.iol.ie/~98com): The story of the United Irishmen's first rebellion against the British is told in multimedia pomp at this small but interesting museum. The museum engages visitors with objects, an audiovisual presentation, and interactive computer programs. If it's nice outside, this is a great place for a picnic.

The museum is on the N30 and N11 next to Vinegar Hill. Admission is €6 adults; €3.50 seniors, students, and kids. It's open May through September Monday through Friday from 9:30 a.m. to 5 p.m. (last admission 4 p.m.); call for hours from October through March. Allow an hour for your visit.

✔ **Kilmore Quay and the Saltee Islands,** on R739, 22km (14 miles) south of Rosslare: This fishing village, featuring some thatched cottages, is a bit down at the heels these days, but there are still several good reasons to visit: Drop into **Kehoe's Pub** (☎ **053-9129-830**), the center of Kilmore Quay's social life and a museum of fascinating marine artifacts discovered on various dives; arrange for a fishing trip (contact Dick Hayes, of Enterprise, at ☎ **053-912-9704** or 087-254-9111); and (best of all) take a trip to the **Saltee Islands,** Ireland's largest bird sanctuary, if the weather is cooperating. Saltee Island trips also are run by Dick Hayes.

✔ **Ros Tapestry,** Priory Court, The Quay, New Ross (☎ **051-445-396**): Calling history buffs and fabric artists! In 1998, a rector at one of New Ross's churches asked a local artist to create tapestries illustrating the history of this Norman town. The request blossomed into a multifaceted project, as local painter Ann Griffin Bernstorff researched the history of the area and painted 15 panels illustrating scenes from the town's past. These panels have been transformed into large, sumptuously embroidered tapestries by over 150 avid embroiderers from the area. At the exhibition, you can view each tapestry as you listen to a digital audio tour that explains the scenes depicted.

Admission is €6 adults, €5 seniors, €4 students and kids. It's open April through September daily from 9:30 a.m. to 6 p.m. (last admission 5 p.m.), October through March daily from 10 a.m. to 5 p.m. (last admission 4 p.m.). Allow 45 minutes for your visit.

✔ **Selskar Abbey,** Westgate Street, Wexford Town: The story behind this ruined abbey is oddly romantic: Our tale begins when Alexander de la Roche left his fiancée behind to join the Crusades. Hearing that he had been killed, his fiancée became a nun. However, de la Roche was very much alive and was so grieved at the state of affairs upon his return that he joined an Augustinian order and founded and endowed the abbey at Selskar. If only they'd had cellphones! It is said that Henry II did penance at the abbey for having Thomas à Becket beheaded. Near the abbey are the ruins of a Church of Ireland church from the 1800s. When the congregation at this church merged with a nearby congregation, the church roof was removed so that no rent would be required on the building.

You're free to roam around the site when the gates are unlocked. If gates are locked, let someone at the Westgate Heritage Center know, and they'll open them for you. Allow 30 minutes for your visit.

✔ **Westgate Heritage Tower,** Westgate Street, Wexford Town (☎ 053-914-6506): Before exploring Wexford Town, you may want to stop by this heritage center, housed in one of the five original gate towers along the Viking city walls. A well-done film, *In Selskar's Shadow,* relates the rich history of Wexford Town, and a gallery on the first floor sells beautiful handcrafted gifts made by Wexford artisans. You can walk the battlements from here to Selskar Abbey.

Tickets to the film cost €3 adults, €1.50 students. Opening hours change from week to week, so call for current information. Allow 45 minutes for your visit.

Shopping in County Wexford

Westgate Design, 22 N. Main St., Wexford Town (☎ 053-912-3787), offers a large selection of Irish crafts, from wool clothing to pottery to jewelry. A family of silver- and goldsmiths runs **Wexford Silver,** 115 N. Main St., Wexford Town (☎ 053-912-1933), which sells finely crafted pieces that make perfect gifts or keepsakes. Also see Westgate Heritage Tower, in the previous section. **Barkers,** 36–40 S. Main St., Wexford Town (☎ 053-912-3159), sells Waterford Crystal, china, and local and international crafts. You'll find Irish gifts, such as Waterford Crystal and Belleek, along with great clothes, at **Carraig Donn,** 3 S. Main St., Wexford Town (☎ 053-912-3651).

Hitting the pubs in County Wexford

Antique Tavern
Enniscorthy

A black-and-white Tudor-style exterior makes this place easy to find. Inside, the dark and cozy pub is full of antiques (hence, the name). Check out the objects that line the walls, from weapons used during the 1798 Rebellion to farm equipment. Try for a spot on the outdoor balcony when the weather's pleasant.

14 Slaney St. ☎ 053-923-3428.

Con Macken's, The Cape of Good Hope
Wexford Town

As you venture into Wexford's famous Bullring area, you're sure to do a double take when you see Macken's: The awning over the entrance advertises a bar, undertaker, and grocery. And it's no joke — you can have a pint, pick up a loaf of bread, and make funeral arrangements in one convenient stop! Irish rebels made Macken's a popular meeting place over the centuries, and mementos from their struggles line the walls. Definitely a place like no other.

The Bullring. ☎ 053-912-2949.

The Sky and the Ground
Wexford Town

This simply decorated, homey pub, is a good bet for traditional Irish music (a special candlelit Irish music session currently takes place on Wednesdays beginning at 9 p.m.), as well as other genres, including American country. Take a seat, nurse a pint, listen to whoever happens to be playing, and chat with the locals — you'll feel like you were born and raised in Wexford.

112 S. Main St. ☎ **053-912-1273.**

Fast Facts: County Wexford

Area Codes

County Wexford's area codes are **051** and **053.**

Emergencies/Police

Dial ☎ **999** for all emergencies.

Genealogical Resources

Contact the Genealogy Centre, Yola Farmstead, Tagoat, County Wexford (☎ 053-913-2610; http://homepage. eircom.net/~yolawexford).

Hospital

Wexford General Hospital is off Newtown Road in Wexford Town (☎ 053-915-0000).

Information

For visitor information, go to the tourist office at Crescent Quay, Wexford Town (☎ 053-912-3111; open year-round); the staff there can also provide reservation services. Seasonal offices (open Apr–Sept) are in Enniscorthy (☎ 054-923-4699) and in New Ross at the Dunbrody Famine Ship (☎ 051-421-857). Another good source is www.wexfordtourism.com.

Post Office

The main post office is on Anne Street, Wexford (☎ 053-912-2031).

Visiting County Waterford and Waterford City

Waterford City (Port Láirge in Gaelic) is the oldest town in Ireland, founded by Viking invaders in the ninth century. It's a pretty and bustling town, but aside from the House of Waterford Crystal, there isn't a whole lot to see.

Outside the city, the county offers lovely coastal villages and ethereal inland mountains.

Getting to and around Waterford City

If you're driving, take the N25 from Cork, the N24 from the west, the N9 and N10 from Kilkenny and points north, the N7 to M9 to N9 from Dublin, and the N25 from Wexford. Lismore is off the N72. A fast and cost-effective route across Waterford Harbour, between Passage East,

County Waterford (16km/10 miles east of Waterford), and Ballyhack, County Wexford (32km/20 miles west of Wexford), is provided by **Passenger East Car Ferry** (☎ 051-38-2480). See "Getting to and around County Wexford," earlier in this chapter, for more details.

Irish Rail (☎ 1-850-366-222; www.irishrail.ie) serves Waterford at Plunkett Station, on Terminus Street, about a ten-minute walk from the city center. **Bus Éireann** (☎ 01-836-6111; www.buseireann.ie) travels year-round to Waterford, Lismore, and other major towns in County Waterford. In Waterford City, buses arrive at the same station as the train: Plunkett Station.

Waterford is an easily walkable city. Stroll up the quays toward Reginald's Tower, take a right, and you're in the heart of town. If you're parking your car on the street, use the Pay-and-Display machines in the city center. A bit outside the city center, the street-parking system involves purchasing a parking disc at a local shop near the block you're parking on. There are many parking lots in the city, with the majority located along the quays right next to the river. Hotels in the city center sometimes have their own parking areas.

Spending the night in County Waterford

Foxmount Country House
$$ Passage East

This 17th-century B&B is only 15 minutes away from Waterford City, but you'll feel as though you're in the middle of nowhere — in a good way. The imposing ivy-covered house sits on a large stretch of stunningly landscaped grounds with grand trees, flowers, and a paddock where four horses and a donkey reside. The house is located on a working dairy farm, so you may catch a glimpse of a herd of cows. Want to relax? Head out to the peaceful herb garden at the back of the house. Looking to stretch your legs? Ramble down one of the dirt roads, past emerald pastures. Rooms have beautiful views and are spacious and elegantly furnished with antiques, and the large bathrooms feature comfortable tubs. Cordial hostess Margaret Kent serves a bang-up breakfast; I especially enjoyed the porridge with honey, brown sugar, and exceptionally fresh cream, and the tasty scrambled eggs. Head down the road for a pint at Jack Meade's pub (reviewed in "Hitting the pubs in County Waterford," later in this section), which looks as if it were transplanted from Middle Earth.

Passage East Road. Take Dunmore East Road (R683) from Waterford City for 6km (3½ miles) until you reach a fork. Take the left fork toward Passage East, and keep right at the next Y junction. Turn right just before the bridge at Jack Meade's pub. ☎ *051-87-4308. Fax: 051-85-4906.* www.foxmountcountryhouse.com. *Parking: Free on-site. Rack rates: €110–130 double. V.*

Waterford City

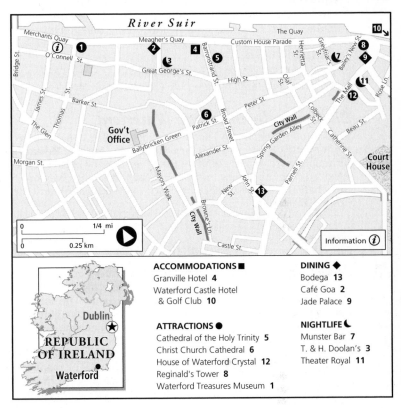

ACCOMMODATIONS ■
Granville Hotel **4**
Waterford Castle Hotel
& Golf Club **10**

ATTRACTIONS ●
Cathedral of the Holy Trinity **5**
Christ Church Cathedral **6**
House of Waterford Crystal **12**
Reginald's Tower **8**
Waterford Treasures Museum **1**

DINING ◆
Bodega **13**
Café Goa **2**
Jade Palace **9**

NIGHTLIFE ☾
Munster Bar **7**
T. & H. Doolan's **3**
Theater Royal **11**

Granville Hotel
$$ **Waterford City**

This is one of those great hotels that is solid in all aspects. The location is central, the staff is kind and helpful, and the breakfast is terrific. The rooms, outfitted with dark wood furnishings and floral prints, are spotless and large.

Meagher Quay (R680). ☎ *051-305-555.* www.granville-hotel.ie. *Parking: In nearby parking lots for about €5 a day. Rack rates: €80–€90 double. AE, MC, V.*

Waterford Castle Hotel & Golf Resort
$$$ **Balinakill**

Staying in this castle is like living a fairy tale. Located on a private island in the River Suir (accessible only by the castle's car ferry), only 3.2km

(2 miles) from Waterford City, the Norman castle and its Elizabethan-style wings are filled with tapestries, large stone fireplaces, antiques, and oak-paneled walls. All the impeccably clean, richly decorated rooms have stunning views. The staff is warm and friendly, and golf lovers will appreciate having a course right in their backyard. Check the Web site for frequent special offers.

The Island. ☎ **051-87-8203.** *Fax: 051-878-203.* www.waterfordcastle.com. *Parking: Free on-site. Rack rates: €108–€200 double. AE, MC, V.*

Dining locally in County Waterford

In addition to the places I list in this section, you can combine your dinner with a river cruise aboard the **Galley Cruising Restaurant.** Although you catch the boat on the River Barrow in New Ross, County Wexford (see the review in "Dining locally in County Wexford," earlier in this chapter), the trip takes you down to the River Suir and through County Waterford.

Bodega

$$$ Waterford City   NEW IRISH/FRENCH

A Spanish wine bar vibe defines this new Waterford restaurant, which is decorated with patio stone, warm amber lighting, built-in wooden wine racks, and strings of lanterns and Christmas lights. The sounds of jazz and Latin music are just audible against the buzz of laughter and clinking glasses. The menu focuses on casual New Irish cuisine prepared with the best French cooking techniques, including the excellent lamb burger with mint crème fraîche, the superb mussels with french fries, and the succulent duck served with berries and red wine sauce. The raspberry sabayon, with crushed berries, mascarpone cheese, raspberry sorbet, and crunchy anisette cookies, has to be one of the best desserts in Ireland.

54 John's St. ☎ **051-844-177.** *Reservations recommended. Main courses: €16–€27. AE, MC, V. Open: Mon–Wed noon to 10 p.m., Thurs–Fri noon to 10:30 p.m., Sat 5:30–10:30 p.m.*

Café Goa

$$ Waterford City   INDIAN

This is a great place to people-watch in Waterford, with a cross-section of the city, from families to club-going friends, passing through. The look here is casual, with abstract paintings in red, black, and gold, and bistro tables and chairs. The restaurant does a first-rate job with the Indian classics, from a mild but delicious tikka masala to the toothsome *aloo gobi* (a chickpea and potato dish) to the outstanding shrimp bhuna, with tomato, spring onions, garlic, ginger, and spices.

36 The Quay. ☎ **051-304-970.** *Main courses: €11–€16. MC, V. Open: Daily 5–11 p.m.*

Jade Palace
$$ Waterford City   CHINESE

Jade Palace offers authentic, mouthwatering Cantonese cuisine in down-town Waterford. This is the kind of place where you tell the server what you think you'd like, let him decide for you, and then stuff yourself silly. The clay pot dishes, such as roast duck served on Asian greens, are espe-cially excellent.

3 The Mall, next to Reginald's Tower in the city center. ☎ *051-855-611. Main courses: €14–€18. AE, MC, V. Open: Mon–Fri 12:30–2:30 p.m. and 5–10:30 p.m., Sat 5–10:30 p.m., Sun 12:30–10:30 p.m.*

The Tannery
$$$ Dungarvan   NEW IRISH

This stylish, contemporary restaurant was an operating tannery until 1995. The kitchen is wide open so that patrons can watch innovative chef Paul Flynn in action. Flynn adds unique twists to whatever dish he's cook-ing, such as roast rump of lamb with spiced carrot, tomato, and chickpea risotto or hot smoked duck served with spiced lentil sauce, chili, pineap-ple, and buttered cabbage. The interior is minimalist — white dishes on unadorned light-wood tables. The fixed-price three-course dinner (€29) is served all evening Tuesday through Friday.

10 Quay St. From Waterford or Cork, take the N25 to Dungarvan. ☎ *058-45-420.* www.tannery.ie. *Reservations recommended. Main courses: €19–€29. AE, MC, V. Open: Tues–Thurs and Sat 6–9:30 p.m., Fri 12:30–2:30 p.m. and 6–9:30 p.m., Sun 12:30–2:45 p.m. and (July–Aug only) 6:30–9 p.m.*

Exploring County Waterford: The top attractions

Waterford Tourist Services' award-winning **Walking Tours of Historic Waterford** (☎ **051-87-3711**) leave mid-March through mid-October daily from the Waterford Treasures Museum at 11:45 a.m. and 1:45 p.m. and from the Granville Hotel, on Meagher Quay, at noon and 2 p.m. Tours run about an hour and cost €7.

Another great walking-tour option, both fun and interesting, is the **From Vikings to Victorians Tour** (☎ **051-304-500**), which covers sights in Waterford's historic quarter. Tours run daily in June, July, and August, starting at 11 a.m. and 2:30, 4:30, and 7 p.m.; they last about an hour and 15 minutes. Meet in the plaza in front of the House of Waterford Crystal, on the Mall. Price is €6 adults, free for kids 15 and under.

Outside of Waterford City, a ride on the Victorian-era narrow-gauge **Waterford & Suir Valley Railway** (☎ **051-384-058;** www.wsrailway. ie), which follows tracks laid down in 1878, is a treat. The railway passes through lovely manor estates and woodland, and along a recently excavated Viking village. The 45-minute round-trip leaves from Kilmeadan Station, right outside Kilmeadan Village on the R680. Fares are €8 adults, €6.50 seniors and students, €3.50 kids. Trains depart hourly May through August Monday through Saturday from 11 a.m. to 4 p.m. (Sun noon to 5 p.m.) and April and September Monday through Saturday from 11 a.m. to 3 p.m. (Sun noon to 4 p.m.).

For self-guided hikes and walks, visit Waterford City's tourist office (see "Fast Facts: County Waterford," at the end of this section) to pick up route maps.

House of Waterford Crystal
Waterford City

What makes crystal shine brighter than regular glass? It's a lead oxite called *litharge*. You'll be able to spout off this fact and many more after a fascinating tour of the House of Waterford Crystal. Sadly, the original Waterford Crystal Factory has been shuttered since 2009, when the bulk of production moved overseas. However, the company has retained several skilled craftspeople who produce the most complex pieces, as well as special orders, for the brand. You'll be shown every step of the meticulous process that goes into the creation of the world-renowned crystal, from the blowing of molten glass to the engraving. You also get the opportunity to ask questions and get up close as a master craftsperson cuts or engraves a piece. Talk about a stressful job: Waterford Crystal has a six-step screening process for every piece that's made. About 45 percent of pieces are destroyed for minor flaws, and only perfect pieces make it into stores, which is why you'll never see Waterford *seconds* (slightly imperfect works). Along the tour, you have a chance to see some unique crystal pieces, including hefty sports trophies. The store here houses the largest selection of Waterford Crystal in the world. Allow two hours for your visit.

The Mall, in the heart of Waterford City. ☎ *051-317-000. Tour: €10 adults, €8 seniors and students, €3.50 kids 5–18, free for kids 4 and under. Tour schedule: June–Sept Mon–Sat 9 a.m.–4:15 p.m., Sun 10:30 a.m.–4:15 p.m.; Oct–May Mon–Fri 9:30 a.m.–3:15 p.m. Showroom open for about 1½ hours after the last tour leaves.*

Lismore Castle Gardens
Lismore

The two gardens here (upper and lower) are wonderfully varied, with riotously bright blossoms, apple trees, contemporary sculptures, and a kaleidoscope of roses. The magical yew tree walk in the lower garden is where Edmund Spenser is said to have written the *Faerie Queen*. The acres of gardens are set against the backdrop of a still-occupied 12th-century castle. Because this is an inhabited castle, you can't tour the inside (however, if you've come into some money, you can stay in the castle when the Duke of Devonshire is not in residence). This is a lovely place for a picnic. Allow 90 minutes for your visit.

Lismore. ☎ *058-54-424. Admission: €8 adults, €4 kids 16 and under. Open: St Patrick's Day to Sept 30 daily 11 a.m.–4:45 p.m.*

Reginald's Tower
Waterford City

Restored to its medieval appearance, this squat round tower was built by a Viking governor in the 12th century and is thought to be Ireland's oldest standing building in continuous use. It has been used in many different capacities — as a mint, a fortress, a prison, and an air-raid shelter. It's said that Norman leader Strongbow married Celtic Aoife (Eva) here, beginning a bond between the Norman invaders and the Celts. Though it's well worth a look from the outside, the three-level museum only houses a small collection of medieval artifacts and is not really worth your time unless you're a die-hard medieval history buff. Guided tours are available on request. Allow five minutes to visit the tower without going in, 30 minutes if you go in.

The Mall. ☎ **051-304-220.** *Admission: €3 adults, €2 seniors, €1 students and kids. Open: June to mid-Sept daily 10 a.m.–6 p.m., mid-Sept to Easter Wed–Sun 10 a.m.–5 p.m., Easter to May daily 10 a.m.–5 p.m. (last admission 30 minutes before closing).*

South East Coastal Drive or Bike

This well-marked 130km (80-mile) drive takes you along the coast through sweet seaside towns and by meandering rivers. At one end of your drive, you'll come upon Tramore, a family-friendly resort area with long stretch of golden sand that's incredibly popular with Irish families for swimming and other water sports. The route officially begins in Wexford Town, but Dunmore East makes a good starting point for a shorter drive (about 82km/51 miles). If you'd like to bike the route, rent a bike from May through August from **Altitudes Cycle,** 22 Ballybricken Green, Waterford City (☎ **051-870-356**).

The end points of the route are Wexford Town and Ardmore. From Wexford Town, take the R733 west and hook up with the R675 after you take the short car ferry ride to Passage East.

The Vee Drive

This winding 18km (11-mile) drive leads you through the lush Knockmealdown Mountains up to a stunning viewpoint of the farmland laid out like a quilt below and the glowing Galtee Mountains beckoning in the distance. The Vee Gap viewpoint, at the highest point of the drive, opens onto a variety of walking trails. Look for the parking lot and a sign mapping out the trails. Allow an hour for the drive, more if you want to hike.

The endpoints of the signposted Vee Drive are Lismore and Clogheen. From Lismore, take the R668 or the R669 (hook up to the R669 via the N72). From Clogheen, take the R668.

Waterford Cathedrals
Waterford City

Two for the price of one (well, actually, they're both free to visit). In the 18th century, architect John Roberts designed both Waterford's Catholic cathedral, the Cathedral of the Holy Trinity, and the town's Anglican cathedral, Christ Church Cathedral. The grand Catholic cathedral features Waterford crystal chandeliers and handsome marble columns topped with gold leaf. The graceful Christ Church Cathedral also boasts lovely marble columns, as well as a beautiful plasterwork ceiling and one of the finest organs in Ireland. Christ Church frequently hosts concerts and recitals (check the Web site).

Cathedral of the Holy Trinity: Barronstrand Street. ☎ *051-874-757. Admission: Free; pictorial guide to the cathedral €2. Open: Mon–Fri 11 a.m.–5 p.m.*

Christ Church Cathedral: Cathedral Square. ☎ *051-858-958.* www.christ churchwaterford.com. *Admission: Free; guided tours €2.50. Open: June–Sept Mon–Fri 9 a.m.–6 p.m., Sat 10 a.m.–4 p.m.; Oct Mon–Fri 10 a.m.–5 p.m., Sat 10 a.m.– 4 p.m.*

Waterford Treasures Museum
Waterford City

This well-done museum, housed in a gorgeously restored granary, presents artifacts that illustrate the history of Waterford from the arrival of the Vikings almost 1,000 years ago up to the present. Interactive audiovisual presentations, including a "ride" on a Viking ship, are engaging and entertaining, though maintenance has been lacking a bit lately. Many of the objects here, indeed, are treasures, from a sword given to Waterford's mayor by King Edward IV to an intricate 12th-century gold brooch, to a variety of Irish silver items. Allow one or two hours for your visit.

Merchant's Quay. ☎ *051-304-500. Admission: €7 adults; €5 seniors, students, and kids; free for kids 4 and under. Open: June–Aug Mon–Sat 9 a.m.–6 p.m., Sun 11 a.m.–6 p.m.; Sept–May Mon–Sat 10 a.m.–5 p.m., Sun 11 a.m.–5 p.m.*

Shopping in Waterford City

Pedestrianized **John Roberts Square** and **Arundel Square** are the focal points for shopping, with loads of stores. Those in the market for crystal may want to pay a visit to the store at the **House of Waterford Crystal** (reviewed earlier in this chapter) and to talented local craftsman **Sean Egan,** who works out of the Waterford Museum of Treasures, on Merchants Quay (☎ **051-304-500**). Do be aware that much of the inventory was not made in Ireland.

Nightlife in County Waterford

Waterford's **Theatre Royal,** on The Mall, between Bank Lane and Mall Lane (☎ 051-874-402; www.theatreroyal.ie), is a grand old theater with an interesting and varied program. To give you an idea of the range of offerings, performances from this summer season included a concert by *Crystal Swing,* Ireland's hottest country group (Ellen Degeneres is a huge fan!); an avant-garde play about a silent-film director; and a performance of *Aladdin* by local dance students. Be sure to leave time to view the beautiful artworks, on loan from the Waterford Municipal Art Collection.

Hitting the pubs in County Waterford

Jack Meade's
Ballycanavan

There are three bars on this site, which is a few miles south of Waterford City. You want the "Antique" bar, located under the stone bridge. This cozy, low-ceilinged pub was built in 1703 and hasn't changed much since. Locals sit at the bar to chat, and crackling fireplaces invite you to stay just a little bit longer. On summer Sundays, point yourself in the direction of the banner reading "BBQ," where you'll find excellent steaks, garlicky mushrooms, and other treats, all cheerfully served at picnic tables. A large beer garden features a family-friendly menu and a children's play area.

Take the R683 east of Waterford City to the little village of Halfway House. ☎ 051-850-950.

The Munster Bar
Waterford City

The Munster (also known as Fitzgerald's) is superbly decorated with Waterford Crystal, antique mirrors, and wood walls taken from the old Waterford toll bridge. This place is a favorite with Waterford locals and serves up some of the best pub food in the South, made with as many local and artisan ingredients as possible.

Baileys New Street. ☎ 051-874-656.

T. & H. Doolan's
Waterford City

The oldest tavern in Waterford, Doolan's has long been considered one of the best establishments in the area. The black-and-white 18th-century pub opens onto a pedestrian street in the center of town and has excellent traditional music sessions most nights, as well as warm fires, delicious pub grub, warm welcomes, and a cheerful crowd. Oh, and the stout is perfect as well. What does the T. & H. stand for? That's for you to find out.

32 Georges St. ☎ 051-841-504.

Fast Facts: County Waterford

Area Codes

County Waterford's area code is **051**.

Emergencies/Police

Dial ☎ **999** for all emergencies.

Genealogical Resources

Contact the Waterford Heritage Genealogical Centre, Jenkins Lane, off Barronstrand Street (near St. Patrick's Church), Waterford City (☎ 051-876-123).

Hospital

Waterford Regional Hospital is on Dunmore Road (R683), Waterford City (☎ 051-848-000).

Information

For visitor information, go to the tourist office in the Granary Building, which also houses the Waterford Treasure Museum, on Merchant's Quay in Waterford City (☎ 051-875-788).

Internet Access

Voyager Internet Cafe, 85 The Quay, Waterford City (☎ 051-843-843), has Internet access and printing capabilities.

Post Office

The main post office is at 100 The Quay, Waterford City (☎ 051-317-312).

Roaming in County Tipperary

County Tipperary and its towns are certainly not bustling in any way whatsoever, but that's what makes this place so special: It's the fantasy of a quiet, rolling, green Ireland come true. Because there are a limited number of attractions, one or two days should suffice here, unless you're looking for a long getaway retreat.

Getting to and around County Tipperary

If you're coming by car, take the M7 to the M8/N8 southwest from Dublin to Cashel and Cahir. From Cork, take the N8/M8 north to Cashel. From Limerick, take the N24 to Cahir and Tipperary. From Tipperary, you can take the N74 to Cashel. **Irish Rail** (☎ **1-850-366-222;** www.irishrail.ie) serves Tipperary, Cahir, and Carrick-on-Suir; and **Bus Éireann** (☎ **01-836-6111;** www.buseireann.ie) travels year-round to Tipperary, Cahir, Cashel, and Carrick-on-Suir, as well as other major towns in County Tipperary.

Spending the night in County Tipperary

Tir Na Nog Bed and Breakfast
$ **Cashel**

If you didn't have any friends in County Tipperary before you got here, you will when you leave. Your hosts, Joan and Tommy Moloney, are friendly, funny, kind, and incredibly helpful, and their house is warm and welcoming. Rooms are simple and bright, and the Irish breakfast is a

Quite a long way to Tipperary

While you're moseying around and hitting the pubs, you may hear the song "It's a Long Way to Tipperary," a happy yet plaintive tune about an Irishman in England missing his home and sweetheart. The song was composed by Englishman Jack Judge, whose grandfather was from Tipperary. Legend has it that the tune was born in an English music hall when a friend challenged Judge to come up with a new song during intermission and to perform it in the second act.

standout. The setting is another perk — peaceful countryside only a five- to ten-minute drive from the Rock of Cashel.

East of the town of Cashel on Dualla Road (R691). ☎ **062-61-350**. *Fax: 062-62-411. www.tirnanogbandb.com. Parking: Free on-site. Rack rates: €70–€75 double. MC, V.*

Dining locally in County Tipperary

Chez Hans
$$$$ Cashel   FRENCH

This is French cuisine at its finest, and it's served in a gorgeous Gothic-style structure that began life as a chapel. From the black-and-white uniformed waitstaff to the artistic presentation of the dishes, everything is professional and elegant. All the dishes are top-notch, especially the seafood offerings, such as seafood cassoulet and Dover sole with a brown butter sauce. Main courses are quite pricey, so I recommend the two-course (€29) and three-course (€35) fixed-price menus, which you can order between 6 and 8 p.m. Tuesday, Wednesday, and Thursday, and between 6 and 7 p.m. Friday. Right next door, Chez Hans's little brother **Café Hans** has you covered for lunch, with flavorful offerings from sandwiches and salads (the open-faced chicken sandwich with curry mayonnaise and cucumbers is a favorite) to hot dishes such as gnocchi with pancetta and spinach.

Moore Lane, off Dullin Road/Lady's Well Street. ☎ **062-61-177**. *Reservations highly recommended. Main courses: €25–€45; early-bird fixed-price menu €29–€35; regular fixed-price menu €60. MC, V. Open: Tues–Sat 6–10 p.m. Closed two weeks in Jan.*

Spearman's Bakery
$ Cashel   CAFE

If everyone could drop into Spearman's once in a while for a pot of tea and a slice of cake, we might come that much closer to world peace. The décor here is simple, but who's focusing on the tablecloths when there are such wonderful homemade sandwiches, panini, and pastries to focus on? I especially recommend the light-as-air pavlova. At press time, Spearman's was closed due to a devastating fire, but the owners were confident that they'd be up and running again soon; by the time you read this, they hope to be back in business.

97 Main St. ☎ *061-61-143. Main courses: €4–€8. Open: Mon–Fri 9 a.m.–5:45 p.m., Sat 9 a.m.–5 p.m.*

Exploring County Tipperary: The top attractions

The **Cashel Heritage Centre**, Main Street (☎ 062-62-511) has a model of the city of Cashel in 1640, accompanied by an audio commentary describing what you're seeing. Entrance is free and the center is open March through October daily 9:30 a.m. to 5:30 p.m., and November through February Monday through Friday 9:30 a.m. to 5:30 p.m. Tourist information is also available here.

The Rock of Cashel
Cashel

The word *rock* doesn't really do justice to this giant limestone outcropping crowned with spectacular medieval ruins.

The Rock of Cashel was the seat of the kings of Munster from about a.d. 360 to 1101 and was probably also a center of Druidic worship at this time. Legend places St. Patrick in Cashel in about a.d. 432 for his famous explanation of the Holy Trinity. He is said to have shown the pagans a shamrock to illustrate the relationship of the Father, Son, and Holy Ghost. Legend also has it that this is the place where St. Patrick converted the local king, King Aenghus, and baptized him. In the 11th century, Ireland's most important high king, Brian Boru, was crowned king of Ireland here.

At the summit of the rock, you can explore the shell of 13th-century St. Patrick's Cathedral, which was gutted in a fire set by Cromwell's troops. You also can visit the 28m-high (92-ft.) round tower, which is well-preserved. Don't miss the Romanesque Cormacs Chapel, located on a dramatic outcrop, which is decorated with carved beasts and human figures (currently open on guided tours only). The unique St. Patrick's Cross (a replica — the original is in the museum) has a carved figure of St. Patrick on one side and Jesus on the other. The roofless cathedral is the largest building on the Rock; it was never restored after Cromwell's men set fire to it (along with the villagers hiding inside). An interpretive center has great views for photos, contains stone carvings and silver religious artifacts, and offers a short audiovisual display. I highly recommend joining one of the tours, which really helps you to envision the life of the buildings. Allow 90 minutes for your visit.

Take the N8 from Dublin or the N74 east from Tipperary to Cashel. ☎ *062-61-437. Admission: €6 adults; €4 seniors, students, and kids. Open: Mid-Mar to mid-June and mid-Sept to mid-Oct daily 9 a.m.–5:30 p.m., mid-June to mid-Sept daily 9 a.m.–7 p.m., mid-Oct to mid-Mar 9 a.m.–4:30 p.m. (last admission 45 minutes before closing).*

Brú Ború Heritage Centre & Theatre
Cashel

Located next to the Rock of Cashel, the Heritage Centre's main attraction is its theater, which resonates with the sounds of well-played traditional Irish music Tuesday through Saturday nights during the summer. An exhibit relates the intriguing history of Irish music (the connection between this place and Brian Ború is that Ború was a harpist). In addition to the theater and exhibit, there is a restaurant and a comprehensive computerized genealogical research center. If you come for the show, which begins at 9 p.m., you also may want to book for the well-done four-course dinner. Allow 30 minutes if you're not seeing a show, a few hours if you are.

Take the N8 from Dublin or the N74 east from Tipperary to the Rock of Cashel. ☎ *062-61-122. Admission: Center free; evening performances €20 adults, €10 kids 11 and under; performances with dinner €50 adults, €25 kids 11 and under. Open: Mid-June to Aug Mon 9 a.m.–5 p.m., Tues–Sat 9 a.m.–11:30 p.m.; Sept to mid-June Mon–Fri 9 a.m.–5 p.m.*

Cahir Castle
Cahir

This was a defensive castle from the 13th to 15th centuries and is one of Ireland's largest and best preserved castles. It sits on an island in the middle of the River Suir. The walls and towers are in excellent condition, and the interior is fully restored. The 15-minute audiovisual presentation is interesting and covers the history of the castle and of the region's other historic sites. Engaging guided tours of the castle are available. Attention, movie buffs: The castle was used as the set for John Boorman's film *Excalibur.* Allow an hour for your visit.

Off the N8 from Cashel or Cork or the N24 from Tipperary. ☎ **052-744-1011.** *Admission: €3 adults, €2 seniors, €1 students and kids. Open: Mid-Mar to mid-June and Sept to mid-Oct daily 9:30 a.m.–5:30 p.m., mid-June to Aug daily 9 a.m.–6:30 p.m., mid-Oct to mid-Mar daily 9:30 a.m.–4:30 p.m.*

Holy Trinity Church and Medieval Walls
Fethard

Sitting along the River Clashawley, the small town of Fethard (pop. less than 1,000) claims the most complete circuit of medieval town walls in Ireland. Enter the walled inner city at the cast-iron gateway on Abbey Street, which opens into the pretty churchyard of Holy Trinity. The views of the heather-strewn valley are best from the top of one of the towers, and the castle-like church itself is a fine example of medieval construction. Allow an hour for your visit.

Take the small road connecting Cashel and Windgap east from Cashel, or go north off the N24 to Fethard. No phone. Admission: Free. Open: No official hours, but the Abbey Street gate of the town wall is often locked. During normal business hours, you can get a key from Whytes grocery store, just a few doors down on Main Street. And, if the church is closed and you want to enter, you can get a key from Dr. Stoke's office at the eastern end of Main Street.

Shopping in County Tipperary

A band of rebel craftsmen left Waterford Crystal in 1988 to start **Tipperary Crystal,** Carrick-on-Suir (☎ **051-640-543**), where they produce top-quality items, just as they did under their former label. These folks are so good that they're the only Irish crystal producer to supply prestigious Tiffany & Co. The visitor center/shop is located off the N24 in Ballynoran, next to Dovehill Castle.

Fast Facts: County Tipperary

Area Codes

County Tipperary's area codes are **052** and **062**.

Emergencies/Police

Dial ☎ **999** for all emergencies.

Genealogy Resources

Contact the Brú Ború Heritage Centre, Rock of Cashel (☎ 062-61-122; Fax: 062-62-700),

or the Tipperary Family History Research Centre, Excel Heritage Centre, Mitchell Street, Tipperary Town (☎ 062-80-555).

Information

A Tourist Office is open year-round at Cashel Heritage Centre, Main Street (☎ 062-62-511).

County Kilkenny

Polish up your old armor and rev up your trusty steed; Kilkenny City in County Kilkenny is one of the best-preserved medieval towns in Ireland, anchored by the majestic 12th-century Kilkenny Castle. The compact city overflows with tourists during the high season, but you can always get a breath of fresh air in the Kilkenny countryside. Save some space in your luggage, because Kilkenny County is one of the craft capitals of Ireland, with stores selling everything from one-of-a-kind gold bracelets to richly colored pottery.

Getting to County Kilkenny

By car, take the N7/M7 to the M9 south from Dublin and points north and east; from the M9, take the N10 into Kilkenny City. From Waterford, take the N9/N10 north; from Cork and the southwest, take the M8 east; and from Limerick and the west take the N24 to the M8. **Irish Rail** (☎ **1-850-366-222;** www.irishrail.ie) serves Kilkenny City and Thomastown. **Bus Éireann** (☎ **01-836-6111;** www.buseireann.ie) travels year-round to Kilkenny City and many other towns in County Kilkenny.

Kilkenny City

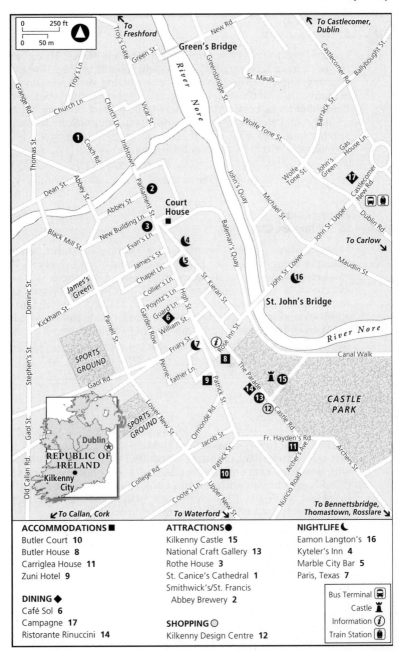

ACCOMMODATIONS ■
Butler Court **10**
Butler House **8**
Carriglea House **11**
Zuni Hotel **9**

DINING ◆
Café Sol **6**
Campagne **17**
Ristorante Rinuccini **14**

ATTRACTIONS ●
Kilkenny Castle **15**
National Craft Gallery **13**
Rothe House **3**
St. Canice's Cathedral **1**
Smithwick's/St. Francis
  Abbey Brewery **2**

SHOPPING ○
Kilkenny Design Centre **12**

NIGHTLIFE ☾
Eamon Langton's **16**
Kyteler's Inn **4**
Marble City Bar **5**
Paris, Texas **7**

Bus Terminal 🚌
Castle ♜
Information ⓘ
Train Station 🚆

Spending the night in County Kilkenny

Abbey House
$ **Thomastown**

Located right across the street from Jerpoint Abbey, this place feels far, far away from Kilkenny City's madding crowds. Abbey House is a stately country home nestled in a peaceful setting incorporating gardens, a stream, and medieval ruins. You get the feeling that owner Helen Blanchfield was born knowing how to be a great hostess. Helen is warm, friendly, and skilled at offering top-notch suggestions for exploring the surrounding area. Plus, she makes a mean Irish breakfast. The house is a few minutes' drive from artsy little Thomastown.

Southwest of Thomastown on the N9. ☎ **056-772-4166.** *www.abbeyhouse jerpoint.com. Parking: Free on-site. Rack rates: €84 double. MC, V.*

Butler Court
$$ **Kilkenny City**

I have a whole stack of accolades for Yvonne and John Dalton, who are hailed as some of the most helpful and genial hosts in Ireland. The Daltons can help you plan your itinerary in Kilkenny City (the center of the medieval town is a ten-minute walk away from the guesthouse) and the surrounding area. Rooms are modern, comfortable, cheerful, and warmly lit, and the continental breakfast (which you'll find in the room) makes a nice break from the usual Irish fry-up. Say hi to Bob the dog.

Patrick Street. ☎ **056-776-1178.** *Fax: 056-779-0767. www.butlercourt.com. Parking: Free in nearby garage. Rack rates: €80–€130 double. MC, V.*

Carriglea House
$ **Kilkenny City**

This B&B has everything: It's a five-minute walk from Kilkenny Castle and the center of town, it has one of the nicest and most helpful proprietors this side of the Atlantic, and it's a beautiful house. Bedrooms are furnished with antiques and are comfortable, airy, and homey. Owner Josephine O'Reilly greets you with tea and cookies in the lovely sitting room. The breakfast is one to write home about, with the usual offerings, plus homemade scones, omelets, and pancakes with maple syrup.

1 Archers Ave., off Castle Road (R700). ☎ **056-776-1629.** *www.carriglea kilkenny.com. Parking: Free on-site. Rack rates: €70–€76 double. Closed Nov–Feb.*

Butler House
$$$ **Kilkenny City**

Not many places could pull off modern abstract artwork alongside intricately decorated Georgian-era plasterwork ceilings, but ivy-covered Butler House does it with style. Built in the 1770s as part of the Kilkenny Castle

Estate, Butler House effortlessly blends the traditional elements of the building with contemporary design. Rooms are spacious, soothing, and airy; each is decorated uniquely, and many feature cream and deep orange colors. Bathrooms are sparkling and up-to-date. Try to book a room overlooking the splendid formal courtyard gardens, with a view of the castle, which is lit up at night. Unless you're someone who can sleep through anything, avoid rooms that face the noisy street. The thoughtful and friendly staff will happily recommend an area restaurant or attraction to suit you, and the excellent location puts you right next to the castle and Kilkenny Design Centre, and only a short walk from most other Kilkenny City attractions. Check the Web site for special offers and packages.

16 Patrick St. ☎ *056-772-2828. Fax: 056-776-5626.* www.butler.ie. *Parking: Free on-site. Rack rates: €120–€180 double. AE, MC, V.*

Zuni Hotel
$$ Kilkenny City

If you're overdosed on ornate, cluttered Victorian bedrooms, rush yourself to Zuni for an antidote of clean, Asian-inspired minimalist décor. The 13 guest rooms here are simply furnished in black, white, and deep red, with beds that make you want to sleep late. The location is fabulous — less than a five-minute walk to Kilkenny's main thoroughfare. The friendly, helpful staff goes above and beyond to make your stay pleasant — when I left my globe-trotting stuffed elephant in one of the rooms, they sent it out to me in Dublin the very next day. Hungry? The hotel's sleek restaurant, one of the most popular in Kilkenny, serves lively dishes, from rare ahi tuna with Japanese condiments to spiced duck breast with port wine *jus.* Packages featuring two nights B&B plus a dinner are often featured on the Web site.

26 Patrick St. ☎ *056-772-3999. Fax: 056-77-5-6400.* www.zuni.ie. *Parking: Free on-site. Rack rates: €80–€120 double. AE, MC, V.*

Dining locally in County Kilkenny

The Zuni Restaurant (see Zuni Hotel in the previous section) is another excellent choice in the city. Kyteler's Inn (see "Hitting the pubs in County Kilkenny," later in this chapter) is a good choice for pub grub. For lovely cafe meals, hit the Kilkenny Design Centre (see the listing under "Shopping in County Kilkenny," later in this chapter).

If you're lucky enough to be in Kilkenny City on a Thursday, swing by the **farmers market** in Market Yard, off John's Bridge Road. Sausages, smoked fish, fresh vegetables, baked goods, and other treats are all there for the buying, and the grounds at Kilkenny Castle are perfect for picnicking. The market is open from 9 a.m. to 2:30 p.m.

Campagne
$$$ Kilkenny City MODERN FRENCH/NEW IRISH

This stylish, cozy restaurant is going to have to build a little nook for all the awards that it's garnering. Each of the heavenly dishes is the result of the marriage between the finest local ingredients and impeccable French-style cooking skills. The ingredients and cooking are so solid that even a relatively straightforward dish such as the John Dory, served with braised fennel, clams, basil, and black olives, is a revelation. Though most dishes are based around meat or fish, the vegetarian dishes are just as classy as the rest of the menu; the current favorite is a fondue of wild mushrooms with asparagus and a poached egg. Remember to look up from your plate once in a while to take in artist Catherine Barron's vibrant, abstracted mural of country life. Early birds get the gourmet equivalent of the worm; you can order from the fixed-priced menus between 6 and 7 p.m. Wednesday through Friday, and 6 and 6:30 p.m. on Saturday.

John's Green, off Wolfe Tone Street. ☎ *056-777-2858. Reservations highly recommended. Main courses: €18–€29. MC, V. Open: Wed–Thurs and Sat 6–10 p.m., Fri 12:30–2:30 p.m. and 6–10 p.m., Sun 12:30–4:30 p.m. (and 6–10 p.m. June–Aug).*

Café Sol
$$ Kilkenny City NEW IRISH

This bright, cheerful, casual spot serves homemade food all day, starting with hearty and scrumptious soups, salads, and sandwiches for lunch, and segueing into a locally sourced, changing dinner menu containing sophisticated-yet-unfussy dishes such as roasted organic goose with stuffing. Several dishes are accented with influences from around the globe, including the Thai-style fishcakes, served with pickled cucumbers, preserved lemon, and a soy dressing. The early-bird specials (€23 for two courses, €27 for three courses) are actually all-evening-bird specials, served daily from 5:30 p.m. until closing. There's another location of this fabulous place on Low Street in Thomastown.

6 William St. ☎ *056-776-4987. Main courses: €15–€19. MC, V. Open: May–Sept and Dec Mon–Thurs 11:30 a.m.–9:30 p.m., Fri–Sat 11:30 a.m.–10p.m., Sun noon to 9 p.m.; Oct–Nov and Jan–Apr Wed–Thurs 11:30 a.m.–9:30 p.m., Fri–Sat 11:30 a.m.–10p.m., Sun noon to 9 p.m.*

Ristorante Rinuccini
$$–$$$ Kilkenny City ITALIAN

Two large Renaissance portraits dominate this restaurant's romantically lit dining room. Italianate mirrors, alabaster fixtures, and wooden wine racks add to the ambience. Service is formal, and guests dress up. The Italian fare is fresh and full of flavor, and the homemade pasta puts dried pasta to shame. The menu runs from traditional pasta dishes to fish and meat offerings such as scallops in a brandy-and-mustard cream sauce. I recommend the bruschetta baked with olive oil and garlic, and the well-spiced, generous meatballs served with pasta.

1 The Parade, opposite Kilkenny Castle. ☎ **056-776-1575.** *Reservations highly recommended. Main courses: Pastas €17–€19, fish and meat dishes €20–€30. AE, DC, MC, V. Open: Mon–Fri noon to 3 p.m. and 5–10 p.m., Sat noon to 3:30 p.m. and 5–10 p.m., Sun noon to 3:30 p.m. and 5–9:30 p.m.*

Exploring County Kilkenny

Pat Tynan leads terrific walking tours through the medieval streets of Kilkenny, relating the history of the area and some local lore. A highlight is the short visit to one of the city's old jail cells. This is a great way to get a sense of the layout of Kilkenny City and a grasp of this region's history. Tours leave from the Kilkenny Tourist Office, located in the Shee Alms House on Rose Street. Departure times are mid-March through October Monday through Saturday at 10:30 a.m. and 12:15, 3, and 4:30 p.m.; Sunday at 11:15 a.m. and 12:30 p.m. Pat will set up tours November through mid-March if you contact him in advance. Tours cost €6 adults, €5.50 seniors and students, free for kids 11 and under. Call ☎ **087-265-1745** to reserve your spot. In 2011, Tynan will begin to offer ghost tours, which promise to be excellent; call for details.

The top attractions

See "Shopping in County Kilkenny," later in this chapter, for information on visiting the workshops of the many high-quality artists and craftspeople who call County Kilkenny home.

Dunmore Cave
Ballyfoyle

An underground river formed these large limestone caverns, which contain some of the most beautiful calcite formations in Ireland. The cave was the site of a Viking massacre in a.d. 928, and Viking artifacts are on display. Guided tours lead you down into the Earth and across catwalks that traverse the caverns. Wear good shoes, and be prepared to climb many stairs up to the surface at the end of your tour. Allow about an hour for your visit.

Castlecomer Road, right off the N78 about 11km (7 miles) north of Kilkenny. ☎ *056-776-7726. Admission: €3 adults, €2 seniors, €1 students and kids. Open: Mar to mid-June and mid-Sept to Oct daily 9:30 a.m.–5 p.m. (last tours 4 p.m.); mid-June to mid-Sept daily 9:30 a.m.–6:30 p.m. (last tour 5 p.m.); Nov–Mar Wed–Sun 9:30 a.m.–5 p.m. (last tour 3 p.m.).*

Kilkenny Castle
Kilkenny City

This 12th-century medieval castle, which was remodeled in Victorian times, cuts quite the storybook-castle profile and is the principal attraction in the town of Kilkenny. Surrounded by 20 hectares (50 acres) of grounds, including rolling parklands, a riverside walk, and formal gardens, the castle was home to the distinguished Butler family from the late 14th century to the mid-20th century. The interior of the castle resembles a

Victorian manor house. Self-guided tours, which average about 45 minutes, take you through restored rooms, where you learn a bit about the Butler dynasty as you admire the 1830s-era furnishings. A highlight of the tour is a visit to the 45m-long (150-ft.) Long Gallery, which houses portraits of the Butler family and has a beamed ceiling gorgeously decorated with painted Celtic knots. The castle's Butler Gallery hosts modern-art exhibits. Be sure to stop by the play area if you have kids. Allow an hour for your visit, more if you want to explore the grounds at leisure.

The Parade. ☎ **056-770-4106.** *Admission: €6 adults, €4 seniors, €2.50 students and kids, free for kids 6 and under. Open: June–Aug daily 9 a.m.–5:30 p.m., Apr–May and Sept daily 9:30 a.m.–5:30 p.m., Mar daily 9:30 a.m.–5 p.m. Last entrance always 45 minute before closing.*

Jerpoint Abbey
Thomastown

This Cistercian abbey is considered one of the best-preserved monastic ruins in the country. It houses Celtic crosses and unique stone carvings of knights and dragons. There's a ton to see as you explore the graveyard and 15th-century cloister grounds. The small visitor center provides information about the history of the carvings and abbey. I highly recommend taking a tour if possible; one can almost always be arranged if you call in advance. Allow an hour for your visit.

Off the Waterford Road (N9), about 4km (2½ miles) southwest of Thomastown. ☎ **056-77-2-4623.** *Admission: €3 adults, €2 seniors, €1 kids. Open: June to mid-Sept daily 10 a.m.–6 p.m., Mar–May and mid-Sept to Oct daily 10 a.m.–5 p.m., Nov daily 10 a.m.–4 p.m. Closed Dec–Feb except for prearranged groups.*

National Craft Gallery
Kilkenny City

If you enjoy innovative crafts and design, pay a visit to this gallery, where changing themed exhibitions (from glass to metalwork) showcase the best new creations from Irish and international artists. Allow 30 minutes for your visit.

Castle Yard (across from Kilkenny Castle), Kilkenny City. ☎ **056-776-1804.** *www.ccoi.ie. Admission: Free. Open: Apr–Dec Tues–Sat 10 a.m.–5:30 p.m., Sun 11 a.m.–5:30 p.m.; Jan–Mar Tues–Sat 10 a.m.–5:30 p.m.*

Smithwick's/St. Francis Abbey Brewery Tour
Kilkenny City

The St. Francis Abbey Brewery has some strong beer-brewing mojo. Fourteenth-century monks brewed ale on this site, and ruby red Smithwick's Ale (pronounced *smith*-icks or *smit*-icks) has been brewed here for over 300 years. The excellent tour first visits the beautiful 13th-century abbey, and then takes in the working brewery, where you may get to meet the official Smithwick's tasters (Homer Simpson's ideal job?). A tutored tasting session and complimentary pint round out the experience. If you have time, check out the exhibit, which uses objects, pictures, and audio to relate the history of the brewery. Brewery tour guests must be 18 or older. Allow 90 minutes for your visit.

Parliament Street, Kilkenny, County Kilkenny. ☎ **056-779-6498.** *Admission: €10. You must be 18 or older to take the tour. Tours leave Tues–Sun at 12:30, 1, 3, and 3:30 p.m. Call to check on times, as these are subject to change depending on the time of year.*

St. Canice's Cathedral
Kilkenny City

This 13th-century church has a beautiful Gothic interior, restored after Cromwell stabled his horses here and destroyed many of the windows, tombs, and monuments in 1650. Check out the handsome stained-glass windows, the four colors of marble used on the floor (green from Connemara, red from Cork, gray from Tyrone, and black from Kilkenny), and the sculpted knight-and-lady effigies on the memorials that pepper the cathedral. The round tower on this site was built around a.d. 849, and you can climb the 167 ancient steps that lead to the top of the tower. This is one of only two round towers that members of the public are allowed to climb, it's worth some huffing and puffing for the phenomenal views. Allow 45 minutes for your visit.

Off St. Canice's Place and Coach Road. ☎ **056-776-4971.** *Admission: Cathedral €4 adults, €3 seniors and students, free for kids 11 and under; round tower €3 adults, €2.50 seniors, students, and kids 12 and over (kids 11 and under are not permitted to climb the tower). Cathedral open: June–Aug Mon–Sat 9 a.m.–6 p.m., Sun 2–6 p.m.; Apr–May and Sept Mon–Sat 10 a.m.–1 p.m. and 2–5 p.m., Sun 2–5 p.m.; Oct–Mar Mon–Sat 10 a.m.–1 p.m. and 2–4 p.m., Sun 2–4 p.m. Tower open: Apr–Sept most days 10 a.m.–10 p.m.; call to confirm.*

More cool things to see and do

✔ **Mount Juliet Golf Course,** on the Waterford-Dublin Road (N9), Thomastown (☎ **056-777-3078**): The par-72 Mount Juliet was host of the Irish Open from 1993 to 1995. The lakes and waterfalls make a picturesque backdrop to this course, called the Augusta of Europe and voted the best inland course in Ireland. Greens fees are €115 to €160.

✔ **Rothe House,** Parliament Street, Kilkenny, County Kilkenny (☎ **056-772-2893**): This example of a successful merchant's home circa 1594 features a small collection of Kilkenny artifacts, including paintings, fossils found on the site, and more. You'll also find a genealogical research center and a sweet little 17th-century-style medieval garden. Exciting restoration work is being done as this book goes to press, and by mid-2011 two more houses will be open to the public and exhibits will tell the stories of the Rothe family and 17th-century Kilkenny. Because of this work, the house will be closed between 2010 and roughly April 2011.

Admission to the house and garden is €5 adults; €4 seniors, students, and kids. For the gardens only, it's €2 adults; €1 seniors, students, and kids. It's open April through October Monday through Saturday from 10:30 a.m. to 5 p.m. and Sunday from 3 to 5 p.m., November through March Monday through Saturday from 10:30 a.m. to 4:30 p.m. Allow 30 minutes for your visit.

Shopping in County Kilkenny

County Kilkenny is a mecca for crafts and design, and the towns of Bennettsbridge (6km/4 miles south of Kilkenny City on the R700), Castlecomer (check out the Castlecomer Estate Yard; north of Kilkenny on the N78), and Thomastown (south of Kilkenny on the R700) are focal points. Here and in surrounding locations, you find the workshops of potters, woodworkers, glass blowers, and other craftspeople. If this interests you, be sure to pick up the *Kilkenny Craft Trail* brochure from the tourist office, which gives you details for and a map directing you to a number of workshops. You can find the same information and map (plus extra information on sales and special events) on the well-done Web site www.madeinkilkenny.ie.

One of the most popular workshops you'll find in Bennettsbridge is **Nicholas Mosse Pottery,** signposted off the R700 (☎ 056-772-7505; www.nicholasmosse.com). Expert potter Mosse uses the River Nore to produce the electricity to fire his pots, and each piece is hand-thrown. The earthenware clay pottery, sold as individual pieces or in sets, is hand-painted with charming country themes such as flowers, fruits and vegetables, and farm animals. The shop also sells Nicholas Mosse glassware and linens, plus furniture, jewelry, and other items from some of Ireland's best craftspeople. Be sure to check out the *seconds* (slightly imperfect works) upstairs for good deals. Also in Bennettsbridge, on Kilkenny Road, check out **Moth to a Flame** (☎ 056-772-7826; www.mothtoaflame.ie), which creates lovely candles, including a line of candles that look like polished river rocks.

In Stoneyford, **Jerpoint Glass** (☎ 056-772-4350; www.jerpointglass.com) creates stunning glass pieces with dashes of vivid color. You can watch glass pieces being blown at the workshop and then browse the selection, from vases to candlesticks.

To the north of Kilkenny Town, Castlecomer is home to several artists and craftspeople, including **Maeve Coulter** (☎ 056-444-0582; www.maevecoulter.com), who creates richly colored fabric pieces as well as prints.

In Kilkenny Town, **Kilkenny Design Centre,** Castle Yard, Kilkenny (☎ 056-77-22-118), stocks a large selection of Ireland's best handcrafted items, including pottery, linen, jewelry, glassware, clothing, fine art, and leatherwork. The excellent cafe provides a respite from deciding what you want to buy. Be sure to visit the **craft workshops** in the converted stables behind the Design Centre, where you can watch craftspeople at work as you browse.

Hitting the pubs in County Kilkenny

For a side of traditional Irish music with your pub experience, book a **Kilkenny Traditional Irish Music Trail** tour (☎ **085-165-8243**; www. kilkennytradtrail.net). You'll be introduced to the music and instruments of Ireland as you pub-hop with Trish and Joe, who are kind, fun, and funny, and also happen to be great traditional musicians. Tours are offered Friday and Saturday nights in June, August, and September, and Thursday, Friday, and Saturday nights in July. The price is €12 adults, €10 students, free for kids 11 and under.

Eamon Langton's
Kilkenny City

This place is a deserved four-time winner of the National Pub of the Year award. It has all the hallmarks of a classic Victorian pub, from a beautiful fireplace to globe lamps. Check out the garden area in back, if the weather permits.

69 John St. ☎ **056-776-5133.**

Kyteler's Inn
Kilkenny City

This coaching inn, established in 1324, is named for Dame Alice Kyteler, the inn's original owner. Kyteler, who buried four husbands, was accused of witchcraft. She fled to England, but her maid was not so lucky — she was burned at the stake. The cozy upstairs bar buzzes with conversation and live music. Downstairs, enjoy some good pub grub in a medieval cellar featuring the original stone walls and columns. You may be graced by the presence of Ms. Kyteler herself — she's rumored to haunt the place, so make sure she doesn't slip anything into your stew.

27 St. Kieran's St. ☎ **056-772-1064.**

Marble City Bar
Kilkenny City

Even if you don't stop for a drink at this friendly, welcoming pub, check out the gorgeous facade of wrought iron, brass, and carved wood, all lit by gas lamps.

In the Langton House Hotel, 67 John St. ☎ **056-776-5133.**

Paris, Texas
Kilkenny City

Round up your friends, and head on down to this spacious saloon straight out of the American West. This place is always hopping and often hosts live music.

92 High St. ☎ **056-776-1822.**

Fast Facts: County Kilkenny

Area Codes
County Kilkenny's area code is **056**.

Emergencies/Police
Dial ☎ **999** for all emergencies.

Genealogy Resources
Contact the Family History Centre at the Rothe House, 16 Parliament St., Kilkenny City (☎ 056-772-2893).

Information
The Tourist Information Office is located in the Shee Alms House, Rose Street (☎ 056-775-1500; www.kilkennytourism.ie).

Internet
You can access the Internet at WEB-Talk, Rose Inn Street, Kilkenny (no phone).

Post Office
The Kilkenny City Post Office is at 73 High St. (☎ 056-776-2327).

Part IV
Counties Cork and Kerry

The 5th Wave   By Rich Tennant

"Let me ask you a question. Are you planning to kiss the Blarney Stone, or ask for its hand in marriage?"

In this part . . .

Cork City (Chapter 15) is a happening big city with the soul of a small town. It has a nice selection of restaurants, an interesting arts scene, proximity to many attractions, and some very friendly locals.

The south and southwest counties certainly have their share of natural beauty, with the gorgeous beaches, seascapes, and hills of West Cork (Chapter 15); the peaceful woodlands and lakes of Killarney National Park (Chapter 16); and the stunning mountains, cliffs, beaches, and sea views of the popular Ring of Kerry and Dingle Peninsula (both in Chapter 16).

Chapter 15

County Cork

County Cork (see the nearby map) occupies the eastern half of Southern Ireland and encompasses young, artsy Cork City; one of Ireland's loveliest golf courses (the Old Head of Kinsale); several historical sights; a number of cute and artsy small towns; and loads of gorgeous, uncrowded countryside to explore by car, foot, or bicycle.

Many travelers breeze into Cork City, look around, stop at Blarney Castle on the way out for a quick smooch, and then head right for Killarney. Big mistake. The city itself is worth a visit, and the stretch of coast from the lovely seaside town of Kinsale to the tip of the Beara Peninsula is just too beautiful to pass up. West Cork offers splendid views of craggy shoreline, seascapes, mountains, and hedges or stone walls dividing the landscape into irregular little farm fields. Artsy little towns and a thriving local food scene are other major draws. I highly recommend this area to people seeking postcard-style Irish scenery away from the crowds (the only exception being Kinsale, which is packed with people during the summer).

East Cork is a lush, gently rolling land with some great attractions, including Fota Wildlife Park. The star of East Cork is the pretty harbor town of Cobh. Stick around a while.

Cork City and East County Cork

The first thing you notice about Corkonians is that they have a fierce pride in their city, which they've nicknamed "The People's Republic of Cork." And they should be proud of Cork; it manages to have a small-town, friendly feel while offering many things that a large city should,

County Cork

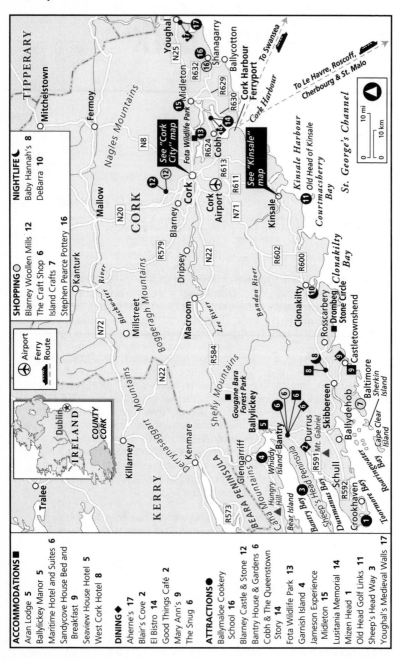

ACCOMMODATIONS ■
Aran Lodge **5**
Ballylickey Manor **5**
Maritime Hotel and Suites **6**
Sandycove House Bed and Breakfast **9**
Seaview House Hotel **5**
West Cork Hotel **8**

DINING ◆
Aherne's **17**
Blair's Cove **2**
El Bistro **14**
Good Things Café **2**
Mary Ann's **9**
The Snug **6**

ATTRACTIONS ●
Ballymaloe Cookery School **16**
Blarney Castle & Stone **12**
Bantry House & Gardens **6**
Cobh & The Queenstown Story **14**
Fota Wildlife Park **13**
Garnish Island **4**
Jameson Experience Midleton **15**
Lusitania Memorial **14**
Mizen Head **1**
Old Head Golf Links **11**
Sheep's Head Way **3**
Youghal's Medieval Walls **17**

SHOPPING ○
Blarney Woollen Mills **12**
The Craft Shop **6**
Island Crafts **7**
Stephen Pearce Pottery **16**

NIGHTLIFE 🍸
Baby Hannah's **8**
DeBarra **10**

Airport ✈
Ferry Route

TIPPERARY
Mitchelstown
Fermoy
Mallow
Kanturk
Millstreet
Macroom
Dripsey
Blarney
CORK
Cork
Cork Airport
Kinsale
Clonakilty
Skibbereen
Ballydehob
Castletownshend
Rosscarbery
Drombeg Stone Circle
Bantry
Durrus
Ballylickey
Glengarriff
Schull
Crookhaven
Dunmanus Bay
Roaringwater Bay
Cape Clear Island
Sherkin Island
Baltimore
Clonakilty Bay
Courtmacsherry Bay
Kinsale Harbour
Old Head of Kinsale
Cork Harbour
Cork Harbour Ferryport
Midleton
Youghal
Shanagarry
Ballycotton

Nagles Mountains
Boggeragh Mountains
Derrynasaggart Mountains
Shehy Mountains
Caha Mountains
Mt. Gabriel
Hungry Hill
Whiddy Island
Bear Island

KERRY
BEARA PENINSULA
Sheep's Head Peninsula
Tralee
Killarney
Kenmare

Gougane Bara Forest Park

Blackwater River
Bandon River
Lee River

St. George's Channel

To Le Havre, Roscoff, Cherbourg & St. Malo
To Swansea

See "Cork City" map
See "Kinsale" map
Fota Wildlife Park

COUNTY CORK
Dublin
IRELAND

N25 N8 N20 N22 N71 N72 N73
R579 R584 R591 R592 R573 R600 R602 R611 R613 R624 R629 R630 R632

10 mi
10 km

including a lively arts scene and quite a few great restaurants. You can take in the major attractions in the city itself in a day or two, but Cork City also makes a great urban base for visiting the surrounding areas. East County Cork, home to popular attractions such as the Fota Wildlife Park, the Blarney Stone and Castle, and the sweet seaside town of Cobh, is easily accessible from Cork City.

The city hosts several large festivals including the popular **Guinness Cork Jazz Festival** (www.guinnessjazzfestival.com) in October.

Getting to Cork City and East County Cork

To get to **Cork City** by car from other large cities, take the N25 (which turns into the N8) west from Waterford, the N20 south from Limerick, or the N22 southeast from Kilkenny. The towns of east County Cork are located off the N25, except Blarney, which is north of Cork City on the N20. If you're driving west from Cobh or east to Cobh from West Cork, you can avoid the snarls of traffic in Cork City by taking the **Cross River Ferry** (☎ 021-481-1485) between Carrigaloe, just outside of Cobh on the east side of the bay and Glenbrook, in Monkstown (about 15km/9 miles southeast of Cork City), on the west side. The scenic trip takes only about five minutes and runs year-round, 7 a.m. to 10 p.m. daily. The cost is €7 round-trip, €4.50 one-way.

Irish Rail (☎ 1-850-366-222; www.irishrail.ie) serves Cork City, Fota, and Cobh regularly; **Bus Éireann** (☎ 01-836-6111; www.bus eireann.ie) serves Cork City, Cobh, Youghal, and other cities throughout County Cork daily. The main bus depot in Cork City is located at Parnell Place, in the middle of the city, and the **Cork Kent** rail station is located on Lower Glanmire Road, about a 20-minute walk northeast of the city center.

Getting around Cork City

The compact downtown area of Cork City surrounds **St. Patrick's Street,** the city's hub for shopping, and **Oliver Plunkett Street,** a great place to begin a Cork City pub crawl.

Cork City is best seen on foot for several reasons: First of all, many of the main downtown areas are open exclusively to pedestrian traffic, and parking nearby can by hard to come by. In addition, the city can be confusing to drive in because the River Lee forks and winds through the city, creating two sets of *quays* (wharves or piers). One-way streets and frequently changing street names are the sour cherries on top. You get the idea — park your car at your hotel or B&B and walk in to explore the compact city center.

Parking in many parts of Cork City runs on the Pay-and-Display system. You purchase time at a Pay-and-Display machine (located along the street), and then display the receipt inside your windshield. Other parts of Cork City still use the disc system, in which you purchase a parking

Cork City

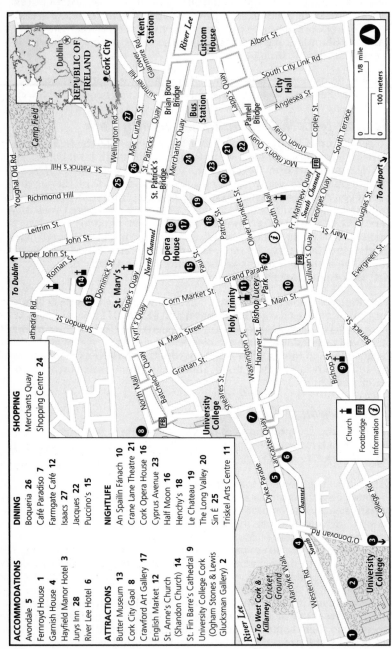

ACCOMMODATIONS
Avondale **5**
Fernroyd House **1**
Garnish House **4**
Hayfield Manor Hotel **3**
Jurys Inn **28**
River Lee Hotel **6**

ATTRACTIONS
Butter Museum **13**
Cork City Gaol **8**
Crawford Art Gallery **17**
English Market **12**
St. Anne's Church
(Shandon Church) **14**
St. Fin Barre's Cathedral **9**
University College Cork
(Ogham Stones & Lewis
Glucksman Gallery) **2**

DINING
Boqueria **26**
Café Paradiso **7**
Farmgate Café **12**
Isaacs **27**
Jacques **22**
Puccino's **15**

NIGHTLIFE
An Spailin Fánach **10**
Crane Lane Theatre **21**
Cork Opera House **16**
Cyprus Avenue **23**
Half Moon **16**
Henchy's **18**
Le Chateau **19**
The Long Valley **20**
Sin É **25**
Triskel Arts Centre **11**

SHOPPING
Merchants Quay
Shopping Centre **24**

Church ✝
Footbridge FB
Information ℹ

disc at a shop (look for the signs) and then display it in your windshield. If you're staying in the city center, you can make use of one of the city's eight multistory parking garages. Some central ones are on Lavitt's Quay (near Paul Lane), North Main Street (near Bachelor's Quay), and off Grand Parade.

After all those warnings about driving in Cork City, I will tell you that it's best to have a car for getting to and from attractions and towns in east County Cork on your own schedule. All the major car-rental companies have offices at Cork Airport (see p. 68 for car-rental contact information).

Bus Éireann (☎ **01-836-6111;** www.buseireann.ie) operates local service from Cork City to neighboring towns such as Blarney, Cobh, and Fota. Most buses leave from the Parnell Place Bus Station in the center of the city. If you need a taxi in Cork City, call **Taxi Co-Op** (☎ **021-427-2222**). If you need a taxi in the outlying towns, call **Blarney Castle Cabs** (☎ **021-438-2222**) in Blarney or **Harbour Cabs** (☎ **021-481-4444**) in Cobh.

Spending the night in Cork City and East County Cork

Avondale
$ **Cork City**

Within five minutes of setting down your bags in your impeccably clean room, you'll feel as if you've lived here for years. Your hosts, Dolores and John, couldn't be nicer and more welcoming, and the house feels peaceful even though you're only a five-minute walk from the boisterous city center. Rooms are uncluttered, with soothing peach and yellow walls, bright contemporary art, cloud-white duvets, and pine furnishings, and the breakfast room offers views of the pretty backyard. The civilized 11:30 a.m. checkout time means that you can sleep in after a lively night at one of Cork City's many pubs. The campus of University College Cork, across the road, offers many picturesque spots for picnics. If Avondale is booked, Fernroyd House is another excellent option.

On Western Road, across from University College Cork. ☎ *021-490-5874.* www.avondalebb.com. *Parking: On the street; free at night, paid during the day. Rack rates: €80 double. MC, V.*

Fernroyd House
$$ **Cork City**

Located on a quiet street about a ten-minute walk from the center of the city, Fernroyd House offers rooms that are simplicity itself, with pretty white quilts on the beds and bright little reading lamps. Hosts Avril and Tony Lyons are helpful and welcoming, going out of their way to make you feel taken care of and offering great advice about what to see and do in Cork. Their breakfasts (with many choices, including Avril's homemade scones) will get you right out of bed in the morning.

4 Donovan O'Rossa Rd., off Western Road. ☎ *021-427-1460.* `www.fernroyd house.com`. *Parking: Free on-site. Rack rates: €80–€85 double. MC, V.*

Garnish House
$$ Cork City

This townhouse B&B just may offer the best breakfast in the city, with a laden buffet table and a restaurant-worthy menu of choices, from cinnamon toast with spiced grapefruit wedges to a fresh salmon and dill tart to the beloved porridge with fresh cream and Baileys liquor. The smallish rooms are sweet and soothing, with brightly painted walls, beds that are an ocean of white sheets and stylish comforters, and a bowl filled with fresh fruit. The B&B is about a 20-minute walk from the heart of Cork City. Check out the beautiful wood-framed photos of Ireland that decorate the house.

Western Road. ☎ *021-427-5111. Fax: 021-427-3872.* `www.garnish.ie`. *Parking: Free on-site. Rack rates: €88–€106 double. AE, MC, V.*

Hayfield Manor Hotel
$$$ Cork City

Every time this hotel comes up in conversation, former guests say the same thing: The staff here is exceptional, willing to help with anything and everything. That's just one more item to add to the ever-growing list of reasons to stay at the Hayfield Manor. Others include the spacious rooms, outfitted with classic printed fabrics and elegant Victorian-style furniture, the old-world library, the lovely spa, and the idyllic afternoon tea. With its tree-lined avenue, you might imagine that this place is located far out in the countryside, but it's actually just a 20- to 25-minute walk from the center of Cork City. Kids are treated as royally as adults here.

Perrott Avenue, off College Road. ☎ *021-484-5900.* `www.hayfieldmanor.ie`. *Parking: Free on-site. Rack rates: €159–€209 double. AE, MC. V.*

Jurys Inn
$$ Cork City

The service is good, and the modern rooms are comfortable, but there's nothing exceptional about Jurys Inn — except the low price and the excellent location, within a few minutes of the city center. A flat rate for up to three adults or two adults and two children per room makes this a good deal for traveling families. Ask for a room away from the street, if you're a light sleeper. Also, if you have a car, be aware that there is little on-site parking, and that parking in the lot near the hotel can become quite expensive.

Anderson's Quay between the Custom House and bus station at the mouth of the north channel. ☎ *021-494-3000. Fax: 021-427-6144.* `www.jurysinns.com`. *Parking: Free on-site (in a very small lot), €8 overnight or €2 per hour during the day in nearby lot. Rack rates: €79–€100 up to three adults or a family of four. Breakfast is not included in all room rates. AE, MC, V.*

River Lee Hotel
$$–$$$ Cork City

Located about a five-minute walk from the city, the large River Lee Hotel feels like a stylish business hotel. Rooms, decorated in muted colors, are spotless and uncluttered, and feature such perks as pillow-top mattresses, under-floor heating in the bathroom, and comprehensive entertainment systems (hide that PlayStation from your kids — or spouse). The Spa is lovely, as is the inviting sitting area, with its soaring ceilings, grand polished stone fireplace, velvety plum-colored couches, and pretty orchids. Service is professional, though not particularly warm.

Western Road, near the University College Cork campus. ☎ **021-425-2700.** *www. doylecollection.com. Parking: Free on-site. Rack rates: €88–€160 double. Breakfast is not included in all room rates. AE, DC, MC, V.*

Dining in Cork City and East County Cork

Also see the English Market (p. 249), which offers a dizzying array of breads, cheeses, fish, meats, baked goods, and more, from which you can create a first-class picnic; and the Long Valley (p. 254), which serves up solid soups and sandwiches for lunch in an atmospheric pub. In addition, the cafe at the Crawford Art Gallery (p. 249) is excellent. If you're in the mood for tapas and wine, head to **Boqueria,** 6 Bridge St. (☎ **021-455-9049**).

Aherne's
$$$$ Youghal   SEAFOOD

This port-town restaurant, with garnet walls and dark wood furnishings, has a reputation for serving some of the freshest and tastiest seafood in this part of the country. New Englanders may never order cod back home again after having it at Aherne's, and the seafood chowder is unmatched. If you're really hungry, go for the award-winning fish and shellfish platter. If you don't want to shell out (pun intended) for the restaurant, the pub food, ranging from stuffed sandwiches to smoked salmon platters, is also a great choice. Aherne's also has nice, simple rooms for rent upstairs.

163 N. Main St. Take the main road to Waterford (N25), and then turn off onto Main Street. ☎ **024-92-424.** *www.ahernes.net. Main courses: €28–€32. AE, MC, V. Open: Bar food daily noon to 10 p.m., restaurant daily 6–9:30 p.m.*

Cafe Paradiso
$$$ Cork City   VEGETARIAN

When Cafe Paradiso opened in 1993, it was one of the first restaurants in Ireland to offer upscale vegetarian cooking. The chefs seek out the best in local cheeses and vegetables, and use a variety of cooking techniques and international influences to create some stunning dishes. Though a few dishes can be a bit bland, you won't even miss meat as you dig in to such gems as the sweet chili-glazed pan-fried tofu with Asian greens in a coconut and lemongrass broth, served with soba noodles, or the pan-fried artichokes with herb breadcrumbs, lemon cream, spinach, caramelized shallots, and sheep-cheese ravioli. The excellent staff manages to create a relaxed atmosphere in a stylish setting of dark wood floors and brushed steel bistro tables. If you feel like climbing into bed after your meal, reserve one of the restaurant's stylish yet homey rooms upstairs.

16 Lancaster Quay. From the city center, head down Washington Street, which turns into Western Road. ☎ *021-427-7939. Reservations recommended. Main courses: €23–€25; fixed-price menus (5:30–7 p.m.) €24 for two courses, €31 for three courses. MC, V. Open: Tues–Thurs 5:30–10 p.m., Fri and Sat noon to 3 p.m. and 5:30–10 p.m.*

El Bistro
$ Cobh CAFE

Looking for a cute place to pop into as you explore Cobh? Check out El Bistro, a bright spot that's always buzzing with families and groups of friends. Food is simple and delicious, from pasta to open-faced sandwiches. I highly recommend the Thai chicken curry.

4 East Beach St. ☎ *021-481-6935. Main courses: €7–€12. No credit cards. Open: Daily 8:30 a.m.–6 p.m.*

Farmgate Café
$$ Cork City IRISH

This buzzy cafe is located on an indoor balcony overlooking the bustling English Market (reviewed under "The top attractions"). You can choose to dine in the dining room with table service or on the balcony where food is served cafeteria-style. Both areas of the cafe serve up excellent traditional Irish dishes plus some contemporary plates, and everything is made with the freshest local ingredients from the market below. This is the place to try *tripe* (the stomach lining of a sheep) and *drisheen* (blood sausages), specialties specific to County Cork. The Irish lamb stew is wonderful, as are the lighter dishes, such as salads and the vegetarian soup of the day. Farmgate is a great place to get a taste of Cork food, and to get a taste of Corkonians themselves, as locals frequent the place.

Upstairs in the English Market (enter on Princes Street or Grand Parade). ☎ *021-427-8134. Main courses: €9–€15. MC, V. Open: Mon–Fri 9–10:30 a.m. and noon to 4 p.m., Sat 9–11 a.m. and noon to 4 p.m.*

Isaacs
$$$ Cork City

An informal restaurant that's trendy but doesn't act like it, Isaacs is an amalgam of contemporary and traditional — much like Cork City itself. Located in a converted Victorian warehouse with a vaulted ceiling, Isaacs has redbrick walls adorned with local art pieces, as well as a chatty evening crowd. The unfussy dishes, from fish cakes with tartar sauce and a green salad to the selection of vegetarian Indian curries, use local seasonal produce and are reliably delicious. The three-course early-bird menu, at €25 (served Thurs–Sat) is a nice deal.

Farm to table: Cooking courses and demonstrations at Ballymaloe Cookery School

Many of the best chefs in Ireland today can trace their culinary roots back to **Ballymaloe Cookery School** (☎ 021-464-6785; www.cookingisfun.ie) located on a 100-acre organic farm. The school was founded by the legendary Darina Allen, who has been one of Ireland's most influential proponents of local, sustainable farming and cooking for over 25 years. Most of the courses at the cooking school are one to two days long, with offerings ranging from "Learn How to Cook Two Fool-proof Dinner Parties in a Day" to "How to Make Homemade Butter, Yogurt, and Cheeses." For those who want to spend more time here, there are five-day courses and a 12-week certificate program. If a cooking class is not in the cards for you, consider making a reservation for the frequent afternoon demonstrations, where you can watch the chefs prepare ten dishes and then sample each dish. You'll also get to take the recipes home. Lured in by the sights, smells, and tastes? You can stay the night in the peaceful Ballymaloe House.

48 McCurtain St. Above the north channel; take a right off of St. Patrick's Hill. ☎ *021-450-3805. Main courses: €17–€27. AE, DC, MC, V. Open: Mon–Sat 12:30–2:30 p.m. and 6–10 p.m., Sun 6–9:30p.m.*

Jacques
$$$ Cork City   CONTINENTAL/NEW IRISH

Twenty-five years in business gives you great connections with the best local suppliers, and Jacques does a beautiful job of treating the fresh seafood, meats, cheese, and vegetables that they receive with respect. The menu changes daily based on the fresh ingredients that beckon the chef that day. My subtly herb-crusted lamb, served with a mint reduction and Moroccan-spiced carrots, was heavenly, as was my husband's cannelloni with spinach, tomatoes, and Irish cheese, and we battled over the last of the lemon, polenta, and almond cake with cream and gingered rhubarb. The choices on the expertly curated wine list are not inexpensive, but they're worth the money. The décor, with a long mirror, muted heather walls, and focused spot lighting, looks a little late-'90s-business-dinner-ish, but you'll barely be paying attention as you dig into the excellent dishes. The three-course fixed-price menu (served Thurs–Sat before 7 p.m. and after 9:30 p.m.) is a steal at €25.

Phoenix Street (a little side street off South Mall between Pembroke and Smith streets). ☎ *021-427-7387. Main courses: €22–€27. AE, MC. V. Open: Mon–Sat 6–10 p.m.*

Puccino's
$ Cork City   CAFE

It was a dark and stormy day. I had just wandered all over the city, and was craving some *banoffee pie* (that wonderful symphony of bananas and toffee on a crumbled cookie crust). And lo and behold, I discovered this casual cafe, home to not only an excellent banoffee pie, but other luscious light dishes including salads, pizzas, baked potatoes, pastas, soups, and an assortment of outstanding breakfast dishes. The cafe also offers a tapas menu, featuring such tasty bites as roasted peppers with feta, garlic mussels, and spicy chorizo. The atmosphere is relaxed, with small groups of friends chatting at the burnished copper tables, and newspaper-readers relaxing on the comfy couches.

9 Paul St. ☎ *021-436-6001. Main courses: €6–€11. MC, V. Open: Mon–Sat 9 a.m.–5 p.m., Sun 9 a.m.–4 p.m.*

Exploring Cork City and East County Cork

Bus Éireann (☎ 01-836-6111; www.buseireann.ie) offers half-day tours of Cork City and Blarney (including the famed castle) on an open-top bus. You have the option of catching a later bus, if you'd like to spend more time in Blarney. Tours leave from and arrive at Parnell Place in Cork City. They depart daily from June through August at 10:10 a.m. and return at 1 p.m. Prices are €11 adults, €9.90 seniors and students, €7.20 kids. Tours won't take place if it's very rainy.

The **Cork City Hop-On/Hop-Off Bus Tour** (☎ 021-430-9090) is a terrific way to see Cork City's attractions. The company operates double-decker buses that visit most of Cork City's major sights. You can get on and off the bus at your leisure, joining the next bus after you've finished exploring each stop. The bus runs from 9:30 a.m. to 5 p.m. and picks up every 45 minutes in May, June, September, and October; every 30 minutes in July and August; and every 90 minutes in March, April, and November. You can board at any of the stops, though the "official" starting place is on Grand Parade, across from the Tourist Office. Prices are €14 adults, €12 seniors and students, €5 kids 5 to 14. You can purchase your ticket at the Tourist Office, from the bus driver, or online at www.corkcity tour.com.

Cork Historic Walking Tours (☎ 085-100-7300; www.walkcork.ie) offers great walking tours that tell the story of Cork City. You can choose a tour that covers the history of the early city (from the city's founding to the end of the medieval period) or one that focuses on the city's history from 1690 to the present. Currently, the tours leave April through September from the Tourism Office on Grand Parade. Tours take place Monday through Friday at 10 a.m. (early history of the city) and 2 p.m. (history of the city from 1690 to the present). Tours cost €10 adults; €5 seniors, students, and kids 14 and younger. Call to confirm times and meeting place, as they change each year.

This is no blarney: The origins of blarney

Wondering just where the old "gift of gab" lore stems from? Well, we've all heard some blarney in our lives, but the person who apparently did it best (and first) was the charismatic Lord of Blarney, Cormac McDermot McCarthy. When Queen Elizabeth asked all Irish lords to effectively sign over their land to the crown, McCarthy was determined not to. For every demand the queen made, he responded with eloquent letters that claimed undying loyalty and dripped with flattery, although he had no intention of giving in to her demands. After receiving yet another crafty letter, the queen, exasperated, proclaimed, "This is all Blarney. What he says, he rarely means." So today, anyone who uses a lot of eloquence and empty phrases and deceives or exaggerates is said to be talking *blarney*.

 If you want to know more about Cobh's maritime history, book one of Michael Martin's superb **Titanic Trail Walking Tours** (☎ 021-481-5211), which will take you to locations connected to the doomed ship, as well as sites linked with the three million emigrants who left from Cobh. Tours leave from the Commodore Hotel, in Cobh, at 11 a.m. and 2 p.m. daily from June through August, and at 11 a.m. in September and May (call for times during the rest of the year). Tours cost €9.50 adults, €4.75 kids 11 and younger. Martin has also started to run fun ghost tours of Cobh (call for reservations) for €15.

The top attractions

Blarney Castle and Stone
Blarney

To kiss or not to kiss, that is the question. Yes, it's touristy, but there is a satisfaction that comes from kissing a hunk of rock that's famous across the world, and there is a fun camaraderie with your fellow smoochers as you wait in line. The Blarney Stone, located at the top of the ruins of a 15th-century castle (after a fair amount of climbing up narrow, twisting stairways), allegedly imparts eloquence, or "the gift of gab," to those daring enough to contort upside down from the parapet walk and kiss it. There are various theories as to the origin of the stone's significance and most are biblical; some say that it was Jacob's Pillow, brought to Ireland by the prophet Jeremiah, while others claim that David hid from Saul behind the rock and that it was brought to Ireland during the Crusades. It's a real feat to lean back into nothing and tip your head to kiss the smooth rock — it may even be a little frightening to people afraid of heights (or germs). It's customary to tip the guy who holds your legs, and you may want to give it over *before* he holds you over the faraway courtyard. Blarney is one of the most fortified castles in Ireland — its walls are 5.5m (18 ft.) thick in some parts. You can climb through the ruins of the castle, exploring various rooms (including the "murder holes") along the way. Don't leave Blarney without seeing the castle grounds, with their pretty gardens. If you have no intention of puckering up and have explored (or will explore) other castle ruins, a trip out here is probably not worth the time. Allow two hours for your visit.

Off the N20 north of Cork City, heading toward Limerick. ☎ *021-438-5252. Bus: You can catch a Bus Éireann round-trip to the castle from the bus station in Cork, at Parnell Place. Admission: €10 adults, €8 seniors and students, €3.50 kids 8–14. Open: June–Aug Mon–Sat 9 a.m.–7 p.m., Sun 9 a.m.–5:30 p.m.; May and Sept Mon–Sat 9 a.m.–6:30 p.m., Sun 9:30 a.m.–5:30 p.m.; Oct–Apr Mon–Sat 9 a.m. to dusk, Sun 9 a.m. to dusk.*

Cobh and The Queenstown Story at Cobh Heritage Centre
Cobh

Cobh (pronounced *cove*) is a lovely seaside town, and a ramble by the harbor and through the streets, with their vividly colored buildings, is a great way to spend a morning or afternoon.

Cobh Harbor was the main point of departure for thousands of starving Irish on their way to North America during the Great Famine and for convicts being sent to Australia. It was also the last port of call for the ill-fated *Titanic* and *Lusitania*. The heritage center, located in a beautiful restored railway station, uses objects, dioramas, text, and sound to relate the stories of these ships and their connections with Cobh. The highlight is the life-size, walk-through replica of the inside of a ship full of convicts bound for Australia. You can almost feel the waves battering the hull. This whole exhibit will be particularly interesting to those whose relatives emigrated through Cobh. Allow an hour for your visit.

Cobh Railway Station. ☎ *021-481-3591. Admission: €7.10 adults, €6 seniors and students, €4 kids. Open: June–Aug Mon–Fri 9:30 a.m.–6 p.m. (last admission 5 p.m.), Sat 9:30 a.m.–6 p.m. (last admission 5 p.m.), Sun 11 a.m.–6 p.m. (last admission 5 p.m.); Sept–May Mon–Sat 9:30 a.m.–5 p.m. (last admission 4 p.m.), Sun 11 a.m.–5 p.m. (last admission 4 p.m.).*

Cork City Gaol
Cork City

The history of Cork City's old jail (*gaol* is pronounced as jail), operational from 1824 to 1923, is brought to life with wax figures of the prisoners who occupied the cells here. You still can see the graffiti on the walls of many of the cells, and an interesting audio tour gives you the background stories for many of the prisoners portrayed here, from those who were relocated to Australia to those who fought for the establishment of an independent Republic of Ireland. This is one of those attractions that achieves that great combination of fun and education. Allow an hour for your visit.

Convent Avenue, in the Sunday's Well neighborhood of Cork City. ☎ *021-430-5022. Admission: €7 adults, €6 seniors and students 18 and over, €6 students 17 and under and kids. Open: Mar–Oct 9:30 a.m.–5 p.m., Nov–Feb 10 a.m.–4 p.m.*

The Shandon Bells Speak

The Shandon Bells, first cast in 1750, each bear an inscription. From highest pitch to lowest, they are as follows:

When us you ring we'll sweetly sing

God preserve the Church and King

Health and prosperity to all our benefactors

Peace and good neighbourhood

Prosperity to the city and trade thereof

We were all cast at Gloucester in England by Abel Rudhall 1750

Since generosity has opened our mouths our tongues shall sing aloud its praise

I to the Church the living call and to the grave do summon all

Crawford Art Gallery
Cork City

The engaging Crawford Art Gallery displays a broad array of art, and hosts intriguing and varied temporary exhibits — the recent *Art in an Age of Anxiety: Terror and the Sublime* exhibit featured works from the late 18th century through the present that explore fears in the face of political upheavals. Highlights of the museum include an extensive collection of classical Greek and Roman sculpture casts, and many 19th- and 20th-century Irish paintings and drawings, including some gems by Jack B. Yeats. Make time for lunch or a snack in the first-rate cafe. Art fans should also check out the **Lewis Glucksman Gallery** at University College Cork (see p. 251). In addition, those interested in seeing works by eminent and emerging Cork artists may want to visit the **Cork Opera House** (call ☎ 021-427-0022 to find out when they'll be open).

Emmet Place. ☎ *021-480-5042.* www.crawfordartgallery.ie. *Admission: Free. Open: Mon–Wed and Fri–Sat 10 a.m.–5 p.m., Thurs 10 a.m.–8 p.m.*

English Market
Cork City

This bustling, stone-floored indoor market, dating from 1788, is one of the best in Ireland. The market was damaged by fire in 1986, but it has been beautifully restored, featuring the original fountain, columns, and cast-iron railings. All sorts of meat, vegetables, fruits, sweets, breads, and prepared foods are sold here, and the market is famous for its alley full of sparkling fresh fish. Here's a suggested shopping list for a gourmet picnic: First, fortify yourself with a cup of rich hot chocolate from the Chocolate Shop; then pick up some cured meats and Irish cheeses from On the Pig's

Back, a loaf of your choice from Alternative Bread Co., and some sushi or dried fish from Kay O'Connell's; finally, grab a bottle of wine from Bubble Brothers or a French soda from Café An Raith. The University College Cork campus, on Western Road, is a gorgeous spot to enjoy your picnic, as is Bishop Lucey Park, a little green park at Grand Parade. If the weather gods are not cooperating with your picnic plans, the Farmgate Café (reviewed in the "Dining in Cork City and East County Cork" section, earlier in this chapter) is the next-best thing. Allow 45 minutes for your visit.

Between Grand Parade and Princes Street. Entrances on Patrick Street, Grand Parade, Oliver Plunkett Street, and Princes Street. Open: Mon–Sat 8 a.m.–6 p.m. Usually closed on public holidays.

Fota Wildlife Park
Carrigtwohill

This place is not Irish in the least, but it's a fascinating attraction, where more than 70 species of exotic wildlife roam relatively freely (except the cheetahs — for both your safety and theirs). Giraffes nibble on leaves, peacocks strut their stuff, zebras nuzzle one another, and *maras* (guinea-pig-type animals from Argentina) bounce along everywhere. Highlights are the monkeys, who love to hoot and show off their amazing acrobatics on rope "vines." Panels with text explain where the animals came from and how they live, always with an eye to conservation (the park does a lot of breeding for conservation), and excellent talks are offered each day. If you can, try to catch the Cheetah Run at 4 p.m., during which the park's cheetahs run with incredible speed to catch their dinner. An open-air train circles the park, but you'll see more by walking. Admission to the wildlife park also includes free admission to the Fota Arboretum, with its collection of temperate and subtropical plants and trees. Allow two hours for your visit.

16km (10 miles) from Cork City toward Cobh off the N25. Take the Cobh/Fota exit and then continue about 5.6km (3½ miles) on the Cobh Road to reach the park. There is also train service on the Cork to Cobh commuter line (www.irishrail.ie).
☎ *021-481-2678. www.fotawildlife.ie. Admission: €14 adults; €9 seniors, students, and kids 15 and under. Open: Mon–Sat 10 a.m.–6 p.m. (last admission 5 p.m.), Sun 11 a.m.–6 p.m. (last admission 5 p.m.). Parking: €3.*

St. Anne's Church (Shandon Church)
Cork City

You know those church bells that ring out over so many Irish towns and cities? Well, here's your chance to play them in one of Cork City's most beloved churches. Enter the church and take a look around the chapel, where you'll find a christening font from 1629 and a small collection of old books (my favorite is the Irish-language bible). Then take the stairs up to the first floor, where you can play the eight bells for all to hear. There are several song cards that tell you how to play various songs on the bells, or you can adapt your own favorites (my husband and I spent considerable time adapting our alma mater's fight song for the bells). A tip: To make the bells easier to ring, pull the ropes out toward you rather than straight down. After you've finished your debut concert, take the spiral staircase up to see the clockworks and the bells themselves. At the end of the spiral staircase, don the hearing protection and take the short, steep staircase out of the belfry and onto the outside terrace of the bell tower for a lovely view of Cork City. When you exit the church, check out the four-sided clock tower. Each side of the tower has a clock and, until the mid-1980s, each clock read a slightly different time, prompting Corkonians to refer to the clock tower as "The Four-Faced Liar." Allow 40 minutes for your visit.

Church Street, off Shandon Street on the north side of the River. ☎ *021-450-5906. Admission: €6 adults, €5 seniors and students. Open: June–Sept Mon–Sat 10 a.m.– 5 p.m., Sun 11:30 a.m.–4:30 p.m.; Mar–May and Oct Mon–Sat 10 a.m.–4 p.m., Sun 11:30 a.m.–3:30 p.m.; Nov–Feb 11 a.m.–3 p.m. Last admission 30 minutes before closing. An Anglican service takes place Sun 10 a.m. and is open to the public.*

St. Fin Barre's Cathedral
Cork City

This cathedral was built on the site of a monastery and university created by St. Fin Barre, Cork City's founder, around a.d. 650. Interesting highlights of the **cruciform** (cross-shaped) cathedral include the one-of-a-kind underground church organ, zodiac symbols on the stained glass, and gilded ceilings. You'll get more out of your visit to this French Gothic–style Anglican cathedral if you take the short informative tour. From September through June, the girls and boys choirs can be heard at 10:15 a.m. and 6 p.m. Sunday services. Allow 30 minutes for your visit.

Dean Street. ☎ **021-496-3387.** *Admission: €4 adults, €2 students and kids. Open: Apr–Nov Mon–Sat 9:30 a.m.–5:30 p.m., Sun 12:30–5 p.m.; Dec–Mar Mon–Sat 10 a.m.– 12:45 p.m. and 2–5 p.m.*

University College Cork: Ogham Stones and the Lewis Glucksman Gallery
Cork City

The University College Cork campus itself, with lush green lawns and gothic-style buildings, would be reason enough to visit. In the Stone Corridor, you can step back about 1,500 years to take in the collection of Ogham stones. The inscriptions on these stones, which are thought to be burial markers, bear the earliest examples of the written language that gave rise to modern Irish Gaelic and the oldest recordings of Irish clan names. Don't miss the computer program that allows you to see what your name would look like in Ogham. Now catapult back to the present to visit the Glucksman Gallery, a contemporary art gallery that mounts diverse, thoughtfully curated exhibitions. You may find anything from a sound and visual art installation focusing on Irish traditional music to an exploration of childhood as portrayed in contemporary photography.

University College Cork is located on Western Road. The Lewis Glucksman Gallery is located near the main Western Road entrance to the campus. The Stone Corridor is connected to the Aula Maxima building that fronts the Main Quadrangle. ☎ 021-490-1844 for the Glucksman Gallery. Admission: Free to the campus and the Stone Corridor; also free to the Glucksman Gallery, although a €5 donation is suggested. Open: Campus and Stone Corridor are open at all times; Glucksman Gallery Tues–Sat 10 a.m.–5 p.m., Sun 2–5 p.m.

Other cool things to see and do

✔ **Butter Museum,** O'Connell Square, Shandon, Cork City (☎ 021-430-0600): This museum traces the history of butter-making and the butter trade (Cork had a booming butter market until the early 20th century) from ancient times to today. The exhibit comprises audio-visual displays, wall text, and butter-related artifacts. If you're one of those people who enjoy museums on quirky subjects (I am one of those people), you'll probably like this place; if not, you'll likely be bored.

Admission is €4 adults, €3 seniors and university students, €2 kids 12 to 16. It's open July and August daily 10 a.m. to 6 p.m., March through October daily 10 a.m. to 5 p.m. Allow 45 minutes for your visit.

✔ *Lusitania* **Memorial,** Cobh Harbour, on the square right by the water: This is an impressive and sobering memorial to the 1,195 people who died aboard the *Lusitania* when it was hit by a German torpedo off the Irish coast in 1915. The sinking of the boat was one of the events that prompted the U.S. to enter World War I. You can see the memorial in a couple minutes.

✔ **Jameson Experience Midleton,** Distillery Road, off Main Street, Midleton, off the N25, east of Cork City and west from Youghal (☎ 021-461-3594): Journey through the history of Irish whiskey. You'll see an interesting audiovisual presentation and parts of this restored 18th-century distillery, including the largest pot still in the world, able to hold an intoxicating 30,000 gallons. The modern distillery here (entrance is not permitted) is the largest in Ireland, producing many different whiskies, including Jameson and Tullamore Dew. At the end of the tour, you get to sample some of the smoothest whiskey ever made. Pick up a bottle to take home and some shot glasses in the souvenir shop.

Admission is €14 adults, €10 seniors and students 18 and over, €8 kids and students 17 and under. Tours in March through October are conducted daily every 35 minutes between 10 a.m. and 4:30 p.m.; November through February tours are conducted Monday through Saturday at 11:30 a.m. and 1, 2:30, and 4 p.m.; Sunday 12:30, 2:30, and 4 p.m. Allow an hour and 15 minutes for your visit.

✔ **Youghal (Medieval Walls),** Youghal Heritage Centre, Market Square, on the N25 east of Midleton (☎ 024-201-70): This lovely little port town is worth a stop to get out, stretch your legs, and see what Dublin may have looked like if it hadn't become the capital of the country. Like Dublin, Youghal (pronounced *yawl*) was settled by the Vikings and later fortified by the Normans, who built a wall around the city, half of which still stands. As you make your way from the main Water Gate along the old wall, you see several towers (originally built close enough to allow guards to shout to one another) and the main arched gate, called Cromwell's Arch because it's believed that Oliver Cromwell ended his bloody campaign here. Don't miss the restored Clock Gate (formerly Trinity Gate) at the southern entrance to the town, once an execution site and prison. The guided tours of the walls and town are excellent.

You may want to top off your stop in Youghal with a trip to the town's long, sandy stretch of beach, located right past the town center.

Tours are €7 adults, €4 students. They leave from the Heritage Centre June through September Monday through Friday at 11 a.m. If you want to book a tour outside of these months, call the center. The Heritage Centre is open May through October daily from 9 a.m. to 5 p.m., and November through April, Monday through Friday from 10 a.m. until 3 p.m. Allow an hour and a half for the tour, 15 minutes for the Heritage Centre.

Shopping in Cork City and East County Cork

County Cork is home to many first-rate craftspeople and artists. **The County Cork Craft Guide,** available free at tourist information offices and some galleries, is a terrific resource, featuring brief profiles on hundreds of craftspeople and information on where to find their work.

Cork is a diverse city for shopping. From the highbrow stores on Patrick's Street to the eclectic mix of small retail shops along Oliver Plunkett Street, you can find everything from designer clothing and linen to gourmet cheeses and homemade crafts. For all sorts of tasty edibles, see the English Market, reviewed in "The top attractions," earlier in this chapter. The **Merchants Quay Shopping Centre** is home to 40 shops, while the upscale department stores **Roches** and **Marks & Spencer** are on Patrick's Street. The **Coal Quay Market** is a fun flea market whose merchants sell all sorts of used books, clothes, and the like. You do have to hunt, but there are some treasures here. The market is held Saturdays from 9 a.m. to 4:30 p.m. and is located on Emmet Place while Coal Quay, on Cornmarket Street, is undergoing renovations.

The **Blarney Woollen Mills,** near Blarney Castle, off the N20, Blarney (☎ 021-451-6111), is the original in a string of famous stores that sell everything from crystal to tweed to, of course, sweaters. **Stephen Pearce Pottery,** on the R629, Shanagarry (☎ 021-464-6807), is the place to go for the popular and unique handmade white-and-terra-cotta earthenware that you see all over.

Nightlife and pubs

Cyprus Avenue, Caroline Street (☎ 021-427-6165; www.cyprus avenue.ie), boasts a packed concert schedule that ranges from folk to indie rock, and everything in between. **Crane Lane Theatre,** Phoenix Street (☎ 021-427-8487; www.cranelanetheatre.com) has great live music almost every night, from jazz to ska to dance. Parts of this venue can be clubby, while others are more relaxed. An eclectic assortment of theater, dance, and concerts make up the offerings at the **Cork Opera House,** Emmet Place (☎ 021-427-0022; www.corkoperahouse.ie). You could find anything from *Fame* to an Irish comedy trio. **The Half Moon,** in the Cork Opera House, Emmet Place (☎ 021-427-0022), stages music, experimental theater, and comedy, though the offerings seem few and far between these days. The **Triskel Arts Centre,** Tobin Street, off Main Street (☎ 021-427-2022; www.triskelart.com), offers a range of concerts, from jazz to traditional Irish.

After the shows let out, hit one of Cork City's many excellent pubs.

An Spailpín Fánach

Open fireplaces, a friendly crowd, and traditional music sessions on most nights make An Spailpín one of the best pubs in town. It's also one of the oldest pubs in Cork and is located opposite the Beamish Brewery, which should give you a good idea what you should order.

28 S. Main St. ☎ 021-427-7949.

Henchy's

A *snug* (a separate room where women were once relegated to drink), a mahogany bar, polished brass, and stained glass characterize this elegant classic pub. The atmosphere here is friendly and welcoming.

40 Saint Luke's St. ☎ 021-450-7833.

Le Chateau

Centrally located in the heart of Cork and built more than 200 years ago, this labyrinthine Victorian-decorated pub with an inexplicably French name is one of the oldest and most-favored places in town. City memorabilia is featured prominently in the many sections and snugs. The Irish coffee is legendary.

93 Patrick St. ☎ 021-427-0370.

The Long Valley

This wonderful watering hole is one of the most popular in Cork, known for excellent (and giant) sandwiches and great conversation. A long bar stretches the length of the room, and historic photos line the walls.

10 Wintrop St., at the corner of Oliver Plunkett Street across from the General Post Office. ☎ 021-427-2144.

Sin É

Friendly conversation and great traditional music sessions are on tap in this cozy pub, so settle in for the long haul.

Coburg Street, off the corner of St. Patrick's Street and MacCurtain Street on Cork City's north side. ☎ 01-450-2266.

Fast Facts: Cork City and East County Cork

Area Codes

Cork City and East County Cork's area codes (or city codes) are **021, 022,** and **024.**

Emergencies/Police

Dial ☎ **999** for all emergencies.

Genealogy Resources

Mallow Heritage Centre, 27–28 Bank Place, Mallow (☎ 022-50-302; www.mallow heritagecentre.com).

Hospital

Cork University Hospital is in Wilton, in Cork City (☎ 021-492-2000).

Information

For the most comprehensive visitor information, go to the Cork Tourist Office, 42 Grand Parade (near Oliver Plunkett Street), Cork (☎ 021-425-5100). Other towns in the area also have tourist offices.

Internet

In Cork City, you can use the Internet at Wired to the World, 28 N. Main St. (☎ 021-453-0383).

Post Office

The General Post Office in Cork is on Oliver Plunkett Street, near Morgan Street (☎ 021-485-1032).

Kinsale and West County Cork

You can feast on some of the finest cuisine in this part of Ireland (especially seafood) in the charming and popular port city of **Kinsale,** which is known as the Gourmet Capital of Ireland. Between meals, wander the winding streets, browse through some terrific little shops, and stroll around the sheltered harbor. Arts fans should definitely look into visiting Kinsale in mid- to late-July during **Kinsale Arts Week** (www.kinsale artsweek.com), an eclectic, beautifully curated week of contemporary music, dance, visual arts, and theater.

Past Kinsale, **West County Cork** looks like a magazine advertisement for Ireland, with fishing villages, cozy pubs (many with excellent music), and awe-inspiring cliffs and craggy coastline. If you're looking for postcard Ireland, with seascapes, hills, and green fields crisscrossed by stone walls, but you want to avoid the crowds, West Cork is a great choice. Towns that are worth a visit include artsy **Clonakilty** and **Ballydehob,** both of which have several galleries; the market town of **Skibbereen,** known for excellent traditional music; **Baltimore,** a port town known for its great restaurants; and **Bantry,** a pretty harbor town with a beautiful manor house and gardens.

Kinsale

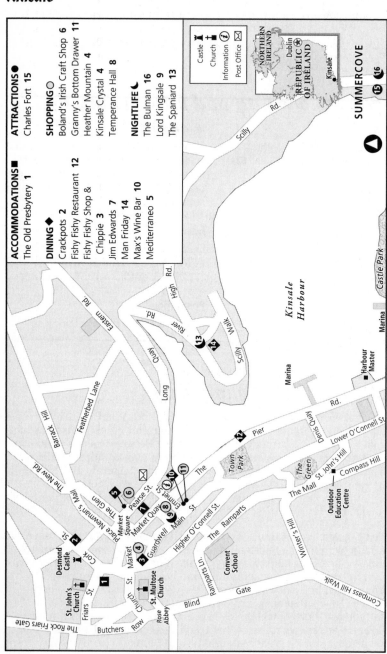

ACCOMMODATIONS■
The Old Presbytery **1**

DINING◆
Crackpots **2**
Fishy Fishy Restaurant **12**
Fishy Fishy Shop &
  Chippie **3**
Jim Edwards **7**
Man Friday **14**
Max's Wine Bar **10**
Mediterraneo **5**

ATTRACTIONS●
Charles Fort **15**

SHOPPING○
Boland's Irish Craft Shop **6**
Granny's Bottom Drawer **11**
Heather Mountain **4**
Kinsale Crystal **4**
Temperance Hall **8**

NIGHTLIFE☽
The Bulman **16**
Lord Kingsale **9**
The Spaniard **13**

Castle ⚔
Church ✝
Information ①
Post Office ⊠

NORTHERN
IRELAND
REPUBLIC
OF IRELAND
Dublin ✪
Kinsale ●

SUMMERCOVE

Getting to Kinsale and West County Cork

To get to Kinsale by car, take the R600 south from Cork or the R605 south from Inishannon. The N71 runs out of Cork City and links many of the major towns in west County Cork. **Bus Éireann** (☎ 01-836-6111) travels year-round to Kinsale, Bantry, and other major towns in west County Cork.

Easy Tours Cork (☎ 021-454-5328; www.easytourscork.com) offers a tours of West Cork that takes you through several small charming villages. Your first stop is Gougane Barra, a peaceful lakeside spot in a forested area that was once home to a sixth-century monastery. You then move on to the little town of Glengarriff, where you'll have the option of taking a short ferry ride to the beautiful gardens on Garnish Island (see p. 265). You finish your day with a stroll and hot beverage in the lovely town of Bantry. The tours run about eight hours, leaving from the Cork City Tourist Office, 42 Grand Parade (near Oliver Plunkett Street) at 9:30 a.m. on Tuesdays and Fridays. Tours run from April through September. Tours are €30 adults, €26 seniors, €23 students, and €16 kids 13 and under.

Spending the night in Kinsale and West County Cork

Manor lords- and ladies-in-training should also take a look at the beautiful accommodations at **Bantry House** (p. 264).

Aran Lodge
$ **Ballylickey (outside of Bantry)**

Cross your fingers for clear weather, because the views of the hills and valleys that surround this simple B&B are delightful. This place feels like a real family home; Joe and Deirdre O'Connell's four kids laugh and play outside, and the cozy rooms are furnished in a down-to-earth country style. It's also earth-friendly — the house has solar panels, utilizes captured rainwater, and has several other environmental measures in place. Deirdre caters to all tastes and appetites at breakfast, offering everything from a full Irish fried breakfast to pancakes to vegetarian options such as quiche. Families will appreciate the large grounds (great for running around), the friendly O'Connell kids, and the laid-back atmosphere. The picnic tables outside are a great place for dinner or lunch. The O'Connells will happily pack a picnic for you, or you can pick up gourmet supplies at Manning's Emporium (see p. 260).

Ballylickey. About 4km (2½ miles) outside of Bantry on the Glengarriff Road (N71). ☎ *027-50-378.* www.aran-lodge.com. *Parking: Free on-site. Rack rates: €70 double. DC, MC, V.*

Ballylickey Manor
$$ **Ballylickey (outside of Bantry)**

Peace is the word that comes mind at this manor house, where old trees arch over the gorgeous landscaped grounds. You can choose to stay either in a room in the manor house or in a small cottage with a bedroom, giant sitting room, and bathroom. Both the rooms and the cottages are serene, airy, and uncluttered, and they're furnished with elegant furniture and Victorian-looking fabrics. Service is professional and gracious, if slightly detached.

Bantry Bay. From Bantry Town, go 4.8km (3 miles) north on the N71 toward Glengarriff. Ballylickey Manor is on the left, facing the water. ☎ **027-50-071.** *Fax: 027-50-124. www.ballylickeymanorhouse.com. Parking: Free on-site. Rack rates: €110– €130 cottages, €130–€180 rooms in the manor house. AE, DC, MC, V. Closed Nov–Apr.*

Maritime Hotel and Suites
$$$ **Bantry**

It was inevitable. As Bantry becomes part of more and more peoples' travel itineraries, the town was bound to invest in a modern luxury hotel. Located right on the harbor in downtown Bantry, this new hotel is all about amenities, with everything from a large pool to a spa to a flat-screen TV in each room. Rooms and bathrooms are spacious and contemporary, with hip little details such as a brown and hot pink throw on each bed. The staff is friendly, helpful, and attentive. If you're staying on a weekend and there is a wedding in the hotel, ask for a room far away from the pulsing music of the function room.

The Square, on Bantry Harbor. ☎ **027-54-700.** *Fax: 027-54-701. www.themaritime. ie. Parking: Free on-site. Rack rates: €100–€150 double. AE, MC, V.*

The Old Presbytery
$$$ **Kinsale**

The uncluttered rooms here are the picture of casual comfort, with unvarnished farmhouse-chic furniture, large windows, and Victorian brass beds laden with a mass of embroidered white pillows and blankets. Just to make sure you're totally relaxed, many of the rooms have claw-foot tubs or Jacuzzis (just ask when you book). The staff is warm and friendly, and the guesthouse has a perfect location within a few minutes of the heart of town yet away from the tour-bus hustle and bustle.

43 Cork St. ☎ **021-477-2027.** *www.oldpres.com. Parking: Free on-site. Rack rates: €100–€170 double. MC, V. Closed Dec–Jan.*

Rivermount House Bed and Breakfast
$$ **Kinsale**

If you cringe at the sight of floral bedspreads and antique furniture, I have just the place for you. Rivermount, located about a ten-minute drive from downtown Kinsale, has a gorgeous super-modern décor in tones of silver, black, gold, and deep purple. Bedrooms have luxurious textured wallpaper and feature contemporary paintings and sculpture, while the light-filled public rooms overlook a quilt of fields below. You'll find thoughtful little details including extra-fluffy towels and access to both 110-volt and 220-volt sockets in each room. Service is kind, and the breakfasts are excellent (try the pancakes with real maple syrup).

Barrell's Cross (signposted off the R600). ☎ *021-477-8033. Fax: 021-477-8225.* `www.rivermount.com`. *Parking: Free on-site. Rack rates: €76–€90 double. Credit cards only accepted through the online booking system. Closed Nov 1–Feb 14.*

Sandycove House Bed & Breakfast
$ Castletownshend

You know you're in Ireland when the view out of your bedroom window is a sweet donkey grazing in the foreground, with cliffs dropping to sapphire waters and a golden crescent of a beach in the background. The views would be enough of a reason to book a stay here; throw in soothing bedrooms with fluffy white duvets and pretty built-in cabinetry and you've got a real gem. Make time for a leisurely breakfast — both because the breakfasts are excellent and because the breakfast room is a glass-paneled conservatory with more of those stunning views. A stay here wouldn't be complete without dinner at the legendary Mary Ann's (see p. 262).

Castletownshend, near Skibbereen. Take the R596 toward Castletownshend. Right before you enter the village, take a right turn to the Coast Road, where you'll find signs guiding you to the house. ☎ **028-36223.** `www.sandycovehouse.com`. *Parking: Free on-site. Rack rates: €70 double. MC, V. Closed Nov to mid-March.*

Seaview House Hotel
$$$$ Ballylickey

This is a classic, small, old-world hotel, where you'll find antique furniture in the bedrooms, an airy conservatory, and impeccably kept gardens. The dinners served in the gracious, antiques-filled dining room are quite good. The menu changes every night, making use of the finest local ingredients in such dishes as lamb with rosemary and Dover sole with lemon butter.

Ballylickey. About 4km (2½ miles) outside of Bantry, on the Glengarriff Road (N71). ☎ **027-50-073.** `www.seaviewhousehotel.com`. *Parking: Free on-site. Rack rates: €140–€210 double. MC, V. Closed mid-Nov to mid-March.*

West Cork Hotel
$$ Skibbereen

What the small town of Skibbereen lacks in jaw-dropping scenery or must-see attractions, it makes up for in the charm of a bustling downtown where locals are friendly and down-to-earth. Similarly, guests come to the West Cork Hotel not for a fabulous spa or a trendy bar, but for the friendly atmosphere and the comfortable, classic style that defines this 150-year-old hotel. The spacious rooms retain much of their "old-world" feel, with patterned carpeting and flowered wallpaper and curtains, while contemporary touches, such as snow-white duvets and gold-striped pillows, bring things up to date. This is the kind of place where locals flood the wood-paneled dining room for the Sunday buffet lunch and the staff can suggest a nice spa in the area. Here's to hoping the West Cork Hotel will always maintain that balance.

On Ilen Street off N71 in Skibbereen. ☎ **028-21-277.** *www.westcorkhotel.com. Parking: Free on-site. Rack rates: €89–€109 double. AE, MC, V.*

Dining locally in Kinsale and West County Cork

In the Bantry area, also see the Seaview House Hotel (p. 259), which offers classic cooking using the finest local ingredients.

In Kinsale, I suggest making restaurant reservations early in the day to avoid disappointment. For a dream picnic, check out the dazzling selection of local cheese, sausages, and more at **Manning's Emporium,** in Ballylickey, on the Glengarriff Road about 3km (2 miles) outside of Bantry (on the way to Glengarriff).

Blair's Cove
$$$$ Durrus CONTINENTAL

For starters, let's talk about the starters — a host of delicious options, arranged buffet-style for you to pick and choose among. Then the main courses arrive. The main course options are mostly fish and meat, such as cod with chive beurre blanc, and rib-eye steak with béarnaise peppercorn sauce, and all are cooked to perfection. Finally, the piano becomes a dessert tray, with an array of delectable sweets. Early-bird deals are offered between 5:30 and 6:45 p.m.; two courses are €30 and three are €40. A €35 Sunday lunch is also offered. The restaurant is housed in a beautifully renovated old stone barn surrounded by acres of lawns and gardens.

Barley Road, 1.6km (1 mile) from Durrus, on the road to Barleycove. ☎ **027-62-913.** *Reservations recommended. Main courses: Full dinner €58, starter buffet and dessert €45. MC, V. Open: Mar 17–Oct 31 Tues–Sat 7–9 p.m., Sun 1–3 p.m.; call for winter hours as they vary.*

Crackpots
$$$ Kinsale NEW IRISH/SEAFOOD

Fresh ingredients are expertly prepared at this warm, candlelit restaurant. Perhaps roasted chicken with a parsley stuffing on cauliflower puree with spring onion sauce whets your appetite? Or maybe you're more intrigued by the seared scallops served with saffron beurre blanc, wilted spinach, and crispy Parma ham? Chandeliers, beautiful paintings, antique mirrors, gorgeous crockery, and the golden glow of candlelight create a setting that is elegant and artsy without being at all stuffy. Wondering about the name? There is a gallery upstairs where you can purchase paintings and dishes like the ones you just ate from.

3 Cork St. ☎ **021-477-2847.** *Reservations recommended. Main courses: €17–€28. AE, MC, V. Open: Mon–Thurs 6–10 p.m., Fri–Sat 1–3 p.m. and 6–10:30 p.m., Sun 1–3 p.m. and 6–10 p.m.*

Fishy Fishy Restaurant and Fishy Fishy Shop & Chippy
$–$$$ **Kinsale**   **SEAFOOD**

One-hundred-and-ninety-seven years of fishing experience. That's the sum you reach when you total up the years that Fishy Fishy's five main fishermen have been plying the waters. Nearly two centuries of experience equals a shop counter full of sparkling-fresh fish. At the shop and chippy, you can place your order at the counter and take a seat at one of the long tables in the casual cafe area to watch as locals come in to buy a few cuts of salmon or a bag of mussels. There are several options on the menu here, but the fish and chips and the tomato-based seafood chowder are the stars. On Crowley's Quay, you'll find Fishy Fishy's more formal restaurant branch, serving up first-rate seafood in simple dishes that let the flavor of the fish shine. The mussels with lemon butter and basil is an excellent choice, as is the smoked salmon platter. It seems that Fishy Fishy may be resting on its laurels (seaweed?) recently, as some have complained of rude service and, on one visit, my crab claws were not the flavorful specimens I had come to expect. Still, this place has built up a reputation for good reason. We'll see what the future holds.

Small restaurant on Guardwell, next to St. Multoge Church; large restaurant on Crowley's Quay. ☎ *021-477-4453 for the cafe,* ☎ *021-4700-415 for the larger restaurant. Reservations highly recommended for dinner. Main dishes: €10–€15 cafe, €15–€30 restaurant. MC, V. Open: Cafe daily noon to 4:30 p.m., restaurant daily noon to 9 p.m. Hours may change in winter, so call ahead.*

Good Things Café
$$$ **Durrus**   **NEW IRISH/SEAFOOD**

It's a little like a fairy tale, encountering this glowing little restaurant after driving stretches of the sparsely populated Beara or Sheep's Head peninsulas. The restaurant has a shabby-chic farmhouse feel, with large stone tables, barn lamps with sparkly flower garlands wrapped around them, mismatched plates, and bookshelves with inspiring cookbooks lining the walls. There is a huge focus on local and organic sources here, and it pays off in the dishes, which can be inventive but never drown out the flavors of the centerpiece. My salad featured unbelievably fresh and tasty baby greens, a local goat cheese and herb cake was served on tomatoes that parted with the vine that day, and the crowning glory, a lobster with herbs and garlic, was trapped by the fisherman down the road. By now, it probably goes without saying that the menu changes all the time. It does, and we're all the luckier because of it.

On Ahakista Road, about 0.5km (⅓ mile) from the town of Durrus. ☎ *027-61-426. Main courses: €15–€28 (lobster €30–€38). MC, V. Open: End of June to mid-Sept Thurs–Mon 12:30–3 p.m. and 6:30–9 p.m.*

Jim Edwards
$$–$$$ **Kinsale**   **PUB GRUB/SEAFOOD**

This cozy bar, with polished wood and nautical décor, serves up mouthwatering, uncomplicated dishes such as rack of lamb, seafood chowder, mussels with garlic crumbs, steaks, and possibly the best crab claws with garlic butter in all of Ireland. There's a popular candlelit restaurant upstairs, serving more upscale versions of the pub favorites (scallops Mornay instead of cod Mornay, for example) but I recommend hanging out in the bar with a pint and some of this superior pub grub.

Market Quay off Emmet Place. ☎ *021-477-2541. Main courses: Pub €13–€18, restaurant €17–€30. AE, MC, V. Open: The pub serves food daily noon to 9:45 p.m., while the restaurant serves from 5:30–9:45 p.m.*

Man Friday
$$$–$$$$ Kinsale   CONTINENTAL/SEAFOOD

Maybe it's the lantern-style lamps casting a warm glow on the wood-and-stone interior, or maybe it's the cozy banquettes, but something makes you want to linger over dinner at this buzzing, romantic restaurant. Maybe it's just that you want to keep eating the fresh, skillfully prepared dishes. The black sole, cooked on the bone, melts in your mouth, and the steak *au poivre* is juicy and full of flavor. You'll be licking the shells if you order the mussels stuffed with buttered breadcrumbs and garlic for starters. But then you'd be missing out on the deep-fried brie with plum and port sauce.

On the Scilly Road. ☎ *021-477-2260. Main courses: €23–€31. Reservations recommended. AE, MC, V. Open: Mon–Sat 6:30–10:15 p.m.*

Mary Ann's
$$$–$$$$ Castletownshend   SEAFOOD

I have eaten many tasty finned creatures, but the best piece of fish I've ever had the pleasure of eating was a melt-in-your-mouth filet of Dover sole at Mary Ann's. And the great thing is, you don't even have to dress up or shell out the big bucks in order to enjoy the best seafood in West Cork. Just have a seat at one of the dark wood tables in this warmly lit, lively pub, and get ready for a slice of seafood heaven. Favorites include simply prepared catch of the day, Dublin Bay prawns, gourmet fish and chips, and, for dessert, sticky toffee pudding. There are excellent nonseafood options as well; my husband polished off his lamb sausages and mashed potatoes before I even had chance to ask for a bite. Don't miss Mary Ann's if you're in the area.

Castletownshend. Take the N71 to Skibbereen and go 8.1km (5 miles) south on the Castletownshend Road (R596). ☎ *028-36-146. Reservations recommended for dinner. Main courses: €18–€35. MC, V. Open: Daily noon to 2:30 p.m. and 6–9 p.m.*

Max's Wine Bar
$$$ Kinsale   SEAFOOD/NEW IRISH

A meal in this intimate, family-run town house restaurant, located in the heart of Kinsale, is one of the best gourmet dining experiences you'll have in the area — as a columnist in the *Irish Independent* wrote, "No visit to Kinsale is complete without a visit to Max's." The French chef, Olivier, has a light hand and a creative mind. He finds the best of Cork's vegetables, fish, and meat, and transforms them into innovative dishes that let the flavors of the ingredients shine. The menu changes all the time, featuring such dishes as heavenly scallops served with three sauces: lentil, celeriac, and lemongrass, and an unforgettable rack of lamb with a cider and apricot reduction. Seafood is definitely the restaurant's strongest point — they serve at least six different catches of the day, and their "symphony of oysters," an array of oysters prepared in different styles, is fantastic. Service is excellent. If you're looking for lunch on a warm summer day, call ahead to make sure that Max's is open; the family will sometimes close for lunch to take their kids to the beach.

Main Street. ☎ *021-477-2443. Reservations recommended. Main courses: €19–€29. MC, V. Open: Mid-June to Aug daily 12:30–2 p.m. and 6–10 p.m., Sept to mid-Dec and mid-Mar to mid-June Wed–Sun 12:30–2 p.m. and 6–10 p.m. Closed mid-Dec to mid-Mar.*

Mediterraneo
$$–$$$ Kinsale

Blues and whites plus small paintings of Italy set the scene in my favorite Italian restaurant in these parts. They've got all the classics down to a science, from penne *all'arrabiata,* with tomato, garlic, and fresh chilies, to tagliatelle with chicken and mushrooms. But the menu doesn't stop there. The restaurant also aces more daring dishes such as risotto with fresh mussels, asparagus, and saffron sauce. Service here is gracious in a way that my grandfather (a career waiter at the Algonquin Hotel in New York) would have appreciated.

7 Pearse St. ☎ *021-477-3844. Main courses: €14–€25. AE, MC, V. Open: Daily 6–11 p.m.*

The Snug
$$ Bantry   IRISH/PUB FOOD

You know that place at home that you go to for dinner when you just want something good in a comfortable setting? This is Bantry's version of that restaurant. Aptly named, the Snug is a cozy and relaxing joint, with warm wood-paneled walls decorated with antique signs, stained glass, tree branches, and a turn-of-the-century bicycle. The food is comfortable too, with options such as roast stuffed chicken, burgers, and tagliatelle bolognaise. If they're in season, go for the strawberries and cream for dessert. The staff is fantastic, and the bartender has tons of stories.

The Square, by the Bantry Habour. ☎ *027-50-057. Main courses: €6–€21. MC, V. Open: Mon–Sat 11 a.m.–9 p.m., Sun 12:30–9 p.m.*

Exploring Kinsale and West County Cork: The top attractions

See p. 257 for information on a bus tour of West Cork that leaves from Cork City.

The **Old Head Golf Links** (☎ 021-477-8444; www.oldhead.com) is a challenging par-72 course located on a stunning outcrop of land surrounded by the Atlantic Ocean, just south of Kinsale. Greens fees are €200 for 18 holes.

The Mizen Head area and the Sheep's Head Peninsula offer great biking. You can rent a bike from **Roycroft's Stores,** in Heron Court, right near the main parking lot in Skibbereen (☎ 028-21-235), or from **Nigel's Bicycle Shop,** on Glengarriff Road in Bantry (☎ 027-52-657).

If you'd like to sail a small yacht in Kinsale's harbor, contact **Sovereign Sailing** (☎ 021-477-4145; www.sovereignsailing.com). Your sailing trip is skippered, and you're more than welcome to sail the boat yourself, relax as the skipper sails, or do a little of each. If you'd prefer touring the harbor on a larger boat, contact **Kinsale Harbour Cruises** (☎ 086-250-5456; www.kinsaleharbourcruises.com). The cruises depart daily on the hour during the summer, and they leave from the area diagonally across the road from Acton's Hotel.

To get a sense of Kinsale history from two excellent tour guides, take **Herlihy's Guided Tour** (☎ 021-477-2873), which leaves from the tourist office at 9:15 a.m. and 11:15 a.m. daily from May through September, and 11:15 a.m. daily October through April. The walk costs €6 adults, €1 kids, and is about 90 minutes long.

In the mood for a creepy, funny adventure? Try the exciting **Kinsale Ghost Tour** (☎ 087-948-0910), which leaves from the Tap Tavern at 9 p.m. all summer and costs €10 adults, €5 kids.

Bantry House and Gardens
Bantry

If I had to choose to visit only one of Ireland's many great houses, Bantry House, built for the earls of Bantry in 1750, would be my pick. This sumptuously furnished house is unique in that there are no velvet ropes guarding the rooms; you're free to wander through the house at will with a written guide that identifies the origins and history of each work of art, decoration, or piece of furniture. There are many treasures within the house, including several tapestries created to celebrate Marie Antoinette's wedding; *The Fruit Market,* a massive painting by Snyders and Rubens; and a rosewood grand piano in the 18m-long (60-ft.) library. Set aside time to explore the vast grounds and lovely gardens, which offer stunning views of Bantry Bay below. The most magnificent panorama of the house, gardens, and bay is afforded by climbing the steep stairs in the garden behind the house. You can recover from your climb with a cup of tea and a piece of cake at the tearoom. Allow two hours for your visit.

If you've fallen in love with Bantry House, you may want to consider staying here for a few nights. B&B rates run from €200 to €300 per night.

On the N71, between Glengarriff and Skibbereen, on the western outskirts of Bantry Town. ☎ **027-50-047.** www.bantryhouse.ie. *Admission: House, gardens, and* *armada center €10 adults, €8 seniors and students, €3 kids 5–16, free for kids 4 and under; gardens only €5 adults, free for kids 13 and under. Open: Mid-Mar to Oct daily 10 a.m.–6 p.m.*

Charles Fort
Kinsale

Military history buffs and view-lovers will both be pleased here. One of Ireland's largest forts, Charles Fort is a star-shaped fortification constructed in the late 17th century. There is a small museum, but the highlight is wandering through the rooms of the fort and along the ramparts, where you are afforded superb views of Kinsale's harbor. To get here, I recommend taking the Scilly Walk, a path that curves along the harbor and through woodlands from Kinsale, offering beautiful views of the water. The walk is roughly 2km (1¼ miles) on relatively flat paths. James Fort (1602) is across the river. Allow about an hour for your visit.

Summer Cove. Scilly Road or coastal walk (signposted and called Salmon Walk from Kinsale) starts at Perryville House, Pearse Street. ☎ 021-477-2263. Admission: €4 adults, €3 seniors, €2 students and kids. Open: Mid-Mar to Oct daily 10 a.m.–6 p.m., Nov to mid-Mar daily 10 a.m.–5 p.m. (last admission one hour before closing).

Driving, biking, or hiking the Beara Peninsula

When you get home, don't forget to tell your friends that the Beara (pronounced *bare*-ah) Peninsula was terribly ugly and boring. That way, the peninsula will remain the wild and unspoiled place that it is now, with magnificent seascapes, and sweeping hills punctuated by ruins (both ancient and more recent) and the pretty, bustling little towns of Allihies and Castletownbere. If you want a peninsula drive like those on the Ring of Kerry or the Dingle Peninsula, but with fewer crowds, the Beara is for you. Be aware that the Beara Peninsula has much less tourist infrastructure than the other two peninsulas (fewer restaurants, hotels, and built-up attractions). The drive around the peninsula (begin your loop around the peninsula either at Kenmare [take the R571] or at Glengarriff [take the R572], making sure to take the cutoff leading to Healy Pass from either Adrigole or Lauragh) takes a whole day if you do it at a leisurely pace. Stops in Allihies and Castletownbere are great ways to break up your journey. Beara Tourism (www.bearatourism.com) provides all the information you need to plan a hiking or bicycle trip on the peninsula. Strong cyclists will enjoy biking the **Beara Way** hiking and bicycling path. Day hikers (and bikers) can join up with the trail for hikes at several points along the loop drive. On a nice day, it's worth extending your drive by a few hours to spend some time exploring the peaceful forest and still sapphire lake at Gougane Barra, off the R584 on the way from Glengarriff towards Ballingeary.

Garnish Island (Ilnacullin Island)

This little island is an amazing sight — an expansive Italian garden of rare trees, vivid flowers, and shrubs set along walkways and pools, all sitting out in the sea on an uninhabited 18-hectare (37-acre) island. Before the owner brought over hundreds of tons of topsoil to grow the exotic plants, the island was bare rock. Half the fun is the short journey getting there on one of the small ferries that serve the island (keep an eye out for basking seals!). Allow 90 minutes for your visit, including the ferry trip.

The Blue Pool Ferry (☎ 027-63-333) leaves from the harbor in Glengarriff every half-hour or so from about 10 a.m. until about 5:30 p.m. and takes 15 minutes to reach the island. Ferries sail Mar–Oct. Round-trip €10 adults, €3 seniors, €5 kids 2–12. ☎ 027-63-040. Admission: €4 adults, €2.60 seniors, €2 students and kids. Open: In all cases, the last landing on the island is one hour before the island closes. May and Sept Mon–Sat 10 a.m.–6:30 p.m., Sun noon to 6:30 p.m.; June Mon–Sat 10 a.m.–6:30 p.m., Sun 11 a.m.–6:30 p.m.; July–Aug Mon–Sat 9:30–6:30 p.m., Sun 11–6:30 p.m.; Apr Mon–Sat 10 a.m.–6:30 p.m., Sun 1–6:30 p.m.; Oct Mon–Sat 10 a.m.–4 p.m., Sun 1–5 p.m. Closed Nov–Mar.

Mizen Head and Mizen Head Fog Signal Station

Located at Ireland's most southwesterly point, Mizen Head seems a little out of the way, but the drive from the east is gorgeous, all beautiful beaches and green hills. At the Mizen Head Visitor Centre, traverse the suspension bridge over craggy cliffs and sea, and climb to the top of Mizen Head for priceless views of the cliffs jutting down to the Atlantic. Keep an eye out for dolphin, whales, basking sharks, seals, and several different species of seabirds, all of which are sighted here. The visitor center provides a good introduction to the area, with small exhibits on lighthouses and fog signal stations, light keepers and their families, and the flora and fauna of the area. Don't miss trying out Navigational Aids Simulator, a virtual-reality program used to train seafarers. *Note:* A new suspension bridge was being constructed as of this writing and should be ready for the public by January 2011. Allow 45 minutes for your visit.

Mizen Head. From Skibbereen, the drive is about an hour. Take the N71 to the R592 in Ballydehob, travel through Schull and Goleen, and then follow signs for the Mizen Head Drive. From the north, follow the N71 to Bantry, take the R591 (marked "Crookhaven") through Durrus and Goleen, and follow the signs for the Mizen Head Drive. ☎ 028-35-115 or 028-35-225. Admission: €4.50 adults, €3.50 seniors and students, free for kids 11 and under. Open: June–Aug daily 10 a.m.–6 p.m., mid-Mar to May and Sept–Oct daily 10:30 a.m.–5 p.m., Nov to mid-Mar Sat–Sun 11 a.m.–4 p.m.

Visiting the West Cork Islands

In addition to the must-see Garnish Island (described earlier), West Cork has several other islands that are worth a visit. Rugged **Cape Clear Island** offers cliffs, bogland, ruins, and a pretty lake, and is home to about 120 year-round residents (most of whom speak Irish as a first language). This is arguably the best place to go birding in Ireland, and you may also spot sea life including whales and dolphins. To get to Cape Clear Island, take the **Cape Clear Island Ferry Service** (☎ 086-346-5110; www.capeclear islandferry.com), which sails the 45-minute trip from Baltimore Harbour. The ferries operate three times daily from April through October, with one additional trip daily in June, July, and August. Though **Dursey**

Island is striking in its own right, with a craggy landscape, great birding, and gorgeous seascapes, getting there and back is half the fun. You'll take a **cable car** from the tip of the Beara Peninsula (the end of the R572) on a ten-minute trip over the sea to the island (don't worry about plunging into the waters below — the car is licensed to hold a cow). The cable car operates Monday through Saturday 9 to 10:30 a.m., 2:30 to 4:30 p.m., and 7 to 7:30 p.m., and Sunday 9 to 10 a.m., 1 to 2 p.m., and 7 to 7:30 p.m.

Hiking part of the Sheep's Head Way

This 89km (55-mile) route was voted the best hike in Ireland by *Country Walking Magazine*. The marked route makes a loop out of the town of Bantry, traveling through vast moorland, through green fields dotted with cottages both inhabited and uninhabited, and along craggy cliffs and sandy beaches. Most hikers take four days to complete the entire hike. If you aren't ready to dedicate four days to a trek (I've promised myself I'll do it next year), I recommend making the loop by car and then getting out to walk sections of the Sheep's Head Way whenever you feel like it. You can start the driving loop at Bantry or at Durrus. Set aside at least half a day for your journey, especially if you want to stop for a short hike at some point. For information on hikes, activities, accommodations and more, check out the well-done Sheep's Head Way Web site (www.the sheepsheadway.ie). For maps of the peninsula, visit the tourist information offices in Skibbereen or Bantry. Those who are hiking the whole Sheep's Head Way will need more detailed maps, so purchase the Ordnance Survey Discovery maps 85 and 88 before your trip at www.osi. ie, or by calling the Ordnance Survey Ireland shop at ☎ **1-802-5300**.

Whale- and Dolphin-Watching Trips
Trips leave from Baltimore or Union Hall

Nic Slocum is a zoologist with over 20 years of whale- and dolphin-watching experience, so you're in for a treat when you take one of his three- to four-hour whale- and dolphin-watching trips. Nic's knowledge is encyclopedic, and he takes every measure to make sure that you're safe and comfortable as you take in the minke whales, fin whales, dolphins, humpback whales, and other species found in the West Cork waters. The species that you'll see depends on the season; minkes are usually around from May through January, while humpbacks usually arrive in August and stay through January. If you're around in late summer, autumn, or early winter, you'll have the chance of encountering humpback whales as well. Nic is an ardent advocate for marine conservation and sustainable tourism, and he works hard to make sure that his trips do not disturb the whales and dolphins. Even if it's a nice day, bring something warm to put on if you get cold, and bring any food or drinks that you might want to snack on. ***Important:*** You must make reservations by phone (☎ **086-120-0027** or 028-33-357) or online (www.whalewatchwestcork.com) to reserve your place on the boat.

Trips leave from Reen Pier (drive to Union Hall and follow the signs from there) or Baltimore Harbor daily at 9 a.m. and 2 p.m. May through August; call for trip times during the other months. The cost is €50 per person.

Kayaking in glowing waters

Atlantic Sea Kayaking offers excellent day paddles, but the magic really begins when you take one of its **Night Time Paddling Tours.** You set out an hour before the sun sets, with the golden glow of the last of daylight illuminating the shores. As night falls, you're treated to a sky full of stars. You make your way to an area known for tiny bioluminescent organisms, which light up in sparkling waves when nudged by the edges of your kayak and paddle or your fingers. The effect is like paddling through a galaxy. The 2½-hour tour is run daily (unless the guides are out of town), and the bioluminescence is at its best in late summer and early autumn. The price is €45 per person, and tours depart from Reen Pier outside Union Hall (near Skibbereen). Book your tour through **Atlantic Sea Kayaking** (☎ 028-210-58; www.atlanticseakayaking.com).

Shopping

As mentioned in the "Cork City and East County Cork" section, County Cork is home to many superb craftspeople and artists. Make a point to pick up *The County Cork Craft Guide,* a free comprehensive guide to galleries and craftspeople in Cork. The guide is available in most tourist offices in the area and in some galleries.

A small craft market in Kinsale's **Temperance Hall,** facing Pier Road, is held Friday, Saturday, and Sunday, selling earrings, homemade soaps, knitted items, and the like. **Boland's Irish Craft Shop,** Pearse Street, Kinsale (☎ 021-477-2161), offers a variety of items including Irish pottery, jewelry, crafts, and clothing. **Granny's Bottom Drawer,** 53 Main St., Kinsale (☎ 021-477-4839), sells traditional linen and lace: pillowcases, placemats, tablecloths, and more, all hand-woven with delicate care. **Heather Mountain,** 15 Market St., Kinsale (☎ 021-477-3384), sells a good selection of Aran sweaters and other Irish-made clothing. **Kinsale Crystal,** Market Street (☎ 021-477-4493), sells faceted crystal pieces that positively glow.

The Craft Shop, Glengarriff Road, Bantry (☎ 027-50-003), offers the best of everything: pottery by Nicholas Mosse and Stephen Pearse; glass by Jerpoint Glass Studio; silver jewelry by Linda Uhleman; plus candles, leatherwork, baskets, and more.

If you're taking the ferry to Cape Clear, Heir, or Sherkin islands, stop off at **Island Crafts,** on the pier in Baltimore (☎ 028-20022), which sells gorgeous knitwear, textile art, pottery, and jewelry, mostly made by craftspeople on the islands.

If you can, try to make it to Bantry for the weekly **Friday market,** which takes place in the town square from about 9:30 a.m. to about 1 p.m. You'll find absolutely everything here, from rugs to roosters. On my last visit, I purchased an old Guinness pub sign, homemade goat cheese, and some fresh vegetables.

Hitting the pubs

Baby Hannah's

You may think you're just popping in for a quick drink at this mid-19th-century pub, but chances are, you'll end up staying for the friendly atmosphere, great conversation, and excellent traditional Irish music. Locals say this pub pulls the best pint in town, so go on, have another.

42 Bridge St., Skibbereen. ☎ **028-22783.**

The Bulman

This pub offers a stunning view of Kinsale Harbor, excellent seafood dishes, a warm stone interior, crackling fires, and music on some nights. What more could you want?

Summercove, Kinsale. On Scilly Road, on the way to Charles Fort from Kinsale. ☎ **021-477-2131.**

De Barra

From top to bottom and inside and out, everything about this lovely traditional pub is authentic. The décor includes hand-painted signs and old-fashioned whiskey jars, and the music is terrific, ranging from traditional Irish with top-notch musicians to the latest heavy metal from West Cork (really!). Check the Web site (www.debarra.ie) to see what's playing when you're in town.

55 Pearse St., Clonakilty. ☎ **023-883-3381.**

Lord Kingsale

A classic black-and-white-exterior pub, Lord Kingsale is a romantic little spot, with small snug areas, and live music almost every night of the week during the summer (weekends and Mon, during the winter). Delicious home-cooked food is served all day long, and a comfortable, lived-in atmosphere draws a pleasant, subdued crowd.

4 Main St., Kinsale. ☎ **021-477-2371.**

The Spaniard

The best part of the Spaniard is the outdoor seating that overlooks the harbor. Inside are cozy turf and log fires and traditional, jazz, folk, and blues music. This fishing-themed pub is built over the ruins of a castle and named in honor of Don Juan del Aquila, commander of the Spanish fleet and ally to the Irish during the Battle of Kinsale in 1601.

On the Scilly Road about half a mile from Kinsale's town center. ☎ **021-477-3303.**

Fast Facts: Kinsale and West County Cork

Area Codes

Kinsale and West County Cork's area codes (or city codes) are **021, 027,** and **028.**

Emergencies/Police

Dial ☎ **999** for all emergencies.

Information

There are many tourist offices around West Cork. The tourist office in Kinsale is located on Pier Road (☎ 021-477-2234;

www.kinsale.ie). In Skibbereen, there is a tourist office on North Street (☎ 028-21-766). In Bantry, the tourist office is at the top of the town square in the Old Courthouse (☎ 027-50-229). This office is open only during the high season (roughly June–Aug).

Internet

Computer Services, Lower O'Connell Street, Kinsale (☎ 021-477-2042), offers Internet access and Wi-Fi.

Chapter 16

County Kerry

In This Chapter

▶ Exploring beautiful Killarney National Park

▶ Taking in the cliffs, sea, and mountains of the Ring of Kerry

▶ Walking, biking, or driving around the gorgeous Dingle Peninsula

▶ Hanging out (perhaps with a dolphin) in funky Dingle Town

C ounty Kerry is not nicknamed "The Kingdom" for nothing. The county encompasses some of the most famous and stunning natural sights in Ireland, including the Ring of Kerry, the Dingle Peninsula, and Killarney National Park. You'll find sea cliffs, rolling green hills, charming seaside villages, and aquamarine lakes. This area has long been one of the centers of Irish culture — many people speak Gaelic as their first language here, and the traditional Irish music and crafts scenes are thriving. Sound like a place you'd like to go? A lot of other people think so, too, making County Kerry one of the most-visited areas in Ireland. During the summer, the town of Killarney (and to a lesser extent Kenmare) swarms with visitors. If this is not your thing, my advice is to plan your vacation for the spring or fall or take some turns off the well-trodden tourist trails. I provide some off-the-beaten-track options in this chapter, such as a mountain drive on the Dingle Peninsula and a hidden farmhouse off the Ring of Kerry.

The brochure *Kerry Gems,* which you can pick up at any Tourist Information office, has many excellent suggestions for exploring this region.

Killarney and Killarney National Park

Killarney National Park is a must-see in this area — a gorgeous park with velvety valleys and deep blue lakes. Killarney Town itself doesn't have any must-see attractions, but it makes a fine base for visiting the park and for beginning or ending your tour of the Ring of Kerry. The town is overrun with visitors in the summer.

County Kerry

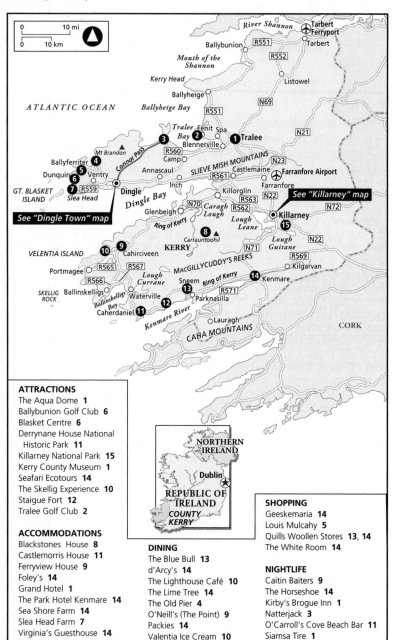

0 10 mi
0 10 km

River Shannon
Tarbert Ferryport
Tarbert
Ballybunion R551
R552
Mouth of the Shannon
Kerry Head
Listowel
Ballyheige
ATLANTIC OCEAN Ballyheige Bay
R551
N69
Tralee Bay Fenit Spa
Mt Brandon Blennerville **1** Tralee
R560 N21
Connor Pass Camp
Ballyferriter **4**
Dunquin **5** Ventry Annascaul SLIEVE MISH MOUNTAINS N23
Castlemaine Farranfore Airport
R561
GT. BLASKET ISLAND **7** R559 Inch Farranfore
Slea Head Dingle Killorglin N22
Dingle Bay R563 See "Killarney" map
See "Dingle Town" map Glenbeigh N70 Caragh Lough R562 N72
Ring of Kerry Lough Leane **15** Killarney
Carrauntoohil **8** N71 Lough Guitane N22
VELENTIA ISLAND **10** **9** Cahirciveen KERRY R569
Portmagee R565 R567 MacGILLYCUDDY'S REEKS Kilgarvan
R566 Lough Currane Sneem Ring of Kerry **14** Kenmare
SKELLIG ROCK Ballinskelligs Waterville **13** R571
Ballinskellig Bay **12** Parknasilla
Caherdaniel **11** Kenmare River Lauragh
CAHA MOUNTAINS CORK

NORTHERN IRELAND

Dublin

REPUBLIC OF IRELAND
COUNTY KERRY

ATTRACTIONS
The Aqua Dome **1**
Ballybunion Golf Club **6**
Blasket Centre **6**
Derrynane House National Historic Park **11**
Killarney National Park **15**
Kerry County Museum **1**
Seafari Ecotours **14**
The Skellig Experience **10**
Staigue Fort **12**
Tralee Golf Club **2**

ACCOMMODATIONS
Blackstones House **8**
Castlemorris House **11**
Ferryview House **9**
Foley's **14**
Grand Hotel **1**
The Park Hotel Kenmare **14**
Sea Shore Farm **14**
Slea Head Farm **7**
Virginia's Guesthouse **14**

DINING
The Blue Bull **13**
d'Arcy's **14**
The Lighthouse Café **10**
The Lime Tree **14**
The Old Pier **4**
O'Neill's (The Point) **9**
Packies **14**
Valentia Ice Cream **10**

SHOPPING
Geeskemaria **14**
Louis Mulcahy **5**
Quills Woollen Stores **13**, **14**
The White Room **14**

NIGHTLIFE
Caitin Baiters **9**
The Horseshoe **14**
Kirby's Brogue Inn **1**
Natterjack **3**
O'Carroll's Cove Beach Bar **11**
Siamsa Tire **1**

Getting to Killarney

To get to Killarney by car, take the N21 southwest from Limerick or the N22 northwest from Cork. From the Ring of Kerry and West Cork, take the N70. To get to Tralee from Killarney, take the N22 north. To continue on to Dingle, take the N86 from Tralee. **Irish Rail** (☎ **1-850-366-222;** www.irishrail.ie) serves Killarney and smaller towns on routes from Dublin, Limerick, Cork, and Galway. Trains arrive daily at the Killarney Railway Station, Railway Road, off East Avenue Road. The **Bus Éireann** (☎ **01-836-6111;** www.buseireann.ie) depot is next to the train station.

Getting around Killarney

Compact Killarney is entirely walkable, and **Tourist Trail** signs point out the highlights of the town. If you have a rental car with you, I recommend parking it at your hotel while you explore town. If you do park your car in town during the day, you need to display a parking disc in your car; discs are available at shops and hotels. There's no bus service within the town, but you can get a taxi at the taxi rank on College Square. For taxi pickup, call **Kerry AutoCabs** (☎ **064-663-7634**) or **Killarney Taxi** (☎ **086-389-5144**). For information on getting around Killarney National Park, see "Exploring Killarney National Park," later in this chapter.

Spending the night in Killarney

In addition to the options listed here, you also may want to check out **The Ross,** Town Centre (☎ **064-663-1855;** www.theross.ie), a swanky hotel in the center of Killarney.

Aghadoe Heights
$$$$ Killarney

Located far from the crowds of Killarney Town, Aghadoe Heights is all about hip luxury. Rooms are meant to be hideaways, with free-standing tubs, plasma TVs, cushy beds, Frette linens, and stunning views of Killarney's lakes and mountains. And then there's the spa, which recently won Best Resort Spa of the Year, and offers all sorts of treatments in slick surroundings (check out the zen relaxation suite). Service is friendly and helpful.

Lakes of Killarney (off N22). ☎ *064-663-1766. Fax: 064-663-1345. Parking: Free on-site. Rack rates: €180–€220 double. AE, MC, V.*

Arbutus Hotel
$$ Killarney

This hotel in the center of town has a traditional Irish feel to it, with cozy chairs arranged around a turf fire in the lobby. Rooms (especially those on the second floor) are large and tastefully furnished with beautiful

Killarney

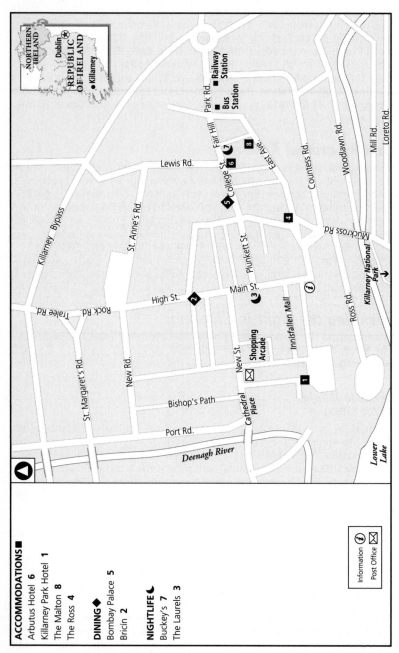

NORTHERN
IRELAND

Dublin

REPUBLIC
OF IRELAND
•Killarney

Railway
Station

Park Rd.

Bus
Station

Fair Hill

Lewis Rd.

College St.

St. Anne's Rd.

Killarney Bypass

East Ave.

Countess Rd.

Woodlawn Rd.

Mill Rd.

Loreto Rd.

Muckross Rd.

Killarney National Park

Plunkett St.

High St.

Main St.

Rock Rd.

Tralee Rd.

Innisfallen Mall

Ross Rd.

New Rd.

St. Margaret's Rd.

New St.

Shopping
Arcade

Cathedral
Place

Bishop's Path

Port Rd.

Deenagh River

Lower
Lake

Information ⓘ
Post Office ⊠

ACCOMMODATIONS ■
Arbutus Hotel **6**
Killarney Park Hotel **1**
The Malton **8**
The Ross **4**

DINING ◆
Bombay Palace **5**
Bricin **2**

NIGHTLIFE ☾
Buckey's **7**
The Laurels **3**

fabrics and furniture. The downstairs Buckley's Pub has an oak-paneled bar, and locals say that the bartenders there pull the best pints of Guinness in town. Good traditional music frequently fills the air. The Arbutus is a family-run hotel (going back three generations), and the entire staff is friendly and willing to help with anything.

College Street. From Main Street, turn onto Plunkett Street (it only goes one way). Plunkett becomes College, and the hotel is at the roundabout where College meets Lewis Road. ☎ **064-663-1037.** *www.arbutuskillarney.com. Parking: In a nearby garage, for a fee. Rack rates: €80–€110 double. Some rates do not include breakfast. MC, V.*

Friar's Glen
$$ **Killarney**

Everything at this bed-and-breakfast is about comfort, from the peat fire that blazes in the lovely sitting room to the soothing guest rooms. Mary and John Fuller welcome you to their grand country home with tea and cookies. The house is located right in Killarney National Park, and the Fullers will happily help you plan your visit. Rooms are large, with windows that look out on the surrounding mountains. Breakfasts are exceptional; be sure to try the banana "fritters," which are actually more like delicate crepes.

Mangerton Road. Coming from Killarney Town, turn left at Molly Darcy's Pub. ☎ **064-663-7500.** *Fax: 064-663-7388. www.friarsglen.ie. Parking: Free on-site. Rack rates: €100–€130 double. MC, V.*

Kathleen's Country House
$$ **Killarney**

This B&B and Friar's Glen are my top choices for those who are country mice rather than city mice. Kathleen's is located about 1.6km (1 mile) outside of Killarney Town, on large grounds filled with gardens. The bright, recently renovated rooms are furnished with antique furniture and original contemporary art. Kathleen herself is warm, friendly, and helpful.

Madam's Height, Tralee Road (N22). ☎ **064-663-2810.** *Fax: 064-663-2340. www.kathleens.net. Parking: Free on-site. Rack rates: €75–€100 double. AE, MC, V. Closed Nov–Feb.*

Killarney Park Hotel
$$$$ **Killarney**

Every inch of this luxurious hotel is a study in old-world elegance, class, and refinement. The Victorian-style lobby has plush couches, armchairs, and several fireplaces, and there's a fully stocked library where you can plan out your day over a cup of tea. Breakfast is served in a vaulted dining room complete with large oil portraits and plush, high-backed chairs. Guest rooms are spacious and tastefully furnished with antiques and sumptuous fabrics.

Kenmare Place, between the railway station and the cineplex. ☎ *064-663-5555.* www.killarneyparkhotel.ie. *Parking: Free on-site. Rack rates: €200–€310 double. Some rates do not include breakfast. AE, MC, V.*

The Malton
$$$ Killarney

This hotel has true classic style. The Victorian décor in the public rooms is polished and ornate, with detailed plasterwork, chandeliers, and inviting fireplaces. Guest rooms are large and traditionally furnished, and overlook the hotel's lush, gorgeously landscaped 8-hectare (20-acre) grounds. Amenities include a leisure center with a heated pool and Jacuzzi, a cocktail bar, 24-hour room service, and a full-service spa. The hotel's just a short walk from the center of town, but it feels worlds away.

Railway Road, off East Avenue Road between the railway station and the tourist office. ☎ **064-663-8000.** www.themalton.com. *Parking: Free on-site. Rack rates: €130–€170 double. AE, MC, V.*

Dining in Killarney Town

Bombay Palace
$$ Killarney INDIAN

After feasting on farmhouse cheeses, baby greens, and other gastronomic staples at sleek "New Irish" establishments, you may just be ready for a change of pace. Bombay Palace offers comfy tapestried chairs, friendly service, and all the usual favorites: chicken biryani, *aloo gobi* (cauliflower and potatoes), warm and fragrant garlic naan, and a sweet mango lassi to wash it all down.

10 College St. ☎ **064-37-755.** *Main courses: €9–€12. AE, MC, V. Open: Daily 5–11 p.m.*

Bricín
$$$ Killarney IRISH

If you're hankering for some hearty, well-made Irish food, you'll definitely want to try this cozy place, furnished with dark wood furniture, raspberry walls, and stained-glass windows. The restaurant specializes in *boxty,* traditional Irish potato pancakes filled with the meat or vegetable filling of your choice. Other options are delicious versions of such tried-and-true Irish dishes as lamb with rosemary.

26 High St. ☎ **064-663-4902.** *Main courses: €19–€26. MC, V. Open: Tues–Sat noon to 3 p.m. and 6–9:30 p.m. Closed late Jan–Feb.*

Exploring Killarney

Killarney Town is a fine place to sleep and eat while absorbing the majestic beauty of nearby Killarney National Park, but be forewarned: The town is thronged with visitors. Though there are a few interesting attractions in Killarney Town, including St. Mary's Cathedral on

Cathedral Place, off Port Road, and St. Mary's Church on Church Place, across from the tourist office, mostly Killarney Town is good for nice lodgings, pubs, and an assortment of shops selling souvenirs of the leprechaun-sitting-on-a-horseshoe-holding-a-shamrock variety.

The **Killarney Tourist Trail** takes you to the highlights of the town, keeping you on track with a series of signposts. The tour begins at the **Killarney Tourist Information Office** on Beech Road (☎ **064-31-633**) and takes about two hours, if you walk at a leisurely pace. To get to the tourist office, take New Street from the center of town and make a left onto Beech Road.

Exploring Killarney National Park

Killarney National Park is a paradise of sapphire lakes studded with grass-covered islands, heather-blanketed mountains towering above bogs, lush forests filled with rhododendron, and paths leading through rocky gaps laced with streams. A road dips and winds through part of the park past the three main lakes, but much of the land is accessible only by hiking, biking, horseback-riding, or riding in a horse-drawn jaunting car, and you'll get the best views and park access without a car. If you do decide to drive along the road, make time to stop at the various viewpoints, and park your car to take some short walks. Without stopping, the drive takes just over an hour, but you should give it at least half a day, because there's so much to see. The main entrance and **visitor center** is at Muckross House (☎ **064-663-1440**; www.killarney nationalpark.ie), where you can find maps and guides detailing hikes and other activities in the park. I definitely recommend stopping here to plan your visit. Admission to the park is free, and the park is open during daylight hours.

Gap of Dunloe

This breathtaking valley is bound on either side by craggy glacial rocks and soaring cliffs, and passes streams and lakes of a deep blue. The gap is accessible only by horse-and-cart, by foot, on horseback, or by bicycle (see the following section, "Exploring the park by foot, bicycle, or horseback," for more information). The best time to take the journey during the high season is early in the morning or late in the afternoon, when a quiet peace descends on an area that can be quite overcrowded.

Ladies View

Ladies View looks out on a stunning panorama of the surrounding mountains and the three lakes. How did it get its name? In the 1800s, Queen Victoria of England made a trip to Killarney and took her entourage through what is now the National Park. The queen's ladies-in-waiting were particularly thrilled with the view from this spot.

Off the N71, near the Upper Lake.

Killarney National Park

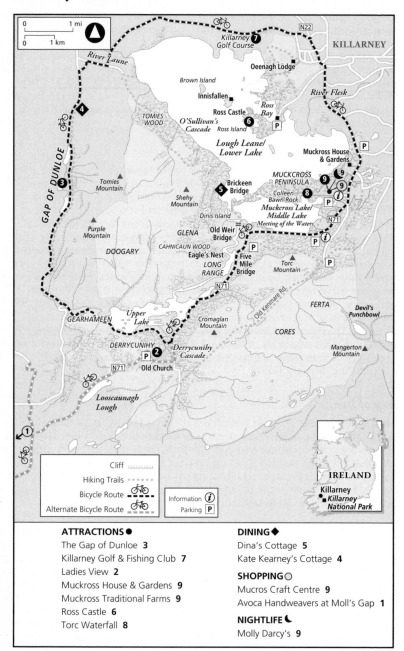

0 ____ 1 mi
0 ____ 1 km

KILLARNEY

N22

Killarney Golf Course **7**

River Laune

Oeenagh Lodge

Brown Island

Innisfallen

River Flesk

Ross Castle

TOMIES WOOD

O'Sullivan's Cascade

Ross Island

Ross Bay

6

Muckross House & Gardens

Lough Leanel Lower Lake

GAP OF DUNLOE

4

3

Tomies Mountain

Brickeen Bridge **5**

Shehy Mountain

MUCKROSS PENINSULA

Colleen Bawn Rock **8**

9

9

9

Muckross Lakel Middle Lake

Purple Mountain

Dinis Island

GLENA

Old Weir Bridge

Meeting of the Waters

N71

DOOGARY

CAHNICAUN WOOD

Eagle's Nest

LONG RANGE

Five Mile Bridge

Torc Mountain

N71

GEARHAMEEN

Upper Lake

Cromaglan Mountain

Old Kenmare Rd.

FERTA

Devil's Punchbowl

DERRYCUNIHY

2

Derrycunihy Cascade

CORES

Mangerton Mountain

N71

Old Church

Looscaunagh Lough

1

IRELAND

Killarney
• Killarney
National Park

Cliff ....
Hiking Trails ••••••
Bicycle Route ᘓ–•–
Alternate Bicycle Route ᘓ–

Information ⓘ
Parking Ⓟ

ATTRACTIONS ●
The Gap of Dunloe **3**
Killarney Golf & Fishing Club **7**
Ladies View **2**
Muckross House & Gardens **9**
Muckross Traditional Farms **9**
Ross Castle **6**
Torc Waterfall **8**

DINING ◆
Dina's Cottage **5**
Kate Kearney's Cottage **4**

SHOPPING ○
Mucros Craft Centre **9**
Avoca Handweavers at Moll's Gap **1**

NIGHTLIFE ☾
Molly Darcy's **9**

Muckross House and Gardens

This Victorian mansion is one of Ireland's finest stately manors. The décor and furnishings of the upper part of the home illustrate the lifestyle of the mid-19th-century gentry, while the basement gives you an idea of the harsher environment the domestic servants endured. A craft center here houses artisans working at traditional crafts such as weaving, bookbinding, and pottery making. The beautiful gardens are known for their rhododendrons, azaleas, and restored Edwardian greenhouses, and the grand lawns are enough to make any suburban homeowner drool with jealousy. Unfortunately, there is restricted accessibility for the disabled. Allow 90 minutes for your visit.

Take Kenmare Road (N71) out of Killarney. ☎ **064-663-1440.** *www.muckross-house.ie. Admission: Muckross House and Gardens alone €7 adults, €5.30 seniors, €3 students and kids; combined ticket for house, gardens, and traditional farms (see the next review) €12 adults, €10 seniors, €6 students and kids. Open: July–Aug 9 a.m.–7 p.m., Sept–June 9 a.m.–5:30 p.m. Last admission always one hour before closing.*

Muckross Traditional Farms

Turn off your cellphone, forget that you stayed in a hotel with electric lighting last night, and immerse yourself in the world of 19th-century rural Ireland. Farms of three sizes (small, medium, and large) occupy the pretty grounds and are populated by folks in period dress who go about their daily tasks: milking cows, cutting hay, gathering eggs from the chickens, harvesting potatoes, and so on. You also find a carpenter's workshop, a saddler's workshop, and a blacksmith's forge, all in operation. You're invited to step inside the farmhouses to enjoy home baking in front of the turf fires, join the farmers in their tasks, watch the craftsmen at work, and ask questions. Allow one to two hours for your visit.

Take Kenmare Road (N71) out of Killarney. ☎ **064-663-1440.** *www.muckross-house.ie. Admission: Farm €7.50 adults, €10 seniors, €6 students and kids; combination tickets for traditional farms with the house and gardens also available (see the previous review). Open: June–Aug daily 10 a.m.–6 p.m.; May and Sept daily 1–6 p.m.; Apr and Oct Sat–Sun 1–6 p.m. Last admission one hour before closing.*

Ross Castle

This fortified castle was built by the O'Donoghue chieftains, probably during the 15th century, and was the last stronghold in the province of Munster to surrender to Cromwell in 1652. What remains today is a huge tower house, surrounded by a wall with four smaller towers at each corner — clearly, fortification was a priority. Inside the tower is a lovely collection of furniture from the 16th and 17th centuries. The castle sits on a peninsula projecting into Lough (pronounced lock) Leane, Killarney's largest lake. The M.V. *Pride of the Lakes* (see "Joining an organized tour," later in this chapter) and other boats leave to explore the lake from the castle. You also can take a pretty lakeside walk between Killarney Town and the castle. Allow an hour for your visit.

Ross Road, off Kenmare Road (N71) about 2km (1¼ miles) outside of Killarney Town. Head south from town on Ross Road. ☎ 064-663-5851. Admission: €6 adults, €4 seniors, €2 students and kids. Open: Mid-Mar to Oct 27 daily 9:30 a.m.–5:45 p.m. Last admission 45 minutes before closing.

Torc Waterfall

This crashing waterfall is just off the N71, near Muckross House and Gardens. You can see the waterfall after a short walk on the lower path, but climb the stone stairs for an even better view.

Take the lower path from Muckross House.

Exploring the park by foot, bicycle, or horseback

If you're looking to explore on your own, pick up detailed maps at the Killarney Park tourist office at Muckross House, or at the Killarney tourist office in town.

✔ **By foot:** There are several signposted trails in the park, including the 2.4km (1½-mile) Blue Pool Nature Trail, which winds through woodlands and past a small lake; the 0.8km (half-mile) Old Boat House Nature Trail, which travels near Muckross Lake; the 2.4km (1½-mile) Mossy Woods Nature Trail, which takes you through woods along low cliffs; and the 4.8km (3-mile) Arthur Young's Walk, which takes you through forest and along the Muckross Peninsula.

My favorite hike involves getting a boat from the Old Boathouse across Muckross Lake to Dina's Cottage (a cute tearoom with beautiful views), and then hiking back along the Muckross Peninsula until you join up with the Arthur Young Trail. This hike should take most people about two hours. The visitor center at Muckross House can provide maps of the trails.

✔ **By bicycle:** Killarney National Park is a cyclist's paradise, with many marked bike trails through both easy and challenging landscapes. Biking through the Gap of Dunloe is a breathtaking experience (in both senses of the word). You can rent a bicycle at the **Bike Shop & Outdoor Store Killarney,** Lower New Street in Killarney Town (☎ **064-663-1282**).

✔ **By horseback:** A guided ride through the park is one of the finest ways to explore the area. **Killarney Riding Stables,** N72, Ballydowney (☎ **064-663-1686**), offers one- to three-hour rides through the park, as well as multiday horseback adventures that travel the Iveragh Peninsula (home to the Ring of Kerry). **Muckross Riding Stables,** on Mangerton Road, in Muckross (☎ **064-663-2238**), also leads horse treks through the park.

Joining an organized tour

If you want to add some structure to your explorations, check out the organized tours in the following list.

✔ **Dero's Killarney National Park Tours:** These tours are terrific ways to see the spectacular Kerry Mountains up close and personal. **Killarney Highlights** is a three-hour bus tour that takes you to all the highlights of Killarney National Park, including Ross Castle, Muckross House and Gardens, Torc Waterfall, Aghadoe, and the Gap of Dunloe. The longer **Gap of Dunloe** tour takes you by bus to Kate Kearney's Cottage (a craft shop) then either on a horse cart or hike through the breathtaking Gap of Dunloe. Once you've emerged on the other side of the gap, you'll take a boat down a river to Ross Castle, where the bus will meet you for your journey back to Killarney Town.

Tours run daily May through September. The Killarney Highlights tour departs at 2:30 p.m. from Dero's Tours office, 22 Main St., Killarney; the Gap of Dunloe tour leaves from the tour office at 10:30 a.m. Call ☎ **064-663-1251,** or go to www.derostours.com to confirm days and times. The Killarney Highlights tour costs €17; the Gap of Dunloe tour costs €50 with the horse-cart ride, €30 without.

✔ **Jaunting-Car Tour:** These horse-drawn buggies are as much a part of Killarney as the lakes and mountains. The drivers will take you through the town and as far as the Gap of Dunloe, and into Killarney National Park as far as Muckross House and Torc Waterfall. The drivers are characters, and pretty persuasive — even if you had no intention of taking one, you could find yourself bouncing in the back of a buggy with a blanket snug around your legs. This adventure is best undertaken in the off season or toward the end of the day, when the Gap of Dunloe is quieter and, thus, much more magical.

You can find jaunting cars all over town — or, rather, they'll find you. If you want to book in advance, contact **Tangney Tours** (☎ **064-663-3358**), though you won't have a problem finding a car in town on a moment's notice. Ask the tourist office or your hotel what to expect price-wise — prices vary based on demand and season. The going rate at press time for a one-hour tour was about €40 per car (up to four people can be taken in one car). Have the driver quote a price before heading out.

✔ **M.V.** *Lily of Killarney* **Waterbus Tour:** This tour leaves from Ross Castle and takes you around Lough Leane, Killarney's largest lake, on a large boat.

Tours leave from the pier at Ross Castle, from March through October (call ☎ **064-663-2638** for times). It costs €10 adults, €5 kids.

If all this green makes you think golf, visit the **Killarney Golf and Fishing Club.** The course is nestled among the beautiful Lakes of Killarney and below the majestic Macgillycuddy's Reeks Mountains. It's on Mahony's Point, Killarney (☎ **064-663-1034;** www.killarney-golf.com). The greens fees are €120 to €130 on the Killeen course, €90 to €100 on the Mahony's Point course, and €60 to €70 on the Lackabane course. Visitors are welcome every day and should make reservations ahead of time.

Shopping in Killarney

Avoca Handweavers, Molls Gap, in Killarney National Park off the N71 (☎ 064-663-4720), has a huge selection of knit and woven clothes, trendy "bohemian-chic fashions," unique jewelry, and crafts. **Mucros Craft Centre,** Muckross House (☎ 064-663-1440), features all sorts of Irish crafts, with the added bonus of on-site studios including a book bindery, a pottery, and a weaving studio.

Hitting the pubs

Buckley's
Killarney

Locals say this pub pulls the best pint of Guinness in town. The interior is oak-paneled, and turf fires make it cozy and welcoming. As the story goes, publican Tim Buckley spent some time in New York but, in the 1920s, he returned to Ireland because he deeply missed his hometown. He created this pub to combine all the great things he missed about Ireland while in the United States; maybe that's why it exudes such Irish comfort. Pub grub is served all day, and frequently you can find traditional music.

College Street. ☎ 064-663-1037.

The Laurels
Killarney

Kate Lee and Con O'Leary's place hasn't changed much over the past century. Secret alcoves and dim, warm lighting make this a great place for a long chat. There is occasional Irish music and dancing in summer.

Main Street. ☎ 064-663-1149.

Molly Darcy's
Killarney

This place has all the trimmings of a cozy, traditional pub, with stone walls, a beamed ceiling, and a thatched roof. It's quite popular with visitors, so move on if you're more interested in mixing with locals.

Muckross Road. In the Muckross Hotel complex across from Muckross House. ☎ 064-662-3400.

Getting the hang of Gaelic football

County Kerry is known for its excellent Gaelic football and rugby teams. If you're interested in seeing a match, check out the schedules on www.gaa.com and www.irishrugby.ie, or call the tourist office in Killarney (☎ 064-663-1633).

Fast Facts: Killarney

Area Code

Most numbers have the area code **064** followed by the numbers **663**.

Emergencies/Police

Dial ☎ **999** for all emergencies.

Genealogical Resources

You best bet is to contact the Kerry County Libraries (☎ 066-712-1200).

Hospital

Killarney Community Hospital is on St. Margaret's Road (☎ 064-663-1076).

Information

For visitor information, go to the Killarney Tourist Office, on Beech Road

(☎ 064-663-1633), open year-round. A great resource is the free publication *Kerry Gems,* which includes useful information such as maps, and events and entertainment listings. It's available at most hotels and guesthouses in town.

Internet Access

Check out the funky Rí-Rá Internet Café, 3 Plunkett St. (☎ 064-663-8729). For free access, head to Killarney Library, Rock Road (☎ 064-663-2655).

Post Office

The main Killarney Post Office is on New Street (☎ 064-663-1461).

The Ring of Kerry and the Iveragh Peninsula

The Ring of Kerry, a 176km (110-mile) circuit around the Iveragh Peninsula, is one of the most popular routes in Ireland. And there are good reasons for its renown: The winding route provides thrilling, dramatic views of the sea and the high inland mountains, and passes through a succession of charming villages, each with its own unique points of interest. Be aware that this is not the place to escape the crowds; the Ring is quite busy, especially during the summer.

Getting to and around the Ring of Kerry

By car, take the N70 south from Tralee or the N71 southwest from Killarney. A car is the best way to get to the Ring of Kerry and the best way to see it all. **Bus Éireann** (☎ 01-836-6111; www.buseireann.com) has limited service from Killarney to Cahersiveen, Waterville, Kenmare, and a few other towns on the Ring.

Railtours Ireland (☎ 01-856-0045; www.railtoursireland.com) runs a one-day tour that leaves from Dublin. You'll take a train to Killarney, and then board a bus for your tour of the Ring of Kerry. Tours cost €109 and leave daily at 7 a.m., returning at 9:15 p.m.

The Ring of Kerry is short enough to drive in a single day, but there are lots of things to see and do throughout the peninsula, and there are many places to spend the night, so I recommend taking two days for the drive. See "Exploring the Iveragh Peninsula and the Ring of Kerry," later in this chapter, for information on how to drive the Ring.

Spending the night on the Iveragh Peninsula and the Ring of Kerry

Blackstones House
$ Glencar

You may feel as though you're staying in a friend's house at this cozy farmhouse B&B. There are no locks on the bedroom doors, and guests can snuggle up with a book and a pot of tea in the family living room or hang out with one of the dogs at the picnic table outside. Rooms have a modern ski-lodge feel to them, with knotty-pine furniture and original watercolors, and all have spectacular views of the swift river that runs through the property (fishing equipment is available at the house), backed by rounded mountains. Hiking opportunities abound, and there are several golf courses nearby, though the isolated location won't suit you if pub-crawling is a priority. Your hosts, Padraig and Breda Breen, are sweet, friendly, and helpful. Evening meals are available on request.

Outside Glencar, off the Killorglin Road. ☎ *066-976-0164. Fax: 066-976-0269.* www. glencar-blackstones.com. *Parking: Free on-site. Rack rates: €60 double. MC, V. Closed Nov–Mar, but they may take guests, if you call in advance.*

Ferryview House
$ Caherciveen

If you're taking your time exploring the Ring of Kerry, Ferryview is a comfortable, homey spot for a rest. Jim and Mary Guirey and their dogs welcome you to the house, which is situated on a picturesque mini-peninsula just minutes away from the ferry to lovely Valentia Island. Rooms are airy and bright, with flower prints and colorful fabrics. Make time to walk to O'Neill's which serves up seafood that was swimming its way through the deep earlier that day.

Renard's Point, Caherciveen (right near the Valentia Island car ferry). ☎ *066-947-2052. Parking: Free on-site. Rack rates: €50–€56 double. No credit cards.*

Foley's
$$ Kenmare

This guesthouse has everything — location, food, music, drink, and comfort — all for a reasonable price. Set in the heart of Kenmare, Foley's is located within walking distance of golf, horseback-riding, and fishing. The downstairs pub is cozy and welcoming, and has excellent traditional Irish music many nights during the summer. Rooms are cute and trendy, with fun, bold wallpaper and fluffy white duvets. Be aware that the central location of the guesthouse means that weekend nights can be noisy.

Henry Street, where the N70 and N71 meet. ☎ *064-664-2162.* www.foleys kenmare.com. *Parking: Free in a nearby lot. Rack rates: €79–€89 double. MC, V.*

The Park Hotel Kenmare
$$$$ **Kenmare**

This grand hotel is beautifully situated, with lawns running down to Kenmare Bay and gorgeous views of the Caha Mountains in the distance. And that's just the outside. The interior is all luxury, all the time, with open fireplaces, high ceilings, rich upholstery, and stunning antiques. The spacious rooms are decorated with sumptuous fabrics and Victorian or Georgian furnishings, and some even boast canopy or four-poster beds. Service is warm and welcoming. The hotel's restaurant serves excellent modern Irish cuisine plus the lauded "Best Breakfast in Ireland," and the fabulous spa, named one of *Condé Nast Traveler*'s top 25 spas in the world, offers a range of treatments. You can even take in a classic movie in the hotel's own 12-seat cinema.

On the R569 in Kenmare, past the golf club. ☎ **064-664-1200.** *www.parkkenmare. com. Parking: Free on-site. Rack rates: €168–€198 double. AE, MC, V. Closed Nov–Mar.*

Sea Shore Farm
$$ **Kenmare**

The selling point of this spacious farmhouse is the unbelievable view of the Bay of Kenmare and the mountains of the Beara Peninsula beyond, visible through the large windows and sliding doors in most rooms. The style of the spacious, uncluttered rooms is sort of a country twist on standard modern hotel décor, with flowery quilts and antique-style furniture. The house is a five- or ten-minute drive from town, but it feels much more secluded, especially when you ramble down to the empty seashore. Hosts Mary Patricia and Owen O'Sullivan are friendly, interesting, and helpful. In fact, every time we're in the area, my dad asks, "Oooh, are we staying with Owen and Pat?"

Tubrid (right outside Kenmare). From Kenmare, take the N71, make a left on N70, and then take another left turn at the sign for Sea Shore Farm. ☎ **064-664-1270.** *www. kenmare.eu/seashore. Parking: Free on-site. Rack rates: €100–€130 double. MC, V. Closed Mid-Nov to Feb.*

Virginia's Guesthouse
$ **Kenmare**

Located right in the center of charming Kenmare, this B&B has some of the kindest owners in these parts. Neil and Noreen Harrington consistently go the extra mile for guests, helping with everything from planning your itinerary in Kerry to finding the best lunch spot. Breakfast is divine, with such interesting options as melted blue cheese over pears, served with crispy (American-style) bacon. The culinary adventure continues at Mulcahy's, the terrific restaurant located under the guesthouse. Rooms are bright, spotless, and simply furnished in blue and beige. Ask for a room away from the street if you're sensitive to noise.

Henry Street. ☎ **064-664-1021.** *Fax: www.virginias-kenmare.com. Parking: Free on the street. Rack rates: €60–€80 double. MC, V.*

Dining in Kenmare and along the Ring

For some great pub dining options, see "Hitting the pubs", later in this section. For gourmet ice cream in a peaceful seaside setting, hit **Valentia Ice Cream,** off R565 near Tinnies, on Valentia Island (☎ 066-947-6864), open daily during the summer. The caramel and pistachio are two of my favorites.

The Blue Bull
$$–$$$ Sneem   SEAFOOD/PUB GRUB

This roadside pub, decorated with old black-and-white prints of Kerry, is known throughout the county for its fresh seafood, so you can't go wrong with the seafood platter. Steaks, hearty soups, and other classic Irish fare, including a delectable Irish stew, round out the menu. Irish music sessions take place several times a week during the high season.

South Square. On the Ring of Kerry, 24km (15 miles) west of Kenmare. ☎ 064-664-5382. Main courses: €8–€22. AE, MC, V. Open: Bar food daily 11:30 a.m.–9:30 p.m., restaurant daily 6–9:30 p.m.

d'Arcy's
$$$ Kenmare   NEW IRISH/SEAFOOD

Come to d'Arcy's for solidly delicious gourmet Irish food, prepared with fresh ingredients by a talented chef and served in a pretty dining room with a big open fireplace. Menu highlights are oysters (served in several different guises), whole grilled lemon sole served with poached grapes and chive beurre blanc, and herb-crusted rack with roast garlic and rosemary *jus*. The set menu is a steal at €29 for three courses. d'Arcy's has worked several environmentally friendly practices into its operation, from buying locally sourced ingredients to collecting rainwater for floor mopping and plant watering.

Main Street. ☎ 064-664-1589. Reservations recommended. Main courses: €15–€26; set menu €29. AE, MC, V. Open: May–Sept Tues–Sun 5–10 p.m., Oct–Jan and mid-Feb to Apr most weekends 5–10 p.m. Closed Jan to mid-Feb.

The Lighthouse Café
$–$$ Valentia Island   IRISH

The indoor area of this cafe is a cute place to sit on a rainy day, but wish hard for a sunny day if you really want to enjoy this place. Pick a table outside and soak in the views of green cliffs running down to the sea below. The menu is not extensive, but the food is fantastic, especially the thick seafood chowder, studded with mussels, smoked haddock, fresh cod, and vegetables. Be sure to try a salad, as the cafe grows many of its vegetables and edible flowers in organic gardens on-site.

Dohilla, Valentia Island (follow signs from Knightstown). ☎ 066-947-6304. Main courses: €6–€18. No credit cards. Open: June–Aug Tues–Thurs and Sun 11 a.m. –7 p.m., Fri–Sat 11 a.m.–10 p.m. Call for hours Sept–May.

The Lime Tree
$$$ **Kenmare   IRISH**

What a genuine place. No slave to trends, the Lime Tree is beloved for its consistent focus on beautifully prepared, straightforward dishes such as rich seafood chowder, expertly steamed mussels, and generous steaks. Meat, fish, and vegetables are fresh and locally sourced, and it shows. The setting is a high-ceilinged stone cottage, and the décor is a marriage of contemporary and country. Service couldn't be nicer.

Shelbourne Street. ☎ **064-41-225.** *Main courses: €18–€28. MC, V. Open: Easter to Oct daily 6:30–10 p.m.*

O'Neill's (The Point)
$$$ **Cahirciveen   SEAFOOD**

At first glance, this might look like your everyday, cozy pub, with model boats, bottles of liquor and jars on shelves lining the walls, and stone floors. But after you settle in, you'll likely note the delicious smells wafting from the kitchen. Toothsome seafood dishes are the specialty — from smoked salmon to deep-fried squid, to crab claws tossed with olive oil, garlic, and chili peppers. O'Neill's owns its own fleet of fishing boats, so you can be sure that your dish was just swimming (or scuttling, in the case of the crabs) that morning. My favorite dish is the hot and cold seafood selection, a sampler plate offering pan-fried hake, deep-fried squid, crab, shrimp, fresh salmon, and smoked salmon.

Renard Point, right near the ferry to Valentia Island. ☎ **066-947-2165.** *Main courses: €17–€24. No credit cards. Open: Apr–Oct Mon–Sat noon to 2 p.m. and 5:30–9:30 p.m., Sun 5:30–9:30 p.m.*

Packies
$$$–$$$$ **Kenmare   IRISH/NEW IRISH**

This hip, cheerful restaurant, with stone walls displaying contemporary local art, serves up delectable dishes that range from traditional Irish to internationally influenced fare. The simple crab claws in garlic butter will have you licking your fingers, and more-adventurous dishes, such as plaice with orange, lime, and cilantro, may have you licking your plate.

Henry Street. ☎ **064-664-1508.** *Reservations recommended. Main courses: €15–€33. MC, V. Open: Mon–Sat 6–10 p.m. May be closed Jan–Mar, so check in advance.*

Exploring the Iveragh Peninsula and the Ring of Kerry

In addition to taking in the glorious views that the Ring of Kerry offers around every bend, history and natural history buffs should enjoy the sights in this section.

The draw of the Ring of Kerry and the Iveragh Peninsula is the breathtaking mountain, cliff, and coastal scenery, best seen by driving or biking for the strong of heart (both physically and metaphorically), with frequent stops for hikes and walks. I highly recommend driving the Ring yourself if you don't mind a lot of twists and turns and the occasional monster tour bus hogging the road.

Tour buses usually drive the Ring counterclockwise, beginning in Killarney or Killorglin and going around to Kenmare. To avoid the buses, begin in Kenmare and go clockwise — that way, you'll be going against the traffic. Another way to beat the tour buses is to hit the road before they do — buses leave Killarney and Killorglin at 9 or 10 a.m.

If you don't think you're up for driving yourself around the Ring, check out the **Railtours Ireland Ring of Kerry Tour** (see "Getting to and around the Ring of Kerry," earlier in this chapter).

If you take the standard counterclockwise route and start in **Killorglin,** known as the gateway to the Ring, the next town you come to is **Glenbeigh,** which is partially surrounded by mountains. At **Rossbeigh,** you first catch sight of the Atlantic. You'll hit the town of **Cahirciveen** before arriving at **Portmagee,** a pretty fishing harbor where you cross the bridge to **Valentia Island.** You'll find interesting sights on the island, including tetrapod footprints left more than 350 million years ago, the **Skellig Experience** (see p. 289), and stunning views complemented by historical information about the area at Geokaun Mountain and Fogher Cliffs. You can depart from here for a boat trip of the Skellig rocks, which rise like cathedrals from the Atlantic and are topped with monastic ruins. I also highly recommend taking the Bray Head hike to an overlook of the Skelligs. To get to Bray Head, start at the Skellig Experience, and then continue on R565 until it hits a *T,* then make a left, and park in the small parking lot at the beginning of the hike. **Ballinskelligs** is a *Gaeltacht,* or Irish-speaking area. If the weather is good, you also may be able to see the Skelligs from here.

Waterville, the next town on the Ring, is known as a fishing resort but has plenty of other sporting attractions to divert you from the drive. In beautiful **Caherdaniel,** you can see the home of Daniel "The Liberator" O'Connell; and nearby **Castlecove** is loaded with sandy beaches. The lovely village of **Sneem,** filled with vividly colored buildings, has mountain and river scenery and is a haven of peace and quiet. **Parknasilla** benefits from the Gulf Stream and has a (comparably) warm climate and even subtropical plants. Finally, the Ring of Kerry ends in the charming, picturesque town of **Kenmare,** where you'll find great hotels, restaurants, shopping, and pubs.

Now, some insider advice: Yes, the Ring is spectacular, but it is only a small part of the Iveragh Peninsula. I highly recommend taking some of the local interior roads through the mountains and hills that make up the center of the peninsula, particularly in the area around gorgeous Caragh Lake. It's amazing how untouched this area is. Instead of tour buses, you may encounter a farmer leading his herd of cows down the road to a different pasture. And you'll certainly encounter incredible scenery. All you need is a good driving map.

Derrynane House National Historic Park
Caherdaniel

This home was where early 19th-century political figure Daniel O'Connell, often called "The Liberator," lived for most of his life. O'Connell was a lawyer and politician who fought for the repeal of anti-Catholic laws, and for the separation of Ireland from Great Britain. The house sits on the coast and boasts extensive gardens. Allow about an hour for your visit.

Right off the Ring, in Caherdaniel. You see a sign 1.6km (1 mile) north of Caherdaniel for parking. ☎ *066-947-5113. Admission: €3 adults, €2 seniors, €1 students and kids. Open: May–Sept daily 10:30 a.m.–6 p.m., Apr and Oct–Nov Wed–Sun 10:30–5 p.m. Last admission 45 minutes before closing.*

Seafari Ecotours

A two- to three-hour cruise aboard this boat, which holds up to 100 people, is the best way to get up close and personal with the many gray seals that call this area home. The cruise is also a great way to see the castles, ruins, and megalithic monuments that line the shores of the bay. Captain Ross is both hilarious and knowledgeable, providing interesting commentary on local geology and history, and pointing out the dolphins, sea otters, and water birds that often frequent the bay along with the seals. If you'd prefer to cruise with a smaller group of travelers, a more intimate cruise (☎ 087-259-2209; www.kenmareanglingandsightseeing.com) explores the bay with just ten passengers.

Leaves from Kenmare Pier (next to the Kenmare suspension bridge), Kenmare. ☎ *064-664-2059. www.seafariireland.com. Price: €20 adults, €18 students 19 and over, €15 students 12–18, €13 kids 11 and under. Frequent departures daily May–Oct; call for information on departures in the off season.*

The Skellig Experience
Valentia Island

The two Skellig rock islands, Skellig Michael and Little Skellig, jut steeply out of the sea about 14km (8 miles) from the Iveragh Peninsula. This heritage center, located on beautiful Valentia Island, has well-done exhibits and audiovisual displays explaining the natural and human history of the Skelligs. You learn about the lives and work of the early Christian monks who created their monastery on Skellig Michael, the history of the Skellig lighthouse and its keepers, and the bird and plant life of the Skelligs. Allow 45 minutes if you're not taking the boat trip.

The visit may inspire you to book one of the center's incredible boat trips out to the islands. If you'd like a chance to explore the monastery ruins on the Skellig Michael, check out the Skellig Michael boat trip, reviewed next.

Take the R565 to Portmagee and Valentia Island. The heritage center is just across the bridge from Portmagee as soon as you cross over onto Valentia Island. ☎ 066-947-6306. Admission: Exhibit only €5 adults, €4 seniors and students, €3 kids 11 and under; exhibit and boat trip €28 adults, €25 seniors and students, €15 kids 11 and under. Open: July–Aug daily 10 a.m–7 p.m., May–June and Sept daily 10 a.m.–6 p.m., Mar–Apr and Oct–Nov Mon–Fri 10 a.m.–5 p.m. Closed Dec–Mar. Boat trips leave most days but are canceled will some frequency due to inclement weather and high seas. Suggested visit: 45 minutes if you are not taking the boat trip.

Skellig Michael Boat Trip and Exploration

This fabulous adventure begins with a 45-minute boat ride to Skellig Michael. Once there, you can climb the steep steps up to the monastery, which was founded in the 6th or 7th century and flourished until the 12th or 13th century. Among the ruins, you'll find a church, a number of small beehive-style huts, and two oratories. In addition to the archaeological marvels, the thousands of nesting gannets on Little Skellig and the many puffins on nearby Puffin Island are quite a sight. The trip lasts about 4½ hours.

Trips depart from Portmagee. Reserve beforehand at ☎ 087-120-9924. Price: €40 per person.

Staigue Fort
Castlecove

This is one impressive ring fort. Not much has changed in the structure since the chieftains of the region lived here around a.d. 300 with their extended family and slaves. Climb the steps inside the fort for some spectacular views, and duck into the elfin-sized storerooms along the interior. There is a visitor center, but it doesn't add much.

Signposted off the N70, west of Castlecove. ☎ 066-75-127. Admission: Free, but suggested donation of €1 adults. Open: Daily 24 hours.

Shopping

Plenty of shops dot the Ring of Kerry, but the best shopping is in the town of Kenmare, which has a variety of specialty shops and several stores selling what the town used to be known for — Kenmare lace.

Geeskemaria, 2 Shelbourne St., Kenmare (☎ 064-664-1410), sells stylish knitwear, jewelry, and silk clothing. **The White Room,** 21 Henry St., Kenmare (☎ 064-664-0600), stocks a fine collection of tablecloths, sheets, nightgowns, and more made with linen and Irish lace. **Quills Woolen Market,** the corner of Market and Main streets, Kenmare (☎ 064-664-1078), has a fine selection of Irish clothing including Aran sweaters, Donegal tweeds, and Irish linen; there's a second location in Sneem, along the Ring of Kerry.

Hitting the pubs

Caitin Baiters
Cahirciveen

This thatched-roof pub is comfortable and cozy, and serves hearty food and a well-pulled pint, both at reasonable prices. Some nights (it's hit-or-miss), there are music sessions.

Kells Bay. From the town's main street, follow the turnoff to Kells Bay; it's on that little road. ☎ **066-947-7614.**

The Horseshoe
Kenmare

A relaxed vibe is on tap at this bar, which fronts an excellent restaurant. Nurse a pint, chat with the locals, and all will be right with the world.

3 Main St., Kenmare. ☎ **064-664-1553.**

O' Carroll's Cove Beach Bar
Caherdaniel

The Ring of Kerry's version of an ocean-side Cancun club, this place is located in a gorgeous cove with a swimming area. By day, families hang out on the beach and pack into the bar for burgers, fish and chips, and the like. By night, the crowds enjoy the nightly live music.

Located off the N70 outside of Caherdaniel. ☎ **066-947-5151.**

The Puck Fair

For three days during the second week of August, Killorglin explodes into a fiesta of music, drinking, storytelling, and general merrymaking during the Puck Fair. A billy goat is crowned King Puck, and the ribbon-bedecked goat presides over the festivities from a high pedestal. The origins of this celebration stretch far back — it's thought to have started as a pagan festival in honor of Lugh, the Celtic sun god. When I asked a Killorglin gent whether he had taken part in the festivities for all three days, he replied "Aye, and three nights." Check out www.puckfair.ie for all sorts of information on the festival.

Fast Facts: The Iveragh Peninsula and the Ring of Kerry

Area Codes

Most numbers on the Ring of Kerry have the area codes **064** or **066**.

Emergencies/Police

Dial ☎ **999** for all emergencies.

Hospital

Kenmare Community Hospital can be reached at ☎ 064-664-1088.

Information

For visitor information, go to the Kenmare Tourist Office at The Square (open summer only).

Internet

You can access the Internet at Kenmare Library, on Shelbourne Street (☎ 064-664-1416).

Tralee and the Dingle Peninsula

Don't tell the Irish Tourism Board, but I think that the Dingle Peninsula is even more beautiful than the Iveragh Peninsula. The Dingle Peninsula generally has a gentler beauty (though, like the Iveragh Peninsula, it also boasts awe-inspiring views of wave-pounded cliffs) and is less clogged with visitors. Long, sandy beaches, hills of a thousand different stunning shades of green divided into a patchwork by old stone walls and hedges, extraordinary pre-Christian ruins, craggy cliffs, and a large *Gaeltacht* (Irish-speaking area) — what more could you want? I also have a special place in my heart for the sweet and funky town of Dingle (also known as An Daingean, the town's Irish name), with its many shops, restaurants, and galleries, and its beautiful views of Dingle Harbor. The town is a busy place in July and August, but it still manages to retain its friendly, artsy, small-town character.

If you're coming to the Dingle Peninsula from another area of Ireland, you may want to stop over in **Tralee** the night before you set out to explore the peninsula. Tralee is pleasant and convenient, though there is not a lot to see or do in the town. If you're traveling without a car, **Deros Tours** (☎ 064-663-1251; www.derostours.com) runs a bus tour that takes you from Tralee along the rugged Dingle coastline, past many of the prehistoric highlights of the peninsula. See p. 300 for more information on tours of the Dingle Peninsula.

Getting to and around Tralee and the Dingle Peninsula

If you're coming by car from Dublin, follow signs for the M7/N7 southwest to Limerick, and then get on the N21 or N69 (Coast Road) to Tralee.

Tralee

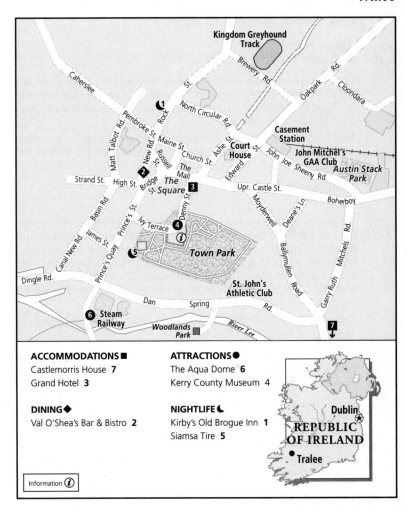

ACCOMMODATIONS ■
Castlemorris House **7**
Grand Hotel **3**

DINING ◆
Val O'Shea's Bar & Bistro **2**

ATTRACTIONS ●
The Aqua Dome **6**
Kerry County Museum **4**

NIGHTLIFE ☾
Kirby's Old Brogue Inn **1**
Siamsa Tire **5**

Information *i*

From the Ring of Kerry and points south, take the N70 to Tralee. From Killarney, Cork, and the east, take the N22. Trains and buses to Tralee arrive at the station on John Joe Sheehy Road (call ☎ **01-836-6111** for bus information, ☎ **1-850-366-222** for train information).

Bus Éireann also provides service to Dingle Town daily; the depot is on Upper Main Street.

Spending the night in Tralee and on the Dingle Peninsula

Alpine House
$ Dingle Town/An Daingean

This guesthouse offers great value. The sizable rooms are comfortable, spotless, and bright; and owners Paul and Caroline are friendly and helpful. The heart of Dingle Town is just a two-minute walk away, and the views of Dingle Bay are splendid.

Mail Road. ☎ **066-915-1250.** *Fax: 066-915-1966.* www.alpineguesthouse.com. *Off the main road (N86). Parking: Free on-site. Rack rates: €70–€110 double. AE, MC, V.*

Castlemorris House
$$ Tralee

A room in a 1790s manor house at these rates? Nope, you're not dreaming. Rooms here are large and elegant, furnished with reproduction antique furniture, but it's the hosts that really make the place. Tony and Ciara Fields are more than willing to help with plans, directions, and anything else that you might need. The breakfasts are excellent, and the location is superb: a ten-minute walk from downtown Tralee and perfect for launching your visit to the Dingle Peninsula.

Tralee (off the N86). ☎ **066-718-0060.** www.castlemorrishouse.com. *Parking: Free on-site. Rack rates: €90–€100 double. MC, V.*

Castlewood House
$$–$$$ Dingle Town

Wow. How do Brian and Helen Heaton manage to maintain such a lovely, elegant B&B, always find time to chat with and help out their guests, and make it all look effortless? The Heatons clearly have a keen eye for design; each room is unique, from an Asian-influenced boudoir with silky fabrics and a Buddha statue, to a cozy hideout with lush carpeting and lovely handmade quilt. The couple has thought of everything — there's even a computer with Internet access just for guests. Breakfasts, with choices from porridge with Bailey's liquor to fresh kippers, are fabulous, and the central location is the icing on the cake.

The Wood (on the west end of Dingle Town). ☎ **066-915-2788.** www.castlewood dingle.com. *Parking: Free on-site. Rack rates: €100–€140 double. MC, V. Closed Jan.*

Grand Hotel
$ Tralee

This hotel is a solid, reliable choice. The staff is warm and helpful, and the public rooms have that great old-world hotel look, with lots of mahogany and ornate plasterwork. Guest rooms are of the standard business-hotel

Dingle Town

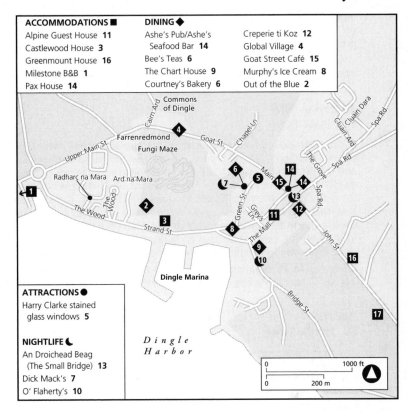

ACCOMMODATIONS ■
Alpine Guest House **11**
Castlewood House **3**
Greenmount House **16**
Milestone B&B **1**
Pax House **14**

DINING ◆
Ashe's Pub/Ashe's
  Seafood Bar **14**
Bee's Teas **6**
The Chart House **9**
Courtney's Bakery **6**

Creperie ti Koz **12**
Global Village **4**
Goat Street Café **15**
Murphy's Ice Cream **8**
Out of the Blue **2**

Commons
of Dingle

Cairn Ard

Cluain Dara

Cluain Ard

Spa Rd.

Farrenredmond
Fungi Maze

Goat St.

Chapel Ln.

The Grove

Spa Rd.

Upper Main St.

Radharc na Mara

Ard na Mara

The Wood

The Wood

Main St.

Green St.

Greys Ln.

Spa Rd.

John St.

Strand St.

The Mall

Bridge St.

Dingle Marina

ATTRACTIONS ●
Harry Clarke stained
  glass windows **5**

NIGHTLIFE ☾
An Droichead Beag
  (The Small Bridge) **13**
Dick Mack's **7**
O' Flaherty's **10**

*Dingle
Harbor*

0   1000 ft
0   200 m

variety, decorated with dignified earth tones. The hotel restaurant, Samuel, is a destination in itself, serving fresh, well-prepared dishes. End your night in the lovely bar, where you'll likely find a convivial mix of locals and visitors.

Denny Street. ☎ **066-712-1499.** *Fax: 066-712-2877. Parking: Free on-site (small lot), or in paid parking lots nearby. Rack rates: €70–€90 double. Some rates do not include breakfast. AE, MC, V.*

Greenmount House
$$ Dingle

Beware: The views of Dingle Bay and Dingle Town from this modern lodging may cause you to delay your day's plans in favor of lingering over breakfast. The house feels more like a small hotel than a B&B, with spacious rooms (those in the bungalow building have sitting areas and balconies), large bathrooms, upscale modern furniture, and extremely comfortable beds. Service is kind and professional, but if you're looking for a lot of warmth and helpful hints from your hosts, you may be better off at Milestone House. Breakfast is amazing in both scope and quality — be sure to try some of the mouthwatering cheeses from the buffet. The main streets of Dingle Town are about a 10- or 15-minute walk away.

John Street. ☎ **066-915-1414.** *www.greenmounthouse.com. Parking: Free on-site. Rack rates: €70–€100 double. MC, V.*

Milestone B&B
$ Dingle Town

It's hard to do anything but gush about the Milestone, which is located a short drive from Dingle Town. The rooms are simple, impeccably clean, and bright, furnished with IKEA-style furniture; the views of Dingle Bay are dazzling; and the breakfasts are excellent. But what sets this B&B apart from the pack are your hosts, Michael and Barbara Carroll. The Carrolls love the Dingle Peninsula, and they know it inside and out. They make it their mission to share their knowledge with their guests, and can often be found helping visitors to plan an itinerary that suits their needs. If this is your first time in Dingle, definitely book a room here.

Milltown, 1km (½ mile) outside of Dingle on the R559. ☎ **066-915-1831.** *www.iol. ie/~milstone. Parking: Free on-site. Rack rates: €70–€80 double. No credit cards.*

Pax House
$$ Dingle Town

The first thing that you notice about this place is the view — it's spectacular. Overlooking the water, with mountains in the distance, Pax House will tempt you to just lounge around on the comfortable balcony all day after enjoying your gourmet breakfast. Inside, rooms are welcoming and homey, furnished with eclectic artwork and lovely fabrics.

Upper John Street. ☎ **066-915-1518.** *www.pax-house.com. Parking: Free on-site. Rack rates: €80–120 double. MC, V. Closed Dec–Feb.*

Slea Head Farm
$ Dunquin

Located on a working farm, this cozy B&B is situated in a rural area between Ventry and Dunquin. The panoramas surrounding the house are pure, gorgeous Ireland: cows and sheep grazing on emerald-green grass, a maze of old stone walls creeping up a gentle hill, and a ruined stone house next door. And the finest views are reserved for travelers whose bedroom windows look out onto the nearby sea and the famed Blasket Islands. Rooms are simple and sweet, with homey touches such as stuffed animals perched on the furniture. The Irish-speaking family who runs the B&B is warm and welcoming.

On the road between Ventry and Dunquin. ☎ **066-915-6120.** *www.sleahead farm.com. Parking: Free on-site. Rack rates: €60–€70 double. MC, V. Closed Oct–Apr.*

Dining locally in Tralee and on the Dingle Peninsula

Dingle Town can be a little pricey for food, so take advantage of the early-bird set menus that almost all restaurants in town offer, usually from about 5:30 p.m. until about 7 p.m.

If you're in town on a Friday from May through October, hit the Dingle Farmer's Market, at the Holyground Car Park in Dingle Town, for bannoffee cupcakes, unbelievable artisan cheese, and all sorts international hot dishes, from Polish to Greek. The market runs from about 9 a.m. until about 2 p.m.

Ashe's Pub/Ashe's Seafood Bar
$$$ Dingle Town   GOURMET PUB FOOD/SEAFOOD

The scene: A traditional pub, with dark wood tables and chairs and warm golden lighting. The supporting players: The friendly manager and helpful staff. The stars: A menu featuring terrific and creative seafood dishes along with Irish pub standards such as beef-and-Guinness stew. Standouts include "tempura of today's catch" served with cilantro aioli and chili sauce; the Spanish fish stew, laced with saffron and fennel; and an out-of-this-world seafood chowder.

Lower Main Street. ☎ *086-804-9563. Reservations recommended. Main courses: €16–€29. MC, V. Open: Food served Mon–Sat noon to 3 p.m. and 6–9 p.m., Sun 5:30–9:30 p.m. (tapas).*

Chart House
$$$$ Dingle Town   NEW IRISH

This place is the culinary equivalent of a spa treatment, with everything from the country décor to the warm service conspiring to create a relaxing atmosphere. The freshest of Irish ingredients are used in the well-executed dishes, which, on my last visit, included such gems as herb-crusted skate with a leek and parmesan risotto, and a seared filet of Kerry beef with dauphinoise potatoes, caramelized shallots, and port wine *jus*. The room is inviting, with stone walls, stained-glass windows, and pine tables set with mismatched pottery. Don't miss the warm sticky toffee pudding.

The Mall. ☎ *066-915-2255. Reservations recommended. Main courses: €20–€30. MC, V. Open: June–Sept daily 6:30–10 p.m.; phone ahead for opening hours in the off season.*

Global Village
$$$$ Dingle Town   NEW IRISH/SEAFOOD

Families, groups of friends, and couples all love this relaxed restaurant. The walls are a sunshine yellow, graced with contemporary oil paintings, and (more important) the food is terrific. The chef is creative in preparing fresh, local ingredients. On my last visit, I had braised beef cheeks with horseradish mashed potatoes and red wine *jus,* and my dad had pan-fried mackerel in an oatmeal crust with a warm potato, butter bean, and orange salad. Check out the early-bird specials, which include two or three courses at a great price.

Upper Main Street. ☎ *066-915-2325. Main courses: €22–€29. AE, MC, V. Open: Mar to mid-Nov daily 5:30–10 p.m.*

Goat Street Café
$$–$$$ Dingle Town   CafE/Vegetarian

This bright little cafe draws its influences from around the world, with lunch offerings such as a warm salad of chorizo, roast pear, and goat cheese, and a Thai green curry served with Basmati rice, and dinner choices that feature the freshest produce and the catches of the day. The service couldn't be nicer, and there are some enticing vegetarian choices.

Main Street. ☎ **066-915-2770.** *Main courses: Dinner €15–€20. AE, MC, V. Open: Mon 10 a.m.–4 p.m., Tues–Sat 10 a.m.–4 p.m. and 5:30–8:30 p.m.*

Sweet treats: Unbeatable ice cream, amazing pastries, and the finest teas

I would consider moving to Dingle Town just for **Murphy's Ice Cream,** Strand Street, Dingle (☎ **066-915-2644**). The smooth confection is made with top-quality ingredients: Kerry cream and milk (thank those cows the next time you drive past them), and the best natural flavorings, such as Madagascar and Organic Mexican Vanilla in the vanilla ice cream, real Champagne and peaches in the Bellini sorbet, Jamaican rum in the rum raisin, and so on. You may want to go for one of the distinctly Irish flavors, such as Irish-cream ice cream, black-currant-and-Guinness sorbet, or brown-bread ice cream. After intense menu research, the delicious, caramel-tinged honeycomb ice cream has emerged as my favorite.

Courtney's Bakery (☎ **066-915-1583**), located in the courtyard next to Dick Mack's Pub on Green Street, sells divine pastries. Its fresh cream and apple concoction is perfection. For something a little more French, seek out **Creperie ti Koz**, 2 John St. (☎ **066-9152-039**), an adorable little cafe decorated in warm sunset orange colors that serves up terrific sweet and savory crepes, plus bubbly Kermé cider.

Bee's Teas, also located in the courtyard next to Dick Mack's Pub on Green Street, just might be the sweetest tea room in the world, serving a well-curated menu of teas and coffees, plus finger sandwiches and baked goods, including sparkly cupcakes. (Really! They're sparkly!) The afternoon tea (€22 per person) can make even the dreariest rainy day better. Bee herself is Dick Mack's (see p. 304) great-granddaughter, and the tea-room is located in her great-granddad's old milking parlor.

The Old Pier
$$$–$$$$ Ballydavid   SEAFOOD/CONTIENTAL

For me, there's something about eating seafood with a view of the sea that makes it taste even better, so I find the Old Pier's view of Smerwick Harbour very satisfying. Though the meat dishes are excellent, it's the seafood dishes — featuring locally caught fish and shellfish — that keep bringing people back. Finned choices range from monkfish scampi-style to black sole served in a butter, lemon, and parsley sauce, while the meat-based selections include the terrific grilled lamb cutlets with currant sauce. Don't expect fancy foams or super-innovative ingredients here; this place is dedicated to classic recipes and cooking methods. The restaurant also operates a B&B.

Located north of Ballydavid on the R559. ☎ **066-915-5242**. *Main courses: €17–€30. MC, V. Open: Dinner orders taken Wed–Mon 6–7:15 p.m. Closed Mid-Nov to Feb.*

Out of the Blue
$$$$ Dingle Town   SEAFOOD

The official name of this place is Out of the Blue Fresh Fish Seafood Only Restaurant, because it serves only dishes that once swam or crawled through the nearby briny deep (though it also offered a vegetarian plate when I was last there). A little pompous, maybe, but Out of the Blue does serve the best seafood in Dingle Town. The chalkboard menu changes depending on the catches of the day. Preparations, such as *skate* (ray wings) with caper butter and haddock on tomato sauce, are relatively simple and allow the flavor of the fish to shine through. The garlic crab claws are unbelievable. The restaurant itself has a Mediterranean feel, with simple pine tables and oil paintings of fish and the sea gracing the walls. Lunch here is much less expensive than dinner.

Waterside. ☎ **066-915-0811**. *Reservations recommended. Main courses: Dinner €23–€34. MC, V. Open: Thurs–Tues noon to 3 p.m. and 6–9:30 p.m. Closed Nov–Mar 17.*

Exploring Tralee and the Dingle Peninsula
If you're interested in a boating trip on Dingle Bay, contact **Dingle Marine Eco Tours,** located at The Pier in Dingle Town. Book in advance at ☎ **086-285-8802.**

The Sleeping Giant?

As you tour the Dingle Peninsula on the Slea Head Drive, keep an eye out for an island that looks like a giant taking a snooze on his back. From most parts of the peninsula, he looks like he's slumbering peacefully. However, on other parts of the peninsula, it appears that he has a dagger embedded in his neck. In those parts, he's known as the Murdered Bishop rather than the Sleeping Giant.

A dazzling tour of the Dingle Peninsula

The big attraction of the Dingle Peninsula is driving, biking, or hiking your way around, taking in the scenery, as well as the many prehistoric ruins. I recommend starting in **Castlemaine** and taking the coastal road (R561 or R559) toward Dingle Town. Along the way, you may want to pay a visit to **Inch Beach,** a long sandy beach with the Atlantic waves on one side and curvy, sea-grass-covered dunes on the other. It's a strange sight to stand on the dunes looking at the vast Atlantic in one direction and grazing cows and sheep in the other. Move on toward **Dingle Town,** which is a great place to spend a night or two before driving the Slea Head Tour.

From Dingle Town, take the gorgeous 48km (33-mile) **Slea Head Tour,** a round-trip circuit that winds along the south coast, past miles and miles of small patchwork fields, up the west end of the peninsula, and then back to Dingle Town. If you prefer two wheels rather than four, this is a great route for biking; you can rent bikes from **Foxy John's,** Main Street, Dingle (☎ **066-915-1316**). You may want to make your first stop at pretty **Ventry Beach,** before visiting the remains of **Dunbeg Fort,** built in 800 b.c. Right near Dunbeg Fort, look out for signs indicating the location of **beehive huts** (known as *clocháin* in Irish), small stone structures that are thought to date from around 1000 b.c. The highlight of the route is **Slea Head,** which features towering cliffs with incredible views of the Atlantic Ocean and the **Blasket Islands** (described later in this section), sandy beaches (though the waters are not safe for swimming), and several trail heads. Visit the village of **Dún Chaoin** (Dunquin), the heart of the Dingle *Gaeltacht* (Irish-speaking area), with its striking views of the Blasket Islands, before checking out the **Blasket Centre** and possibly taking a boat trip to Great Blasket Island. You may then want to have lunch at Tig Áine and move on to visit **Clogher Strand,** a small beach with beautiful stones that look as though they're decorated with maps from some undiscovered land (the beach is located off the second turn after the Louis Mulcahy pottery shop). Next stop: **Gallarus Oratory,** an astoundingly intact seventh-century Christian church built without any sort of mortar. Adventurers will want to depart from the Slea Head Drive at Feothanagh, driving east (and up) on narrow mountain roads through breathtaking **Conor Pass,** where you'll be rewarded with thrilling panoramic view of the entire peninsula, plus views of several peaceful glacial lakes. Wind your way down to the picture-postcard fishing villages of **Cloghane** and **Brandon.** From there, you can drive east past unspoiled sandy beaches, cute fishing villages, and farmland. *Note:* Only confident drivers should attempt the Conor Pass route, as it's a triple threat of winding, narrow, and steep.

This route will take you a whole day. I recommend staying in Dingle Town or west of Dingle Town on the nights before and after your drive or bike ride.

If you're visiting Dingle Peninsula without a car (and even if you have a car), **Denis Ryan** (☎ **086-325-2996;** www.dingletours.com) takes travelers out to explore the archeology and scenery of the peninsula in his cab. Tours start at €20 per person.

Hiking the Dingle Peninsula

The Dingle Way leaves from Tralee and makes a 153km (95-mile) circuit of the peninsula. The trail winds through beaches and farmland and along cliffs. For day-hikers, there is a beautiful stretch between Dunquin and Ballyferriter, and another going northeast out of Féohanagh. Get your hands on the *Dingle Way Map Guide* (available at tourist offices and shops in the area) before you begin the trail.

Another great hiking trail, the Pilgrim's Route (48km/30 miles), meanders through the fields of the peninsula, connecting many of the peninsula's interesting early Christian sites. The ascent to Mount Brandon's summit, located at the end of the route, is difficult but spectacular. Pick up a Pilgrim's Route map (available at tourist offices and shops in the area) before you begin the trail.

The Aqua Dome
Tralee

If your kids don't think they've been on vacation if they haven't gotten a chance to submerge themselves in water, this indoor water park is the place to go. Kids can splash around in the kiddie pools, fly down sky-high slides, and battle raging rapids — all under one roof. Meanwhile, adults can relax in the sauna dome, which has two saunas, a steam room, a cool pool, and a sun bed. The main pool is for the whole family, and next door is an over-16-only "health suite," with hot tubs and a sauna. If you or your kids get sick of the water, there's also a mini–golf course, remote-controlled trucks and boats, and a giant trampoline.

Dingle Road (next to the steam railway heading out of town). ☎ **066-712-9150.** *Admission: €15 adults; €12 seniors, students, and kids; free for kids 1 and under. Open: Mon–Fri 10 a.m.–10 p.m., Sat–Sun 10 a.m.–8 p.m. (9 p.m. in July and the first half of Aug).*

Blasket Centre (Ionad an Bhlascaoid Mhóir)
Dunquin (Dún Chaoin)

This heritage center, on the tip of the Dingle Peninsula, celebrates the Blasket Islands, which lie a few miles from the mainland. Great Blasket, the largest of the islands, was home to a Gaelic-speaking community until the 1950s. Photographs, a video presentation, and other exhibits illustrate the lives of the Blasket Islanders, who farmed and fished for sustenance and have a rich storytelling and musical tradition. Much of the museum focuses on the literary achievements of the Blasket Islanders — several autobiographies and collections of Blasket Island tales were published with great success. The exhibits, while very well done, are heavy on text, so younger kids may be bored. There are incredible views of the islands through the large windows in the center. If you're interested in visiting the

Blasket Islands, see the information in the next review. Allow 90 minutes for your visit.

Village of Dunquin (right off the R559). ☎ **066-915-6444.** *Admission: €4 adults, €3 seniors, €2 students and kids. Open: Apr–Oct daily 10 a.m.–6 p.m. Last admission 45 minutes before closing time.*

Blasket Islands

Intrigued by what you've seen and heard at the Blasket Centre? There's only one thing to do: Book a trip to peaceful Great Blasket Island, where you can walk amongst the ruins of the village, hike the *green road*s (roads that have been reclaimed by grass), and watch seals (and sometimes dolphins, porpoises, shark, and whales) from the white sand beaches.

The Blasket Island Ferry departs from Dunquin Harbour. ☎ **086-335-3805.** *Ferries depart several times daily Apr–Sept 30 starting at 10 a.m.; call for off-season sailing times. Reservations recommended. Tickets: €25 round-trip adults, €15 round-trip kids 11 and under.*

Harry Clarke Stained-Glass Windows at Díseart
Dingle

This Irish Cultural Centre contains a treasure of Irish art — six magnificent stained-glass windows created by master stained-glass artist Harry Clarke in 1922. The windows depict scenes from the Bible, with glowing colors and tremendous detail, especially in the animated faces of the subjects. An audio tour gives you the details on the history of Clarke and the windows, and explains the scene portrayed in each window. On your way in or out of Díseart, check to see if the center is holding any of its frequent cultural events.

Off Green Street, behind St. Mary's Church. ☎ **066-915-2476.** *Admission: €3.50. Open: Daily 9 a.m.–5 p.m.*

Fungie the Dolphin
Dingle

Dingle's most famous resident, Fungie the Dolphin, is a friendly, playful dolphin who has been hanging out around the waters of Dingle Bay since 1984. He's not in captivity, so theoretically he could take off for bluer waters at any time, but he's stuck around for more than two decades, so odds are good that he's in Dingle to stay. Fungie seems to love playing with humans, and if you take a boat tour to see him (there are separate trips for swimmers and nonswimmers), you'll likely be treated to a display of arcing jumps and up-close encounters as Fungie swims alongside the boat. Plus, you'll have wonderful views of serene Dingle Bay. If you're up for it, I recommend going whole-hog and renting a wetsuit and snorkel gear so that you can play with Fungie in the water. Floating peacefully in the blue water of Dingle Bay and seeing this winsome creature eye-to-eye are worth the initial shock of climbing into the cool water.

The Pier. ☎ **066-915-2626** *for boat trips, 066-915-1146 for wetsuit rental. Call to pick up a wetsuit and make reservations the day before for swimming trips. Cost: Boat trip €16 adults, €8 kids 2–12, free for kids 1 and under; swimming trip €25; wetsuit €20. You can buy tickets for the boat ride at the tourist office on the Pier. Call for times and to reserve a spot.*

Other cool things to see and do

Try some of these activities to get yourself out into the bracing Dingle air:

- ✔ **Golfing:** On Sandhill Road, you'll find **Ballybunion Golf Club** (☎ **068-27-146;** www.ballybuniongolfclub.ie), a seaside club with two excellent 18-hole, par-71 courses. The newer course was fashioned by the legendary Robert Trent Jones, though the Old Course is the more challenging of the two. Greens fees are €140 to €180 for the Old Course and €55 to €75 for the newer course. Visitors are welcome daily, provided you call to book in advance.

  The par-71 **Tralee Golf Club,** located at West Barrow, Ardfert, in Tralee (☎ **066-713-6379;** www.traleegolfclub.com), is the original European Arnold Palmer–designed course. This course is set against an amazing backdrop, framed by a river, the sea, and the crumbling castles of Ardfert. Greens fees are €180 from May through October, and €90 the rest of the year. Visitors are welcome from May through October every day except Sunday. Visitors are not permitted on Sundays or on Wednesdays in June, July, and August. You must book in advance either over the phone or on the Web site.

- ✔ **Horseback riding:** Mountain and beach rides are available through **Dingle Horse Riding** (☎ **087-133-8084;** www.dinglehorse riding.com), located a mile outside of Dingle Town.

- ✔ **Kerry County Museum,** Ashe Memorial Hall, Denny Street, Tralee (☎ **066-712-7777**): Kerry's history unfolds before you at this well-done heritage center. Exhibits cover everything from myths and legends of the county to local music to Gaelic football.

  Admission is €8 adults, €6.50 students, €5 kids. It's open May through August daily from 9:30 a.m. to 5:30 p.m.; September through April Tuesday through Saturday 9:30 a.m. to 5 p.m. Last admission is one hour before closing. Allow 90 minutes for your visit.

Irish folk theater

Siamsa Tire, Town Park, Tralee (☎ **066-712-3055;** www.siamsatire.com), performs theater that celebrates the rich dance, music, and folklore traditions of Ireland.

Shopping

Dingle Town is home to many artists, making it a fabulous place to buy contemporary fine art as well as crafts. In addition, there are some great pottery shops along roadsides throughout the Dingle Peninsula; just drop in when you come across them.

Brian de Staic, Green Street, Dingle (☎ 066-915-1298), offers unique handcrafted gold jewelry. Many of his pieces incorporate Celtic designs. **Dingle Record Shop,** Green Street (across from St. Mary's Church; ☎ 087-298-4550), owned by the wonderful Mazz O'Flaherty, is a great place to buy traditional music recordings. Out on the peninsula, well-known craftsman **Louis Mulcahy** (☎ 066-915-6229) creates lustrous pieces of pottery. Mulcahy's workshop is located about 4km (2½ miles) west of Ballyferriter.

Hitting the pubs

The Dingle Peninsula, and Dingle Town in particular, is a great place for music. Drop into most any pub during the summer, and you'll hear tin whistles, fiddles, pipes, and other instruments going strong.

An Droichead Beag (The Small Bridge)
Dingle Town

The trifecta of a warren of dimly lit rooms, year-round top-notch Irish music, and warm crowds makes this one of my favorite pubs in this part of Ireland.

Main Street. ☎ 066-915-1723.

Dick Mack's
Dingle Town

Beloved Dick Mack's retains an aura of times gone by — years ago, pubs often doubled as providers of other essential services; this one served as a cobbler's shop, and one side of the pub still holds the leatherworking tools of the late owner. Hang out with locals at the bar — there's always great *craic* — or duck into the little snug for a quiet chat.

Green Street. ☎ 066-915-1960.

Kirby's Brogue Inn
Tralee

This bright-yellow alehouse has dubbed itself "your landmark in Tralee." Given the great atmosphere and food, it probably will be. Its quaint exterior gives way to a wonderful old pub inside, where you'll hear traditional Irish music and jazz in the summers, and where you can chow down on great pub grub all day.

Rock Street. ☎ 066-712-3357.

Natterjack
Castlegregory

This old pub, which concentrates more on great traditional music and food than on the latest trend in décor, is a perfect place to stop in for a bite and a refreshing pint after the drive to the north end of the peninsula. The pub offers a kids' menu and a beer garden in summer.

The West End. ☎ **066-713-9491.**

O'Flaherty's
Dingle Town

You can count on the music in O'Flaherty's to be good — the owner frequently performs. Check out the posters and clippings that line the walls to get a real feel for Dingle Town. Everything about this place screams *authentic,* and the locals who frequent it often chat in Irish Gaelic. It's big and open, with a stone-flagged floor.

Bridge Street. ☎ **066-915-1983.**

Fast Facts: Tralee and Dingle Peninsula

Area Code
The main area code for Tralee and Dingle is **066.**

Emergencies/Police
Dial ☎ **999** for all emergencies.

Hospital
In Tralee, the Tralee General Hospital is off the N69 (☎ **066-718-4000**). In Dingle, the Dingle District Hospital is located in St. Elizabeth's, on the north side of town (☎ 066-915-1455).

Information
For visitor information in Tralee, go to the Tralee Tourist Office at Ashe Memorial Hall, Denny Street, Tralee (☎ 066-712-1288), which is open year-round. The Dingle Tourist Office is on Strand Street in Dingle Town (☎ 066-915-1188).

Internet
Dingle Internet Cafe, Lower Main Street, Dingle (☎ 066-915-2478), has Internet access and printing capabilities.

Part V
The West and the Northwest

The 5th Wave   By Rich Tennant

In this part . . .

You can't beat the West and Northwest for their sheer diversity of landscapes. In Clare (Chapter 17), take in the vertiginous Cliffs of Moher, which plummet down to the sea; the rocky moonscape of the Burren, studded with a rainbow of wildflowers; and the county's sandy beaches. Up in County Galway (Chapter 18), explore the wild lakes, bogs, mountains, and beaches of Connemara. Mayo (Chapter 19) offers gorgeous heather-covered islands, beaches, and a continuation of the Connemara landscape of bogs, cliffs, and mountains, while travelers to Sligo (Chapter 19) will find lakes, beaches, and woodlands, many connected in some way with poet William Butler Yeats. If you want to get way off the well-trodden track, head up to wild, sparsely populated County Donegal (Chapter 20) and explore the craggy coastline, towering cliffs, sandy beaches, and impressive mountains of the region.

And I haven't even mentioned the cities and towns in these parts. Westport in County Mayo (Chapter 19) and Clifden in County Galway (Chapter 18) are two of the most charming, bustling, and picturesque towns in Ireland. Sligo Town (Chapter 19), a friendly little town with a healthy arts scene, makes a nice base for exploring sights associated with Yeats, while Ennis is a small town with winding medieval streets and a dizzying choice of top-notch traditional Irish music. And compact Galway City (Chapter 18) may turn out to be your favorite city in Ireland, with its beautiful location on the shores of Galway Bay and Lough Corrib; its strong art, music and theater scenes; and its packed-to-the-rafters pubs.

Chapter 17

Counties Limerick and Clare

Many people know **County Limerick** through Frank McCourt's *Angela's Ashes,* in which Limerick City is depicted as a sodden and sullen place. Yes, it rains in Limerick (as it does all over the West of Ireland), but you may be surprised by the new restaurants and shops that are popping up in the city. Though it's still not a destination city, Limerick is worth a brief stop if you're interested in any of the attractions in the area. Near Limerick City, **Adare** is a sweet little village of restored thatched-roof cottages with some excellent restaurants.

Sure, **County Clare** is famous for the sheer, breathtaking Cliffs of Moher. But this county is no one-trick pony. In the north, you'll find the rocky moonscape of the Burren, with all sorts of wildflowers poking up through the gaps in the vast stone fields. Where else can you find Arctic and tropical wildflowers growing side by side? In the south are long sandy stretches of beach backed by rolling green hills. And throughout the county are charming towns and villages whose pubs ring to the rafters with some of the best traditional music in all of Ireland.

County Limerick: Limerick City and Adare

County Limerick has never exactly been the tourist hub of the country, but many visitors to Ireland pass through at some point. Those who have read Frank McCourt's *Angela's Ashes* often picture **Limerick City** as a town wracked with poverty, unemployment, alcoholism, and rain — lots of rain. "Out in the Atlantic Ocean," McCourt wrote, "great sheets of rain gathered to drift slowly up the River Shannon and settle forever in Limerick. . . . The rain drove us to the church — our refuge, our strength, our only dry place. . . . Limerick gained a reputation for piety, but we knew it was only the rain."

The whole west of Ireland does get its fair share of rain, but you'll be surprised to see how different the Limerick of today is from the Limerick McCourt remembered from his youth. The city has been pulling itself up from near dilapidation and is slowly becoming a bustling place with some good restaurants and shopping (especially clothes shopping), plus a first-rate art and history museum and a handful of historic sights. Some places in the city still fit McCourt's descriptions, but these are becoming fewer and fewer, as funky cafes open up in previously boarded-up buildings, and so on. If you're interested in any of the attractions in or near the city, the city makes a fine base; otherwise, I would skip it — Dublin, Cork, Belfast, and Galway are more lively large cities, and parts of Limerick can be a bit dangerous at night, though crime in the city seems to be on the way down.

With its main street of thatched-roof cottages sporting window boxes full of flowers, narrow streets, and ruined ivy-covered churches, the pretty little town of **Adare** (pronounced uh-*dare*) looks like a set for a movie about old Ireland. The town is clearly geared for tourism, and you find no lack of fellow travelers enjoying the little shops, excellent restaurants, and handful of historic sights. You don't need more than a day to explore.

Getting to County Limerick

Shannon International Airport (☎ 061-71-2000; www.shannon airport.com), located on the N19, off the N18, south of Ennis and 24km (15 miles) west of Limerick City, receives direct flights from North America, Europe, and Britain (see Chapter 6 for more information), as well as flights from within Ireland. Rental-car company desks are located at Shannon Airport's Arrivals Hall. All the major car-rental companies listed in Chapter 7 are represented there. **Bus Éireann** (☎ 01-836-6111; www.buseireann.ie) offers service from Shannon to the many destinations in the area (including Limerick City itself). In addition, **J. J. Kavanagh & Sons** (☎ 0818-333-222; www.jjkavangh.ie) runs a bus service from Shannon Airport to Dublin Airport that stops at the University of Limerick, in the city. Taxis also run from Shannon into Limerick City for about €45.

Getting to and around Limerick City

If you're coming by car, Limerick City can be reached by the N20 from Cork, the N21 from Tralee, the N24 from Tipperary, the M6 to N7 from Dublin, or the N18 from Ennis and Galway. By the time you read this, the M7 highway from Dublin straight to Limerick may be in place.

Counties Limerick and Clare

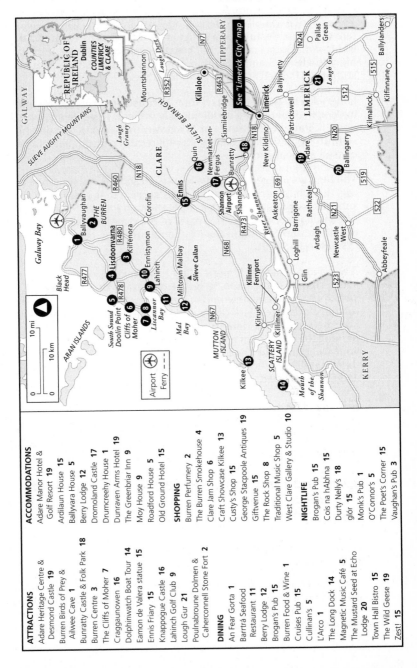

ATTRACTIONS
Adare Heritage Centre & Desmond Castle **19**
Burren Birds of Prey & Ailwee Cave **1**
Bunratty Castle & Folk Park **18**
Burren Centre **3**
The Cliffs of Moher **7**
Craggaunowen **16**
Dolphinwatch Boat Tour **14**
Eamon de Valera statue **15**
Ennis Friary **15**
Knappogue Castle **16**
Lahinch Golf Club **9**
Lough Gur **21**
Poulnabroune Dolmen & Caherconnell Stone Fort **2**

DINING
An Fear Gorta **1**
Barrtrá Seafood Restaurant **11**
Berry Lodge **12**
Brogan's Pub **15**
Burren Food & Wine **1**
Cruises Pub **15**
Cullinan's **5**
L'Arco **5**
The Long Dock **14**
Magnetic Music Café **5**
The Mustard Seed at Echo Lodge **20**
Town Hall Bistro **15**
The Wild Geese **19**
Zest! **15**

ACCOMMODATIONS
Adare Manor Hotel & Golf Resort **19**
Ardilaun House **15**
Ballyvara House **5**
Berry Lodge **12**
Dromoland Castle **17**
Drumcreehy House **1**
Dunraven Arms Hotel **19**
The Greenbriar Inn **9**
Moy House **9**
Roadford House **5**
Old Ground Hotel **15**

SHOPPING
Burren Perfumery **2**
The Burren Smokehouse **4**
Clare Jam Shop **6**
Craft Showcase Kilkee **13**
Custy's Shop **15**
George Stacpoole Antiques **19**
Giftvenue **15**
The Rock Shop **8**
Traditional Music Shop **5**
West Clare Gallery & Studio **10**

NIGHTLIFE
Brogan's Pub **15**
Cois na hAbhna **15**
Durty Nelly's **18**
glór **15**
Monk's Pub **1**
O'Connor's **5**
The Poet's Corner **15**
Vaughan's Pub **3**

Irish Rail (☎ 1-850-366-222; www.irishrail.ie) services Limerick City from Dublin, Cork, Killarney, and other cities throughout Ireland. Trains arrive at Colbert Station, on Parnell Street within walking distance of most destinations in Limerick City. **Bus Éireann** (☎ 01-836-6111; www.buseireann.ie) has daily service to Limerick City and most towns in County Limerick. The bus station is the same as the train station, at Parnell Street in Limerick City.

Limerick City is best seen on foot, because one-way streets and continuing construction make it ridiculously difficult to get from point A to point B. Park at your hotel or in a downtown parking lot and hoof it from sight to sight. Parking on city streets requires discs that can be purchased at local shops.

The best way of getting to the major attractions outside the city is by car, though Limerick has a local bus service that covers the city's suburbs — running from Colbert Station on Parnell Street — and Bus Éireann has service to other parts of the county. You also can catch a cab at Colbert Station in the city center at night, or call **City Taxi** at (☎ 086-815-5655).

A word about safety: Limerick City has a history of gang-related violence, though it seems to be on the decline as of this writing. Take the same precautions you would in most big cities. Always take a taxi back to your hotel after dark (it's a good idea to leave the pubs about half an hour before closing time to ensure that you get a taxi quickly), park in a parking lot if you're in a less busy part of town or at night, don't put your wallet in your back pocket, and keep an eye on belongings. Other than that, locals recommend avoiding Southill, at the junction of N20 and Childers Road.

Getting to and around Adare

By car, take the N21 southwest from Limerick City. **Bus Éireann** (☎ 01-836-6111) runs through Adare. The town itself is completely walkable.

Spending the night in Limerick City and Adare

The Mustard Seed at Echo Lodge (see p. 314) also offers splendid, antiques-furnished rooms.

Adare Manor Hotel and Golf Resort
$$$$ **Adare**

This tremendous castle-like manor house is one of the most beautiful properties in Ireland. There is nothing subtle about it — the structure was designed to reflect a variety of Irish and English homes admired by the first owners, the Lord and Lady Dunraven. It is an amalgam of styles, with turrets, 52 chimneys, and stone gargoyles gracing its exterior. The public rooms are breathtaking, especially the giant hall inspired by the Hall of Mirrors at Versailles. Opulent fabrics, hand-carved woodwork and stone, and gorgeous views of a river characterize the bedrooms. And I haven't even mentioned the 226-hectare (840-acre) grounds, which include a Robert Trent Jones–designed golf course (home to the Irish Open in 2007, 2008, and 2009), a trout-filled river, formal French gardens, sweeping parklands, and majestic trees. A spa on the premises rounds out the offerings. The hotel attracts many travelers from the United States, so it's not the place to bump elbows with locals. The separate "Golf Villas" are popular with larger groups who want the convenience of several bedrooms, a kitchen, and a den; prices at this time are €330 to €600 per night for a three-bedroom option.

Off the N21. ☎ **061-60-5200,** *or* ☎ **800-462-3273** *in the U.S.* www.adaremanor. ie. *Parking: Free on-site. Rack rates: €300–€440. AE, MC, V.*

Dunraven Arms Hotel
$$$ Adare

Built in 1792 and located across the street from the thatched cottages of little Adare, this is a classic "old-style" hotel with loads of character. Rooms are well-kept and spacious, outfitted with the lovely fabrics and antique furniture. Modern conveniences include a pool, a sauna, and a gym, plus a new 200-person conference center. Service is welcoming and friendly. Skip the restaurant; there's much higher-quality food to be had in this area. The hotel often offers excellent Internet-only rates on its Web site, so check there before calling to make a reservation.

Main Street (N21). ☎ **061-60-5900.** *Fax: 061-39-6541.* www.dunravenhotel. com. *Parking: Free on-site. Rack rates: €90–€160 double. MC, V.*

Limerick Strand Hotel
$$ Limerick City

This has got to be one of the best of Ireland's new breed of modern, independent hotels. Located across the river from the center of Limerick, it seems to please everyone, from families to business travelers to couples. Rooms are stylish, decorated in vibrant colors, with fluffy white duvets, silky pillows, and abstract paintings. My room had a coffee-and-orange color scheme, with crushed-velvet lounge chairs. Everything is spotless, including the nicely sized bathroom (each has a tub with a shower). The options are excellent for breakfast in the dining room, but you also can choose to reserve a room without breakfast or you can order breakfast to your room (for a small fee). A health club, spa, hair salon, and air-conditioning in each room are other perks. Reserve on the Internet for the best rates.

On the corner of Limerick Street and Patrick Street, Limerick City. ☎ **061-421-800.** www.strandhotellimerick.ie. *Parking: €5 per day on-site. Rack rates: €72–€92. Breakfast not included in some rates. AE, MC. V.*

Dining locally in Limerick City and Adare

For lunch in Limerick, the **Sage Cafe,** 67–68 Catherine St. (☎ 061-409-458), serves excellent dishes made with all sorts of local products. **Dolan's Pub** (see p. 319) has great hearty Irish dishes for lunch and dinner, and **Locke Bar** (see p. 319) serves some nice seafood.

Copper and Spice
$$ Limerick City INDIAN/THAI

This popular, relaxed restaurant does a bang-up job with both Thai and Indian standards, such as its best-selling chicken makhani. Excellent vegetarian options include such treats as okra with crunchy spiced onions, *saag aloo* (a spinach and potato dish), and *Bombay aloo* (potatoes cooked in a beautifully spiced tomato sauce). The chefs adjust spiciness levels according to your preference, and they aren't afraid to turn up the heat if you ask them. The space has an elegant, South Asian feel, with red plush banquettes, large Impressionist paintings in fiery colors, and hammered-copper glasses and pitchers on each table. The €25 three-course meal is quite a deal.

2 Cornmarket Row. ☎ **061-31-3620.** *Main courses: €11–€19. MC, V. Open: Wed–Sun 5–10:30 p.m.*

The Mustard Seed at Echo Lodge
$$$$ Ballingarry NEW IRISH

The surroundings are gorgeous enough to distract you, but even endless gardens, a splashing fountain, and a beautiful country manor can't take away the impact of the food at the Mustard Seed. You'll spend a bit more than at many other places mentioned in this book, but you'll get a true gourmet meal in return. Organic vegetables (from the restaurant's own garden), fruits, and cheeses, combined with local meats and fish, are the foundation of the creative dishes. The menu changes all the time. Some of the gems in the past have included pan-fried filets of sea bass with caramelized endive, onion velouté, and an avocado and sweet corn salsa; and the imaginative breast of Barbary duck on a bed of buttered greens, served with lime and vanilla mashed potatoes and chocolate oil. The atmosphere is calm and gracious. Sunday through Thursday, a three-course fixed-price meal can be ordered between 6:45 p.m. and 7:45 p.m. for €38.

Newcastlewest Road, Echo Lodge. From Limerick City, take the N21 southwest to Adare, and then the R519 south to Ballingarry. ☎ **069-68-508.** *Reservations recommended. Main courses: €63 four-course fixed-price dinner. AE, MC, V. Open: Daily 6:30–9 p.m. Usually closed Mon in winter (call to check).*

The Wild Geese
$$$$ Adare NEW IRISH

Just to give you an idea of the kind of restaurant this is, when the gracious server came around with the bread basket, in addition to the usual white

---

The birth of Irish coffee

It was a dark and stormy night (really!) in 1943 and a handful of passengers had just landed in Limerick as a stopover between the U.S. and mainland Europe on a grueling flight. The chef at the airport's cafe, Joseph Sheridan, whipped up a concoction of coffee, cream, and Irish whisky to warm the passengers. They loved it, and legend has it that one impressed passenger asked, "Is this Brazilian coffee?", to which Sheridan responded, "No, it's Irish coffee." Here's the basic recipe:

1. **Warm a stem glass.**

2. **Add 2 teaspoons brown sugar and a splash of whiskey.**

3. **Fill almost to the top with hot black coffee, and stir well.**

4. **Pour lightly whipped cream slowly on top so that it floats.**

---

and wheat rolls, we were offered banana rolls, which turned out to be excellent. The chef here is not afraid to use his locally sourced ingredients with a sense of fun and daring. The menu changes, but expect main courses such as a breast of corn-fed chicken stuffed with brie and sun-dried tomatoes, wrapped in pancetta and served with a wild-mushroom risotto, and appetizers such as the onion-and-parmesan tartlet studded with raisins. The interior is simple and candlelit, and the mood is convivial. The fixed-price menu is a terrific deal at €29 for two courses and €35 for three courses. The sumptuous Sunday lunch is €20 for two courses and €25 for three courses.

Rose Cottage, Main Street. ☎ *061-39-6451. Reservations recommended. Main courses: €28–€30. AE, DC, MC, V. Open: Tues–Sat 6:30–10 p.m., Sun 12:30–2:30 p.m. Closed for two weeks mid-Jan.*

Exploring Limerick City and Adare

Limerick City has enough interesting sights to make a full day of sightseeing. Adare really only has one attraction — the Heritage Centre — but it's a pretty place to wander around for a couple hours.

Joining an organized tour

The *Angela's Ashes* **Walking Tour** covers many sights mentioned in Frank McCourt's popular novel. Tours leave daily at 2:30 p.m. from the Tourist Office at Arthur's Quay if enough people have reserved places. Book by calling **Noel Curtain** (☎ **087-235-1339**) or the **Tourist Office** (☎ **061-31-7522**). Tours cost €10. Noel also offers excellent historical walking tours on request.

If you'd rather see the town on your own, pick up the well-done walking maps at the Tourist Office. There is one brochure for the medieval section of the city, and another that contains several other routes.

For something totally different, check out the seven-day barge cruises offered on the ***Shannon Princess*** (☎ **087-251-4809;** www.shannon princess.com). You'll visit several different towns and cities while sleeping and eating (gourmet meals) on the luxuriously outfitted barge.

Seeing the top attractions

Adare Heritage Centre and Desmond Castle
Adare

A little museum at the Heritage Centre does a nice job of presenting the tumultuous history of Adare through displays, text, and audiovisual presentations. You'll find out about the monasteries that used to exist here, the battles that took place in the town, and the history of the Desmond Castle. The highlight is the model of Adare during the Middle Ages; various areas light up in sync with a 20-minute narration. A 20-minute video also presents the town as it is today, which is interesting, but I suggest you spend the time seeing the real thing instead. The Heritage Centre is also the starting point for tours of Desmond Castle, a handsome ruin of a medieval fortified castle. Tours take place daily from June 1 through September 20, as long as there is demand. The cost is €6 adults, €5 seniors and kids, free for kids 10 and younger. Stop into the craft and knitwear shops on the premises, and pop into the cafe for some fresh-baked bread. Books are available if you want to know more about the area, and there is a tourist information desk on-site. This place should give you a sense of what else you want to see and do in and around town. Allow 30 minutes for a visit to the Heritage Centre, an hour for the tour of the castle.

Main Street. ☎ *061-39-6666. Admission: €4.50 adults; €3.50 seniors, students, and kids; free for kids 10 and under. Open: Tourist Information daily 9 a.m.–5 p.m.; exhibit Mar–Dec daily 9:30 a.m.–5 p.m., Jan–Feb Mon–Fri 10 a.m.–4 p.m., Sat–Sun 10 a.m.– 5 p.m.*

Hunt Museum
Limerick City

Located in Limerick's beautifully refurbished Custom House, this museum's art collection was generously donated by the Hunt family and includes many world-class pieces that occasionally go out on loan to international exhibitions. The range of art is extremely wide, with Picasso and da Vinci works; medieval paintings, jewelry, and crystal; ancient Egyptian, Greek, Olmec, and Roman pieces; and a great deal of Irish art and artifacts from as far back as prehistoric times. Highlights include a gold cross once owned by Mary Queen of Scots, and a menu designed by Picasso. The fabulous shop in the lobby sells classy souvenirs, and the museum restaurant serves light meals. Allow an hour and a half to two hours for your visit.

The Custom House, Rutland Street (next to Arthur's Quay, on the River Shannon). ☎ *061-31-2833. Admission: €8 adults, €6.25 seniors and students, €4.25 kids. Open: Mon–Sat 10 a.m.–5 p.m., Sun 2–5 p.m.*

Lough Gur
Southeast of Limerick City

Burial mounds, a wedge tomb, a dwelling built between 500 and 1000 a.d., a 4,000-year-old stone circle (the largest in Ireland), and other treasures surround a glittering lake, or *lough* (pronounced lock) at this rich archeological site, which was continuously inhabited from prehistoric to late medieval times. An interpretive center, housed in authentic-looking Stone Age huts right on the location of the original settlement, features models of unearthed tools, weapons, and pottery, plus audiovisual displays and text about different aspects of the site. You can explore on your own with a map from the visitor center or take a tour of the site. Tours are held from June through August on Sunday at 11 a.m. (walking) and 4 p.m. (walking and bus); call the interpretive center directly or Michael Quinlan (☎ 087-273-9199) to book a summer tour or to arrange an off-season tour. Allow 45 minutes for your visit.

Lough Gur. 11km (7 miles) southeast of Limerick City, off the R512. ☎ 061-385-186. Admission: Interpretive center €5 adults, €3.30 seniors and kids; grounds free. Open: Interpretive center May–Sept daily 10 a.m.–5 p.m. (last admission 4:30 p.m.); grounds year-round.

More cool things to see and do

- ✔ **Georgian House & Gardens,** 2 Pery Sq. (☎ 061-314-130): Limerick City was home to several beautifully furnished Georgian homes in the 1700s. This home has been restored and filled with furniture and décor of the era. After touring the house (you can explore on your own or with a tour), check out the garden, which has been planted exactly as it was in the 1700s.

  Admission is €6 adults; €4 seniors, students, and kids; free for kids 4 and under. It's open Monday through Friday 10 a.m. to 4 p.m. Allow 45 minutes for your visit.

- ✔ **King John's Castle,** east of Thomond Bridge, at the corner of Nicholas and Castle streets, Limerick City (☎ 061-41-1201): This impressive fortress, on the banks of the River Shannon, was the brainchild of King John, who commissioned it in 1210. Clearly a place built to keep people out, this castle is one of the finest examples of a fortified Norman structure in Ireland. Leave time to see the pre-Norman houses that have been excavated below the castle.

  Admission is €9 adults, €6.65 seniors and students, €5.50 kids. (*Note:* I feel that this attraction overcharges for what it offers — you don't get to see many areas of the castle — so if you're going to see other castles, you may want to skip this one.) It's open daily from 10 a.m. to 5 p.m. (last admission 4 p.m.) Call to double-check hours in the winter months. Allow 45 minutes for your visit.

- ✔ **St. Mary's Cathedral,** Bridge Street, one block south of King John's Castle on Nicholast Street, Limerick City (☎ 061-31-0293): Built in the 12th century, this building is the oldest in Limerick City. The rounded Romanesque doorway is a remnant of the original church. Inside are many beautiful 15th-century carvings in black oak.

Admission is free, but the suggested donation is €2. It's open Monday through Friday from 9:30 a.m. to 4:30 p.m.; visitors are also welcome to attend Sunday Mass. Allow 30 minutes for your visit, longer if you attend Mass.

✔ **Treaty Stone,** O'Callaghan Strand, across the Thomond Bridge, facing King John's Castle across the Shannon, Limerick City: This noble slab of limestone is reportedly the place where the Treaty of Limerick was signed in 1691,ending the war between supporters of William of Orange and supporters of King James II. You can see the stone in a few minutes.

Shopping

Limerick, like nearly all of Ireland's major cities, is a hub of shopping for the surrounding region. The main city thoroughfares, **O'Connell Street** and **William Street,** are lined with small shops and department stores. The city has some excellent clothing stores, day spas, and salons on these streets and on Cruises Street. **O'Mahony's,** 120 O'Connell St., Limerick (☎ **061-41-8155**), has a great selection of books, maps, and stationery. You can catch up on your Joyce or write friends back home in style.

The **Milk Market,** at the corner of Wickham and Ellen streets, is a restored medieval marketplace. Bordered by the original city walls, this thriving market offers all sorts of prepared food, crafts, and flowers on Friday from 11 a.m. to 7 p.m. Saturday from 8 a.m. to 4 p.m. is foodie heaven, with everything from local cheeses to lovely warm crepes. Sunday sees the Variety Market, with all sorts of crafts, art, and antiques for sale. The weekend markets are complemented by surrounding stalls and stores, mostly selling food, that are open from Wednesday through Sunday.

In **Adare,** on the main street, Michelina and George Stacpoole sell high-fashion knitwear, great old Irish prints and postcards, paintings, and a vast selection of antiques in **George Stacpoole Antiques** (☎ **061-39-6409;** www.stacpooles.com).

A day at the races or the rugby match

Horse-racing is extremely popular in Ireland. You can get in on the action in Limerick at the **Limerick Racecourse** (☎ **061-32-0000;** www.limerickraces.ie), or visit www.hri.ie to see the racing schedules for the entire country. The newly renovated **Thomond Park Stadium,** about a ten-minute walk from the city center, is the home turf of the excellent Munster Rugby team. For information on which teams are playing and where, check www.irishrugby.ie or call ☎ **01-647-3800.**

Hitting the pubs

Before a night out, you may want to catch a film, play, or concert at **Belltable Arts Centre,** 69 O'Connell St. or 36 Cecil St. (☎ **061-31-9866;** www.belltable.ie). Just call or check the site to see what's going on when you're in town.

Dolan's Pub
Limerick City

Music lovers Mick and Valerie Dolan opened this warm and friendly pub so that Irish musicians could have a welcoming place to play every night of the week. You'll find traditional Irish sessions starting at about 9:30 p.m. daily, plus Irish set-dancing classes (open to drop-ins) Tuesday at 7:30 p.m. The setting is classic Irish pub, with polished wood and stone floors. The pub has proved so popular that the Dolans have opened the upstairs space for small performances and the adjacent Dolan's Warehouse, which has a great gig list that includes jazz, rock, punk, blues, and occasionally theater or comedy performances, including shows by such stars as Arlo Guthrie and the Irish band Kila.

3–4 Dock Rd. ☎ **061-314-483.** *www.dolanspub.com.*

The Locke Bar
Limerick City

Dating back to 1724, The Locke is one of Limerick City's oldest and best pubs, and it has a great location, too. It sits right on the bank of the river, amid some of the city's oldest landmarks: the Old Custom House (now the Hunt Museum) and the Old Court House. When weather permits, there's seating across the street on the quay. Inside, you can warm up at the open fires and listen to traditional music every Tuesday and Wednesday night, and piano music each Friday and Saturday. The atmosphere is friendly and buzzy, and the pub serves great seafood dishes, including several oyster options.

3 George's Quay. ☎ **061-41-3733.**

South's Pub
Limerick City

Made famous by Frank McCourt's *Angela's Ashes,* this pub still basks in the fame bestowed by the Pulitzer Prize–winning author. The walls bear newspaper accounts of the local uproar that occurred when the book was published — many Limerick natives objected to the negative light it cast on their city. (Of course, there are also those who consider McCourt the local boy who made good.) Star element aside, South's is a gorgeous pub — all wood, marble bar, and snugs. During the day, nice lunches are served.

The Crescent, O'Connell Avenue (right near the Jesuit church). ☎ **061-31-8850.**

Fast Facts: County Limerick

Area Codes

County Limerick's area code is **061**.

Emergencies/Police

Dial ☎ **999** for all emergencies.

Hospital

St. John's Hospital (☎ 061-46-2222) is on St. John's Square, Limerick.

Information

For visitor information in Limerick City, go to the tourist center at Arthur's Quay (☎ 061-31-7522). In Adare, visit the Adare Heritage Centre, Main Street (☎ 061-39-6666).

Post Office

The General Post Office is on Post Office Lane, off Cecil Street, Limerick City (☎ 061-21-2055).

County Clare

County Clare sometimes gets lost somewhere between the dazzle of counties Galway and Kerry, but people who skip this county are missing out on some of Ireland's finest scenery and several interesting historic (and prehistoric) attractions. They're also missing out on great little towns and villages that are less visited than those in counties Galway and Kerry. In the north lies one of my favorite places in Ireland: the Burren, a strange and breathtaking sea of cracked limestone that is home to several archeological sights and an incredible range of plant life, including species that normally thrive only in Arctic or tropical climates. To the south, there are the famed sheer Cliffs of Moher, and a stretch of long sandy beaches backed by gently rolling farmland. Other attractions include two completely restored and furnished castles from the Middle Ages, and several ancient sights. Clare doesn't have any large cities, but it's dotted with charming towns and villages. **Ballyvaughan** (pronounced bally-*vah*-hon) makes a great base for exploring the Burren, while **Doolin, Lahinch** (pronounced *luh*-hinch is some places and luh-*hinch* in others), and tiny **Milltown Malbay** are good options if you're exploring the Clare coast. **Ennis,** the main town in the county, is a great choice if you'd like a larger town as a base while exploring Clare. The medieval streets are bustling and lively, with a mix of locals and visitors, and there is excellent traditional music every night.

Getting to and around County Clare

Shannon International Airport (☎ **061-71-2000;** www.shannon airport.com), located on the N19, off the N18, about 24km (15 miles) south of County Clare's main town of Ennis and 24km (15 miles) west of Limerick, welcomes direct flights from North America, England, and other locations in Ireland. See Chapter 6 for more information on the airport.

If you're coming by car, take the N18 north from Limerick or south from Galway to Ennis. Rental-car company desks at Shannon Airport's Arrivals Hall represent all the major car-rental companies listed in Chapter 7.

If you'd like to go directly from Kerry to Clare (or vice versa), instead of taking the longer route that goes through Limerick, **Shannon Ferries** (☎ **065-905-3124;** www.shannonferries.com) runs a car ferry connecting Tarbert, County Kerry, with Killimer, County Clare. The ferry runs April through September Monday through Saturday from 7 a.m. to about 9 p.m., and Sunday from about 9 a.m. to about 9 p.m.; October through March Monday through Saturday from 7 a.m. to 7 p.m. and Sunday from 9:30 a.m. until 7 p.m. In June, July, and August ferries depart from both Killimer and Tarbert every half-hour; the rest of the year, ferries leave on the hour from Killimer and on the half-hour from Tarbert. The trip costs €17 one-way and €28 round-trip for a car with passengers. Reservations are not necessary.

Irish Rail (☎ **1-850-366-222;** www.irishrail.ie) serves Ennis at the Ennis Rail Station on Quinn Road. **Bus Éireann** (☎ **01-836-6111;** www.buseireann.ie) travels year-round to Ennis, Ballyvaughan, Doolin, Kilkee, and several other towns in County Clare. You can walk to the city center from the bus and train station.

Spending the night in County Clare

Ardilaun House
$ Ennis

This is a great B&B for those who want to be near the hustle and bustle of Ennis without being in the middle of it. Located a 15- to 20-minute walk from the town center, Ardilaun offers simple, tidy rooms with stylish quilts and (in most rooms) windows that look out onto the River Fergus. Your hosts, the Purcells, are kind and accommodating, and they cook up a nice Irish breakfast.

Off the Gort Road (R458) a bit north of the town of Ennis. ☎ **065-682-2311.** www.ardilaun.com. *Parking: Free on-site. Rack rates: €50–€75 double. MC, V.*

Ballyvara House
$$ Doolin

This guesthouse, which is more like a little hotel than a B&B, seems to have everything. Location? Yup. The house is situated in the countryside (say hello to the resident ponies) and is half a mile from the delightful little village of Doolin, known for its traditional music, and just a ten-minute drive from the Burren. Good food? Check. The breakfast menu includes such treats as crepes and omelets, and the house chef prepares interesting and delicious dinners. Helpful hosts? You got it. Becky and John Flanagan know the area and can help you figure out the best itinerary. Rooms are spacious, sparkling clean, and bright, and bathrooms feature spa or Jacuzzi tubs.

Off the R479 to Doolin Village. ☎ **065-707-4467.** *Fax: 065-707-4868.* www.ballyvarahouse.ie. *Parking: Free on-site. Rack rates: €100–€120 double. MC, V. Open all summer, but call to find out about spring and fall — the proprietors open the house according to demand during these seasons.*

Berry Lodge
$$ Annagh, Miltown Malbay

This is a must-stay for any serious gourmet. Originally a well-known cooking school, this 17th-century country house near the sea now offers surprisingly inexpensive accommodations as well. The rooms are simple and colorfully decorated, but the real draw of the place is the food, grown and caught locally. You'll definitely want to have dinner, and you may want to consider taking one of the cooking classes — special weekend rates combine rooms with classes. Views of farmlands and sea are spectacular. Book online for a 10 percent discount on room rates.

From Quilty (south), continue north on the N67 for about 2.4km (1½ miles) and take the third right to find the house. From Milltown Malbay (North), take the N67 south for about 3.2km (2 miles), cross the bridge, and then take the second left. ☎ **065-708-7022.** www.berrylodge.com. *Parking: Free on-site. Rack rates: €90–€96 double. MC, V.*

Dromoland Castle
$$$$ Newmarket-on-Fergus

If you've ever had fantasies of living in a castle, this place is calling your name. The 19th-century building (built to replace the original 16th-century structure) has all the round and square towers and crenellations that fairy tales have embedded in the collective Western subconscious. Public spaces and rooms are magnificently decked out with crystal chandeliers, portraits, and oak paneling, and bedrooms are spacious and furnished with fine fabrics. Ask for a room in the main wing, as rooms in the newer wings, though still beautiful, feel more like standard hotel rooms than castle suites. The hotel and picturesque grounds have everything that modern royalty could require, including a spa, an excellent golf course, fishing, boating, gardens, restaurants, a falconer offering lessons on flying Harris hawks, and a gracious and helpful staff. Dromoland is located near Shannon Airport, making it the perfect first or last night's stop in Ireland. Check the Web site for special packages and offers.

Located on the R458 (signposted off the N18). ☎ **061-36-8144,** *or* ☎ **800-346-7007** *in the U.S. Fax: 061-36-3355.* www.dromoland.ie. *Parking: Free on-site. Rack rates: €320–€450 double. AE, DC, MC, V.*

Drumcreehy House
$$ Ballyvaughan

Drumcreehy is a fantastic choice for travelers who want to explore the Burren. The wide selection of delicious breakfast offerings, served in a cheerful dining room, will fuel you for a day of hiking, and the location is right near some of the best hiking on the Burren. After you've returned from your explorations of the rocky landscape, chill out in your bright and spacious room or over tea in the antiques-furnished sitting room. Each bedroom is painted in a lovely shade and furnished with country-style furniture. Your hosts, Bernadette and Armin, can advise you on every-thing from where to dine in the area to how to experience the Burren.

Outside of Ballyvaughan on the N67. ☎ **065-707-7377.** *Fax: 065-707-7379.* www. drumcreehyhouse.com. *Parking: Free on-site. Rack rates: €84–€100 double. MC, V.*

Moy House
$$$$ Lahinch

Warning: This country house hotel may throw a wrench in your plans for all-day sightseeing. You wake up early, planning to hit the sights after a quick breakfast. You figure that you'll come back for dinner at the house that night and then turn in relatively early so that you can do more sight-seeing tomorrow. Here's what actually happens: You linger over the excel-lent breakfast and then lounge on one of the couches in the pretty Georgian-style reading room, listening to the Atlantic waves right outside the window. You go out to sightsee (the Cliffs of Moher are only a 15-minute drive), and then linger over an exceptional three-course dinner that combines French techniques with Irish ingredients. After dinner, you chat with fellow travelers over a drink from the honor bar, and you finally roll into bed in your cozy room, which is furnished with Georgian and Victorian antique furniture and elegant fabrics. Check the Web site for special offers and packages.

Off the N67 south of the village of Lahinch. ☎ **065-708-2800.** *Fax: 065-708-2500.* www. moyhouse.com. *Parking: Free on-site. Rack rates: €225–€280. AE, MC, V.*

Old Ground Hotel
$$$ Ennis

This busy hotel is located right in the middle of Ennis, so you can just pop up from a rollicking night of traditional music in the fabulous hotel pub (see "Hitting the pubs," later in this chapter) or a dinner in the excellent Town Hall restaurant, and fall into your exceptionally comfortable bed, with its fluffy white duvet. The atmosphere is relaxed and unpretentious, with a kind and helpful staff.

O'Connell Street. ☎ **065-682-8127.** www.flynnhotels.ie. *Parking: Free on-site (though the parking lot is small). Rack rates: €119–€170 double. Some rates do not include breakfast. AE, MC, V.*

Roadford House
$ Doolin

Marian and Frank Sheedy (and Beans, the dog) are consummate hosts, warm and down-to-earth, helping visitors with whatever they need. The B&B is located on a quiet hillside only a few minutes' walk from several of Doolin's popular pubs. Rooms are large, airy, and simply outfitted with pine furnishings, and windows overlook the rolling farmland. Breakfast is exceptional, which makes sense, given that Marian and Frank also run an excellent restaurant on-site (definitely book for dinner there at least once).

Doolin. ☎ **065-707-5050.** *www.roadfordrestaurant.com. Parking: Free on-site. Rack rates: €60–€78 double. MC, V.*

The Greenbriar Inn
$$ Lahinch

Looking for a place to relax after playing golf? This guesthouse couldn't be closer to the renowned links at the Lahinch Golf Club. Rooms are spotless and simply furnished with pretty antique-style pine furniture, and the bustling resort village of Lahinch is just a short walk down the road. Your host Victor, who runs the guesthouse with his wife Margaret, has a great dry sense of humor and loads of information about what to see and do in the area.

On the Ennistymon Road, just outside the village of Lahinch. ☎ **065-708-1242.** *www.greenbrierinn.com. Parking: Free on-site. Rack rates: €90–€170 double. MC, V. Closed Jan–Feb.*

Dining locally in County Clare

In Ennis, **Zest!** on Market Place (☎ **065-682-1014**) is a stylish new cafe selling fresh lunches and baked goods along with gourmet food items. The sandwich of organic smoked salmon with lemon-dill cream cheese, cucumbers, and red onions makes my list of best sandwiches ever. Also in Ennis, **Brogan's Pub** (see p. 336) serves good pub grub. If you'd like to listen to Irish music sessions here, having dinner is a great way to claim a good seat. On O'Connell Street in Ennis, **O'Connors Bakery** (☎ **065-682-2860**) makes divine baked goods.

Berry Lodge (p. 322) is one of the best restaurants in all of Clare, and **Roadford Restaurant** (p. 323) is a winner in Doolin.

An Fear Gorta
$ Ballyvaughan   CAFE/BAKERY

Legend has it that those who step on *fear gortach* (hungry grass) will be doomed to a perpetual and insatiable hunger. Perhaps I grazed a patch of the grass, or perhaps it was just a long morning spent hiking on the Burren, but I was quite hungry as I entered this sweet and casual tea room, with its large garden and conservatory. Fortunately, my excellent open-faced salmon sandwich and large slice of fresh-baked chocolate cake soothed my hunger beautifully. The tearoom serves light dishes, including soups and salads, and a dizzying array of wonderful homemade cakes.

Main Street, on the harbor. ☎ **065-707-7157.** *Main courses: €4–€9. No credit cards. Open: May–Sept daily 11 a.m.–6 p.m.*

Barrtrá Seafood Restaurant
$$$ Lahinch   SEAFOOD

This small and homey restaurant is down a little farm road, overlooking
Liscannor Bay. The friendly staff serves some of the freshest fish and
shellfish on the west coast, all prepared with simple and innovative
sauces, spices, or herbs that highlight the taste of the fish, such as the
delicious cod with orange and ginger sauce. The wine list is extensive, and
the desserts, such as the pear and almond tart, are delicious.

*Off the N67. Go 3.2km (2 miles) south of Lahinch on the Lahinch/Miltown Malbay
coast road (N67), until you see the small road to the restaurant. ☎ 065-708-1280.
Reservations highly recommended. Main courses: €15–€30; fixed-price dinners
€30–€40. AE, MC, V. Open: June–Aug daily 5:30–9:30 p.m. Call to ask about hours
outside of the summer months.*

Burren Food & Wine
$$ Ballyvaugan   IRISH

A lunch or afternoon tea here is the perfect restorative after a hike on the
Burren. Owner Cathleen Connole is dedicated to using as much local produce as possible in the cafe's fresh-as-can-be, beautifully presented
dishes. My friends started their lunch with a fabulous mushroom soup
made from mushrooms picked that morning, while I chose the seafood
chowder, packed with hunks of fresh fish. We then shared the wonderful
local cheese plate (the St. Tola's goat cheese is out of this world) and the
artfully arranged local smoked fish plate. We finished of with a pavlova, a
tough choice given that there are several homemade dessert options. The
setting is a 200-year-old stone cottage with a wood ceiling and shelves
loaded with wines and gourmet gifts (the cafe sells Christmas hampers
Nov–Dec). You can book a traditional afternoon tea in advance, and keep
an eye out for Irish Party Evenings, which attract local musicians and
poets.

*Off the N67 on Corkscrewhill Road, about 3.2km (2 miles) outside Ballyvaughan.
☎ 065-707-7046. Main courses: €10–€15. Open: June–Aug daily 11:30 a.m.–5 p.m.
Call for Irish Party Evening dates and times.*

Cullinan's
$$$ Doolin   SEAFOOD/NEW IRISH

The chefs at Cullinan's use fresh local ingredients to create beautiful, cre-
ative, perfectly prepared dishes such as oven-roasted filet of Clare lamb
loin served with spiced couscous and garlic aioli, and plump pan-seared
scallops with baby spinach fondue, a chorizo disc, and a balsamic and
black pepper reduction. The excellent food is complemented by the set-
ting: an airy, elegant white room with two walls of windows looking out
onto green fields. The early-bird fixed-price menus, served between 6 and
7 p.m., are a nice option at €25 for two courses or €30 for three courses.

*On the R479, Doolin. ☎ 065-707-4183. Reservations recommended. Main courses:
€21–€27. MC, V. Open: Easter to Oct Thurs–Sat and Mon–Tues 6–9:15 p.m.*

M'Lady: Do you fancy a medieval banquet at a castle?

Okay, it's very, very touristy, but the **Medieval Banquet** at 15th-century **Bunratty Castle** is also quite fun. Your evening begins in the Mead Hall of the castle, a grand space featuring handsome 15th- and 16th-century tapestries and furnishings. You're greeted by your butler for the evening, who explains the history of the castle. Then you enjoy a glass or two of mead (yum!), and meet the Earl and Lady of the evening, selected from the crowd. You then head downstairs to the banquet hall, where you sit at long, dark wood tables lit by candles to enjoy your family-style four-course meal (spiced parsnip soup; spare ribs with honey and whiskey sauce; breast of chicken with apple and mead sauce; a fruit mousse; and plenty of mead, wine, and water). Entertainment, in the form of lovely madrigal singing, harp playing, and fiddling, takes place throughout dinner and after dessert, and it's quite good. Knappogue Castle (see p. 332) offers a slightly smaller version of the banquet, but why not go whole hog!

Bunratty also offers Traditional Irish Nights, which aim to replicate a night of music and dinner in old Ireland, I recommend skipping these, as the real McCoy can be found in hundreds, if not thousands, of pubs across Ireland every night.

Reservations are required for the banquets; call ☎ **061-711-200** or book online at www. shannonheritage.com. The Bunratty banquet costs €60 adults; the Knappogue banquet costs, €57 adults. Kids 12 and under get discounted rates. Call in advance or check online for the frequent special deals. Set aside two and a half hours for the entire experience.

Cruises Pub
$$ Ennis   IRISH

The staff at this cozy, authentic pub is the living embodiment of Irish hospitality, serving up a wide range of well-done dishes, from superb lamb stew to excellent pizzas and calzones to salmon with lemon-dill sauce, plus a selection of vegetarian dishes. The interior is dim and traditional, with beautiful carved wood; open fireplaces; tin signs on the wall; and shelves filled with old and weathered miscellany, from jugs and bottles to books. There's top-quality traditional Irish music many nights. Another great spot for pub food in Ennis is **Brogan's** (see p. 336).

Abbey Street. ☎ *065-684-1800. Main courses: €10–€19. MC, V. Open: Sun–Thurs 12:30 p.m. to midnight, Fri–Sat 12:30 p.m.–1:30 a.m. (food served until 9 p.m. daily).*

Magnetic Music Café
$ Doolin   CAFE

Stop into this adorable cafe for a snack or a light lunch (perhaps the Mediterranean Medley, a platter of meats, cheeses, and Mediterranean vegetables). Inside you'll be surrounded by the sounds of Irish music (the cafe sells all sort of traditional Irish music CDs), while outside, in the garden, you may chance upon the cafe's golden lab, Molly. Candlelit concerts are held here during the summer.

Fisherstreet, Doolin. ☎ **065-707-4988.** *Main courses: €6–€9. Open: June–Aug daily 11 a.m.–8 p.m., Apr–May and Sept–Oct daily 11 a.m.–5 p.m.*

L'Arco
$$ Ballyvaughan ITALIAN

If you're looking for something different from the seafood and New Irish cuisine of Clare, check out L'Arco, a sprawling Italian restaurant situated somewhat incongruously in the little town of Ballyvaughan. The large room is divided into cozy smaller spaces, including an elevated area that's perfect for a large family or group of friends. The setting is a lovely combination of Italian and Irish — the stone building retains its old wooden beams, while the deep red and black color scheme is pure Italy. Pasta is the dish to get here, from the popular spinach ricotta ravioli in sage and butter sauce, to the penne Amatriciana, with its spicy tomato sauce, cherry tomatoes, and pancetta (the pizzas aren't as good).

On Main Street in Ballyvaughan (pass through the arch next to Quinn's Craftshop). ☎ **065-708-3900.** *Reservations suggested. Main courses: €13–€22. MC, V. Open: Mon–Sat 5:30–9:30 p.m., Sun 5–9 p.m. Call during the winter, as hours may vary.*

The Long Dock
$$ Carrigaholt SEAFOOD/TRADITIONAL IRISH

"Okay, so which of the nine types of fish landed today should I order? Or should I go with one of the menu choices like herb-crusted cod with creamed leeks or red snapper with garlic, chili, and ginger butter? What about a traditional dish like bacon and cabbage in parsley sauce?" These are questions that everyone must face at this terrific, seafood-focused pub. I always end up with the fresh fish, such as the stunning lemon sole with garlic butter that I had the last time. Once you emerge from your appetizer and main course decision-making process, you're tossed into indecision again as you encounter the dessert menu. I can only offer the opinion that the Long Dock Mess, a pile of cream, fruit, and meringue, is heavenly, as is the legendary sticky toffee pudding. The setting is quintessential Irish pub, with beamed ceilings, fisherman's lamps, stone floors, and warm wood paneling. Lovely photos of the nearby estuary and shore grace the walls.

On The Mall on Clare Road, Carrigaholt. ☎ **065-905-8106.** *Main courses: €12–€25. MC, V. Open: Daily 11 a.m.–9 p.m.*

Town Hall Bistro
$$$ Ennis NEW IRISH

Located in the middle of Ennis, this popular restaurant manages to be elegant without being at all stodgy. Dressy couples and groups of friends dine here, but the chefs had no trouble whipping up an impromptu kid-friendly feast for a toddler dining with her family. The setting is a grand, candelit old town hall with high ceilings, large oil paintings, sculptures, and deep eggplant-colored banquettes. The Town Hall serves fresh Irish ingredients in dishes that are creative but not far-fetched, such as baked pork filet with peach and thyme stuffing and a cider reduction, and filet of hake with leeks and fennel, served with new potatoes and tarragon beurre blanc.

O'Connell Street. ☎ **065-689-2333.** *Reservations suggested during the summer and on weekend nights. Main courses: €21–€26. AE, MC, V. Open: Daily 10 a.m.–5 p.m. and 6–10 p.m.*

Exploring County Clare

A car, by far, is the best way to explore this area. However, if you're car-less, several bus companies run tours of the Burren, the Cliffs of Moher, and other attractions in Clare out of Galway City. For details on the various tours, call or visit the **Galway Tourist Office** (also known as Ireland West Tourism or Aras Fáilte) on Forster Street City (☎ **091-53-77-00;** www.discoverireland.ie/west). **The Burren Wild Tour Bus** (☎ **087-877-9565;** www.burrenwalks.com) is a favorite for touring the area; you'll depart from Galway, stop at the Cliffs of Moher, and take a guided walk in the Burren. The trip leaves daily at 10 a.m. from the bus station on Fairgreen Road in Galway and costs €25 adults, €22 students. You can book online or by phone, or purchase tickets at the Galway Tourist Office.

During the summer, the Clare Museum, off O'Connell Square in Ennis, hosts free lunchtime **Irish music concerts** featuring different masters of Irish music Wednesday from 1 p.m. to 2 p.m. Check www.richesof clare.com or contact the **Arts Office** at ☎ **065-689-9091** to find out who's playing when you're there.

The top attractions

Bunratty Castle and Folk Park
Bunratty

This medieval castle, built in 1425 and pillaged many times, is one of Ireland's biggest attractions. Great care has been taken to ensure that the interior is as it was in the 15th century, with furnishings and tapestries that reflect the era. Great halls and tiny stairways characterize the castle, and the dungeon is quite eerie. On the castle grounds is the Bunratty Folk Park, an interesting re-creation of a 19th-century Irish village. You can poke your head into farmhouses from all different parts of the country (the differences are striking), a blacksmith's forge, and a watermill, and go down a typical 19th-century village street, visiting the post office, school, pawn shop, doctor's house, printers, hardware shop, and pub. Costumed interpreters help the village come to life. At night, Bunratty Castle hosts huge medieval banquets (see p. 326). Allow at least two hours for your visit.

On the N18, north of Limerick. The short exit ramp off the N18 takes you to the entrance of the castle. ☎ **061-711-200.** *Admission: €16 adults (€12 in the off season), €9.45 seniors, €10 students, €9 kids. Admission is a flat €8 if you're also coming to the banquet. Open: Jan–May & Sept–Dec daily 9 a.m.–5:30 p.m. (last admission 4:15); June–Aug Mon–Fri 9 a.m.–5:30 p.m. (last admission 4:15), Sat–Sun 9 a.m.–6 p.m. (last admission 5:15). Last admission to castle is 4 p.m. daily year-round.*

The Burren
Northwest County Clare

Don't miss this awesome phenomenon — a vast expanse of cracked limestone, stretching as far as the eye can see, that's home to a variety of unique plants and animals. The name *Burren* comes from the Irish *bhoireann,* which means "a rocky place," and the "rocky" designation is totally accurate. Expansive fields of broken limestone slabs cover a maze of underground caves. The water that seeps up through cracks in the rock supports a wide and spectacular variety of flowers and plants, including species that usually thrive only in the Arctic or Mediterranean. Lizards, badgers, frogs, stoats, and numerous birds call the Burren home. In addition, 26 species of butterflies have been seen here, including one that's indigenous to the area: the lovely and rare Burren Green. The Burren is at its most colorful, with tons of wildflowers, in May, June, and early July, but you'll find a variety of flora year-round. Despite the lack of soil, humans have lived in the area from the Neolithic period through the present, leaving behind a variety of structures, from 5,000-year-old *dolmen* (burial monuments) and ancient cooking sites to medieval and more recent churches, houses, and graveyards. Though there is much to be enamored with at ground level, don't forget to look up at the glorious views of Clare and Galway Bay from the high points in the Burren.

The best way to explore the Burren is by hiking (or "walking" as it's called in Ireland). It's a great idea to begin your explorations at **The Burren Centre** (see p. 331), to get information on various options for hiking on the Burren. I recommend taking a guided hike first — the terrain is rough and a guide can help you truly understand the history, geology, and biology of this amazing place. There are two tour guides that I highly recommend and they have completely different styles.

Warm and kind, **Tony Kirby** (☎ **065-682-707** or 087-292-5487; www.heartofburrenwalks.com) is a scholar of the Burren. Tony loves the area in a way that is both deeply personal and academic. To wit, Tony has published an excellent book detailing walks in the Burren and he's always up on the latest research papers about the area. Tony's tours of the limestone pavement leave from the Burren Centre Thursday through Sunday and Tuesday at 2:30 p.m. On Wednesday, Tony leads a different tour that takes you through a grassy valley, along old stone walls and flowering hedge rows, to see several historical sites, from a Neolithic ring fort to a medieval church. The tours leave at 10 a.m. from Burren Food & Wine. Both tours cost €20, and kids 15 and younger are free.

Shane Connolly (☎ **065-707-7168**), grew up in the Burren. He is fiery in his love for the Burren and shares his vast knowledge of the history, folklore, animal and plant life, and geology of the area in a way that makes you feel as if he was born knowing it. He's also quite funny. Call Shane for details about various walks and to book.

After you've taken a guided tour, strike out on your own for more exploration; the peace and stillness that you'll find climbing around on the Burren with only your travel companions is incredible. My top choices for **independent hikes** are the marked two-and-a-half-hour **Mullaghmore loop** route (to get here, turn right in Kilnaboy before the church, drive 4km/2½ miles, take another right turn, drive 0.8km/half a mile, and park at the side of the road where the trailhead begins), and the area along the R477 near Oughtdarra and Poulnagun. The Mullaghmore loop claims to be "very difficult," but anyone who is reasonably fit shouldn't have a problem. For the R477 area, just find an area that appeals to you, park the car somewhere off the road, and explore to your heart's content. If you'd like a longer journey, the stunning **Burren Way** is a 26-mile hike that takes you through the heart of the Burren and along the **Cliffs of Moher.**

It's worth packing a pair of hiking shoes with ankle support and rugged soles if you're planning on hiking in the Burren. Also, check yourself for ticks when you return from a hike, as they like to hang out in this area.

Burren Birds of Prey Centre and Ailwee Cave
The Burren

Though it was added to the attractions at Aillwee Cave recently, the Burren Birds of Prey Centre is the real star here. The center is home to a number of birds, from tiny owls to huge falcons. If the weather is good, don't miss the **Flying Displays** at noon and 3 p.m. (and more often in the summer), when several birds are brought into an outdoor show area to fly free.

Though it's expensive, I can't recommend the **Hawk Walk** highly enough. A falconer will give you brief instructions on how to hold and call back your Harris hawk, and then you'll move into the woods to fly the hawk for about an hour. The sight of the hawk zooming through the trees toward you, and the feeling of her gentle landing on your gloved hand makes this one of those I'll-remember-it-for-the-rest-of-my-life experiences.

The cave here was discovered in the 1940s when a farmer's dog disappeared; the farmer followed the dog's path and not only recovered his dog but also discovered this large network of passageways. The cave is interesting, though not breathtaking like other caves you may have visited. Your guide will point out the hibernation chambers of the now-extinct Irish brown bear, a few small stalagmites and stalactites, and a pretty curtain formation. The highlight is a waterfall that crashes into a pool below. If you're pressed for time, see the birds instead of the cave. Tours leave every half-hour during open hours.

The farm shop is worth a visit to taste and purchase Burren Gold Cheese and homemade fudge (both produced right in the shop), as well as a nice assortment of other gourmet products from the region.

Painting the Burren

The **Burren Painting Centre**, Lisdoonvarna (☎ **065-707-4208;** www.burren paintingcentre.com), offers courses in painting. Every day, a different painting location around the Burren or the Atlantic coast is chosen, from an ancient burial site on the rocks of the Burren to a streetscape in one of the small towns in the area, and expert tutors provide feedback and instruction. Courses can last anywhere from two to six days, and you can stay at the center or at a B&B or hotel in the area.

Allow two hours for your visit if you plan to see the cave and the birds.

Off the R480, south of Ballyvaughan. ☎ *065-707-7036. Admission: €17 adults, €15 seniors and students, €10 kids; the admission price covers both attractions. Open: July–Aug daily 10 a.m.–6:30 p.m., Sept –Nov 23 and Jan–June daily 10 a.m.–5:30 p.m.*

Burren Centre
Kilfenora

With a visitor desk dedicated to providing information on the Burren, this is a great place to get your bearings. A well-done movie and small exhibit are a nice introduction to the natural and social history of the area.

Kilfenora. ☎ *065-708-8030. Admission: Information area free; exhibit and movie €6 adults, €5 seniors and students, €4 kids 6–15, free for kids 5 and under. Open: June–Aug daily 9:30 a.m.–5:30 p.m., mid-Mar to May and Sept to mid-Nov daily 10 a.m.–5 p.m.*

The Cliffs of Moher

Spectacular doesn't begin to describe the view from these breathtaking sheer cliffs. At places, they rise more than 213m (700 ft.) above the crashing Atlantic and stretch for miles in both directions. On the highest cliff is **O'Brien's Tower,** which was built in the 1800s as a viewing point for visitors. It's worth paying the €2 to climb the tower; from the top you can see the Clare coast, the Aran Islands, and, on a clear day, mountains as far away as Kerry and Connemara., When the strong wind blows in, it can be a bit harrowing up there, so stay behind the barriers at all times. The cliffs can be touristy during the high season; be prepared for Irish fiddlers in the parking lot and so on. If you're looking for cliffs that are almost as spectacular but don't draw as many visitors, head up to the towering cliffs of Slieve League (p. 398).

At the flashy visitor center you'll find a permanent interpretative exhibit called the *Atlantic Edge.* The exhibit is relatively small, featuring a 3-D movie that makes you feel as if you're soaring over the Cliffs, pictures of and quotations from people associated with this area, and some interactive pieces dealing with the science of the Cliffs. The €4.95 adult admission price is a little steep for such a small display, so I would only go if you know that you usually enjoy this type of exhibit.

One of the best ways to appreciate the grandeur of the Cliffs of Moher is to see them from the ocean. **Cliffs of Moher Cruises** (☎ **065-707-5949;** www.cliffs-of-moher-cruises.com) makes one-hour trips along the Cliffs daily at noon and 3 p.m. between April 1 and October 31 (weather permitting). During the summer months, book ahead of time to ensure a spot on the boat. Tours cost €20 and there is usually a €5 discount for booking online. Allow 45 minutes for your visit.

Off the R478, on the Atlantic coast. Take the R487 northwest from Lahinch or south-west from Lisdoonvarna. ☎ *061-708-6141. Parking: €8. Admission to visitor center: €4.95 adults; €3.95 seniors and students, €2.95 kids 4–16. Open: Cliffs are always accessible; visitor center June 9 a.m.–7:30 p.m., July–Aug 9 a.m.–9:30 p.m., May and Sept 9 a.m.–7 p.m., Mar and Oct 9 a.m.–6 p.m., Apr 9 a.m.–6:30 p.m., Nov–Feb 9:15 a.m.–5 p.m.*

Knappogue Castle
Quinn

This imposing 15th-century castle has seen its share of history. Built by the McNamaras, it was the pride of the tribe, which dominated the area for 1,000 years. But the stronghold had its troubles. In the 1700s, Cromwell's troops occupied the castle for ten years, and during the War of Independence in the early 1920s, revolutionary forces camped within its walls. The castle has been extraordinarily refurbished, and the interior is overflowing with 15th-century antiques and period furnishings. Don't miss the beautiful walled garden in back. This castle also hosts a medieval banquet. Allow an hour for your visit.

Just off the Ennis-Killmury Road (R469) southeast from Ennis. ☎ *061-36-0788. Admission: €6 adults, €3.50 seniors and students, €3.40 kids. Open: May–Sept daily 10 a.m.–4:30p.m. (last admission 4 p.m.).*

Poulnabrone Dolmen and Caherconnell Stone Fort
The Burren

The Poulnabrone Dolmen consists of a huge capstone supported by two standing stones. One of the most photographed sights in Ireland, the dolmen is an ancient burial monument dating back almost 6,000 years Don't be embarrassed about humming the *Flintstones* theme song in your head during your visit. Just down the road is the beautifully preserved large stone ring fort of Caherconnell. Recent excavations at the sight have yielded exciting finds, including the skeleton of a woman buried in the 15th century, and pottery that was dated to 3700 b.c. If you'd like to learn more about what life was like in prehistoric Ireland, check out Craggaunowen (p. 333).

The Burren. Off the R480, south from Ballyvaughan. Poulnabrone Dolmen is always accessible. Open: Caherconnell Mar–June and Sept–Oct 10 a.m.–5 p.m., July–Aug 10 a.m.–6 p.m.

More cool things to see and do

✔ **Clare Museum,** Arthur's Row, off O'Connell Square, Ennis (☎ 065-682-3382): If you're interested in history, drop into this well-done, compact museum, which houses an interesting assortment of artifacts from prehistoric times up to the 20th century, including a telegram from Irish politician Éamon de Valera to his wife and three Bronze Age musical instruments.

Admission to the museum is free. The museum is generally open Tuesday through Saturday from 9:30 a.m. to 1 p.m. (last admission 12:30 p.m.) and from 2 to 5:30 p.m. (last admission 4:30 p.m.). Call ahead to be sure. Allow 30 to 45 minutes for your visit.

✔ **Craggaunowen,** off the N18, near the village of Quin (☎ 061-711-200): This small living history museum gives you an insight into prehistoric and early Christian Ireland. You'll find an ancient ring fort and reproductions of Bronze Age dwellings. Costumed interpreters demonstrate ancient cooking and farming techniques, and craftspeople are often on hand to demonstrate weaving and pottery-making. It's a little overpriced for its size, but definitely unique.

Admission is €9 adults, €6.85 seniors and students, €5.50 kids. It's open May through September daily from 10 a.m. to 5 p.m. (last admission 4 p.m.). Allow 45 minutes for your visit.

✔ **Dolphinwatch Boat Tour** (☎ 065-905-8156; www.dolphinwatch.ie): More than 100 bottleneck dolphins occupy the area where the Shannon River flows into the Atlantic Ocean, and this two-hour boat trip gives you the chance to see them up close and personal as they swim, feed, play, and (if you're very lucky) jump. The dolphins breed here, and sightings of young dolphin calves are not uncommon. Sea birds are abundant here as well, including gannets, guillemots, razorbills, and peregrine falcons. You must call and book ahead of time (you'll get a refund if the trip is canceled due to bad weather).

The trip leaves from the port village of Carrigaholt four times daily during July and August and most days from April through June and September through October, weather permitting. Tickets cost €24 adults, €12 kids ages 4 to 15, €6 kids ages 2 to 3, and free for kids 1 and under.

✔ **Éamon de Valera Statue,** in Ennis town park, off Gort Road (R352): Éamon de Valera, Irish freedom fighter, prime minister, and later president of the Republic of Ireland, is honored with a bronze statue in Ennis. De Valera was born in New York, and only his American citizenship kept him from facing the firing squad after his part in the Easter Rising of 1916. You can see the statue in a few minutes.

✔ **Ennis Historical Walking Tour** (☎ 087-648-3714): This excellent historical walking tour has it all: politics, ghosts, murders, and rebellions. It's a great way to spend a morning in town.

Tours leave from the Ennis Tourist Office (located in the Temple Gate Hotel courtyard) May through October Monday, Tuesday, Thursday, Friday, and Saturday at 11 a.m. and last about an hour and 15 minutes. They cost €8 adults; kids with parents are free.

✔ **Ennis Friary,** Abbey Street (☎ 065-682-9100): This 13th-century Franciscan abbey was a well-known seat of learning in medieval times, home to more than 1,000 friars and students. Though the building fell to ruin after it was abandoned in the 1692, parts of it have been restored, and you'll find beautiful statues, bas-reliefs, tombs, and carvings.

Admission is €3 adults, €2 seniors, €1 students and kids. It's open April through mid-September daily from 10 a.m. to 6 p.m., mid-September through October daily from 10 a.m. to 5 p.m. Allow 45 minutes for your visit.

✔ **Lahinch Golf Club,** Lahinch (☎ 065-708-1003; www.lahinchgolf.com): The high elevation of the world-class par-72 Old Course provides amazing views of the sea. Watch your ball — local goats are known to cross the fairway. If the fee for the Old Course is too rich for your blood, try the par-70 Castle Course, which many golfers say is nearly as interesting. Check online for substantial discounts on both courses.

Both courses are open daily, except when there's a tournament. Book your tee time in advance. Monday through Friday, greens fees on the Old Course are €100; Saturday and Sunday, they're €125. Greens fees on the Castle Course are €30.

Shopping

Ennis offers some great shopping, including several clothing boutiques with beautiful and interesting selections. You'll find most of these shops on O'Connell Street. One of the best traditional Irish music shops in Ireland is **Custy's Shop,** in Cookes Lane off O'Connell Street, Ennis (☎ 065-682-1727). Not only will you find the best CDs and tune books here, but you're also likely to encounter the many local musicians who come in to chat with the owner and staff. **Giftvenue,** 36 Abbey St., Ennis (☎ 065-686-7891), is the best store in the area for Galway Crystal and Belleek pottery — that thin white pottery decorated with shamrocks; plus, it has top-notch customer service.

Created 40 years ago, the **Burren Perfumery,** Carran (☎ 065-708-9102), uses local flora to create unique fragrances. To get there, take the R480 to the Carran turnoff and follow the signs. In addition to the shop, there is a nice tearoom and a pretty herb garden here. The **West Clare Gallery & Studio,** on the main street in Ennistymon, is open daily showing gorgeous paintings by Phillip Morrison and Eamon Doyle. **Craft Showcase Kilkee,** O'Connell Street, Kilkee (☎ 065-905-6880), sells crafts from ceramics and sheepskin rugs to Celtic jewelry and baskets. The store is on the main Kilkee-Kilrush Road, on the right from Kilkee city center. **The Rock Shop,** in Liscannor, near the Cliffs of Moher (☎ 065-708-1930)

Local edible souvenirs

The Burren Smokehouse, Lisdoonvarna (☎ 065-707-4432), is a gourmet store selling the finest smoked Irish Atlantic salmon, trout, mackerel, and eel. You can watch the process of smoking at the visitor center. Perhaps not so much a take-home souvenir as an eat-while-in-Ireland souvenir, **St. Tola's goat cheeses,** produced by Inagh Farmhouse Cheese, in Inagh, are legendary. They can be found at the Burren Smokehouse, and at local farmer's markets and stores. To see the goat farm and watch cheese-making in action, book a tour in advance at ☎ 065-683-6633. For something sweet, **The Clare Jam Shop,** on the R478 south of Doolin (☎ 065-707-4778), sells a variety of luscious jams, marmalades, jellies, and chutneys.

displays and sells minerals and fossils. **The Traditional Music Shop,** Doolin (☎ 065-707-4407), sells beautiful Irish instruments, plus a large variety of Irish music CDs — a great souvenir is a beginner tin whistle.

Nightlife in County Clare

If you've ever wanted to try Irish set dancing (a partnered form of dance that resembles American square dancing), get yourself over to **Cois na hAbhna,** Gort Road (☎ 065-682-4276), on a Wednesday night. Classes run between 9 p.m. and 11 p.m. Call to confirm — times and venue may change.

Ennis's fabulous performing arts complex **glór,** on the Causeway Link, off Friar's Walk or Francis Street (☎ 065-684-3103; www.glor.ie), offers music, theater, dance, and visual arts. This place books many of the finest traditional Irish music legends, so be sure to find out which musicians are performing while you're around.

In Doolin, check out **Magnetic Music** (☎ 065-707-4988; www.magnetic-music.com) for terrific traditional Irish music concerts.

Hitting the pubs

A note about traditional Irish music in Clare: First of all, there's a whole lot of it. Great sessions take place all over the county (ask around, especially in music shops, since venues and times change frequently). **Doolin** used to be the go-to answer when visitors asked where to find the best music. Unfortunately, it has been a bit of a victim of its own success; pubs are often crowded with visitors and the music can be uneven, from excellent to poor. **Miltown Malbay** is a good bet early in the week while **Ennistymon** (pronounced ennis-*tie*-min) is sure to have great music from Thursday through Sunday. If you want to be guaranteed great music on any night of the week, Ennis is your best bet. If the **Kilfenora Ceili Band** or the **Tulla Ceili Band** are playing near you in Clare, go! Also, see the excellent **Cruises Pub,** under "Where to dine in County Clare," earlier in this chapter.

Brogan's Pub
Ennis

Great pub food, friendly people, lovely Irish traditional music, and a pretty, warmly lit interior. Need I say more?

24 O'Connell St. ☎ **065-682-9480.**

Durty Nelly's
Bunratty

Since 1620, this world-famous tavern has been a thirst-quencher for everyone from the guards who once protected Bunratty Castle to the tourists who explore it today. The interior looks like it hasn't changed over the centuries, with sawdust-strewn floors, low lighting from lanterns, and traditional music sessions that commence at any time in any room of the pub. Though it offers food, this place is better for a drink than for a meal.

In the Bunratty Castle complex. Take the N18 north from Limerick. ☎ **061-36-4861.**

Monk's Pub
Ballyvaughan

Peat fires burn and rustic furnishings invite you to take a seat at this pub overlooking Ballyvaughan Harbor. It's right on the water, and good pub grub is served all day (the seafood chowder is unbelievable). Music fills the air on many weekends.

Main Street. ☎ **065-707-7059.**

O'Connor's
Doolin

The same family has run this combination pub and market for more than 150 years. The pub sits amid a row of thatched fisherman cottages and really comes to life at night with traditional Irish music. If this proves too packed (it seems everyone knows about O'Connor's), head up to McGann's, nearby on Lisdoonvarna Road.

Off the N67, west of Lisdoonvarna. ☎ **065-707-4168.**

The Poet's Corner
Ennis

This beautiful, welcoming pub, in the Old Ground Hotel, plays host to locals and visitors alike. The Irish music sessions here (Thurs–Sun) are a force to be reckoned with.

O' Connell Street. ☎ **065-682-8127.**

Vaughan's Pub
Kilfenora

The old stone barn is the place to be for Irish set dancing (akin to American square dancing) to the tunes of a top-notch band on Thursdays at 10 p.m. and Sundays at 9 p.m. Hang out, remember not to gawk (this is a locals place, not at all a showplace for visitors), and join in if someone offers to teach you a set. You'll have a blast.

Off Main Street on the R481. ☎ **065-708-8004.**

Fast Facts: County Clare

Area Codes

County Clare's area codes (or city codes) are **061** and **065**.

Emergencies/Police

Dial ☎ **999** for all emergencies.

Genealogy Resources

Contact the Clare Heritage Centre, Church Street, Corofin (☎ 065-683-7955).

Hospital

Ennis Hospital is on Gort Road (☎ 065-686-3100).

Information

There are tourist information offices in many towns in Clare, most of which are open only during the summer. A good place to start is Ennis Tourist Office, next to the Temple Gate Hotel in Ennis (☎ 065-682-8366); it's open year-round.

Post Office

There are post offices in all towns in Clare. In Ennis, there is a post office on Market Street (☎ 065-682-9697).

Chapter 18

County Galway: Galway City, the Aran Islands, and Connemara

. . . .

In This Chapter

▶ Hearing some great traditional Irish music in Galway City

▶ Dining in the best restaurants in the West

▶ Visiting the peaceful Aran Islands, bastions of tradition

▶ Exploring the vast boglands, mountains, and coastlines of Connemara (and meeting some sweet Connemara ponies!)

. . . .

*C*ounty Galway is a winning combination of the fun and bustle of Galway City with its great music, pubs, restaurants, and shops; the wild and breathtaking mountain-and-bog landscape of Connemara; the peaceful Aran Islands; picturesque small towns; and one of the largest *Gaeltachts* (Irish-speaking regions) in the country.

Galway City

Buzzing Galway City serves as a gateway to the rest of the county. It's a fabulous city to explore, with a youthful university population; constant street entertainment; a robust arts scene; loads of traditional Irish music; and a great variety of both trendy and traditional places to eat, sleep, drink, and shop. They certainly don't roll up the sidewalks at 9 p.m. here; the center of the city is usually lively into the wee hours of the morning. The city has a gorgeous location, set on peaceful Galway Bay, which is home to a number of swans, and the River Corrib, a favored fishing location. The only thing that Galway City doesn't have is major sights within the city; there are places to visit, but there aren't any must-see attractions. The medieval center of the city is so tiny that you'll know your way around in no time.

County Galway

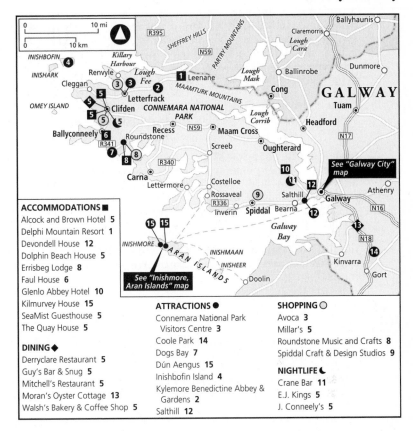

ACCOMMODATIONS ■

Alcock and Brown Hotel **5**
Delphi Mountain Resort **1**
Devondell House **12**
Dolphin Beach House **5**
Errisbeg Lodge **8**
Faul House **6**
Glenlo Abbey Hotel **10**
Kilmurvey House **15**
SeaMist Guesthouse **5**
The Quay House **5**

DINING ◆

Derryclare Restaurant **5**
Guy's Bar & Snug **5**
Mitchell's Restaurant **5**
Moran's Oyster Cottage **13**
Walsh's Bakery & Coffee Shop **5**

ATTRACTIONS ●

Connemara National Park
  Visitors Centre **3**
Coole Park **14**
Dogs Bay **7**
Dún Aengus **15**
Inishbofin Island **4**
Kylemore Benedictine Abbey &
  Gardens **2**
Salthill **12**

SHOPPING ○

Avoca **3**
Millar's **5**
Roundstone Music and Crafts **8**
Spiddal Craft & Design Studios **9**

NIGHTLIFE ☾

Crane Bar **11**
E.J. Kings **5**
J. Conneely's **5**

Galway loves its festivals and celebrations. The stars of the events calendar are the excellent **Galway Arts Festival** (two weeks in mid-July), the insanely popular **Galway Horse Races** (usually the last week in July), and the **Galway Oyster Festival** (in late September), which sees over 100,000 local oysters going down the hatches of locals and visitors alike.

If you're driving or going to a festival, I recommend giving the city itself a day or two and two nights unless you're looking for an urban base as you explore Connemara, the Burren (see Chapter 17), or the Aran Islands during the day. If you're traveling without a car, Galway City is a great place to spend a few days; the city has a compact, pedestrian-friendly layout and many excellent guided tours leave from the city to explore Connemara, the Aran Islands, the Burren, and other destinations in counties Galway and Clare.

Getting to and around Galway City

Aer Lingus (☎ 0818-365-000; www.aerlingus.com) has daily service from Dublin into Galway Airport, in Carnmore (☎ 091-75-5569; www.galwayairport.com). The best way to get into town from the airport is by taxi. Cabs line up right outside the terminal building and the trip into Galway City should cost about €15. **Big-O-Taxi-co** (☎ 091-58-5858) is partnered with Galway Airport and offers frequent, reliable service.

If you're driving to Galway City from Dublin, take the M4 to the M6. If you'd like to rent a car in Galway, try **Budget** (☎ 091-566-376), on Eyre Square.

Irish Rail (☎ 1-850-366-222; www.irishrail.ie) travels from Dublin and several other points to Ceannt Station (pronounced ky-*ant* and also known as plain old "Galway Station"), located right off Eyre Square, in the center of Galway. **Bus Éireann** (☎ 01-836-6111; www.buseireann.ie) also travels from several towns to Ceannt Station. The private coach service **CityLink** (☎ 1-890-28-08-08; www.citylink.ie) travels between Galway and Dublin and offers several nonstop journeys. The rail trip from Dublin takes about two and a half hours, as does the non-stop CityLink service. The Bus Éireann trip takes about three and a half hours.

Galway City is best seen on foot. The town is compact, and the heart is pedestrian-only, so a car wouldn't do you much good. If you do take a car into the city, know that parking in Galway City is sparse and that street parking requires a Pay-and-Display card, available at Pay-and-Display machines around the city. Galway has good local bus service that covers the city's suburbs, running from the city center (either from Ceannt Station or from the Tourist Office on Eyre Square) out to Salthill and the coastal towns. Contact **Galway City Direct Bus Company** (☎ 091-860-814; www.citydirectgalway.ie) or **Bus Éireann** (☎ 01-836-6111; www.buseireann.ie) for schedules and fares. You can pick up a taxi on Eyre Square or by calling a taxi company such as **Abby Taxis** (☎ 091-533-333) or **Cara Cabs** (☎ 091-563-939).

The main drags in Galway City are Shop Street, Middle Street, William Street, High Street, Abbeygate Street, and the streets around **Eyre Square** (*Eyre* is pronounced *air*). Though the Claddagh neighborhood may look far away on city maps, in reality this buzzy area is only a five- to ten-minute walk from the city center over one of the Corrib River bridges.

Spending the night in Galway City

Try to book your accommodations well in advance if you'll be visiting during the Galway Arts Festival (mid-July) and Galway Races (late July).

Galway City

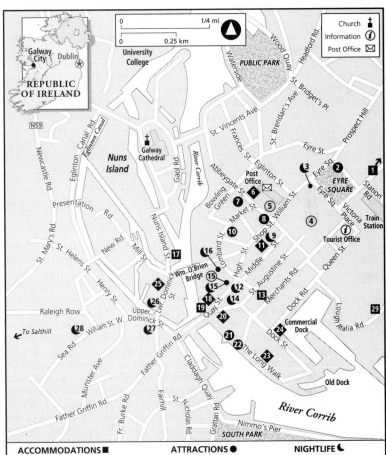

ACCOMMODATIONS ■
the g **29**
the house hotel **13**
Jurys Inn Galway **17**
Petra House **1**
St. Martin's Bed & Breakfast **19**

DINING ◆
Ard Bia Café & Restaurant at
    Nimmos **23**
Cava **25**
Couch Potatas **6**
Goya's Café **20**
Kirwan's Lane **20**
The Malt House **11**
McDonagh's Seafood House **18**
Wa Café **24**

ATTRACTIONS ●
Browne Doorway **2**
Collegiate Church of
    St. Nicholas **10**
Eyre Square **2**
Galway City Museum **22**
Lynch Memorial
    Window **7**
Lynch's Castle **8**
Spanish Arch **21**

SHOPPING ○
Eyre Square Shopping
    Centre **4**
Thomas Dillon's **15**
The Treasure Chest **5**

NIGHTLIFE ☾
Crane Bar **28**
Druid Theatre
    Company **12**
The Kings Head **9**
Monroe's Tavern **27**
The Quays **14**
Róisín Dubh **26**
The Skeff Bar **3**
Tig Neachtain **16**

Devondell House
$$ Galway City

Berna Kelly should run a school for aspiring B&B hosts and hostesses. Warm and welcoming, she greets every guest with a tea tray filled with home-baked treats and is happy to help you plan your days in Galway and the surrounding area. Her home is cozy and sparkling clean, and rooms are homey and comfortable, with white quilts and crisp Irish linens. You may not want to make any sightseeing plans for the morning because Berna's incredible breakfast, which is served at two tables so that you can chat with your fellow guests, invites lingering. The options are endless, from delicious stewed pears, plums, rhubarb, and other fruits to a comprehensive cheese plate to fruit smoothies. And that's just the preamble to the main course! The house is about a 20-minute walk from the heart of Galway City and is within walking distance of the seafront.

47 Devon Park, off Salthill Road Lower. ☎ **091-528-306.** *www.devondell.com. Parking: Free on the street. Rack rates: €80–€90 double. No credit cards. Closed Nov–Feb.*

the g
$$$$ Galway City

Okay, you already know that this has to be a hip hotel, because the name of the place is in lowercase letters. "But just how hip is it?" you ask. Well, you enter the dramatic black-glass lobby to find a wall-length aquarium filled with tropical fish, and a huge neon sign reading: "This must be the place." And, indeed, it is. Dreamed up by couture hat designer Philip Treacy (Camilla Parker Bowles is just one of his famous clients), the hotel is luxurious and theatrical, like the set of a glamorous avant-garde film. Treacy blends ultramodern design elements, such as movie scenes projected silently on the wall of the Grand Salon, with unexpected natural touches (many inspired by the coast of Connemara). The effect is over-the-top and dazzling. Set aside time to spend in all the public lounges, from the Grand Salon, with its impossibly high ceilings, glass-and-silver sphere installation, and tables filled with Swarovski crystal bits; to the Blue Room, which has rich purple and amber velvet couches and chairs. The spa offers all sorts of treatments and is another beauty, with a flock of origami fabric cranes gliding over the hot tub, which is lit in green. The restaurant, headed up by culinary star Stefan Matz, serves New Irish cuisine in an *Alice in Wonderland*–esqe setting of oversized candy-colored armchairs and giant purple banquettes. The bedrooms are simpler than the rest of the hotel, decorated in cool whites and creams, with a space-age-style lamp that looks like it could cook breakfast for you and a bed that feels like a cloud. Service is exceptional. The hotel often has special offers available on its Web site, and even if you're not staying at the hotel, you can still take in the public rooms during afternoon tea, evening cocktails, or dinner. The Dinner and a Movie package (€30) is quite popular, offering a two-course meal in one of the lounges and a free ticket to a movie in the nearby EYE Cinema.

Wellpark. ☎ **091-865-200.** *Fax: 091-865-203.* www.theghotel.ie. *Parking: Free self-parking on-site, €10 valet. Rack rates: €160–€240 double. AE, MC, V.*

Glenlo Abbey Hotel
$$$$ Galway City

Located about 3.2km (2 miles) outside Galway City, this 1740s manor house is the picture of gracious living. The hotel is surrounded by peaceful grounds, including its own 9-hole golf course, and the interior is furnished with luxurious fabrics, antiques, and hand-carved furniture. The spacious guest rooms boast lovely fabrics, marble bathrooms, and pastoral views. The Pullman Restaurant, which serves meals in two retired *Orient Express* cars, is definitely worth a visit. Check the Web site for frequent specials and packages.

Bushypark, right off the N59, west of Galway City. ☎ **091-526-666.** www.glenlo. com. *Parking: Free on-site. Rack rates: €250–€400 double. Some rates do not include breakfast. AE, MC, V.*

The House Hotel
$$$ Galway City

I could get used to a house like this — a funky, quiet oasis in the heart of a lively city. An antidote to cookie-cutter accommodations, each of the hotel's 40 rooms is uniquely decorated with contemporary fabrics and furnishings. Open the door to one room and you might find a cranberry-colored corduroy bed throw, while the next room may feature cream-and-white silk patchwork pillows. Though none of the rooms is cramped, I recommend upgrading from the standard rooms if space is a priority. The staff is genuinely friendly and willing to go the extra mile for guests; one happy visitor reports that the staff sent up complimentary chocolates when they learned that she and her husband were on their honeymoon. The expansive lounge, decorated with bright velvet couches and well-tended orchids, is always full of guests relaxing and chatting.

On Lower Merchants Road. ☎ **091-538-900.** *Fax: 091-568-262.* www.thehouse hotel.ie. *Parking: Discounted rates at a garage nearby. Rack rates: €140–€200 double. Some rates do not include breakfast. AE, MC, V.*

Jurys Inn Galway
$$–$$$ Galway City

Location, location, location. This hotel, part of the reliable Jurys chain, is situated in a terrific spot, right on the edge of the hopping heart of the city, near the pretty River Corrib (the river that separates the city center from the surrounding areas). Rooms are of the standard hotel variety, with pine furnishings and warm colors. A restaurant downstairs serves full meals, and the hotel's pub is a jovial place to chat over a drink (and perhaps listen to some live music). If you're a light sleeper, ask for a room away from the main street. If you can book early online, you're likely to encounter some very low rates.

Quay Street. ☎ **091-566-444.** *Fax: 091-568-415.* www.jurysinns.com. *Parking: About €10 per day, close to the hotel. Rack rates: €70–€164 double. Some rates do not include breakfast. AE, MC, V.*

Petra House
$$ **Galway City**

This is a great place to stay if you want to be close to the buzz of the city but not in the middle of it. The city center is an easy ten-minute walk and there is parking for those who have a car. Owners Joan and Frank Maher are perfect B&B hosts — friendly and helpful without being intrusive. Rooms are simple and spotless, with pine furnishings and colorful bed-spreads, and breakfast is excellent, offering many vegetarian options, fresh fruit salad, home-baked brown bread, and lots of other treats.

29 College Rd. ☎ **091-566-580.** *Fax: 091-566-580. Parking: Free on-site. Rack rates: €80–€120 double. MC, V.*

St. Martin's Bed and Breakfast
$ **Galway City**

Who could pass up a bed-and-breakfast where you're greeted at breakfast by two friendly puppies named Millie and Rambo? Mille, Rambo, and your kind hostess, Mary, will give you a warm welcome, and Mary will help you plan your Galway visit. If stylish room décor is important to you, try Devondell instead (it's comfortable and cozy, but pretty plain-Jane here); if a central location is what you're seeking, this is your place. St. Martin's is located on a quiet street, less than a five-minute walk from the hustle and bustle of downtown Galway.

2 Nuns Island. ☎ **091-568-286.** *Parking: €5 per day, in a nearby lot. Rack rates: €60–€70 double. No credit cards.*

Dining in Galway City

If you're in the mood for something sweet, try **Goyas Cafe,** 2–3 Kirwan's Lane (☎ **091-567-010**), which offers up incredible cakes and tarts, along with generous mugs of tea, coffee, and hot chocolate, in an airy, sky-blue-ceilinged cafe. If you're feeling virtuous, you can have a bowl of soup or a toasted sandwich before the main event, but save room for the orange Madeira, or the fudge cake, or the baked cheesecake, or. . . .

For a fun afternoon tea or dinner in surroundings that are equal parts trendy and luxurious, check out the offerings at **the g** (see p. 342). For a different kind of afternoon snack, get a piping-hot bowl of miso soup and a sushi roll, Japanese sandwich, or Japanese pastry at the pretty little **Wa Café,** 13 New Dock St. (☎ **091-895-850**), open daily from 11:30 a.m. until 9 p.m.

If a sit-down restaurant with simple burgers and sandwiches is what you crave, **The Skeff Bar** (see p. 353) is a good choice.

Ard Bia at Nimmos
$–$$$ **Galway City**   **CAFE/NEW IRISH**

Located in an old stone house on the fast-flowing River Corrib, this place has two different personalities: At lunch, artsy types fill the bright, contemporary country-style space, chatting over giant pots of tea and tasty dishes such as a goat cheese, pickled beet, and toasted walnut salad with onion marmalade, or a smoked chicken, brie, and avocado sandwich dressed with apricot chutney. At dinner, things get a bit more sophisticated as the restaurant serves up inventive seasonal New Irish dishes such as Irish beef filet with a root vegetable and thyme gratin, stout-braised shallots, and port *jus;* and the catch of the day served with an olive, sorrel, and potato salad, braised fennel, and grilled asparagus. Check out the paintings and other art throughout the restaurant and cafe; the owner is an avid collector. The set menus, at €27 for two courses and €35 for three courses, are quite a steal.

Long Walk, through the Spanish Arch. ☎ *091-539-897. Reservations recommended. Main courses: Cafe €7–€12, restaurant €17–€23. AE, MC, V. Open: Cafe Wed–Fri noon to 3 p.m., Sat 10 a.m.–3:30 p.m., Sun noon to 7 p.m.; restaurant Tues–Sat 6–10 p.m.*

Cava
$$$ **Galway City**   **SPANISH TAPAS**

You know a restaurant is serious about its tapas when part of its interior decorating scheme involves the prominent display of dry-cured ham shanks. The space is beautiful and eclectic, with high ceilings; walls painted stucco-style in blue, white, and coffee colors; baroque sconces; and low shelves displaying old wooden boxes that used to hold Spanish fig-and-almond cakes. Though the restaurant serves excellent main courses at lunch and dinner, the menu of over 50 tapas, served from noon until 10 p.m., is just too wonderful to pass up. Some of my group's favorites included the mackerel marinated with sherry vinegar, the pan-fried chorizo and potato dish, the white beans with wild mushrooms, the Serrano ham and Manchego cheese plate, and the duck with plum and honey. Prepare to be stuffed. But also be prepared to order the creamy pistachio ice cream for dessert.

51 Lower Dominick St. ☎ *091-539-884. Reservations highly recommended. Tapas: €5–€15 per plate (three tapas plates per person is usually plenty). Main courses: €19–€29. MC, V. Open: Daily noon to 5 p.m. and 6–10 p.m. (later Fri–Sat).*

Couch Potatas
$ **Galway City**   **BAKED POTATOES**

This casual baked-potato joint is constantly bustling with chatty 20- and 30-somethings. Sit down at one of the wood tables in the white-walled, wood-ceilinged restaurant, and select your spud. There is something to please everyone (as long as you like potatoes), from the Venice by Night, a potato filled with tuna, corn, peppers, tomato sauce, onions, mushrooms, and mozzarella cheese, to the Nora Barnacle, a potato stuffed with strips of chicken breast and served with a creamy garlic sauce. There are a few nonpotato appetizers and salads if you're feeling starched out. Be sure to check out the paintings of spuds as famous movie characters (the intrepid-looking Batman potato is my favorite) while you wait for your order. The casual atmosphere and fun meal choices make this a great place for families.

40 Upper Abbeygate St. ☎ *091-561-664. Main courses: €8–€9. No credit cards. Open: Mon–Sat noon to 9:30 p.m., Sun 12:30–9:30 p.m.*

Kirwan's Lane
$$$ Galway City   CONTINENTAL-NEW IRISH

Not only do I recommend this upscale, candlelit restaurant, but so does the entire group who sat next to me: They couldn't stop raving about the food and proclaimed their meal the best they had eaten in Ireland. The décor on the lower floor is modern and Scandinavian-looking, while the upper floor is painted with vivid reds and yellows. Dishes feature the freshest of ingredients, and some borrow Indian, southern European, and Asian spices, condiments, and cooking techniques, such as the roast duck with fried polenta, glazed fresh figs, and star anise *jus.* Other dishes are straight-up New Irish, such as the pan-fried local salmon with leek and potato puree and asparagus. The several vegetarian dishes are very classy, including such treats as a fennel and zucchini "osso buco" served with saffron couscous. Finish up with the heavenly French-chocolate cake served with pistachio ice cream if it's on the menu.

Kirwan's Lane (the small lane next to McDonagh's Restaurant, off Quay Street). ☎ *091-568-266. Reservations recommended. Main courses: €18–€28. AE, DC, MC, V. Open: Daily 12:30–2:30 p.m. and 6–10 p.m.*

The Malt House
$$$–$$$$ Galway City   CONTINENTAL/NEW IRISH

This Galway institution has undergone a massive overhaul. Gone are the carpets and other trappings of old-world Continental dining. In their place is an airy, modern restaurant with a relaxed feel. The mission of the Malt House is to serve locally sourced, in-season dishes, and the chef and owner have worked hard to find the best producers in the region. These local ingredients are highlighted in dishes such as the appetizer of wild nettle soup with Guinness cream and fresh baked soda bread, and the main course of local spring lamb with organic carrots, chard, and rosemary *jus.* Prices on the a la carte menu may induce slight sticker shock, but the €25 two-course and €30 three-course fixed-price menus will soften the blow.

15 High Street, in a little courtyard near the Kings Head Pub. ☎ *091-567-866. Main courses: €19–€32. AE, MC. V. Open: Daily noon to 3 p.m. and 5:30–10 p.m.*

McDonagh's Seafood House
$–$$ Galway City SEAFOOD

Fish doesn't get fresher or better than at this popular place, where rope ladders twist across the ceiling and murals of old fish markets in Galway decorate the walls. The McDonaghs, who've been at it for four generations, have had plenty of practice in the trade. There's a great sit-down restaurant, but for the true McDonagh's experience, I recommend visiting the top-notch fish-and-chips shop in the front of the restaurant, grabbing a bench outside, and watching the world pass by as you dig into your moist and delicious cutlet of fish. If you're curious about curry chips (French fries with curry sauce), this is the place to try them. Also, if you're a homesick Scot, you can get your haggis fix here.

22 Quay St. (beside Jurys Inn, near the Spanish Arch). ☎ *091-56-5001. Main courses: €13–€20; fish and chips €4–€9. AE, DC, MC, V. Open: Restaurant Mon–Sat 5–10 p.m.; fish-and-chips counter Mon–Sat noon to 11 p.m., Sun 4–10 p.m.*

Moran's Oyster Cottage
$$$ Kilcolgan SEAFOOD

This is possibly the best place in Ireland for oysters. Moran's has been run by the same family for six generations and is dedicated to serving the very best oysters along with a well-pulled pint. If you are not a friend of the bivalve, there are other options on the menu, from chili-spiced prawns to baked salmon. All these treats are served overlooking the weir, which is frequented by swans.

The Weir, Kilcolgan. 10 miles south of Galway on the N6, outside the village of Clarenbridge. ☎ *091-796-113. Main courses: €20–€24 (€39 for lobster). AE, MC, V. Open: Food served daily noon to 10 p.m. (pub open later on weekends).*

Exploring Galway City: The top attractions

Galway doesn't have any don't-leave-Ireland-without-seeing-it attractions; it's more of a place to wander around, enjoy the excellent street performers who flock to the city in the summer, shop a little, and take advantage of the fabulous restaurant and nightlife scenes.

The compact heart of Galway is a pedestrian area that begins west of Eyre Square. The main street here starts as William Street at Eyre Square and then changes names many times before hitting the River Corrib.

Galway has a whole lot of history and many legends, so I recommend taking a walking tour. Check out **Galway Tours** (☎ 086-402-1819); they conduct tours daily any time between 9 a.m. and 7 p.m., so call to let them know what works for you. If you'd rather explore the city by bus, the **Galway City Tour** (☎ 091-566-566) departs May through September daily at 11 a.m. from the Galway bus station, off Forster Street. Looking for a darker perspective on the city? Try the creepy **Galway Night Tour** (☎ 091-566-566), a bus tour that leaves from the bus station off Forster Street on Friday at 9 p.m. Book in advance for all tours. Here are some attractions that you may want to look out for as you wander the city.

The 14 tribes

You may hear Galway City referred to as the City of the Tribes. This nickname comes from the 14 wealthy merchant families, mostly from England, that took control of this area and established Galway City between the 13th and 16th centuries. The last names of the "tribes" are Athy, Blake, Bodkin, Browne, D'Arcy, Deane, Ffont, Ffrench, Joyce, Kirwan, Lynch, Martyn, Morris, and Skerritt. You'll see past and present evidence of these families all around Galway City, from 700-year-old streets that retain family names to contemporary Galwegians who wear these last names with pride. To give you an idea of the enduring presence of these families, 64 members of the Lynch family have served as mayors of Galway over the last 500 years. Angela Lynch, the latest in the line, served until 1998. For a look at the coat of arms of each family, check out the 14 flags in Eyre Square.

Browne Doorway

Looking pretty odd at the head of Eyre Square, the Browne Doorway is a towering stone archway that's connected to nothing. Dating from 1627, the doorway comes from an old mansion on Lower Abbeygate Street, and features the coat of arms for the Browne and Lynch families, 2 of the original 14 families who founded Galway City.

Located on the northwest side of Eyre Square.

Collegiate Church of St. Nicholas

Christopher Columbus is rumored to have prayed in this well-preserved medieval church before setting sail for the New World. Built in 1324, the church changed hands from Protestant to Catholic several times over the centuries; it has been Protestant for the last 300 years and continues to enjoy a sizable Protestant congregation. You'll find beautiful stone carvings, plaques bearing all sorts of interesting eulogies, gargoyles, and a tombstone dating from 1280. Sadly, many of the faces on the angel sculptures were removed by Cromwell's army in the 1650s.

Corner of Mainguard Street and Lombard Street. ☎ **091-564-648.** *Admission: Free. Open: Mar–Dec daily 9 a.m.–7 p.m., Jan–Feb daily 9 a.m.–5 p.m.*

Eyre Square

This giant grassy square has been restored and is a hangout for locals and travelers alike. If you're in the area, Eamon O'Doherty's spectacular modern sculpture of an old Galway hooker ship, the 14 flags featuring the coat of arms for each of Galway's founding families (see p. 348), and the Browne Doorway (see p. 348) are all worth a look.

Galway City Museum

If it's a rainy day and you want to hang out somewhere dry, spend an hour or so in the Galway City Museum, which has several decent, though text-heavy, exhibits on the history of the area. Be sure to check out the beautiful Galway hooker boat on the ground floor.

Spanish Arch. ☎ *091-532-460. Admission: Free. Open: June–Aug Tues–Sat 10 a.m.–5 p.m., Mon 2–5 p.m.; Sept–May Tues–Sat 10 a.m.–5 p.m.*

Lynch's Castle (AIB Bank)

If this isn't the first castle you've seen in Ireland, you may expect something . . . well, larger. This 15th-century home of the legendary Lynch family was restored and now houses a bank, though you can still marvel at the coats of arms, gargoyles, and the Spanish-style stonework on the exterior.

Upper Abbeygate Street (between Shop and Market streets).

Lynch Memorial Window

The Lynch Memorial Window, with a skull-and-crossbones carving underneath, is set into a wall just above a Gothic doorway on Market Street. Legend has it that James Lynch FitzStephen, unyielding magistrate and mayor of Galway, earned his place in dictionaries when he condemned and executed his own son (convicted of murder) in 1493 as a demonstration that the law does not bend even under family ties. For many years, people thought that this incident explained the origins of the word *lynch*. In recent years, however, evidence has emerged that this story is most likely apocryphal. Though the event was supposed to have taken place in 1493, the stonework of the windows is from the 1500s. As one skeptic said, "You can't hang a 15th-century man out of a 16th-century window."

Market Street (one block northwest of Eyre Square), next to the Collegiate Church of St. Nicholas.

Spanish Arch

This stone arch was built in 1519 to protect Galway City's docks from looting. No one is quite sure how the Spanish Arch got its present name. Most people believe that it derives its moniker from the Spanish ships that traded with Galway in the 16th and 17th centuries. Others say it got its name from the Spanish Armada ships that wrecked nearby, and still others say that the arch got its name when a Spanish sailor was found murdered near the arch in the 18th century.

Between Wolfe Tone Bridge and the Long Walk, at the mouth of the River Corrib.

The swans of the River Corrib

The waters of Lough (pronounced lock) Corrib, the largest lake in the Republic of Ireland, run through the River Corrib to join the sea at the edge of Galway City. Go down to the pier, near the Spanish Arch, to see the huge flock of mute swans who make their home here, and keep an eye out for fluffy gray signets.

Walking the Salthill Promenade

This fun resort strip makes for a fun day with very pretty bay views. Walk along the 3.2km-long (2-mile) promenade, eat fast food, play arcade games, splash in the bay, visit the Leisureland amusement park, and maybe say hi to the local fish and rays at Atlantaquaria on the Seafront Promenade. It's local tradition to kick the wall at the very end of the promenade for good luck. No one knows why, though my favorite theory is that the kick expresses the walker's disappointment that she's prevented from continuing her beautiful stroll on the promenade.

Take Father Griffin Rd. (R336) southwest from the city center for about 3km (2 miles). It will turn into Whitestrand Rd. and then into the Promenade. **City Direct Galway** *(☎ 091-860-814) runs several bus trips between Eyre Square and various points along the Salthill promenade Mon–Fri.*

A short side trip from Galway City

Coole Park
Gort

The house and grounds here were once home to Lady Gregory — writer, friend of many an Irish luminary, and cofounder of Dublin's Abbey Theatre. The grounds are now a nature reserve; red deer, red squirrels, stoats, otters, several species of waterfowl, and other animals make it their home. There are beautiful wooded trails where you'll encounter a variety of wildflowers, including orchids. In addition, there are several *turloughs* (lakes that appear and disappear with the seasons) and lush gardens. One of the most interesting parts of the park is the Autograph Tree, which bears the carved initials of such famous people as George Bernard Shaw; Oliver St. John Gogarty; Sean O'Casey; and William Butler Yeats, Lady Gregory's friend and partner in creating the Abbey Theatre. In the courtyard, you'll find the visitor center, housed in a restored stable. Two interesting presentations on the history of Coole Park are shown here, and a restaurant serves filling lunch dishes and great desserts. Guided tours of the park are available if you book in advance. Die-hard William Butler Yeats fans also may want to pop into **Thoor Ballylee** (☎ 091-63-1436), Yeats's summer home, located off the N66 a few miles north of Gort. Call to make sure it's open — it's been closed recently due to flood damage. Allow two hours for your visit.

Take the N6 east out of Galway to the N18; north of Gort, follow the signs. ☎ *091-63-1804. Admission: Free. Open: Park open year-round; visitor center Apr and Sept 1–19 Wed–Sun 10 a.m.–5 p.m., May–Aug daily 10 a.m.–5 p.m.*

Shopping in Galway City

Galway City is home to lot of shops, and you're bound to find items to suit your taste as you stroll around the heart of the city. A great souvenir to buy in Galway is a Claddagh ring — you know, the ones with two hands clasping a heart topped with a crown. The design is very popular in the Galway area, and numerous stores sell these rings. **Thomas**

Inspired by Coole Park

The trees are in their autumn beauty,

The woodland paths are dry,

Under the October twilight the water

Mirrors a still sky.

—William Butler Yeats, from the poem "The Wild Swans at Coole"

Dillon's, 1 Quay St., near the Spanish Arch (☎ **091-566-365**), claims to be the original maker and is worth a stop for the small homemade Claddagh museum (a little rough around the edges but interesting all the same), even if you aren't in the market for a ring. See the sidebar "The Claddagh ring," later in this chapter, for the lore surrounding the ring.

Kennys Bookshop & Art Galleries, located in Liosbán Retail Park off Tuam Road (R334) east of the downtown area (☎ **091-709-350**), is a well-loved Galway institution, selling all sorts of wonderful books, gorgeous original art, and prints. Though the store has moved to a location that's a bit outside the city center, it's well worth seeking out. You also can get your Kennys fix through its online bookstore and gallery at www.kennys.ie.

The Treasure Chest, 31–33 William St. (☎ **091-563-862**), has just about every Irish gift item you could want under one roof — Waterford Crystal, Royal Tara china, Belleek china, Claddagh rings, Aran knitwear, linen, and more. **MacEocagain/Galway Woollen Market,** 21 High St. (☎ **091-56-2491**), specializes in Aran hand-knits and other knitwear, linen, lace, sheepskins, and jewelry. If you want to experience an Irish mall, **Eyre Square Shopping Centre** has more than 50 shops under one glass roof.

 If you're around on a Saturday from 8 a.m. to 6 p.m. or a Sunday from 2 to 6 p.m., get ready to drool over the food and the crafts at the **Galway Market,** near St. Nicholas's Church, right off of Shop Street. There's plenty of prepared food for sale, from curry to crepes, so stick around for lunch. From December 14 to 24 there is a craft market here from 10 a.m. to 6 p.m.

Enjoying Galway City nightlife

Galway has some excellent theater and live music that you can take in before hitting one of the pubs listed in this section. **Róisín Dubh,** on Dominick Street across the Corrib River (☎ **091-586-540;** www.roisindubh.net), books spectacular bands and singers, from traditional Irish musicians to singer-songwriters to alternative country bands to jazz ensembles to rock groups. **Monroe's Tavern** (see the listing later in this

The Claddagh ring

Claddagh rings feature two hands holding a heart, which is topped by a crown. The hands symbolize friendship, the crown symbolizes loyalty, and the heart represents love.

Though the origins of the ring are debated, rings of this style have been around since Roman times. The name comes from the Claddagh, one of the oldest fishing villages in Ireland, which occupied the west bank of the Corrib Estuary, right across from the center of the city. The explanation for the association between this area and the ring holds that Richard Joyce, a native of Galway, was captured by Algerian pirates on his way to the West Indies in the 1680s. Once in Algeria, he was sold as a slave to a rich Moorish goldsmith who trained him in the craft. Upon his release and return to Galway in 1689, Joyce became a goldsmith and developed the Claddagh ring based on a design he had encountered in Algeria. This story is supported by the fact that many Claddagh rings from the early 1700s bear Joyce's initials.

According to tradition, the wearer wears the ring with the crown pointing toward the fingertips to show that he or she is in love or married. If the wearer is unattached, he or she wears the ring with the heart pointing toward the fingertips. In the Galway area, the ring often serves as a woman's engagement or wedding ring.

To learn more about the Claddagh ring, visit the little museum at Thomas Dillon's shop, located at 1 Quay St., near the Spanish Arch.

section) has similarly eclectic offerings, from traditional Irish music to U2 tribute bands. If the Irish dance and music show *Fuaim Chonamara* is performing at Monroe's while you're in Galway, try to get tickets. **Galway Cathedral,** off Eglinton Street across the Salmon Weir Bridge from the city center (☎ 091-531-438; www.galwaycathedral.ie) hosts superb classical musicians on Thursday nights at 8 p.m. in July and August.

The stellar **Druid Theatre Company,** Druid Lane, off Quay Street (☎ 091-568-660; www.druid.ie), presents inventive performances of 20th-century and new Irish plays.

For information on what's going on in pubs, clubs, theaters, and more, check out www.galwayentertainment.ie.

For a different kind of entertainment, visit **Dunguaire Castle,** right outside the village of Kinvara (☎ 061-711-200), for its cheesy-yet-fun **medieval banquet,** held nightly from May through September at 5:30 p.m. and 8:45 p.m. The banquet lasts a little more than two hours and features a four-course dinner and entertainment, including Irish songs, stories, and poetry. The usual prices are €59 adults, €49 kids 9 to 12, €28 kids 6 to 9, and free for kids 5 and under. Booking in advance is essential.

Crane Bar

This is arguably the best place in Galway City for traditional Irish music. Casual sessions take place every night with some of the best musicians in town. The décor is nothing special, but it won't matter once you get carried along on the current of jigs and reels.

2 Sea Rd., Salthill (less than a mile out of Galway City center). ☎ **091-587-419.** *www. thecranebar.com.*

The Kings Head

The Middle Ages live on in the Kings Head. The building has been in existence since at least 1612 and retains its original medieval fireplaces and windows. Every bit of the place looks the part of a 400-year-old pub, and there's history galore associated with this place — a chat with the barkeep will reveal some of the stories. Spread over three floors, the pub features music almost every night; there's an emphasis on Irish traditional music, but you also may find a DJ or a great cover band. To secure a seat before the music starts come for some of the great pub grub or pizza. And don't forget to take your picture sitting on the throne next to the downstairs fireplace.

15 High St., at the corner of Shop Street and Quay Street. ☎ **091-56-6630.** *www. thekingshead.ie.*

Monroe's Tavern

Feeling footloose? Set in an old house with low ceilings and timber floors, locals pack this place every Monday night at 9 p.m. for set dancing — a partnered form of Irish dance that resembles American square dancing. There's music every night, either more casual offerings in the bar downstairs or more formal shows, from rock to traditional Irish, upstairs at Monroe's Live. Monroe's serves excellent pub food.

Dominick Street. ☎ **091-58-3397.** *www.monroes.ie.*

The Quays

No trip to Galway is complete without a stop at this lively pub. The interior is furnished with features imported from a medieval French church, including stained glass, Gothic arches, and carved wood. Traditional Irish sessions are often found downstairs, while the upstairs usually features rock bands and is packed to the gills late into the night. The pub grub is quite tasty.

Quay Street and Chapel Lane. ☎ **091-56-8347.**

The Skeff Bar

This pub, which encompasses six bars, is a good place for conversation. It incorporates all different kinds of décor: Some parts look like an upper-class drawing room, with elegant couches, coffee tables, stained glass, and Persian rugs; other parts are distinctly Irish pub, with low stools, snugs, and fireplaces. The straightforward food (burgers, chicken fingers, and so on) is good, and there's often a DJ on weekends.

Eyre Square. ☎ **091-56-3173.**

Tíg Neachtain

This is the real deal. This cozy pub, in a building that dates from the Middle Ages, is filled with old snugs that have seen infinite pints of Guinness and been party to countless late-night conversations. There is music (mostly traditional Irish) here on Sundays. The name of the pub is pronounced tig *nock*-tin.

17 Cross St. ☎ **091-568-820.**

The Aran Islands

The Aran Islands — Inis Mor (Inishmore), Inis Meáin (Inishmaan), and Inis Oirr (Inisheer) — are beautiful havens of traditional Irish culture: Most islanders speak Irish Gaelic as a first language, and many still don traditional Aran sweaters with their jeans. Each of the islands has a different personality, although all are excellent for those who love to explore by foot. Visitors arrive at Inishmore, the largest and most developed of islands, by the boatload during the summer to explore the pre-Christian and Christian monuments and ruins. **Dún Aengus,** a huge prehistoric stone fort perched on sheer cliffs, is the main attraction. Inishmaan is the second-largest and least-visited island, with beautiful hilly landscapes and the strongest Irish cultural tradition of the three islands; Inisheer is the smallest of the islands and is a great place to bike or meander along beaches, wildflower meadows, and a maze of old stone walls.

If you're going to come to the Aran Islands, I highly recommend spending the night. The true personality of the islands (and the islanders) seems to emerge only after the day-trippers have gone back to the mainland.

For more information on the islands, check out www.aranislands.ie.

Getting to and around the Aran Islands

The most common way to get to the Arans is by ferry. **Aran Island Ferries** (☎ **091-56-8903;** www.aranislandferries.com), which has an office at the Galway Tourist Office on Forster Street off Eyre Square, operates ferries that depart from Ros á Mhil (Rossaveal) Pier in Connemara (the bus trip from Queen Street in Galway City to Ros á Mhil is included in the price, but you must book the bus in advance). Prices are €25 adults, €20 seniors and students, €13 kids. The ferries depart several times daily, year-round, unless the weather is awful. The ferries call at each of the islands, with the most popular (and busiest) port being Kilronan (Cill Rónáin), on Inishmore. Aran Island Ferries travel between Inisheer and Inishmaan; if you want to travel between other combinations of islands, you need to travel back to Ros á Mhil first. You

Inishmore, Aran Islands

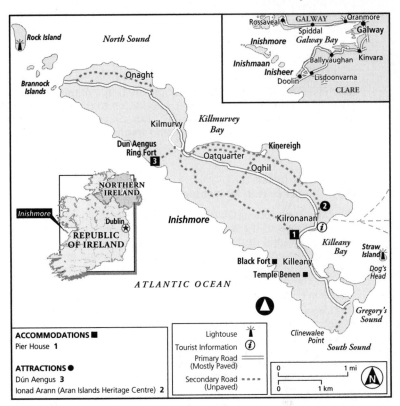

must check in for the ferry at least half an hour before your departure time; if you're driving, leave Galway City for the pier an hour before check-in time. From April through September, you also can travel to the Aran Islands by ferry from Doolin, in County Clare, on **Doolin Ferries** (☎ 065-707-4455; www.doolinferries.com), although this trip is recommended only for those who are very strong of stomach.

If you'd rather fly, **Aer Arann** (☎ 091-59-3034; www.aerarannislands. ie) takes off from Connemara airport, about 29km (18 miles) west of Galway City (a bus from the city is available to the airport; just ask when you book), and flies to all three islands; its most popular flights land in Kilronan (Cill Rónáin), on Inishmore. The ten-minute flights are the shortest scheduled flights in the world. Prices are currently €45 round-trip adults, €37 round-trip students, and €25 round-trip kids 12 and under. Check the Web site for discounts.

You can't bring your car to the Arans, and there are no car rentals, so when you reach the islands, you have a couple choices: You can rent a bike near the piers on Inisheer and Inishmore, hire a driver and minibus or a bumpy horse and cart, or walk (especially easy on little Inisheer and Inishmaan). Walking and biking maps are available at the Galway City Tourist Office, online at www.aranislands.ie, and at the **visitor center** in Kilronan, on Inishmore (☎ **099-61-263**).

Spending the night on the Aran Islands

Each island has several B&Bs; for information, contact the **Galway Tourist Office** (☎ **091-53-77-00**). In addition to the option listed in this section, other favorites are **Man of Aran**, on Inishmore (☎ **099-61-301**; www.manofarancottage.com), and **Radharc An Chlair**, on Inisheer (☎ **099-75-019**).

Kilmurvey House
$$ Kilmurvey (Cill Mhuirbhigh), Inishmore

The stunning fort of Dún Aengus is practically in your backyard at this grand 18th-century house. Treasa and Bertie Joyce are model hosts: friendly, helpful and very knowledgeable about the island. Rooms are sweetly furnished in a flowery Victorian style, and guests have access to two peaceful lounges. The breakfasts are terrific and will whet your appetite for the optional dinner, crafted with local fish, meat, and vegetables and served five nights a week.

In Kilmurvey (Cill Mhuirbhigh), on Inishmore. ☎ **099-61-397**. *Rack rates: €90–€110 double. MC, V. Closed Nov–Mar.*

Exploring the Aran Islands

The Arans are attractions in and of themselves. Rent a bike, flag a pony cart or minivan, or lace up your sneakers, and poke around these beautiful islands. If you're on Inishmore, the heritage center, **Ionad Arann**, in Kilronan (Cill Rónáin) (☎ **099-61-355**), is a good place to begin your visit to the island. The center offers exhibits investigating the culture, history, and geography of the islands. Admission is €4 adults, €2.50 students, and €2 seniors and kids. It's open April, May, September, and October daily from 11 a.m. to 5 p.m., and June through August daily 10 a.m. to 7 p.m.

Dún Aengus
Kilmurvey (Cill Mhuirbhigh), Inishmore

This well-preserved immense Bronze Age stone fort stretches over 4.4 hectares (11 acres) and is set on a sheer cliff overlooking the Atlantic Ocean. The fort is composed of three dry-stone walls, set one inside the other. The former use of the fort is still unknown, though the most popular theories are that the fort was used for defense or for druid ceremonies and rituals. Views of Connemara, Galway Bay, and the Burren are superb from the innermost wall. The visitor center provides interesting background on the fort, and guided tours are available upon request. You can

The origins of the Aran sweater

Aran sweaters may be one of Ireland's biggest exports today, but they came from humble beginnings. Originally, the almost-waterproof wool sweaters were knit by the women of the Aran Islands to ensure that the islands' fishermen stayed warm and dry (the waterproofing comes from natural oils from the sheep's skin, which remain on the wool). The various stitches on the sweater signify different ideas and objects, from a honeycomb stitch that symbolizes hard work to a diamond stitch that represents the desire for success.

get a minibus to and from the sight, though if you have time to hike the 10km (6½-mile) route (takes about two and one-half hours one-way), you'll be rewarded with gorgeous sea views and paths that skirt wildflower fields. Allow one or two hours for your visit.

In Killmurvey (Cill Mhuirbhigh), 7km (4½ miles) west of Kilronan. Admission: €3 adults, €2 seniors, €1 students and kids. Open: Mar–Oct daily 10 a.m.–6 p.m., Nov–Feb daily 10 a.m.–4 p.m.

Traditional Crafts Classes
If you're crafty, contact **Mairéad Sharry** in Lurgan Village, Inishere at ☎ **099-75101** or fromsheeptoshawl@gmail.com to set up a workshop in spinning, weaving, dyeing, knitting, or felting. Sharry is flexible and will arrange workshops from one day to several days based on your schedule. Prices vary.

Shopping
If you've held out long enough, now's your chance to buy an authentic, often-copied-but-never-reproduced, hand-knit fisherman's sweater on the Aran Islands. Numerous shops sell these sweaters.

Connemara

If I had to pick my favorite place for scenery in Ireland, I'd pick the area west of Galway City, known as Connemara (pronounced cah-nuh-*mar*-a). Though it doesn't have the sheer cliffs that many visitors seek in Ireland, Connemara offers some of the most stunning and varied scenery in the country. It's a wild and untamed place of still glacial lakes, stands of evergreens, towering mountains covered in mantles of short velvety grass in shades of green and purple, endless quiet boglands, beaches, and granite moorlands. In addition, it's home to Killary Harbor, a dazzling fjord that reflects mirror images of the surrounding mountains. A large part of Connemara is a *Gaeltacht* (pronounced *gwale*-tokt in this area) — an area where many people use Irish Gaelic as often as English, and where most road signs will be in Irish. Keep an eye out for the rugged little Connemara ponies, which are native to Ireland.

There are only a few towns of any size in this region. The roughly 1,800-person town of **Clifden** (An Clochán) is the unofficial capital of Connemara. Nestled in a valley at the foot of the Twelve Bens mountain range, the town's lively center and beautiful location make it a popular base for visitors both from Ireland and abroad. A quieter option is **Roundstone** (Cloch na Rón), a bustling and charming little fishing village.

Getting to and around Connemara

The best way to see Connemara is by driving, and then picking areas to hike and bike around. See p. 363 for information for my favorite routes in Connemara. **Bus Éireann** (☎ 01-836-6111; www.buseireann.ie) serves Clifden and other towns in the region. See p. 362 for more information on touring Connemara without a car.

Spending the night in Connemara

If you know that you want to take advantage of this region's incredible lake and river fishing, book a room at **Delphi Lodge** (see p. 366).

Alcock & Brown Hotel
$ **Clifden**

This large hotel is named after John Alcock and Arthur Brown, who, in 1919, landed in a Clifden bog after completing the first nonstop transatlantic flight. Set right in the center of Clifden, the hotel is now a great liftoff location for touring the spectacular landscape of Connemara. Rooms are of the typical large hotel variety — clean, spacious, and bright, but lacking in any real character. The bar, which often hosts traditional Irish music and dance, is a lively and cozy place to relax after a day of sightseeing, and the restaurants serves excellent seafood.

Town Square, in the center of town. ☎ *095-21-880. Fax: 095-21-883.* www.alcock andbrownhotel.com. *Parking: €8 per day on-site. Rack rates: €49–€89 double. Breakfast is not included in the rate. AE, DC, MC, V.*

Delphi Mountain Resort
$$$ **Leenane**

Take the best summer camp ever and merge it with a well-appointed, eco-friendly hotel and you've got the Delphi Mountain Resort. The setting, a 162-hectare (400-acre) forest framed by the dramatic Mweelrea and Twelve Bens mountain ranges, will knock your socks off. And though you can enjoy the views through the hotel's windows while sipping tea and munching on fresh-baked scones, one of the best things about the Delphi Mountain Resort is that the staff offers the opportunity to get out into all that beautiful wilderness with a range of activities. You can choose from about 20 activity options, including surfing lessons off a nearby beach, ocean kayaking, flying through the air on a zipline, and challenging yourself on the high ropes course. The hotel is a joy to return to after your adventures, with bedrooms that are simple oases of white walls, pine furniture, and impeccable snow-colored bed linens, and two lovely lounge areas with comfy, deep couches and mountain views. Treat yourself to a massage, body wrap, or facial in the spa — you deserve it after a day of outdoor activities! Finish your day with a meal at the restaurant, which focuses on using as many local ingredients as possible in dishes such as Connemara sea trout with ginger, spring onions, soy sauce, hoisin, and sesame oil, served on a bed of local snap peas. Bliss.

Note: Families may appreciate the two-bedroom suites, which can accommodate two adults and up to three kids.

Outside of Leenane. At Leenane, follow signs for Westport for about 3.2km (2 miles), take a left turn at the sign for Delphi, travel another 8km (5 miles), passing Aasleagh Falls on your right. Delphi Mountain Resort is on your left. ☎ **095-42-208.** *Fax: 095-42-223.* www.delphimountainresort.com. *Parking: Free on-site. Rack rates: €138–€158 double, €300 suite. AE, MC, V.*

Dolphin Beach House
$$$ Clifden

This is a top contender for my favorite place to stay in all of Ireland, and everyone I meet who has also stayed here has either extended their stay or wished they could. Though it's a quick drive from lively downtown Clifden, the house seems worlds away, with views of the ocean and a short path garden leading down to a beach covered in smooth rocks of all sizes and colors (I found a geode there!). Your hosts, Clodagh and her husband Darragh, couldn't be sweeter or more helpful. It's clear that the house is decorated by someone with a strong artistic streak; every piece of furniture and every object seems chosen for its beauty, from the dark wood sleigh bed in the stunning Bay View bedroom to the artfully arranged clamshells that we found on an outdoor table. The two lounges, one bright and airy, and the other cozy and warm, invite lingering. The artistry extends to the kitchen, where Clodagh prepares incredible breakfasts and simple, fresh dinners. Can I move in?

Lower Sky Road, about 5km (3 miles) outside the center of Clifden. ☎ **095-21-204.** *Fax: 095-22-935.* www.dolphinbeachhouse.com. *Parking: Free on-site. Rack rates: €130–€180 double. Dinner €40 (book in advance). MC, V. Children 12 and over are welcome.*

Errisbeg Lodge
$$ Roundstone

This peaceful B&B has views of the Errisbeg Mountains and the Atlantic Ocean, both of which are close at hand. Nature-lovers take note: The B&B has a vast amount of land (as proprietors Jackie and Shirley King like to say, "We have a national park in our backyard"). You can wander through the gardens, say hello to the Kings' sweet Connemara ponies and donkey; stroll and shell-hunt on the nearby smooth, sandy beaches (Dogs Bay is especially beautiful); and climb Errisbeg Mountain for panoramic views of the area. Rooms are simple and airy, with pine furnishings, king-size beds in many rooms, and pretty comforters. The Kings are incredibly friendly and enthusiastic about sharing this beautiful location with their guests. Kids will love running around the grounds and playing with the ponies.

Ballyconneely-Roundstone Road (R341), 1.5km (1 mile) west of Roundstone, opposite Gurteen Beach. ☎ **095-35-807.** www.errisbeglodge.com. *Parking: Free on-site. Rack rates: €85–€100 double. No credit cards. Closed Nov to mid-Mar.*

Faul House
$ Ballyconneely

About half of the Faul House's guests are return visitors, which makes complete sense given the warmth and friendliness of owners Kathleen and Michael Conneely. Kathleen and Michael are a compendium of Connemara knowledge (Michael grew up on this land) and are genuinely happy to help visitors develop an itinerary that suits their individual needs and interests. The house is located on a peaceful country lane and has miles of land, where you'll find the Conneelys' donkeys and sweet Connemara ponies. You'll definitely want to make time to explore the property, visit the animals, and walk down to the sea. The house has a gentle, welcoming feel about it, with a turf fire burning in the living room and bedrooms that are simple and airy, decorated with hand-painted watercolors and sporting king-size beds. Breakfast is fantastic, particularly the scrambled eggs blanketed with fresh smoked salmon.

Ballyconneelly Road, 2km (1¼ miles) southwest of Clifden. ☎ **095-21-239.** *Fax: 095-21-998.* www.faulhouse.com. *Parking: Free on-site. Rack rates: €70–€80 double. No credit cards. Closed Nov–Mar 15.*

Sea Mist House
$$ Clifden

This place has a serene and homey feel that you may not expect in the middle of the bustling town of Clifden. The bedrooms are furnished in a modern country style, with a chic combination of burgundies, creams, and golds, and you'll find original art and interesting furnishings throughout the house. Plan extra time in the morning to linger over the excellent breakfasts (including such treats as pancakes and scrambled eggs with feta cheese) in the glass-walled conservatory.

Parking is limited, so if you're staying in Clifden during the day, it may be wise to leave your car at its space and explore the town on foot.

Seaview Street. ☎ **095-21441.** www.seamisthouse.com. *Parking: Free on-site (but only three spaces) or paid on the street. Rack rates: €80–€120 double. MC, V. Closed midweek Nov–Feb.*

The Quay House
$$$ Clifden

The décor here is certainly not your run-of-the-mill prints of Ireland and Victorian-reproduction tables. Owners Paddy and Julia Foyle have furnished this grand restored harbor master's house with bold, artistic choices, including zebra, tiger, and other animal skins; dramatic paintings in gilded frames; and glass chandeliers. One wall of the airy conservatory breakfast room is decorated with the lids of silver serving platters. Bedrooms are spacious and individually furnished, running from ornate Victorian-style quarters to rooms that look like they belong in a chic hunting lodge in Africa. Birders many want to ask for the Bird Room, featuring several stuffed parrots. Six suites have balconies and four have fireplaces. Paddy and Julia have a deep knowledge of the area and are always happy to advise visitors on outdoor activities, dining, drives, and so on. The house is located a ten-minute walk from the town of Clifden. Check the Web site for special offers.

Parking is limited, so you may have to park on the street.

Beach Road. ☎ *095-21-369.* www.thequayhouse.com. *Parking: Free on-site (limited) or free on the street. Rack rates: €150–€180 double. MC, V. Closed mid-Nov to mid-Mar.*

Dining locally in Connemara
Browns, located in the Alcock & Brown Hotel (reviewed earlier in this chapter), has a good Irish menu that features seafood.

Derryclare Restaurant
$$–$$$ Clifden SEAFOOD/IRISH

Warm and cozy is the name of the game here. Candles in cast-iron holders cast a golden glow on the dark, shiny wood tables and benches, and weathered signs decorate the walls. The restaurant buzzes with conversation and laughter from a convivial crowd that runs from couples to large families. Dishes are made with the freshest ingredients, simply prepared and boasting some inspired sauces and spices. My tagliatelle with olive oil, cherry tomatoes, and herbs was delicious, and the couple next to me was enjoying braised Connemara lamb shank *au jus.* Enjoy vegetables, such as buttery creamed carrots and perfectly steamed broccoli, with your meal.

Market Street. ☎ *095-21-440. Main courses: €14–€24. MC, V. Open: Daily noon to 10 p.m.*

Guy's Bar & Snug
$$ Clifden PUB FOOD/NEW IRISH

My favorite place for dinner in Clifden, Guy's is the place to go for top-notch pub food, such as golden fish and chips and burgers, plus more upscale dishes like duck-leg confit served with *colcannon* (mashed potatoes with spring onions) and a port wine *jus*. The kicker? Everything, including the excellent specials, is served at pub-food prices. The pub is composed of several rooms, with various nooks and crannies, including several snugs with doors. The setting is a combination of old and new, with well-loved country-style tables graced with white pillar candles, old wainscoting painted in stylish sage and cinnamon colors, and funky lamps hanging over the bar. The staff is down-to-earth and friendly, and rooms buzz with the chatter and laughter of couples, families, and small groups of friends.

Main Street. ☎ **095-21-130**. *Main courses: €13–€16. MC, V. Open: Food served daily 10 a.m.–9 p.m.*

Mitchell's Restaurant
$$$ Clifden   SEAFOOD/IRISH

Seafood is the staple of this stylish restaurant. Expect dishes such as baked filet of salmon with parsley mashed potatoes and creamed leeks, and pan-fried brill with sun-dried tomato mashed potatoes and chive sauce. Steaks and stews (including a luscious Connemara lamb stew) are also on offer, and noteworthy lighter meals, including pastas, quiche, and salads, are served during the day. The interior juxtaposes contemporary sleekness with ornate and rustic touches — contemporary paintings hang right next to an elaborately carved altar.

Market Street, in the center of town. ☎ **095-21-867**. *Reservations recommended on weekends and during the summer. Main courses: €17–€27. AE, MC, V. Open: Daily noon to 10 p.m. (last orders at 9:30 p.m.).*

Walsh's Bakery and Coffee Shop
$ Clifden   BAKERY/CAFE

Yes, you can have a nice light lunch here, including salads and terrific toasted sandwiches (the chicken, stuffing, and cranberry sauce is a favorite), but what you're really here for is the heavenly baked goods. I had an near-existential crisis trying to decide between the melt-in-your-mouth Napoleon and the tangy rhubarb square. Luckily, I averted the angst of deciding by getting both. Problem solved!

Market Street. ☎ **095-21-283**. *Sandwiches and baked goods: €3–€7. Open: Daily 8:30 a.m.–6 p.m. or later.*

Exploring Connemara

If you're car-less, you can choose among several guided day-tours of Connemara that begin and end in Galway City. You can hit Galway City's tourist office on Forster Street, off Eyre Square, to figure out which one suits you. Some choices include **Galway Tour Company** (☎ 091-566-566; www.galwaytourcompany.com), which offers day tours of Connemara that start and end in Galway City and **Bus Éireann's** (☎ 01-836-6111; www.buseireann.ie) Connemara Bus Tour.

Hiking in Connemara is a treat. If you're up for something difficult, the loop hike up and down **Mweelrea,** the highest mountain in this area of Ireland, rewards you with unbelievable sea, beach, cliff, and mountain views. The route starts at the northwestern end of Doo Lough, along R335 15km (9⅓ miles) northwest of Leenane and 13km (8 miles) south of Louisburgh. Get your hands on OSI map no. 37 (☎ **01-860-6778;** www. osi.ie) for this 12km (7½-mile) hike, which takes most people about seven hours. For an easier option (minus a short steep scramble) with mountain and fjord views, hike the 10km (6¼-mile) route along **Killary Harbour,** also marked on the OSI map no. 37. A good place to start the hike is at the pier at Rosroe. The hike takes roughly four hours. You can order maps of the walks online or buy them *before you leave Galway City* from the **Map Store** in the Galway County Council Buildings on Prospect Hill (☎ **091-509-152**). For something shorter, there are two beautiful and gentle loop walks at Kylemore Abbey (see listing later in this chapter), and Connemara National Park (also see listing later in this chapter) has several excellent hiking options. **Inishbofin Island** (see listing later in this chapter) is a walker and hiker's paradise. **Michael Gibbons Walking,** Market Street, Clifden (☎ **095-21-379**), offers a number of well-done guided hikes in Connemara; call for a schedule and prices (closed in winter).

The following are two gorgeous **Connemara driving and biking routes.** You can rent bikes from **John Mannion,** Bridge Street, Clifden (☎ **095-211-60**). You're more likely to enjoy these routes if you're an experienced cyclist, because they have inclines and are shared with cars.

✔ **Tour 1:** My favorite driving route through Connemara takes you past shimmering lakes, along the wild and proud Twelve Bens mountains, and through purple-hued bogs. You'll also travel through the moody boglands around Connemara National Park, follows the N59 from Galway City through Moycullen and Oughterard to Maam Cross, where you pick up the R336 toward Leenaun (also known as Leenane). Turn onto narrow R334 (off the N59 to the west of Leenuan/Leenane) toward Recess for jaw-dropping mountain scenery. When you join up again with the N59 near Recess, take the N59 west to the junction with the R341, and follow the R341 along the coast to Roundstone, a cute fishing village that makes a good stop for a snack or for lunch. Continue on the R341 toward Ballyconnelly, stopping to take in Dogs Bay (see listing later in this chapter) and Gorteen Bay, two pristine beaches. Both are signposted off the R341, at the most southerly point. Then take the R341 back up to Clifden. Definitely dedicate a whole day for the drive, especially if you'll be stopping.

Though the entire route is not recommended for bicyclists, a full-day loop covers most of the westerly section of the route, starting in Clifden, taking the N59 to the R341 and then hooking back up with the N54 to get back to Clifden.

Another beautiful biking route, taking about three hours on average and covering 40km (25 miles), uses the R341 to loop from Clifden through Ballyconneely and Roundstone, and back to Clifden.

✔ **Tour 2:** The Sky Road, signposted out of Clifden, is aptly named. You feel like you're flying as the road climbs higher and higher over farmland and sea cliffs. This is a great though tough looping bike route, covering 16km (10 miles) and taking a little less than two hours on average.

There are several **pony-trekking** outfitters in Connemara, and **Errislannan Manor** (☎ 095-21-133; www.errislannanmanor.com) is one of the finest, offering guided rides across Connemara's moors and coastland Monday through Friday mornings. To get there, take the Ballyconneely Road south out of Clifden. The Errislannan Manor is signposted on the road about 6.5km (4 miles) outside of Clifden. Rates are €35 per hour; call to arrange the time for your trek.

The top attractions

The biggest attraction of Connemara is the landscape itself, so dedicate time to explore it. There are several suggestions for enjoying the countryside earlier in the chapter, as well as in the "More cool things to see and do" section.

Connemara National Park and Visitor Centre
Letterfrack

Some of most beautiful scenery in Connemara is contained in this 2,000-hectare (5,000-acre) park. Vast bogland cloaks this area, and four of the mountains in the impressive Twelve Bens range are within its boundaries, including Benbaun, the highest of the 12, which reaches 720m (2,400 ft.). There are 4,000-year-old prehistoric structures, rare flowers, and a herd of Connemara ponies. The clearly marked trails take you up through the boglands, revealing beautiful panoramas of the sea and the undulating hills. This is the kind of beauty that many find to be subtle rather than striking — the bogland reveals its splendor to those who walk slowly and look carefully. There are three loop walks within the park. Those who take the challenging Diamond loop will be rewarded with splendid views of the land and sea. The Visitor Centre (on the N59) has fascinating exhibits on the history of the area and on all things bog-related, and an audiovisual show on the park. The center also organizes nature trail walks (call in advance to see when they're being offered). Wear sturdy shoes and socks that you don't mind getting dirty (bogland is quite soggy). Allow several hours for your visit.

Off the Clifden-Westport Road (N59). ☎ *095-41-323. Admission: Free. Open: Park year-round, Visitor Centre Mar–Oct daily 9 a.m.–5:30 p.m.*

A little bogged down

Just south of Clifden, you'll find the Derrygimlagh Bog, where British pilots John Alcock and Arthur Brown "landed" after completing the first successful nonstop transatlantic flight. The pilots thought the soft green field looked like a perfect place to land, until they touched down and found that the grass covered a soggy, spongy bog. Not the most graceful landing, but both aviators emerged unscathed. A monument commemorating the arrival marks the bog, and you can walk a short path to the original landing spot.

Inishbofin Island

Sort of a mini-Ireland unto itself, Inishbofin is an outdoors person's paradise, with paths rambling through green farm fields peppered with wildflowers and ruins from the Neolithic times through the 20th century. The island is hugged by lovely sandy beaches with safe swimming and a rainbow array of shells, and the clear waters attract snorkelers and divers. The island is home to several species of seabirds as well as the elusive and endangered corncrake. Several small towns offer dining and accommodations choices, and it's well worth staying the night for rollicking Irish music and fresh, simple dinners. Allow five hours for a trip to the island.

Off the coast of Ireland from Cleggan. There are multiple daily ferry crossings to the island year-round. To plan your visit, call ☎ 095-45-895 or visit www.inishbofin.com. To contact the ferry company call ☎ 095-45-819. Currently, a ferry departs Cleggan daily at 11:30 a.m. in addition to several other departure times on various days. Similarly, there is a daily departure from Inishbofin at 5 p.m., in additional to other departure times on various days. Round-trip fares are €20 adults, €10 kids 5–12, €5 kids 3–5.

Kylemore Abbey & Walled Gardens
Kylemore

Sitting in a stunning setting at the base of the mountains and on the shores of a lake, this abbey looks like a storybook castle — and it is, in a way. An English tycoon had the gorgeous neo-Gothic building constructed for his adored wife and sold it to the duke and duchess of Manchester upon her death. Several owners later, a group of nuns escaping the horrors of World War I in Belgium took up residence and converted it into an abbey. The nuns used to run a girls' boarding school here; the last class graduated in 2010. You can visit the striking main hall and reception rooms, and walk along the lake to the gorgeous restored neo-Gothic church (wave hello to the small colony of bats that calls the chapel home). The star of the abbey is the magnificent walled Victorian garden, which slopes up on either side like an open book and contains an astounding assortment of vegetables, fruits, and flowers. Have a look inside the greenhouse, a restored version of one in a series of connecting greenhouses that originally stood in the garden (in Victorian times, the lady of the house and her friends were treated to the unique pleasure of eating a fresh banana in the dead of winter — quite an unusual delicacy at that time). There are two delightful walks, one through woodlands and one along the lake; and you can reward yourself for your efforts at the pretty restaurant, which makes use of the produce grown in the garden. The abbey is also known for its pottery; you can watch it being created and purchase some in the craft shop. Allow about two hours for your visit.

On the Clifden-Westport Road (N59), east of Letterfrack. ☎ **095-41-146.** *www.kylemoreabbey.com. Admission: Summer €12 adults, €9 seniors, €8 students, free for kids 11 and under; winter €8 adults, €7 seniors, €6.50 students, free for kids 11 and under. Open: Mar–June daily 9 a.m.–6 p.m., July–Aug daily 9 a.m.–7 p.m., Sept–Oct daily 9:30 a.m.–6 p.m., Nov–Feb daily 10 a.m.–4:30 p.m.*

More cool things to see and do

✔ **Cruising Lough Corrib** (☎ **092-46-029;** www.corribcruises.com): Take a round-trip cruise on lovely Lough Corrib, Ireland's largest lake. You cruise from Oughterard (*uk*-tuh-rard), in County Galway, to Cong Village, in County Mayo, where you can gaze upon the exterior of the beautiful 13th-century Ashford Castle and explore the village, featured in *The Quiet Man.* Along the way, you stop on Inchagoill Island for a guided tour of the fifth-century ruins there.

Cruises leave from the pier in Oughterard June through August Wednesday through Monday at 10:45 a.m. (but the owners can arrange cruises for larger groups outside of these months); they take about 5 hours and 45 minutes. They cost €28 adults, €14 kids 5 to 15, free for kids 4 and under. Book in advance — cruises fill up quickly.

✔ **Dogs Bay,** off the R341, west of Roundstone Village: You'll certainly see dogs taking their owners for walks on this perfect crescent of a beach. You'll also find lovely shells and some of the finest and softest white sand in Ireland here. Allow 45 minutes for your visit.

✔ **Fishing:** The area around Leenane in Connemara is probably the best place in Ireland for river and lake fishing. The Erriff River system is world-famous for salmon, brown trout, and sea-trout fly-fishing; Glencullin Lough is a favorite for salmon and sea trout; and Derrintin Lough holds the promise of brown trout. Pike, eel and mackerel also are found throughout the region. The fishing season runs from early February through late September. Permits and information on equipment rental, guides, and permit acquisition is available from the **Western Regional Fisheries Board** (☎ **091-563-110;** www.wrfb.ie). If you're an experienced angler and you want to fish in Connemara, book a room at **Delphi Lodge,** outside of Leenane (☎ **095-42-222;** www.delphilodge.ie), a grand 1830s country-house hotel that offers fly-fishing equipment, excellent guides, occasional beginner courses, and access to many top-notch fishing areas. The house offers a lovely dinner where conversations run to the watery variety. If it's good enough for Prince Charles, it's probably good enough for the rest of us.

✔ **Killary Fjord Cruise** (☎ **091-566-736;** www.killarycruises. com): This 90-minute cruise is a nice option for exploring the narrow, glassy body of water, which mirrors surrounding mountains. There are many ways to explore the fjord and surrounding mountains by foot, by bicycle, and by car, but this is the best option if you want to sit and relax as the scenery glides by.

Cruises leave from Nancy's Point, 2km (1¼ miles) west of Leenane off the N59. They cost €21 adults, €17 seniors and students, €10 kids, free for kids 3 and under. Kids of any age cruise free on Friday, Saturday, and Sunday, and there are always discounts if you book online. Cruises leave June through August daily at 10:30 a.m. and 12:30, 2:30, and 4:30 p.m.; May and September daily at 10:30 a.m and 12:30 and 2:30 p.m.; and April and October daily at 12:30 p.m. and 2:30 p.m. Barbecue cruises are offered at 7 p.m. on Fridays and Saturdays in July and August.

✔ **Outdoor activities at Delphi Mountain Resort,** outside of Leenane (☎ **095-42-208;** www.delphimountainresort.com): This hotel (see p. 358) is also home to an adventure center that offers over 20 guided activities, from surfing and kayaking to rock climbing, hiking, and ziplining.

At Leenane, follow the signs for Westport for about 3.2km (2 miles), and then take a left turn at the sign for Delphi. Travel another 8km (5 miles), passing Aasleagh Falls on your right. Delphi Mountain Resort is on your left.

You can choose one water activity or two land activities per session. The per-session rates are €45 adults, €25 kids. There are discounts if you book more than one session. The morning session runs from 9:30 a.m. to 12:30 p.m.; the afternoon session, from 2 to 5 p.m.

✔ **Walking or biking to Omey Island:** Yes, you read that right. When the tide is out, you can take a beautiful walk on the seafloor from the mainland to the island, with the sea views on both sides of the marked walk and little gem-like shells strewn along the way. Once on the island, there are pretty walks and several ruins to explore. Park the car at Claddaghduff on the mainland, and then roughly follow the marker poles across the seafloor. Give yourself about 20 minutes to walk from the mainland to island.

Important: You *must* check the tide charts to plan your visit. Cross around the peak of low tide so that you don't get stranded on the island or on the seafloor walk.

½ dog + ½ otter = 1 Dobhar-Chú

On Omey Island, keep your eyes out for the Dobhar-Chú, also known as the "Master Otter," a mythical water-dwelling creature (or creatures?) that is said to resemble both an otter and a dog. The Kinlough Stone, in County Leitrim, is a 1722 gravestone depicting the Dobhar-Chú, which is said to have killed the grave's occupant, Grace Connolly. Legend has it that her husband killed the Dobhar-Chú, but the giant otter's mate then rose out of the water and chased the man down. Irish artist Sean Corcoran and his wife say that they sighted the Dobhar-Chú on Omey Island in 2003.

Shopping in Connemara

The Spiddal Craft and Design Studios, in Spiddal, west of Galway City on the R336, houses craftspeople who make and sell a variety of crafts, from pottery to candles. One of the stars of the studio complex is **Máire Ní Thaidhg** (☎ 086-814-2530), who hand-weaves scarves, shawls, and wall hangings in vibrant colors. Owner Malachy Kearns and his staff at **Roundstone Music and Crafts,** in Roundstone (☎ 095-35-808; www.bodhran.com), make and sell a large and high-quality selection of *bodhráns* (Irish drums). Malachy is something of a celebrity: He made the drums for the *Riverdance* ensemble and is featured on an Irish postage stamp. **Millar's,** Main Street, Clifden (☎ 095-21-038), sells beautiful trendy handmade clothing, tweeds, and interesting jewelry and knick-knacks. **Avoca,** in Letterfrack (☎ 095-41-058), sells all sorts of beautiful Irish crafts, furnishings, and clothing.

Hitting the pubs

Guy's Bar and Snug (see p. 361) is another terrific pub with traditional Irish music sessions on some nights. There are frequent traditional Irish music concerts throughout Connemara, so keep your eyes open for posters, and ask around town and at local tourist offices for information.

E. J. Kings
Clifden

Almost anyone who's been to Clifden is familiar with E. J. Kings, because when you go, you can't forget it. Always packed and humming, Kings has many floors, and in the high season, music fills the air. Seafood is the feature of the fantastic pub-food menu, but there's also good traditional fare. When it's cold, a welcoming fire warms the pub, and in nice weather, the outdoor patio is the hottest spot. The atmosphere in Kings is relaxed, and you're sure to get a warm welcome from the chatty staff.

The Square. ☎ 095-21-330.

J. Conneely's Bar
Clifden

J. Conneely's has great seafood, amazing views of the Atlantic from the balcony, a well-pulled pint of Guinness, and nightly Irish traditional music sessions. I'll let that sentence speak for itself.

Market Street. ☎ **095-22-733.**

Fast Facts: County Galway

Area Codes

County Galway's area codes (or city codes) are **091, 095,** and **099.**

Emergencies/Police

Dial ☎ **999** for all emergencies.

Genealogy Resources

Contact the Galway Family History Society West, on Ashe Road in Galway City (☎ 091-860-464).

Hospital

University College Hospital is on Newcastle Road, Galway City (☎ 091-52-42-22).

Information

For visitor information and reservation services for Galway City and the whole of County Galway, go to the Galway Tourist Office (also known as Ireland West Tourism or Aras Fáilte), Forster Street (on Eyre Square), Galway City www.ireland west.ie). It's open year-round.

Internet

NetAccess, Olde Malte Arcade, off High Street, Galway (☎ 091-395-725), has high-speed Internet access.

Post Office

Galway City's main post office is at 3 Eglinton St., Galway City (☎ 091-53-4727).

Chapter 19

Counties Mayo and Sligo

. . . .

In This Chapter

▶ Imagining the past at the ancient ruins at Carrowmore and Carrowkeel
▶ Watching falcons fly (and petting an owl)
▶ Driving and hiking through stunning mountain, coastal, and bogland scenery

. . . .

*A*long with Connemara, counties **Mayo** and **Sligo** are my favorite places in the Republic of Ireland to enjoy gorgeous landscapes, outdoor activities, and ancient sights — all without the crowds that you find in other parts of the country. County Donegal is similar in these respects, but Mayo and Sligo throw in the bonus of a fairly wide selection of good restaurants, accommodations, and shopping.

Sparsely populated **Mayo** (rhymes with *hay*-o) is one of the unsung beauties of Ireland, boasting stunning mountains and coastlines; a glassy fjord; beautiful islands; many remarkable Neolithic, Bronze Age, and Iron Age sights; and miles of moody bogland. Charming **Westport** is a great place to base yourself, and a night on **Achill Island** is sure to please outdoorsy travelers, from hikers to surfers to beach-walkers.

Like Mayo, **Sligo** (pronounced *sly*-go) has quite a varied landscape, with flat-topped mountains, rolling farmland, long sandy beaches, and sea cliffs. This is the county that William Butler Yeats loved so, and you'll find no shortage of Yeats-related sights here. Sligo is also jam-packed with impressive Neolithic sights, from tombs to ancient stone walls. If you want to base yourself in a town, little **Sligo Town** is a good choice, with a nice selection of restaurants, shops, and attractions, including a medieval abbey and a modern art museum.

County Mayo

Getting to and around County Mayo

If you're driving from Dublin, take the N5 to Castlebar and Westport in County Mayo. From Galway, take the N17 to meet the N5 in County Mayo. **Irish Rail** (☎ 1-850-366-222; www.irishrail.ie) serves Westport, Foxford, Claremorris, Ballina, and Castlebar. **Bus Éireann** (☎ 01-836-6111; www.buseireann.ie) travels to Westport, Cong, Ballina, and several other towns in County Mayo.

Counties Mayo and Sligo

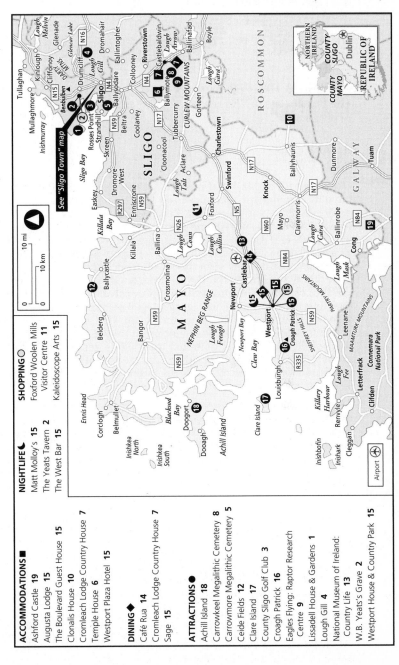

ACCOMMODATIONS ■
Ashford Castle **19**
Augusta Lodge **15**
The Boulevard Guest House **15**
Clonalis House **10**
Cromleach Lodge Country House **7**
Temple House **6**
Westport Plaza Hotel **15**

DINING ◆
Café Rua **14**
Cromleach Lodge Country House **7**
Sage **15**

ATTRACTIONS ●
Achill Island **18**
Carrowkeel Megalithic Cemetery **8**
Carrowmore Megalithic Cemetery **5**
Ceide Fields **12**
Clare Island **17**
County Sligo Golf Club **3**
Croagh Patrick **16**
Eagles Flying: Raptor Research
   Centre **9**
Lissadell House & Gardens **1**
Lough Gill **4**
National Museum of Ireland:
   Country Life **13**
W.B. Yeats's Grave **2**
Westport House & Country Park **15**

NIGHTLIFE ◖
Matt Molloy's **15**
The Yeats Tavern **2**
The West Bar **15**

SHOPPING ○
Foxford Woolen Mills
   Visitor Centre **11**
Kaleidoscope Arts **15**

Aer Arann (☎ **0818-210-210**; www.aerarann.com) has daily flights from Dublin into **Knock Airport,** in Charlestown, County Mayo (☎ **094-936-8100**; www.knockairport.com).

Mickey's Cabs (☎ **087-222-6227**) provides taxi service in the Westport area.

Spending the night in County Mayo

The Bervie (see p. 375) is a perfect choice for travelers visiting gorgeous Achill Island.

Ashford Castle
$$$$ **Cong**

Okay, time for a quiz: What do Fred Astaire, Joan Baez, and Jerry Springer have in common? If you answered that they've all stayed at luxurious Ashford Castle, you're correct. Perched on the banks of sapphire Lough (pronounced lock) Corrib and surrounded by 140 hectares (350 acres) of woodlands and gardens, this is a great place to indulge dreams of living in a castle. The castle itself incorporates a mix of architectural time periods and styles: The original structure dates from 1228, with a French-chateau-style addition added in the 18th century and two Victorian wings added in the 19th century. The interior is sumptuously decked out with carved oak paneling, crystal chandeliers, gorgeous oil paintings, and lush fabrics. The standard doubles have the nice fabrics and solid, dark wood furniture that you might expect at an upscale hotel, but they don't have the grandeur of the public rooms. This complex feels like a resort, with golf, fishing, archery, tennis, horseback riding, spa treatments, two gourmet restaurants, and many other offerings (including an on-site school of falconry). The staff goes above and beyond for guests.

Take the R346 to Cross, and turn left at the church, going toward Cong. Ashford Castle is on the left side of the road before you reach the village of Cong. ☎ *094-954-6003, or* ☎ *800-346-7007 within the U.S. Fax: 094-954-6260.* www.ashford.ie. *Parking: Free on-site. Rack rates: €350–€430 double. AE, DC, MC, V.*

Augusta Lodge
$ **Westport**

A nice choice if you want to stay a bit outside of town (a 15-minute walk), Augusta Lodge offers spotless, contemporary bedrooms with sunny yellow walls and country-style pine furnishings. Dave O'Regan is a hands-on proprietor with many helpful hints for seeing the area. Dave is also a golf devotee, so he's an especially great resource for those who want to know more about the various courses in Ireland. There's even a little mini-golf course out front for you to practice your swing.

Golf Links Road. Take the N59 north of Westport's town center; the guesthouse is one of the first houses after you turn left onto Golf Links Road. ☎ *098-28-900. Fax: 098-28-995.* www.augustalodge.ie. *Parking: Free on the street. Rack rates: €70–€80 double. AE, MC, V.*

The Boulevard Guest House
$ Westport

Could this place be more pleasant? My favorite B&B in Westport, the Boulevard is located right near the center of town. Each of the homey, bright, uncluttered rooms is artistically decorated in different shades of one color (I really like the green room) and graced with a framed picture that complements the hues. White and pine country-style furniture rounds out the look. You're invited to spend time in the simple and pretty common areas, including a delightful little courtyard where you may have a chance to chat with Sadie and Noreen, your kind and friendly hosts.

South Mall. ☎ *098-25-138.* www.boulevard-guesthouse.com. *Rack rates: €80–€90 double. Parking: Free on the street. No credit cards.*

Clonalis House
$$$$ Castlrea, County Roscommon

Just over the County Mayo border is the Victorian Italianate mansion and ancestral home of the O'Conors of Connacht, descendants of Ireland's high kings. Everything is old-world elegance here, from the leather-bound books lining the walls of the library to the four-poster beds. Don't miss famous Irish bard Turlough O'Carolan's harp. Your hosts, Pyers and Marguerite O'Conor-Nash, will gladly chat about the family history or the area attractions over whiskey by the fireplace. The beautiful, expansive grounds are heaven for visitors who like to walk and explore, and the house dinner is excellent. If you're an O'Conor (or O'Connor) yourself, you'll find the library and historical heirlooms of particular interest.

Take the N60 west from Castlerea or east from Ballyhaunis. ☎ *094-962-0014.* www.clonalis.com. *Parking: Free on-site. Rack rates: €190–€220 double. MC, V. Closed Oct–Mar.*

Westport Plaza Hotel
$$$ Westport

There are so many terrific things about this hotel. Rooms are spacious and plush, with incredibly comfortable beds, and every bathroom features a Jacuzzi tub. Then there's the restaurant, which does a beautiful job with fresh ingredients, offering creative dishes such as pan-fried halibut filet with a fennel-and-Pernod coulis. Add the spa, with soothing treatments at reasonable rates, and the welcoming and helpful staff, and you've got a true top-notch hotel.

Castlebar Street. ☎ *098-51-166. Fax: 098-51-133.* www.westportplazahotel. ie. *Parking: Free on-site. Rack rates: €140–€210. AE, MC, V.*

Dining locally in County Mayo
Restaurant Merlot, at the Westport Plaza Hotel (see p. 373) is another terrific choice for a night out.

Café Rua
$ Castlebar CAFE

If you want to taste some of County Mayo's finest local produce, it's worth the short drive from Westport for lunch or a snack at this adorable cafe in bustling, workaday Castlebar. The space is outfitted with mismatched tables and chairs and red-and-white polka-dot tablecloths, and it's always buzzing. Aran and Colleen McMahon source everything possible from the area. The seasonal Best of the West Plate features Connemara smoked salmon, lovely brown bread, locally produced cheeses and butter, a fresh-picked salad, and glasses of sparkling elderflower cordial. There is a selection of lovely home-baked desserts, and a kids' menu is available on request.

New Antrim Street, Castlebar. ☎ *094-928-6072. Main courses: €7–€12. MC, V. Open: Mon–Sat 9 a.m.–6 p.m.*

Sage
$$$ Westport ITALIAN

Handmade pastas in the middle of a small town in the West of Ireland? You've got it, courtesy of local Sarah Hudson and her Sardinian husband Davide Donnalia. The challenge is deciding which dish to order at this stylish, casual place: Do you go for the linguine de mare with calamari, tiger prawns, and mussels, or the melt-in-your-mouth slow-roasted pork belly served on Italian beans, or the ravioli in creamy sage sauce. . . .

10 High St. ☎ *098-56-700. Main courses: €17–€23. MC, V. Open: Tues–Sun 5:30–10 p.m.*

Exploring County Mayo

Also see p. 363 for information about **Killary Harbour,** a fjord that divides County Galway from County Mayo.

The top attractions

Achill Island
County Mayo

Shhh. . . . Many Irish people would like to keep this place a secret, because it's one of their favorite destinations for gorgeous cliffs and coastal scenery, golden beaches, great hiking, and all sorts of water sports, from surfing to kayaking. At 22km (13 miles) long and 19km (12 miles) wide, Achill (pronounced *ah*-kul) is Ireland's largest offshore island and offers one of the country's most diverse and most beautiful landscapes — a paradise for hikers and walkers. Swimming, fishing, kayaking, windsurfing, scuba diving, and surfing are other popular activities.

The island's stunning coastal and cliff scenery is best seen by taking the twisty **Atlantic Drive** (signposted off the bridge that connects the mainland to the island). For a moodier sort of beauty, take the route down the middle of the island through vast fields of bog. Turn off this route to see the **deserted village**, in **Slievemore**, a haunting area of nearly 100 ruined cottages that used to be used by farmers but are believed to have been abandoned due to the Great Famine. Look up at **Slievemore Mountain,** which often has strange cloud formations hovering over it.

At the far end of the island, don't miss **Keem Bay,** a crescent of fine sand surrounded by piles of rocks (fun for scrambling) and green hills that end abruptly in sea cliffs. Swimming is safe and peaceful here. A hike from Keem Bay along the ridgeline of the cliffs will reward you with panoramas of the rocky outcroppings at **Achill Head** and the jaw-dropping cliffs at **Croaghaun** (*Cruachán* in Irish). The whole hike takes about five hours. Wear good shoes and take rain gear since the weather changes quickly here. Finally, on a clear day, the lookout from the TV towers on top of **Minaun Mountain** (*Barr an Mhionnán* in Irish) offers stunning views of Achill Island itself, the ocean, and several other islands. The steep drive up the mountain is not for the faint-hearted.

There are no real towns to speak of on the island, though B&Bs, restaurants, and shops are sprinkled here and there. Because most of Achill's draw is its terrific scenery and outdoor activities, it may not be worth the trip if it's raining hard. For more information about Achill Island, contact **Achill Tourism** (☎ 098-47-353; www.achilltourism.com). If you'd like to spend the night on the island, the **Bervie** (☎ 098-43-114; www.bervie-guesthouse-achill.com), a guesthouse on the sea, is a great spot.

Céide Fields
Ballycastle, County Mayo

This is one of the world's most extensive Stone Age ruins, with a dwelling area, grazing grounds, stone walls, planting fields, and megalithic tombs from nearly 6,000 years ago. However, you'll have to do a lot of imagining here. A bog (which is quite a sight, in and of itself, with beautiful plants and flowers) now covers most of the ruins. Just a few areas have been uncovered to show where the fields were partitioned by stone walls for growing food and grazing animals. Tools and pottery also have been unearthed and are on display in the interpretive center, where films and exhibits do a nice job of explaining the history of the area. The well-done tour is the best way to get a real sense of the site, so wear shoes that you don't mind getting dirty. The fields back up to some of the most captivating cliffs and rock formations in the country. Allow an hour for your visit.

Take the R314 coastal road north from Ballina, 8.1km (5 miles) west of Ballycastle. ☎ *096-43-325. Admission: €4 adults, €3 seniors, €2 students and kids. Open: Apr–May and Oct daily 10 a.m.–5 p.m., June–Sept daily 10 a.m.–6 p.m.*

Clare Island
Clew Bay, County Mayo

The 20- to 30-minute trip over to Clare Island on the little ferry is a bit like taking a time machine to the rural Ireland of the past. The island offers miles of walking and biking trails through patchwork fields divided by old stone walls, velvety green hills, a sandy beach with excellent swimming, and some terrific historical sights. History buffs will be delighted to find the ruins of a castle that belonged to 1600s pirate queen Grace (Granuaile) O'Malley's family, a 12th-century Cistercian abbey with beautiful medieval wall paintings (Granuaile is thought to be buried in the O'Malley crypt here), and a 19th-century Napoleonic signal tower. The castle is right near the ferry dock, and the abbey is about a 45-minute walk (one-way). Get the key to the abbey from Bernie Winters, who lives in the cottage across the street. You can rent bicycles near the ferry dock. Save this one for a dry day, as it's just not worth it in the rain. Allow two to four hours for your visit, depending on what you want to see.

O'Malley Ferries (☎ 098-25-045; www.omalleyferries.com*) runs ferries several times daily (weather permitting) from Roonagh Pier. Follow signs from Louisburgh, off the R335. Tickets: Round-trip €15 adults, €12 students, €8 kids 10–16, €5 kids 5–10, free for seniors with travel passes and kids 4 and under. Call or check online for sailing times.*

Croagh Patrick
Murrisk, County Mayo

According to legend, St. Patrick achieved divine inspiration on this pyramid-shaped mountain after praying and fasting for 40 days. On the last Sunday of July, more than 25,000 devout Catholics climb the 762m (2,500-ft.) mountain (some barefoot) in honor of their patron saint. There are stunning views of Mayo and Clew Bay from the mountaintop. The climb takes most people about three and a half hours round-trip and is tough work (wear shoes with soles that grip) but not impossible. If you can make it to the saddle, a flat stretch about 610m (2,000 ft.) up, you'll be rewarded with spectacular panoramic views and avoid the most difficult part of the climb. A visitor center on the Pilgrim's trail at the base of the mountain in Murrisk sells crafts and mementos and offers information on the mountain, a restaurant, and hot showers. Allow three to five hours for your visit, depending on your speed.

Between Louisburgh and Westport, off the R395. ☎ 098-64-114 for Croagh Patrick Tourist Information. Admission: Free. Open: Daylight hours.

National Museum of Ireland: Country Life
Castlebar, County Mayo

Surrounded by pretty gardens, this museum features well-crafted, interesting exhibits on life in rural Ireland since 1850. You'll find artifacts, such as spinning wheels and clothing, alongside video footage of country traditions. The museum works hard to make sure that visitors come away with a real sense of the people behind the objects. This place is definitely worth a stop if you're interested in the history and culture of rural Ireland.

Off the N5, in Turlough village, 8km (5 miles) east of Castlebar, County Mayo. ☎ 094-903-1755. www.museum.ie. *Admission: Free. Open: Tues–Sat 10 a.m.–5 p.m., Sun 2–5 p.m.*

More cool things to see and do in County Mayo

✔ **Beach walk from Silver Strand (Thallabawn) to White Strand:** It's hard to decide where to focus your attention as you trek along these beaches. Do you take in the sand dunes, or do you gaze out at the mountains of Mayo and Connemara? Do you sift the sand for delicate shells, or do you pause on a rocky outcropping to search the seascape for dolphins? What a luxurious dilemma. To get here, follow the silver strand/killadoon signs from Louisburgh.

✔ **Fishing:** What's your poison — salmon, trout, pike, perch? Contact the Ballina branch of **Inland Fisheries Ireland** (☎ 096-22-788; www.fisheriesireland.ie) for information about Mayo and Sligo's many places to fish.

✔ **Westport House & Country Park,** right outside of Westport's center (☎ 098-27-766): Fans of Georgian architecture will appreciate this limestone house, which has long belonged to the Browne family, descendents of 16th-century pirate queen Grace (Granuaile) O'Malley. It's a grand residence, featuring beautiful original furnishings and architectural details from the late 18th and 19th centuries. You'll find high ceilings, an extraordinary white marble staircase, portraits of the Brownes, and a dining room full of antiques, including Irish silver and Waterford Crystal. The extensive grounds are (somewhat incongruously) a small amusement park, offering log flume rides, swan pedal boats, two giant slides, a pitch-'n'-putt, a castle bounce, and more. If Granuaile were alive today, she might be proud of the high price of admission — another form of plundering perhaps?

You can get to the house either from the R335 or from Golf Links Road (look for signs on both routes). Admission to the house is €12 adults, €7.50 seniors, €9 students, €6.50 kids 3 and up, free for kids 2 and under; a combination ticket for the house and amusement park is €22 adults, €12 seniors, €20 students, and €19 kids. The house is open June through September daily from 10 a.m. to 5:30 p.m.; it may be open during Easter week, May, and October, but call for hours. The amusement park is open Easter week daily from 10:30 a.m. to 5:30 p.m., June daily from 11 a.m. to 4 p.m., and July and August daily from 10:30 a.m. to 5:30 p.m. Plan on an hour for the house, more if you'll be visiting the amusement park.

Shopping in County Mayo

The locally famous and beautifully colored Foxford wool tweeds, rugs, blankets, and much more can be found at **Foxford Woolen Mills Visitor Centre,** Foxford (from Westport take the N5 northeast to the N58 north; ☎ 094-925-6756). **Kaleidoscope Arts**, Bridge Street, Westport (☎ 086-853-3073), is a beautifully curated shop selling lovely contemporary paintings, pottery, and jewelry by Irish artists and craftspeople.

Hitting the pubs in County Mayo

Matt Molloy's
Westport, County Mayo

If you like traditional Irish music, this pub is worth visiting. It was started by the flutist from the famous band the Chieftains, who are often credited with the revival in Irish folk music. The back room features music nearly every night — Molloy himself sometimes stops in for a session when he's in town. Get here early to get a good seat because everyone seems to know about this place.

Bridge Street. ☎ **098-26-655.**

The West Bar
Westport, County Mayo

If the noise and crowds at Matt Molloy's have reached intolerable levels, check out the West, a friendly, cozy, old-style pub.

Bridge Street. ☎ **098-25-886.**

Fast Facts: County Mayo

Area Codes

County Mayo area codes are **092, 094, 096, 097,** and **098.**

Emergencies/Police

Dial ☎ **999** for all emergencies.

Genealogy Resources

Contact the North Mayo Heritage Centre, on Enniscoe Estate, Castlehill, near the town of Crossmolina (☎ 096-31-809), or the South Mayo Family History Research Centre, Main Street, Ballinrobe (☎ 094-954-1214).

Hospital

Mayo General Hospital is on Westport Road in Castlebar (☎ 094-902-1733).

Information

There are several tourist offices in various towns in County Mayo. A comprehensive tourist office, open year-round, is located on James Street in Westport (☎ 098-25-711; www.discoverireland.ie/west).

Internet

Gavins DVD & Internet, Bridge Street, Westport (☎ 098-264-61), has inexpensive Internet service.

Post Office

Almost every town has a post office. A centrally located post office is on North Mall in Westport (☎ 098-25-475).

County Sligo

Getting to and around County Sligo

From Dublin, take the N4 to Sligo; from Galway, take the N17; and from Donegal, take the N15.

Irish Rail (☎ 1-850-366-222; www.irishrail.ie) serves Sligo Town (at Lord Edward Street), Collooney, Ballymote, and Boyle in County Sligo. **Bus Éireann** (☎ 01-836-6111; www.buseireann.ie) serves Ballymote, Sligo Town, Tubbercurry, Collooney, and several other towns in County Sligo. There is also local service between Sligo Town and the beaches at Rosses Point.

Aer Arann (☎ 0818-210-210; www.aerarann.com) has daily flights from Dublin into Sligo Airport, in Strandhill (☎ 071-916-8280; www.sligoairport.com).

Sligo Town can be a very frustrating place to drive due to the river that runs through town and the many one-way streets. I recommend parking outside the downtown area and exploring on foot. If you do decide to park in Sligo, you can use the Pay-and-Display machines if you're parking on the street, or one of the large parking garages. Taxis in Sligo Town line up on Quay Street. **Ace Cabs** (☎ 071-914-4444) is a reliable taxi service if you need a pickup.

Spending the night in County Sligo

Sligo Town doesn't have any standout hotels right now. If you have your heart set on staying in a hotel in town, fine options are **Riverside Suites Hotel**, JFK Parade Road (☎ 071-914-8080; www.riversidesuiteshotelsligo.com), with a pretty location on the river in town and the bonus of well-outfitted kitchens in each suite; and **Park Hotel Sligo** (☎ 071-919-040; www.sligoparkhotel.com), a large and slightly dated hotel with a friendly staff located a few minutes' drive south of Sligo Town on Pearse Road.

Check out the "Sligo Town" map for locations of accommodations there.

Cromleach Lodge Country House
$$$ Castlebaldwin, County Sligo

A real hideaway, this modern inn overlooks large Lough Arrow and is surrounded by gentle countryside. This is a place for peaceful rambles around the hills, and the owners, husband-and-wife Moira and Christy, are virtual encyclopedias on the best walks and hikes in the area. If you're in the market for some relaxation, spend a leisurely afternoon enjoying the views of the lake and its little islands from the glass-walled sun porch. The more expensive bedrooms are furnished in a country style with Victorian touches, while the less expensive rooms are uncluttered and contemporary, with stylish fabrics and IKEA-esque furnishings. The lauded restaurant serves beautiful meals made with local ingredients and may very well provide one of the most memorable meals of your trip.

Take the N4 south from Sligo Town toward Boyle to Lough Arrow in Castlebaldwin. ☎ *071-916-5155.* www.cromleach.com. *Parking: Free on-site. Rack rates: €110–€180 double. AE, DC, MC, V.*

Lisadorn
$ Sligo Town, County Sligo

This stately home is at the end of a flower-lined drive, a perfect welcome to a lovely guesthouse. Rooms are large and brightly furnished, and the place offers amazing hospitality and comfort for the cost. Lisadorn has a great location, only a five-minute drive from town and a ten-minute drive from the seaside and beaches at Rosses Point.

Donegal Road. From the center of town, take the N15 north. ☎ **071-91-43-417.** *Fax: 071-91-46-418. Parking: Free on the street. Rack rates: €70 double. No credit cards.*

Temple House
$$$ Ballymote, County Sligo

I'm trying to figure out if there is any possible way that I could be related to the Percevals, who have lived on these breathtaking 400 hectares (1,000 acres) of land since 1665. If I were, say, a second-cousin twice-removed, perhaps I could return regularly to their expansive 1825 manor and again experience the kind of warmth that makes one feel like a member of the family. The splendor of the grounds and the house alone would make this one of the finest places to stay in Ireland, but it's the feeling that you're an honored guest of your hosts, Roderick and Helena Perceval, and their family (including the past generations, who look out from portraits and photographs throughout the house) that draws me so strongly to the place. A perfect day at Temple House: Wake up in your canopy bed in your vast room (some are bigger than my entire Brooklyn apartment was), surrounded by rich brocade draperies, gilt mirrors, gleaming mahogany furnishings, and family heirlooms. Head down to breakfast in the grand dining room, and then take a stroll with Fudge, Darcy, and Treacle (the house dogs) around the gorgeous property, checking out the ruins of a 12th-century Knights Templar castle, rowing a boat on the lake (and perhaps trying your luck with the giant pike), and wandering miles of forest trails. Finish your day with a delicious three-course dinner (available Mon–Sat with reservations beforehand), served at the immense table in the dining room (€45); gatherings have the feel of a dinner party.

Ballymote. Signposted from the N17, near Ballinacarrow. ☎ **071-918-3329.** *Fax: 071-918-3808.* www.templehouse.ie. *Parking: Free on-site. Rack rates: €150–€180 double. MC, V. Open: Apr–Nov.*

Treetops Bed and Breakfast
$ Sligo Town, County Sligo

Artsy folks will want to make extra time to look around this terrific bed-and-breakfast, where original contemporary Irish paintings, drawings, and sculpture grace the walls and surfaces. Your hosts couldn't be kinder and more helpful, and they cook your Irish breakfast to perfection. The contemporary rooms are spotless and cozy. You get the best of both worlds

Sligo Town

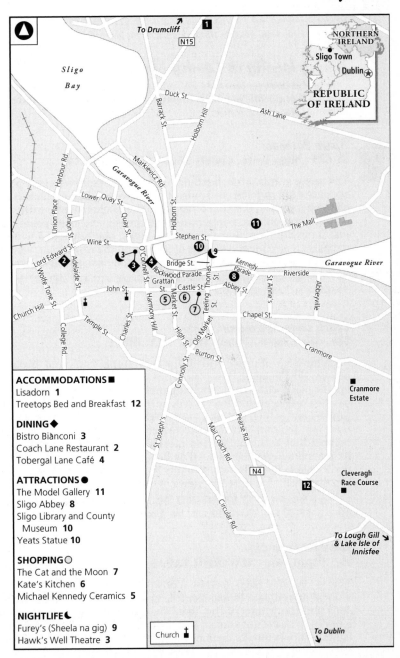

To Drumcliff

1

N15

Sligo Bay

Duck St.

Barack St.

Holborn Hill

Ash Lane

NORTHERN IRELAND

Sligo Town

Dublin

REPUBLIC OF IRELAND

Harbour Rd.

Marklevicz Rd.

Garavogue River

St. Union

Lower Quay St.

Union Place

Union St.

Quay St.

Stephen St.

11

The Mall

Wine St.

Lord Edward St.

Adelaide St.

2

3

3

O'Connell St.

Rockwood Parade

4

10

Bridge St.

9

Kennedy Parade

Riverside

Garavogue River

Wolfe Tone St.

Grattan St.

John St.

Castle St.

Thomas St.

8

Abbey St.

St. Anne's

Abbeyville

Church Hill

College Rd.

Temple St.

Charles St.

Harmony Hill

Market St.

5

6

7

High St.

Old Market St.

Teeling St.

Chapel St.

Cranmore

Connolly St.

Burton St.

St. Joseph's

Mail Coach Rd.

Pearse Rd.

N4

Cranmore Estate

Cleveragh Race Course

Circular Rd.

12

To Lough Gill & Lake Isle of Innisfee

ACCOMMODATIONS ■
Lisadorn **1**
Treetops Bed and Breakfast **12**

DINING ◆
Bistro Biànconi **3**
Coach Lane Restaurant **2**
Tobergal Lane Café **4**

ATTRACTIONS ●
The Model Gallery **11**
Sligo Abbey **8**
Sligo Library and County
  Museum **10**
Yeats Statue **10**

SHOPPING ○
The Cat and the Moon **7**
Kate's Kitchen **6**
Michael Kennedy Ceramics **5**

NIGHTLIFE ☾
Furey's (Sheela na gig) **9**
Hawk's Well Theatre **3**

Church ✝

To Dublin

in the location: You're about a ten-minute walk from downtown Sligo on a quiet, peaceful road.

Cleveragh Road, off Pearse Road (R287). ☎ **071-916-0160.** www.sligobandb. com. *Parking: Free on-site. Rack rates: €74 double. MC, V.*

Dining locally in County Sligo

One of the best restaurants in County Sligo, **Cromleach Lodge** (p. 379) offers a wonderful New Irish menu in a dining room with views of the surrounding countryside.

Bistro Bianconi
$$–$$$ Sligo Town, County Sligo   ITALIAN/PIZZA

The menu at this large, bustling Italian restaurant includes no fewer than six pages full of different kinds of pizza, from a Cajun chicken pizza with sliced peppers and smoked bacon to the Michelangelo, with mozzarella, caramelized onions, pepperoni, goat cheese, and basil pesto. And that's just the pizza. The bistro also offers steak, chicken, and a wide selection of pastas. Families and groups of friends fill the restaurant, which is decorated in trattoria style, with Roman busts, mosaics, and columns.

44 O'Connell St. ☎ **071-914-1744.** *Main courses: €12–€23. AE, MC, V. Open: Daily 12:30–3 p.m. and 5:30–10 p.m.*

Coach Lane Restaurant
$$$ Sligo Town, County Sligo   NEW IRISH

Imagine a farmhouse, with brick and stone walls and broad wooden beams. Now imagine that your hippest friend has just moved in, decorating the place with just the right quantity of stylish touches like white pillar candles, vases of wildflowers, gilt mirrors, and garnet silk curtains. That's Coach Lane, which serves a varied New Irish menu that emphasizes fresh meat and seafood in dishes like seared scallops with a mint and pea puree or beef filet with shallot and merlot *jus.* The restaurant also excels at Italian-influenced dishes such as linguini with clams in a white wine and garlic sauce. Specials include many fresh fish dishes. Ask for a table on the top floor, which has pretty views of the town below.

1–2 Lord Edward St. ☎ **071-916-2417.** *Main courses: €20–€28. AE, DC, MC, V. Open: Mon–Sat 5–10 p.m., Sun 4–10 p.m.; bar food served daily 3–10 p.m.*

Tobergal Lane Cafe
$$ Sligo Town   NEW IRISH/TAPAS

This is just what Sligo needed: A down-to-earth restaurant that uses loads of local ingredients in excellent dishes. The menus change with the seasons and the whims of the chef. The cafe puts as much effort into light lunches (a butternut squash and goat cheese sandwich was a recent highlight) as it puts into its evening menu, which includes both Irish-influenced tapas, such as a chorizo and cheese bruschetta, and main courses such as duck confit with a red wine glaze.

On Tobergal Lane (off O'Connell Street). ☎ **071-914-6599.** *Main courses: €14–€23. MC, V. Open: June–Sept daily 10 a.m.–10 p.m., Oct–May Tues–Sun 10 a.m.–9 p.m.*

Exploring County Sligo

If you're a Yeats fan without a car, luck is on your side, because **Discover Sligo Tours** (☎ **071-914-7488**) offers excellent narrated bus tours of the Sligo area and of sights associated with Yeats.

The top attractions

Carrowkeel Megalithic Cemetery
Carrowkeel (near Castlebaldwin), County Sligo

Okay, you're going to have to work hard to get to this vast mountaintop field of passage tombs (like those at Newgrange but smaller), but if you love archaeology and ancient history adventures, it's so worth it. There are no tour guides, no brochures, no gift shops selling T-shirts that say, "My grandma went to Carrowkeel and all I got was this shirt." There's just peace, unbelievable views of the Sligo countryside, and a large collection of roughly 5,000-year-old tombs, some covered by turf (look for mounds) and some completely exposed. Things get even cooler. You can go down the passage into two of the larger exposed tombs. Bring a flashlight if possible so that you can check out the stonework, including the massive capstone on the first tomb you encounter.

To get here, follow signs from the N4. When you get to the farm gate (look for the no shooting sign near it), open it, drive through, and close it behind you and continue to follow the signs. If you're a confident driver and it's not raining, go past the first parking area to drive the narrow, twisty road up the mountain and then park in the little pullout (there's a pedestrians only sign). If you'd rather not attempt the road, you can walk up the mountain from the lower parking area. From the pedestrians only sign, look for the paths (there are several) to scramble up to the tombs. I wouldn't attempt the road by car if it has been or is raining a lot. Allow 90 minutes for your visit.

I highly recommend visiting Carrowmore (see the next review) before exploring Carrowkeel; the guided tour at Carrowmore will help you to picture what might have taken place at Carrowkeel.

Carrowmore Megalithic Cemetery
Carrowmore, County Sligo

You may imagine that you hear the whispers and see the ritual fires of generations past as you tour this ancient group of *passage tombs* (burial mounds with entrance passageways) and *dolmen* (tombs composed of one rock lying flat across other standing rocks), which are spread out over a great grassy field ringed by mountains. This is the largest collection of megalithic tombs in Ireland, and some of the oldest tombs in the country

The mystery of Queen Maeve

Legend has it that the great Celtic warrior Queen Maeve (first century A.D.) ordered her followers to bring her body to Sligo and bury her standing up and facing down her enemies to the north. She is said to stand within a tomb atop Knocknarea Mountain, one of the impressive ring of mountains that surround Carrowmore (see the description of Carrowmore earlier in this chapter). The unmistakable loaf-shaped outline of the passage tomb can be seen from almost every location in Sligo. Some say Queen Maeve was a mythic goddess; others say she was a very real and ruthless Celtic queen. Archaeologists speculate that the Knocknarea tomb contains much older megalithic remains. But still, the tomb remains undisturbed in respect for Maeve, and, thus far, there are no plans to excavate it.

In Sligo, there is a custom of adding a stone to the tomb, ostensibly to "keep away the fairies," though many say the custom may have originated as a way to make sure that Maeve stays put in her resting place.

You can hike up to the tomb in about 45 minutes. Park at the base of the mountain, accessible off the R292, southwest of Sligo Town. You'll need good shoes, as there is a bit of a scramble toward the top.

are found here, including one that's estimated to be more than 7,000 years old. The Carrowmore area is only a small portion of a vast local group of such tombs; look at the bumps at the tops of the surrounding mountains to locate other tombs. Definitely take the free guided tour; the exceptionally knowledgeable guides bring the site to life, painting a picture of the activities that may have taken place here thousands of years ago, and discussing various theories surrounding the creation and use of these tombs. A restored cottage houses exhibits and information related to the site. Allow 90 minutes for your visit.

If you enjoy your explorations here, I highly recommend that you visit **Carrowkeel** (see previous review).

Located off the R292, going west out of Sligo Town. ☎ 071-916-1534. Admission: €3 adults, €2 seniors, €2 students and kids. Open: Apr to mid-Oct daily 10 a.m.–6 p.m. (last admission 5 p.m.).

Drive around Lough Gill
Drumcliff, County Sligo

Serene, azure Lough Gill makes many appearances in Yeats's poems. You may be inspired to jot down a few lines of poetry yourself as you make the 42km (26-mile) drive around this gorgeous lake, stopping to ramble along the nature trails and gaze at the island of Innisfree, made famous in Yeats's poem "The Lake Isle of Innisfree." On the north side of the lake drive, you may want to stop to take a guided tour of the beautiful 17th-century **Parke's Castle**, Fivemilebourne, Leitrim (☎ 071-916-4149). On the north side of the lake, the Hazelwood Sculpture Trail is a beautiful walk along the lake, although the large wood sculptures that it's named for have fallen into disrepair. On the south side of the lake, Slish Wood is a lovely 3.2km (2-mile) lakeside trail. Take along some food for the ducks and swans. You also can take boat rides on the lake (see p. 386). Allow 90 minutes or more for your drive, depending on how often you stop.

Go south from Sligo Town 1.6km (1 mile). Take Stephen Street in Sligo Town, which turns into the N16; turn right onto the R286, and follow the signs.

Eagles Flying: Irish Raptor Research Centre
Ballymote, County Sligo

If having a flying falcon's wing graze your hair isn't an amazing experience, I don't know what is. The highlights of this beautiful sanctuary for birds of prey are the daily hour-long free-flying demonstrations (11 a.m., 3 p.m.), when falconers fly eagles, hawks, owls, and falcons over your head as they explain the behaviors and characteristics of each bird. You'll get a chance to pet an owl during the demonstration, and you can wander the grounds before or after the show, getting another look at the birds and petting and feeding some of the other animals, including ferrets, donkeys, chicks, and a friendly pig. Allow 90 minutes for your visit.

Portinch, Ballymote. Follow directions for Temple House (p. 380), and then turn left at the gate of Temple House. ☎ *071-918-9310. Admission: €9 adults, €8 students, €5.50 kids 3–16, free for kids 2 and under. Open: Apr–Nov 7 10:30 a.m.–12:30 p.m. and 2:30–4:30 p.m. (demonstrations daily during these months at 11 a.m. and 3 p.m.)*

Lissadell House and Gardens
Drumcliff, County Sligo

William Butler Yeats called Lissadell House "that old Georgian mansion," which is quite the understatement. This grand square stone house was owned by the Gore-Booth family, friends of Yeats. One of the Gore-Booth daughters was Countess Markievicz (she married a Polish count), who took part in the Easter Rising of 1916; she was the first woman elected to the British House of Commons and the first woman cabinet member in the Irish Dáil (Parliament). Her sister, Eva, was a poet. Highlights of the house include

---

A Sligo-style seaweed spa treatment

Getting into a bathtub filled with warm water and seaweed may not be the first thing that you think of when you picture a relaxing bath, but that may be because you haven't experienced the moisturizing and calming properties of a hot bath strewn with fresh Irish seaweed. **Voya Seaweed Baths & Spa,** in Strandhill, right outside of Sligo Town (☎ **071-916-8686**), offers private seaweed baths, plus massages, facials, and other spa fare.

a grand marble staircase; paintings and engravings by Countess Markievicz, John Butler Yeats (father to William and Jack), and Percy French; and a collection of Regency books. The restored upper walled garden (a kitchen garden) and 0.8-hectare (2-acre) Alpine Garden are magnificent. Definitely make time for a snack or lunch at the tearoom. *Note:* Lissadell House and Gardens was closed for almost a year due to a dispute between the owners of the house and the Sligo County Council. It looks like the matter has been resolved, but call first or check online to make sure that the house and gardens are open. Allow two and a half hours for your visit.

In Drumcliff, signposted off the N15, between Sligo and Donegal. ☎ **071-916-3150.** www.lissadellhouse.com. *Admission: House tour and gardens €12 adults, €6 kids; house tour only €6 adults, €3 kids; gardens only €5 adults, €2.50 kids. Open: Daily 10:30 a.m.–6 p.m. (last tour 5 p.m.).*

Lough Gill Cruise
Lough Gill, County Sligo

Relax on *The Rose of Innisfree* as you cruise Loch Gill and view the isle of Innisfree, made famous in the eponymous poem by William Butler Yeats. Snacks and drinks are on offer, and Yeats's poetry is recited live. The company also offers sunset cruises and a music and dinner cruise.

Cruises leave from Parke's Castle, located 11km (7 miles) from Sligo Town, on the R286. ☎ **071-916-4266.** *Admission: Poetry cruise €15 adults, €7.50 kids. There are several cruises daily from Easter through October. Call for departure times and to make reservations.*

The Model Gallery
Sligo Town, County Sligo

The Yeats family legacy is a cornerstone of the collection at this excellent museum, which features many paintings by Jack Yeats and his father, John Yeats, in addition to the works of many other 20th-century and contemporary Irish artists. The gallery also curates popular temporary shows by current cutting-edge contemporary Irish and international artists, and offers a jam-packed schedule of gallery talks, music, and film. Allow about 90 minutes for your visit.

The Mall. ☎ **071-914-1405.** www.themodel.ie. *Admission: Free. Open: Tues–Wed and Fri–Sat 10 a.m.–5:30 p.m., Thurs 10 a.m.–8 p.m., Sun noon to 5 p.m.*

Sligo Abbey
Sligo Town, County Sligo

This is the city's only surviving medieval building, constructed in the mid-13th century for Dominican monks. Inside are carvings and tomb sculptures. The highlight is the superbly carved high altar from the 15th century, the only one of its kind in a monastic church in Ireland. The abbey burned down in 1414 and was damaged again in the 1641 Rebellion. According to local legend, worshippers saved the abbey's silver bell from thieves by putting it in Lough Gill. Some say that those free from sin can hear the bell's toll from under the waves. The abbey is always cool inside, even in warm weather, so you may want to bring a jacket. Allow 45 minutes for your visit.

Abbey Street, 1 block south of Kennedy Parade in the center of Sligo Town. ☎ *071-914-6406. Admission: €3 adults, €2 seniors, €1 students and kids. Open: Apr to mid-Oct daily 10 a.m.–6 p.m., mid-Oct to Oct 31 Fri–Sun 9:30 a.m.–4:30 p.m. (last admission 45 minutes before closing).*

More cool things to see and do in County Sligo

✓ **Beach horseback rides:** Everyone has a dream of riding a noble steed across a golden stretch of sand, right? Fulfill that dream with a one- to five- hour guided ride leaving from **Island View Riding Stables**, in Grange (☎ **071-916-6156;** www.islandviewriding stables.com). The stables cater to everyone from novices to experienced riders.

✓ **County Sligo Golf Club,** Rosses Point, County Sligo (☎ **071-917-7134;** www.countysligogolfclub.ie): This par-71 course challenges even top players, but dabblers can have fun playing it, too. It's set between striking Atlantic beaches and the flat-topped mountain of Benbulben. The course is open daily, but you have to reserve your tee time in advance (the club recommends at least three weeks during high season, to ensure that you get a time). There is a dress code for the course. The greens fee is €70.

✓ **Sligo Library and County Museum,** Stephen Street, County Sligo (☎ **071-911-1850;** www.sligolibrary.ie): Arise and go now, William Butler and Jack B. Yeats fans and Countess Constance Markievicz fans, to see this collection of photographs, letters, prints, portraits, drawings, and broadsheets that relate to the Yeatses and Markievicz. Admission is free, and the museum is open Tuesday through Saturday from 9:30 a.m. to 5 p.m. (until 8 p.m. Thurs). Allow 45 minutes for your visit.

✓ **William Butler Yeats's grave,** 8km (5 miles) north of Sligo, on the main Donegal Road (N15): Yeats died in France, but, in 1948, his remains were brought to rest in Sligo, the place he always considered home. His grave in the Drumcliff churchyard is near a beautiful Celtic high cross. On the grave is an epitaph Yeats wrote: "Cast a cold eye on life, on death. Horseman pass by." Look out for an installation in front of the church incorporating Yeats's poem "He Wishes for the Cloths of Heaven." You can see the grave in a few minutes.

✓ **The Yeats Statue,** Stephen Street, just across Hyde Bridge in Sligo Town: One of the more interesting statues in Ireland is a cartoonish likeness of Sligo's famous poet near the banks of the Garavogue River, in Sligo Town. Scrawled over his entire figure are the words of his own verse. You can see the statue in a few minutes.

Two splendid drives

In County Sligo, hook up with the N17, south of Sligo Town, and take it in the direction of Ballinacarrow. After you've gone through Ballinacarrow, look out for the sign for Temple House. At the sign, make a right in the direction of Killoran, taking the road through the unspoiled Ox Mountains (keep following signs pointing towards Ladies' Brae). The road will open onto a panoramic view of patchwork fields rippling down to Sligo Bay, with the distinctive flat-topped Ben Bulben Mountain rising at the far end of the bay. Take a left when you reach the N59, and then a right onto the Coast Road, following signs for Aughris Head. Your destination is Maggie Maye's Beach Bar, at Aughris Strand, where you can have a pint on an unspoiled rocky beach with gorgeous views of Ben Bulben and Knocknarea (see the nearby sidebar "The mystery of Queen Maeve"). To get back to the main roads, leave the Coast Road for the N59, which is much simpler to follow.

The following scenic route takes you from County Mayo to Connemara: Take the R335 out of Westport. You'll drive past Clew Bay, studded with tiny grass-green islands, and the bottom of the pyramid-shaped Croagh Patrick (described earlier). Continue through the steep and windswept bogland of Doolough Pass, and along glassy Killary Fjord, which reflects the surrounding mountains. You may want to stop at powerful Aasleagh Falls. From here, you can either continue on into Connemara on the N59 (a gorgeous route in itself) or retrace the route back to Westport.

Shopping in County Sligo

The Cat and The Moon, 4 Castle St., Sligo Town (☎ **071-914-3686**), sells gorgeous Irish handcrafted jewelry, glass, textile art, and more. Check out the art gallery on the first floor. **Michael Kennedy Ceramics,** Market Street (☎ **071-914-8844**), sells Kennedy's gorgeous pottery, which is inspired by the sea, landscapes, plants, and flowers of the West of Ireland. Stop into **Kate's Kitchen,** 3 Castle St., Sligo Town (☎ **071-914-3022**), for picnic food: meats, cheeses, salads, pâté, homemade bread, Irish chocolates, and preserves; the store also sells an array of luxurious soaps and lotions.

Hitting the pubs in County Sligo

Before a Sligo Town pub crawl, you may want to take in a performance by the excellent **Blue Raincoat Theatre Company** (☎ **071-917-0431**; www. blueraincoat.com), which performs modern European classics. Irish plays are prominently featured, including short pieces by Yeats. At **Hawk's Well Theatre,** Temple Street (☎ **071-916-1518**; www.hawkswell.com), offerings range from classic Irish plays to new dance works.

Furey's (Sheela na gig)
Sligo Town, County Sligo

Created by members of the traditional Irish music supergroup Dervish, this pub has great *craic* (fun) and music, from traditional to jazz, almost every night of the week.

Bridge Street. ☎ **071-914-3825.**

The Yeats Tavern
Drumcliff Bridge, County Sligo

Just a short walk from the grave of poet William Butler Yeats, this pub, also known as Davis's Restaurant @ The Yeats Tavern, is a popular watering hole for locals and visitors alike. Inside, you find plenty of Yeats memorabilia and quotes from his works. This place features good pub grub, as well as a restaurant for more formal dining.

Drumcliff Bridge. Go 8.1km (5 miles) out of Sligo Town on the main Donegal Road. ☎ **071-916-3117.**

Fast Facts: County Sligo

Area Codes
071 and **074** for County Sligo.

Emergencies/Police
Dial ☎ **999** for all emergencies.

Genealogy Resources
Contact the Sligo Heritage and Genealogy Society, Temple Street, Sligo Town (☎ 071-914-3728).

Hospital
Sligo General Hospital is on The Mall in Sligo Town (☎ 071-917-1111).

Information
There are several tourist offices in various towns in Sligo. A comprehensive tourist office, open year-round, is located on Temple Street in Sligo Town (☎ 071-916-1201; www.sligotourism.ie).

Internet
Cafe Online, Stephen Street, Sligo Town (☎ 071-914-4892), is a comprehensive Internet cafe.

Post Office
Almost every town has a post office. A centrally located and large post office is on Wine Street, Sligo (☎ 071-915-9273).

Chapter 20

County Donegal

This county has wild natural beauty in spades, plus several areas where Gaelic culture thrives (especially the Atlantic Peninsula and the peninsula north of Donegal Bay). It's less visited than most of the other coastal counties, which means that you'll have fewer choices for accommodations, attractions, and restaurants. What you get in return are gorgeous landscapes without the crowds. The county has many different faces. The **peninsula north of Donegal Bay** is stunning, with mountains, rolling pastureland, charming little towns, and the towering sea cliffs of **Slieve League** (the highest in Ireland). The towns on the south side of Donegal Bay are seaside resorts frequented mostly by Irish vacationers; and some, such as Bundoran, are pretty tacky. **Glenveagh National Park** boasts forests, several sparkling lakes, a castle, and an entire herd of red deer. The **Atlantic Highlands** (in the north) and the **Inishowen Peninsula** are wild landscapes, vast and breathtaking, with mountains, woodland, cliffs, and the ever-present crashing of the ocean.

There isn't one specific area known for man-made sights; instead, you'll come across a variety of attractions, including a prehistoric fort and a house packed with art treasures, as you explore this little-visited corner of the country.

The second largest town in the county, **Donegal Town,** is a nice, walkable village along the River Eske. There are no big attractions in town (other than the castle), so it isn't worth spending more than a morning or afternoon exploring, but it makes a good point of departure for touring the coast clockwise.

For the record, Donegal is pronounced dun-ee-*gawl.*

County Donegal

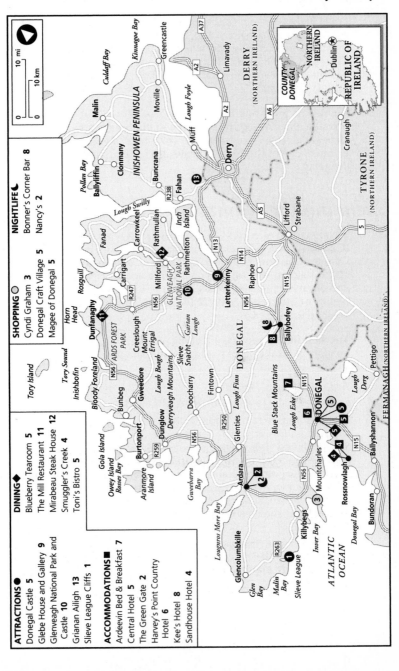

ATTRACTIONS ●
Donegal Castle **5**
Glebe House and Gallery **9**
Glenveagh National Park and
Castle **10**
Grianan Ailigh **13**
Slieve League Cliffs **1**

ACCOMMODATIONS ■
Ardeevin Bed & Breakfast **7**
Central Hotel **5**
The Green Gate **2**
Harvey's Point Country
Hotel **6**
Kee's Hotel **8**
Sandhouse Hotel **4**

DINING ◆
Blueberry Tearoom **5**
The Mill Restaurant **11**
Mirabeau Steak House **12**
Smuggler's Creek **4**
Toni's Bistro **5**

SHOPPING ○
Cyndi Graham **3**
Donegal Craft Village **5**
Magee of Donegal **5**

NIGHTLIFE ♪
Bonner's Corner Bar **8**
Nancy's **2**

Getting to and around County Donegal

Local flights come into Donegal Airport, Letterkenny (☎ **074-954-8284;** www.donegalairport.ie), located 65km (40 miles) from Donegal Town. If you come by car, you can take the N15 north from Sligo. **Bus Éireann** (☎ **1-850-366-222;** www.buseireann.ie) travels year-round to Donegal Town, Ballyshannon, Ardara, Letterkenny, and other towns in County Donegal.

There's no local bus service in Donegal Town, but you can easily walk through and around the town if you don't have a car. Exploring County Donegal is best done with a car (or a bike, if you're a strong biker) because one of the biggest draws is traveling through the natural scenery.

Spending the Night

If you need to stay right in Donegal Town, the **Central Hotel** (☎ **074-972-1027;** www.centralhoteldonegal.com) is a decent choice. Doubles run from €90 to €100. However, if possible I encourage you stay outside town, where you'll find a great assortment of charming and often inexpensive B&Bs. If you're interested in renting a cottage, house, or apartment, call ☎ **087-619-0240,** or visit www.donegal selfcatering.ie.

The Mill Restaurant (see "Dining in County Donegal," later in this chapter) is a pleasant place to stay in Dunfanaghy.

Ardeevin Guest House

$ Lough Eske (outside of Donegal Town)

Perhaps angsty teens should be required to spend a night at Ardeevin, where it seems impossible not to be cheerful. The spacious, airy rooms are furnished in a bright, sweet country style with such touches as an antique vanity sporting a Victorian-era brush, comb, and mirror set. Your friendly, very professional hosts serve breakfast (one of the tastiest Irish breakfasts I've ever had) in a dining room decorated with polished dark-wood furniture, small sparkling chandeliers, and pink glassware. Be sure to check out the views of Lough (pronounced lock) Eske from the front of the house.

Take the N15 from Donegal Town, toward Letterkenny and Derry, for 4km (2½ miles). Take the second left turn after the Skoda car dealership, and then follow the signs for Ardeevin. ☎ *074-972-1790.* http://ardeevin.tripod.com. *Parking: Free on-site. Rack rates: €65–€70 double. No credit cards.*

The Green Gate
$$ Ardara

If you want Jacuzzi bathtubs and luxury linens, this is not the place for you. However, if you're interested in a truly unusual, bohemian lodging, with stunning views of green hills and ocean, this just may be your kind of place. Follow the slightly enigmatic symbols of a green gate from the town of Ardara to the remote hilltop location, where you'll be warmly greeted by Paul Chatenoud, an eccentric, kind, sometimes flirtatious character who was drawn to Donegal from Paris over 20 years ago. Meeting Paul, who is full of stories and tips on the best-kept secrets of Donegal, is half of the reason to come here. The other half of the reason is to sleep in a real live cottage (one with a traditional thatched roof and one with an old slate roof), and to appreciate the spare but artistic design of the rooms and property. Breakfast is served outside on a tree stump, and my room featured a ship's lantern set into a recess in the wall and a haiku-like note on the mirror in the bathroom reading: "The water is brown . . . It is normal."

Ardara. To reach the B&B from Ardara, follow the Green Gate signs. ☎ **074-954-1546.** www.thegreengate.eu. *Parking: Free on-site. Rack rates: €90–€110 double. No credit cards.*

Harvey's Point Country Hotel
$$$–$$$$ Lough Eske (outside of Donegal Town)

Ask the locals about Harvey's Point and they'll answer with a smile. This well-known hotel is beautifully situated right on the shores of Lough Eske, with water views in abundance. Rooms remind me of those that you see on tours of manor houses, with gorgeous wallpaper, four-poster beds, and opulent furnishings. And everything is kept in tip-top condition (I dare you to find a chip in the paint). There is a great attention to detail — turndown service leaves a small box of chocolates on your pillow, and the service is exceptional.

Lough Eske. Follow signs from Donegal Town. ☎ **074-972-2208.** www.harveyspoint.com. *Parking: Free on-site. Rack rates: €160–€200 double. AE, MC, V.*

Kee's Hotel
$$ Stranorlar/Ballybofey

This charming historic coaching inn is in a great location for exploring County Donegal. The staff is warm and friendly, and the rooms are big and comfortable (though a bit dated), with views of the grand Blue Stack Mountains. Guests can use the gym and the pool, and then relax in front of one of the hotel's open fireplaces. The restaurant serves excellent food, and bikes are available for rent. The hotel often runs special deals, so check the Web site. Be aware that the towns of Stranorlar and Ballybofey are small and quiet, so you'll definitely want a car or bike for transportation.

Take the N15 northeast from Donegal Town to where it meets the N13. ☎ **074-913-1018.** *Fax: 074-913-1917.* www.keeshotel.ie. *Parking: Free on-site. Rack rates: €70–€90 double. MC, V.*

Sandhouse Hotel
$$$ **Rossnowlagh**

This oceanside fishing lodge turned hotel is all about the peaceful location, with breathtaking views of the ocean and a fantastic surfing beach. Rooms are large, simple, and clean, and the staff couldn't be nicer. Don't leave without taking a dip in the Jacuzzi. Splurging on a room with a view of the Atlantic Ocean and Donegal Bay is worth it.

Rossnowlagh Beach (off the R231 about 8km/5 miles northwest of Ballyshannon). ☎ *071-985-1777. Fax: 071-985-2100.* www.sandhouse-hotel.ie. *Parking: Free on-site. Rack rates: €140–€150 double. AE, MC, V.*

Dining in County Donegal

Nancy's (see "Hitting the Pubs" later in this chapter), in Ardara, serves excellent seafood dishes. *Fresh* and *local* are not just buzzwords at **Aroma Cafe,** at the Donegal Craft Village (see "Shopping," later in this chapter), which serves up excellent lunches. The menu is creative, ranging from white wine risotto with chargrilled chicken and seared asparagus to the ever-popular chimichangas.

Blueberry Tearoom
$ **Donegal Town   IRISH/CAFE**

Decorated with plates and teapots, this cute and cozy restaurant has the feel of a cottage tearoom out in the countryside. Dishes are simple and fresh, and the menu runs the gamut from a grilled goat-cheese salad to a sandwich of turkey, stuffing, and cranberry sauce on brown bread. For the very hungry, hearty specials such as a roast beef dinner with Yorkshire pudding are served. Save room for the homemade desserts.

Castle Street. ☎ *074-972-2933. Main courses: €7–€13. No credit cards. Open: Mon–Sat 9 a.m.–7 p.m.*

Mirabeau Steak House
$$ **Ramelton   STEAK**

With the most courteous of service, and a setting that feels as if you're in someone's dining room, this restaurant seems to be a portal to a kinder, more decorous time. The menu includes nice dishes such as duck *á l'orange* and grilled lamb cutlets, but it's the juicy, perfectly cooked steaks that are the real stars here. I particularly recommend the peppered filet with garlic butter, grilled medium-rare. Sides (which are big enough to feed at least two) are terrific versions of dishes that you'd find in many American households circa 1950: Waldorf salad, dauphine potatoes, cauliflower Mornay, and the like. Everything is served at a leisurely pace in a burgundy room featuring a richly colored tapestry, a fire in the hearth, candlelight, and a wall-to-wall Persian carpet.

The Mall, Ramelton. ☎ **074-915-1138.** *Main courses: €12–€20. MC, V. Open: Fri–Sun 6–10 p.m.*

Smuggler's Creek
$$$ Rossnowlagh   IRISH/SEAFOOD

The view itself is enough to make a meal at Smuggler's Creek memorable. From the conservatory dining room, which sits atop a cliff, you can look out at Donegal Bay, and, if your timing's good, you may catch a fantastic sunset. The room feels rustic, with stone walls and old wooden beams. The menu is devoted to fresh, unfussy dishes, such as the excellent steak with sautéed mushrooms and onions, and a whiskey pepper sauce. Not surprisingly, seafood is a specialty here. The fish specials change depending on what's fresh.

About 0.5km (¼ mile) off the R231, off the main Sligo-Donegal road (N15). Take the little, no-name side road from the R231 to get closer to the water. Signs won't let you miss the turnoff. ☎ **071-985-2367.** *Main courses: €13–€25. MC, V. Open: June to mid-Sept daily 1–9:30 p.m. or so, mid-Sept–May Thurs–Sun 1–9:30 p.m.*

The Mill Restaurant
$$$ Dunfanaghy   CONTINENTAL/SEAFOOD

This is the kind of fine dining that feels very relaxed. You don't have to worry about your unfamiliarity with yuzu-glazed goose breast or wonder if the folks at the next table are commenting that your dress is "so last season." The staff is friendly, the fixed-price menu is straightforward, and the room is relaxing, furnished with antiques, and overlooking a lovely lake. The well-crafted dishes make use of local and seasonal offerings, especially seafood. The menu changes often, proffering such choices as pan-fried pollock with homemade tagliatelle, buttered leeks, anchovies, and a chive-butter sauce; and rib-eye steak with wild mushrooms and béarnaise sauce.

Located on the N56, 0.8km (½ mile) west of the village of Dunfanaghy. ☎ **074-913-6985.** *Main courses: Fixed-price menu €44. Kids' menu available. MC, V. Open: Tues–Sun 7–10 p.m. (last orders at 9 p.m.).*

Toni's Bistro
$ Donegal Town

Donegal Town tends to have a plethora of expensive, decent restaurants for dinner but doesn't do very well in the less expensive realm. If you're looking for filling, inexpensive food, head down Main Street to Toni's for sandwiches, soups, burgers, and salads. A cross between a coffeehouse and a diner, this place has exposed stone walls and features photos of Ireland.

3 Main St. ☎ **074-972-5682.** *Main courses: €10–€13. MC, V. Open: Mon–Sat 9:30 a.m.–9 p.m., Sun 10:30 a.m.–9 p.m.*

Exploring County Donegal

In Ardara, you can rent bikes from **Byrne's,** West End (☎ **074-954-1658**). In Letterkenny, **Church Street Cycles** (☎ **074-912-6204**) is located on Church Lane off Main Street.

The top attractions

Donegal Castle
Donegal Town

Built in the 15th century by the O'Donnell clan chieftain, this impressive castle sits beside the River Eske. Inside, lovely furnishings include Persian rugs and French tapestries — 17th-century additions from the last owner, Sir Basil Brooke, who also added an extension with ten gables and a large bay window. Free half-hour guided tours are available. Allow an hour for your visit.

Off the Diamond in Donegal Town. ☎ *074-972-2405. Admission: €4 adults, €3 seniors, €2 students and kids. Open: Mid-Apr to mid-Sept daily 10 a.m.–6 p.m. (last admission 5:15 p.m.), mid-Sept to mid-Apr Thurs–Mon 9:30–4:30 p.m. (last admission 3:45 p.m.).*

Exploring the Donegal Bay coastline

The peninsula north of Donegal Bay is one of my very favorite places in all of Ireland. It has gorgeous rolling green pastures, wild mountains, thatched-roof cottages, stunning sea cliffs, sweet and friendly little towns, and excellent traditional music. What more could you want? I recommend taking the N56 west from Donegal Town, and then linking up with the R263 to loop around the peninsula. Though the roads are very narrow (one car width only) and twisty, you'll be rewarded with splendid panoramas and a real feel for rural Irish culture. For a stop along the way, definitely check out **Slieve League,** the highest sea cliffs in Europe. The town of **Glencolumbkille,** way out on the peninsula, has an atmosphere infused with Gaelic culture. Most people here speak both Gaelic and English, and the traditional music is fabulous. At the **Glencolumbkille Folk Village** (☎ **074-973-0017**), you can explore life in the rural Ireland of centuries past. For my money, the best-kept secret in Ireland is **Port,** a small abandoned farm town perched on green hills overlooking the sea. To get to Port from Glencolumbkille, go to the top of the main street, and turn left. When you get to a T-junction, turn right, and start to look for the signs for Port. You also can get to Port by taking the N56 south of Ardara, and then taking a right turn after Bracky Bridge. A nonlooping coastal walk at Port provides dazzling views of small cliffs and waves crashing against rock formations. You could end your day in the cute town of Ardara (pronounced ar-*dra),* which has many crafts and tweed shops, and **Nancy's,** a cozy little specimen of a pub that serves terrific seafood dishes (reviewed later in this chapter).

Though you could drive the peninsula in one day, I recommend two. If you're an experienced hiker, you may want to hike around the perimeter of the peninsula. If you prefer a shorter walk, you can join up with the coastal trail at several places along the coast, including Glencolumbkille, Port, and Magheera. Another option for the strong-legged is to explore the peninsula by bicycle; you can rent bikes in Ardara at **Byrne's** (☎ 074-954-1658).

Glebe House and Gallery
Churchill, Letterkenny

This house was the pride and joy of artist, art collector, and world traveler Arthur Derek Hill, who filled his space with over 300 works of art. The collection is eclectic, ranging from paintings of Mt. Fuji by famed Japanese painter Hokusai, to Tiffany lamps, and from costume designs by Cecil Beatton to a Renoir painting. Decorative details, including William Morris wallpaper and curtains, pull the collection together. Don't miss the paintings by James Dixon, a celebrated self-taught painter from Ireland's remote Tory Island, and check out the call bells in the kitchen, left over from the time when the house was a hotel. If the weather is nice, you many want to explore the surrounding grounds. You can see the house only on guided tours, which leave every half-hour. Across from the house is a gallery that features 19th- and 20th-century works, including sculpture by Picasso and paintings by Degas and Jack B. Yeats. Allow 90 minutes for your visit.

Off the R251, about 18km (11 miles) west of the town of Letterkenny. ☎ **074-913-7071.** *Admission: €3 adults, €2 seniors, €1 students and kids. Open: July–Aug daily 11 a.m.–6 p.m., June and Sept Sat–Thurs 11 a.m.–6:30 p.m. Last tour always leaves at 5:30 p.m.*

Glenveagh National Park and Castle
Churchill, Letterkenny

This National Park is a beauty, with more than 16,000 hectares of wilderness encompassing valleys and glens, lakes, dense woodlands, bogland, and the highest mountain in Donegal: Mount Errigal. Encounters with flora and fauna are often highlights of a visit; keep an eye out for a herd of red deer on the bog, an array of plant life, and all sorts of birds, including golden eagles.

The park is centered on an impressive castle built in 1870 by John George Adair, who obnoxiously decided to kick 224 tenants off the land to create his estate. Tours take you through the grand rooms, which contain the furnishings left by the last owner, Henry McIlhenny, an American philanthropist and art collector. Near the castle is an assortment of handsome themed gardens, some featuring exotic plants and flowers. The tearoom at the castle is a charming spot for a warm drink and some light food.

The visitor center (check out the roof!) has an audiovisual show about the park and information on the various trails and any guided hikes that are taking place. If you have time for only one trail, I recommend the View Point Trail, which goes through forest and opens onto a picturesque panorama of the castle and sparking Lough Veagh. If you're visiting in the summer months, either take bug spray or purchase some from one of the machines in the archway leading to the gardens. Allow three or four hours for your visit.

Northwest from Letterkenny, on the main road to Kilmacrennan (N56). ☎ **074-913-7090.** www.glenveaghnationalpark.ie. *Admission: Park free; shuttle bus to and from the parking lot to the castle and gardens €3 adults, €2 seniors, students, and kids; castle tours €5 adults, €3 seniors, €2 students and kids. Open: Park year-round daily; visitor center Mar–Oct daily 10 a.m.–6 p.m., Nov–Feb daily 9 a.m.–5 p.m.; castle daily 10 a.m.–5 p.m. Call for tour times in winter when they're less frequent.*

Sliabh Liag (Slieve League Cliffs)
Southwest County Donegal

The movie-poster slogan for the cliffs of Slieve League (pronounced shleev-*leeg*) would read: "If you liked the Cliffs of Moher, you'll love the cliffs of Slieve League!" These sea cliffs are among the highest in Europe, and they're breathtaking, literally and figuratively. From Teelin, follow the signs for the cliffs, which may be in English or Irish. You'll encounter a farm gate (close it behind you) and take the narrow, winding road up to the top of the cliffs, with options to park at two parking lots. Most visitors decide to hike the 3km (1¾ miles) from the first parking lot to the second (follow the signs for the Coastal Trail), both because the hike itself offers gorgeous views and because you avoid white-knuckling it along the rest of the scarily narrow and twisting road. Views from Bunglass Point, at the second parking lot, are dazzling. From here, you have the option of hiking a path that hugs the cliffs, climbing even higher. Parts of this path are extremely challenging and should be attempted only by experienced climbers and hikers. Stop and turn around, if you feel at all uncomfortable. Sturdy shoes and a bottle of water are essential for anyone visiting the cliffs, regardless of whether you're planning to hike. Keep a close watch on kids — many areas lack guardrails. I recommend spending about two hours here, especially if you're interested in hiking.

If you'd like to see the cliffs from the ocean, call ☎ **087-628-4688** to arrange a boat trip with **Nuala Star Teelin.** From March through October, boats depart daily from Teelin Pier every two hours from 10 a.m. to 6 p.m. (call to confirm and reserve a spot); outside of these months, trips can be scheduled if you call a few days in advance.

Other cool things to see and do

- ✔ **Climbing Mt. Errigal:** A climb up Donegal's highest peak rewards you with gorgeous views of the surrounding area. Call the **Glenveagh National Park Visitor Center (☎ 074-913-7090).**

- ✔ **Driving the Inishowen Peninsula:** It's wild and woolly country up here, with lonely mountains, windswept pastureland, and panoramic sea views. You need a good solid day (and a good map) to make the loop around the coast of the peninsula.

✔ **Grianan Ailigh:** History and myths surround this ancient stone ring fort. Some say that the fort belonged to Tuatha de Danaan, a mythical group, heavily linked with magic, who are said to have occupied Ireland before the Celts. It's located off the N13, northeast from Letterkenny, or west from Derry, in Burt, Inishowen. Allow 20 minutes for your visit.

Shopping

At **Donegal Craft Village,** on the Ballyshannon-Sligo Road in Donegal Town (☎ 074-972-2225), a collective of artisans create and sell a range of crafts: glass, jewelry, paintings, weavings, batik, and more. There's an excellent cafe here called **Aroma Cafe. Magee of Donegal,** on the Diamond in Donegal Town (☎ 074-972-2660), is the best source for famous Donegal tweed.

Cyndi Graham, whose studio is located near the Castlemurray House Hotel, St. John's Point, off the N56 outside of Dunkineely (☎ 074-973-7072), hand-weaves all sorts of items featuring colors inspired by the surrounding land and sea.

Hitting the Pubs

Bonner's Corner Bar
Ballybofey

If you're hankering for a pint and some conversation, go to Corner, with its warm and comfortable brick interior. This is a no-nonsense Irish pub, where you can find plenty of friendly locals engaged in lively chats.
Main Street at Glenfinn Street. ☎ 074-913-1361.

Nancy's
Ardara

Hobbits would feel right at home at Nancy's, a warren of cozy, warmly lit rooms that are packed to the gills with knickknacks; copper kettles and pots; and an eclectic assortment of tables, benches, stools, and chairs (my favorite being the old sewing-machine table). Pub ownership has passed through seven generations of the same family, and the crowd is always a jovial, talkative mix of locals and visitors. Excellent seafood is served here, including oysters, crab claws in garlic butter, and Charlie's Supper, a dish of shrimp and smoked salmon in a chili, garlic, and lemon sauce.
Front Street, Ardara. ☎ 074-954-1187.

Fast Facts: County Donegal

Area Codes

Area codes (or city codes) are **071** and **074**.

Emergencies/Police

Dial ☎ **999** for all emergencies.

Genealogy Resources

Contact Donegal Ancestry, The Quay, Ramelton, Letterkenny (☎ 074-915-1266; www.donegalancestry.com).

Hospital

Donegal Community Hospital is on Ballybofey Road (☎ 074-972-1019).

Information

For visitor information, go to the Letterkenny Tourist Office, on Neal T. Blaney Road in Letterkenny (☎ 074-912-1160; www.discoverireland.ie/northwest).

Internet

There is an Internet cafe over the Blueberry Tearoom, Castle Street, Donegal Town (☎ 074-972-2933).

Post Office

There are post offices in most town and villages. In Donegal Town, the main post office is on Tirconaill Street (☎ 074-973-1030).

Part VI
Northern Ireland

The 5th Wave **By Rich Tennant**

In this part . . .

Northern Ireland has as much splendor and beauty as the Republic with a fraction of the visitors, making it an excellent choice for travelers who don't like crowds. The green folds of the Mourne Mountains (Chapter 23) beg to be hiked, and travelers from all over the world come to clamber over the strange six-sided columns of basalt at the Giant's Causeway (Chapter 22). The North Antrim coast (Chapter 22) is a dramatic landscape of cliffs, beaches, and sea. Farther south, County Fermanagh (Chapter 21) boasts two giant lakes with many islands.

In addition to natural beauty, Northern Ireland offers two exciting cities: Belfast (Chapter 22) and Derry (Chapter 21). Belfast has a great arts scene (including first-rate traditional music), a bunch of excellent restaurants, a terrific museum, and some lovely Victorian architecture. Being a university town, Belfast also has no lack of places to party, from old-world pubs to trendy clubs. After many years of relentless political strife, Derry is emerging as a city with a lot to offer, including many historical sights, a burgeoning nightlife scene, and a growing calendar of arts events.

Chapter 21

Counties Derry, Fermanagh, and Tyrone

● ●

In This Chapter

▶ Exploring Derry's walls and the Bogside Murals
▶ Living in 19th-century Ireland and America: The Ulster American Folk Park
▶ Touring the Marble Arch Caves
▶ Hiking and strolling through woodlands at Florence Court

● ●

*T*hese three counties offer diverse attractions, a rolling landscape filled with lakes, and a warm welcome. This is an ideal place for those who have seen some of the major attractions of the North and the Republic and want to have a leisurely, relaxing vacation without crowds.

It's a very exciting time to be in Derry/Londonderry City, as the city is experiencing a rebirth after the Troubles. In fact, the city was named the European Capital of Culture for 2013. You'll find many historical sights, excellent historical museums, great pubs, and an up-and-coming arts scene. The pretty county of Tyrone, with its farmlands, cottages, and the gentle Sperrin Mountains, is known mainly for the excellent Ulster American Folk Park. County Fermanagh offers a huge and peaceful lake with 154 islands, several manor houses with beautiful grounds, and the bustling little town of Enniskillen.

For an update on safety and the political situation in Northern Ireland, see the introduction to Chapter 22.

Getting to Counties Derry, Fermanagh, and Tyrone

The **City of Derry (Eglinton) Airport** (☎ **028-7181-0784;** www. cityofderryairport.com) is 12km (7 miles) from the city and served by **Aer Arann** (☎ **1-818-210-210** in Ireland ☎ 0870-876-7676 in the U.K.; www.aerarann.com) and **Ryanair** (☎ **0818-303-030** in Ireland, 0871-246-0000 in the U.K.; www.ryanair.com). The easiest way to get to Derry from the airport is to take a cab. The fare is £12 to the city center.

To get to Derry by car from Donegal, take the N15 to Strabane, and then take the A5 north. To get to Enniskillen from Sligo, take the N16 (which becomes the A4 in Northern Ireland) east. To get to Omagh from Derry or Strabane, go south on the A5; from Enniskillen, go north on the A32. If you rented your car in the Republic, check with your rental company to make sure that you don't need extra insurance to drive into Northern Ireland.

Northern Ireland Railways (☎ **028-9066-6630;** www.nirailways. co.uk) services Derry year-round, and **Ulsterbus** (☎ **028-9066-6630;** www.ulsterbus.co.uk) travels year-round to Derry, Omagh, Enniskillen, and other major towns in counties Derry, Tyrone, and Fermanagh.

County Derry

Inhabited since the sixth century, **Derry/Londonderry City** is one of the oldest cities in Ireland. This small, walled city has seen its share of turmoil and heartbreak, from the siege led by Catholic King James's army in 1688, to the many Irish emigrants who set out from Derry for America in the 18th and 19th centuries, to the horrors and violence of the Troubles in the 20th century. Things have been basically peaceful in Derry for a while now, though 2009 and 2010 saw a surge of political violence. The city is a fun and vibrant place on its way up, with strong nightlife, a thriving cultural scene, and many restored historical sights and well-done museums.

Spending the night in County Derry

The "Derry/Londonderry City" map can help you locate accommodations and attractions. Be aware that there are not as many accommodations in Derry/Londonderry City as there are in cities in the South, so be sure to book in advance if possible.

Abbey Bed & Breakfast
$ **Derry/Londonderry City**

The Abbey feels like your own comfortable home in Derry City. Your hosts are friendly and helpful, and the rooms are decorated in a warm, contemporary fashion, with cute touches such as a beautiful vase in one room and funky striped comforters in another. You'll be right in the Bogside neighborhood, near the walls and near Waterloo Street, one of Derry's best pub streets (though the house remains blissfully quiet).

4 Abbey St. ☎ **028-7127-9000.** *www.abbeyaccommodation.com. Parking: Free in nearby public lot. Rack rates: £60 double. AE, MC, V.*

Counties Derry, Fermanagh, and Tyrone

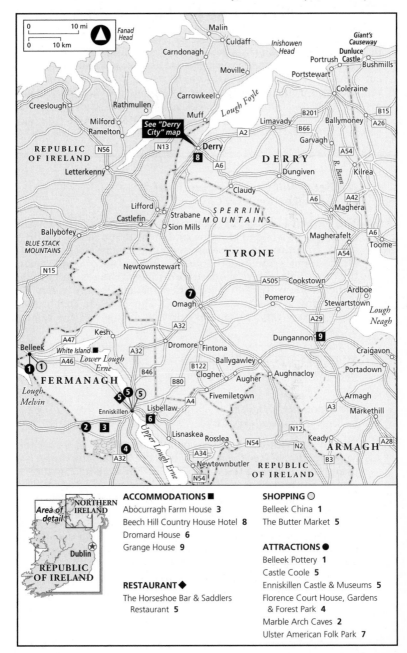

ACCOMMODATIONS ■
Abocurragh Farm House **3**
Beech Hill Country House Hotel **8**
Dromard House **6**
Grange House **9**

RESTAURANT ◆
The Horseshoe Bar & Saddlers
  Restaurant **5**

SHOPPING ○
Belleek China **1**
The Butter Market **5**

ATTRACTIONS ●
Belleek Pottery **1**
Castle Coole **5**
Enniskillen Castle & Museums **5**
Florence Court House, Gardens
  & Forest Park **4**
Marble Arch Caves **2**
Ulster American Folk Park **7**

Derry or Londonderry?

The name used for the city tends to depend on where the speaker stands politically. Unionists (who want to remain under the English crown) call it Londonderry, while Nationalists (who want to become part of the Republic of Ireland) call it Derry. You'll notice that Derry is usually the name used for the city in the Republic of Ireland, while Londonderry is more commonly used in Northern Ireland. Newscasters often try to avoid trouble by calling the city "Derry/Londonderry" (said as "Derry-stroke-Londonderry" since the slash sign is known as a "stroke" here). Gerry Anderson, a popular TV and radio broadcaster, has taken to calling the city "Stroke City."

The Beech Hill Country House Hotel
$$ **Derry/Londonderry City**

This elegant 1729 country house is the perfect place for relaxation. Stroll the gorgeous wooded grounds, and then curl up before the fire with a cup of tea. Or hit the sauna, steam room, or Jacuzzi after working out in the fitness room. About half of the 28 rooms are decorated in Georgian style; the other half feature modern furnishings. The restaurant offers terrific dishes made with fresh ingredients including locally caught seafood and home-grown seasonal vegetables. The hotel is just outside Derry/Londonderry City, within easy driving distance of the region's biggest attractions.

32 Ardmore Rd. Take the A6 south out of the city toward Belfast and follow the signs. ☎ **028-7134-9279.** *Fax: 028-7134-5366.* www.beech-hill.com. *Parking: Free on-site. Rack rates: £85–£115 double. MC, V.*

The Merchant's House
$ **Derry/Londonderry City**

Owned and run by the same people who do such a fine job with the Saddler's House (see the next review), the Merchant's House is an elegant, beautifully restored Georgian B&B within walking distance of the city center. The home has high ceilings and intricate plasterwork, and the bedrooms are spacious and painted in warm, vivid colors. Flames in the fireplace flicker on the walls of the comfortable parlor. Having breakfast in the polished Georgian dining room, you may think you've slipped back in time. Your hosts are incredibly knowledgeable about the city and can help you plan an itinerary that will suit your needs and interests.

16 Queen St. ☎ **028-7126-9691.** *Fax: 028-7126-6913.* www.thesaddlershouse.com. *Parking: Free on-site. Rack rates: £50–55 double. MC, V.*

Derry/Londonderry City

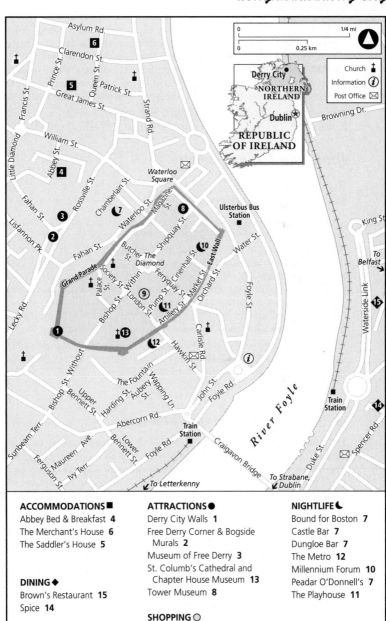

ACCOMMODATIONS ■
Abbey Bed & Breakfast **4**
The Merchant's House **6**
The Saddler's House **5**

DINING ◆
Brown's Restaurant **15**
Spice **14**

ATTRACTIONS ●
Derry City Walls **1**
Free Derry Corner & Bogside
  Murals **2**
Museum of Free Derry **3**
St. Columb's Cathedral and
  Chapter House Museum **13**
Tower Museum **8**

SHOPPING ○
Austins **9**

NIGHTLIFE ☾
Bound for Boston **7**
Castle Bar **7**
Dungloe Bar **7**
The Metro **12**
Millennium Forum **10**
Peadar O'Donnell's **7**
The Playhouse **11**

The Saddler's House
$ Derry City

You'll feel right at home in this cozy Victorian B&B, with its guest common room, selection of books in each bedroom, and tasty breakfasts served in a light-flooded space. Rooms aren't huge, but they're certainly big enough to move around in and charmingly furnished in a way that makes them seem more like rooms in someone's home than rooms in a guest lodging. The location is terrific, within a ten-minute walk of the heart of the city.

36 Great James St. ☎ *028-7126-9691. Fax: 028-7126-6913.* www.thesaddlers house.com. *Parking: Free on-site. Rack rates: £45–£55 double. MC, V.*

Dining in County Derry

Brown's Restaurant
$$$ Derry/Londonderry City   NEW IRISH

This sleek, modern restaurant, decorated with neutral colors, zebra-print curtains, and Art Deco touches, serves some of the best cuisine in these parts, made with the freshest locally sourced ingredients. Groups of friends and couples come to feast on dishes such as grilled Toulouse sausages with baked borlotti beans, olive oil mash, and aged balsamic vinegar, and local chicken with sautéed spring vegetables and a pea-and-mint purée. The menu changes frequently, so you never know what kind of delicious new offerings you'll find. A great early-bird menu is available Tuesday through Friday between 6 p.m. and 7:30 p.m.

1 Bond's Hill, Waterside (right off the A5 on the east side of the river, across from the old station). ☎ *028-7134-5180. Main courses: £12–£21. MC, V. Open: Tues–Fri noon to 2:30 p.m. and 5:30–10:30 p.m., Sat 5:30–10:30 p.m.*

Spice
$$ Derry/Londonderry City   NEW IRISH

This well-named restaurant seamlessly weaves flavors from around the world into dishes made with the best in Irish meats, fish, and vegetables. The five-spice and coriander lamb shank has a great depth of flavor, and the Thai mashed potatoes, laced with cilantro and coconut milk, make an addictive side dish. There are a few straightforward options as well, including a warm chicken Caesar salad and a sautéed salmon dish. The atmosphere is elegant and unpretentious, and the service is excellent. Couples and groups of friends relax in the dusky-purple room, which is graced with contemporary art and oversize vases of dried flowers. If it's on the menu, the Malteser Hot Toffee Meringue is a must-try mess of sugary goodness!

162 Spencer Rd., Waterside (on the east side of the river). ☎ *028-7134-4875. Main courses: £10–£15 (more for steak). Open: Mon–Sat 12:30–10 p.m., Sun 5–9 p.m.*

Digging into an Ulster Fry

What's the difference between a traditional Irish breakfast in the Republic and an Ulster Fry? Well, along with your fried egg, sausage, bacon, black pudding, fried tomatoes, and toast, you often get *soda farls* and *potato cakes*. Soda farls are pieces of soft bread, fluffed with soda and buttermilk; potato cakes are made with mashed potatoes, flour, and butter. They're both fried up with the rest of the breakfast and are delicious.

Exploring County Derry

Most of the attractions to be seen in County Derry are in the walled **Derry/Londonderry City.** A walking tour is the best way to get to know the city and its complicated background. In my opinion, the best tour of the city walls and the Bogside Murals is offered by **Derry City Tours** (☎ **027-7127-1996** or 0771-293-7997; try to get Martin as your guide). Tours leave at 10 a.m., noon, and 2 p.m. every day from the Tourist Information Centre, 44 Foyle St. (☎ **028-7126-7284**); they cost £4. The Tourist Information Centre is a great place to find out the city's frequent events and festivals.

Derry City Walls
Derry/Londonderry City

Derry is one of the few European cities that still has intact city walls. The walls, 7.9m (26 ft.) high and about 9.1m (30 ft.) thick, were built in 1618 and succeeded in keeping Derry safe from many attacks. In fact, the walls have never been breached, earning Derry the cheeky nickname "The Maiden City." I highly recommend walking the city walls. You can walk the parapet on your own (a few staircases at different points along the walls take you to the top), or you can take one of the excellent tours described in the introduction to this section.

Free Derry Corner and the Bogside Murals
Derry/Londonderry City

Bogside is one of the Catholic neighborhoods in Derry that has seen the worst of the Catholic–Protestant conflict. In 1969, a local man painted the words *You are now entering Free Derry* on a wall at the corner of Fahan and Rossville streets. This act and the slogan became a symbol of resistance to British Rule. The Bogside Murals were created by a collective of three artists who began working together in 1993. These murals depict events in Derry/Londonderry since 1968, and include, among others, a mural of Annette McGavigan, the first child victim of the Troubles; a mural of a young petrol bomber; and mural depicting the events of Bloody Sunday, when 13 civil-rights marchers were shot by British soldiers. The best way to see the murals is with the artists who painted them. Tom Kelly, William

Kelly, and Kevin Hasson lead tours of and presentations about the murals from their studio/gallery, the Peoples Gallery. Allow an hour to an hour and a half for your visit.

Bogside area. The artists give tours of the murals from the Peoples Gallery, 46 William St., where presentations on the murals are given daily. Admission: Peoples Gallery free. Tours: €10. Open: Peoples Gallery daily 10 a.m.–5 p.m. (presentations given hourly). Tours: Daily 11 a.m., 2 and 4 p.m. Call ☎ 028-7137-3842 to reserve a spot on the tour.

Museum of Free Derry
Derry/Londonderry City

This is required visiting for anyone who wants to understand the Troubles. Posters, photographs, and other objects from the Derry civil-rights movement of the '60s and the early Troubles era in the '70s are on view, and the staff is incredibly knowledgeable.

55 Glenfada Park, off Rossville Street. ☎ 028-7136-0880. Admission: £3 adults; £2 seniors, students, and kids. Open: Oct–May Mon–Fri 9:30 a.m.–4:30 p.m.; Apr–June Mon–Fri 9:30 a.m.–4:30 p.m., Sat 1–4 p.m.; July–Sept Mon–Fri 9:30 a.m.–4:30 p.m., Sat–Sun 1–4 p.m.

St. Columb's Cathedral and Chapter House Museum
Derry/Londonderry City

This Gothic Anglican cathedral — named for St. Columb, founder of Derry — towers above the city walls. It houses many memorials and relics from the 1688–1689 siege of Derry, when the city's Protestant population held out against the forces of Catholic King James II for 105 days, helping secure the throne for Protestant King William III. Points of interest include stained glass that tells the story of the siege, and the tremendous mortar ball that King James fired over the city walls, embedded with a note asking the people of Derry to surrender (they refused). The little Chapter House Museum at the back of the cathedral displays artifacts of the city's history, including the original keys to the city gates, and shows an audiovisual presentation relating the history of the city. Allow 45 minutes for your visit.

London Street. ☎ 028-7126-7313. Admission: £2. Open: Apr–Sept daily 9 a.m.–5 p.m., Oct–Mar daily 9 a.m.–1 p.m. and 2–4 p.m.

A story of hope

For many years, the mural depicting Annette McGavigan, the first child victim of the Troubles, had a black-and-white butterfly representing the unsure future of the peace process. In the summer of 2006, the artists decided to add vivid colors to the butterfly to symbolize their confidence in the continuing success of the process and their delight in the city's revitalization.

Tower Museum
Derry/Londonderry City

This well-done museum really gets at the heart of Derry history, covering events and daily life from prehistoric times to the present day. In the Story of Derry exhibit, you'll find everything from Stone Age tools recovered in the area to a life-size diorama of a woman creating shirt collars — a task that kept many families financially afloat during the early 20th century. The museum has added an excellent exhibit focused on artifacts recovered from a Spanish Armada ship that wrecked nearby. Part of a cittern, olive oil jugs, and ship fittings are just some of the objects that you'll find in the display. The museum is housed in the O'Doherty Tower, a replica of the 16th-century medieval fort that stood on this spot. Allow an hour for your visit.

Union Hall Place. ☎ **028-7137-2411.** *Admission: £4 adults; £2.50 seniors, students, and kids. Open: July–Aug Mon–Sat 10 a.m.–5 p.m. (last admission 4:30 p.m.), Sept–June Tues–Sat 10 a.m.–4:30 p.m.*

Shopping in Derry/Londonderry City

The Victorian-era department store **Austins,** The Diamond (☎ **028-7126-1817**), is a city landmark, specializing in clothes, perfume, china, crystal, and linens. The cafe on the third floor has a great view of the city.

Nightlife in Derry/Londonderry City

The Playhouse, 5–7 Artillery St. (☎ **028-7126-8027;** www.derryplayhouse.co.uk), presents local, national, and international plays, music, and dance. The **Millennium Forum,** Newmarket Street (☎ **028-7126-4455;** www.millenniumforum.co.uk), offers a program of plays, dance, and musicals, including children's shows.

Hitting the pubs

Want to hear traditional Irish music in Derry/Londonderry? Head to **Waterloo Street,** just outside the city walls in front of Butcher and Castle Gates. Some of the best pubs for informal sessions lie along this route. In particular, the **Dungloe Bar** (☎ **028-7126-7716**), **Bound for Boston** (☎ **028-7127-1315**), **Castle Bar** (☎ **028-7126-6018**), and **Peadar O'Donnell's and The Gweedore Bar** (☎ **028-7137-2138**) are great places to have a pint. As in other large cities, take a cab back to your B&B or hotel after dark, especially after the pubs close.

The Metro
Derry/Londonderry City

Plenty of little alcoves and mementos from across the globe make the Metro an interesting stop. The pub sits in the shadow of the old city walls and serves a mean beef Guinness stew.

3–4 Bank Place. ☎ **028-7126-7401.**

Counties Fermanagh and Tyrone

Island-studded **Lough Erne** (*lough* is pronounced lock) is the center-piece of County Fermanagh, serving as a destination for boaters and anglers, while County Tyrone is home to the gentle Sperrin Mountains and what is arguably Ireland's finest outdoor living museum.

Spending the night in Counties Fermanagh and Tyrone

Abocurragh Farm Guesthouse
$ **Letterbreen, Enniskillen, Fermanagh**

On my last visit to this welcoming country guesthouse, we stood outside in the dusk talking about international politics and conflicts with one of our hosts as he fixed his tractor. It was a peculiar feeling to be chatting about such things in this setting, which is incredibly peaceful. The house is located in the middle of the mountains on a working dairy farm. Rooms are bright and clean, combining contemporary pine furnishings with Victorian and country-style touches, and many have beautiful views of the house gardens and the mountains. Foodies will love the breakfast options, which range from cinnamon-flavored porridge with honey, cream, or Irish whiskey to oak-smoked salmon with scrambled eggs.

Letterbreen. Take the A4 out of Enniskillen through Letterbreen. Go 3.2km (2 miles) out of Letterbreen, and you'll see a sign on the left for the guesthouse; turn left. ☎ **028-6634-8484.** *www.abocurragh.com. Parking: Free on-site. Rack rates: £60–£65. MC, V.*

Dromard House
$ **Tamlaght, Enniskillen, County Fermanagh**

A warm welcome; a tranquil setting overlooking a valley with grazing cows; and sweet, simple, country-style rooms . . . what more could you want from a countryside bed-and-breakfast? Your friendly hosts, Sharon and Clive, can point you toward all the best attractions in the area, or you can just relax on the property, taking a walk through the woods, curling up on the giant porch swing overlooking the valley, and watching a movie in the cozy sitting room. Your hosts have kids of their own and are happy to accommodate families. The B&B is quite green: Clive is an organic farmer who has won awards for his sustainable practices, wood stoves provide hot water and heat in the house, and bicycle rental (with maps, helmets, and locks) is available for $5 a day.

Tamlaght. Take the A4 southeast from Enniskillen toward Tamlaght. ☎ **028-6638-7250.** *www.dromardhouse.com. Parking: Free on-site. Rack rates: £58 double. MC, V.*

Grange House
$$ **Dungannon, County Tyrone**

Oh, the porridge. Perhaps half the reason to stay at this grand former Quaker meetinghouse is the Bushmills porridge offered for breakfast. This heavenly concoction is made with Bushmills whiskey, heavy cream, and a topping of brown sugar. Delicious. The other reasons to stay here are not too shabby either: kind and professional hosts, beautiful grounds, the charming floral rooms (dolls and doilies abound), and the inn's proximity to the excellent Ulster American Folk Park.

7 Grange Rd. 1.6km (1 mile) from M1 Junction 15 on the A29 to Moy/Armagh. ☎ *028-8778-4212.* www.grangelodgecountryhouse.com. *Parking: Free on-site. Rack rates: £88 double. MC, V.*

Dining in Counties Fermanagh and Tyrone

The Horseshoe Pub, Saddlers Restaurant, and Saddlers Bistro & Wine Bar
$–$$$ Enniskillen, County Fermanagh   EUROPEAN

The Saddlers empire just keeps expanding, with the addition of a new wine bar to the offerings. The food is hearty, delicious, and varied at the restaurant, wine bar, and pub, but I recommend dining in the pub, which is a real locals' place, with groups of friends discussing the news, older men who seem to live on their bar stools, and kids running around. Horse lovers will delight at the equestrian décor. Steaks are the specialty at all the venues, and with good reason — their filet with garlic butter could give Peter Luger a run for its money, and the T-bone topped with sautéed onions is known far and wide. At the pub, you'll also find burgers, a mixed grill, fish and chips, salads, and more. The restaurant serves standards, as well as more adventurous dishes such as a pork filet pan-fried in cream sauce with peaches and caramelized apples, and monkfish with a vanilla dressing. The slick wine bar and bistro serves a menu that borrows from both the pub and the restaurant, with many appetizers that are great for a snack accompanying a glass of wine.

66 Belmore St. ☎ *028-6632-6223. Main courses: Pub £3.75–£12 (T-bone and mixed grill €16), restaurant and bistro/wine bar £11–£19. MC, V. Food served: Pub daily 11 a.m.–11 p.m.; wine bar/bistro and restaurant Mon–Sat 5–11 p.m., Sun 12:30–10 p.m.*

Exploring counties Fermanagh and Tyrone

Fermanagh is famous for long and narrow **Lough Erne.** For canoeing, sailing, and kayaking on the lake, contact **Share Village,** Castle Island, Enniskillen (☎ **028-6772-2122;** www.sharevillage.org). For guided fly-fishing on Lough Erne, contact **Erne Angling** (☎ **078-8447-2121**).

Erne Tours (☎ **028-6632-2882**) offers a two-hour boat tour of Lower Lough Erne River aboard the 56-seater *Kestrel.* The trip is fully narrated and covers a good deal of the nature and history of the lake. It includes a 45-minute stop at **Devenish Island,** where you can get off and explore monastic ruins dating to the sixth century, including a beautifully preserved round tower. Trips last about 1¾ hours and depart from Round "O" Jetty, at Brook Park in Enniskillen, signposted off A46. Tours operate daily in July and August at 10:30 a.m., 12:15 p.m., 2:15 p.m., and 4:15

p.m.; in June daily at 2:15 p.m. and 4:15 p.m.; and in May, September, and October Tuesday, Saturday, and Sunday at 2:15 p.m. and 4:15 p.m. Prices are £10 adults, £9 seniors, and £6 kids 9 and under.

Hikers will want to explore Florence Court Forest Park and the grounds at Castle Coole (described later in this chapter). For hikers and bicyclists who love solitude, the gentle **Sperrin Mountains** in County Tyrone are paradise. Contact **Sperrins Tourism (☎ 028-8674-7700**; www.sperrinstourism.com) for comprehensive information about the area.

Belleek Pottery Tours
Belleek, County Fermanagh

Belleek is Ireland's oldest and most famous pottery works. Though most Belleek is no longer produced here, you can still watch highly trained craftspeople create and decorate the famous thin bone china (30-minute guided tours are given every several times on weekdays) and explore a museum covering the history of Belleek pottery. If you want to take some pottery home with you, the showroom stocks the complete range of Belleek products. Allow an hour for your visit.

Main Street, Belleek. Take the A46 northeast from Enniskillen. ☎ **028-6865-9300.** *Admission: Free. Tours: £4 adults, £3 kids. Open: Visitor Center July–Oct Mon–Fri 9 a.m.–6 p.m., Sat 10 a.m.–6 p.m., Sun noon to 6 p.m.; Mar–June Mon–Fri 9 a.m.–5:30 p.m., Sat 10 a.m.–5:30 p.m., Sun 2–5:30 p.m.; Nov–Dec Mon–Fri 9 a.m.–5:30 p.m., Sat 10 a.m.–5:30 p.m.; Jan–Feb Mon–Fri 9 a.m.–5:30 p.m. Tours: Every half-hour Mon–Fri 9:30 a.m.–12:15 p.m. and 1:45–4 p.m. (last tour Fri 3 p.m.).*

Castle Coole
Enniskillen, County Fermanagh

This 18th-century neoclassical-style house was completely refurbished by the state and is open for guided tours. Most of the stone fittings and fixtures are from England, and, extraordinarily, almost all the original furniture is in place. The opulent State Bedroom has a bed that was specially made for King George IV to use during his 1821 visit to Ireland. Other highlights are a Chinese-style sitting room, the gorgeous woodwork and fireplaces throughout the house, and the servants' quarters downstairs. Save some time to explore the surrounding 600-hectare (1,500-acre) woodlands. The 1.6km (1-mile) looped Lake Walk is especially beautiful and offers chances to see all sorts of wildlife, from otters and badgers to shiny blue kingfishers. Keep an eye out for the current Earl of Belmore, who lives in the Garden House. Allow an hour for your visit.

Off the Belfast-Enniskillen road (A4) about 1.6km (1 mile) out of Enniskillen. ☎ **028-6632-2690.** *Admission: House £5.50 adults, £2.50 kids; grounds £3.50 per car. Open: House Mar–May and Sept Sat–Sun 11 a.m.–5 p.m. (daily Apr 2–11), June Fri–Wed 11 a.m.–5 p.m., July–Aug daily 11 a.m.–5 p.m. (last house admission always one hour before closing); grounds Mar–Oct daily 10 a.m.–7 p.m., Nov–Feb daily 10 a.m.–4 p.m.*

Enniskillen Castle Museums
Enniskillen, County Fermanagh

This 15th-century castle, once the stronghold of powerful Irish chieftains, sits majestically in the west end of town, overlooking the River Erne. The castle contains a county museum with exhibits on the area's history, wildlife, landscape, and crafts, including pieces from the nearby Belleek pottery factory. A smaller museum uses uniforms, weapons, and medals to relate the story of the Royal Inniskilling Fusiliers — a town militia that fought against James II in 1688. Allow 90 minutes for your visit.

At the west end of town, on Wellington Road. ☎ *028-6632-5000.* www.enniskillen castle.co.uk. *Admission: £3.50 adults; £2.50 seniors, students, and kids. Open: May–June and Sept Mon–Sat 2–5 p.m.; July–Aug Tues–Fri 10 a.m.–5 p.m., Sat–Mon 2–5 p.m.; Oct–Apr Mon 2–5 p.m., Tues–Fri 10 a.m.–5 p.m.*

Florence Court House, Gardens, and Forest Park
Enniskillen, County Fermanagh

Fans of Georgian houses will want to make a stop at Florence Court House, which was built in the mid-18th century for the lord of this area. Highlights include the rococo plasterwork in the dining room, the many family heirlooms and portraits, and the majestic staircase. You can see the house by guided tour only.

The extensive grounds are a gorgeous place for a hike, with marked trails through a contrasting collection of landscapes, from open mountain to bogland to forest to old estate woodland. Trails range from an easy stroll through the woods to an 8km (5-mile) forest trek. All the trails are accessible from the information booth next to the parking lots. A lovely tearoom is open for refreshments after your hike. Allow about an hour to see the house, longer if you want to explore the grounds.

Signposted off the A32, about 13km (8 miles) south of Enniskillen. ☎ *028-6634-8249. Admission: House tour £5 adults, £2 kids; grounds £3.25 adults, €1.75 kids, €7.75 families. Open: House mid-Mar to Apr and Oct 11 a.m.–5 p.m. (daily Apr 2–11), May–June and Sept Wed–Mon 11 a.m.–5 p.m., July–Aug daily 11 a.m.–5 p.m. (last tour is always one hour before closing); grounds Mar–Oct daily 10 a.m.–7 p.m., Nov–Feb daily 10 a.m.–4 p.m.*

Marble Arch Caves
Florencecourt, County Fermanagh

Exploring the UNESCO-recognized Marble Arch Caves is like traveling to another world. Guides lead you on foot through the winding passages and echoing chambers of the caves, pointing out stalactites, stalagmites, curtains, and all sorts of other mineral formations, and offering detailed information on the natural history of the caves. For much of the way, you'll follow the bends of an underground river; my favorite part of the tour is seeing a collection of stalactites reflected perfectly in the still water below like a lost city. The short boat ride at the beginning of the tour is another highlight, as you glide silently through some of the smaller chambers.

The Marble Arch Caves are very popular, so it's wise to book ahead. Also, it gets pretty chilly down under, so bring a sweater. If there's been heavy rain, the caves occasionally close for safety reasons, so call if there's been bad weather. Finally, it's important to wear comfortable shoes and to be in decent shape — you'll be walking and climbing stairs for the bulk of the tour. Allow 75 minutes for the tour, two hours total if you're interested in the exhibit and audiovisual presentation as well.

Marlbank Scenic Loop. Off the A35, 19km (12 miles) south of Enniskillen. When you're in the village of Florencecourt, near the border of Northern Ireland and the Republic, there is a loop road that takes you out to the caves, with plenty of signs to point the way. ☎ **028-6634-8855.** www.marblearchcaves.net. *Admission: £8 adults, £5.25 seniors and students, £5 kids 17 and under. Open: Mid-Mar to June and Sept daily 10 a.m.–6 p.m. (last tour leaves at 4:30 p.m.), July–Aug daily 10 a.m.–6:30 p.m. (last tour leaves at 5 p.m.).*

Ulster American Folk Park
Castletown, County Tyrone

This immensely interesting and engaging outdoor museum covers 40 acres and features actual rebuilt 18th- and 19th-century buildings from Ireland and America, from a Pennsylvania log farmhouse to an Irish-Catholic mass house (a home used as a church). You begin your tour in Ireland, and then stroll through a re-created 19th-century Irish street to board a replica of a 19th-century ship bound for America. When you exit, you're in the America of the 18th and 19th centuries. You can interact with the costumed interpreters stationed throughout the park, who illustrate and explain life during these times. You'll be offered snacks made from old recipes, get a scolding if you slouch at your desk in the schoolhouse, learn traditional crafts, and get a chance to buy sweets at a late-1800s shop. If you're not getting a chance to interact with the interpreters as much as you'd like, I recommend tagging along behind a school group to watch the interpreters in action. Though the park attracts families, groups of adults tend to love it, too.

The Folk Park has an excellent lineup of events, including American Independence Day celebrations in July, an Appalachian and Bluegrass music festival in September, and a Halloween Festival in October. Allow at least three hours for your visit — there's a lot to see, and the park is large.

Mellon Road. Off the A5, 4.7km (3 miles) north of Omagh. Look for the signs. ☎ **028-8224-3292.** www.nmni.com. *Admission: £6.50 adults; £4 seniors, students, and kids; free for kids 4 and under. Open: Mar–Sept Tues–Sun 10 a.m.–5 p.m.; Oct–Feb Tues–Fri 10 a.m.–4 p.m., Sat–Sun 11 a.m.–4 p.m.*

Shopping in County Fermanagh

The **Butter Market,** Down Street, Enniskillen (☎ **028-6632-3837**), has studio workshops where local craftspeople make and sell all sorts of art, including pottery, jewelry, photography, and more.

Fast Facts: Counties Derry, Fermanagh, and Tyrone

Area Code

The area code (or city code) for Derry, Fermanagh, and Tyrone is **028.**

Emergencies/Police

Dial ☎ **999** for all emergencies.

Genealogy Resources

In County Derry, contact the Genealogy Centre, Harbour Musuem, Harbour Square, Derry City (☎ 028-7137-7331). For counties Tyrone and Fermanagh, contact Heritage World, 26 Market Sq., Dungannon, County Tyrone (☎ 028-8772-4187).

Hospital

Altnagelvin Hospital (☎ 028-7134-5171) is on Glenshane Road in Derry.

Information

In Derry, go to the tourist office at 44 Foyle St. (☎ 028-7137-7577); it's open year-round. In County Tyrone, contact the Omagh Tourist Information Centre at Strule Arts Centre, Townhall Square, Omagh (☎ 028-8224-7831). The Fermanagh Tourist Information Centre is located on Wellington Road in Enniskillen (☎ 028-6632-3110).

Chapter 22

Belfast and County Antrim

In This Chapter

▶ Exploring the Belfast's Botanical Gardens

▶ Experiencing Belfast's many Victorian-era pubs

▶ Clambering around on the amazing Giant's Causeway

▶ Bringing out your inner adventurer on a rope bridge

*Y*ou get the best of both worlds in this county: Belfast is a dynamic city, where great restaurants, accommodations, arts venues, pubs, and clubs occupy beautiful Victorian and Edwardian buildings. Outside of the city, you get the stunning cliffs and glens of the North Antrim and the extraordinary hexagonal basalt columns of the Giant's Causeway.

A word about safety: Instances of political violence in Northern Ireland have decreased from the height of the Troubles. However, there are still flare-ups from time to time, and the summer of 2010 saw an increase in violent incidents. Although it would be a shame to miss the beauty and people of Northern Ireland, it is important to be aware of the situation. Check for alerts and warnings on travel to Northern Ireland at the Department of State's Web site (http://travel.state.gov), and keep alert in larger towns and cities. Do not initiate or engage in conversations about Northern Irish politics. Until the situation is solidly peaceful, I advise against coming to Northern Ireland during the days surrounding July 12, when Unionist associations hold their parades and violence tends to flare up. See Chapter 2 for information about the political situation in Northern Ireland, past and present.

Belfast and the Surrounding Area

Belfast is a hopping city, full of university students and, thus, full of hot restaurants and hotels and even hotter clubs and bars. Belfast is also a beautiful city, with many lovely examples of Victorian and Edwardian architecture. Top attractions include a Victorian-era botanical garden, one of the best indoor markets in Ireland, an eclectic museum, tours of the area where the *Titanic* was built, and the rich art and music scenes. The city is in the midst of revitalizing its waterfront for the celebration of the centenary of *Titanic*'s completion, so look out for all sorts of new attractions in that area beginning in the summer of 2012.

County Antrim

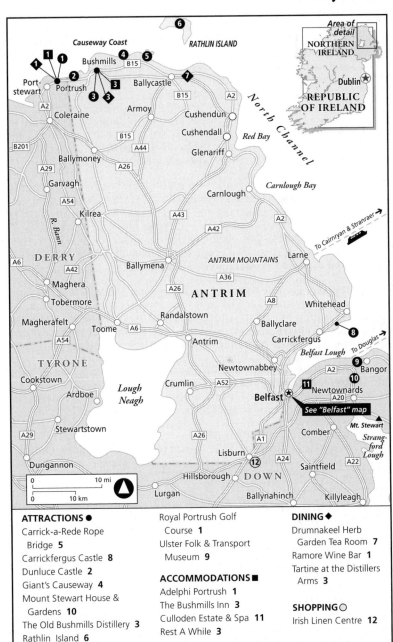

Causeway Coast

RATHLIN ISLAND

Bushmills

Port-
stewart   Portrush

Ballycastle

Armoy   Cushendun

Coleraine   Cushendall   *Red Bay*

Glenariff

Ballymoney

Garvagh   *Carnlough Bay*

Carnlough

Kilrea

R. Bann

North Channel

To Cairnryan & Stranraer →

DERRY   Larne

Ballymena   ANTRIM MOUNTAINS

Maghera

Tobermore   **ANTRIM**   Whitehead

Magherafelt   Randalstown

Toome   Ballyclare

Antrim   Carrickfergus

TYRONE   Newtownabbey   To Douglas →

Cookstown   *Belfast Lough*   Bangor

Ardboe   *Lough*   Crumlin   **Belfast**   Newtownards
        Neagh   See "Belfast" map

Stewartstown   Comber   *Mt. Stewart*
                        *Strang-
                        ford
                        Lough*

Dungannon   Lisburn

Hillsborough   **DOWN**   Saintfield

Lurgan   Ballynahinch   Killyleagh

0   10 mi
0   10 km

*Area of
detail*
NORTHERN
IRELAND

Dublin ★
REPUBLIC
OF IRELAND

ATTRACTIONS ●
Carrick-a-Rede Rope
 Bridge **5**
Carrickfergus Castle **8**
Dunluce Castle **2**
Giant's Causeway **4**
Mount Stewart House &
 Gardens **10**
The Old Bushmills Distillery **3**
Rathlin Island **6**

Royal Portrush Golf
 Course **1**
Ulster Folk & Transport
 Museum **9**

ACCOMMODATIONS ■
Adelphi Portrush **1**
The Bushmills Inn **3**
Culloden Estate & Spa **11**
Rest A While **3**

DINING ◆
Drumnakeel Herb
 Garden Tea Room **7**
Ramore Wine Bar **1**
Tartine at the Distillers
 Arms **3**

SHOPPING ○
Irish Linen Centre **12**

Getting to Belfast and County Antrim

Continental, bmi, easyJet, and more airlines fly into **Belfast International Airport** (☎ 028-9448-4848; www.belfastairport.com), about 31km (19 miles) from Belfast. The **George Best Belfast City Airport** (☎ 028-9093-9093; www.belfastcityairport.com) handles flights within the U.K. and to and from the Republic. To get to the city center from Belfast International Airport, take the Airport Express Bus 300, which runs 24 hours a day and takes 30 to 40 minutes. The buses leave every 15 to 30 minutes during the day and every 40 to 60 minutes all night. The fare is £7 one-way, £10 round-trip. Taxis are also available and rates are posted in the airport. From Belfast City Airport, take a cab (the fare should be about £8), or the Airport Express 600, which departs every 20 minutes between 5:30 a.m. and 10 p.m. and costs £2 one-way or £3 round-trip.

If you're coming to Belfast from Britain or Scotland, consider the ferry. **Norfolk Line Irish Sea Ferries** (☎ 0871-230-0330 in Britain, or ☎ 01-819-2999 in the Republic; www.norfolkline-ferries.co.uk) takes eight hours from Liverpool to Belfast. **Stena Line** (☎ 44-8448-758-759 in Britain, 44-8445-768-768 in Northern Ireland, 01-204-7777 in the Republic; www.stenaline.com) runs ferries from Stranraer, Scotland, to Belfast that make the crossing in two hours.

If you're coming by car from Dublin, take the M1 (which becomes the A1) north to Belfast. To get to the Antrim Coast from Belfast, take the A2, which runs along the entire coast. If you're driving from the Republic into Northern Ireland, make sure you notify your rental-car company, because extra insurance is occasionally required.

Irish Rail (☎ 1-850-366-222; www.irishrail.ie) and **Northern Ireland Railway** (☎ 888-274-8724 or 028-9066-6630; www.nirailways.co.uk) trains travel from Dublin's Connolly Station to Belfast's Central Station daily and connect many towns in Northern Ireland.

Ulsterbus (☎ 028-9066-6630; www.translink.co.uk) runs buses to and from towns all over Northern Ireland, including Belfast, Larne, Ballycastle, Bushmills, and several other towns. Ulsterbus also provides service between Belfast and Dublin.

Getting around Belfast and the surrounding area

You can easily navigate much of central Belfast on foot. For longer journeys, a bus service, called **Metro** (☎ 028-9066-6630; www.translink.co.uk/Metro.asp), provides service throughout the city. Most of the Metro bus routes make a stop at Donegall Square, in the city center. If you know that you want to use the bus several times in one day, go for the Metro Day ticket, available from all Metro drivers. If you'll be in Belfast for several days, consider purchasing a Smartlink card; you can buy one that allows unlimited travel for a week, or one that provides a discount when you pay for several journeys in advance. Smartlink cards are available at local shops (look for the smartlink sign) and at the

Metro kiosk in Donegall Square. See "Exploring Belfast and the surrounding area," later in this chapter, for information on bus tours in Belfast.

You also can get around Belfast and the area by bike. You can rent a bike at **McConvey Cycles,** 183 Ormeau Rd. (☎ **028-9033-0322;** www.rentabikebelfast.com). With your rental, you'll receive a free helmet and great information on touring the area.

If you need a cab, look for the **taxi ranks** at Central Station, both bus stations, and at City Hall. The metered cabs in Northern Ireland are standardized London-style black taxis with yellow discs on the windshield. I recommend that you take the standard cabs rather than nonmetered cabs. If you do take a nonmetered cab, ask for the price of the journey when you first enter the cab so that you don't get taken for a monetary ride in addition to a taxi ride. If you need a cab, try **Gransha Taxis** (☎ **028-9060-2092**).

Areas that have been hot spots for political violence are the Ardoyne and Shankill Road areas, northwest of the city center, and the Falls Road area, west of the city center. Depending on the political situation when you're in town, you may want to avoid these areas unless you're with a black taxi tour.

Spending the night in Belfast and the surrounding area

Benedicts of Belfast
$$ Belfast

I feel a little like an infomercial, telling you that Benedicts seems like it's "too good to be true." But it does. The hotel offers ridiculously reasonable rates given its central location, and the elegant, contemporary rooms, with their cloud-like beds, are kept in beautiful condition. The staff is friendly and helpful, and the classy bar and restaurant serve up excellent Continental fare in a lively atmosphere. And if you order now, they'll throw in a free set of steak knives! (No, not really.)

7–21 Bradbury Place, Shaftesbury Square, off the A1 (Great Victoria Street), at Donegal Road. ☎ *028-9059-1999. Fax: 028-9059-1990. www.benedictshotel.co.uk. Bus: 1, 29, 71, 83, or 84. Parking: In a nearby garage £7 for 24 hours. Rack rates: £80 double. AE, MC, V.*

Culloden Estate and Spa
$$$ Holywood, County Down

The Culloden, located near the Ulster Folk and Transport Museum, is a government-rated five-star hotel — and it deserves every point on those stars. A former 19th-century mansion, the hotel is surrounded by almost 5 hectares (12 acres) of beautiful, secluded gardens and the picturesque Holywood Hills. Bedrooms are elegantly decorated with modern

Belfast

NORTHERN IRELAND

Belfast

Dublin

REPUBLIC OF IRELAND

ACCOMMODATIONS ■
Benedicts of Belfast **24**
Europa Hotel **20**
Malmaison **9**
Premier Inn & Suites **22**
Ten Square **16**

DINING ◆
Benedicts of Belfast **24**
Cayenne **23**
The Ginger Bistro **21**
Marks & Spencer **11**
St. George's Market **13**
Zen **15**

ATTRACTIONS ●
Albert Memorial Clock **7**
Belfast Botanic Gardens **26**
City Hall **14**
Titanic Dock & Pump House **8**
Ulster Museum **27**
W5: Whowhatwhere-whenwhy **8**

SHOPPING ○
Smyth's Irish Linen **2**
spaceCRAFT **10**
St. George's Market **12**
The Steensons **17**

NIGHTLIFE ☾
Black Box **6**
Crown Liquor Saloon **19**
Duke of York **5**
The Garrick **12**
Grand Opera House **18**
The John Hewitt **4**
Kelly's Cellars **3**
Madison's Café Bar **25**
Madden's Bar **1**

† St. Anne's Cathedral

Smithfield Market

Castle Court Centre

Albert Square

Queen Elizabeth Bridge

Queen's Bridge

Botanic Rail Station

Shaftesbury Square

Queen's University

BOTANIC GARDENS

North of Ireland Sport Club

River Lagan

Church †
Information ⓘ

0   1/4 mi
0   0.25 km

furnishings, and the beds are legendary for their comfort. The public rooms are filled with stunning antiques, Louis XV chandeliers, and decorative plasterwork. A terrific spa offers all sorts of treatments. Service is impeccable. Would former British prime ministers Tony Blair and John Major have stayed here if it weren't?

Right off the A2 going toward Bangot, about 6 miles northeast of Belfast in County Down. ☎ **028-9042-1066.** *www.hastingshotels.com. Parking: Free on-site. Rack rates: £125–£175 double. AE, DC, MC, V.*

Europa Hotel
$$–$$$$ **Belfast**

You can't beat the location of the Europa: in the heart of Belfast, right next to the Grand Opera House and near the bustling Golden Mile, which is lined with historic buildings. Former President Bill Clinton apparently agrees, because this is where he decided to stay on two of his trips to Northern Ireland. The spacious rooms are immaculate. You'll find huge beds that invite sleeping in, lush fabrics, and sparkling chrome and glass bathrooms. The staff has an encyclopedic knowledge of Belfast, making this a great choice for a first-time visitor. Definitely book on the Web site, which offers deep discounts.

Great Victoria Street. From the M1 or M2 motorways, follow the Westlink and then take the Grovesnor Road exit. ☎ **028-9027-1066.** *www.hastingshotels.com. Bus: 82, 83, 84, 85, or Centrelink (100). Parking: In nearby parking garages about £14. Rack rates: £85–£210 double. AE, DC, MC, V.*

Killead Lodge
$ **Belfast**

Craving a country hideaway while you explore Belfast? Located about 20 minutes from the city center and right near Belfast International Airport, Killead Lodge could be summed up in a word: *cheerful*. Rooms, painted a warm honey yellow, feature comfortable beds and flat-screen TVs, and several cats frequent the back garden. Breakfast is ample and satisfying, and your hosts are willing to help with anything. If you stay here, definitely check out Spice, a very good Indian restaurant located nearby at 106 Ballyrobin Rd.

25 Killead Rd., Aldergrove, Crumlin. ☎ **028-9445-9896.** *www.killeadlodge.com. Parking: Free on-site. Rack rates: £60–£70 double. MC, V.*

Malmaison
$$–$$$ **Belfast**

This trendy, sophisticated lodging is the definition of a boutique hotel. It's housed in two converted 1867 grain warehouses that retain gorgeous architectural details, including old wood and steel beams, and it offers incredibly friendly, professional, and personal service. The theatrical rooms are outfitted in black, gold, and deep garnet hues and have an Asian feel. Staff wouldn't reveal their celebrity guests, but it seems like the type of place Madonna would visit. I could just picture her shooting pool on the purple pool table in the fabulous Samson suite, or snagging a lime from the artfully placed bowl near the elevators. The hotel is designed to anticipate every need, with height-of-comfort beds, speedy room service, minibars (rare in these parts), and power showers.

34–38 Victoria St. From the M3, take the Queen's Bridge across the river, and make a right onto Victoria Street. ☎ *028-9022-0200.* www.malmaison-belfast.com. *Bus: 8, 13, 13B, 21, 155, 160, 161, or Centrelink (100). Parking: In nearby parking garages about £20 per day. Rack rates: £85–£125 double. Some rates don't include breakfast. AE, DC, MC, V.*

Premier Inn & Suites
$ **Belfast**

Premier Inn is a great choice if you know that you're going to be out exploring a lot and just want a clean, reliable place to rest your head. This branch of a large U.K. hotel chain has a great location that's midway between central Belfast and the Botanic Avenue/Queens University area (where the botanical gardens, Ulster Museum, and several great restaurants are located). The young staff is incredibly helpful and friendly; I asked the front-desk clerk where I could find a Laundromat, and he offered to throw my clothes into one of the hotel's washing machines and then bring them up to me later that afternoon. Rooms can be on the small side but are comfortable, neat as a pin, and quiet. Family rooms are an amazing deal; they can accommodate two adults and two kids 14 and under and are currently only £60 without breakfast. My only complaint is the bizarre blueish lighting in the rooms, which made me feel a little bit like I was staying in a fish tank. There is a second Belfast branch at 2–6 Waring St.

Alfred Street. ☎ **0871-527-8000** *in the U.K., 044-158-256-7890 outside the U.K.* www.premierinn.com. *Parking: £14 for 24 hours on-site. Rack rates: £45–£65 double. Many rates do not include breakfast. AE, MC, V.*

Ten Square
$$$ **Belfast**

The designers of this Asian-style, minimalist hotel in central Belfast wouldn't know the meaning of the word *clutter*. Rooms are a study in simple elegance, with vases of fresh flowers and low beds covered with white comforters. The staff is friendly, warm, and well-versed in all that Belfast has to offer. You don't have to go far for nourishment; the hotel restaurant, The Grill, serves up good food.

10 Donegall Sq. S. ☎ **028-9024-1001.** *Fax: 028-9024-3210.* www.tensquare.co.uk. *Bus: 82, 83, 84, 85, or Centrelink (100). Parking: In a nearby public garage £12 for 24 hours. Rack rates: £140–£150 double. AE, MC, V.*

Dining in Belfast and the surrounding area

See also Benedicts of Belfast, mentioned in the previous section.

If you're in the city on a Friday, Saturday, or Sunday, eat your way through **St. George's Market,** an indoor market on East Bridge Street, between Victoria Street and Oxford Street. The market is huge and you'll find everything from excellent paella at the Lemon Tree Taperia booth to a dizzying array of amazing baked goods (I dream about the watermelon cupcakes I had there). The Friday market is open 6 a.m. until 2 p.m., the Saturday market is open 9 a.m. until 3 p.m., and the Sunday market is open 10 a.m. to 4 p.m.

For lunch on a nice day, grab a bite from **Marks & Spencer,** 48 Donegall Place, and join the rest of Belfast on the grass by City Hall.

For the best pub food in Belfast, check out **John Hewitt,** 51 Donegall St., and **The Garrick,** 29 Chichester St. Both of these pubs host excellent traditional Irish music sessions several times a week.

Cayenne
$$$ Belfast   FUSION/NEW IRISH

This wonderful restaurant was one of the first stars in Belfast's constellation of excellent fusion eateries. It's still going strong, serving dishes that combine ingredients in unexpectedly delicious ways, such as the appetizer of cinnamon quail with carrot, honey, and ginger salad. You can't go wrong with any of the main courses, from duck breast *au poivre* with roasted wild mushrooms, to lobster and monkfish in a Thai yellow curry with mango, basil, and rice noodles. Service is friendly and professional, and the crowd is always in high spirits.

7 Ascot House, Shaftesbury Square. ☎ *028-9033-1532. Reservations recommended. Bus: 1, 29, 71, 83, or 84. Main courses: £14–£23. AE, MC, V. Open: Mon–Wed and Sat 5–10 p.m., Thurs–Fri noon to 2:15 p.m. and 5–10 p.m., and Sun noon to 4 p.m. and 5–10 p.m.*

The Ginger Bistro
$$$ Belfast   NEW IRISH/FUSION

I've coined a new term expressly for this restaurant, and that is *mellegance,* an amalgam of *mellow* and *elegance* that perfectly describes the atmosphere here. The setting is a high-ceilinged room with exposed steel beams and pipes, warmly lit by Moroccan lanterns, Japanese paper lamps, and tea lights. Chef Simon McCance is a devotee of local ingredients, and he uses these fresh items in lovely dishes that are often accented by Indian and Asian spices, sauces, and cooking techniques. The short menu changes often and always features excellent vegetarian choices in addition to the meat and seafood options. On a recent visit, I had an appetizer of fried squid with homemade sweet chili dip, and a heavenly main course of tandoori monkfish served with mint and lime couscous, spicy tomato chutney, crispy onions, and garlic yogurt. The pre-theater menu, served Monday through Friday from 5 p.m. to 6:45 p.m., is a terrific deal. Service is relaxed and professional.

7–8 Hope St., off Great Victoria Street at the junction with Bruce Street. ☎ 02-9024-4421. Main courses: £14–£18 (steak £22). AE, MC, V. Open: Mon 5–9 p.m., Tues–Thurs noon to 3 p.m. and 5–9:30 p.m., Fri–Sat noon to 3 p.m. and 5–10 p.m.

Zen
$$–$$$ **Belfast** **JAPANESE/JAPANESE FUSION**

Calling all sushi-holics: This hip spot is the place to get your raw-fish-and-vinegared-rice fix in Belfast. Bartenders shake martinis behind the glass bar lit with blue lights, and club-gear-clad 20-somethings strut through the high-ceilinged, dramatic space, which is decorated with carved Japanese wooden screens, black lacquer tables, and a large shiny Buddha. I always order sushi here, but the menu also features an array of cooked Japanese dishes, from vegetable curry to chicken teriyaki to more adventurous options such as duck samosas.

If you're in the market for a less formal Japanese meal, check out buzzing **Sakura Sushi,** 62 Botanic Ave. (☎ **028-9043-9590**), which offers cooked entrees and an excellent, slightly spicy miso soup, in addition to a great "sushi train."

55–59 Adelaide St. ☎ 028-9023-2244. Bus: 58, 59, 69, 69A, 70, 71, 89, 90, 91, 92, 95, or Centrelink (100). Reservations recommended for dinner on weekends Main courses: £10–£20. MC, V. Open: Mon–Fri noon to 3 p.m. and 5–11:30 p.m., Sat 5:30 p.m.–1 a.m., Sun 1:30–10:30 p.m.

Exploring Belfast and the surrounding area

The **Belfast Welcome Centre**, 47 Donegall Place (☎ **028-9024-6609**) is worth a visit. This comprehensive tourist information office has great information on what's happening when you're in town and can book tickets for tours, events, and the like.

If you're in town Friday, Saturday, or Sunday, check out **St. George's Market**, indoors on East Bridge Street (see "Dining in Belfast and the surrounding areas" for more information).

City Sightseeing Belfast (☎ **028-9077-0900;** www.belfastcitysight seeing.com) operates hop-on/hop-off open-top bus tours of Belfast that stop at the city's top attractions (your ticket is good for 48 hours, so can hop off one bus and join another later at each attraction). Knowledgeable guides do an excellent job of explaining the city's history from the 18th century through the present day. Tours depart daily every hour from 10:30 a.m. until 4:30 p.m., so if you decide to get off the bus at an attraction, plan to pick up the next bus an hour later. All tours leave from Chichester Street at Victoria Square. Prices are £13 adults, £11 seniors and students, and £6 kids ages 4 to 12. You can buy tickets at city center hotels, at the Belfast Welcome Centre, and online. Discounts are available for online bookings.

Local experts lead two terrific 90-minute walking tours that depart from the Belfast Welcome Centre (the main tourist information office), at 47

Donegall Place. On the **Historic Belfast Walking Tour,** your guide will relate over 300 years of Belfast history as he or she takes you through the city, pointing out everything from *Titanic*-related sights to the extravagant Victorian city hall. The tour departs on Wednesdays, Fridays, and Sundays at 2 p.m. year-round. The **Blackstaff Way Tour** is an excellent introduction to the heart of Belfast, taking in most of the city's main streets. The tour departs at 11 a.m. every Saturday. Both tours fill up quickly, so book in advance through the Belfast Welcome Centre (☎ 028-9024-6609). Each of the tours costs £6.

Belfast Black Taxi Tours (☎ 028-9064-2264; www.belfasttours.com) offers the best look at the rocky history of the city, which saw much of the violence during the height of the Troubles in the '70s, '80s, and early '90s. Your guide will explain the ins and outs of the Troubles as you view the many political murals found in the hearts of the sectarian neighborhoods, including Protestant Shankill Road and Catholic Falls Road. Tours cost £25 for one or two passengers, £10 each for three or more passengers.

Don't miss touring the sights associated with the ***Titanic.*** Highlights include the immense dry dock where the finishing touches were put on the ship before her fateful journey, and the pump house, which pumped water out of the dry dock at lightning speeds (and where you'll have the chance to handle some of the tools used to build the *Titanic*). Access to the pump house is via guided tour only. You can take the entire 2½-hour Titanic Walking Tour, which introduces you to an array of sights associated with the birth of the *Titanic,* or you can join the tour for the last hour to visit the dry dock and pump house only.

Titanic Walking Tour tickets are available from the Belfast Welcome Centre, online at www.titanicwalk.com, or at the starting point of the tour. The longer tours depart from the **Odyssey Complex,** on Queen's Quay, daily at 11 a.m. and 2 p.m., and cost £12 adults and £11 seniors and students. If you'd like to join the tour for the last hour, meet at the **Pump House Café and Visitors Centre,** Queens Road (☎ 028-9033-0844) at 12:30 p.m. or 2 p.m. (plus 3:45 p.m. June–Aug). The hour-long portion of the tours costs £6 adults, £4 kids 5–16. The pump house is about a 40-minute walk from the city center; buses 26 and 26B provide service regularly from Donegal Square West (Belfast City Hall).

Finally, enjoy the best of Belfast's formidable collection of historical pubs on the **Belfast Pub Tour** (see "Hitting the pubs" toward the end of this chapter).

The top attractions

Belfast's Murals
Belfast

Northern Ireland has a tradition of public mural painting that dates to the early 1970s. Though some murals are not political or religious in nature, many depict Unionist or Loyalist political beliefs. The most compelling of Belfast's murals are found along the Loyalist (and primarily Catholic) Falls Road and along the Unionist (and primarily Protestant) Shankill Road and Sandy Row. I've provided directions to all three spots here, but because of flare-ups in violence over the past few years, I urge you to explore the murals with a guide. Belfast Black Taxi Tours (see earlier in this chapter) is an excellent choice.

To reach Falls Road from the center of the city, head north on Donegall Place, turn left on Castle Street, go straight ahead down Divis Road and cross Westlink to Falls Road. To find Shankill Road, head north on Donegall Place and Royal Avenue, turn left on Peter's Hill and cross Westlink Road. To find Sandy Row, go south on Great Victoria Street, make a right on Donegall Pass Road, and then another right up Sandy Row.

Belfast Botanic Gardens
Belfast

These lovely gardens have a lot to offer. When it's in bloom (June–July), the large rose garden is so dazzling and so varied that it almost doesn't seem real. Then there's the Palm House, an 1840s greenhouse that looks like a mini-palace of cast iron and glass, and houses all sorts of exotic plants. But my very favorite place is the Tropical Ravine, a large green-house built in 1889. Pull hard on the door, and enter into a tropical won-derland of flowering vines, orchids, and ponds. The Tropical Ravine is not particularly well kept, but that's part of its charm. As the little boy behind me said to his grandparents: "It's an adventure!" A picnic on one of the grassy lawns makes a great treat after exploring. Allow 45 minutes for your visit.

Entrance on Botanic Avenue. ☎ *028-9027-0611. Admission: Free. Open: Grounds daily 7:30 a.m. to sunset or 9 p.m., whichever comes first; Palm House and Tropical Ravine Apr–Sept Mon–Fri 10 a.m. to noon and 1–4:45 p.m., Sat–Sun 1–4:45 p.m., Oct–Mar Mon–Fri 10 a.m. to noon and 1–3:45 p.m., Sat–Sun 1–3:45 p.m.*

City Hall
Belfast

Modeled on St. Paul's Cathedral in London, Belfast's City Hall was built in 1888 after Queen Victoria conferred city status on Belfast. The building is made of Portland stone, with a central copper dome that rises 52m (173 ft.) into the sky and is visible for miles. In front, there is a statue of the queen and a memorial to the victims of the *Titanic*, which was built in a Belfast shipyard. Free tours of City Hall are given daily, and there is an interesting little exhibit on the many inventions that have emerged from this city. Allow 45 minutes for your visit.

Donegall Square. ☎ *028-9027-0456, ext. 2618. Bus: 58, 59, 69, 69A, 70, 71, 89, 90, 91, 92, 95, or Centrelink (100). Admission: Free. Tours: Mon–Fri 11 a.m., 2 and 3 p.m.; Sat 2 and 3 p.m.*

The Leaning (Clock) Tower of Belfast

Among Belfast's many beautiful Victorian buildings is the **Albert Memorial Clock,** at Queen's Square, built in 1865. The land that the tower was built on has sunk over the years, so that the tower now leans 1.25 meters (4 ft.) off the vertical.

Mount Stewart House and Gardens
Newtownards, County Down

Though its interior is grand, with a fabulous entrance hall and the famous George Stubbs painting *Hambletonian,* this impressive 18th-century mansion almost pales in comparison with the spectacular gardens surrounding it. Check out the Shamrock Garden, which has an Irish-harp-shaped topiary and a flower bed shaped like a red hand (the emblem of Ulster) enclosed in a hedge shaped like a shamrock. Spanish and Italian gardens are in the back, and a colorful sunken garden sits in the east yard. Allow 1 hour for your visit.

On Portaferry Road, 5km (3 miles) southeast of Newtownards, along the Ards Peninsula. ☎ *028-4278-8387. Admission: House and garden £7.80 adults, £3.90 kids; gardens only £5.90 adults, £2.90 kids. Open: House mid-Mar to Oct 31 Thurs–Tues 11 a.m.–6 p.m., gardens daily year-round 10 a.m.–6 p.m., formal gardens Mar 13– Oct 31 daily 10 a.m.–6 p.m.*

Ulster Folk and Transport Museum
Holywood, County Down

This is one of those attractions that kids and adults both love. This truly excellent museum is composed of two very different parts: In the giant Transport Galleries is a stunning collection of trains, cars, buses, trams, motorcycles, and bicycles, featuring all sorts of gems from a Victorian bicycle to a section of the first railway in Ireland to a DeLorean car (that famous *Back to the Future* vehicle), along with interesting text and displays about the various forms of transportation. A flight exhibit explores the history and science of flight using interactive science displays, artifacts related to the history of flight (including some actual aircraft), and a popular eight-person flight simulator.

The other half of this attraction is a well-done living museum of Ireland in the early 1900s. The museum has re-created a town and a rural area, rebuilding actual period buildings from all over Ireland on this site. Costumed interpreters carry out the tasks of daily life in many of these buildings — you can watch them cook over an open hearth, spin wool, work metal, print the town newspaper, make lace, and so on; and often, you can try your hand at these activities with them. Don't miss the sweet (in both senses of the word) candy store in the town area. You must walk from building to building, so if it's raining hard, you may want to skip this part of the attraction. The museum hosts all sorts of events year-round. Allow at least three hours if you're visiting both museums; you could reasonably spend five or six hours here.

Off the A2, 11km (7 miles) east of Belfast in Holywood, County Down. ☎ **028-9042-8428.** *Admission: Folk museum and transport museum individually £6.50 adults, £4 seniors, students, and kids, free for kids 4 and under; combined admission £8 adults, £4.50 seniors, students, and kids, free for kids 4 and under. Open: Mar–Sept Tues–Sun 10 a.m.–5 p.m.; Oct–Feb Tues–Fri 10 a.m.–4 p.m., Sat–Sun 11 a.m.–4 p.m.*

Ulster Museum
Belfast

The newly renovated Ulster Museum could not be more different from its pre-renovation predecessor. The old museum was a jumble of treasures; you would find a dusty chunk of amethyst behind a stuffed tiger, or a mysterious piece of pottery with no text to explain it. The new museum is sleek, immaculate, and relatively user-friendly. Though many locals feel that the new museum is a bit soulless compared with its former version, they also admit that it has been designed beautifully. Upon entering, visit the first gallery (on your left), which has been curated to give you a taste of what the museum offers so that you can decide what areas you want to focus on. There are many gems in the building; some of my favorites are the Egyptian mummy, the jeweled salamander pendant recovered from a Spanish Armada wreck, the *Edmontosaurus* dinosaur skeleton, the heart-breaking Famine ration tickets, the well-preserved stuffed birds, and the key to the Annesley synagogue, founded by Jewish Belfast citizens who had escaped the Russian pogroms of the 19th century. Allow at least two hours for your visit.

In the Botanic Gardens, which are located off of Botanic Avenue. ☎ **0845-608-0000.** *www.nmni.com. Admission: Free. Open: Tues–Sun 10 a.m.–5 p.m.*

More cool things to see and do

✔ **Carrickfergus Castle,** Marine Highway, Antrim Street, off the A2 in Carrickfergus, County Antrim (☎ **028-9335-1273**): During this impressive, well-preserved castle's 800-year history, it grew from a small castle to an unequaled Norman fortress. Tours are self-guided, with strategically placed information boards bringing the castle's exciting history to life. A highlight is a walk along the parapets, looking out to sea. During the first two weeks of August, the castle and grounds are home to a lively medieval fair and crafts market.

Admission is £3 adults, £1.50 seniors and kids. It's open Easter through September daily from 10 a.m. to 6 p.m., October through Easter daily 10 a.m. to 4 p.m. Last admission 30 minutes before closing. Allow an hour for your visit.

✔ **W5: Whowhatwherewhenwhy,** 2 Queen's Quay (in the Odyssey Center), Belfast (☎ **028-9046-7700;** www.w5online.co.uk; Bus: 94): Jutting out over the city's waterfront, this well-maintained interactive science and art museum has all sorts of things to do, hear, and see, from an exhibit where you can create your own animation to a super-cool stringless harp that uses lasers to detect the location and motion of your hands. The only things that are lacking from this otherwise excellent venue are clear explanations of the science behind the exhibits. The museum is best for kids 4 through 10.

To get there, cross Queen Elizabeth Bridge from city center, make the first left, and follow the instructions on parking. Admission is £7.50 adults, £6 seniors and students, £5.50 kids 3 to 15, free for kids 2 and younger. It's open July and August daily 10 a.m. to 6 p.m.; September through June Monday through Thursday 10 a.m. to 5 p.m., Friday and Saturday 10 a.m. to 6 p.m., and Sunday noon to 6 p.m. Last admission is always one hour before closing time. Allow a couple hours for your visit.

Shopping in Belfast

Belfast's City Hall is a perfect landmark for the shopping district, which is just across the street. There, you'll find posh (and expensive) British department stores, Irish shops, and some North American chains. **St. George's Market** (see "Dining in Belfast") is one of the best markets in Ireland, selling everything from baked goods to paintings.

Space CRAFT Gallery, up an escalator to the second floor of the Fountain Center, on College Street (☎ **028-9032-9342**), displays works by some of the best craftspeople from Northern Ireland and the Republic. You'll find everything from inexpensive collages to break-the-bank jewelry. **The Steensons** (Bill and Christina), in Bedford House, Bedford Street (☎ **028-9024-8269**), sell celebrated contemporary gold and silver jewelry. **Smyth's Irish Linens,** 65 Royal Ave. (☎ **028-9024-2232**), sells a full stock of Irish linens. Much more than just a shop, the **Irish Linen Centre,** Market Square, Lisburn (about 16km/10 miles from Belfast; ☎ **028-9266-0074**), relates the history of the famous Ulster linen and conducts hand-weaving demonstrations — and, of course, sells plenty of Irish linen, from coats to clothes.

Enjoying nightlife in Belfast

For a performance before the pub-hopping begins, you have several great options. The **Grand Opera House**, Great Victoria Street (☎ **028-9024-1919;** www.goh.co.uk), presents musicals, concerts, and plays with broad appeal, while the **Black Box,** 18–22 Hill St. (☎ **028-9024-4400;** www.blackboxbelfast.com), hosts an eclectic assortment of crackerjack musicians, from traditional Irish music greats to top-notch blues groups.

This is definitely a town that knows how to party, especially on the weekends. Belfast has a hot and happening nightlife, with lots of clubs in addition to the usual pubs. Scuffles sometimes break out as the night wears on, so take a cab back to your hotel, especially after the pubs close.

Hitting the pubs

Belfast has some of Ireland's finest pubs, many authentically Victorian. The company that produces the famed Bailey's Irish Cream hosts a good **Belfast Pub Tour** that covers six of the best pubs in the city, most with traditional music. The tour lasts about two hours and meets May through October Thursday at 7 p.m. and Saturday at 4 p.m., upstairs at the Crown Liquor Saloon, at 46 Great Victoria St. To ensure a spot on the tour, call ☎ **028-9268-3665** in advance. Tours cost £6.

Crown Liquor Saloon

Unquestionably the most famous pub in Belfast, and perhaps the most beautiful in Ireland, the Crown is owned by the state (by the National Trust, to be exact). The traditional interior is gorgeous, with hand-painted tiles, carved wood, brass fittings, and gas lamps — truly a perfect Irish watering hole. The local Strangford Lough (pronounced lock) oysters are excellent. You may want to find a seat early — the Crown fills up most evenings.

46 Great Victoria St. ☎ **028-9024-3187.** *Bus: 82, 83, 84, 85, or Centrelink (100).*

Kelly's Cellars

Not only is this the oldest continuously used licensed pub in Belfast, but Kelly's was also the popular meeting place for the United Irishmen, who organized the 1798 Rebellion. The name is misleading; Kelly's Cellars is a two-storied building with a stone-floored bar downstairs, decorated with all sorts of memorabilia, and a restaurant upstairs. Despite its popularity, Kelly's remains a locals place, filled with interesting characters and often featuring great traditional music. If you get hungry, try the incredible Black Velvet Steak Pie.

30 Bank St. ☎ **028-9032-4835.** *Bus: 80, 81, or Centrelink (100).*

Madison's Café Bar

One of the city's newest and most stunning bars, Madison's is named for the modern hotel in which it's housed. Featuring an Art Nouveau theme and sporting a striking copper-and-ceramic bar top, it's a sophisticated and hip gathering place for young professionals and students. There's a club downstairs that's great for dancing.

59–63 Botanic Ave. ☎ **028-9050-9800.** *Bus: 82, 83, 85, 89, 90, 91, or 92.*

Best pubs for traditional music

Some of the best pubs in Belfast to get those toes a-tappin' include **Madden's Bar,** Berry Street, right next to the Castlecourt Shopping Centre (☎ **028-9024-4114;** music almost every night); the **Duke of York,** 11 Commercial Court, off Lower Donegall Street (☎ **028-9024-1062;** traditional music Thurs and often on other nights); the **John Hewett,** 51 Donegall St. (☎ **028-9023-3768;** music many nights); and **Kelly's Cellars** (see review earlier in this chapter).

North Antrim

North Antrim is a place of dramatic beauty, with sheer sea-pounded cliffs, pristine green valleys, and the spectacular weirdness of the Giant's Causeway. Outdoorsy folks will have a ball. I recommend driving the coastal route along the Antrim Glens, starting at the town of Larne and heading north. The drive takes you along sleepy seaside towns, picturesque crescents of sand, and stunningly green fields, and deposits you at most of the top sights in this area.

If you don't have a car and you want an easy way see the Antrim countryside, take advantage of the Antrim tour run by **CitySightseeing Belfast** (☎ **028-9031-5333;** www.belfastcitysightseeing.com). The tour takes you to the Giant's Causeway, Carrickfergus Castle, Dunluce Castle, and the Bushmills Distillery. Tours depart daily at 9:30 a.m.; return at 6:30 p.m.; and cost £25 adults, £18 kids 10 and under.

If you're interested in taking a guided overnight bike tour of Antrim, check out the offerings at **Irish Cycle Tours** (☎ **066-712-8733;** www.irishcycletours.com).

Spending the night in North Antrim

Adelphi Portrush
$$$　**Portrush**

The Adelphi is located in the center of Portrush, a vacation town of amusement centers that has become a little ragged around the edges. The Adelphi itself is calm and composed, with every detail well thought out by its proprietors, who are passionate not only about giving guests a great experience but also about making their hotel eco-friendly. This attention to detail is evidenced in the heated stones on the floor of the Jacuzzi area, the laden breakfast table, the extensive menu of treatments at the spa, and the earth-friendly LEDs that light much of the hotel. The spacious rooms have the feel of rooms at a business hotel, with plush red carpeting and finely crafted pine furniture, and many have great views of either town or sea. Try to score a room on the fourth floor, where several rooms showcase the hotel's original oak beams. The Giant's Causeway, Dunluce Castle, Carrick-A-Read Rope Bridge, and several golf courses are easily accessible by car from the hotel.

61–71 Main St. ☎ *028-7082-5544.* www.adelphiportrush.com. *Parking: Free in a nearby public lot. Rack rates: £105–£125 double. MC, V.*

The Bushmills Inn
$$$–$$$$　**Bushmills**

The warm glow of a turf fire greets you when you enter this fantastic inn, with its grand staircase, gas lamps, and many antiques. You have a choice between the quaint, individually decorated rooms in the Coaching Inn and the much larger and newer rooms in the Mill House. The cozy library and the oak-beamed loft living room may tempt you to skip sightseeing for a day and curl up by the fire with one of the inn's excellent Irish coffees (made, of course, with premium Bushmills whiskey). Tasty Irish and New Irish cuisine is served in the restaurant.

Located on the A2 (called Dunluce Road in Bushmills), on the banks of the Bush River. ☎ **028-2073-3000.** www.bushmillsinn.com. *Parking: Free on-site. Rack rates: £138–£178 double. AE, MC, V.*

Rest A While
$ Bushmills

This two-room bed-and-breakfast gets rave reviews for its hosts, Gail and Ross Torrens, who strike that wonderful balance of being kind and helpful without being at all intrusive. They clearly care about the preferences of each guest, as evidenced by the wide selection on the breakfast menu. The location is also balanced — windows look out onto pretty green fields and a lovely garden, even though the B&B is right outside the bustling little town of Bushmills. Rooms are simply decorated and sweet, with pretty comforters and wood rocking chairs in each. Families with older children will appreciate the family room setup: a double bed for parents and bunk beds for two kids.

90 Castlenagree Rd. Off Straid Road (B17), about 1km (⅔ mile) east of the town of Bushmills. ☎ **028-207-32869.** *Parking: Free on-site. Rack rates: £50–£60 double. MC, V.*

Dining in County Antrim

Drumnakeel Herb Garden Tea Room
$ Ballyvoy (outside of Ballycastle) CAFE

This lovely garden cafe is the perfect place to relax over a simple lunch or snack. Delicious soups, salads (with edible flowers if you're lucky), sandwiches, and baked goods are on offer. Dishes are made with herbs and vegetables grown in the garden, so that cucumber in your salad may have been photosynthesizing just hours before.

Follow signs in Ballyvoy, which is a couple of miles east of Ballycastle on the A2. ☎ **028-2076-3350.** *Main courses: £3–£7. Open: July–Aug Mon–Fri 11 a.m.–5 p.m.*

Ramore Wine Bar
$$ Portrush GLOBAL

Pack yourself in with what feels like the rest of the town of Portrush for some casual, well-done grub. You'll find everyone, from couples on dates to families, at the pine bistro tables, chowing down on such options as burgers, a lamb kabob with peppers and onions, and an excellent Thai green curry. The menu is extensive, with many fish dishes in addition to the meat and chicken offerings, and more than one vegetarian option (rare in these parts). Try to get a seat at one of the large windows, which overlook the hustle and bustle of the oceanfront and harbor. And don't miss the banoffee pie (toffee, bananas, and meringue) for dessert.

Harbour Road, off Main Street and Kerr Street. ☎ **028-7082-4313.** *Main courses: £9–£15. Open: Mon–Thurs 12:15–2:15 p.m. and 5–10 p.m., Fri 12:15–2:15 p.m. and 5–10:30 p.m., Sat 12:15–2:15 p.m. and 4:45–10:30 p.m., Sun 12:30–3 p.m. and 5–8:45 p.m.*

Tartine at the Distillers Arms
$$ Bushmills   NEW IRISH

It used to be hard to find a good meal at a good value in Bushmills. With the opening of the newly revitalized Tartine, this is no longer true. Old stone walls, contemporary paintings, and funky purple lamps conspire to create a setting that is romantic without being at all stuffy. The menu ranges from New Irish comfort food such as braised lamb shank served with *champ* (mashed potatoes with green onions), roasted root vegetables and red wine *jus,* to more adventurous options such as a whole roast sea bass stuffed with lemon and fennel, served with sweet potatoes and a Spanish tomato sauce. There are usually two vegetarian options on the menu. As for dessert, I have three words for you: Sticky. Toffee. Pudding.

In the Distillers Arms Hotel, 140 Main St. ☎ **028-2073-1044.** *Main courses: £10–£16. AE, MC, V. Open: July–Aug Mon–Thurs 5–9 p.m., Fri–Sun 12:30–3 p.m. and 5–9 p.m.; Sept–June Wed–Fri 5–9 p.m., Sat 12:30–2:30 p.m. and 5–9:30 p.m., Sun 12:30–2:30 p.m. and 5–9 p.m.*

Exploring North Antrim

I highly recommend taking the A2, a spectacular coastal drive along sea-splashed cliffs and by small coastal towns with picturesque harbors. Major attractions along the road include the Giant's Causeway, the Dunluce Castle ruins, and the Carrick-A-Rede Rope Bridge (all reviewed later in this section).

My top choice for a **day hike** is the stunning 7.7km (4.8-mile) hike between the parking lot at the Giant's Causeway Visitors Centre and the parking lot at Dunseverick Castle, which rewards hikers with panoramic views of the causeway and jaw-dropping cliff scenery. In summer, you can take the Causeway Rambler (bus no. 376) back to your starting point. You can print directions from www.walkni.com (search for the North Antrim Cliff Path to Dunseverick Castle), order Ordnance Survey sheets 4 and 5 from www.ordnancesurvey.co.uk or by phone at ☎ **44-23-8079-2912,** or purchase the fabulous "Walking Tours" packet from Causeway Coast & Glens Tourism at 11 Lodge Rd., Coleraine (☎ **028-7032-7720;** www.causewaycoastandglens.com)

Those looking for long-distance hikes should check out the **Ulster Way,** the **Moyle Way,** and the **Causeway Coast Path.** For more trail information, check out *Walk Northern Ireland,* available at most tourist offices and as a PDF on www.discovernorthernireland.com (click "Things to See & Do," and then click "Walking," for trail maps and details).

For the birds: Rathlin Island

In the past, Rathlin's strategic position between Ireland and Scotland made it the site of many battles. Today, the tiny, boomerang-shaped island off the coast of Ballycastle is a peaceful place and the home of thousands of seabirds and only about 100 people. Storytelling, song, and music flourish here, and islanders are happy to welcome visitors.

On the eastern end of the island is Bruce's Cave, where the Scottish King Robert the Bruce hid after being defeated by the English. For information on the island, check out www.northantrim.com/rathlin_island.htm; for the ferry schedule, contact the Rathlin Island Ferry ticket office (☎ **028-2076-9299**; www.rathlinbally castleferry.com).

Golfers will certainly want to try **Royal Portrush,** Dunluce Road, Portrush, County Antrim (☎ **028-7082-2311;** www.royalportrush golfclub.com). The excellent 18-hole **Dunluce Course** offers amazing seaside views of the northern Antrim Coast, while the underrated **Valley Course** has beautiful inland views. Par is 72 on both courses. From April through October, fees for the Dunluce Course are £125 during the week and £140 on weekends; November through March, they're £60 daily. From April through October, fees for the Valley Course are £35 during the week and £40 on the weekend; November through March, they're £25 daily. For the Dunluce Course, guests are welcome daily except for mornings on Mondays and Saturdays, and afternoons on Wednesdays and Fridays. Visitors are welcome on the Valley Course after 10:50 a.m. on weekdays and after 2 p.m. on weekends. Book your tee time well in advance, especially for the Dunluce Course.

Carrick-A-Rede Rope Bridge
Larrybane

Here's one for the Indiana Jones in all of us! This heart-stopping rope bridge, spanning a chasm 18m (60 ft.) wide, is not for the fainthearted: It wiggles and shakes underfoot as the sea crashes 24m (80 ft.) below; no matter how brave you are, you're in for a scare. It's worth it, though — the views of coastal cliffs and the sea from the area are dazzling, and on a clear day you can see all the way to the coast of Scotland. Seabirds nest on the cliffs of the island, and you can often see them hovering in the wind. There is a 1km (⅔ mile) walk to the bridge. Allow 30 minutes for your visit.

Off the B15 (look for the signs). ☎ *028-2076-9839. Admission: £5.40 adults, £2.90 kids. Open: Mar–May 23 and Sept–Oct daily 10 a.m.–6 p.m.; May 24–Aug daily 10 a.m.–7 p.m.; Nov–Dec daily 10 a.m.–3:30 p.m. Last entry to rope bridge 45 minutes before closing.*

Dunluce Castle
Bushmills

These gorgeous castle ruins, mostly dating from the late 16th century, perch precariously over the sea (so precariously, in fact, that part of the main house plunged into the sea below in 1639). You can explore at will, discovering ruined fireplaces, round towers, and picture windows that frame the sea and sky, and imagining the lives of the powerful Scottish family that lived in this dramatic place. I recommend getting an information sheet from the visitor center before entering the ruins; it's full of interesting details. Guided tours can be arranged with advance notice. Allow 45 minutes for your visit.

Dunluce Road. Take the A2 about 5.6km (3½ miles) east of Portrush. ☎ **028-2073-1938**. *Admission: £2 adults, £1 seniors and kids, free for kids 3 and under. Open: Easter to Sept daily 10 a.m.–5:30 p.m., Oct to Easter daily 10 a.m.–4 p.m.*

Giant's Causeway
Bushmills

This is one of Ireland's strangest and most awesome sights. The Giant's Causeway is a 4.8km (3-mile) stretch of roughly 40,000 tightly packed, mostly hexagonal basalt rock columns of varying heights — some up to 12m (40 ft.) tall — that jut up from the foot of a cliff and eventually disappear under the sea. Experts will tell you that the causeway was formed by the quick cooling of an ancient volcanic eruption, but according to legend, Finn MacCool built the causeway as a path across the sea to reach his girlfriend on a Scottish island. (An aside: In 1842, the writer William Thackeray noted in his *Irish Sketch Book,* "Mon Dieu! And I have traveled a hundred and fifty miles to see that?" Just goes to show, even the eighth wonder of the world can't please everybody!) Though a shuttle bus is available, I recommend walking down to the biggest concentration of columns. Allow at least 90 minutes for your visit, more if you'll be hiking.

Off the A2 along the North Antrim Coast. ☎ **028-2073-1855**. *Parking: £6. Open: Visitor center Mar–Oct daily 10 a.m.–5 p.m., Nov–Feb daily 10 a.m.–4:30 p.m. You can hike the causeway at any time (no admission fee).*

The Old Bushmills Distillery
Bushmills

A thorough and well-guided tour of the world's oldest distillery, which still produces whiskey, awaits you at Bushmills. One highlight: a room so heady with whiskey fumes that the workers have to get a ride home at the end of the day because they've inhaled so much alcohol. (No fear; a couple of minutes won't affect you.) The shop has every Bushmills product you can imagine, from fudge to golf towels and, of course, every kind of whiskey the distillery makes. The tour ends with a taste test. Allow two and a half hours for your visit.

Main Street. On the A2 along the North Antrim Coast. ☎ **028-2073-3218**. *Admission: £6 adults, £5 seniors and students 18 and over, £3 kids 8–17; kids 7 and under are not* *permitted on the tour. Open: Apr–June and Oct Mon–Sat 9:15 a.m.–5 p.m., Sun noon to 5 p.m.; July–Sept Mon–Sat 9:15 a.m.–5 p.m., Sun 11 a.m.–5 p.m.; Nov–Feb Mon–Fri 10 a.m.–3:30 p.m., Sat–Sun 12:30–3:30 p.m.; Mar Mon–Sat 10 a.m.–5 p.m., Sun noon to 4 p.m. The last tour is always at 4 p.m., and tours run roughly every 30 minutes.*

Fast Facts: Belfast and County Antrim

Area Codes

The area code for all of Northern Ireland is **028,** if you're calling from within the U.K., and **048,** if you're calling from outside the U.K.

Emergencies/Police

Dial ☎ **999** for all emergencies.

Genealogy Resources

Visit or contact the Ulster Historical Foundation, 49 Malone Rd., Belfast (☎ 028-9066-1988; www.ancestry ireland.com).

Hospital

The Belfast City Hospital is at 51 Lisburn Rd. (A1; ☎ 028-9032-9241).

Information

For visitor information, go to the Belfast Welcome Center at 47 Donegall Place (☎ 028-9024-6609; www.gotobelfast. com).

Internet

Check out Revelations Internet Cafe in Ascot House, 27 Shaftesbury Sq. (☎ 028-9032-0337).

Post Office

There are two centrally located post offices in Belfast, one at 26–32 High St., at Bridge Street, and the other at 12–16 Bridge St.

Chapter 23

County Down

· ·

In This Chapter

▶ Hiking in the Mourne Mountains
▶ Rock-climbing, canoeing, and more
▶ Golfing at Royal County Down
▶ Paying respects to St. Patrick

· ·

*T*he stars of **County Down** are the velvety green and purple Mourne Mountains. The Mournes are the highest mountains in Northern Ireland, their rounded peaks reaching over 610m (2,000 ft.). A hiking and walking paradise, the sparsely populated mountains are threaded with trails that range in intensity from easy riverside strolls to strenuous boulder scrambles. This just may be the Irish and Northern Irish country landscape that you pictured before you got here, with weathered stone walls and farmhouses, sheep gamboling in the folds of the hills, lazy cows, wind-swept mountain gaps, and winding rivers. The stone Mourne Wall, built between 1904 and 1922, connects the 15 mountain peaks, snaking gracefully over rocky cliffs and up heather-covered crests.

The mountains roll down to the coastal area, where tacky-though-charming seaside towns, such as Newcastle, invite lolling on the sandy beaches, sauntering down the street with an ice cream cone, and rattling the bones of your traveling companions in bumper cars at the many amusement complexes.

In a completely different vein, this area, including County Armagh to the west, is where St. Patrick planted the seeds of Irish Christianity in the fifth century. The saint is though to be buried in the churchyard at Downpatrick Cathedral, reviewed later in this chapter.

For information on safety in Northern Ireland, see the note in Chapter 21.

I include the reviews for Culloden Estate and Spa, Mount Stewart House and Gardens, and the Ulster Folk and Transport Museum, which are actually in County Down, in Chapter 22 because they're easy side trips from Belfast, so check out that chapter, too.

County Down

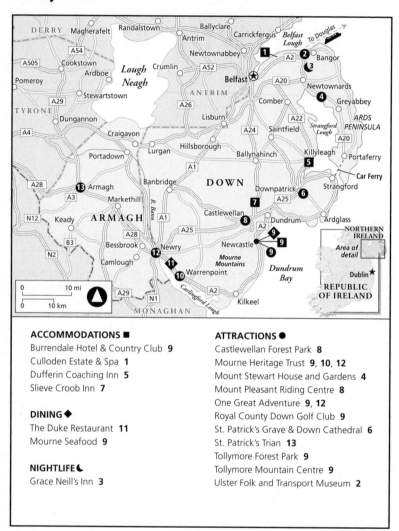

ACCOMMODATIONS ■
Burrendale Hotel & Country Club **9**
Culloden Estate & Spa **1**
Dufferin Coaching Inn **5**
Slieve Croob Inn **7**

DINING ◆
The Duke Restaurant **11**
Mourne Seafood **9**

NIGHTLIFE ◖
Grace Neill's Inn **3**

ATTRACTIONS ●
Castlewellan Forest Park **8**
Mourne Heritage Trust **9**, **10**, **12**
Mount Stewart House and Gardens **4**
Mount Pleasant Riding Centre **8**
One Great Adventure **9**, **12**
Royal County Down Golf Club **9**
St. Patrick's Grave & Down Cathedral **6**
St. Patrick's Trian **13**
Tollymore Forest Park **9**
Tollymore Mountain Centre **9**
Ulster Folk and Transport Museum **2**

Getting to County Down

The nearest airports are in Belfast, which is also the destination for ferries from England and Scotland (see Chapter 22 for information on those methods).

If you're coming by car from Dublin, take the M1 north to Newry (the M1 becomes the A1 in Northern Ireland). From Newry, take the A28 to Armagh. To get to the coast from Newry, take the A2 southeast (the A2 runs along the entire coast). If you're driving from Ireland into Northern Ireland, make sure you notify your rental-car company because extra insurance is occasionally required.

Irish Rail (☎ 1850-366-222; www.irishrail.ie) and **Northern Ireland Railways** (☎ 028-90-66-66-30; www.nirailways.co.uk) serve Newry, Portadown, Lurgan, Lisburn, Bangor, and other towns in Down year-round. **Ulsterbus** (☎ 028-90-66-66-30; www.translink.co.uk/ulsterbus) travels year-round to Newry, Portadown, and other major towns in county Armagh and Down.

Spending the Night in County Down

Burrendale Hotel, Country Club & Spa
$$$ Newcastle

This modern hotel is great for families. The clean, up-to-date rooms are nothing special in the décor department, but the amenities and location are perfect for kids. There is a nice restaurant with plenty of kid-friendly dishes, a large indoor pool, and a hot tub. The town of Newcastle seems made for families, with plenty of ice cream shops and amusement complexes. Work off that ice cream while hiking the Mourne Mountains, walking along the sandy beaches, and visiting the two nearby parks. Golfers also will be thrilled with the location: There are 15 courses nearby — including one of the best on the island, Royal County Down. Check online for the hotel's frequent packages and deals.

51 Castlewellan Rd. (off the A2 toward Downpatrick). ☎ **028-4372-2599.** *Fax: 028-4372-2328.* www.burrendale.com. *Parking: Free on-site. Rack rates: £140 double. AE, MC, V.*

Dufferin Coaching Inn
$$ Killyleagh

This stately inn, dating from 1803, is located in the shadow of Killyleagh Castle in the little town of Killyleagh, on the road between Downpatrick and Belfast. The seven bedrooms are bright, spacious, and elegantly furnished, and each has unique details, such as a king-size four-poster bed or a marble fireplace. The inn is much larger than it looks from the outside, with a pub, a library, and a guest lounge, plus a restaurant that features Irish cooking. Service is exceptionally warm and friendly, and the breakfast is fit for a (very hungry) king and queen. The inn is very popular, so reserve early.

33 High St. (Killyleagh is off the A20). ☎ **028-4482-1134.** *Fax: 028-4482-1102.* www.dufferincoachinginn.com. *Parking: Free on the street and in a nearby lot. Rack rates: £60–£90 double. AE, MC, V.*

Slieve Croob Inn
$ Castlewellan

If you aren't stirred by the setting of this lodging, restaurant, and bar complex, surrounded by verdant rolling hills, you need to check your pulse. Located where an old farmhouse used to stand, the modern inn has a simple mountain-lodge look to it. The spacious rooms are outfitted with pine furniture, landscape prints, and doors painted forest green. But it doesn't really matter what the rooms look like when there are trails and lanes that virtually begin at the front door, some leading to vistas of Newcastle Bay. The cozy bar and restaurant has gorgeous views, and the breakfast chefs make a mean poached egg.

Seeconnell, 119 Clonvaraghan Rd. (look for signs 1.6km/1 mile north of Castlewellan, on the A25). ☎ *028-4377-1412. Fax: 028-4377-1162.* www.nireland.com/slievecroob. *Parking: Free on-site. Rack rates: £65 double. MC, V.*

Dining in County Down

For out-of-this-world pub grub, drop in to Grace Neills (see "Hitting the Pubs," toward the end of this chapter).

The Duke Restaurant
$$ Warrenpoint NEW IRISH/SEAFOOD

Fresh, flavorful ingredients are at the root of the dishes served at this busy, jovial restaurant. Main courses range from meat dishes to vegetarian options, and although all are excellent, the gems of the menu are the dishes incorporating local seafood. The menu changes frequently; recent hits included grilled turbot with wilted bok choy and prawn bisque cream, and turbot with sautéed Savoy cabbage and an Armagh cider sauce.

Above the Duke Bar, 7 Duke St. (Warrenpoint is 9.7km/6 miles southeast of Newry, on the A2). ☎ *028-4175-2084. Main courses: £12–£16. MC, V. Open: Tues–Sat 6–10 p.m., Sun 5:30–9p.m.*

Mourne Seafood
$$ Newcastle IRISH/SEAFOOD

Being by the sea always puts me in the mood for fresh seafood, and this restaurant, with seafood dishes that change daily, proved the perfect answer to my cravings. The lunch menu is straightforward and solid, featuring choices like smoked salmon sandwiches, burgers, and fish and chips. At dinner, expect everything from the simple (divine mussels in a white wine sauce) to the more complex (a caramelized filet of salmon with fried crab linguini, chili, and chorizo oil). Those who are not seafood fans should be pleased with the steak and chicken options. The restaurant has a casually elegant feel, with contemporary art gracing the walls and spherical red paper lamps hanging from the ceiling. The service is exceptional.

107 Central Promenade. ☎ *028-4372-6401. Main courses: £7.50–£15. MC, V. Open: July–Aug Mon–Thurs 12:30 –9:30 p.m., Fri–Sat noon to 9:30 p.m.; Sept–May Fri–Sun noon to 9 p.m.*

Exploring County Down

Be sure to lace those walking shoes tightly, because County Down is a playground for nature lovers, with myriad hiking trails; all sorts of outdoor activities; and a dreamy setting of rivers, woods, and purple-green mountains. The Down Cathedral and the Aquarium are good rainy-day options.

The Mourne Mountains

In my opinion, the finest way to see this beautiful area is to take a hike along one of the many trails. You can access the Mourne Mountains along the A2, getting off at Newcastle, Kilkeel, Rostrevor, Warrenpoint, or any other town in the area.

Be aware that the word *walk* is used instead of *hike* in the Republic and Northern Ireland. Anything from a gentle ramble to a tough scramble over boulders may be called a *walk,* so ask for specifics.

The **Mourne Heritage Trust** offers information on hiking in several tourist information centers, including one at 10–14 Central Promenade, Newcastle, County Down (☎ 028-4372-2222); one in the Town Hall on Church Street in Warrenpoint, County Down (☎ 028-4175-2256); and one on Bank Parade in Newry, County Down (☎ 028-3026-8877). The centers are open most days during the summer; they offer all sorts of maps and information, plus a series of talks on various facets of the area and guided weekend hikes.

The *Mourne Country Outdoor Pursuits Map,* published by the Ordnance Survey of Northern Ireland, is an excellent detailed topographical map that has many trails marked. I also recommend purchasing *Mourne Mountain Walks,* a packet of ten laminated cards featuring maps and detailed instructions for ten of the area's best hikes. The Mourne Heritage Web site (www.mournelive.com) is an excellent resource for various hiking ideas, as well as other pertinent information.

The **Mourne Rambler** and **Kilkeel Rambler** bus service (☎ 028-9066-2222; www.translink.co.uk) makes circuits of the mountains with many stops; this is a great choice if you want to take a one-way hike and then take the bus back to your departure point.

One of my favorite routes is the **hike to Hare's Gap,** which takes you on a gentle, winding path uphill, with a scramble over large boulders before you reach the gap and a section of the graceful Mourne Wall. There are breathtaking views of the countryside as you ascend, and Hare's Gap is the starting point for a number of other excellent trails that take you higher and deeper into the mountains. Find the route at the parking lot along Trassey Road at the northern foot of Clonachullion Hill. Turn left upon exiting the parking lot, and you see the gate and stile that mark the beginning of the hike. The round-trip hike should take about three and a half hours.

For all hikes, good shoes, rain gear, and water are essential. If you're hiking alone (or even if you're not), it's a good idea to let someone know where you're planning on hiking and when you plan to return.

If you want to develop or improve upon your hiking skills, **Tollymore Mountain Centre,** Bryansford, Newcastle (☎ **028-4372-2158;** www. tollymore.com), offers a range of instructional courses geared to everyone, from beginner to experienced hikers.

You can do more than just hike in the Mourne Mountains. Here are some more options for outdoor activities:

✔ In addition to courses in hiking, **Tollymore Mountain Centre,** Bryansford, Newcastle (☎ **028-4372-2158;** www.tollymore.com), offers numerous rock-climbing, canoeing, and kayaking instructional courses in the area, ranging from one to three days. The center offers accommodations (spare but functional) for guests who are taking courses. **One Great Adventure** (☎ **0844-770-5477;** www.onegreatadventure.com) is another excellent outfitter that offers courses in all the activities mentioned earlier, plus mountain biking. There are locations at the Castlewellan Forest Park and on Main Street in the village of Annalong, in Newry.

✔ For information on **canoeing** in this region and in other areas of Northern Ireland, you can contact the **Canoe Association of Northern Ireland** (☎ **028-907-38884;** www.cani.org.uk).

✔ Little traffic and gorgeous vistas make the Mournes, especially around Castwellan, prime **cycling** territory. **Ross Cycle,** 44 Clarkhill Rd., signposted from the Clough-Castlewellan Road outside Castlewellan (☎ **028-4377-8029**), rents bicycles. You can park and ride or get the bike delivered to you.

✔ Point your putter in the direction of the excellent Championship and Annesley links courses at **Royal County Down Golf Club,** 36 Golf Links Rd., Newcastle (☎ **028-4372-3314;** www.royalcountydown.org). Both courses are challenging, full of sand dunes covered in heather and gorse. The stunning backdrops are Mourne Mountains and a sparking bay. Visitors are welcome on the Championship course on Mondays, Tuesdays, Thursdays (morning only), Fridays, and Sundays, and on the Annesley links at all times except Saturday mornings. Fees for the Championship course are £50 to £100 from November through April and £145 to £180 from May through October. In contrast, fees for the Annesley links are £20 November through March and £25 April through October.

✔ The **Mount Pleasant Riding Centre,** on Bannonstown Road, Castlewellan (☎ **028-4377-8651;** www.mountpleasantcentre.com), offers horseback treks on car-free forest trails. Visitors with some riding experience also can trek on the beach.

Other top attractions in County Down

Castlewellan Forest Park
Castlewellan

This 460-hectare (1,137-acre) wooded park just begs you to stroll around, enjoying the trout-filled lake, wooded paths, and views of a Scottish baronial-style castle on the grounds. The highlight is the gorgeous Annesley Garden and Arboretum, a splendid collection of trees and flowering shrubs from around the world, studded with fountains, ponds, and greenhouses. Don't miss the Peace Maze, one of the longest and largest hedge mazes in the world. Give yourself lots of time — my family was in there for a couple of hours. The Grange Coffee House is a sweet little spot for a light lunch and sells heavenly bite-size apple tarts. There is an area for tent campers and for trailers (called *caravans* in Ireland), if you want to spend the night. Allow about two and a half hours.

Entrance is across from the marketplace in the town of Castlewellan. ☎ **028-4377-8664.** *Admission: £2 adults on foot, 50p kids on foot, £4.20 per car. Open: Daily 10 a.m. to sunset.*

St. Patrick's Grave and Down Cathedral
Downpatrick

Sitting atop the Hill of Down is Down Cathedral, a small and austere church built in the 18th and 19th centuries in the style of its 13th- and 16th-century predecessors (buildings of religious significance have stood here for the past 1,800 years). Legend has it that the little churchyard here contains the remains of Ireland's patron saint, St. Patrick — a rock slab with the word *Patric* across it marks the spot. To find out more about St. Patrick and the interesting history of this area, walk over to the well-done **Down County Museum,** on the Mall, at English Street, in Downpatrick (☎ **028-4461-5218**), open Monday through Friday 10 a.m. to 5 p.m., Saturday and Sunday 1 to 5 p.m. (free admission). **St. Patrick's Trian Visitor Centre**, 40 English St., Armagh City, (☎ **028-3752-1801**) also does a nice job of telling St. Patrick's story. Armagh City is located in County Armagh, the western neighbor of County Down. Allow 20 minutes for your visit, unless you're also visiting the museum.

Down Cathedral, 33 Cathedral St. ☎ **028-4461-4922.** *Admission: Free. Open: Mon–Sat 9:30 a.m.–4:30 p.m., Sun 2–5 p.m.*

Tollymore Forest Park
Newcastle

This 480-hectare (1,200 acre) forest park has a bit of a fairy-tale feel to it. There are several garden follies, including a barn built in the style of a gothic castle and a range of wildlife from the area, including foxes, badgers, and otters. Amble along the river, perhaps stopping for a picnic, or break a sweat on one of the mountain trails. Allow one to three hours, depending on what you want to do.

Tullybrannigan Road (follow the signs from B180, 3.2km/2 miles north of Newcastle). ☎ **028-4372-2428**. *Admission: £2 adults on foot, 50p kids on foot, £4.20 per car. Open: Daily 10 a.m. to dark.*

Hitting the Pubs in County Down

Grace Neill's Inn
Donaghadee

Many pubs claim to be the oldest in Ireland, but this one, established in 1611, really is. Don't believe me? *Guinness World Records* says so, and those people know their pubs. Grace Neill herself was the proprietress of the pub in the mid- to late-1800s, known for greeting her guests with a welcoming kiss on the cheek and for smoking a pipe. More than one staff member claims that several unexplained occurrences are courtesy of Grace's ghost. The old part of the tavern practically defines what an Irish pub should look like, and even though it's been extended to include a lounge and conservatory, the whole place keeps the old-school style. The pub grub here is fabulous.

33 High St. (Donaghadee is off the A2, near Bangor). ☎ **028-9188-4595.**

Fast Facts: County Down

Area Code
The area code of County Down is **028**. When calling from the Republic of Ireland, dial **048**.

Emergencies
Dial ☎ **999** for all emergencies.

Hospital
In addition to Belfast's many hospitals, Downe Hospital, 2 Struell Wells Rd., Downpatrick (☎ 028-4461-3311), is a good choice.

Information
There are several tourist information centers in County Down. One of the best is at 10–14 Central Promenade, Newcastle (☎ 028-4372-2222).

Part VII
The Part of Tens

The 5th Wave   By Rich Tennant

"Douglas, it's time we talked about this beer paraphernalia hobby of yours."

In this part . . .

The Part of Tens is all about giving you a couple fun extras.

In Chapter 24, I list ten traditional Irish dishes and beverages that you shouldn't miss, from home-baked brown bread to Guinness.

If you're wondering what to bring home from Ireland, check out Chapter 25. I describe some of the best authentically Irish products sold on the island and point you toward the finest places to buy them.

Chapter 24

Top Ten Traditional Irish Dishes and Drinks

In This Chapter

▶ Breaking some brown bread
▶ Digging into a traditional breakfast
▶ Sipping Guinness

*T*hough most Irish cities now offer everything from sushi to margaritas, you'll have no trouble finding these traditional Irish dishes and drinks.

Apple and Rhubarb Tarts

The world would be a happier place if everyone sat down a few days a week to a rhubarb or apple tart, served with a dollop of fresh cream.

Brown Bread

Earthy brown bread is the perfect vehicle for fresh Irish butter, as well as the ideal implement for scooping up the dregs of your soup or stew.

Guinness

Does the thick black stuff really need an introduction? See Chapter 2 for more about the lifeblood of Ireland.

Hard Cider

Sweet and refreshing, a glass or pint of cider is the perfect way to cool down on a warm, lazy evening.

Irish Breakfast

You won't need lunch after chowing down on a traditional Irish breakfast. In its most complete form, the Irish breakfast in the Republic features bacon, eggs, sausages, fried tomatoes, fried mushrooms, baked beans, *black pudding* (a sausage that gets its color from pig's or cow's blood), and *white pudding* (a similar sausage, but without the blood). In the North, the traditional breakfast plate (called an Ulster Fry) has everything you find in the Republic's version, with the addition of two kinds of bread — soda bread and potato bread (sometimes called potato farls).

Irish Farmhouse Cheeses

Smoky Gubbeen cheese from County Cork, creamy Cashel Blue cheese, all kinds of goat cheese — I could go on and on. . . .

Irish Stew

The cornerstones of hearty, stick-to-your-ribs Irish stew are juicy pieces of lamb, cubed potatoes, and onions, but you could spend a lifetime cataloging the subtle variations in recipes across the country — a sprinkling of parsley here, a handful of carrots there, and so on.

Irish Whiskey

Irish whiskey is different from Scotch whisky in several ways. The malt barley for Scotch is dried using peat smoke, but the malt barley used in Irish whiskey is dried in a warm, closed oven, preserving the integrity of the barley flavor. In addition, Irish whiskey is distilled three times, which gives it a smoothness that connoisseurs claim is unrivaled.

Potatoes (and Curry Chips)

It wouldn't be a book about Ireland without mention of the humble tuber that served as a staple on the island for centuries. The Irish have created a number of delicious potato-based dishes, including *champ* (potatoes mashed with milk and green onions or leeks) and *boxty* (grilled potato pancakes). My favorite potato-related dish is *chips* (french fries) doused in curry sauce, available at many fish-and-chip shops.

Seafood

The Irish have embraced the fact that they're surrounded by waters rife with delicious creatures. The shellfish is spectacular, and the catch of the day is sure to be delicious (I've developed a love for brill). A standout is Irish salmon — you can find it in a variety of forms, from simple smoked slices to moist filets bathed in dazzling sauces.

Chapter 25

The Top Ten Items to Buy in Ireland

In This Chapter

▶ Purchasing the best Irish souvenirs
▶ Supporting local craftspeople

*1*reland is a shopper's paradise, offering everything from one-of-a-kind pottery to rare books.

Remember that one of the best things you can do to help the environment and support the local economy is to buy items that are made by craftspeople in Ireland. Not only are you helping a local artist to do what he loves, but you're also saving the fuel used to transport imported items. Read the labels carefully — I almost bought what I thought was a hand-knit Irish sweater, only to find on closer examination that it was factory-made abroad.

Books

Ireland is one literary place. Check out the newest releases from Irish authors or hunt through used bookshops for treasures.

CDs

Relive the *craic* of a late night in the pub with an Irish music CD (see Chapter 2 for recommendations). In Dublin, Claddagh Records (see Chapter 11) is a great place to get your collection started.

Chocolate and Candy

Bring home a bag of your new favorite sweets, such as the red-cherry cables you'll see me clutching on my way through Customs.

Irish Whiskey

Just think: You can sit back and sip the smooth water of life while recalling your trip to Ireland. If you get to the Old Jameson Distillery (see Chapter 11), you can even have a bottle personalized.

Jewelry

Ireland is home to numerous talented silversmiths and goldsmiths. One of the most popular souvenirs is the Claddagh ring — a ring with two hands clasping a heart that's topped with a crown (see Chapter 18).

Linen

You can find the famous snow-white Irish linen in all sorts of forms, from tablecloths to bed sheets to summer dresses.

Musical Instruments

I can't think of a better souvenir from Ireland than a tin whistle. It's inexpensive, light, truly Irish, and relatively easy to play (buy a tutor book along with it). Custy's Traditional Music Shop (see Chapter 17) sells all sorts of Irish instruments.

Pottery

High-quality pottery is abundant in Ireland, with designs running the gamut from the country-style painted pottery of Nicholas Mosse (see Chapter 14) to modern raku pieces.

Sweaters

You can thank all those sheep for Ireland's beautiful sweaters. There is a breathtaking range of offerings, from chic cashmere turtlenecks to thick oatmeal-colored Aran sweaters.

Tweed

Like those battered tweed hats that many farmers wear? Though you can find tweed items throughout Ireland, County Donegal is the home to some of the finest, and Magee of Donegal (see Chapter 20) is tweed heaven.

Appendix

Quick Concierge

○ ○

Fast Facts

ATMs

ATMs (often called *cash points*) are located all over the country, even in the smallest towns.

Credit Cards

Visa and MasterCard are the most commonly accepted credit cards, followed by American Express. Diners Club usually is not accepted. If your credit card is lost or stolen, call one of the following emergency numbers from Ireland: For American Express, ☎ 1-336-393-1111 (collect) in the Republic and in Northern Ireland; for Master Card, ☎ 1-800-55-7378 in the Republic, or ☎ 0800-96-4767 in Northern Ireland; and for Visa, ☎ 1-800-55-8002 in the Republic or ☎ 0800-89-1725 in Northern Ireland.

Customs

From outside the European Union, you can't bring firearms, ammunition, explosives, narcotics, pornography, meat, milk, plants, or animals into Ireland. Also, you may bring in no more than 200 cigarettes, 1 liter of liquor, and 2 liters of wine.

For information on U.S. Customs restrictions on what you can bring home from Ireland, read the brochure *Know Before You Go,* at www.cbp.gov/xp/cgov/travel/vacation/kbyg. Canadian travelers can find out about Customs restrictions by reading the *I Declare*

document at http://cbsa-asfc.gc.ca/publications/pub/bsf5056-eng.html. Australian travelers can check out the Quick Guide to Customs link at www.customs.gov.au, and New Zealanders can find Customs information at www.customs.govt.nz.

Dentists and Doctors

If you need to see a dentist or doctor, ask the concierge or host at your hotel or guesthouse for a recommendation. Otherwise, contact your local consulate for a recommendation. Many cities and larger towns have walk-in clinics for non-life-threatening treatment. Expect to pay for treatment upfront and to ask your insurance company for reimbursement after the fact. For more information about staying healthy, see Chapter 10.

Driving

You must have a valid driver's license from your home country to drive in Ireland. Always remember that the Irish drive on the left side of the road. Distances in the Republic are measured in kilometers, while distances in Northern Ireland are measured in miles. The speed limit in the Republic is 120kmph (75 mph) on motorways 100kmph (60 mph) on National roads, and 50 kmph (30 mph) on other roads. In Northern Ireland, the speed limit on motorways is 70 mph, while the speed limit on other roads is 60 mph, going down to 30 mph in cities and towns.

For more on driving in Ireland, see Chapter 7.

Drugstores

Drugstores are usually called *chemists* or *pharmacies.*

Pack prescription medications (in their original-label vials) in your carry-on luggage. Bring along copies of your prescriptions, in generic form rather than under a brand name, in case you need a refill.

Electricity

The standard electrical current is roughly 220 volts in the Republic of Ireland and roughly 240 volts in Northern Ireland. The Republic and Northern Ireland use three-pronged plugs unique to Ireland, so you'll need an adaptor. If you bring non-Irish appliances, you also may need a transformer, though many laptops and some other appliances have built-in transformers. You usually can buy adaptors and transformers at hardware or travel stores.

Embassies and Consulates

The American Embassy is at 42 Elgin Rd., Ballsbridge, Dublin 4 (☎ 01-668-8777 or 01-668-9612); the American Consulate is in Danesfort House at 223 Stranmillis Rd., in Belfast (☎ 028-9038-6100). The Canadian Embassy is at 7–8 Wilton Terrace, Dublin 2 (☎ 01-234-4000); the British Embassy is at 29 Merrion Rd., Dublin 4 (☎ 01-205-3700); and you can find the Australian Embassy at Fitzwilton House, Wilton Terrace, Dublin 2 (☎ 01-664-5300).

Emergencies

For the police, fire, ambulance, or other emergencies, dial ☎ **999**. A law-enforcement officer is called a *garda* or guard; in the plural, it's *gardai* (pronounced *gar*-dee), or simply *the guards.*

Internet Access

You'll find Wi-Fi access in most hotels and B&Bs. Check the "Fast Facts" section of each destination chapter for information on local Internet cafes.

Liquor Laws

You must be 18 or older to be served alcoholic beverages. Those 18 and over can purchase alcoholic beverages by the bottle at liquor stores, off-license shops (look for the signs), and most supermarkets. Ireland has very severe laws and penalties regarding driving while intoxicated.

Maps

If you're driving, a good driving map or a GPS/satellite navigation system is essential. My favorite map is the Ordnance Survey's *Ireland Touring Map,* available at http://leisure.ordnancesurvey.co.uk. For local maps, visitor centers are your best bet.

Post Office

Post offices in the Republic and Northern Ireland are easy to spot: Look for a bright-green storefront with the town name across it in the Republic, or a bright red storefront, also sporting the town name, in Northern Ireland. You can find post office locations at www.anpost.ie for the Republic and www.postoffice.co.uk in the North.

Restrooms

Restrooms are called *toilets* and are marked with international symbols. Some public restrooms use the Gaelic words *fir* (men) and *mna* (women).

Safety

Though Ireland's large cities are generally safe, you still need to take reasonable precautions. Always take a taxi back to your hotel late at night, especially in Dublin. In addition, leave your passport and other important documents in your hotel room, always lock car doors, and don't carry loads of cash.

See Chapter 22 for information on political violence in Northern Ireland, which ebbs and flows. For the most up-to-date safety recommendations for the region, check the U.S. Department of State Travel Warning section at http://travel.state.gov.

Smoking

Smoking is banned in pubs, restaurants, clubs, stores, public transportation, and taxis throughout Ireland. In addition, some accommodations don't allow smoking; check before making a reservation.

Telephone

To call Ireland from anywhere in the world, dial the international access code (011 from the United States and Canada, 0011 from Australia, and 00 from the United Kingdom and New Zealand) and then the country code (Ireland is 353; Northern Ireland is 44), followed by the city code without the initial zero (for example, you dial 1 for the Dublin city code, even though it's listed in this book as 01) and the number. *Two exceptions:* When calling Northern Ireland from elsewhere in the United Kingdom, dial 028 and the local eight-digit number. When calling Northern Ireland from the Republic, replace the 028 prefix with 048.

To call the Republic from Northern Ireland, dial 00-353 and then the city code (leaving off the zero) and number.

To call locally in the Republic of Ireland and Northern Ireland, just dial the number direct. You need to include the city code when calling from town to town in the Republic; in Northern Ireland, you can just dial the eight-digit local number. For local operator assistance in Ireland, dial ☎ 10 in the Republic or ☎ 100 in Northern Ireland.

To make international calls from Ireland, dial the international access code (00), followed by the country code (1 for the United States and Canada, 44 for the United Kingdom, 61 for Australia, and 64 for New Zealand), the area or city code, and then the local number. So, to call the U.S. number 718-000-0000, you'd dial 00-1-718-000-0000.

From the Republic of Ireland, dial ☎ 11818 for international directory assistance or ☎ 114 for operator assistance with international calls. From Northern Ireland, dial ☎ 153 for international directory assistance or ☎ 155 for operator assistance with international calls.

See Chapter 10 for information on calling cards, cellphones, and more.

Time Zone

Ireland is five time zones ahead of the eastern United States (when it's noon in New York, it's 5 p.m. in Ireland), except for a week or so when daylight savings begins and ends, when the gap increases by one hour.

Tipping

Tips of about 12 percent to 15 percent are expected at restaurants. It is not customary to tip bartenders at pubs unless you receive table service.

For porters or bellhops, tip €1 or £1 per piece of luggage. For taxi drivers, round up to the nearest euro or pound. For more about tipping, see Chapter 5.

Weather Updates

The best site on the Web for Ireland's weather forecasts is www.ireland.com/weather.

Airline and Car Rental Numbers and Web Sites

Airlines

Aer Lingus
☎ 800-474-7424 in the U.S. and Canada
☎ 0871-718-5000 in the U.K.
☎ 0818-365-000 in Ireland
www.aerlingus.com

Air Canada
☎ 888-247-2262 in the U.S. and Canada
www.aircanada.ca

American Airlines
☎ 800-433-7300 in the U.S.
www.aa.com

bmi
☎ 01-332-648-181 outside the U.K.
☎ 0844-8484-888 in the U.K.
www.flybmi.com

Continental Airlines
☎ 800-231-0856 in the U.S. and Canada
www.continental.com

Delta Air Lines
☎ 800-221-1212 in the U.S. and Canada
www.delta.com

Ryanair
☎ 0818-30-30-30 in the Republic
☎ 0871-246-0000 in the U.K.
☎ 353-1-248-0856 outside the U.K. or Ireland
www.ryanair.com

United Airlines
☎ 800-864-8331 in the U.S. and Canada
www.united.com

Car-rental agencies

Alamo
☎ 877-222-9075
www.alamo.com

Argus
☎ 212-372-7266 in the U.S.
☎ 647-724-5103 in Canada
☎ 023-888-3002 in the Republic
☎ 0844-330-2584 in the U.K.
www.argus-rentacar.com

Avis
☎ 800-331-1212 in the U.S. and Canada
☎ 044-8445-818181 in the U.K.
☎ 021-428-1111 in the Republic
www.avis.com

Budget
☎ 800-472-3325 in the U.S.
☎ 800-268-8900 in Canada
☎ 084-4544-3455 in the U.K.
www.budget.com

Dan Dooley
☎ 800-331-9301 in the U.S. and Canada
☎ 0800-282-189 in the U.K.
☎ 062-53-103 in the Republic
www.dan-dooley.ie

Europcar
www.europcar.ie

Hertz
☎ 800-654-3001 in the U.S.
www.hertz.com

National
☎ 877-222-9058 in the U.S. and
Canada
www.nationalcar.com

Index

USINESS, CAREERS & PERSONAL FINANCE

ccounting For Dummies,
Edition*
3-0-470-24600-9

ookkeeping Workbook
r Dummies†
3-0-470-16983-4

mmodities For Dummies
3-0-470-04928-0

ing Business in China For Dummies
3-0-470-04929-7

E-Mail Marketing For Dummies
978-0-470-19087-6

Job Interviews For Dummies,
3rd Edition*†
978-0-470-17748-8

Personal Finance Workbook
For Dummies*†
978-0-470-09933-9

Real Estate License Exams For Dummies
978-0-7645-7623-2

Six Sigma For Dummies
978-0-7645-6798-8

Small Business Kit For Dummies,
2nd Edition*†
978-0-7645-5984-6

Telephone Sales For Dummies
978-0-470-16836-3

USINESS PRODUCTIVITY & MICROSOFT OFFICE

cess 2007 For Dummies
3-0-470-03649-5

cel 2007 For Dummies
3-0-470-03737-9

fice 2007 For Dummies
8-0-470-00923-9

utlook 2007 For Dummies
8-0-470-03830-7

PowerPoint 2007 For Dummies
978-0-470-04059-1

Project 2007 For Dummies
978-0-470-03651-8

QuickBooks 2008 For Dummies
978-0-470-18470-7

Quicken 2008 For Dummies
978-0-470-17473-9

Salesforce.com For Dummies,
2nd Edition
978-0-470-04893-1

Word 2007 For Dummies
978-0-470-03658-7

DUCATION, HISTORY, REFERENCE & TEST PREPARATION

rican American History
r Dummies
'8-0-7645-5469-8

lgebra For Dummies
'8-0-7645-5325-7

lgebra Workbook For Dummies
'8-0-7645-8467-1

rt History For Dummies
'8-0-470-09910-0

ASVAB For Dummies, 2nd Edition
978-0-470-10671-6

British Military History For Dummies
978-0-470-03213-8

Calculus For Dummies
978-0-7645-2498-1

Canadian History For Dummies,
2nd Edition
978-0-470-83656-9

Geometry Workbook For Dummies
978-0-471-79940-5

The SAT I For Dummies,
6th Edition
978-0-7645-7193-0

Series 7 Exam For Dummies
978-0-470-09932-2

World History For Dummies
978-0-7645-5242-7

OOD, HOME, GARDEN, HOBBIES & HOME

ridge For Dummies, 2nd Edition
'8-0-471-92426-5

oin Collecting For Dummies,
nd Edition
78-0-470-22275-1

ooking Basics For Dummies,
rd Edition
78-0-7645-7206-7

Drawing For Dummies
978-0-7645-5476-6

Etiquette For Dummies,
2nd Edition
978-0-470-10672-3

Gardening Basics For Dummies*†
978-0-470-03749-2

Knitting Patterns For Dummies
978-0-470-04556-5

Living Gluten-Free For Dummies†
978-0-471-77383-2

Painting Do-It-Yourself
For Dummies
978-0-470-17533-0

HEALTH, SELF HELP, PARENTING & PETS

nger Management For Dummies
78-0-470-03715-7

nxiety & Depression Workbook
or Dummies
'78-0-7645-9793-0

ieting For Dummies, 2nd Edition
78-0-7645-4149-0

og Training For Dummies,
nd Edition
'78-0-7645-8418-3

Horseback Riding For Dummies
978-0-470-09719-9

Infertility For Dummies†
978-0-470-11518-3

Meditation For Dummies
with CD-ROM, 2nd Edition
978-0-471-77774-8

Post-Traumatic Stress Disorder
For Dummies
978-0-470-04922-8

Puppies For Dummies,
2nd Edition
978-0-470-03717-1

Thyroid For Dummies,
2nd Edition†
978-0-471-78755-6

Type 1 Diabetes For Dummies*†
978-0-470-17811-9

---

* Separate Canadian edition also available
† Separate U.K. edition also available

vailable wherever books are sold. For more information or to order direct: U.S. customers visit www.dummies.com or call 1-877-762-2974.
J.K. customers visit www.wileyeurope.com or call (0) 1243 843291. Canadian customers visit www.wiley.ca or call 1-800-567-4797.

 **WILEY**

INTERNET & DIGITAL MEDIA

AdWords For Dummies
978-0-470-15252-2

**Blogging For Dummies,
2nd Edition**
978-0-470-23017-6

**Digital Photography All-in-One
Desk Reference For Dummies,
3rd Edition**
978-0-470-03743-0

**Digital Photography For Dummies,
5th Edition**
978-0-7645-9802-9

**Digital SLR Cameras & Photography
For Dummies, 2nd Edition**
978-0-470-14927-0

**eBay Business All-in-One Desk
Reference For Dummies**
978-0-7645-8438-1

eBay For Dummies, 5th Edition*
978-0-470-04529-9

eBay Listings That Sell For Dummies
978-0-471-78912-3

Facebook For Dummies
978-0-470-26273-3

**The Internet For Dummies,
11th Edition**
978-0-470-12174-0

**Investing Online For Dummies,
5th Edition**
978-0-7645-8456-5

**iPod & iTunes For Dummi
5th Edition**
978-0-470-17474-6

MySpace For Dummies
978-0-470-09529-4

Podcasting For Dummies
978-0-471-74898-4

**Search Engine Optimizati
For Dummies, 2nd Edition**
978-0-471-97998-2

Second Life For Dummies
978-0-470-18025-9

**Starting an eBay Business
For Dummies,3rd Edition***
978-0-470-14924-9

GRAPHICS, DESIGN & WEB DEVELOPMENT

**Adobe Creative Suite 3 Design
Premium All-in-One Desk Reference
For Dummies**
978-0-470-11724-8

**Adobe Web Suite CS3 All-in-One
Desk Reference For Dummies**
978-0-470-12099-6

AutoCAD 2008 For Dummies
978-0-470-11650-0

**Building a Web Site For Dummies,
3rd Edition**
978-0-470-14928-7

**Creating Web Pages All-in-One Desk
Reference For Dummies,
3rd Edition**
978-0-470-09629-1

**Creating Web Pages For Dummies,
8th Edition**
978-0-470-08030-6

Dreamweaver CS3 For Dummies
978-0-470-11490-2

Flash CS3 For Dummies
978-0-470-12100-9

Google SketchUp For Dummies
978-0-470-13744-4

InDesign CS3 For Dummies
978-0-470-11865-8

**Photoshop CS3 All-in-One
Desk Reference For Dummies**
978-0-470-11195-6

Photoshop CS3 For Dummies
978-0-470-11193-2

**Photoshop Elements 5
For Dummies**
978-0-470-09810-3

SolidWorks For Dummies
978-0-7645-9555-4

Visio 2007 For Dummies
978-0-470-08983-5

**Web Design For Dummies,
2nd Edition**
978-0-471-78117-2

**Web Sites Do-It-Yourself
For Dummies**
978-0-470-16903-2

**Web Stores Do-It-Yourself
For Dummies**
978-0-470-17443-2

LANGUAGES, RELIGION & SPIRITUALITY

Arabic For Dummies
978-0-471-77270-5

Chinese For Dummies, Audio Set
978-0-470-12766-7

French For Dummies
978-0-7645-5193-2

German For Dummies
978-0-7645-5195-6

Hebrew For Dummies
978-0-7645-5489-6

Ingles Para Dummies
978-0-7645-5427-8

Italian For Dummies, Audio Set
978-0-470-09586-7

Italian Verbs For Dummies
978-0-471-77389-4

Japanese For Dummies
978-0-7645-5429-2

Latin For Dummies
978-0-7645-5431-5

Portuguese For Dummies
978-0-471-78738-9

Russian For Dummies
978-0-471-78001-4

Spanish Phrases For Dummies
978-0-7645-7204-3

Spanish For Dummies
978-0-7645-5194-9

**Spanish For Dummies,
Audio Set**
978-0-470-09585-0

The Bible For Dummies
978-0-7645-5296-0

Catholicism For Dummies
978-0-7645-5391-2

**The Historical Jesus
For Dummies**
978-0-470-16785-4

Islam For Dummies
978-0-7645-5503-9

**Spirituality For Dummies,
2nd Edition**
978-0-470-19142-2

NETWORKING AND PROGRAMMING

ASP.NET 3.5 For Dummies
978-0-470-19592-5

C# 2008 For Dummies
978-0-470-19109-5

Hacking For Dummies, 2nd Edition
978-0-470-05235-8

**Home Networking
For Dummies, 4th Edition**
978-0-470-11806-1

Java For Dummies, 4th Edition
978-0-470-08716-9

**Microsoft® SQL Server™ 2008
All-in-One Desk Reference For Dummies**
978-0-470-17954-3

**Networking All-in-One Desk Reference
For Dummies, 2nd Edition**
978-0-7645-9939-2

**Networking For Dummies,
8th Edition**
978-0-470-05620-2

**SharePoint 2007
For Dummies**
978-0-470-09941-4

**Wireless Home Networking
For Dummies, 2nd Edition**
978-0-471-74940-0